Online Access for *Concepts of Programming Languages*

Thank you for purchasing a new copy of ***Concepts of Programming Languages***, **Eighth Edition**. Your textbook includes six months of prepaid access to the book's Companion Website. This prepaid subscription gives you full access to all student support areas, including:

- An online language reference library, complete with reference material, links to compilers and the best Web sites for each supported language.
- Online lecture notes to reinforce the concepts in the textbook.
- Self-assessment quizzes to test your knowledge.

To access the *Concepts of Programming Languages* Companion Website for the first time:
You will need to register online using a computer with an Internet connection and a Web browser. The process takes just a couple of minutes and only needs to be completed once.

1. Go to **http://www.aw-bc.com/sebesta** to begin.
2. Click the **Register** button.
3. Use a coin to scratch off the gray coating below and reveal your student access code.* *Do not use a knife or other sharp object, which can damage the code.*

4. On the registration page, enter your student access code. Do not type the dashes. You can use lowercase or uppercase.
5. Follow the on-screen instructions. If you need help at any time during the online registration process, simply click the **Need Help?** icon.
6. Once your personal Login Name and Password are confirmed, you can begin using the *Concepts of Programming Languages* Companion Website!

To log into this Website after you've registered:
You only need to register for this Companion Website once. After that, you can access the site by going to http://www.aw-bc.com/sebesta and providing your Login Name and Password when prompted.

IMPORTANT: The access code on this page can only be used once to establish a subscription to the *Concepts of Programming Languages*, Eighth Edition Companion Website. This subscription is valid for six months upon activation, and is not transferable. If this access code has already been scratched off, it may no longer be valid. If this is the case, you can purchase a subscription by going to http://www.aw-bc.com/sebesta and clicking the **Get Access** button on the login page and following the instructions provided.

concepts of
Programming
Languages

Eighth Edition

Robert W. Sebesta

University of Colorado at Colorado Springs

concepts of
Programming
Languages

Eighth Edition

PEARSON

Addison
Wesley

Boston San Francisco New York
London Toronto Sydney Tokyo Singapore Madrid
Mexico City Munich Paris Cape Town Hong Kong Montreal

Publisher	Greg Tobin
Acquisitions Editor	Matt Goldstein
Editorial Assistant	Maurene Goo
Associate Managing Editor	Jeffrey Holcomb
Senior Production Supervisor	Marilyn Lloyd
Senior Marketing Manager	Michelle Brown
Marketing Assistant	Sarah Milmore
Media Producer	Bethany Tidd
Cover Designer	Joyce Cosentino Wells

Cover Image © Rocky Mountain Reflections Photography, Inc. Winter photography of Pikes Peak and Garden of the Gods, Colorado Springs, Colorado.

Senior Manufacturing Buyer	Carol Melville
Production Services	WestWords PMG

Many of the designations used by manufacturers and sellers to distinguish their products are claimed as trademarks. Where those designations appear in this book, and the publisher was aware of a trademark claim, the designations have been printed in initial caps or all caps.

The programs and applications presented in this book have been included for their instructional value. They have been tested with care but are not guaranteed for any particular purpose. Neither the publisher nor the author offers any warranties or representations, nor do they accept any liabilities with respect to the programs or applications.

Library of Congress Cataloging-in-Publication Data

Sebesta, Robert W.
    Concepts of programming languages / Robert W. Sebesta.—8th ed.
      p. cm.
    Includes bibliographical references and index.
    ISBN-13: 978-0-321-49362-0
    ISBN-10: 0-321-49362-1
    1. Programming languages (Electronic computers) I. Title.

QA76.7.S43 2007
005.13--dc22   2007006846

ISBN-13: 978-0-321-49362-0
ISBN-10: 0-321-49362-1

1 2 3 4 5 6 7 8 9 10-CRW-10 09 08 07

Preface

Changes for the Eighth Edition

The goals, overall structure, and approach of this eighth edition of *Concepts of Programming Languages* remain the same as those of the seven earlier editions. The principal goals are to introduce the main constructs of contemporary programming languages and to provide the reader with the tools necessary for the critical evaluation of existing and future programming languages. An additional goal is to prepare the reader for the study of compiler design, by providing an in-depth discussion of programming language structures, presenting a formal method of describing syntax, and introducing approaches to lexical and syntatic analysis.

The eighth edition evolved from the seventh through two basic kinds of changes. First, to maintain the currency of the material, some of the discussion of older programming languages has been replaced by material on newer languages. Discussions of the unique control structures of Python and Ruby were added to Chapter 8. Ruby blocks and iterators are now covered in Chapter 9. Support for abstract data types in Python and Ruby is discussed in Chapter 11, along with support for generic classes in Java 5.0 and C# 2005. An overview of Ruby support for object-oriented programming has been added to Chapter 12. The second kind of changes are minor changes, primarily to improve clarity, which were made to a large number of sections of the book.

The Vision

This book describes the fundamental concepts of programming languages by discussing the design issues of the various language constructs, examining the design choices for these constructs in some of the most common languages, and critically comparing design alternatives.

Any serious study of programming languages requires an examination of some related topics, among which are formal methods of describing the syntax and semantics of programming languages, which are covered in Chapter 3. Also, implementation techniques for various language constructs must be considered: Lexical and syntax analysis are discussed in Chapter 4, and implementation of subprogram linkage is covered in Chapter 10. Implementation of some other language constructs is discussed in various other parts of the book.

The following paragraphs outline the contents of the eighth edition.

Chapter Outlines

Chapter 1 begins with a rationale for studying programming languages. It then discusses the criteria used for evaluating programming languages and language constructs. The primary influences on language design, common design trade-offs, and the basic approaches to implementation are also examined.

Chapter 2 outlines the evolution of most of the important languages discussed in this book. Although no language is described completely, the origins, purposes, and contributions of each are discussed. This historical overview is valuable, because it provides the background necessary to under-standing the practical and theoretical basis for contemporary language design. It also motivates further study of language design and evaluation. In addition, because none of the remainder of the book depends on Chapter 2, it can be read on its own, independent of the other chapters.

Chapter 3 describes the primary formal method for describing the syntax of programming language—BNF. This is followed by a description of attribute grammars, which describe both the syntax and static semantics of languages. The difficult task of semantic description is then explored, including brief introductions to the three most common methods: operational, axiomatic, and denotational semantics.

Chapter 4 introduces lexical and syntax analysis. This chapter is targeted to those colleges that no longer require a compiler design course in their curricula. Like Chapter 2, this chapter stands alone and can be read independently of the rest of the book.

Chapters 5 through 14 describe in detail the design issues for the primary constructs of the imperative languages. In each case, the design choices for several example languages are presented and evaluated. Specifically, Chapter 5 covers the many characteristics of variables, Chapter 6 covers data types, and Chapter 7 explains expressions and assignment statements. Chapter 8 describes control statements, and Chapters 9 and 10 discuss subprograms and their implementation. Chapter 11 examines data abstraction facilities. Chapter 12 provides an in-depth discussion of language features that support object-oriented programming (inheritance and dynamic method binding), Chapter 13 discusses concurrent program units, and Chapter 14 is about exception handling, along with a brief discussion of event handling.

The last two chapters (15 and 16) describe two of the most important alternative programming paradigms: functional programming and logic programming. Chapter 15 presents an introduction to Scheme, including descriptions of some of its primitive functions, special forms, and functional forms, as well as some examples of simple functions written in Scheme. Brief introductions to ML, and Haskell are given to illustrate some different kinds of functional language. Chapter 16 introduces logic programming and the logic programming language, Prolog.

To the Instructor

In the junior-level programming language course at the University of Colorado at Colorado Springs, the book is used as follows: We typically cover Chapters 1 and 3 in detail, and though students find it interesting and beneficial reading, Chapter 2 receives little lecture time due to its lack of hard technical content. Because no material in subsequent chapters depends on Chapter 2, as noted earlier, it can be skipped entirely, and because we require a course in compiler design, Chapter 4 is not covered.

Chapters 5 through 9 should be relatively easy for students with extensive programming experience in C++, Java, or C#. Chapters 10 through 14 are more challenging and require more detailed lectures.

Chapters 15 and 16 are entirely new to most students at the junior level. Ideally, language processors for Scheme and Prolog should be available for students required to learn the material in these chapters. Sufficient material is included to allow students to dabble with some simple programs.

Undergraduate courses will probably not be able to cover all of the last two chapters in detail. Graduate courses, however, should be able to completely discuss the material in those chapters by skipping over parts of the early chapters on imperative languages.

Supplemental Materials

The following supplements are available to all readers of this book at *www.aw.com/cssupport*.

- A set of lecture note slides. PowerPoint® slides are available for each chapter in the book.
- PowerPoint® slides containing all the figures in the book.

To reinforce learning in the classroom, to assist with the hands-on lab component of this course, and/or to facilitate students in a distance learning situation, access the Companion Website at *www.aw.com/sebesta*. This site contains:

- Mini-manuals (approximately 100-page tutorials) on a handful of languages. These proceed on the assumption that the student knows how to program in some other language, giving the student enough mation to complete the chapter materials in each language. Currently the site includes manuals for C++, C, Java and Smalltalk.

- Self-assessment quizzes. Students can complete a series of multiple-choice and fill-in-the-blank exercises to check their understanding of each chapter.

Solutions to many of the problem sets are available to qualified instructors on our Instructor Resource Center at *www.aw-bc.com/irc*. Please contact your local Addison-Wesley sales representative or send an email to *computing@aw.com* for more information.

Language Processor Availability

Processors for and information about some of the programming languages discussed in this book can be found at the following Web sites:

C, C++, Fortran, and Ada	*gcc.gnu.org*
C#	*microsoft.com*
Java	*java.sun.com*
Haskell	*haskell.org*
Scheme	*www.plt-scheme.org/software/drscheme*
Perl	*www.perl.com*
Python	*www.python.org*
Ruby	*www.ruby-lang.org/en/*

JavaScript is included in virtually all browsers; PHP is included in virtually all Web servers.

All this information is also included on the companion Web site.

Acknowledgments

The suggestions from outstanding reviewers contributed greatly to this book's present form. In alphabetical order, they are:

I-ping Chu,	*DePaul University*
Amer Diwan,	*University of Colorado*
Stephen Edwards,	*Virginia Tech*
Nigel Gwee,	*Southern University–Baton Rouge*
K. N. King,	*Georgia State University*
Donald Kraft,	*Louisiana State University*
Simon H. Lin,	*California State University–Northridge*
Mark Llewellyn,	*University of Central Florida*

Bruce R. Maxim,	*University of Michigan–Dearborn*
Gloria Melara,	*California State University–Northridge*
Frank J. Mitropoulos,	*Nova Southeastern University*
Euripides Montagne,	*University of Central Florida*
Bob Neufeld,	*Wichita State University*
Amar Raheja,	*California State Polytechnic University–Pomona*
Hossein Saiedian,	*University of Kansas*
Neelam Soundarajan,	*Ohio State University*
Paul Tymann,	*Rochester Institute of Technology*
Cristian Videira Lopes,	*University of California–Irvine*
Salih Yurttas,	*Texas A&M University*

Special thanks are due to two reviewers who thoroughly analyzed the manuscript and provided many detailed comments, Amer Diwan and Bob Neufeld. Numerous other people provided input for the previous editions of *Concepts of Programming Languages* at various stages of its development. All of their comments were useful and greatly appreciated. In alphabetical order, they are: Vicki Allan, Henry Bauer, Carter Bays, Manuel E. Bermudez, Peter Brouwer, Margaret Burnett, Paosheng Chang, Liang Cheng, John Crenshaw, Charles Dana, Barbara Ann Griem, Mary Lou Haag, John V. Harrison, Eileen Head, Ralph C. Hilzer, Eric Joanis, Leon Jololian, Hikyoo Koh, Jiang B. Liu, Meiliu Lu, Jon Mauney, Robert McCoard, Dennis L. Mumaugh, Michael G. Murphy, Andrew Oldroyd, Young Park, Rebecca Parsons, Steve J. Phelps, Jeffery Popyack, Raghvinder Sangwan, Steven Rapkin, Hamilton Richard, Tom Sager, Joseph Schell, Sibylle Schupp, Mary Louise Soffa, Neelam Soundarajan, Ryan Stansifer, Steve Stevenson, Virginia Teller, Yang Wang, John M. Weiss, Franck Xia, and Salih Yurnas.

Matt Goldstein, Editor, Maurene Goo, Editorial Assistant, and Marilyn Lloyd, Senior Production Supervisor of Addison-Wesley, and Tammy King and Bethann Thompson at WestWords, all deserve my gratitude for their efforts to produce the eighth edition both quickly and carefully.

About the Author

Robert Sebesta is an Associate Professor Emeritus in the Computer Science Department at the University of Colorado–Colorado Springs. Professor Sebesta received a B.S. in applied mathematics from the University of Colorado in Boulder and M.S. and Ph.D. degrees in Comptuer Science from the Pennsylvania State University. He has taught computer science for more than 36 years. His professional interests are the design and evaluation of programming languages, compiler design, and software testing methods and tools.

Contents

Preliminaries

Before we begin discussing the concepts of programming languages, we must consider a few preliminaries. First we explain some reasons why computer science students and professional software developers should study general concepts of language design and evaluation. This discussion is valuable for those who believe that a working knowledge of one or two programming languages is sufficient for computer scientists. The major programming domains are then briefly described. Next, because the book evaluates language constructs and features, we present a list of criteria that can serve as a basis for such judgments. The two major influences on language design, machine architecture and program design methodologies, are then discussed. After that, the various categories of programming languages are introduced. Next we describe a few of the major trade-offs that must be considered during language design.

Because this book is also about the implementation of programming languages, this chapter includes an overview of the most common approaches to implementation. Finally, we briefly describe a few examples of programming environments and discuss their impact on software production.

1.1 Reasons for Studying Concepts of Programming Languages

It is natural for students to wonder how they will benefit from the study of programming language concepts. After all, many other topics in computer science are worthy of serious study. The following is what we believe to be a compelling list of potential benefits of studying concepts of programming languages:

- *Increased capacity to express ideas*. It is widely believed that the depth at which people can think is influenced by the expressive power of the language in which they communicate their thoughts. Those with only a weak understanding of natural language are limited in the complexity of their thoughts, particularly in depth of abstraction. In other words, it is difficult for people to conceptualize structures they cannot describe, verbally or in writing.

  Programmers in the process of developing software are similarly constrained. The language in which they develop software places limits on the kinds of control structures, data structures, and abstractions they can use; thus the forms of algorithms they can construct are likewise limited. Awareness of a wider variety of programming language features can reduce such limitations in software development. Programmers can increase the range of their software development thought processes by learning new language constructs.

  It might be argued that learning the capabilities of other languages does not help a programmer who is forced to use a language that lacks those capabilities. That argument does not hold up, however, because often language constructs can be simulated in other languages that do not support those constructs directly. For example, a C programmer who had learned the structure and uses of associative arrays in Perl (Wall et al., 2000), might design structures that simulate associative arrays in that language. In other words, the study of programming language concepts builds an appreciation for valuable language features and encourages programmers to use them.

- *Improved background for choosing appropriate languages.* Many professional programmers have had little formal education in computer science; rather, they have learned programming on their own or through in-house training programs. Such training programs often teach only one or two languages that are directly relevant to the current projects of the organization. Many other programmers received their formal training in the distant past. The languages they learned then are no longer used, and many features now available in programming languages were not widely known. The result of this is that many programmers, when given a choice of languages for a new project, continue to use the language with which they are most familiar, even if it is poorly suited to the projects. If these programmers were familiar with a wider range of languages and language constructs, they would be better able to choose the language that includes the features that best address the characteristics of the problem at hand.

  Some of the features of one language often can be simulated in another language. However, it is always better to use a feature whose design has been integrated into a language than to use a simulation of that feature, which is often less elegant, more cumbersome, and less safe in a language that does not support it.

- *Increased ability to learn new languages.* Computer programming is still a relatively young discipline, and design methodologies, software development tools, and programming languages are still in a state of continuous evolution. This makes software development an exciting profession, but it also means that continuous learning is essential. The process of learning a new programming language can be lengthy and difficult, especially for someone who is comfortable with only one or two languages and has never examined programming language concepts in general. Once a thorough understanding of the fundamental concepts of languages is acquired, it becomes far easier to see how these concepts are incorporated into the design of the language being learned. For example, programmers who understand the concepts of object-oriented programming will have a much easier time learning Java (Arnold et al., 2006) than those who have never used those concepts.

  The same phenomenon occurs in natural languages. The better you know the grammar of your native language, the easier you will find it to learn a second natural language. Furthermore, learning a second language also has the beneficial side effect of teaching you more about your first language.

  The TIOBE Programming Community issues an index (`http://www.tiobe.com/tiobe_index/index.htm`) that is an indicator of the relative popularity of programing languages. For example, according to the index, Java, C, and C++ were the three most popular languages in use in January 2007. However, dozens of other languages were being fairly widely used at that time. The index data also show that the distribution of usage of progamming languages is always changing. Both the length of the list of languages in use and the dynamic nature of the statistics imply that every software developer frequently must learn different languages.

Finally, it is essential that practicing programmers know the vocabulary and fundamental concepts of programming languages so they can read and understand programming language descriptions and promotional literature for languages and compilers. These are the sources of information needed to both choose and learn a language.

- *Better understanding of the significance of implementation.* In learning the concepts of programming languages, it is both interesting and necessary to touch on the implementation issues that affect those concepts. In some cases, an understanding of implementation issues leads to an understanding of why languages are designed the way they are. This knowledge in turn leads to the ability to use a language more intelligently, as it was designed to be used. We can become better programmers by understanding the choices among programming language constructs and the consequences of those choices.

    Certain kinds of program bugs can be found and fixed only by a programmer who knows some related implementation details. Another benefit of understanding implementation issues is that it allows us to visualize how a computer executes various language constructs. In some cases, some knowledge of implementation issues provides hints about the relative efficiency of alternative constructs that may be chosen for a program. For example, programmers who know little about the complexity of the implementation of subprogram calls often do not realize that a small subprogram that is frequently called can be a highly inefficient design choice.

    Because this book touches on only a few of the issues of implementation, the previous two paragraphs also serve well as rationale for studying compiler design.

- *Better use of languages that are already known.* Many contemporary programming languages are large and complex. Accordingly, it is uncommon for a programmer to be familiar with and use all of the features of a language they frequently employ. By studying the concepts of programming languages, programmers can learn about previously unknown and unused parts of the languages they already use and begin to use those features.

- *Overall advancement of computing.* Finally, there is a global view of computing that can justify the study of programming language concepts. Although it is usually possible to determine why a particular programming language became popular, many believe, at least in retrospect, that the most popular languages are not always the best available. In some cases, it might be concluded that a language became widely used, at least in part, because those in positions to choose languages were not sufficiently familiar with programming language concepts.

For example, many people believe it would have been better if ALGOL 60 (Backus et al., 1963) had displaced Fortran (Metcalf, et al., 2004) in the early 1960s, because it was more elegant and had much better control statements than Fortran, among other reasons. That it did not is due partly to the programmers and software development managers of that time, many of whom did not clearly understand the conceptual design of ALGOL 60. They found its description difficult to read (which it was) and even more difficult to understand. They did not appreciate the benefits of block structure, recursion, and well-structured control statements, so they failed to see the benefits of ALGOL 60 over Fortran.

Of course, many other factors contributed to the lack of acceptance of ALGOL 60, as we will see in Chapter 2. However, the fact that computer users were generally unaware of the benefits of the language played a significant role.

In general, if those who choose languages were better informed, perhaps better languages would eventually squeeze out poorer ones.

1.2 Programming Domains

Computers have been applied to a myriad of different areas, from controlling nuclear power plants to providing video games in mobile phones. Because of this great diversity in computer use, programming languages with very different goals have been developed. In this section, we briefly discuss a few of the areas of computer applications and their associated languages.

1.2.1 Scientific Applications

The first digital computers, which appeared in the 1940s, were used and indeed invented for scientific applications. Typically, scientific applications have simple data structures but require large numbers of floating-point arithmetic computations. The most common data structures are arrays and matrices; the most common control structures are counting loops and selections. The early high-level programming languages invented for scientific applications were designed to provide for those needs. Their competition was assembly language, so efficiency was a primary concern. The first language for scientific applications was Fortran. ALGOL 60 and most of its descendants were also intended for use in this area, though they were designed to be used in other related areas also. For some scientific applications where efficiency is the primary concern, like those that were common in the 1950s and 1960s, no subsequent language is significantly better than Fortran.

1.2.2   Business Applications

The use of computers for business applications began in the 1950s. Special computers were developed for this purpose, along with special languages. The first successful high-level language for business was COBOL (ISO/IEC, 2002), the initial version of which appeared in 1960. It is still the most commonly used language for these applications. Business languages are characterized by facilities for producing elaborate reports, precise ways of describing and storing decimal numbers and character data, and the ability to specify decimal arithmetic operations.

There have been few developments in business application languages outside the development and evolution of COBOL. Therefore, this book includes only limited discussions of the structures in COBOL.

1.2.3   Artificial Intelligence

Artificial intelligence (AI) is a broad area of computer applications characterized by the use of symbolic rather than numeric computations. Symbolic computation means that symbols, consisting of names rather than numbers, are manipulated. Also, symbolic computation is more conveniently done with linked lists of data rather than arrays. This kind of programming sometimes requires more flexibility than other programming domains. For example, in some AI applications the ability to create and execute code segments during execution is convenient.

The first widely used programming language developed for AI applications was the functional language LISP (McCarthy et al., 1965), which appeared in 1959. Most AI applications developed prior to 1990 were written in LISP or one of its close relatives. During the early 1970s, however, an alternative approach to some of these applications appeared—logic programming using the Prolog (Clocksin and Mellish, 2003) language. More recently, some AI applications have been written in systems languages such as C. Scheme (Dybvig, 2003), a dialect of LISP, and Prolog are introduced in Chapters 15 and 16, respectively.

1.2.4   Systems Programming

The operating system and all of the programming support tools of a computer system are collectively known as its **systems software.** Systems software is used almost continuously and so must be efficient. Therefore, a language for this domain must provide fast execution. Furthermore, it must have low-level features that allow the software interfaces to external devices to be written.

In the 1960s and 1970s, some computer manufacturers, such as IBM, Digital, and Burroughs (now UNISYS), developed special machine-oriented high-level languages for systems software on their machines. For IBM mainframe computers, the language was PL/S, a dialect of PL/I; for Digital, it was

BLISS, a language at a level just above assembly language; for Burroughs, it was Extended ALGOL.

The UNIX operating system is written almost entirely in C (ISO, 1999), which has made it relatively easy to port, or move, to different machines. Some of the characteristics of C make it a good choice for systems programming. It is low-level, execution-efficient, and does not burden the user with many safety restrictions. Systems programmers are often excellent programmers and do not believe they need such restrictions. Some nonsystems programmers, however, find C to be too dangerous to use on large, important software systems.

1.2.5 Web Software

The World Wide Web is supported by an eclectic collection of languages, ranging from markup languages, such as XHTML, which is not a programming language, to general-purpose programming languages, such as Java. Because of the pervasive need for dynamic Web content, some computation capability is often included in the technology of content presentation. This functionality can be provided by embedding programming code in an XHTML document. Such code is often in the form of a scripting language, such as JavaScript or PHP. Alternatively, the XHTML document can request the execution of a separate program on the Web server to provide dynamic content. Such programs can be written in virtually any programming language. There are also some markup-like languages that have been extended to include constructs that control document processing, which are discussed in Section 1.5 and in Chapter 2.

1.3 Language Evaluation Criteria

As noted previously, the purpose of this book is to examine carefully the underlying concepts of the various constructs and capabilities of programming languages. We will also evaluate these features, focusing on their impact on the software development process, including maintenance. To do this, we need a set of evaluation criteria. Such a list of criteria is necessarily controversial, because it is virtually impossible to get even two computer scientists to agree on the value of some given language characteristic relative to others. In spite of these differences, most would agree that the criteria discussed in the following subsections are important.

Some of the characteristics that influence three of the four most important of these criteria are shown in Table 1.1, and the criteria themselves are discussed in the following sections.[1] Note that only the most important

---

1. The fourth primary criterion is cost, which is not included in the table because it is relatively unrelated to the other three criteria and the characteristics that influence them.

Table 1.1 Language evaluation criteria and the characteristics that affect them.

| | CRITERIA | | |
Characteristic	READABILITY	WRITABILITY	RELIABILITY
Simplicity	•	•	•
Orthogonality	•	•	•
Control structures	•	•	•
Data types and structures	•	•	•
Syntax design	•	•	•
Support for abstraction		•	•
Expressivity		•	•
Type checking			•
Exception handling			•
Restricted aliasing			•

characteristics are included in the table, mirroring the discussion in the following subsections. One could probably make the case that if one considered less important characteristics, virtually all table positions could include "bullets."

Note that some of these criteria are broad and somewhat vague, such as writability, whereas others are specific language constructs, such as exception handling. Although the discussion might seem to imply that the criteria have equal importance, that implication is not intended, and it is clearly not the case.

1.3.1 Readability

Perhaps one of the most important criteria for judging a programming language is the ease with which programs can be read and understood. Before 1970, software development was largely thought of in terms of writing code. The primary positive characteristics of programming languages were efficiency and machine readability. Language constructs were designed more from the point of view of the computer than of computer users. In the 1970s, however, the software life cycle concept (Booch, 1987) was developed; coding was relegated to a much smaller role, and maintenance was recognized as a major part of the cycle, particularly in terms of cost. Because ease of maintenance is determined in large part by the readability of programs, readability became an important measure of the quality of programs and programming languages. This was an important juncture in the evolution of programming languages. There was a distinct crossover from a focus on machine orientation to a focus on human orientation.

Readability must be considered in the context of the problem domain. For example, if a program that describes a computation is written in a language not designed for such use, the program may be unnatural and convoluted, making it unusually difficult to read.

The following subsections describe characteristics that contribute to the readability of a programming language.

1.3.1.1 Overall Simplicity

The overall simplicity of a programming language strongly affects its readability. A language that has a large number of basic constructs is more difficult to learn than one with a smaller number of them. Programmers who must use a large language often learn a subset of the language and ignore its other features. This learning pattern is sometimes used to excuse the large number of language constructs, but that argument is not valid. Readability problems occur whenever the program's author has learned a different subset from that subset with which the reader is familiar.

Another complicating characteristic of a programming language is **feature multiplicity**—that is, having more than one way to accomplish a particular operation. For example, in Java a user can increment a simple integer variable in four different ways:

```
count = count + 1
count += 1
count++
++count
```

Although the last two statements have slightly different meaning from each other and from the others in some contexts, all four have the same meaning when used as stand-alone expressions. These variations are discussed in Chapter 7.

A third potential problem is **operator overloading,** in which a single operator symbol has more than one meaning. Although this is often useful, it can lead to reduced readability if users are allowed to create their own overloading and do not do it sensibly. For example, it is clearly acceptable to overload + to use it for both integer and floating-point addition. In fact, this overloading simplifies a language by reducing the number of operators. However, suppose the programmer defined + used between single-dimensioned array operands to mean the sum of all elements of both arrays. Because the usual meaning of vector addition is quite different from this, it would make the program more confusing for both the author and the program's readers. An even more extreme example of program confusion would be a user defining + between two vector operands to mean the difference between their respective first elements. Operator overloading is further discussed in Chapter 7.

Simplicity in languages can, of course, be carried too far. For example, the form and meaning of most assembly language statements are models of simplicity, as you can see when you consider the statements that appear in the next section. This very simplicity, however, makes assembly language programs less readable. Because they lack more complex control statements, program structure is less obvious; because the statements are simple, far more of them are required than in equivalent programs in a high-level language. These same arguments apply to the less extreme case of high-level languages with inadequate control and data-structuring constructs.

1.3.1.2 Orthogonality

Orthogonality in a programming language means that a relatively small set of primitive constructs can be combined in a relatively small number of ways to build the control and data structures of the language. Furthermore, every possible combination of primitives is legal and meaningful. For example, consider data types. Suppose a language has four primitive data types (integer, float, double, and character) and two type operators (array and pointer). If the two type operators can be applied to themselves and the four primitive data types, a large number of data structures can be defined.

The meaning of an orthogonal language feature is independent of the context of its appearance in a program. (The name *orthogonal* comes from the mathematical concept of orthogonal vectors, which are independent of each other.) Orthogonality follows from a symmetry of relationships among primitives. Pointers should be able to point to any type of variable or data structure. The lack of orthogonality leads to exceptions to the rules of the language. For example, if pointers were not allowed to point to arrays, many of those possibilities would be eliminated.

We can illustrate the use of orthogonality as a design concept by comparing one aspect of the assembly languages of the IBM mainframe computers and the VAX series of superminicomputers. We consider a single simple situation: adding two 32-bit integer values that reside in either memory or registers and replacing one of the two values with the sum. The IBM mainframes have two instructions for this purpose, which have the forms

```
A  Reg1, memory_cell
AR Reg1, Reg2
```

where `Reg1` and `Reg2` represent registers. The semantics of these are

```
Reg1 ← contents(Reg1) + contents(memory_cell)
Reg1 ← contents(Reg1) + contents(Reg2)
```

The VAX addition instruction for 32-bit integer values is

```
ADDL  operand_1, operand_2
```

whose semantics is

```
operand_2 ← contents(operand_1) + contents(operand_2)
```

In this case, either operand can be a register or a memory cell.

The VAX instruction design is orthogonal in that a single instruction can use either registers or memory cells as the operands. There are two ways to specify operands, which can be combined in all possible ways. The IBM design is not orthogonal. Only two operand combinations are legal out of four possibilities, and the two require different instructions, A and AR. The IBM design is more restricted and therefore less writable. For example, you cannot add two values and store the sum in a memory location. Furthermore, the IBM design is more difficult to learn because of the restrictions and the additional instruction.

Orthogonality is closely related to simplicity: The more orthogonal the design of a language, the fewer exceptions the language rules require. Fewer exceptions mean a higher degree of regularity in the design, which makes the language easier to learn, read, and understand. Anyone who has learned a significant part of the English language can testify to the difficulty of learning its many rule exceptions (for example, *i* before *e* except after *c*).

As examples of the lack of orthogonality in a high-level language, consider the following rules and exceptions in C. Although C has two kinds of structured data types, arrays and records (**struct**s), records can be returned from functions but arrays cannot. A member of a structure can be any data type except **void** or a structure of the same type. An array element can be any data type except **void** or a function. Parameters are passed by value, unless they are arrays, in which case they are, in effect, passed by reference (because the appearance of an array name without a subscript in a C program is interpreted to be the address of the array's first element).

As an example of context dependence, consider the C expression

```
a + b
```

This expression often means that the values of **a** and b are fetched and added together. However, if a happens to be a pointer, that affects the value of b. For example, if a points to a float value that occupies four bytes, then the value of b must be scaled—in this case multiplied by 4—before it is added to a. Therefore, the type of a affects the treatment of the value of b. The context of b affects its meaning.

Too much orthogonality can also cause problems. Perhaps the most orthogonal programming language is ALGOL 68 (van Wijngaarden et al., 1969). Every language construct in ALGOL 68 has a type, and there are no restrictions on those types. In addition, most constructs produce values. This combinational freedom allows extremely complex constructs. For example, a conditional can appear as the left side of an assignment, along with declarations and other assorted statements, as long as the result is an address. This extreme form of orthogonality leads to unnecessary complexity. Furthermore, because languages require a large number of primitives, a high degree of orthogonality results in an explosion of combinations. So, even if the combinations are simple, their sheer numbers lead to complexity.

Simplicity in a language, therefore, is at least in part the result of a combination of a relatively small number of primitive constructs and a limited use of the concept of orthogonality.

Some believe that functional languages offer a good combination of simplicity and orthogonality. A functional language, such as LISP, is one in which computations are made primarily by applying functions to given parameters. In contrast, in imperative languages such as C, C++, and Java, computations are usually specified with variables and assignment statements. Functional languages offer potentially the greatest overall simplicity, because they can accomplish everything with a single construct, the function call, which can be combined with other function calls in simple ways. This simple elegance is the reason why some language researchers are attracted to functional languages as the primary alternative to complex nonfunctional languages such as C++. Other factors, such as efficiency, however, have prevented functional languages from becoming more widely used.

1.3.1.3 Control Statements

The structured-programming revolution of the 1970s was in part a reaction to the poor readability caused by the inadequate control statements of some of the languages of the 1950s and 1960s. In particular, it became widely recognized that indiscriminate use of goto statements severely reduces program readability. A program that can be read from top to bottom is much easier to understand than a program that requires the reader to jump from one statement to some nonadjacent statement in order to follow the execution order. For example, consider the following nested loops, written in C:

```
while (incr <  20) {
   while (sum <= 100) {
      sum += incr;
   }
   incr++;
}
```

If C did not have its **while** statement, as was the case with early versions of Fortran, this code would be written as follows:

```
loop1:
  if (incr >= 20) go to out;
loop2:
 if (sum >  100) go to next;
  sum += incr;
  go to loop2;
next:
  incr++;
  go to loop1;
out:
```

The versions of BASIC and Fortran that were available in the early 1970s lacked the control statements that allow strong restrictions on the use of gotos, so writing highly readable programs in those languages was difficult. Most programming languages designed since the late 1960s, however, have included sufficient control statements, so the need for the goto statement has been greatly reduced, if not eliminated. Therefore, the control statement design of a language is now a less important factor in readability than it was in the past.

Of course, poorly structured programs can be written in any language, and the inclusion of a goto statement in a language practically invites one to write such programs. Therefore, while adequate control statements allow a language to be used to write well-structured and readable programs, the mere presence of such statements certainly does not guarantee that programs will be readable.

1.3.1.4 Data Types and Structures

The presence of adequate facilities for defining data types and data structures in a language is another significant aid to readability. For example, suppose a numeric type is used for an indicator flag because there is no Boolean type in the language. In such a language, we might have an assignment such as

```
timeOut = 1
```

whose meaning is unclear, whereas in a language that includes Boolean types, we would have

```
timeOut = true
```

whose meaning is perfectly clear. Similarly, record data types provide a method for representing employee records that is more readable than using a collection of similar arrays, one for each data item in an employee record, which is the required method in a language without records. For example, in Fortran 95, an array of employee records might be stored in the following arrays:

```
Character (Len = 30):: Name (100)
Integer:: Age (100), Employee_Number (100)
Real:: Salary (100)
```

Then a particular employee is represented by the elements of these four arrays with the same subscript value.

1.3.1.5 Syntax Design

The syntax, or form, of the elements of a language has a significant effect on the readability of programs. The following are two examples of syntactic design choices that affect readability:

- *Identifier forms*. Restricting identifiers to very short lengths detracts from readability. If identifiers can have six characters at most, as in Fortran 77, it is often impossible to use connotative names for variables. A more extreme example is the original American National Standards Institute (ANSI) BASIC (ANSI, 1978b), in which an identifier could consist only of a single letter or a single letter followed by a single digit. Other design issues concerning identifier forms are discussed in Chapter 5.

- *Special words*. Program appearance and thus program readability are strongly influenced by the forms of a language's special words (for example, **while, class,** and **for**). Especially important is the method of forming compound statements, or statement groups, primarily in control constructs. Some languages have used matching pairs of special words or symbols to form groups. C and its descendants use braces to specify compound statements. All of these languages suffer because statement groups are always terminated in the same way, which makes it difficult to determine which group is being ended when an **end** or } appears. Fortran 95 and Ada make this clearer by using a distinct closing syntax for each type of statement group. For example, Ada uses **end if** to terminate a selection construct, and **end loop** to terminate a loop construct. This is an example of the conflict between simplicity that results in fewer reserved words, as in C++, and the greater readability that can result from using more reserved words, as in Ada.

  Another important issue is whether the special words of a language can be used as names for program variables. If so, the resulting programs can be very confusing. For example, in Fortran 95, special words such as Do and End are legal variable names, so the appearance of these words in a program may or may not connote something special.

- *Form and meaning*. Designing statements so that their appearance at least partially indicates their purpose is an obvious aid to readability. Semantics, or meaning, should follow directly from syntax, or form. In some cases, this principle is violated by two language constructs that are identical or similar in appearance but have different meanings, depending perhaps on context. In C, for example, the meaning of the reserved word **static** depends on the context of its appearance. If used on the definition of a variable inside a function, it means the variable is created at compile time. If used on the definition of a variable that is outside all functions, it means the variable is visible only in the file in which its definition appears; that is, it is not exported from that file.

One of the primary complaints about the shell commands of UNIX (Raymond, 2004) is that their appearance does not always suggest their function.

For example, the meaning of the UNIX command `grep` can be deciphered only through prior knowledge, or perhaps cleverness and familiarity with the UNIX editor, ed. Its appearance connotes nothing to UNIX beginners. (In ed, the command */regular_expression/* searches for a substring that matches the regular expression. Preceding this with g makes it a global command, specifying that the scope of the search is the whole file being edited. Following the command with p specifies that lines with the matching substring are to be printed. So g/*regular_expression*/p, which can obviously be abbreviated as `grep`, prints all lines in a file that contain substrings that match the regular expression.)

1.3.2 Writability

Writability is a measure of how easily a language can be used to create programs for a chosen problem domain. Most of the language characteristics that affect readability also affect writability. This follows directly from the fact that the process of writing a program requires the programmer frequently to reread the part of the program that is already written.

As is the case with readability, writability must be considered in the context of the target problem domain of a language. It is simply not reasonable to compare the writability of two languages in the realm of a particular application when one was designed for that application and the other was not. For example, the writabilities of COBOL and Fortran are dramatically different for creating a program to deal with two-dimensional arrays, for which Fortran is ideal. Their writabilities are also quite different for producing financial reports with complex formats, for which COBOL was designed.

The following subsections describe the most important characteristics influencing the writability of a language.

1.3.2.1 Simplicity and Orthogonality

If a language has a large number of different constructs, some programmers might not be familiar with all of them. This situation can lead to a misuse of some features and a disuse of others that may be either more elegant or more efficient, or both, than those that are used. It may even be possible, as noted by Hoare (1973), to use unknown features accidentally, with bizarre results. Therefore, a smaller number of primitive constructs and a consistent set of rules for combining them (that is, orthogonality) is much better than simply having a large number of primitives. A programmer can design a solution to a complex problem after learning only a simple set of primitive constructs.

On the other hand, too much orthogonality can be a detriment to writability. Errors in programs can go undetected when nearly any combination of primitives is legal. This can lead to absurdities in code that cannot be discovered by the compiler.

1.3.2.2 Support for Abstraction

Briefly, **abstraction** means the ability to define and then use complicated structures or operations in ways that allow many of the details to be ignored. Abstraction is a key concept in contemporary programming language design. This is a reflection of the central role that abstraction plays in modern program design methodologies. The degree of abstraction allowed by a programming language and the naturalness of its expression are therefore very important to its writability. Programming languages can support two distinct categories of abstraction, process and data.

A simple example of process abstraction is the use of a subprogram to implement a sort algorithm that is required several times in a program. Without the subprogram, the sort code would have to be replicated in all places where it was needed, which would make the program much longer and more tedious to write. More important, if the subprogram were not used, the code that used the sort subprogram would be cluttered with the sort algorithm details, greatly obscuring the flow and overall intent of that code.

As an example of data abstraction, consider a binary tree that stores integer data in its nodes. Such a binary tree would usually be implemented in a language that does not support pointers and dynamic storage management with a heap, such as Fortran 77, as three parallel integer arrays, where two of the integers are used as subscripts to specify offspring nodes. In C++ and Java, these trees can be implemented by using an abstraction of a tree node in the form of a simple class with two pointers (or references) and an integer. The naturalness of the latter representation makes it much easier to write a program that uses binary trees in these languages than to write one in Fortran 77. It is a simple matter of the problem solution domain of the language being closer to the problem domain.

The overall support for abstraction is clearly an important factor in the writability of a language.

1.3.2.3 Expressivity

Expressivity in a language can refer to several different characteristics. In a language like APL (Gilman & Rose, 1984), it means that there are very powerful operators that allow a great deal of computation to be accomplished with a very small program. It more commonly means that a language has relatively convenient, rather than cumbersome, ways of specifying computations. For example, in C, the notation `count++` is more convenient and shorter than `count = count + 1`. Also, the **and then** Boolean operator in Ada is a convenient way of specifying short-circuit evaluation of a Boolean expression. The inclusion of the **for** statement in Java makes writing counting loops easier than with the use of **while,** which is also possible. All of these increase the writability of a language.

1.3.3 Reliability

A program is said to be reliable if it performs to its specifications under all conditions. The following subsections describe several language features that have a significant effect on the reliability of programs in a given language.

1.3.3.1 Type Checking

Type checking is simply testing for type errors in a given program, either by the compiler or during program execution. Type checking is an important factor in language reliability. Because run-time type checking is expensive, compile-time type checking is more desirable. Furthermore, the earlier errors in programs are detected, the less expensive it is to make the required repairs. The design of Java requires checks of the types of nearly all variables and expressions at compile time. This virtually eliminates type errors at run time in Java programs. Types and type checking are discussed in depth in Chapters 5 and 6.

One example of how failure to type check, at either compile time or run time, has led to countless program errors is the use of subprogram parameters in the original C language (Kernighan and Ritchie, 1978). In this language, the type of an actual parameter in a function call was not checked to determine whether its type matched that of the corresponding formal parameter in the function. An **int** type variable could be used as an actual parameter in a call to a function that expected a **float** type as its formal parameter, and neither the compiler nor the run-time system would have detected the inconsistency. For example, because the bit string that represents the integer 23 is essentially unrelated to the bit string that represents a floating-point 23, if an integer 23 is sent to a function that expects a floating-point parameter, any uses of the parameter in the function will of course produce nonsense. Furthermore, such problems are often difficult to diagnose.[2] The current version of C has eliminated this problem by requiring all parameters to be type checked. Subprograms and parameter-passing techniques are discussed in Chapter 9.

1.3.3.2 Exception Handling

The ability of a program to intercept run-time errors (as well as other unusual conditions detected by the program), take corrective measures, and then continue is an obvious aid to reliability. This language facility is called **exception handling.** Ada, C++, and Java include extensive capabilities for exception handling, but such facilities are practically nonexistent in many widely used languages, including C and Fortran. Exception handling is discussed in Chapter 14.

---

2. In response to this and other similar problems, UNIX systems include a utility program named `lint` that checks C programs for such problems.

1.3.3.3 Aliasing

Loosely defined, **aliasing** is having two or more distinct names that can be used to access the same memory cell. It is now widely accepted that aliasing is a dangerous feature in a programming language. Most programming languages allow some kind of aliasing—for example, two pointers set to point to the same variable, which is possible in most languages. In such a program, the programmer must always remember that changing the value pointed to by one of the two changes the value referenced by the other. Some kinds of aliasing, as described in Chapters 5 and 9, can be prohibited by the design of a language.

In some languages, aliasing is used to overcome deficiencies in the language's data abstraction facilities. Other languages greatly restrict aliasing to increase their reliability.

1.3.3.4 Readability and Writability

Both readability and writability influence reliability. A program written in a language that does not support natural ways to express the required algorithms will necessarily use unnatural approaches. Unnatural approaches are less likely to be correct for all possible situations. The easier a program is to write, the more likely it is to be correct.

Readability affects reliability in both the writing and maintenance phases of the life cycle. Programs that are difficult to read are difficult both to write and to modify.

1.3.4   Cost

The ultimate total cost of a programming language is a function of many of its characteristics.

First, there is the cost of training programmers to use the language, which is a function of the simplicity and orthogonality of the language and the experience of the programmers. Though more powerful languages need not be harder to learn, they often are.

Second is the cost of writing programs in the language. This is a function of the writability of the language, which depends in part on its closeness in purpose to the particular application. The original efforts to design and implement high-level languages were driven by the desire to lower the costs of creating software.

Both the cost of training programmers and the cost of writing programs in a language can be significantly reduced in a good programming environment. Programming environments are discussed in Section 1.8.

Third is the cost of compiling programs in the language. A major impediment to the early use of Ada was the prohibitively high cost of running the first-generation Ada compilers. This problem was diminished by the appearance of better Ada compilers.

Fourth, the cost of executing programs written in a language is greatly influenced by that language's design. A language that requires many run-time type checks will prohibit fast code execution, regardless of the quality of the compiler. Although execution efficiency was the foremost concern in the design of early languages, it is now considered to be less important.

A simple trade-off can be made between compilation cost and execution speed of the compiled code. **Optimization** is the name given to the collection of techniques that compilers may use to decrease the size and/or increase the execution speed of the code they produce. If little or no optimization is done, compilation can be done much faster than if a significant effort is made to produce optimized code. The extra compilation effort results in faster code execution. The choice between the two alternatives is influenced by the environment in which the compiler will be used. In a laboratory for beginning programming students, who use a great deal of compiling time but little code execution time (their programs are small and they must execute correctly only once), little or no optimization should be done. In a production environment, where compiled programs are executed many times, it is better to pay the extra cost to optimize the code.

The fifth factor in the cost of a language is the cost of the language implementation system. One of the factors that explains the rapid acceptance of Java is that free compiler/interpreter systems have been available for it since soon after its design was first released. A language whose implementation system is either expensive or runs only on expensive hardware will have a much smaller chance of ever becoming widely used. For example, the high cost of first-generation Ada compilers helped prevent Ada from becoming popular in the early days.

Sixth is the cost of poor reliability. If the software fails in a critical system, such as a nuclear power plant or an X-ray machine for medical use, the cost could be very high. The failures of noncritical systems can also be very expensive in terms of lost future business or lawsuits over defective software systems.

The final consideration is the cost of maintaining programs, which includes both corrections and modifications to add new capabilities. The cost of software maintenance depends on a number of language characteristics; primarily, readability. Because maintenance is often done by individuals other than the original author of the software, poor readability can make the task extremely challenging.

The importance of maintainability of software cannot be overstated. It has been estimated that for large software systems with relatively long lifetimes, maintenance costs can be as high as two to four times as much as development costs (Sommerville, 2005).

Of all the contributors to language costs, three are most important: program development, maintenance, and reliability. Because these are functions of writability and readability, these two evaluation criteria are, in turn, the most important.

Of course, a number of other criteria could be used for evaluating programming languages. One example is **portability,** or the ease with which programs can be moved from one implementation to another. Portability is most strongly influenced by the degree of standardization of the language. Some languages, such as BASIC, are not standardized at all, making programs in these languages very difficult to move from one implementation to another. Standardization is a time-consuming and difficult process. A committee began work on producing a standard version of C++ in 1989. It was approved in 1998.

Generality (the applicability to a wide range of applications) and **well-definedness** (the completeness and precision of the language's official defining document) are two other criteria.

Most criteria, particularly readability, writability, and reliability, are neither precisely defined nor exactly measurable. Nevertheless, they are useful concepts and they provide valuable insight into the design and evaluation of programming languages.

A final note on evaluation criteria: Language design criteria are weighed differently from different perspectives. Language implementors are concerned primarily with the difficulty of implementing the constructs and features of the language. Language users are worried about writability first and readability later. Language designers are likely to emphasize elegance and the ability to attract widespread use. These characteristics sometimes conflict with one another.

1.4 Influences on Language Design

In addition to those factors described in Section 1.3, several other factors influence the basic design of programming languages. The most important of these are computer architecture and program design methodologies.

1.4.1 Computer Architecture

The basic architecture of computers has had a profound effect on language design. Most of the popular languages of the past 50 years have been designed around the prevalent computer architecture, called the von Neumann architecture, after one of its originators, John von Neumann (pronounced "von Noyman"). These languages are called **imperative** languages. In a von Neumann computer, both data and programs are stored in the same memory. The central processing unit (CPU), which executes instructions, is separate from the memory. Therefore, instructions and data must be piped, or transmitted, from memory to the CPU. Results of operations in the CPU must be moved back to memory. Nearly all digital computers built since the 1940s have been based on the von Neumann architecture. The overall structure of a von Neumann computer is shown in Figure 1.1.

Because of the von Neumann architecture, the central features of imperative languages are variables, which model the memory cells; assignment statements, which are based on the piping operation; and the iterative form of repetition, which is the most efficient way to implement repetition on this

Figure 1.1

The von Neumann
computer architecture

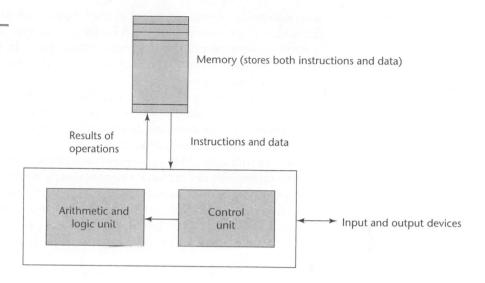

Memory (stores both instructions and data)

Results of operations

Instructions and data

Arithmetic and logic unit

Control unit

Input and output devices

Central processing unit

architecture. Operands in expressions are piped from memory to the CPU, and the result of evaluating the expression is piped back to the memory cell represented by the left side of the assignment. Iteration is fast on von Neumann computers because instructions are stored in adjacent cells of memory and repeating the execution of a section of code requires only a simple branch instruction. This efficiency discourages the use of recursion for repetition, although recursion is sometimes more natural.

The execution of a machine code program on a von Neumann architecture computer occurs in a process called the **fetch-execute cycle.** As stated earlier, programs reside in memory but are executed in the CPU. Each instruction to be executed must be moved from memory to the processor. The address of the next instruction to be executed is maintained in a register called the **program counter.** The fetch-execute cycle can be simply described by the following algorithm:

initialize the program counter
repeat forever
    fetch the instruction pointed to by the program counter
    increment the program counter to point at the next instruction
    decode the instruction
    execute the instruction
end repeat

The "decode the instruction" step in the algorithm means the instruction is examined to determine what action it specifies. Program execution terminates when a stop instruction is encountered, although on an actual computer a stop instruction is rarely executed. Rather, control transfers from the operating system to a user program for its execution and then back to the operating system when the user program execution is complete. In a computer system in which more than one user program may be in memory at a given time, this process is far more complex.

As stated earlier, a functional, or applicative, language is one in which the primary means of computation is applying functions to given parameters. Programming can be done in a functional language without the kind of variables that are used in imperative languages, without assignment statements, and without iteration. Although many computer scientists have expounded on the myriad benefits of functional languages, such as Scheme, it is unlikely that they will displace the imperative languages until a non–von Neumann computer is designed that allows efficient execution of programs in functional languages. Among those who have bemoaned this fact, the most eloquent has been John Backus, the principal designer of the original version of Fortran (Backus, 1978).

The parallel-architecture machines that have appeared over the past 25 years hold some promise for speeding the execution of functional programs, but so far it has not been enough to make them competitive with imperative programs. In fact, although there are elegant ways of using parallel architectures to execute functional programs, most parallel machines are used for imperative programs, particularly those written in dialects of Fortran.

In spite of the fact that the structure of imperative programming languages is modeled on a machine architecture, rather than on the abilities and inclinations of the users of programming languages, some believe that using imperative languages is somehow more natural than using a functional language.

1.4.2 Programming Methodologies

The late 1960s and early 1970s brought an intense analysis, begun in large part by the structured-programming movement, of both the software development process and programming language design.

An important reason for this research was the shift in the major cost of computing from hardware to software, as hardware costs decreased and programmer costs increased. Increases in programmer productivity were relatively small. In addition, progressively larger and more complex problems were being solved by computers. Rather than simply solving sets of equations to simulate satellite tracks, as in the early 1960s, programs were being written for large and complex tasks, such as controlling large petroleum-refining facilities and providing worldwide airline reservation systems.

The new software development methodologies that emerged as a result of the research of the 1970s were called top-down design and stepwise refinement. The primary programming language deficiencies that were discovered were incompleteness of type checking and inadequacy of control statements (requiring the extensive use of gotos).

In the late 1970s, a shift from procedure-oriented to data-oriented program design methodologies began. Simply put, data-oriented methods emphasize data design, focusing on the use of abstract data types to solve problems.

For data abstraction to be used effectively in software system design, it must be supported by the languages used for implementation. The first language to provide even limited support for data abstraction was SIMULA 67 (Birtwistle et al., 1973), although that language certainly was not propelled to popularity because of it. The benefits of data abstraction were not widely recognized until the early 1970s. However, most languages designed since the late 1970s support data abstraction. Data abstraction is discussed in detail in Chapter 11.

The latest step in the evolution of data-oriented software development, which began in the early 1980s, is object-oriented design. Object-oriented methodology begins with data abstraction, which encapsulates processing with data objects and controls access to data, and adds inheritance and dynamic method binding. Inheritance is a powerful concept that greatly enhances the potential reuse of existing software, thereby providing the possibility of significant increases in software development productivity. This is an important factor in the increase in popularity of object-oriented languages. Dynamic (run-time) method binding allows more flexible use of inheritance.

Object-oriented programming developed along with a language that supported its concepts: Smalltalk (Goldberg and Robson, 1989). Although Smalltalk never became as widely used as some other languages, support for object-oriented programming is now part of most popular imperative languages, including Ada 95 (ARM, 1995), Java, and C++. Object-oriented concepts have also found their way into functional programming in CLOS (Bobrow et al., 1988) and logic programming in Prolog++ (Moss, 1994). Language support for object-oriented programming is discussed in detail in Chapter 12.

Procedure-oriented programming is, in a sense, the opposite of data-oriented programming. Although data-oriented methods now dominate software development, procedure-oriented methods have not been abandoned. On the contrary, a good deal of research has occurred in procedure-oriented programming in recent years, especially in the area of concurrency. These research efforts brought with them the need for language facilities for creating and controlling concurrent program units. Ada, Java, and C# include such capabilities. Concurrency is discussed in detail in Chapter 13.

All of these evolutionary steps in software development methodologies led to new language constructs to support them.

1.5 Language Categories

Programming languages are often categorized into four bins: imperative, functional, logic, and object-oriented. However, we do not consider languages that support object-oriented programming to form a separate category of languages. We have described how the most popular languages that support object-oriented programming grew out of imperative languages. Although the object-oriented software development paradigm differs greatly from the procedure-oriented paradigm usually used with imperative languages, the extensions to an imperative language required to support object-oriented programming are not overwhelming. For example, the expressions, assignment statements, and control statements of C and Java are nearly identical. (On the other hand, the arrays, subprograms, and semantics of Java are very different from those of C.) Similar statements can be made for functional languages that support object-oriented programming.

Another kind of language, the visual languages, is a subcategory of the imperative languages. The most popular visual language is Visual BASIC (Schneider, 1999), which is now being replaced by Visual BASIC .NET (Deitel, et al., 2002). These languages (or their implementations) include capabilities for drag-and-drop generation of code segments. Such languages were once called fourth-generation languages, though that name has now fallen out of use. The visual languages provide a simple way to generate graphical user interfaces to programs. For example, in Visual BASIC, the code to produce a display of a form control, such as a button or text box, can be created with a single keystroke. These capabilities are now available in all of the .NET languages.

Some authors refer to scripting languages as a separate category of programming languages. However, languages in this category are bound together more by their implementation method, partial or full interpretation, than by a common language design. The languages that are typically called scripting languages, among them Perl, JavaScript, and Ruby, are imperative languages in every sense.

A logic programming language is an example of a rule-based language. In an imperative language, an algorithm is specified in great detail, and the specific order of execution of the instructions or statements must be included. In a rule-based language, however, rules are specified in no particular order, and the language implementation system must choose an execution order that produces the desired result. This approach to software development is radically different from those used with the other three categories of languages and clearly requires a completely different kind of language. Prolog, the most commonly used logic programming language, and logic programming are discussed in Chapter 16.

In recent years, a new category of languages has emerged, the markup/programming hybrid languages. Markup languages are not programming languages. For instance, XHTML, the most widely used markup language, is used to specify the layout of information in Web documents. However, some programming capability has crept into some extensions to XHTML and XML. Among these are the Java Server Pages Standard Tag Library (JSTL) and eXtensible Stylesheet Language Transformations (XSLT). Both of these are briefly introduced in Chapter 2. Those languages cannot be compared to any of the complete programming languages, and therefore will not be discussed after Chapter 2.

A host of special-purpose languages have appeared over the past 40 years. These range from Report Program Generator (RPG), which is used to produce business reports, to Automatically Programmed Tools (APT), which is used for instructing programmable machine tools, to General Purpose Simulation System (GPSS), which is used for systems simulation. This book does not discuss special-purpose languages, primarily because of their narrow applicability and the difficulty of comparing them with other languages.

1.6 Language Design Trade-offs

The programming language evaluation criteria described in Section 1.3 provide a framework for language design. Unfortunately, that framework is self-contradictory. In his insightful paper on language design, Hoare (1973) states that "there are so many important but conflicting criteria, that their reconciliation and satisfaction is a major engineering task."

Two criteria that conflict are reliability and cost of execution. For example, the Java language definition demands that all references to array elements be checked to ensure that the index or indices are in their legal ranges. This step adds a great deal to the cost of execution of Java programs that contain large numbers of references to array elements. C does not require index range checking, so C programs execute faster than semantically equivalent Java programs, although Java programs are more reliable. The designers of Java traded execution efficiency for reliability.

As another example of conflicting criteria that leads directly to design trade-offs, consider the case of APL. APL includes a powerful set of operators for array operands. Because of the large number of operators, a significant number of new symbols had to be included in APL to represent the operators. Also, many APL operators can be used in a single long, complex expression. One result of this high degree of expressivity is that, for applications involving many array operations, APL is very writable. Indeed, a huge amount of computation can be specified in a very compact program. Another result is that APL programs have very poor readability. A compact and concise expression has a certain mathematical beauty but is difficult for anyone other than the person who wrote it to understand. The well-known author Daniel McCracken once noted that it took him four hours to read and understand a four-line APL program (McCracken, 1970). The designer of APL traded readability for writability.

The conflict between writability and reliability is a common one in language design. The pointers of C++ can be manipulated in a variety of ways, which leads to highly flexible addressing of data. Because of the potential reliability problems with pointers, they are not included in Java.

Examples of conflicts among language design (and evaluation) criteria abound; some are subtle, others are obvious. It is therefore clear that the task of choosing constructs and features when designing a programming language requires many compromises and trade-offs.

1.7 Implementation Methods

As described in Section 1.4.1, two of the primary components of a computer are its internal memory and its processor. The internal memory is used to store programs and data. The processor is a collection of circuits that provides a realization of a set of primitive operations, or machine instructions, such as those for arithmetic and logic operations. In most computers, some of these instructions, which are sometimes called macroinstructions, are actually implemented with a set of instructions called microinstructions, which are defined at an even lower level. Because microinstructions are never seen by software, they will not be discussed further here.

The machine language of the computer is its set of instructions. In the absence of other supporting software, its own machine language is the only language that most hardware computers "understand." Theoretically, a computer could be designed and built with a particular high-level language as its machine language, but it would be very complex and expensive. Furthermore, it would be highly inflexible, because it would be difficult (though not impossible) to use it with other high-level languages. The more practical machine design choice implements in hardware a very low-level language that provides the most commonly needed primitive operations and requires system software to create an interface to programs in higher-level languages.

A language implementation system cannot be the only software on a computer. Also required is a large collection of programs, called the operating system, which supplies higher-level primitives than those of the machine language. These primitives provide system resource management, input and output operations, a file management system, text and/or program editors, and a variety of other commonly needed functions. Because language implementation systems need many of the operating system facilities, they interface to the operating system rather than directly to the processor (in machine language).

The operating system and language implementations are layered over the machine language interface of a computer. These layers can be thought of as virtual computers, providing interfaces to the user at higher levels. For example, an operating system and a C compiler provide a virtual C computer. With other compilers, a machine can become other kinds of virtual computers. Most computer systems provide several different virtual computers. User programs form another layer over the top of the layer of virtual computers. The layered view of a computer is shown in Figure 1.2.

The implementation systems of the first high-level programming languages, constructed in the late 1950s, were among the most complex software systems of that time. In the 1960s, intensive research efforts were made to understand and formalize the process of constructing these high-level language implementations. The greatest success of those efforts was in the area of syntax analysis, primarily because that part of the implementation process is an application of parts of automata theory and formal language theory that were then well understood.

Figure 1.2

Layered interface of virtual computers, provided by a typical computer system

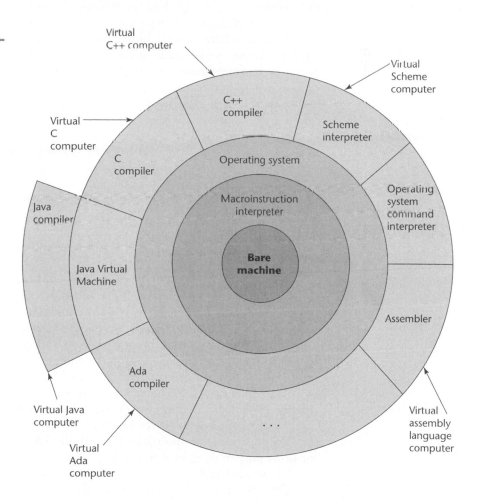

1.7.1 Compilation

Programming languages can be implemented by any of three general methods. At one extreme, programs can be translated into machine language, which can be executed directly on the computer. This method is called a **compiler implementation,** and has the advantage of very fast program execution, once the translation process is complete. Most production implementations of languages such as C, COBOL, and Ada are by compilers.

The language that a compiler translates is called the **source language.** The process of compilation and program execution takes place in several phases, the most important of which are shown in Figure 1.3.

The lexical analyzer gathers the characters of the source program into lexical units. The lexical units of a program are identifiers, special words, operators, and punctuation symbols. The lexical analyzer ignores comments in the source program, because the compiler has no use for them.

The syntax analyzer takes the lexical units from the lexical analyzer and uses them to construct hierarchical structures called **parse trees.** These parse trees represent the syntactic structure of the program. In many cases, no actual parse tree structure is constructed; rather, the information that would be required to build a tree is generated and used directly. Both lexical units and parse trees are further discussed in Chapter 3. Both lexical analysis and syntax analysis, or parsing, are discussed in Chapter 4.

The intermediate code generator produces a program in a different language, at an intermediate level between the source program and the final output of the compiler, the machine language program.[3] Intermediate languages sometimes look very much like assembly languages and in fact sometimes are actual assembly languages. In other cases, the intermediate code is at a level somewhat higher than an assembly language. The semantic analyzer is an integral part of the intermediate code generator. The semantic analyzer checks for errors that are difficult if not impossible to detect during syntax analysis, such as type errors.

Optimization, which improves programs (usually in their intermediate code version) by making them smaller or faster or both, is often an optional part of compilation. In fact, some compilers are incapable of doing any significant optimization. This type of compiler would be used in situations where execution speed of the translated program is far less important than compilation speed. An example of such a situation is a computing laboratory for beginning programmers. In most commercial and industrial situations, execution speed is more important than compilation speed, so optimization is routinely desirable. Because many kinds of optimization are difficult to do on machine language, most optimization is done on the intermediate code.

The code generator translates the optimized intermediate code version of the program into an equivalent machine language program.

The symbol table serves as a database for the compilation process. The primary contents of the symbol table are the type and attribute information of each user-defined name in the program. This information is placed in the

---

3. Note that the words *program* and *code* are often used interchangeably.

Figure 1.3

The compilation process

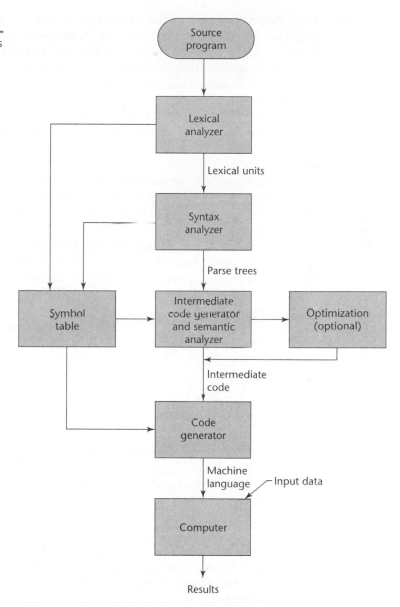

symbol table by the lexical and syntax analyzers and is used by the semantic analyzer and the code generator.

   As stated previously, although the machine language generated by a compiler can be executed directly on the hardware, it must nearly always be run along with some other code. Most user programs also require programs from the operating system. Among the most common of these are programs for input and output. The compiler builds calls to required system programs when they are needed by the user program. Before the machine language programs produced by a compiler can be executed, the required programs from the operating system must be found and linked to the user program. The linking operation connects the user program to the system programs by placing the addresses of the entry points of the system programs in the calls to them in the user program. The user and system code together are sometimes called a **load module,** or **executable image.** The process of collecting system programs and linking them to user programs is called **linking and loading,** or sometimes just **linking.** It is accomplished by a systems program called a **linker.**

In addition to systems programs, user programs must often be linked to previously compiled user programs that reside in libraries. So the linker not only links a given program to system programs, it may also link it to other user programs.

The speed of the connection between a computer's memory and its processor usually determines the speed of the computer, because instructions often can be executed faster than they can be moved to the processor for execution. This connection is called the **von Neumann bottleneck;** it is the primary limiting factor in the speed of von Neumann architecture computers. The von Neumann bottleneck has been one of the primary motivations for the research and development of parallel computers.

1.7.2   Pure Interpretation

Pure interpretation lies at the opposite end (from compilation) of implementation methods. With this approach, programs are interpreted by another program called an interpreter, with no translation whatever. The interpreter program acts as a software simulation of a machine whose fetch-execute cycle deals with high-level language program statements rather than machine instructions. This software simulation obviously provides a virtual machine for the language.

Pure interpretation has the advantage of allowing easy implementation of many source-level debugging operations, because all run-time error messages can refer to source-level units. For example, if an array index is found to be out of range, the error message can easily indicate the source line and the name of the array. On the other hand, this method has the serious disadvantage that execution is 10 to 100 times slower than in compiled systems. The primary source of this slowness is the decoding of the high-level language statements, which are far more complex than machine language instructions (although there may be fewer statements than instructions in equivalent machine code). Furthermore, regardless of how many times a statement is executed, it must be decoded every time. Therefore, statement decoding, rather than the connection between the processor and memory, is the bottleneck of a pure interpreter.

Another disadvantage of pure interpretation is that it often requires more space. In addition to the source program, the symbol table must be present during interpretation. Furthermore, the source program may be stored in a form designed for easy access and modification rather than one that provides for minimal size.

Although some simple early languages of the 1960s (APL, SNOBOL, and LISP) were purely interpreted, by the 1980s, the approach was rarely used on high-level languages. However, in recent years, pure interpretation has made a significant comeback with some Web scripting languages, such as JavaScript and PHP, which are now widely used. The process of pure interpretation is shown in Figure 1.4.

Figure 1.4

Pure interpretation

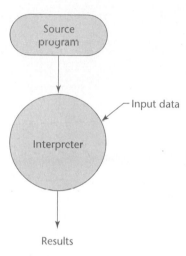

1.7.3   Hybrid Implementation Systems

Some language implementation systems are a compromise between compilers and pure interpreters; they translate high-level language programs to an intermediate language designed to allow easy interpretation. This method is faster than pure interpretation because the source language statements are decoded only once. Such implementations are called **hybrid implementation systems.**

The process used in a hybrid implementation system is shown in Figure 1.5. Instead of translating intermediate language code to machine code, it simply interprets the intermediate code.

Perl is implemented with a hybrid system. Perl programs are partially compiled to detect errors before interpretation and to simplify the interpreter.

Initial implementations of Java were all hybrid. Its intermediate form, called **byte code,** provides portability to any machine that has a byte code interpreter and an associated run-time system. Together, these are called the Java Virtual Machine. There are now systems that translate Java byte code into machine code for faster execution.

Figure 1.5

Hybrid implementation
system

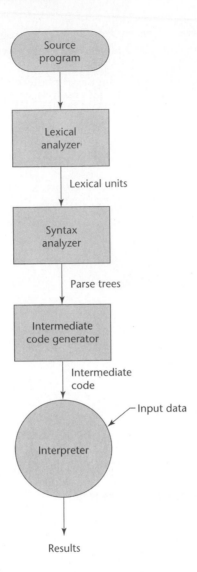

A Just-in-Time (JIT) implementation system initially translates programs to an intermediate language. Then, during execution, it compiles intermediate language methods into machine code when they are called. The machine code version is kept for subsequent calls. JIT systems are now widely used for Java programs. Also, the .NET languages are all implemented with a JIT system.

Sometimes an implementor may provide both compiled and interpreted implementations for a language. In these cases, the interpreter is used to develop and debug programs. Then, after a (relatively) bug-free state is reached, the programs are compiled to increase their execution speed.

1.7.4   Preprocessors

A **preprocessor** is a program that processes a program immediately before the program is compiled. Preprocessor instructions are embedded in programs. The preprocessor is essentially a macro expander. Preprocessor instructions are commonly used to specify that the code from another file is to be included. For example, the C preprocessor instruction

```
#include myLib.c
```

causes the preprocessor to copy the contents of `myLib.c` into the program at the position of the `#include`.

Other preprocessor instructions are used to define symbols to represent expressions. For example, one could use

```
#define max(A, B) ((A) > (B) ? (A) : (B))
```

to determine the largest of two given expressions. For example, the expression

```
x = max(2 * y, z / 1.73);
```

would be expanded by the preprocessor to

```
x = ((2 * y) > (z / 1.73) ? (2 * y) : (z / 1.73);
```

Notice that this is one of those cases where expression side effects can cause trouble. For example, if either of the expressions given to the `max` macro have side effects—such as `z++`—it could cause a problem. Because one of the two expression parameters is evaluated twice, this could result in `z` being incremented twice by the code produced by the macro expansion.

1.8   Programming Environments

A programming environment is the collection of tools used in the development of software. This collection may consist of only a file system, a text editor, a linker, and a compiler. Or it may include a large collection of integrated tools, each accessed through a uniform user interface. In the latter case, the development and maintenance of software is greatly enhanced. Therefore, the characteristics of a programming language are not the only measure of the software development capability of a system. We now briefly describe several programming environments.

UNIX is an older programming environment, first distributed in the middle 1970s, built around a portable multiprogramming operating system. It provides a wide array of powerful support tools for software production and maintenance in a variety of languages. In the past, the most important feature absent from UNIX was a uniform interface among its tools. This made it more difficult to learn and to use. However, UNIX is now often used through a graphical user interface (GUI) that runs on top of UNIX. Examples of UNIX GUIs are the Solaris Common Desktop Environment (CDE), GNOME, and KDE. These GUIs make the interface to UNIX appear similar to that of Windows and Macintosh systems.

Borland JBuilder is a programming environment that provides an integrated compiler, editor, debugger, and file system for Java development, where all four are accessed through a graphical interface. JBuilder is a complex and powerful system for creating Java software.

The latest step in the evolution of software development environments is represented by Microsoft Visual Studio.NET, a large and elaborate collection of software development tools, all used through a windowed interface. This system can be used to develop software in any one of the five .NET languages: C#, Visual BASIC .NET, JScript (Microsoft's version of JavaScript), J# (Microsoft's version of Java), or managed C++.

SUMMARY

The study of programming languages is valuable for a number of important reasons: It increases our capacity to use different constructs in writing programs, enables us to choose languages for projects more intelligently, and makes learning new languages easier.

Computers are used in a wide variety of problem-solving domains. The design and evaluation of a particular programming language is highly dependent on the domain in which it is to be used.

Among the most important criteria for evaluating languages are readability, writability, reliability, and overall cost. These will be the basis on which we examine and judge the various language features discussed in the remainder of the book.

The major influences on language design have been machine architecture and software design methodologies.

Designing a programming language is primarily an engineering feat, in which a long list of trade-offs must be made among features, constructs, and capabilities.

The major methods of implementing programming languages are compilation, pure interpretation, and hybrid implementation.

Programming environments have become important parts of software development systems, in which the language is just one of the components.

REVIEW QUESTIONS

1. Why is it useful for a programmer to have some background in language design, even though he or she may never actually design a programming language?

2. How can knowledge of programming language characteristics benefit the whole computing community?

3. What programming language has dominated scientific computing over the past 45 years?

4. What programming language has dominated business applications over the past 45 years?

5. What programming language has dominated artificial intelligence over the past 45 years?

6. In what language is UNIX written?

7. What is the disadvantage of having too many features in a language?

8. How can user-defined operator overloading harm the readability of a program?

9. What is one example of a lack of orthogonality in the design of C?

10. What language used orthogonality as a primary design criterion?

11. What primitive control statement is used to build more complicated control statements in languages that lack them?

12. What construct of a programming language provides process abstraction?

13. What does it mean for a program to be reliable?

14. Why is type checking the parameters of a subprogram important?

15. What is aliasing?

16. What is exception handling?

17. Why is readability important to writability?

18. How is the cost of compilers for a given language related to the design of that language?

19. What has been the strongest influence on programming language design over the past 50 years?

20. What is the name of the category of programming languages whose structure is dictated by the von Neumann computer architecture?

21. What two programming language deficiencies were discovered as a result of the research in software development in the 1970s?

22. What are the three fundamental features of an object-oriented programming language?

23. What language was the first to support the three fundamental features of object-oriented programming?

24. What is an example of two language design criteria that are in direct conflict with each other?

25. What are the three general methods of implementing a programming language?

26. Which produces faster program execution, a compiler or a pure interpreter?

27. What role does the symbol table play in a compiler?

28. What does a linker do?

29. Why is the von Neumann bottleneck important?

30. What are the advantages in implementing a language with a pure interpreter?

PROBLEM SET

1. Do you believe our capacity for abstract thought is influenced by our language skills? Support your opinion.

2. What are some features of specific programming languages you know whose rationales are a mystery to you?

3. What arguments can you make for the idea of a single language for all programming domains?

4. What arguments can you make against the idea of a single language for all programming domains?

5. Name and explain another criterion by which languages can be judged (in addition to those discussed in this chapter).

6. What common programming language statement, in your opinion, is most detrimental to readability?

7. Java uses a right brace to mark the end of all compound statements. What are the arguments for and against this design?

8. Many languages distinguish between uppercase and lowercase letters in user-defined names. What are the pros and cons of this design decision?

9. Explain the different aspects of the cost of a programming language.

10. What are the arguments for writing efficient programs even though hardware is relatively inexpensive?

11. Describe some design trade-offs between efficiency and safety in some language you know.

12. What major features would a perfect programming language include, in your opinion?

13. Was the first high-level programming language you learned implemented with a pure interpreter, a hybrid implementation system, or a compiler? (You would not necessarily know this without research.)

14. Describe the advantages and disadvantages of some programming environment you have used.

15. How do type declaration statements for simple variables affect the readability of a language, considering that some languages do not require them?

16. Write an evaluation of some programming language you know, using the criteria described in this chapter.

17. Some programming languages—for example, Pascal—have used the semicolon to separate statements, while Java uses it to terminate statements. Which of these, in your opinion, is most natural and least likely to result in syntax errors? Support your answer.

18. Many contemporary languages allow two kinds of comments: one in which delimiters are used on both ends (multiple-line comments), and one in which a delimiter marks only the beginning of the comment (one-line comments). Discuss the advantages and disadvantages of each of these with respect to our criteria.

Evolution of the Major Programming Languages

This chapter describes the development of a collection of programming languages, exploring the environment in which each was designed and focusing on the contributions of the language and the motivation for its development. Overall language descriptions are not included; rather, we discuss only some of the new features introduced by each language. Of particular interest are the features that most influenced subsequent languages or the field of computer science.

This chapter does not include an in-depth discussion of any language feature or concept; that is left for later chapters. Brief, informal explanations of features will suffice for our trek through the development of these languages.

This chapter discusses a wide variety of languages and language concepts that will not be familiar to many readers. Furthermore, these topics are discussed in detail only in later chapters. Those who find this unsettling may prefer to delay reading this chapter until the rest of the book has been studied.

The choice as to which languages to discuss here was subjective, and many readers will unhappily note the absence of one or more of their favorites. However, to keep this historical coverage to a reasonable size, it was necessary to leave out some languages that some regard highly. The choices were based on our estimate of each language's importance to language development and the computing world as a whole. We also include brief discussions of some other languages that are referenced later in the book.

The organization of this chapter is as follows: The initial versions of languages generally are discussed in chronological order. However, subsequent versions of languages appear with their initial version, rather than in later sections. For example, Fortran 2003 is discussed in the section with Fortran I (1956). Also, in some cases languages of secondary importance that are related to a language that has its own section appear in that section.

This chapter includes listings of 14 complete example programs, each in a different language. None of these programs are described in this chapter; they are meant simply to illustrate the appearance of programs in these languages. Readers familiar with any of the common imperative languages should be able to read and understand most of the code in these programs, except those in LISP, COBOL, and Smalltalk. (The LISP example is discussed in Chapter 15.) The same problem is solved by the Fortran, ALGOL 60, PL/I, BASIC, Pascal, C, Perl, Ada, Java, JavaScript, and C# programs. Note that most of the contemporary languages in this list support dynamic arrays, but because of the simplicity of the example problem, we did not use them in the example programs. Also, in the Fortran 95 program, we avoided using the features that could have avoided the use of loops altogether, in part to keep the program simple and readable and in part just to illustrate the basic loop structure of the language.

Figure 2.1 is a chart of the genealogy of the high-level languages discussed in this chapter.

2.1 Zuse's Plankalkül

The first programming language discussed in this chapter is highly unusual in several respects. For one thing, it was never implemented. Furthermore,

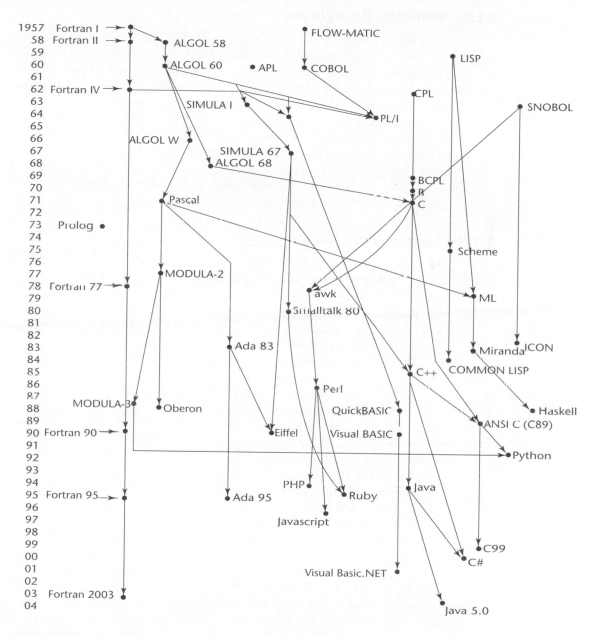

Figure 2.1   Genealogy of common high-level programming languages

although developed in 1945, its description was not published until 1972. Because so few people were familiar with the language, some of its capabilities did not appear in other languages until 15 years after its development.

2.1.1 Historical Background

Between 1936 and 1945, the German scientist Konrad Zuse (pronounced "Tsoo-zuh") built a series of complex and sophisticated computers from electromechanical relays. By early 1945, the war had destroyed all but one of his latest models, the Z4, so he moved to a remote Bavarian village, Hinterstein, and his research group members went their separate ways.

Working alone, Zuse embarked on an effort to develop a language for expressing computations, a project he had begun in 1943 as a proposal for his Ph.D. dissertation. He named this language Plankalkül, which means program calculus. In a lengthy manuscript dated 1945 but not published until 1972 (Zuse, 1972), Zuse defined Plankalkül and wrote algorithms in the language for a wide variety of problems.

2.1.2 Language Overview

Plankalkül was remarkably complete, with some of its most advanced features in the area of data structures. The simplest data type in Plankalkül was the single bit. From the bit type were built types for integer and floating-point numeric types. The floating-point type used twos-complement notation and the "hidden bit" scheme currently used to avoid storing the most significant bit of the normalized fraction part of a floating-point value.

In addition to these usual scalar types, Plankalkül included arrays and records. The records could include nested records.

Although the language had no explicit goto, it did include an iterative statement similar to the Ada **for**. It also had the command **Fin** with a superscript that specified a jump out of a given number of iteration loop nestings or to the beginning of a new iteration cycle. Plankalkül included a selection statement, but it did not allow an else clause.

One of the most interesting features of Zuse's programs was the inclusion of mathematical expressions showing the relationships between program variables. These expressions stated what would be true during execution at the points in the code where they appeared. These are very similar to the assertions used in Java and in axiomatic semantics, which is discussed in Chapter 3.

Zuse's manuscript contained programs of far greater complexity than any written prior to 1945. Included were programs to sort arrays of numbers; test the connectivity of a given graph; carry out integer and floating-point operations, including square root; and perform syntax analysis on logic formulas that had parentheses and operators in six different levels of precedence. Perhaps most remarkable were his 49 pages of algorithms for playing chess, a game in which he was not an expert.

If a computer scientist had found Zuse's description of Plankalkül in the early 1950s, the single aspect of the language that would have hindered its implementation as defined would have been the notation. Each statement consisted of either two or three lines of code. The first line was most like the statements of current languages. The second line, which was optional, contained the subscripts of the array references in the first line. It is interesting to note that the same method of indicating subscripts was used by Charles Babbage in programs for his Analytical Engine in the middle of the nineteenth century. The last line of each Plankalkül statement contained the type names for the variables mentioned in the first line. This notation is quite intimidating when first seen.

The following example assignment statement, which assigns the value of the expression A[4]+1 to A[5], illustrates this notation. The row labeled V is for subscripts, and the row labeled S is for the data types. In this example, 1.n means an integer of *n* bits:

```
  | A + 1 => A
V | 4        5
S | 1.n      1.n
```

We can only speculate on the direction that programming language design might have taken if Zuse's work had been widely known in 1945 or even 1950. It is also interesting to consider how his work might have been different had he done it in a peaceful environment surrounded by other scientists, rather than in Germany in 1945 in virtual isolation.

2.2 Minimal Hardware Programming: Pseudocodes

First, note that the word *pseudocode* is used here in a different sense than its contemporary meaning. We call the languages discussed in this section pseudocodes because that's what they were named at the time they were developed and used (the late 1940s and early 1950s). However, they are clearly not pseudocodes in the contemporary sense.

The computers that became available in the late 1940s and early 1950s were far less usable than those of today. In addition to being slow, unreliable, expensive, and having extremely small memories, the machines of that time were difficult to program because of the lack of supporting software.

There were no high-level programming languages or even assembly languages, so programming was done in machine code, which is both tedious and error-prone. Among its problems is the use of numeric codes for specifying instructions. For example, an ADD instruction might be specified by the code 14 rather than a connotative textual name, even if only a single letter. This makes programs very difficult to read. A more serious problem is absolute addressing, which makes programs very difficult to modify. For example, suppose we have a machine language program that is stored in memory. Many of the instructions in such a program refer to other locations within the program, usually to reference data or to indicate the targets of branch instructions. Inserting an instruction at any position in the program other than at the end invalidates the correctness of all instructions that refer to addresses beyond the insertion point, because those addresses must be increased to make room for the new instruction. To make the addition correctly, all those instructions that refer to addresses that follow the addition must be found and modified. A similar problem occurs with deletion of an instruction. In this case, however, machine languages often include a "no operation" instruction that can replace deleted instructions, thereby avoiding the problem.

These are standard problems with all machine languages and were the primary motivations for inventing assemblers and assembly languages. In addition, most programming problems of that time were numerical and required floating-point arithmetic operations and indexing of some sort to allow the convenient use of arrays. Neither of these capabilities, however, was included in the architecture of the computers of the late 1940s and early 1950s. These deficiencies naturally led to the development of somewhat higher-level languages.

2.2.1   Short Code

The first of these new languages, named Short Code, was developed by John Mauchly in 1949 for the BINAC computer, which was one of the first successful stored-program electronic computers. Short Code was later transferred to a UNIVAC I computer (the first commercial electronic computer sold in the United States) and, for several years, was one of the primary means of programming those machines. Although little is known of the original Short Code because its complete description was never published, a programming manual for the UNIVAC I version did survive (Remington-Rand, 1952). It is safe to assume that the two versions were very similar.

The words of the UNIVAC I's memory had 72 bits, grouped as 12 six-bit bytes. Short Code consisted of coded versions of mathematical expressions that were to be evaluated. The codes were byte-pair values, and most equations fit into a word. Some of the codes were

```
01  -        06  abs value    1n  (n+2)nd power
02  )        07  +            2n  (n+2)nd root
03  =        08  pause        4n  if <= n
04  /        09  (            58  print and tab
```

Variables, or memory locations, were named with byte-pair codes, as were locations to be used as constants. For example, X0 and Y0 could be variables. The statement

```
X0 = SQRT(ABS(Y0))
```

would be coded in a word as 00 X0 03 20 06 Y0. The initial 00 was used as padding to fill the word. Interestingly, there was no multiplication code; multiplication was indicated by simply placing the two operands next to each other, as in algebra.

Short Code was not translated to machine code; rather, it was implemented with a pure interpreter. At the time, this process was called *automatic programming*. It clearly simplified the programming process, but at the expense of execution time. Short Code interpretation was approximately 50 times slower than machine code.

2.2.2 Speedcoding

In other places, interpretive systems were being developed that extended machine languages to include floating-point operations. The Speedcoding system developed by John Backus for the IBM 701 is an example of such a system (Backus, 1954). The Speedcoding interpreter effectively converted the 701 to a virtual three-address floating-point calculator. The system included pseudoinstructions for the four arithmetic operations on floating-point data, as well as operations such as square root, sine, arc tangent, exponent, and logarithm. Conditional and unconditional branches and input/output conversions were also part of the virtual architecture. To get an idea of the limitations of such systems, consider that the remaining usable memory after loading the interpreter was only 700 words and that the add instruction took 4.2 milliseconds to execute. On the other hand, Speedcoding included the novel facility of automatically incrementing address registers. This facility did not appear in hardware until the UNIVAC 1107 computers of 1962. Because of such features, matrix multiplication could be done in 12 Speedcoding instructions. Backus claimed that problems that could take two weeks to program in machine code could be programmed in a few hours using Speedcoding.

2.2.3 The UNIVAC "Compiling" System

Between 1951 and 1953, a team led by Grace Hopper at UNIVAC developed a series of "compiling" systems named A-0, A-1, and A-2 that expanded a pseudocode into machine code subprograms in the same way as macros are expanded into assembly language. The pseudocode source for these "compilers" was still quite primitive, although even this was a great improvement over machine code because it made source programs much shorter. Wilkes (1952) independently suggested a similar process.

2.2.4 Related Work

Other means of easing the task of programming were being developed at about the same time. At Cambridge University, David J. Wheeler developed a method of using blocks of relocatable addresses to partially solve the problem of absolute addressing (Wheeler, 1950), and later, Maurice V. Wilkes (also at Cambridge) extended the idea to design an assembly program that could combine chosen subroutines and allocate storage (Wilkes et al., 1951, 1957). This was indeed an important and fundamental advance.

We should also mention that assembly languages, which are quite different from the pseudocodes mentioned, evolved during the early 1950s. However, they had little impact on the design of high-level languages.

2.3 The IBM 704 and Fortran

Certainly one of the greatest single advances in computing came with the introduction of the IBM 704 in 1954, in large measure because its capabilities prompted the development of Fortran. One could argue that if it had not been IBM with the 704 and Fortran, it would soon thereafter have been some other organization with a similar computer and related high-level language. However, IBM was the first with both the foresight and the resources to undertake these developments.

2.3.1 Historical Background

One of the primary reasons why interpretive systems were tolerated from the late 1940s to the mid-1950s was the lack of floating-point hardware in the available computers. All floating-point operations had to be simulated in software, a very time-consuming process. Because so much processor time was spent in software floating-point processing, the overhead of interpretation and the simulation of indexing were relatively insignificant. As long as floating-point had to be done by software, interpretation was an acceptable expense. However, many programmers of that time never used interpretive systems, preferring the efficiency of hand-coded machine (or assembly) language. The announcement of the IBM 704 system, with both indexing and floating-point instructions in hardware, heralded the end of the interpretive era, at least for scientific computation. The inclusion of floating-point hardware removed the hiding place for the cost of interpretation.

Although Fortran is often credited with being the first compiled high-level language, the question of who deserves credit for implementing the first such language is somewhat open. Knuth and Pardo (1977) give the credit to Alick E. Glennie for his Autocode compiler for the Manchester Mark I computer. Glennie developed the compiler at Fort Halstead, Royal Armaments Research Establishment, in England. The compiler was operational by September 1952. However, according to John Backus (Wexelblat, 1981, p. 26), Glennie's Autocode was so low-level and machine oriented that it should not be considered a compiled system. Backus gives the credit to Laning and Zierler at Massachusetts Institute of Technology.

The Laning and Zierler system (Laning and Zierler, 1954) was the first algebraic translation system to be implemented. By algebraic, we mean that it translated arithmetic expressions, used function calls for mathematical functions, and included arrays. The system was implemented on the MIT Whirlwind computer, in experimental prototype form, in the summer of 1952, and in a more usable form by May 1953. The translator generated a subroutine call to code each formula, or expression, in the program. The source language was easy to read, and the only actual machine instructions included were for branching. Although this work preceded the work on Fortran, it never escaped MIT.

In spite of these earlier works, the first widely accepted compiled high-level language was Fortran. The following subsections chronicle this important development.

2.3.2 Design Process

Even before the 704 system was announced in May 1954, plans were begun for Fortran. By November 1954, John Backus and his group at IBM had produced the report titled "The IBM Mathematical FORmula TRANslating System: FORTRAN" (IBM, 1954). This document described the first version of Fortran, which we refer to as Fortran 0, prior to its implementation. It also boldly stated that Fortran would provide the efficiency of hand-coded programs and the ease of programming of the interpretive pseudocode systems. In another burst of optimism, the document stated that Fortran would eliminate coding errors and the debugging process. Based on this premise, the first Fortran compiler included little syntax error checking.

The environment in which Fortran was developed was as follows: (1) Computers had small memories and were slow and relatively unreliable; (2) the primary use of computers was for scientific computations; (3) there were no existing efficient ways to program computers; (4) because of the high cost of computers compared to the cost of programmers, speed of the generated object code was the primary goal of the first Fortran compilers. The characteristics of the early versions of Fortran follow directly from this environment.

2.3.3 Fortran I Overview

Fortran 0 was modified during the implementation period, which began in January 1955 and continued until the release of the compiler in April 1957. The implemented language, which we call Fortran I, is described in the first Fortran *Programmer's Reference Manual*, published in October 1956 (IBM, 1956). Fortran I included input/output formatting, variable names of up to six characters (it had been just two in Fortran 0), user-defined subroutines, although they could not be separately compiled, the If selection statement, and the Do loop statement.

All of Fortran I's control statements were based on 704 instructions. It is not clear whether the 704 designers dictated the control statement design of Fortran I or whether the designers of Fortran I suggested these instructions to the 704 designers.

There were no data-typing statements in the Fortran I language. Variables whose names began with I, J, K, L, M, and N were implicitly integer type, and all others were implicitly floating-point. The choice of the letters for this convention was based on the fact that at that time integers were used primarily as subscripts, and scientists usually used i, j, and k for subscripts. In a moment of generosity, Fortran's designers threw in the three additional letters.

The most audacious claim made by the Fortran development group during the design of the language was that the machine code produced by the compiler would be about as efficient as what could be produced by hand.[1] This, more than anything else, made skeptics of potential users and prevented a great deal of interest in Fortran before its actual release. To almost everyone's surprise, however, the Fortran development group nearly achieved its goal in efficiency. The largest part of the 18 worker-years of effort used to construct the first compiler had been spent on optimization, and the results were remarkably effective.

The early success of Fortran is shown by the results of a survey made in April 1958. At that time, roughly half of the code being written for 704s was being done in Fortran, in spite of the extreme skepticism of most of the programming world only a year earlier.

2.3.4   Fortran II

The Fortran II compiler was distributed in the spring of 1958. It fixed many of the bugs in the Fortran I compilation system and added some significant features to the language, the most important being the independent compilation of subroutines. Without independent compilation, any change in a program requires that the entire program be recompiled. Fortran I's lack of independent-compilation capability, coupled with the poor reliability of the 704, placed a practical restriction on the length of programs to about 300 to 400 lines (Wexelblat, 1981, p. 68). Longer programs had a poor chance of being compiled completely before a machine failure occurred. The capability of including precompiled machine language versions of subprograms shortened the compilation process considerably.

2.3.5   Fortrans IV, 77, 90, 95, and 2003

A Fortran III was developed, but it was never widely distributed. Fortran IV, however, became one of the most widely used programming languages of its time. It evolved over the period 1960 to 1962 and was standardized as Fortran 66 (ANSI, 1966), although that name is rarely used. Fortran IV was an improvement over Fortran II in many ways. Among its most important additions were explicit type declarations for variables, a logical If construct, and the capability of passing subprograms as parameters to other subprograms.

---

1. In fact, the Fortran team believed that the code generated by their compiler could be no less than half as fast as handwritten machine code, or the language would not be adopted by users.

Fortran IV was replaced by Fortran 77, which became the new standard in 1978 (ANSI, 1978a). Fortran 77 retained most of the features of Fortran IV and added character string handling, logical loop control statements, and an If with an optional Else clause.

Fortran 90 (ANSI, 1992) is dramatically different from Fortran 77. The most significant additions were dynamic arrays, records, pointers, a multiple selection statement, and modules. Also, Fortran 90 subprograms can be recursively called.

A new concept that is included in the Fortran 90 definition is that of removing language features from earlier versions. While Fortran 90 includes all of the features of Fortran 77, it has two lists of features that may be eliminated in future versions of Fortran. The obsolescent-features list has features that may be eliminated in the next version of Fortran after 90.

Fortran 90 included two simple syntactic changes that altered the appearance of both programs and the literature describing the language. First, the required fixed format of code, which required the use of specific character positions for specific parts of statements, was dropped. For example, statement labels could appear only in the first five positions and statements could not begin before the seventh position. This rigid formatting of code was designed around the use of punch cards. The second change was that the official spelling of FORTRAN became Fortran. This change was accompanied by the change in convention of using all uppercase letters for keywords and identifiers in Fortran programs. Now, the convention is that only the first letter of keywords and identifiers is uppercase.

Fortran 95 (INCITS/ISO/IEC, 1997) continued the evolution of the language, but only a few changes were made. Among other things, a new iteration construct, Forall, was added to ease the task of parallelizing Fortran programs.

The latest version of Fortran, Fortran 2003 (Metcalf et al., 2004), adds parameterized derived types, support for object-oriented programming, procedure pointers, and interoperability with the C programming language.

2.3.6 Evaluation

The original Fortran design team thought of language design only as a necessary prelude to the critical task of designing the translator. Further, it never occurred to them that Fortran would be used on computers not manufactured by IBM. Indeed, they were forced to consider building Fortran compilers for other IBM machines only because the successor to the 704, the 709, was announced before the 704 Fortran compiler was released. The effect that Fortran has had on the use of computers, along with the fact that all subsequent programming languages owe a debt to Fortran, are indeed impressive in light of the modest goals of its designers.

One of the features of Fortran I, and all of its successors before 90, that allows highly optimizing compilers is that the types and storage for all variables are fixed before run time. No new variables or space can be allocated during run time. This is a sacrifice of flexibility to simplicity and efficiency. It eliminates the possibility of recursive subprograms and makes it difficult to implement data structures that grow or change shape dynamically. Of course, the kinds of programs that were being built at the time of the development of the early versions of Fortran were primarily numerical in nature and were simple in comparison with recent software projects. Therefore, the sacrifice was not a great one.

The overall success of Fortran is difficult to overstate: It dramatically changed forever the way computers are used. This is, of course, in large part due to its being the first widely used high-level language. In comparison with concepts and languages developed later, early versions of Fortran suffer in a variety of ways, as should be expected. After all, it would not be fair to compare the performance and comfort of a 1910 Model T Ford with the performance and comfort of a 2007 Ford Mustang. Nevertheless, in spite of the inadequacies of Fortran, the momentum of the huge investment in Fortran software, among other factors, has kept it among the most widely used of all high-level languages.

Alan Perlis, one of the designers of ALGOL 60, said of Fortran in 1978, "Fortran is the *lingua franca* of the computing world. It is the language of the streets in the best sense of the word, not in the prostitutional sense of the word. And it has survived and will survive because it has turned out to be a remarkably useful part of a very vital commerce" (Wexelblat, 1981, p. 161).

The following is an example of a Fortran 95 program:

```
! Fortran 95 Example program
!  Input:   An integer, List_Len, where List_Len is less
!              than 100, followed by List_Len-Integer values
!  Output:  The number of input values that are greater
!              than the average of all input values
Implicit none
Integer Dimension(99) :: Int_List
Integer :: List_Len, Counter, Sum, Average, Result
Result= 0
Sum = 0
Read *, List_Len
If ((List_Len > 0) .AND. (List_Len < 100)) Then
! Read input data into an array and compute its sum
   Do Counter = 1, List_Len
      Read *, Int_List(Counter)
      Sum = Sum + Int_List(Counter)
   End Do
! Compute the average
   Average = Sum / List_Len
! Count the values that are greater than the average
   Do Counter = 1, List_Len
      If (Int_List(Counter) > Average) Then
         Result = Result + 1
```

```
      End If
    End Do
! Print the result
    Print *, 'Number of values > Average is:', Result
Else
    Print *, 'Error - list length value is not legal'
End If
End Program Example
```

2.4 Functional Programming: LISP

The first functional programming language was invented to provide language features for list processing, the need for which grew out of the first applications in the area of artificial intelligence (AI).

2.4.1 The Beginnings of Artificial Intelligence and List Processing

Interest in AI appeared in the mid-1950s in a number of places. Some of this interest grew out of linguistics, some from psychology, and some from mathematics. Linguists were concerned with natural language processing. Psychologists were interested in modeling human information storage and retrieval, as well as other fundamental processes of the brain. Mathematicians were interested in mechanizing certain intelligent processes, such as theorem proving. All of these investigations arrived at the same conclusion: Some method must be developed to allow computers to process symbolic data in linked lists. At the time, most computation was on numeric data in arrays.

The concept of list processing was developed by Allen Newell, J. C. Shaw, and Herbert Simon. It was first published in a classic paper that describes one of the first AI programs, the Logical Theorist,[2] and a language in which it could be implemented (Newell and Simon, 1956). The language, named IPL-I (Information Processing Language I), was never implemented. The next version, IPL-II, was implemented on a Rand Corporation Johnniac computer. Development of IPL continued until 1960, when the description of IPL-V was published (Newell and Tonge, 1960). The low level of the IPL languages prevented their widespread use. They were actually assembly languages for a hypothetical computer, implemented with an interpreter, in which list-processing instructions were included. The first implementation was on the obscure Johnniac machine, another factor that kept the IPL languages from becoming popular.

The contributions of the IPL languages were in their list design and their demonstration that list processing was feasible and useful.

---

2. Logical Theorist discovered proofs for theorems in propositional calculus.

IBM became interested in AI in the mid-1950s and chose theorem proving as a demonstration area. At the time, the Fortran project was still under way. The high cost of the Fortran I compiler convinced IBM that their list processing should be attached to Fortran, rather than in the form of a new language. Thus, the Fortran List Processing Language (FLPL) was designed and implemented as an extension to Fortran. FLPL was used to construct a theorem prover for plane geometry, which was then considered the easiest area for mechanical theorem proving.

2.4.2 LISP Design Process

John McCarthy of MIT took a summer position at the IBM Information Research Department in 1958. His goal for the summer was to investigate symbolic computations and develop a set of requirements for doing such computations. As a pilot example problem area, he chose differentiation of algebraic expressions. From this study came a list of language requirements. Among them were the control flow methods of mathematical functions: recursion and conditional expressions. The only available high-level language of the time, Fortran I, had neither of these.

Another requirement that grew from the symbolic-differentiation investigation was the need for dynamically allocated linked lists and some kind of implicit deallocation of abandoned lists. McCarthy simply would not allow his elegant algorithm for differentiation to be cluttered with explicit deallocation statements.

Because FLPL did not support recursion, conditional expressions, dynamic storage allocation, or implicit deallocation, it was clear to McCarthy that a new language was required.

When McCarthy returned to MIT in the fall of 1958, he and Marvin Minsky formed the MIT AI Project, with funding from the Research Laboratory for Electronics. The first important effort of the project was to produce a system for list processing. It was to be used initially to implement a program proposed by McCarthy called the Advice Taker.[3] This application became the impetus for the development of the list-processing language LISP. The first version of LISP is sometimes called "pure LISP" because it is a purely functional language. In the following section, we describe the development of pure LISP.

2.4.3 Language Overview

2.4.3.1 Data Structures

Pure LISP has only two kinds of data structures: atoms and lists. Atoms are either symbols, which have the form of identifiers, or numeric literals. The

---

3. Advice Taker represented information with sentences written in a formal language and used a logical inferencing process to decide what to do.

concept of storing symbolic information in linked lists is natural and was used in IPL-II. Such structures allow insertions and deletions at any point, operations that were then thought to be a necessary part of list processing. It was eventually determined, however, that LISP programs rarely require these operations.

Lists are specified by delimiting their elements with parentheses. Simple lists, in which elements are restricted to atoms, have the form

```
(A B C D)
```

Nested list structures are also specified by parentheses. For example, the list

```
(A (B C) D (E (F G)))
```

is composed of four elements. The first is the atom A; the second is the sublist (B C); the third is the atom D; the fourth is the sublist (E (F G)), which has as its second element the sublist (F G).

Internally, lists are usually stored as single-linked list structures, in which each node has two pointers and represents a list element. A node containing an atom has its first pointer pointing to some representation of the atom, such as its symbol or numeric value, or the pointer to a sublist. A node for a sublist element has its first pointer pointing to the first node of the sublist. In both cases, the second pointer of a node points to the next element of the list. A list is referenced by a pointer to its first element.

The internal representations of the two lists shown earlier are depicted in Figure 2.2. Note that the elements of a list are shown horizontally. The last element of a list has no successor, so its link is NIL, which is represented in Figure 2.2 as a diagonal line in the element. Sublists are shown with the same structure.

2.4.3.2 Processes in Functional Programming

LISP was designed as a functional programming language. All computation in a purely functional program is accomplished by applying functions to arguments. Neither the assignment statements nor the variables that abound in imperative language programs are necessary in functional language programs. Furthermore, repetitive processes can be specified with recursive function calls, making iteration (loops) unnecessary. These basic concepts of functional programming make it significantly different from programming in an imperative language.

2.4.3.3 The Syntax of LISP

LISP is very different from the imperative languages, both because it is a functional programming language and because the appearance of LISP programs is so different from those in languages like Java or C++. For example,

Figure 2.2

Internal representation
of two LISP lists

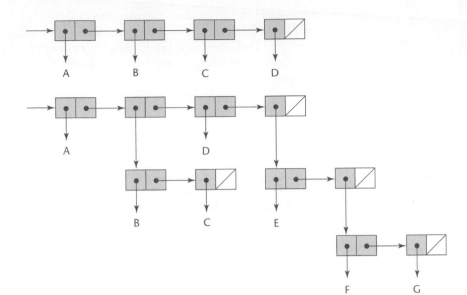

the syntax of Java is a complicated mixture of English and algebra, while
LISP's syntax is a model of simplicity. Program code and data have exactly the
same form: parenthesized lists. Consider again the list

```
(A B C D)
```

When interpreted as data, it is a list of four elements. When viewed as code, it
is the application of the function named A to the three parameters B, C, and D.

2.4.4 Evaluation

LISP completely dominated AI applications for a quarter of a century. Much
of the cause of LISP's reputation for being highly inefficient has been eliminated. Many contemporary implementations are compiled, and the resulting
code is much faster than running the source code on an interpreter. In addition to its success in AI, LISP pioneered functional programming, which has
proven to be a lively area of research in programming languages. As stated in
Chapter 1, many programming language researchers believe functional programming is a much better approach to software development than procedural programming using imperative languages.

   The following is an example of a LISP program:

```
;   LISP Example function
;   The following code defines a LISP predicate function
;   that  takes two lists as arguments and returns True
;   if the two lists are equal, and NIL (false) otherwise
```

```
(DEFUN equal_lists (lis1 lis2)
  (COND
    ((ATOM lis1) (EQ lis1 lis2))
    ((ATOM lis2) NIL)
    ((equal_lists (CAR lis1) (CAR lis2))
              (equal_lists (CDR lis1) (CDR lis2)))
    (T NIL)
  )
)
```

2.4.5 Two Descendants of LISP

Two dialects of LISP are now commonly used, Scheme and COMMON LISP. These are briefly discussed in the following subsections.

2.4.5.1 Scheme

The Scheme language emerged from MIT in the mid-1970s (Dybvig, 2003). It is characterized by its small size, its exclusive use of static scoping (discussed in Chapter 5), and its treatment of functions as first-class entities. As first-class entities, Scheme functions can be the values of expressions and elements of lists; they can be assigned to variables, passed as parameters, and returned as the values of function applications. Early versions of LISP did not provide all of these capabilities, nor did they use static scoping.

As a small language with simple syntax and semantics, Scheme is well suited to educational applications, such as courses in functional programming and general introductions to programming. Scheme is described in some detail in Chapter 15.

2.4.5.2 COMMON LISP

During the 1970s and early 1980s, a large number of different dialects of LISP were developed and used. This led to the familiar problem of portability. COMMON LISP (Graham, 1996) was created in an effort to rectify this situation. COMMON LISP was designed by combining the features of several dialects of LISP developed in the early 1980s, including Scheme, into a single language. Being such an amalgam, COMMON LISP is a large and complex language. Its basis, however, is pure LISP, so its syntax, primitive functions, and fundamental nature come from that language.

Recognizing the flexibility provided by dynamic scoping as well as the simplicity of static scoping, COMMON LISP allows both. The default scoping for variables is static, but by declaring a variable to be **special,** that variable becomes dynamically scoped.

COMMON LISP has a large number of data types and structures, including records, arrays, complex numbers, and character strings. It also has a form of packages for modularizing collections of functions and data providing access control.

COMMON LISP is further described in Chapter 15.

2.4.6 Related Languages

ML (*Meta*Language; Ullman, 1998) was originally designed in the 1980s by Robin Milner at the University of Edinburgh as a metalanguage for a program verification system named Logic for Computable Functions (LCF; Milner et al., 1990). ML is primarily a functional language, but it also supports imperative programming. Unlike LISP and Scheme, the type of every variable and expression in ML can be determined at compile time.[4] Types are associated with objects rather than names. Types of expressions are inferred from the context of the expression, as discussed in Chapter 7.

Unlike LISP and Scheme, ML does not use the parenthesized functional syntax that originated with lambda expressions. Rather, the syntax of ML resembles that of the imperative languages such as Java and C++.

Miranda was developed by David Turner at the University of Kent in Canterbury, England, in the early 1980s (Turner, 1986). Miranda is based partly on the languages ML, SASL, and KRC. Haskell (Hudak and Fasel, 1992) is based in large part on Miranda. Like Miranda, it is a purely functional language, having no variables and no assignment statement. Another distinguishing characteristic of Haskell is its use of lazy evaluation. This means that no expression is evaluated until its value is required. This leads to some surprising capabilities in the language.

Both ML and Haskell are briefly discussed in Chapter 15.

2.5 The First Step Toward Sophistication: ALGOL 60

ALGOL 60 has had a great influence on subsequent programming languages and is therefore of central importance in any historical study of languages.

2.5.1 Historical Background

ALGOL 60 was the result of efforts to design a universal language for scientific applications. By late 1954, the Laning and Zierler algebraic system had been in operation for over a year, and the first report on Fortran had been published. Fortran became a reality in 1957, and several other high-level languages were being developed. Most notable among them were IT, which was designed by Alan Perlis at Carnegie Tech, and two languages for the UNIVAC computers, MATH-MATIC and UNICODE. The proliferation

---

4. While this is true, ML functions can be generic, meaning their parameter types and return types can be different for different calls.

of languages made communication among users difficult. Furthermore, the new languages were all growing up around single architectures, some for UNIVAC computers and some for IBM 700-series machines. In response to this language proliferation, several major computer user groups in the United States, including SHARE (the IBM scientific user group) and USE (UNIVAC Scientific Exchange, the large-scale UNIVAC scientific user group), submitted a petition to the Association for Computing Machinery (ACM) on May 10, 1957, to form a committee to study and recommend action to create a universal programming language. Although Fortran might have been a candidate, it could not become a universal language, because at the time it was solely owned by IBM.

Previously, in 1955, GAMM (a German acronym for Society for Applied Mathematics and Mechanics) had also formed a committee to design one universal, machine-independent, algorithmic language for use on all kinds of computers. The desire for this new language was in part due to the Europeans' fear of being dominated by IBM. By late 1957, however, the appearance of several high-level languages in the United States convinced the GAMM subcommittee that their effort had to be widened to include the Americans, and a letter of invitation was sent to ACM. In April 1958, after Fritz Bauer of GAMM presented the formal proposal to ACM, the two groups officially agreed to a joint language design project.

2.5.2   Early Design Process

GAMM and ACM sent four members each to the first design meeting. The meeting, which was held in Zurich from May 27 to June 1, 1958, began with the following goals for the new language:

- The syntax of the language should be as close as possible to standard mathematical notation, and programs written in it should be readable with little further explanation.

- It should be possible to use the language for the description of algorithms in publications.

- Programs in the new language must be mechanically translatable into machine language.

The first goal indicates that the new language was to be used for scientific programming, which was the primary computer application area at that time. The second was something entirely new to the computing business. The last goal is an obvious necessity for any programming language.

Depending on how it is viewed, the Zurich meeting produced either momentous results or endless arguments. Actually, it did both. The meeting itself involved innumerable compromises, both among individuals and between the two sides of the Atlantic. In some cases, the compromises were not so much over great issues as they were over spheres of influence. The question of whether to use a comma (the European method) or a period (the American method) for a decimal point is one example.

2.5.3   ALGOL 58 Overview

The language designed at the Zurich meeting was named the International Algorithmic Language (IAL). It was suggested during the design that the language be named ALGOL, for ALGOrithmic Language, but the name was rejected because it did not reflect the international scope of the committee. During the following year, however, the name was changed to ALGOL, and the language subsequently became known as ALGOL 58.

In many ways, ALGOL 58 was a descendant of Fortran, which is quite natural. It generalized many of Fortran's features and added several new constructs and concepts. Some of the generalizations had to do with the goal of not tying the language to any particular machine, and others were attempts to make the language more flexible and powerful. A rare combination of simplicity and elegance emerged from the effort.

ALGOL 58 formalized the concept of data type, although only variables that were not floating-point required explicit declaration. It added the idea of compound statements, which most subsequent languages incorporated. Some features of Fortran that were generalized were the following: Identifiers were allowed to have any length, as opposed to Fortran I's restriction to six or fewer characters; any number of array dimensions was allowed, unlike Fortran I's limitation to no more than three; the lower bound of arrays could be specified by the programmer, whereas in Fortran it was implicitly 1; nested selection statements were allowed, which was not the case in Fortran I.

ALGOL 58 acquired the assignment operator in a rather unusual way. Zuse used the form

expression => variable

for the assignment statement in Plankalkül. Although Plankalkül had not yet been published, some of the European members of the ALGOL 58 committee were familiar with the language. The committee dabbled with the Plankalkül assignment form but, because of arguments about character set limitations,[5] the greater-than symbol was changed to a colon. Then, largely at the insistence of the Americans, the whole statement was turned around to the form

variable := expression

The Europeans preferred the opposite form, but that would be the reverse of Fortran.

---

5. The card punches of that time did not include the greater-than symbol.

2.5.4 Reception of the ALGOL 58 Report

Publication of the ALGOL 58 report (Perlis and Samelson, 1958) in December 1958 was greeted with a good deal of enthusiasm. In the United States, the new language was viewed more as a collection of ideas for programming language design than as a universal standard language. Actually, the ALGOL 58 report was not meant to be a finished product but rather a preliminary document for international discussion. Nevertheless, three major design and implementation efforts used the report as their basis. At the University of Michigan, the MAD language was born (Arden et al., 1961). The U.S. Naval Electronics Group produced the NELIAC language (Huskey et al., 1963). At System Development Corporation, JOVIAL was designed and implemented (Shaw, 1963). JOVIAL, an acronym for Jules' Own Version of the International Algebraic Language, represents the only language based on ALGOL 58 to achieve widespread use (Jules was Jules I. Schwartz, one of JOVIAL's designers). JOVIAL became widely used because it was the official scientific language for the U.S. Air Force for a quarter of a century.

The rest of the U.S. computing community was not so kind to the new language. At first, both IBM and its major scientific user group, SHARE, seemed to embrace ALGOL 58. IBM began an implementation shortly after the report was published, and SHARE formed a subcommittee, SHARE IAL, to study the language. The subcommittee subsequently recommended that ACM standardize ALGOL 58 and that IBM implement it for all of the 700-series computers. The enthusiasm was short-lived, however. By spring 1959, both IBM and SHARE, through their Fortran experience, had had enough of the pain and expense of getting a new language started, both in terms of developing and using the first-generation compilers and in terms of training users in the new language and persuading them to use it. By the middle of 1959, both IBM and SHARE had developed such a vested interest in Fortran that they decided to retain it as *the* scientific language for the IBM 700-series machines, thereby abandoning ALGOL 58.

2.5.5 ALGOL 60 Design Process

During 1959, ALGOL 58 was furiously debated in both Europe and the United States. Large numbers of suggested modifications and additions were published in the European *ALGOL Bulletin* and in *Communications of the ACM*. One of the most important events of 1959 was the presentation of the work of the Zurich committee to the International Conference on Information Processing, for there Backus introduced his new notation for describing the syntax of programming languages, which later became known as BNF (for Backus–Naur form). BNF is described in detail in Chapter 3.

In January 1960, the second ALGOL meeting was held, this time in Paris. The work of this meeting was to debate the 80 suggestions that had been formally submitted for consideration. Peter Naur of Denmark had become heavily involved in the development of ALGOL, even though he had not been a member of the Zurich group. It was Naur who created and published the *ALGOL Bulletin*. He spent a good deal of time studying Backus's paper that introduced BNF and decided that BNF should be used to describe formally the results of the 1960 meeting. After making a few relatively minor changes to BNF, he wrote a description of the new proposed language in BNF and handed it out to the members of the 1960 group at the beginning of the meeting.

2.5.6 ALGOL 60 Overview

Although the 1960 meeting lasted only six days, the modifications made to ALGOL 58 were dramatic. Among the most important new developments were the following:

- The concept of block structure was introduced. This allowed the programmer to localize parts of programs by introducing new data environments, or scopes.

- Two different means of passing parameters to subprograms were allowed: pass by value and pass by name.

- Procedures were allowed to be recursive. The ALGOL 58 description was unclear on this issue. Note that although this recursion was new for the imperative languages, LISP had already provided recursive functions in 1959.

- Stack-dynamic arrays were allowed. A stack-dynamic array is one for which the subscript range or ranges are specified by variables, so that the size of the array is set at the time storage is allocated to the array, which happens when the declaration is reached during execution. Stack-dynamic arrays are described in detail in Chapter 6.

Several features that might have had a dramatic impact on the success or failure of the language were proposed but rejected. Most important among these were input and output statements with formatting, which were omitted because they were thought to be too machine-dependent.

The ALGOL 60 report was published in May 1960 (Naur, 1960). A number of ambiguities still remained in the language description, and a third meeting was scheduled for April 1962 in Rome to address the problems. At this meeting the group dealt only with problems; no additions to the language were allowed. The results of this meeting were published under the title "Revised Report on the Algorithmic Language ALGOL 60" (Backus et al., 1963).

2.5.7 Evaluation

In some ways, ALGOL 60 was a great success; in other ways, it was a dismal failure. It succeeded in becoming, almost immediately, the only acceptable formal means of communicating algorithms in computing literature, and it remained for more than 20 years the sole language for publishing algorithms. Every imperative programming language designed since 1960 owes something to ALGOL 60. In fact, most are direct or indirect descendants; examples are PL/I, SIMULA 67, ALGOL 68, C, Pascal, Ada, C++, and Java.

The ALGOL 58/ALGOL 60 design effort included a long list of firsts. It was the first time that an international group attempted to design a programming language. It was the first language that was designed to be machine-independent. It was also the first language whose syntax was formally described. This successful use of the BNF formalism initiated several important fields of computer science: formal languages, parsing theory, and BNF-based compiler design. Finally, the structure of ALGOL 60 affected machine architecture. In the most striking example of this, an extension of the language was used as the systems language of a series of large-scale computers, the Burroughs B5000, B6000, and B7000 machines, which were designed with a hardware stack to implement efficiently the block structure and recursive subprograms of the language.

On the other side of the coin, ALGOL 60 never achieved widespread use in the United States. Even in Europe, where it was more popular than in the United States, it never became the dominant language. There are a number of reasons for its lack of acceptance. For one thing, some of the features of ALGOL 60 turned out to be too flexible; they made understanding difficult and implementation inefficient. The best example of this is the pass-by-name method of passing parameters to subprograms, which is explained in Chapter 9. The difficulties of implementing ALGOL 60 are evidenced by Rutishauser's statement in 1967 that few if any implementations included the full ALGOL 60 language (Rutishauser, 1967, p. 8).

The lack of input and output statements in the language was another major reason for its lack of acceptance. Implementation-dependent input/output made programs difficult to port to other computers.

One of the most important contributions to computer science that is associated with ALGOL 60, BNF, was also a factor in its lack of acceptance. Although BNF is now considered a simple and elegant means of syntax description, to the world of 1960 it seemed strange and complicated.

Finally, although there were many other problems, the entrenchment of Fortran among users and the lack of support by IBM were probably the most important factors in ALGOL 60's failure to gain widespread use.

The ALGOL 60 effort was never really complete, in the sense that ambiguities and obscurities were always a part of the language description (Knuth, 1967).

The following is an example of an ALGOL 60 program:

```
comment ALGOL 60 Example Program
  Input:  An integer, listlen, where listlen is less than
          100, followed by listlen-integer values
  Output: The number of input values that are greater than
          the average of all the input values  ;
```

```
begin
  integer array intlist [1:99];
  integer listlen, counter, sum, average, result;
  sum := 0;
  result := 0;
  readint (listlen);
  if (listlen > 0) ∧ (listlen < 100) then
    begin
comment Read input into an array and compute the average;
    for counter := 1 step 1 until listlen do
      begin
      readint (intlist[counter]);
      sum := sum + intlist[counter]
      end;
comment Compute the average;
    average := sum / listlen;
comment Count the input values that are > average;
    for counter := 1 step 1 until listlen do
      if intlist[counter] > average
        then result := result + 1;
comment Print result;
    printstring("The number of values > average is:");
    printint (result)
    end
  else
    printstring ("Error—input list length is not legal");
end
```

2.6 Computerizing Business Records: COBOL

The story of COBOL is in a sense the opposite of that of ALGOL 60. Although it has been used more than any other programming language, COBOL has had little effect on the design of subsequent languages, except for PL/I. It may still be the most widely used language,[6] although it is difficult to be sure one way or the other. Perhaps the most important reason why COBOL has had little influence is that few have attempted to design a new language for business applications since it appeared. That is due in part to how well COBOL's capabilities meet the needs of its application area. Another reason is that a great deal of growth in business computing over the past 30 years has occurred in small businesses. In these businesses, very little software development has taken place. Instead, most of the software used is purchased as off-the-shelf packages for various general business applications.

---

6. In the late 1990s, in a study associated with the Y2K problem, it was estimated that there were approximately 800 million lines of COBOL in use in the 22 square miles of Manhattan.

2.6.1 Historical Background

The beginning of COBOL is somewhat similar to that of ALGOL 60, in the sense that the language was designed by a committee of people meeting for relatively short periods of time. The state of business computing at the time, which was 1959, was similar to the state of scientific computing several years earlier, when Fortran was being designed. One compiled language for business applications, FLOW-MATIC, had been implemented in 1957, but it belonged to one manufacturer, UNIVAC, and was designed for that company's computers. Another language, AIMACO, was being used by the U.S. Air Force, but it was only a minor variation of FLOW-MATIC. IBM had designed a programming language for business applications, COMTRAN (COMmercial TRANslator), but it had not yet been implemented. Several other language design projects were being planned.

2.6.2 FLOW-MATIC

The origins of FLOW-MATIC are worth at least a brief discussion, because it was the primary progenitor of COBOL. In December 1953, Grace Hopper at Remington-Rand UNIVAC wrote a proposal that was indeed prophetic. It suggested that "mathematical programs should be written in mathematical notation, data processing programs should be written in English statements" (Wexelblat, 1981, p. 16). Unfortunately, it was impossible in 1953 to convince nonprogrammers that a computer could be made to understand English words. It was not until 1955 that a similar proposal had some hope of being funded by UNIVAC management, and even then it took a prototype system to do the final convincing. Part of this selling process involved compiling and running a small program, first using English keywords, then using French keywords, and then using German keywords. This demonstration was considered remarkable by UNIVAC management and was a prime factor in their acceptance of Hopper's proposal.

2.6.3 COBOL Design Process

The first formal meeting on the subject of a common language for business applications, which was sponsored by the Department of Defense, was held at the Pentagon on May 28 and 29, 1959 (exactly one year after the Zurich ALGOL meeting). The consensus of the group was that the language, then named CBL (for Common Business Language), should have the following general characteristics. Most agreed that it should use English as much as possible, although a few argued for a more mathematical notation. The language must be easy to use, even at the expense of being less powerful, in order to broaden the base of those who could program computers. In addition to making the language easy to use, it was believed that the use of English would allow managers to read programs. Finally, the design should not be overly restricted by the problems of its implementation.

One of the overriding concerns at the meeting was that steps to create this universal language should be taken quickly, as a lot of work was already being done to create new business languages. In addition to the existing languages, RCA and Sylvania were working on their own business applications languages. It was clear that the longer it took to produce a universal language, the more difficult it would be for the language to become widely used. On this basis, it was decided that there should be a quick study of existing languages. For this task, the Short Range Committee was formed.

There were early decisions to separate the statements of the language into two categories—data description and executable operations—and to have statements in these two categories reside in different parts of programs. One of the debates of the Short Range Committee was over the inclusion of subscripts. Many committee members argued that subscripts were too complex for the people in data processing, who were thought to be uncomfortable with mathematical notation. Similar arguments revolved around whether arithmetic expressions should be included. The final report of the Short Range Committee, which was completed in December 1959, described the language that was later named COBOL 60.

The language specifications for COBOL 60, published by the Government Printing Office in April 1960 (Department of Defense, 1960), were described as "initial." Revised versions were published in 1961 and 1962 (Department of Defense, 1961, 1962). The language was standardized by the American National Standards Institute (ANSI) group in 1968. The next three revisions were standardized by ANSI in 1974, 1985, and 2002. The language continues to evolve today.

2.6.4 Evaluation

The COBOL language originated a number of novel concepts, some of which eventually appeared in other languages. For example, the DEFINE verb of COBOL 60 was the first high-level language construct for macros. More important, hierarchical data structures (records), which first appeared in Plankalkül, were first implemented in COBOL. They have been included in most of the imperative languages designed since then. COBOL was also the first language that allowed names to be truly connotative, because it allowed both long names (up to 30 characters) and word-connector characters (hyphens).

Overall, the data division is the strong part of COBOL's design, whereas the procedure division is relatively weak. Every variable is defined in detail in the data division, including the number of decimal digits and the location of the implied decimal point. File records are also described with this level of detail, as are lines to be output to a printer, which makes COBOL ideal for printing accounting reports. Perhaps the most important weakness of the original procedure division was in its lack of functions. Versions of COBOL prior to the 1974 standard also did not allow subprograms with parameters.

Our final comment on COBOL: It was the first programming language whose use was mandated by the Department of Defense (DoD). This mandate came after its initial development, because COBOL was not designed specifically for the DoD. In spite of its merits, COBOL probably would not have survived without that mandate. The poor performance of the early compilers simply made it too expensive to use. Eventually, of course, compilers became more efficient and computers became much faster and cheaper, and had much larger memories. Together, these factors allowed COBOL to succeed, inside and outside DoD. Its appearance led to the electronic mechanization of accounting, an important revolution by any measure.

The following is an example of a COBOL program. This program reads a file named BAL-FWD-FILE that contains inventory information about a certain collection of items. Among other things, each item record includes the number currently on hand (BAL-ON-HAND) and the item's reorder point (BAL-REORDER-POINT). The reorder point is the threshold number of items on hand at which more must be ordered. The program produces a list of items that must be reordered as a file named REORDER-LISTING.

```
IDENTIFICATION DIVISION.
PROGRAM-ID. PRODUCE-REORDER-LISTING.

ENVIRONMENT DIVISION.
CONFIGURATION SECTION.
SOURCE-COMPUTER. DEC-VAX.
OBJECT-COMPUTER. DEC-VAX.
INPUT-OUTPUT SECTION.
FILE-CONTROL.
    SELECT BAL-FWD-FILE   ASSIGN TO READER.
    SELECT REORDER-LISTING  ASSIGN TO LOCAL-PRINTER.

DATA DIVISION.
FILE SECTION.
FD  BAL-FWD-FILE
    LABEL RECORDS ARE STANDARD
    RECORD CONTAINS 80 CHARACTERS.

01  BAL-FWD-CARD.
    02 BAL-ITEM-NO         PICTURE IS 9(5).
    02 BAL-ITEM-DESC       PICTURE IS X(20).
    02 FILLER              PICTURE IS X(5).
    02 BAL-UNIT-PRICE      PICTURE IS 999V99.
    02 BAL-REORDER-POINT   PICTURE IS 9(5).
    02 BAL-ON-HAND         PICTURE IS 9(5).
    02 BAL-ON-ORDER        PICTURE IS 9(5).
    02 FILLER              PICTURE IS X(30).
```

```
FD  REORDER-LISTING
    LABEL RECORDS ARE STANDARD
    RECORD CONTAINS 132 CHARACTERS.

01  REORDER-LINE.
    02 RL-ITEM-NO            PICTURE IS Z(5).
    02 FILLER               PICTURE IS X(5).
    02 RL-ITEM-DESC         PICTURE IS X(20).
    02 FILLER               PICTURE IS X(5).
    02 RL-UNIT-PRICE        PICTURE IS ZZZ.99.
    02 FILLER               PICTURE IS X(5).
    02 RL-AVAILABLE-STOCK PICTURE IS Z(5).
    02 FILLER               PICTURE IS X(5).
    02 RL-REORDER-POINT     PICTURE IS Z(5).
    02 FILLER               PICTURE IS X(71).

WORKING-STORAGE SECTION.
01  SWITCHES.
    02 CARD-EOF-SWITCH      PICTURE IS X.
01  WORK-FIELDS.
    02 AVAILABLE-STOCK      PICTURE IS 9(5).

PROCEDURE DIVISION.
000-PRODUCE-REORDER-LISTING.
    OPEN INPUT BAL-FWD-FILE.
    OPEN OUTPUT REORDER-LISTING.
    MOVE "N" TO CARD-EOF-SWITCH.
    PERFORM 100-PRODUCE-REORDER-LINE
        UNTIL CARD-EOF-SWITCH IS EQUAL TO "Y".
    CLOSE BAL-FWD-FILE.
    CLOSE REORDER-LISTING.
    STOP RUN.

100-PRODUCE-REORDER-LINE.
    PERFORM 110-READ-INVENTORY-RECORD.
    IF CARD-EOF-SWITCH IS NOT EQUAL TO "Y"
        PERFORM 120-CALCULATE-AVAILABLE-STOCK
        IF AVAILABLE-STOCK IS LESS THAN BAL-REORDER-POINT
            PERFORM 130-PRINT-REORDER-LINE.

110-READ-INVENTORY-RECORD.
    READ BAL-FWD-FILE RECORD
        AT END
            MOVE "Y" TO CARD-EOF-SWITCH.

120-CALCULATE-AVAILABLE-STOCK.
```

```
    ADD BAL-ON-HAND BAL-ON-ORDER
        GIVING AVAILABLE-STOCK.

130-PRINT-REORDER-LINE.
    MOVE SPACE                TO REORDER-LINE.
    MOVE BAL-ITEM-NO          TO RL-ITEM-NO.
    MOVE BAL-ITEM-DESC        TO RL-ITEM-DESC.
    MOVE BAL-UNIT-PRICE       TO RL-UNIT-PRICE.
    MOVE AVAILABLE-STOCK      TO RL-AVAILABLE-STOCK.
    MOVE BAL-REORDER-POINT TO RL-REORDER-POINT.
    WRITE REORDER-LINE.
```

2.7 The Beginnings of Timesharing: BASIC

BASIC (Mather and Waite, 1971) is another programming language that has enjoyed widespread use but has gotten little respect. Like COBOL, it has largely been ignored by computer scientists. Also, like COBOL, in its earliest versions it was inelegant and included only a meager set of control statements.

BASIC was very popular on microcomputers in the late 1970s and early 1980s. This followed directly from two of the main characteristics of BASIC: It is easy for beginners to learn, especially those who are not science oriented, and its smaller dialects can be implemented on computers with very small memories. When the capabilities of microcomputers grew and other languages were implemented, the use of BASIC waned. A strong resurgence in the use of BASIC began with the appearance of Visual Basic (Microsoft, 1991) in the early 1990s.

2.7.1 Design Process

BASIC (Beginner's All-purpose Symbolic Instruction Code) was originally designed at Dartmouth College (now Dartmouth University) in New Hampshire by two mathematicians, John Kemeny and Thomas Kurtz, who were involved in the early 1960s in producing compilers for a variety of dialects of Fortran and ALGOL 60. Their science students had little trouble learning or using those languages in their studies. However, Dartmouth was primarily a liberal arts institution, where science and engineering students made up only about 25 percent of the student body. It was decided in the spring of 1963 to design a new language especially for liberal arts students. This new language would use terminals as the method of computer access. The goals of the system were:

1. It must be easy for nonscience students to learn and use.
2. It must be pleasant and friendly.
3. It must provide fast turnaround for homework.
4. It must allow free and private access.
5. It must consider user time more important than computer time.

The last goal was indeed a revolutionary concept. It was based at least partly on the belief that computers would become significantly cheaper as time went on, which, of course, they did.

The combination of the second, third, and fourth goals led to the time-shared aspect of BASIC. Only with individual access through terminals by numerous simultaneous users could these goals be met in the early 1960s.

In the summer of 1963, Kemeny began work on the compiler for the first version of BASIC, using remote access to a GE 225 computer. Design and coding of the operating system for BASIC began in the fall of 1963. At 4:00 A.M. on May 1, 1964, the first program using the timeshared BASIC was typed in and run. In June, the number of terminals on the system grew to 11, and by fall it had ballooned to 20.

2.7.2   Language Overview

The original version of BASIC was very small and, oddly, was not interactive: There was no means of getting input data from the terminal. Programs were typed in, compiled, and run, in a sort of batch-oriented way. The original BASIC had only 14 different statement types and a single data type—floating-point. Because it was believed that few of the targeted users would appreciate the difference between integer and floating-point types, the type was referred to as "numbers." Overall, it was a very limited language, though quite easy to learn.

2.7.3   Evaluation

The most important aspect of the original BASIC was that it was the first widely used language that was used through terminals connected to a remote computer.[7] Terminals had just begun to be available at that time. Before then, most programs were entered into computers through either punched cards or paper tape.

Much of the design of BASIC came from Fortran, with some minor influence from the syntax of ALGOL 60. Later it grew in a variety of ways, with little or no effort made to standardize it. The American National Standards Institute issued a Minimal BASIC standard (ANSI, 1978b), but this represented only the bare minimum of language features. In fact, the original BASIC was very similar to Minimal BASIC.

Although it may seem surprising, Digital Equipment Corporation used a rather elaborate version of BASIC named BASIC-PLUS to write significant portions of their largest operating system for the PDP-11 minicomputers, RSTS, in the 1970s.

BASIC has been criticized for the poor structure of programs written in it, among other things. By the evaluation criteria discussed in Chapter 1, spe-

---

7. LISP initially was used through terminals, but it was not widely used in the early 1960s.

cifically readability and reliability, the language does indeed fare very poorly. Clearly, the early versions of the language were not meant for and should not have been used for serious programs of any significant size. Later versions are much better suited to such tasks.

The resurgence of BASIC in the 1990s was driven by the appearance of Visual BASIC (VB). VB became widely used in large part because it provided a simple way of building graphical user interfaces (GUIs), hence the name Visual BASIC. Visual Basic .NET, or just VB .NET, is one of Microsoft's .NET languages. Although it is a significant departure from VB, it will probably displace the older language over the next few years. Perhaps the most important difference between VB and VB .NET is that VB .NET fully supports object-oriented programming. It is possible that VB users will migrate to a different language, such as C# (see Section 2.19), rather than learn VB .NET, especially since all of the .NET languages have access to the GUI construction tools of VB.

The following is an example of a BASIC program:

```
REM   BASIC Example Program
REM   Input:  An integer, listlen, where listlen is less
REM              than 100, followed by listlen-integer values
REM   Output: The number of input values that are greater
REM              than the average of all input values
  DIM intlist(99)
  result = 0
  sum = 0
  INPUT listlen
  IF listlen > 0 AND listlen < 100 THEN
REM  Read input into an array and compute the sum
    FOR counter = 1 TO listlen
      INPUT intlist(counter)
      sum = sum + intlist(counter)
    NEXT counter
REM  Compute the average
    average = sum / listlen
REM  Count the number of input values that are > average
    FOR counter = 1 TO listlen
      IF intlist(counter) > average
        THEN result = result + 1
    NEXT counter
REM  Print the result
    PRINT "The number of values that are > average is:";
          result
  ELSE
    PRINT "Error—input list length is not legal"
  END IF
END
```

User Design and Language Design

ALAN COOPER

Best-selling author of *About Face: The Essentials of User Interface Design*, Alan Cooper also had a large hand in designing what can be touted as the language with the most concern for user interface design, Visual Basic. For him, it all comes down to a vision for humanizing technology.

SOME INFORMATION ON THE BASICS

How did you get started in all of this? I'm a high-school dropout with an associate degree in programming from a California community college. My first job was as a programmer for American President Lines (one of the United States's oldest ocean transportation companies) in San Francisco. Except for a few months here and there, I've remained self-employed.

What is your current job? Founder and Chairman of Cooper, the company that humanizes technology (www.cooper.com).

What is or was your favorite job? Interaction design consultant.

You are very well known in the fields of language design and user interface design. Any thoughts on designing languages versus designing software, versus designing anything else? It's pretty much the same in the world of software: Know your user.

ABOUT THAT EARLY WINDOWS RELEASE

In the 1980s, you started using Windows and have talked about being lured by its plusses: the graphical user interface support and the dynamically linked library that let you create tools that configured themselves. What about the parts of Windows that you eventually helped shape? I was very impressed by Microsoft's inclusion of support for practical multitasking in Windows. This included dynamic relocation and interprocess communications.

MSDOS.exe was the shell program for the first few releases of Windows. It was a terrible program, and I believed that it could be improved dramatically, and I was the guy to do it. In my spare time, I immediately began to write a better shell program than the one Windows came with. I called it Tripod. Microsoft's original shell, called MSDOS.exe, was one of the main stumbling blocks to the initial success of Windows. Tripod attempted to solve the problem by being easier to use and to configure.

When was that "Aha!" moment? It wasn't until late in 1987, when I was interviewing a corporate client, that the key design strategy for Tripod popped into my head. As the IS manager explained to me his need to create and publish a wide range of shell solutions to his disparate user base, I realized the conundrum that there is no such thing as an ideal shell. Every user would need their own personal shell, configured to their own needs and skill levels. In an instant, I perceived the solution to the shell design problem: It would be a shell construction set; a tool where each user would be able to construct exactly the shell that he or she needed for a unique mix of applications and training.

What is so compelling about the idea of a shell that can be individualized? Instead of me telling the users what the ideal shell was, they could design their own, personalized ideal shell. With a customizable shell, a programmer would create a shell that was powerful and wide-ranging, but also somewhat dangerous, whereas an IT manager would create a shell that could be given to a desk clerk that exposed only those few application-specific tools that the clerk used.

How did you get from writing a shell program to collaborating with Microsoft? Tripod and Ruby are the same thing. After I signed a deal with Bill Gates, I changed the name of the prototype from Tripod to Ruby. I then used the Ruby prototype as prototypes should be used: as a disposable model for constructing release-quality code. Which is what I did. MS took the release version of Ruby and added QuickBASIC to it, creating VB. All of those original innovations were in Tripod/Ruby.

> *MSDOS.exe was the shell program for the first few releases of Windows. It was a terrible program, and I believed that it could be improved dramatically, and I was the guy to do it. In my spare time, I immediately began to write a better shell program than the one Windows came with.*

RUBY AS THE INCUBATOR FOR VISUAL BASIC

Let's revisit your interest in early Windows and that DLL feature. The DLL wasn't a thing, it was a facility in the OS. It allowed a programmer to build code objects that could be linked to at run time as opposed to only at compile time. This is what allowed me to invent the dynamically extensible parts of VB, where controls can be added by third-party vendors.

The Ruby product embodied many significant advances in software design, but two of them stand out as exceptionally successful. As I mentioned, the dynamic linking capability of Windows had always intrigued me, but having the tools and knowing what to do with them were two different things. With Ruby, I finally found two practical uses for dynamic linking, and the original program contained both. First, the language was both installable and could be extended dynamically. Second, the palette of gizmos could be added to dynamically.

Was your language in Ruby the first to have a dynamic linked library and to be linked to a visual front end? As far as I know, yes.

Using a simple example, what would this enable a programmer to do with his or her program? Purchase a control, such as a grid control, from a third-party vendor, install it on his or her computer, and have the grid control appear as an integral part of the language, including the visual programming front end.

Why do they call you "the father of Visual Basic"? Ruby came with a small language, one suited only for executing the dozen or so simple commands that a shell program needs. However, this language was implemented as a chain of DLLs, any number of which could be installed at run time. The internal parser would identify a verb and then pass it along the chain of DLLs until one of them acknowledged that it knew how to process the verb. If all of the DLLs passed, there was a syntax error. From our earliest discussions, both Microsoft and I had entertained the idea of growing the language, possibly even replacing it altogether with a "real" language. C was the candidate most frequently mentioned, but eventually, Microsoft took advantage of this dynamic interface to unplug our little shell language and replace it entirely with QuickBasic. This new marriage of language to visual front end was static and permanent, and although the original dynamic interface made the coupling possible, it was lost in the process.

SOME FINAL COMMENTS ON NEW IDEAS

In the world of programming and programming tools, including languages and environments, what projects most interest you? I'm interested in creating programming tools that are designed to help users instead of programmers.

What's the most critical rule, famous quote, or design idea to keep in mind? Bridges are not built by engineers. They are built by ironworkers.

Similarly, software programs are not built by engineers. They are built by programmers.

2.8 Everything for Everybody: PL/I

PL/I represents the first large-scale attempt to design a language that could be used for a broad spectrum of application areas. All previous and most subsequent languages have focused on one particular application area, such as science, artificial intelligence, or business.

2.8.1 Historical Background

Like Fortran, PL/I was developed as an IBM product. By the early 1960s, the users of computers in industry had settled into two separate and quite different camps, scientific and business. From the IBM point of view, scientific programmers could use either the large-scale 7090 or the small-scale 1620 IBM computers. This group used floating-point and arrays extensively. Fortran was the primary language, although some assembly language was also used. They had their own user group, SHARE, and had little contact with anyone who worked on business applications.

For business applications, people used the large 7080 or the small 1401 IBM computers. They needed the decimal and character string data types, as well as elaborate and efficient input and output facilities. They used COBOL, although in early 1963 when the PL/I story begins, the conversion from assembly language to COBOL was far from complete. This category of users also had its own user group, GUIDE, and seldom had contact with scientific users.

In early 1963, IBM planners perceived the beginnings of a change in this situation. The two widely separated computer user groups were moving toward each other in ways that were thought certain to create problems. Scientists began to gather large files of data to be processed. This data required more sophisticated and more efficient input and output facilities. Business applications people began to use regression analysis to build management information systems, which required floating-point data and arrays. It began to appear that computing installations would soon require two separate computers and technical staffs, supporting two very different programming languages.[8]

These perceptions quite naturally led to the concept of designing a single universal computer that would be capable of doing both floating-point and decimal arithmetic, and therefore both scientific and business applications. Thus was born the concept of the IBM System/360 line of computers. Along with this came the idea of a programming language that could be used for both business and scientific applications. For good measure, features to support systems programming and list processing were thrown in. Therefore, the new language was to replace Fortran, COBOL, LISP, and the systems applications of assembly language.

---

8. At the time, large computer installations required both full-time hardware and full-time system software maintenance staff.

2.8.2   Design Process

The design effort began when IBM and SHARE formed the Advanced Language Development Committee of the SHARE Fortran Project in October 1963. This new committee quickly met and formed a subcommittee called the 3×3 Committee, so named because it had three members from IBM and three from SHARE. The 3×3 Committee met for three or four days every other week to design the language.

As with the Short Range Committee for COBOL, the initial design was scheduled for completion in a remarkably short time. Apparently, regardless of the scope of a language design effort, in the early 1960s the prevailing belief was that it could be done in three months. The first version of PL/I, which was then named Fortran VI, was supposed to be completed by December, less than three months after the committee was formed. The committee pleaded successfully on two different occasions for extensions, moving the due date back to January and then to late February 1964.

The initial design concept was that the new language would be an extension of Fortran IV, maintaining compatibility, but that goal was dropped quickly along with the name Fortran VI. Until 1965, the language was known as NPL, an acronym for New Programming Language. The first published report on NPL was given at the SHARE meeting of March 1964. A more complete description followed in April, and the version that would actually be implemented was published in December 1964 (IBM, 1964) by the compiler group at the IBM Hursley Laboratory in England, which was chosen to do the implementation. In 1965, the name was changed to PL/I to avoid the confusion of the name NPL with the National Physical Laboratory in England. If the compiler had been developed outside the United Kingdom, the name might have remained NPL.

2.8.3   Language Overview

Perhaps the best single-sentence description of PL/I is that it included what were then considered the best parts of ALGOL 60 (recursion and block structure), Fortran IV (separate compilation with communication through global data), and COBOL 60 (data structures, input/output, and report-generating facilities), along with an extensive collection of new constructs, all somehow blended together. Because PL/I is now a nearly dead language, we will not attempt, even in an abbreviated way, to discuss all the features of the language, or even its most controversial constructs. Instead, we will mention briefly some of the language's contributions to the pool of knowledge of programming languages.

PL/I was the first programming language to have the following facilities:

- Programs were allowed to create concurrently executing subprograms. Although this was a good idea, it was poorly developed in PL/I.

- It was possible to detect and handle 23 different types of exceptions, or run-time errors.

- Subprograms were allowed to be used recursively, but the capability could be disabled, allowing more efficient linkage for nonrecursive subprograms.
- Pointers were included as a data type.
- Cross sections of arrays could be referenced. For example, the third row of a matrix could be referenced as if it were a vector.

2.8.4   Evaluation

Any evaluation of PL/I must begin by recognizing the ambitiousness of the design effort. In retrospect, it appears naive to think that so many constructs could have been combined successfully. However, that judgment must be tempered by acknowledging that there was little language design experience at the time. Overall, the design of PL/I was based on the premise that any construct that was useful and could be implemented should be included, with insufficient concern about how a programmer could understand and make effective use of such an array of constructs and features. Edsger Dijkstra, in his Turing Award Lecture (Dijkstra, 1972), made one of the strongest criticisms of the complexity of PL/I: "I absolutely fail to see how we can keep our growing programs firmly within our intellectual grip when by its sheer baroqueness the programming language—our basic tool, mind you!—already escapes our intellectual control."

In addition to the problem with the complexity due to its large size, PL/I suffered from a number of what are now considered to be poorly designed constructs. Among these were pointers, exception handling, and concurrency, although we must point out that in each of these cases the construct had not appeared in any previous language.

In terms of usage, PL/I must be considered at least a partial success. In the 1970s, it enjoyed significant use in both business and scientific applications. It was also widely used during that time as an instructional vehicle in colleges, primarily in several subset forms, such as PL/C (Cornell, 1977) and PL/CS (Conway and Constable, 1976).

The following is an example of a PL/I program:

```
/* PL/I PROGRAM EXAMPLE
   INPUT:   AN INTEGER, LISTLEN, WHERE LISTLEN IS LESS THAN
              100, FOLLOWED BY LISTLEN-INTEGER VALUES
   OUTPUT:  THE NUMBER OF INPUT VALUES THAT ARE GREATER THAN
              THE AVERAGE OF ALL INPUT VALUES     */
PLIEX: PROCEDURE OPTIONS (MAIN);
  DECLARE INTLIST (1:99) FIXED.
  DECLARE (LISTLEN, COUNTER, SUM, AVERAGE, RESULT) FIXED;
  SUM = 0;
  RESULT = 0;
  GET LIST (LISTLEN);
  IF (LISTLEN > 0) & (LISTLEN < 100) THEN
    DO;
```

```
/* READ INPUT DATA INTO AN ARRAY AND COMPUTE THE SUM */
    DO COUNTER = 1 TO LISTLEN;
      GET LIST (INTLIST (COUNTER));
      SUM = SUM + INTLIST (COUNTER);
    END;
/* COMPUTE THE AVERAGE */
    AVERAGE = SUM / LISTLEN;
/* COUNT THE NUMBER OF VALUES THAT ARE > AVERAGE */
    DO COUNTER = 1 TO LISTLEN;
      IF INTLIST (COUNTER) > AVERAGE THEN
        RESULT = RESULT + 1;
    END;
/* PRINT RESULT */
    PUT SKIP LIST ('THE NUMBER OF VALUES > AVERAGE IS:');
    PUT LIST (RESULT);
    END;
  ELSE
    PUT SKIP LIST ('ERROR—INPUT LIST LENGTH IS ILLEGAL');
  END PLIEX;
```

2.9 Two Early Dynamic Languages: APL and SNOBOL

The structure of this section is different from that of the other sections of the chapter because the languages discussed here are so different. Neither APL nor SNOBOL were based on any previous language, and neither had much influence on later mainstream languages.[9] Some of the interesting features of APL are discussed later in the book.

In appearance and in purpose, APL and SNOBOL are very different. They share two fundamental characteristics, however: dynamic typing and dynamic storage allocation. Variables in both languages are essentially untyped. A variable acquires a type when it is assigned a value, at which time it assumes the type of the value assigned. Storage is allocated to a variable only when it is assigned a value, because before that there is no way to know the amount of storage that will be needed.

2.9.1   Origins and Characteristics of APL

APL (Brown et al., 1988) was designed around 1960 by Kenneth E. Iverson at IBM. It was not originally designed to be an implemented programming language, but rather was intended to be a vehicle for describing computer architecture. APL was first described in the book from which it gets its name, *A*

---

9. However, they have some imfluence on some nonmainstream languages (J is based on APL, ICON is based on SNOBOL, and AWK is partially based on SNOBOL).

Programming Language (Iverson, 1962). In the mid-1960s, the first implementation of APL was developed at IBM.

APL has a large number of powerful operators, which created a problem for implementors. The first means of using APL was through IBM printing terminals. These terminals had special print balls that provided the odd character set required by the language. One reason APL has so many operators is that it allows arrays to be manipulated as units. For example, the transpose of any matrix is done with a single operator. The large collection of operators provides very high expressivity but also makes APL programs difficult to read. This led people to think of APL as a language that is best used for "throw-away" programming. Although programs can be written quickly, they should be discarded after being used because they would be difficult to maintain.

APL has been around for 40 years and is still used today, though not widely. Furthermore, it has not changed a great deal over its lifetime.

2.9.2   Origins and Characteristics of SNOBOL

SNOBOL (pronounced "snowball"; Griswold et al., 1971) was designed in the early 1960s by three people at Bell Laboratories: D. J. Farber, R. E. Griswold, and I. P. Polonsky (Farber et al., 1964). It was designed specifically for text processing. The heart of SNOBOL is a collection of powerful operations for string pattern matching. One of the early applications of SNOBOL was for writing text editors. Because the dynamic nature of SNOBOL makes it slower than alternative languages, it is no longer used for such programs. However, SNOBOL is still a live and supported language that is used for a variety of text-processing tasks in a number of different application areas.

2.10 The Beginnings of Data Abstraction: SIMULA 67

Although SIMULA 67 never achieved widespread use and had little impact on the programmers and computing of its time, some of the constructs it introduced make it historically important.

2.10.1   Design Process

Two Norwegians, Kristen Nygaard and Ole-Johan Dahl, developed the language SIMULA I between 1962 and 1964 at the Norwegian Computing Center (NCC). They were primarily interested in using computers for simulation, but also worked in operations research. SIMULA I was designed exclusively for system simulation and was first implemented in late 1964 on a UNIVAC 1107 computer.

As soon as the SIMULA I implementation was completed, Nygaard and Dahl began efforts to extend the language by adding new features and modifying some existing constructs in order to make the language useful for general-purpose applications. The result of this work was SIMULA 67, whose design was first presented publicly in March 1967 (Dahl and Nygaard, 1967). We will discuss only SIMULA 67, although some of the features of interest in SIMULA 67 are also in SIMULA I.

2.10.2 Language Overview

SIMULA 67 is an extension of ALGOL 60, taking both block structure and the control statements from that language. The primary deficiency of ALGOL 60 (and other languages at that time) for simulation applications is the design of its subprograms. Simulation requires subprograms that are allowed to restart at the position where they previously stopped. Subprograms with this kind of control are known as **coroutines** because the caller and called subprograms have a somewhat equal relationship with each other, rather than the rigid master/slave relationship they have in imperative languages.

To provide support for coroutines in SIMULA 67, the class construct was developed. This was an important development because the concept of data abstraction began with it. The basic idea of a class is that a data structure and the routines that manipulate that data structure are packaged together. Furthermore, a class definition is only a template for a data structure and as such is distinct from a class instance, so a program can create and use any number of instances of a particular class. Class instances can contain local data. They can also include code that is executed at creation time, which can initialize some data structure of the class instance.

A more thorough discussion of classes and class instances is presented in Chapter 11. It is interesting to note that the important concept of data abstraction was not developed and attributed to the class construct until 1972, when Hoare (1972) recognized the connection.

2.11 Orthogonal Design: ALGOL 68

ALGOL 68 was the source of several new ideas in language design, some of which were subsequently adopted by other languages. We include it here for that reason, even though it never achieved widespread use in either Europe or the United States.

2.11.1 Design Process

The development of the ALGOL family did not end when the revised report appeared in 1962, although it was six years until the next design iteration was published. The resulting language, ALGOL 68 (van Wijngaarden et al., 1969), was dramatically different from its predecessor.

One of the most interesting innovations of ALGOL 68 was one of its primary design criteria: orthogonality. Recall our discussion of orthogonality in

Chapter 1. The use of orthogonality resulted in several innovative features of ALGOL 68, one of which is described in the following section.

2.11.2 Language Overview

One important result of orthogonality in ALGOL 68 was its inclusion of user-defined data types. Earlier languages, such as Fortran, included only a few basic data structures. PL/I included a larger number of data structures, which made it harder to learn and difficult to implement, but it obviously could not provide an appropriate data structure for every need.

The approach of ALGOL 68 to data structures was to provide a few primitive types and structures and allow the user to combine those primitives into a large number of different structures. This provision for user-defined data types was carried over to some extent into all of the major imperative languages designed since then. User-defined data types are valuable because they allow the user to design data abstractions that fit particular problems very closely. All aspects of data types are discussed in Chapter 6.

As another first in the area of data types, ALGOL 68 introduced the kind of dynamic arrays that will be termed *implicit heap-dynamic* in Chapter 5. A dynamic array is one in which the declaration does not specify subscript bounds. Assignments to a dynamic array cause allocation of required storage. In ALGOL 68, dynamic arrays are called **flex** arrays.

2.11.3 Evaluation

ALGOL 68 includes a significant number of features that had not been previously used. Its use of orthogonality, which some may argue was overdone, was nevertheless revolutionary.

ALGOL 68 repeated one of the sins of ALGOL 60, however, and it was an important factor in its limited popularity. The language was described using an elegant and concise but also unknown metalanguage. Before one could read the language-describing document (van Wijngaarden et al., 1969), he or she had to learn the new metalanguage, called van Wijngaarden grammars. To make matters worse, the designers invented a collection of words to explain the grammar and the language. For example, keywords were called *indicants*, substring extraction was called *trimming*, and the process of procedure execution was called a *coercion of deproceduring*, which might be *meek*, *firm*, or something else. It is natural to contrast the design of PL/I with that of ALGOL 68. ALGOL 68 achieved writability by the principle of orthogonality: a few primitive concepts and the unrestricted use of a few combining mechanisms. PL/I achieved writability by including a large number of fixed constructs. ALGOL 68 extended the elegant simplicity of ALGOL 60, whereas PL/I simply threw together the features of several languages to attain its goals. Of course, it must be kept in mind that the goal of PL/I was to provide a unified tool for a broad class of problems; on the other hand, ALGOL 68 was targeted to a single class: scientific applications.

PL/I achieved far greater acceptance than ALGOL 68, due largely to IBM's promotional efforts and the problems of understanding and implementing ALGOL 68. Implementation was a difficult problem for both, but PL/I had the resources of IBM to apply to building a compiler. ALGOL 68 enjoyed no such benefactor.

2.12 Some Early Descendants of the ALGOLs

All imperative languages, including the imperative/object-oriented languages such as C++ and Java, owe some of their design to ALGOL 60 and/or ALGOL 68. This section discusses some of the early descendants of these languages.

2.12.1 Simplicity by Design: Pascal

2.12.1.1 Historical Background

Niklaus Wirth (Wirth is pronounced "Virt") was a member of the International Federation of Information Processing (IFIP) Working Group 2.1, which was created to continue the development of ALGOL in the mid-1960s. In August 1965, Wirth and C. A. R. ("Tony") Hoare contributed to that effort by presenting to the group a somewhat modest proposal for additions and modifications to ALGOL 60 (Wirth and Hoare, 1966). The majority of the group rejected the proposal as being too small an advance over ALGOL 60. Instead, a much more complex revision was developed, which eventually became ALGOL 68. Wirth, along with a few other group members, did not believe that the ALGOL 68 report should have been released, based on the complexity of both the language and the metalanguage used to describe it. This position later proved to have some validity because the ALGOL 68 documents, and therefore the language, were indeed found to be challenging by the computing community.

The Wirth and Hoare version of ALGOL 60 was named ALGOL-W. It was implemented at Stanford University and was used primarily as an instructional vehicle, but only at a few universities. The primary contributions of ALGOL-W were the value-result method of passing parameters and the **case** statement for multiple selection. The value-result method is an alternative to ALGOL 60's pass-by-name method. Both are discussed in Chapter 9. The **case** statement is discussed in Chapter 8.

Wirth's next major design effort, again based on ALGOL 60, was his most successful: Pascal.[10] The original published definition of Pascal appeared in 1971 (Wirth, 1971). This version was modified somewhat in the

---

10. Pascal is named after Blaise Pascal, a sevententh-century French philosopher and mathematician who invented the first mechanical adding machine in 1642 (among other things).

implementation process and is described in Wirth (1973). The features that are often ascribed to Pascal in fact came from earlier languages. For example, user-defined data types were introduced in ALGOL 68, the **case** statement in ALGOL-W, and Pascal's records are similar to those of COBOL and PL/I.

2.12.1.2 Evaluation

The largest impact of Pascal was on the teaching of programming. In 1970, most students of computer science, engineering, and science were introduced to programming with Fortran, although some universities used PL/I, languages based on PL/I, and ALGOL-W. By the mid-1970s, Pascal had become the most widely used language for this purpose. This was quite natural, although perhaps not predictable, because Pascal was designed specifically for teaching programming. It was not until the late 1990s that Pascal was no longer the most commonly used language for teaching programming in colleges and universities.

Because Pascal was designed as a teaching language, it lacks several features that are essential for many kinds of applications. The best example of this is the impossibility of writing a subprogram that takes as a parameter an array of variable length. Another example is the lack of any separate compilation capability. These deficiencies naturally led to many nonstandard dialects, such as Turbo Pascal.

Pascal's popularity, for both teaching programming and other applications, was based primarily on its remarkable combination of simplicity and expressivity. Although there are some insecurities in Pascal, it is still a relatively safe language, particularly when compared with Fortran or C. By the mid-1990s, the popularity of Pascal was on the decline, both in industry and in universities, primarily due to the rise of Modula-2, Ada, and C++, all of which included features not available in Pascal.

The following is an example of a Pascal program:

```
{Pascal Example Program
  Input:  An integer, listlen, where listlen is less than
          100, followed by listlen-integer values
  Output: The number of input values that are greater than
          the average of all input values }
program pasex (input, output);
  type intlisttype = array [1..99] of integer;
  var
    intlist : intlisttype;
    listlen, counter, sum, average, result : integer;
  begin
  result := 0;
  sum := 0;
  readln (listlen);
```

```
    if ((listlen > 0) and (listlen < 100)) then
      begin
  { Read input into an array and compute the sum }
      for counter := 1 to listlen do
        begin
        readln (intlist[counter]);
        sum := sum + intlist[counter]
        end;
  { Compute the average }
      average := sum / listlen;
  { Count the number of input values that are > average }
      for counter := 1 to listlen do
        if (intlist[counter] > average) then
          result := result + 1;
  { Print the result }
      writeln ('The number of values > average is:',
                result)
      end { of the then clause of if (( listlen > 0 ... }
    else
      writeln ('Error—input list length is not legal')
end.
```

2.12.2   A Portable Systems Language: C

Like Pascal, C contributed little to the previously known collection of language features, but it has been widely used over a long period of time. Although originally designed for systems programming, C is well suited for a wide variety of applications.

2.12.2.1 Historical Background

C's ancestors include CPL, BCPL, B, and ALGOL 68. CPL was developed at Cambridge University in the early 1960s. BCPL is a simple systems language developed by Martin Richards in 1967 (Richards, 1969).

The first work on the UNIX operating system was done in the late 1960s by Ken Thompson at Bell Laboratories. The first version was written in assembly language. The first high-level language implemented under UNIX was B, which was based on BCPL. B was designed and implemented by Thompson in 1970.

Neither BCPL nor B is a typed language, which is an oddity among high-level languages, although both are much lower-level than a language such as Java. Being untyped means that all data are considered machine words, which, although extremely simple, leads to many complications and insecurities. For example, there is the problem of specifying floating-point rather than integer arithmetic in an expression. In one implementation of BCPL, the variable operands of a floating-point operation were preceded by periods. Variable operands not preceded by periods were considered to be integers. An alternative to this would have been to use different symbols for the floating-point operators.

This problem, along with several others, led to the development of a new typed language based on B. Originally called NB but later named C, it was designed and implemented by Dennis Ritchie at Bell Laboratories in 1972 (Kernighan and Ritchie, 1978). In some cases through BCPL, and in other cases directly, C was influenced by ALGOL 68. This is seen in its **for** and **switch** statements, in its assigning operators, and in its treatment of pointers.

The only "standard" for C in its first decade and a half was the book by Kernighan and Ritchie (1978).[11] Over that time span, the language slowly evolved, with different implementors adding different features. In 1989, ANSI produced an official description of C (ANSI, 1989), which included many of the features that implementors had already incorporated into the language. This standard was updated in 1999 (ISO, 1999). This new version includes a few significant changes to the language. The 1989 version, which has long been called ANSI C, should now be called C89; we will refer to the 1999 version as C99.

2.12.2.2 Evaluation

C has adequate control statements and data-structuring facilities to allow its use in many application areas. It also has a rich set of operators that provide a high degree of expressiveness.

One of the most important reasons why C is both liked and disliked is its lack of complete type checking. For example, in versions before C99, functions could be written for which parameters were not type checked. Those who like C appreciate the flexibility; those who do not like it find it too insecure. A major reason for its great increase in popularity in the 1980s was that a compiler for it was part of the widely used UNIX operating system. This inclusion in UNIX provided an essentially free and quite good compiler that was available to programmers on many different kinds of computers.

The following is an example of a C program:

```
/* C Example Program
   Input:  An integer, listlen, where listlen is less than
           100, followed by listlen-integer values
   Output: The number of input values that are greater than
           the average of all input values */
void main (){
  int intlist[98], listlen, counter, sum, average, result;
  sum = 0;
  result = 0;
```

---

11. This language is often referred to as "K & R C."

```
    scanf("%d", &listlen);
   if ((listlen > 0) && (listlen < 100)) {
/* Read input into an array and compute the sum */
     for (counter = 0; counter < listlen; counter++) {
       scanf("%d", &intlist[counter]);
       sum += intlist[counter];
       }
/* Compute the average */
     average = sum / listlen;
/* Count the input values that are > average */
     for (counter = 0; counter < listlen; counter++)
       if (intlist[counter] > average) result++;
/* Print result */
     printf("Number of values > average is:%d\n", result);
     }
   else
     printf("Error—input list length is not legal\n");
   }
```

2.12.3 A (Somewhat) Related Language: Perl

This subsection briefly discusses the origins and characteristics of Perl. Perl certainly does not ideally fit in this subsection—it is related to the ALGOL languages only through C, and even then only in its syntax and basic control statements. However, Perl does not fit well in any other section of this chapter, either, and though its importance does not warrant its own section, it should not be ignored.

2.12.3.1 Historical Background

Scripting languages have evolved over the past 25 years. Early scripting languages were used by putting a list of commands, called a **script,** in a file to be executed. The first of these languages, named sh (for shell), began as a small collection of commands that were interpreted as calls to system subprograms that performed utility functions, such as file management and simple file filtering. To this basis were added variables, control flow statements, functions, and various other capabilities, and the result is a complete programming language. One of the most powerful and widely known of these is ksh (Bolsky and Korn, 1995), which was developed by David Korn at Bell Laboratories.

Another scripting language is awk, developed by Al Aho, Brian Kernighan, and Peter Weinberger at Bell Laboratories (Aho et al., 1988). awk began as a report-generation language but later became a more general-purpose language. Tcl is an extensible scripting language developed by John Ousterhout at the University of California at Berkeley (Ousterhout, 1994). Tcl is now combined with Tk, a language that provides a method of building GUIs.

The Perl language, developed by Larry Wall, was originally a combination of sh and awk. Perl has grown significantly since its beginnings, and is now a powerful, though still somewhat primitive, programming language. Although it is still often called a scripting language, it is actually more similar to a typical imperative language, since it is always compiled, at least into an intermediate language, before it is executed. Furthermore, it has all the constructs to make it applicable to a wide variety of areas of computational problems.

2.12.3.2 Characterizing Features

Perl has a number of interesting features, only a few of which are mentioned in this chapter and discussed in the remainder of the book.

Variables in Perl are statically typed and implicitly declared. There are three distinctive namespaces for variables, denoted by the first character of the variables' names. All scalar variable names begin with dollar signs ($), all array names begin with at signs (@), and all hash names (hashes are briefly described below) begin with percent signs (%). This convention makes variable names in programs more readable than those of any other programming language.

Perl includes a large number of implicit variables. Some of them are used to store Perl parameters, such as the particular form of newline character or characters that are used in the implementation. Implicit variables are commonly used as default parameters to built-in functions and default operands for some operators. The implicit variables have distinctive—though cryptic— names, such as $! and @_. The implicit variables' names, like the user-defined variable names, use the three namespaces, so $! is a scalar.

Perl's arrays have two characteristics that set them apart from the arrays of the common imperative languages. First, they have dynamic length, meaning that they can grow and shrink as needed during execution. Second, arrays can be sparse, meaning that there can be gaps between the elements. These gaps do not take space in memory and the iteration statement used for arrays, **foreach,** iterates over the missing elements.

Perl includes associative arrays, which are called **hashes.** These data structures are indexed by strings and are implicitly controlled hash tables. The Perl system supplies the hash function and increases the size of the structure when necessary.

2.12.3.3 Evaluation

Perl is a powerful but somewhat dangerous language. Its scalar type stores both strings and numbers, which are normally stored in double-precision floating-point form. Depending on the context, numbers may be coerced to strings and vice versa. If a string is used in numeric context and the string cannot be converted to a number, zero is used and there is no warning or error message for the user. This effect can lead to errors that are not detected by the compiler or run-time system. Array indexing cannot be checked, because there is no set subscript range for any array. References to nonexistent elements return **undef**, which is interpreted as zero in numeric context. So there is also no error detection in array element access.

Perl's initial use was as a UNIX utility for processing text files. It was and still is widely used as a UNIX system administration tool. When the World Wide Web appeared, Perl achieved widespread use as a Common Gateway Interface language for use with the Web, although that use of Perl is now declining. Perl is now used as a general-purpose language for a variety of applications, such as computational biology and artificial intelligence.

The following is an example of a Perl program:

```
# Perl Example Program
# Input:  An integer, $listlen, where $listlen is less
#           than 100, followed by $listlen-integer values.
# Output: The number of input values that are greater than
#           the average of all input values.
($sum, $result) = (0, 0);
$listlen = <STDIN>;
if (($listlen > 0) && ($listlen < 100)) {
# Read input into an array and compute the sum
  for ($counter = 0; $counter < $listlen; $counter++) {
    $intlist[$counter] = <STDIN>;
  } #- end of for (counter ...
# Compute the average
  $average = $sum / $listlen;
# Count the input values that are > average
  foreach $num (@intlist) {
    if ($num > $average) { $result++; }
  } #- end of foreach $num ...
# Print result
  print "Number of vlues > average is: $result \n";
} #- end of if (($listlen ...
else {
  print "Error--input list length is not legal \n";
}
```

2.13 Programming Based on Logic: Prolog

Simply put, logic programming is the use of a formal logic notation to communicate computational processes to a computer. Predicate calculus is the notation used in current logic programming languages.

Programming in logic programming languages is nonprocedural. Programs in such languages do not state exactly *how* a result is to be computed but rather describe the necessary form and/or characteristics of the result.

What is needed to provide this capability in logic programming languages is a concise means of supplying the computer with both the relevant information and an inferencing process for computing desired results. Predicate calculus supplies the basic form of communication to the computer, and the proof method, named resolution, developed first by Robinson (1965), supplies the inferencing technique.

2.13.1 Design Process

During the very early 1970s, Alain Colmerauer and Phillippe Roussel in the Artificial Intelligence Group at the University of Aix-Marseille, together with Robert Kowalski of the Department of Artificial Intelligence at the University of Edinburgh, developed the fundamental design of Prolog. The primary components of Prolog are a method for specifying predicate calculus propositions and an implementation of a restricted form of resolution. Both predicate calculus and resolution are described in Chapter 16. The first Prolog interpreter was developed at Marseille in 1972. The version of the language that was implemented is described in Roussel (1975). The name Prolog is from *pro*gramming *log*ic.

2.13.2 Language Overview

Prolog programs consist of collections of statements. Prolog has only a few kinds of statements, but they can be complex.

One common use of Prolog is as a kind of intelligent database. This application provides a simple framework for discussing the Prolog language.

The database of a Prolog program consists of two kinds of statements: facts and rules. Examples of fact statements are:

```
mother(joanne, jake).
father(vern, joanne).
```

which state that joanne is the mother of jake, and vern is the father of joanne.

An example of a rule statement is

```
grandparent(X, Z) :- parent(X, Y), parent(Y, Z).
```

which states that it can be deduced that X is the grandparent of Z if it is true that X is the parent of Y and Y is the parent of Z, for some specific values for the variables X, Y, and Z.

The Prolog database can be interactively queried with goal statements, an example of which is

```
father(bob, darcie).
```

which asks if bob is the father of darcie. When such a query, or goal, is presented to the Prolog system, it uses its resolution process to attempt to determine the truth of the statement. If it can conclude that the goal is true, it displays "true." If it cannot prove it, it displays "false."

2.13.3   Evaluation

In the 1980s, there was a relatively small group of computer scientists who believed that logic programming provided the best hope for escaping from the complexity of imperative languages, and also from the enormous problem of producing the large amount of reliable software that was needed. So far, however, there are two major reasons why logic programming has not become more widely used. First, as with some other nonimperative approaches, programs written in logic languages thus far have proven to be highly inefficient relative to equivalent imperative programs. Second, it has been shown to be an effective approach for only a few relatively small areas of application: certain kinds of database management systems and some areas of AI.

There is a dialect of Prolog that supports object-oriented programming — Prolog++ (Moss, 1994). Logic programming and Prolog are described in greater detail in Chapter 16.

2.14 History's Largest Design Effort: Ada

The Ada language is the result of the most extensive and most expensive language design effort ever undertaken. The following paragraphs briefly describe the evolution of Ada.

2.14.1   Historical Background

The Ada language was developed for the Department of Defense (DoD), so the state of their computing environment was instrumental in determining its form. By 1974, over half of the applications of computers in DoD were embedded systems. An embedded system is one in which the computer hardware is embedded in the device it controls or for which it provides services. Software costs were rising rapidly, primarily because of the increasing complexity of systems. More than 450 different programming languages were in use for DoD projects, and none of them was standardized by DoD. Every defense contractor could define a new and different language for every contract.[12] Because of this language proliferation, application software was rarely reused. Furthermore, no software development tools were created (because

---

12. This result was largely due to the widespread use of assembly language for embedded systems, along with the fact that most embedded systems used specialized processors.

they are usually language dependent). A great many languages were in use, but none was actually suitable for embedded systems applications. For these reasons, the Army, Navy, and Air Force each independently proposed in 1974 the development of a single high-level language for embedded systems.

2.14.2 Design Process

Noting this widespread interest, Malcolm Currie, Director of Defense Research and Engineering, in January 1975, formed the High-Order Language Working Group (HOLWG), initially headed by Lt. Col. William Whitaker of the Air Force. The HOLWG had representatives from all of the military services and liaisons with Great Britain, France, and West Germany. Its initial charter was to:

- Identify the requirements for a new DoD high-level language.

- Evaluate existing languages to determine whether there was a viable candidate.

- Recommend adoption or implementation of a minimal set of programming languages.

In April 1975, the HOLWG produced the Strawman requirements document for the new language (Department of Defense, 1975a). This was distributed to military branches, federal agencies, selected industrial and university representatives, and interested parties in Europe.

The Strawman document was followed by Woodenman (Department of Defense, 1975b) in August 1975, Tinman (Department of Defense, 1976) in January 1976, Ironman (Department of Defense, 1977) in January 1977, and finally Steelman (Department of Defense, 1978) in June 1978.

After a tedious process, the many submitted proposals for the language were narrowed down to four finalists, all of which were based on Pascal. In May 1979, the Cii Honeywell/Bull language design proposal was chosen from the four finalists as the design that would be used. The Cii Honeywell/Bull design team in France, the only foreign competitor among the final four, was led by Jean Ichbiah.

In the spring of 1979, Jack Cooper of the Navy Materiel Command recommended the name for the new language, Ada, which was then adopted. The name commemorates Augusta Ada Byron (1815–1851), Countess of Lovelace, mathematician, and daughter of poet Lord Byron, who is generally recognized as being the world's first programmer. She worked with Charles Babbage on his mechanical computers, the Difference and Analytical Engines, writing programs for several numerical processes.

The design and the rationale for Ada were published by ACM in its *SIGPLAN Notices* (ACM, 1979) and distributed to a readership of more than 10,000 people. A public test and evaluation conference was held in October 1979 in Boston, with representatives from over 100 organizations from the United States and Europe. By November, more than 500 language reports had been received from 15 different countries. Most of the reports suggested small modifications rather than drastic changes and outright rejections. Based on the language reports, the next version of the requirements specification, the Stoneman document (Department of Defense, 1980a), was released in February 1980.

A revised version of the language design was completed in July 1980 and was accepted as MIL-STD 1815, the standard *Ada Language Reference Manual*. The number 1815 was chosen because it was the year of the birth of Augusta Ada Byron. Another revised version of the *Ada Language Reference Manual* was released in July 1982. In 1983, the American National Standards Institute standardized Ada. This "final" official version is described in Goos and Hartmanis (1983). The Ada language design was then frozen for a minimum of five years.

2.14.3 Language Overview

This sub-section briefly describes four of the major contributions of the Ada language.

Packages in the Ada language provide the means for encapsulating data objects, specifications for data types, and procedures. This, in turn, provides the support for the use of data abstraction in program design, as described in Chapter 11.

The Ada language includes extensive facilities for exception handling, which allow the programmer to gain control after any one of a wide variety of exceptions, or run-time errors, has been detected. Exception handling is discussed in Chapter 14.

Program units can be generic in Ada. For example, it is possible to write a sort procedure that uses an unspecified type for the data to be sorted. Such a generic procedure must be instantiated for a specified type before it can be used, which is done with a statement that causes the compiler to generate a version of the procedure with the given type. The availability of such generic units increases the range of program units that might be reused, rather than duplicated, by programmers. Generics are discussed in Chapters 9 and 11.

The Ada language also provides for concurrent execution of special program units, named tasks, using the rendezvous mechanism. Rendezvous is the name of a method of intertask communication and synchronization. Concurrency is discussed in Chapter 13.

2.14.4 Evaluation

Perhaps the most important aspects of the design of the Ada language to consider are the following:

- Because the design was competitive, there was no limit on participation.
- The Ada language embodies most of the concepts of software engineering and language design of the late 1970s. Although one can question the

actual methods used to incorporate these features, as well as the wisdom of including such a large number of features in a language, most agree that the features are valuable.

- Although many people did not initially realize it, the development of a compiler for the Ada language was a difficult task. Only in 1985, almost four years after the language design was completed, did truly usable Ada compilers begin to appear.

The most serious criticism of Ada in its first few years was that it was too large and too complex. In particular, Hoare (1981) has stated that it should not be used for any application where reliability is critical, which is precisely the type of applications for which it was designed. On the other hand, others have praised it as the epitome of language design for its time. In fact, even Hoare eventually softened his view of the language.

The following is an example of an Ada program:

```
-- Ada Example Program
-- Input:  An integer, List_Len, where List_Len is less
--            than 100, followed by List_Len-integer values
-- Output: The number of input values that are greater
--            than the average of all input values
with Ada.Text_IO, Ada.Integer.Text_IO;
use Ada.Text_IO, Ada.Integer.Text_IO;
procedure Ada_Ex is
  type Int_List_Type is array (1..99) of Integer;
  Int_List : Int_List_Type;
  List_Len, Sum, Average, Result : Integer;
begin
  Result:= 0;
  Sum := 0;
  Get (List_Len);
  if (List_Len > 0) and (List_Len < 100) then
-- Read input data into an array and compute the sum
    for Counter := 1 .. List_Len loop
      Get (Int_List(Counter));
      Sum := Sum + Int_List(Counter);
    end loop;
-- Compute the average
    Average := Sum / List_Len;
-- Count the number of values that are > average
    for Counter := 1 .. List_Len loop
      if Int_List(Counter) > Average then
        Result:= Result+ 1;
      end if;
    end loop;
-- Print result
```

```
      Put ("The number of values > average is:");
      Put (Result);
      New_Line;
    else
      Put_Line ("Error—input list length is not legal");
    end if;
end Ada_Ex;
```

2.14.5 Ada 95

Two of the most important new features of Ada 95 are described briefly in the following paragraphs. In the remainder of the book, we will use the name Ada 83 for the original version and Ada 95 (its actual name) for the later version when it is important to distinguish between the two versions. In discussions of language features common to both versions, we will use the name Ada. The Ada 95 standard language is defined in ARM (1995).

The type derivation mechanism of Ada 83 is extended in Ada 95 to allow adding new components to those inherited from a base class. This provides for inheritance, a key ingredient in object-oriented programming languages. Dynamic binding of subprogram calls to subprogram definitions is accomplished through subprogram dispatching, which is based on the tag value of derived types through classwide types. This feature provides for polymorphism, another principal feature of object-oriented programming. These features of Ada 95 are discussed in Chapter 12.

The rendezvous mechanism of Ada 83 provided only a cumbersome and inefficient means of sharing data among concurrent processes. It was necessary to introduce a new task to control access to the shared data. The protected objects of Ada 95 offer an attractive alternative to this. The shared data is encapsulated in a syntactic structure that controls all access to the data, either by rendezvous or by subprogram call. The new features of Ada 95 for concurrency and shared data are discussed in Chapter 13.

It is widely believed that the popularity of Ada 95 suffered because the Department of Defense no longer requires its use in military software systems. There are, of course, other factors that have hindered its growth in popularity. Most important among these is the widespread acceptance of C++ for object-oriented programming, which occurred before Ada 95 was released.

2.15 Object-Oriented Programming: Smalltalk

Smalltalk was the first programming language that fully supported object-oriented programming. It is therefore an important part of any discussion of the evolution of programming languages.

2.15.1   Design Process

The concepts that led to the development of Smalltalk originated in the Ph.D. dissertation work of Alan Kay in the late 1960s at the University of Utah (Kay, 1969). Kay had remarkable foresight in predicting the future availability of powerful desktop computers. Recall that the first microcomputer systems were not marketed until the mid-1970s, and they were only remotely related to the machines envisioned by Kay, which were seen to execute a million or more instructions per second and contain several megabytes of memory. Such machines, in the form of workstations, became widely available only in the early 1980s.

Kay believed that desktop computers would be used by nonprogrammers and thus would need very powerful human-interfacing capabilities. The computers of the late 1960s were largely batch oriented and were used exclusively by professional programmers and scientists. For use by nonprogrammers, Kay determined, a computer would have to be highly interactive and use sophisticated graphics in its interface to users. Some of the graphics concepts came from the LOGO experience of Seymour Papert, in which graphics were used to aid children in the use of computers (Papert, 1980).

Kay originally envisioned a system he called Dynabook, which was meant to be a general information processor. It was based in part on the Flex language, which he had helped design. Flex was based primarily on SIMULA 67. Dynabook used the paradigm of the typical desk, on which there are a number of papers, some partially covered. The top sheet is often the focus of attention, with the others temporarily out of focus. The display of Dynabook would model this scene, using screen windows to represent various sheets of paper on the desktop. The user would interact with such a display both through a keyboard and by touching the screen with his or her fingers. After the preliminary design of Dynabook earned him a Ph.D., Kay's goal became to see such a machine constructed.

Kay found his way to the Xerox Palo Alto Research Center (Xerox PARC) and presented his ideas on Dynabook. This led to his employment there and the subsequent birth of the Learning Research Group at Xerox. The first charge of the group was to design a language to support Kay's programming paradigm and implement it on the best personal computer then available. These efforts resulted in an "Interim" Dynabook, consisting of the Xerox Alto hardware and the Smalltalk-72 software. Together, they formed a research tool for further development. A number of research projects were conducted with this system, including several experiments to teach programming to children. Along with the experiments came further developments, leading to a sequence of languages that ended with Smalltalk-80. As the language grew, so did the power of the hardware on which it resided. By 1980, both the language and the Xerox hardware nearly matched the early vision of Alan Kay.

2.15.2 Language Overview

The Smalltalk world is populated by nothing but objects, from integer constants to large complex software systems. All computing in Smalltalk is done by the same uniform technique: sending a message to an object to invoke one of its methods. A reply to a message is an object, which either returns the requested information or simply notifies the sender that the requested processing has been completed. The fundamental difference between a message and a subprogram call is this: A message is sent to a data object, specifically to one of the methods defined for the object. The called method is then executed, often modifying the data of the object to which the message was sent; a subprogram call is a message to the code of a subprogram. Usually the data to be processed by the subprogram is sent to it as a parameter.[13]

In Smalltalk, object abstractions are classes, which are very similar to the classes of SIMULA 67. Instances of the class can be created and are then the objects of the program.

The syntax of Smalltalk is unlike that of any other programming language, in large part because of the use of messages, rather than arithmetic and logic expressions and conventional control statements. One of the Smalltalk control constructs is illustrated in the example in the next subsection.

2.15.3 Evaluation

Smalltalk has done a great deal to promote two separate aspects of computing, graphical user interfaces and object-oriented programming. The windowing systems that are now the dominant method of user interfaces to software systems grew out of Smalltalk. Today, the most significant software design methodologies and programming languages are object oriented. Although the origin of some of the ideas of object-oriented languages came from SIMULA 67, they reached maturation only in Smalltalk. It is clear that Smalltalk's impact on the computing world is extensive and will be long-lived.

The following is an example of a Smalltalk class definition:

```
"Smalltalk Example Program"
"The following is a class definition, instantiations of
which can draw equilateral polygons of any number of sides"
class name                    Polygon
superclass                    Object
instance variable names       ourPen
numSides
sideLength
"Class methods"
  "Create an instance"
```

---

13. It is of course true that a method call can also pass data to be processed by the called method.

```
new
    ^ super new getPen

"Get a pen for drawing polygons"
getPen
    ourPen <- Pen new defaultNib: 2

"Instance methods"
"Draw a polygon"
draw
    numSides timesRepeat: [ourPen go: sideLength;
                               turn: 360 // numSides]

"Set length of sides"
length: len
    sideLength <- len

"Set number of sides"
sides: num
    numSides <- num
```

2.16 Combining Imperative and Object-Oriented Features: C++

The origins of C were discussed in Section 2.12; the origins of Smalltalk were discussed in Section 2.15. C++ builds language facilities on top of C to support much of what Smalltalk pioneered. C++ has evolved from C through a sequence of modifications to improve its imperative features and to add constructs to support object-oriented programming.

2.16.1   Design Process

The first step from C toward C++ was made by Bjarne Stroustrup at Bell Laboratories in 1980. Modifications to C included the addition of function parameter type checking and conversion and, more significantly, classes, which are related to those of SIMULA 67 and Smalltalk. Also included were derived classes, public/private access control of inherited components, constructor and destructor methods, and friend classes. During 1981, inline functions, default parameters, and overloading of the assignment operator were added. The resulting language was called C with Classes and is described in Stroustrup (1983).

It is useful to consider some goals of C with Classes. The primary goal was to provide a language in which programs could be organized as they could be organized in SIMULA 67, that is, with classes and inheritance. A second important goal was that there should be no performance penalty relative to C. For example, array index range checking was not even considered because a significant performance disadvantage, relative to C, would result. A third goal of C with Classes was that it could be used for every application for which C could be used, so virtually none of the features of C would be removed, not even those considered to be unsafe.

By 1984, this language was extended by the inclusion of virtual methods, which provide dynamic binding of method calls to specific method definitions; method name and operator overloading; and reference types. This version of the language was called C++. It is described in Stroustrup (1984).

In 1985, the first available implementation appeared: a system named Cfront, which translates C++ programs into C programs. This version of Cfront and the version of C++ it implemented were named Release 1.0. It is described in Stroustrup (1986).

Between 1985 and 1989, C++ continued to evolve, based largely on user reactions to the first distributed implementation. This next version was named Release 2.0. Its Cfront implementation was released in June 1989. The most important features added to C++ Release 2.0 were support for multiple inheritance (classes with more than one parent class) and abstract classes, along with some other enhancements. Abstract classes are described in Chapter 12.

Release 3.0 of C++ evolved between 1989 and 1990. It added templates, which provide parameterized types, and exception handling. The current version of C++, which was standardized in 1998, is described in ISO (1998).

In 2002, Microsoft released its .NET computing platform, which includes a new version of C++, named Managed C++, or MC++. MC++ extends C++ to provide access to the functionality of the .NET Framework. The additions include properties, delegates, interfaces, and a reference type for garbage-collected objects. Properties are discussed in Chapter 11. Delegates are introduced in Section 2.19. Because .NET does not support multiple inheritance, neither does MC++.

2.16.2   Language Overview

C++ provides two constructs that define types, classes, and structs, with little difference between the two. In practice, structs that include method definitions are rarely used. Multiple inheritance is supported. In C++, methods are often called member functions.

Because C++ has both functions and methods, it supports both procedural and object-oriented programming.

Operators in C++ can be overloaded, meaning the user can create operators for existing operators on user-defined types. C++ methods can also be overloaded, meaning the user can define more than one method with the same name, provided either the numbers or types of their parameters are different.

Dynamic binding in C++ is provided by virtual methods. These methods define type-dependent operations, using overloaded methods, within a collection of classes that are related through inheritance. A pointer to an object of class A can also point to objects of classes that have class A as an ancestor. When this pointer points to an overloaded virtual method, the method of the current type is chosen dynamically.

Both methods and classes can be templated, which means that they can be parameterized. For example, a method can be written as a templated method to allow it to have versions for a variety of parameter types. Classes enjoy the same flexibility.

C++ includes exception handling that is significantly different from that of Ada. One difference is that hardware-detectable exceptions cannot be handled. The exception-handling constructs of Ada and C++ are discussed in Chapter 14.

2.16.3 Evaluation

C++ rapidly became and remains a very popular language. One factor in its popularity is the availability of good and inexpensive compilers. Another factor is that it is almost completely backward compatible with C (meaning that C programs can be, with few changes, compiled as C++ programs), and in most implementations it is possible to link C++ code with C code—and thus relatively easy for the many C programmers to learn C++. Finally, at the time C++ first appeared, when object-oriented programming began to receive widespread interest, C++ was the only language that was available that was suitable for large commercial software projects.

On the negative side, because C++ is a very large and complex language, it clearly suffers drawbacks similar to those of PL/I. It inherited most of the insecurities of C, which make it less safe than languages such as Ada and Java.

The object-oriented features of C++ are described in far more detail in Chapter 12.

2.16.4 A Related Language: Eiffel

Eiffel is another hybrid language with both imperative and object-oriented features (Meyer, 1992). Eiffel was designed by a single person, Bertrand Meyer, who is French but lives in California. The language includes features to support abstract data types, inheritance, and dynamic binding, so it fully supports object-oriented programming. Perhaps the most distinguishing feature of Eiffel is the integrated use of assertions to enforce the "contract" between subprograms and their callers. It is an idea that was born in Plankalkül but ignored by most other languages designed since then. It is natural to compare Eiffel to C++. Eiffel is smaller, simpler, and safer than C++ but has nearly equal expressivity and writability. The reasons for the soaring popularity of C++, while Eiffel has had much more limited use, are not difficult to determine. C++ was clearly the easiest way for software development organizations to move to object-oriented programming, because in many cases their developers already knew C. Eiffel enjoyed no such easy path to adoption. Also, for the first few years that use of C++ spread, the Cfront system was available and inexpensive. During its early years, Eiffel compilers were less available and more expensive. C++ had the backing of the prestigious Bell Laboratories, whereas Eiffel was backed by Bertrand Meyer and his relatively small software company, Interactive Software Engineering.

2.16.5   Another Related Language: Delphi

Delphi (Lischner, 2000) is a hybrid language, similar to C++ in that it was created by adding object-oriented support, among other things, to an existing imperative language, Pascal. Many of the differences between C++ and Delphi are a result of the predecessor languages and the surrounding programming cultures from which they are derived. Because C is a powerful but potentially unsafe language, C++ also fits that description, at least in the areas of array subscript range checking, pointer arithmetic, and its numerous type coercions. Likewise, because Pascal is more elegant and safer than C, Delphi is more elegant and safer than C++. Delphi is also less complex than C++. For example, Delphi does not allow user-defined operator overloading, generic subprograms, and parameterized classes, all of which are part of C++.

Delphi, like Visual C++, provides a graphical user interface (GUI) to the developer and simple ways to create GUI interfaces to applications written in Delphi. Delphi was designed by Anders Hejlsberg, who had previously developed the Turbo Pascal system. Both of these were marketed and distributed by Borland. Hejlsberg was also the lead designer of C#.

2.17   An Imperative-Based Object-Oriented Language: Java

Java's designers started with C++, removed numerous constructs, changed some, and added a few others. The resulting language provides much of the power and flexibility of C++, but in a smaller, simpler, and safer language.

2.17.1   Design Process

Java, like many programming languages, was designed for an application for which there appeared to be no satisfactory existing language; in the case of Java, however, it was actually a sequence of applications, the first of which was the programming of embedded consumer electronic devices, such as toasters, microwave ovens, and interactive TV systems. It may not seem that reliability would be an important factor in the software for a microwave oven. If an oven had malfunctioning software, it probably would not pose a grave danger to anyone and probably would not lead to large legal settlements. However, if the software in a particular model was found to be erroneous after a million units had been manufactured and sold, their recall would entail significant cost. Therefore, reliability *is* an important characteristic of the software in consumer electronic products.

In 1990, Sun Microsystems decided that neither of the two programming languages they had considered, C and C++, would be satisfactory for developing software for consumer electronic devices. Although C was relatively small, it did not provide support for object-oriented programming, which they deemed a necessity. C++ supported object-oriented programming, but it was judged to be too large and complex, in part because it also supported procedure-oriented programming. It was also believed that neither C nor C++ provided the necessary level of reliability. The design of Java was guided by the fundamental goal of providing greater simplicity and reliability than they believed were provided by C++.

Although the initial impetus for Java was consumer electronics, none of the products with which it was used in its early years were ever marketed. When the World Wide Web became widely used, starting in 1993, largely because of the new graphical browsers, Java was found to be a useful tool for Web programming. In particular, Java applets, which are relatively small Java programs whose output can be included in displayed Web documents, quickly became very popular in the middle to late 1990s. In its first few years in public use, the Web was Java's most common application.

The Java design team was headed by James Gosling, who had previously designed the UNIX emacs editor and the NeWS windowing system.

2.17.2 Language Overview

As we stated earlier, Java is based on C++ but was specifically designed to be smaller, simpler, and more reliable. Like C++, Java has both classes and primitive types. Java arrays are instances of a predefined class, whereas in C++ they are not, although many C++ users build wrapper classes for arrays to add features like index range checking, which is implicit in Java.

Java does not have pointers, but its reference types provide some of the capabilities of pointers. These references are used to point to class instances. All objects are allocated on the heap. While pointers and references may seem a great deal alike, there are some important semantic differences. Pointers point to memory locations, but references point to objects. This makes any kind of arithmetic on references nonsense, eliminating that error-prone practice. The distinction between a pointer's value and the value to which it points is the responsibility of the programmer in many languages, in which pointers sometimes must be explicitly dereferenced. References are always implicitly dereferenced, when necessary. So they behave more like ordinary scalar variables.

Java has a primitive Boolean type named **boolean,** used mainly for the control expressions of its control statements (such as **if** and **while**). Unlike C and C++, arithmetic expressions cannot be used for control expressions.

One significant difference between Java and many of its predecessors that support object-oriented programming, including C++, is that it is not possible to write stand-alone subprograms in Java. All Java subprograms are methods and are defined in classes. Furthermore, methods can be called only through a class or object. One consequence of this is that while C++ supports both procedural and object-oriented programming, Java supports only object-oriented programming.

Another important difference between C++ and Java is that C++ supports multiple inheritance directly in its class definitions. Some feel multiple inheritance leads to more complexity and confusion than it is worth. Java supports only single inheritance of classes, although some of the benefits of multiple inheritance can be gained by using its interface construct.

Among the C++ constructs that were not copied into Java are structs and unions.

Java includes a relatively simple form of concurrency control through its **synchronize** modifier, which can appear on methods and blocks. In either case, it causes a lock to be attached. The lock ensures mutually exclusive access or execution. In Java it is relatively easy to create concurrent processes, which in Java are called *threads*.

Java uses implicit storage deallocation for its objects, often called **garbage collection.** This frees the programmer from needing to explicitly delete objects when they are no longer needed. Programs written in languages that do not have garbage collection often suffer from what is sometimes called memory leakage, which means that storage is allocated but never deallocated. This can obviously lead to eventual depletion of all available storage.

Unlike C and C++, Java includes assignment type coercions (implicit type conversions) only if they are widening (from a "smaller" type to a "larger" type). So **int** to **float** coercions are done across the assignment operator, but **float** to **int** coercions are not.

2.17.3 Evaluation

The designers of Java did well at trimming out excess and/or unsafe features of C++. For example, the elimination of half of the assignment coercions that are done in C++ was clearly a step toward higher reliability. Index range checking of array accesses also makes the language safer. The addition of concurrency enhances the scope of applications that can be written in the language, as do the class libraries for applets, graphical user interfaces, database access, and networking.

Java's portability, at least in intermediate form, has often been attributed to the design of the language, but it is not. Any language could be translated to an intermediate form and "run" on any platform that had a virtual machine for that intermediate form. The price of this kind of portability is the cost of interpretation, which traditionally has been about an order of magnitude more than execution of machine code. The initial version of the Java interpreter, called the Java Virtual Machine (JVM), indeed was at least 10 times slower than equivalent compiled C programs. However, many Java programs are now translated to machine code before being executed, using Just-in-Time (JIT) compilers. This makes the efficiency of Java programs competitive with that of programs in compiled languages such as C++.

The use of Java increased faster than that of any other programming language. Initially, this was due to its value in programming dynamic Web documents. Another is that the compiler/interpreter system for Java has been free and easy to obtain on the Web. It is clear that one of the reasons for Java's rapid rise to prominence is simply that programmers like its design. There were always some developers who thought C++ was simply too large and complex to be practical and safe. Java offered them an alternative that has much of the power of C++, but in a simpler, safer language. Java is now widely used in a variety of different applications areas.

The most recent version of Java, which appeared in 2004 and was first called Java 1.5, but later renamed Java 5.0, includes a few significant additions. These include an enumeration class, generics, and a new iteration construct.

The following is an example of a Java program:

```java
// Java Example Program
//  Input: An integer, listlen, where listlen is less
//         than 100, followed by length-integer values
// Output: The number of input data that are greater than
//         the average of all input values
import java.io.*;
class IntSort {
public static void main(String args[]) throws IOException {
  DataInputStream in = new DataInputStream(System.in);
  int listlen,
      counter,
      sum = 0,
      average,
      result = 0;
  int[] intlist = new int[99];
  listlen = Integer.parseInt(in.readLine());
  if ((listlen > 0) && (listlen < 100)) {
/* Read input into an array and compute the sum  */
    for (counter = 0; counter < listlen; counter++) {
      intlist[counter] =
            Integer.valueOf(in.readLine()).intValue();
      sum += intlist[counter];
    }
/* Compute the average */
    average = sum / listlen;
/* Count the input values that are > average */
    for (counter = 0; counter < listlen; counter++)
      if (intlist[counter] > average) result++;
/* Print result */
      System.out.println(
          "\nNumber of values > average is:" + result);
  }  //** end of then clause of if ((listlen > 0) ...
```

```
        else System.out.println(
                "Error—input list length is not legal\n");
    }  //** end of method main
}  //** end of class IntSort
```

2.18 Scripting Languages: JavaScript, PHP, Python, and Ruby

Use of the Web exploded in the mid-1990s after the first graphical browsers appeared. The need for computation associated with HTML documents, which by themselves are completely static, quickly became critical. Computation on the server end was made possible with the Common Gateway Interface (CGI), which allowed HTML documents to request the execution of programs on the server, with the results of such computations returned to the browser in the form of HTML documents. Computation on the browser end became available with the advent of Java applets. Both of these approaches are now slowly being replaced by newer technologies, in large part with the use of scripting languages. This section briefly discusses two of the most popular of these, JavaScript, which is an HTML-resident client-side scripting language, and PHP, which is an HTML-resident server-side scripting language. This section also briefly discusses two other scripting languages, Python and Ruby. Python and Ruby were not created just for Web applications, though they are used for CGI programming.

Note that Perl is often considered to be a scripting language, but Perl is in fact much more like C than a typical scripting language. Perl is discussed in Section 2.12.3.

2.18.1 Origins and Characteristics of JavaScript

JavaScript (Flanagan, 1998), which was originally named LiveScript, was developed at Netscape. In late 1995, LiveScript became a joint venture of Netscape and Sun Microsystems and its name was changed to JavaScript. JavaScript has gone through extensive evolution, moving from version 1.0 to version 1.5 by adding many new features and capabilities. A language standard for JavaScript was developed in the late 1990s by the European Computer Manufacturers Association (ECMA) as ECMA-262. This standard has also been approved by the International Standards Organization (ISO) as ISO-16262. Microsoft's version of JavaScript is named JScript .NET.

Although a JavaScript interpreter could be embedded in many different applications, its most common use is embedded in Web browsers. JavaScript code is embedded in HTML documents and interpreted when the documents are displayed. The primary uses of JavaScipt in Web programming are to validate form input data and create dynamic HTML documents.

In spite of its name, JavaScript is related to Java only through the use of similar syntax. Java is strongly typed, but JavaScript is dynamically typed (see

Chapter 5). JavaScript's character strings and its arrays have dynamic length. Because of this, array indices are not checked for validity, although this is required in Java. Although Java fully supports object-oriented programming, JavaScript supports neither inheritance nor dynamic binding of method calls to methods.

One of the most important uses of JavaScript is for dynamically creating and modifying HTML documents. JavaScript defines an object hierarchy that matches a hierarchical model of an HTML document, which is defined by the Document Object Model. Elements of an HTML document are accessed through these objects, providing the basis for dynamic control of the elements of documents.

Following is an example of a JavaScript script. Its appearance is odd, because it is embedded in an HTML document. This program can be run with any Web browser that includes a recent version of a JavaScript interpreter.

```
<?xml version="1.0" encoding="utf-8"?>
<!DOCTYPE html PUBLIC "-//w3c//DTD XHTML 1.1 //EN"
   "http://www.w3.org/TR/xhtml11/DTD/xhtml11-strict.dtd">
<!-- example.html
     Input: An integer, listLen, where listLen is less
            than 100, followed by listLen-numeric values
     Output: The number of input values that are greater
            than the average of all input values
     -->
<html xmlns = "http://www.w3.org/1999/xhtml">
<head><title> Example </title>
</head>
<body>
<script type = "text/javascript">
<!--
var intList = new Array(99);
var listLen, counter, sum = 0, result = 0;

listLen = prompt (
        "Please type the length of the input list", "");
if ((listLen > 0) && (listLen < 100)) {
// Get the input and compute its sum
   for (counter = 0; counter < listLen; counter++) {
      intList[counter] = prompt (
                      "Please type the next number", "");
      sum += parseInt(intList[counter]);
   }
// Compute the average
   average = sum / listLen;
// Count the input values that are > average
   for (counter = 0; counter < listLen; counter++)
```

```
      if (intList[counter] > average) result++;
// Display the results
   document.write("Number of values > average is: ",
                result, "<br />");
} else
   document.write(
      "Error - input list length is not legal <br />");
// -->
</script>
</body>
</html>
```

2.18.2 Origins and Characteristics of PHP

PHP (Converse and Park, 2000) was developed by Rasmus Lerdorf, a member of the Apache Group, in 1994. Its initial motivation was to provide a tool to help Lerdorf track visitors to his personal Web site. In 1995, he developed a package called Personal Home Page Tools, which became the first publicly distributed version of PHP. Originally, PHP was an acronym for Personal Home Page. Later, its user community began using the recursive name PHP: Hypertext Preprocessor, which subsequently forced the original name into obscurity. PHP is now developed, distributed, and supported as an open-source product. PHP processors are resident on most Web servers.

PHP is an HTML-embedded server-side scripting language specifically designed for Web applications. PHP code is interpreted on the Web server when an HTML document in which it is embedded has been requested by a browser. PHP code usually produces HTML code as output, which replaces the PHP code in the HTML document. Therefore, a Web browser never sees PHP code.

PHP is similar to JavaScript, in its syntactic appearance, the dynamic nature of its strings and arrays, and its use of dynamic typing. PHP's arrays are a combination of JavaScript's arrays and Perl's hashes.

The original version of PHP did not support object-oriented programming, but that support was added in the second release. However, PHP does not support abstract classes or interfaces, destructors, or access controls for class members.

PHP allows simple access to HTML form data, so form processing is easy with PHP. PHP provides support for many different database management systems. This makes it an excellent language for building programs that need Web access to databases.

2.18.3   Origins and Characteristics of Python

Python (Lutz & Ascher, 2004) is a relatively recent object-oriented interpreted scripting language. Its initial version was designed by Guido van Rossum at Stichting Mathematisch Centrum in the Netherlands in the early 1990s. Its development is now being done by the Python Software Foundation. Python is being used for the same kinds of applications as Perl: system administration, CGI programming, and other relatively small tasks. Python is an open-source system and is available for most common computing platforms. The industry-standard distribution for Windows is available at `www.activestate.com/Products/ActivePython`. Implementations for other platforms are available from `www.python.org`, which also has extensive information regarding Python.

Python's syntax is not based directly on any commonly used language. It is type checked, but dynamically typed. Instead of arrays, Python includes three kinds of data structures: lists, immutable lists, which are called **tuples,** and hashes, which are called **dictionaries.** There is a collection of list methods, such as `append`, `insert`, `remove`, and `sort`, as well as a collection of methods for dictionaries, such as `keys`, `values`, `copy`, and `has_key`. Python also supports list comprehensions, which originated with the Haskell language. List comprehensions are discussed in Section 15.8.

Python is object oriented, includes the pattern-matching capabilities of Perl, and has exception handling. Garbage collection is used to reclaim objects when they are no longer needed.

Support for CGI programming, and form processing in particular, is provided by the `cgi` module. Modules that support cookies, networking, and database access are also available.

One of the more interesting features of Python is that it can be easily extended by any user. The modules that support the extensions can be written in any compiled language. Extensions can add functions, variables, and object types. These extensions are implemented as additions to the Python interpreter.

2.18.4   Origins and Characteristics of Ruby

Ruby (Thomas et al., 2005) was designed by Yukihiro Matsumoto (aka Matz) in the early 1990s and released in 1996. Since then it has continually evolved. The motivation for Ruby was dissatisfaction of its designer with Perl and Python. Although both Perl and Python support object-oriented programming, neither is a pure object-oriented language, at least in the sense that both have primitive (nonobject) types and both support functions.

The primary characterizing feature of Ruby is that it is a pure object-oriented language, just as is Smalltalk. Every data value is an object and all operations are via method calls. The operators in Ruby are only syntactic mechanisms to specify method calls for the corresponding operations.

Because they are methods, they can be redefined. All classes, predefined or user defined, can be subclassed.

Both classes and objects in Ruby are dynamic in the sense that methods can be dynamically added to either. This means that both classes and objects can have different sets of methods at different times during execution. So, different instantiations of the same class can behave differently. Collections of methods, data, and constants can be included in the definition of a class.

The syntax of Ruby is related to that of Eiffel and Ada. There is no need to declare variables, because dynamic typing is used. The scope of a variable is specified in its name: A variable whose name begins with a letter has local scope; one that begins with '@' is an instance variable; one that begins with a '$' has global scope. A number of features of Perl are present in Ruby, including implicit variables with silly names, such as $_.

As is the case with Python, any user can extend and/or modify Ruby. Ruby is culturally interesting because it is the first programming language designed in Japan that has achieved relatively widespread use.

2.19 A C-Based Language for the New Millennium: C#

C#, along with the new development platform .NET,[14] was announced by Microsoft in 2000. In January 2002, production versions of both were released.

2.19.1   Design Process

C# is based on C++ and Java, but includes some ideas from Delphi and Visual BASIC. Its lead designer, Anders Hejlsberg, also designed Turbo Pascal and Delphi, which explains the Delphi parts of the heritage of C#.

The purpose of C# is to provide a language for component-based software development, specifically for such development in the .NET Framework. In this environment, components from a variety of languages can be easily combined to form systems. All of the .NET languages, which include C#, Visual Basic .NET, Managed C++, J# .NET, and JScript .NET, use the Common Type System (CTS). The CTS provides a common class library. All types in all five .NET languages inherit from a single class root, `System.Object`. Compilers that conform to the CTS specification create objects that can be combined into software systems. All five .NET languages are compiled into the same intermediate form, Intermediate Language (IL).[15] Unlike Java, however, the IL is never interpreted. A Just-in-Time compiler is used to translate IL into machine code before it is executed.

---

14. The .NET development system is briefly discussed in Chapter 1.

15. Initially, IL was called MSIL (for Microsoft Intermediate Language), but apparently many people thought that name was too long.

2.19.2 Language Overview

Many believe that one of Java's most important advances over C++ lies in the fact that it excludes some of C++'s features. For example, C++ supports multiple inheritance, pointers, structs, **enum** types, operator overloading, and a goto statement, but Java includes none of these. The designers of C# obviously disagreed with this wholesale removal of features, for all of these except multiple inheritance have been brought back in the new language.

To the credit of C#'s designers, however, in several cases, the C# version of a C++ feature has been improved. For example, the **enum** types of C# are safer than those of C++, because they are never implicitly converted to integers. This allows them to be more type-safe. The **struct** type was changed significantly, resulting in a truly useful construct, whereas in C++ it serves virtually no purpose. In C#, a struct is a lightweight class that does not support inheritance or subclassing. However, C# structs can implement interfaces and have constructors. They are value types, which means they are allocated on the run-time stack and are directly accessed, rather than being accessed through references. All C# primitive types are implemented as structs.

C# takes a stab at improving the **switch** statement that is used in C, C++, and Java. In those languages, there is no implicit branch at the end of the selectable segments of code, which has caused innumerable programming errors. In C#, every nonempty case segment must end with an unconditional branch statement. So, if you want control to flow from one case segment to the next, it is necessary to use a goto statement to branch to the next case segment.

Although C++ includes function pointers, they share the lack of safety that is inherent in C++'s pointers to variables. C# includes a new type, delegates, which are both object-oriented and type-safe method references. Delegates are used for implementing event handlers and callbacks.[16] Callbacks are implemented in Java with interfaces; in C++, method pointers are used.

In C#, methods can take a variable number of parameters, as long as they are all the same type. This is specified by the use of a formal parameter of array type, preceded by the **params** reserved word.

Both C++ and Java use two distinct typing systems, one for primitives and one for objects. In addition to being confusing, this leads to a frequent need to convert values between the two systems, for example, to put a primitive value into a collection that stores objects. C# makes the conversion between values of the two typing systems partially implicit through the implicit boxing and unboxing operations, which are discussed in detail in Chapter 12.[17]

Among the other features of C# are rectangular arrays, which are not supported in most programming languages, and a **foreach** statement, which is an iterator for arrays and collection objects. A similar **foreach** statement is

---

16. When an object calls a method of another object and needs to be notified when that method has completed its task, the called method calls its caller back. This call is the callback.

17. This feature was added to Java in Java 5.0.

found in Perl, PHP, and Java 5.0. Also, C# includes properties, which are an alternative to public data members. Properties are specified as data members with get and set methods, which are implicitly called when references and assignments are made to the associated data members.

2.19.3 Evaluation

C# was meant to be an advance over both C++ and Java as a general-purpose programming language. Although it can be argued that some of its features are a step backward, C# clearly includes some constructs that move it beyond its predecessors.

The primary intended application of C# is as the main language in the .NET environment. It is far too early to say with any certainty that C# will succeed in attracting a large number of users. However, given the huge effort being made by Microsoft to sell .NET, it appears that its chances at becoming widely used are excellent. Furthermore, some of its features will surely become adopted by programming languages of the near-term future.

The following is an example of a C# program:

```csharp
// C# Example Program
// Input:  An integer, listlen, where listlen is less than
//         100, followed by listlen-integer values.
// Output: The number of input values that are greater
//         than the average of all input values.
using System;
public class Ch2example {
  static void Main() {
    int[] intlist;
    int listlen,
        counter,
        sum = 0,
        average,
        result = 0;
    intList = new int[99];
    listlen = Int32.Parse(Console.readLiine());
    if ((listlen > 0) && (listlen < 100)) {
// Read input into an array and compute the sum
      for (counter = 0; counter < listlen; counter++) {
        intList[counter] = Int32.Parse(Console.readLine());
        sum += intList[counter];
      } //- end of for (counter ...
// Compute the average
      average = sum / listlen;
// Count the input values that are > average
      foreach (int num in intList)
        if (num > average) result++;
```

```
// Print result
    Console.WriteLine(
        "Number of values > average is:" + result);
  } //- end of if ((listlen ...
  else
    Console.WriteLine(
        "Error--input list length is not legal");
  } //- end of method Main
} //- end of class Ch2example
```

2.20 Markup/Programming Hybrid Languages

A markup/programming hybrid language is a markup language in which some of the elements can specify programming actions, such as control flow and computation. The following subsections introduce two such hybrid languages, XSLT and JSP.

2.20.1 XSLT

eXtensible Markup Language (XML) is a metamarkup language. Such a language is used to define markup languages. XML-derived markup languages are used to define data documents, which are called XML documents. Although XML documents are human-readable, they are processed by computers. This processing sometimes consists of only transformations to forms that can be effectively displayed or printed. In many cases, such transformations are to HTML, which can be displayed by a Web browser. In other cases, the data in the document is processed, just as with other forms of data files.

One of the ways XML documents are transformed for display is with another markup language, eXtensible Stylesheet Language Transformations (XSLT) (www.w3.org/TR/XSLT). The transformations of XSLT can specify programming-like operations. Therefore, XSLT is a markup/programming hybrid language. XSLT was defined by the World Wide Web Consortium (W3C) in the late 1990s.

An XSLT processor is a program that takes as input an XML data document and an XSLT document (which is also in the form of an XML document). In this processing, the XML data document is transformed to another XML document,[18] using the transformations described in the XSLT document. The XSLT document specifies transformations by defining templates, which are data patterns that could be found by the XSLT processor in the XML input file. Associated with each template in the XSLT document are its transformation instructions, which specify how the matching data is to be

---

18. The output document of the XSLT processor could also be in HTML or plain text.

transformed before being put in the output document. So, the templates (and their associated processing) act as subprograms, which are "executed" when the XSLT processor finds a pattern match in the data of the XML document.

XSLT also has programming constructs at a lower level. For example, a looping construct is included, which allows repeated parts of the XML document to be selected. There is also a sort process. These lower-level constructs are specified with XSLT tags, such as `<for-each>`.

2.20.2   JSP

The "core" part of the Java Server Pages Standard Tag Library (JSTL) is another markup/programming hybrid language, though its form and purpose are different from those of XSLT. Before discussing JSTL, it is necessary to introduce the ideas of servlets and Java Server Pages (JSP). A **servlet** is a Java class that resides on and is executed on a Web server system. The execution of a servlet is requested by a markup document being displayed by a Web browser. The servlet's output, which is in the form of an HTML document, is returned to the requesting browser. A program that runs in the Web server process, called a **servlet container,** controls the execution of servlets. Servlets are commonly used for form processing and for database access.

JSP is a collection of technologies designed to support dynamic Web documents and provide other processing needs of Web documents. When a JSP document, which is often a mixture of HTML and Java, is requested by a browser, the JSP processor program, which resides on a Web server system, converts the document to a servlet. The document's embedded Java code is copied to the servlet. The plain HTML is copied into Java statements that output it as is. The JSTL markup in the JSP document is processed, as discussed in the following paragraph. The servlet produced by the JSP processor is run by the servlet container.

The JSTL defines a collection of XML action elements that control the processing of the JSP document on the Web server. These elements have the same form as other elements of HTML or XML. One of the most commonly used JSTL control action elements is `if`, which specifies a Boolean expression as an attribute.[19] The content of the `if` element (the text between the opening tag (`<if>`) and its closing tag (`</if>`)) is markup code that will be included in the output document only if the Boolean expression evaluates to true. The `if` element is related to the C/C++ `#if` preprocessor command. The JSP container processes the JSTL markup parts of JSP documents in a way that is similar to how the C/C++ preprocessor processes C and C++ programs. The preprocessor commands are instructions for the preprocessor to specify how the output file is to be constructed from the input file. Similarly, JSTL

---

19. An attribute in HTML, which is embedded in the opening tag of an element, provides further information about that element.

control action elements are instructions for the JSP processor to specify how to build the XML output file from the XML input file.

One common use of the `if` element is for the validation of form data submitted by a browser user. Form data is accessible by the JSP processor and can be tested with the `if` element to ensure that it is sensible data. If not, the `if` element can insert an error message for the user in the output document.

For multiple selection control, JSTL has `choose`, `when`, and `otherwise` elements. JSTL also includes a `forEach` element, which iterates over collections, which typically are form values from a client. The `forEach` element can include `begin`, `end`, and `step` attributes to control its iterations.

SUMMARY

We have investigated the development and the development environments of a number of the more important programming languages. This chapter should have given the reader a good perspective on current issues in language design. We hope to have set the stage for an in-depth discussion of the important features of contemporary languages.

BIBLIOGRAPHIC NOTES

Perhaps the most important source of historical information about the development of programming languages is *History of Programming Languages*, edited by Richard Wexelblat (1981). It contains the developmental background and environment of 13 important programming languages, as told by the designers themselves. A similar work resulted from a second "history" conference, this time published as a special issue of *ACM SIGPLAN Notices* (ACM, 1993a). In this work, the history and evolution of 13 more programming languages are discussed.

The paper "Early Development of Programming Languages" (Knuth and Pardo, 1977), which is part of the *Encyclopedia of Computer Science and Technology*, is an excellent 85-page work that details the development of languages up to and including Fortran. The paper includes example programs to demonstrate the features of many of those languages.

Another book of great interest is *Programming Languages: History and Fundamentals*, by Jean Sammet (1969). It is a 785-page work filled with details of 80 programming languages of the 1950s and 1960s. Sammet has also published several updates to her book, such as *Roster of Programming Languages for 1974–75* Sammet (1976).

REVIEW QUESTIONS

1. In what year was Plankalkül designed? In what year was that design published?

2. What two common data structures were included in Plankalkül?

3. How were the pseudocodes of the early 1950s implemented?

4. Speedcoding was invented to overcome two significant shortcomings of the computer hardware of the early 1950s. What were they?

5. Why was the slowness of interpretation of programs acceptable in the early 1950s?

6. What hardware capability that first appeared in the IBM 704 computer strongly affected the evolution of programming languages? Explain why.

7. In what year was the Fortran design project begun?

8. What was the primary application area of computers at the time Fortran was designed?

9. What was the source of all of the control flow statements of Fortran I?

10. What was the most significant feature added to Fortran I to get Fortran II?

11. What control flow statements were added to Fortran IV to get Fortran 77?

12. Which version of Fortran was the first to have any sort of dynamic variables?

13. Which version of Fortran was the first to have character string handling?

14. Why were linguists interested in artificial intelligence in the late 1950s?

15. Where was LISP developed? By whom?

16. In what way are Scheme and COMMON LISP opposites of each other?

17. What dialect of LISP is used for introductory programming courses at some universities?

18. What two professional organizations together designed ALGOL 60?

19. In what version of ALGOL did block structure appear?

20. What missing language element of ALGOL 60 damaged its chances for widespread use?

21. What language was designed to describe the syntax of ALGOL 60?

22. On what language was COBOL based?

23. In what year did the COBOL design process begin?

24. What data structure appeared in COBOL that originated with Plankalkül?

25. What organization was most responsible for the early success of COBOL (in terms of extent of use)?

26. What user group was the target of the first version of BASIC?
27. Why was BASIC an important language in the early 1980s?
28. PL/I was designed to replace what two languages?
29. For what new line of computers was PL/I designed?
30. What features of SIMULA 67 are now important parts of some object-oriented languages?
31. What innovation of data structuring was introduced in ALGOL 68 but is often credited to Pascal?
32. What design criterion was used extensively in ALGOL 68?
33. What language introduced the **case** statement?
34. What operators in C were modeled on similar operators in ALGOL 68?
35. What are two characteristics of C that make it less safe than Pascal?
36. What is a nonprocedural language?
37. What are the two kinds of statements that populate a Prolog database?
38. What is the primary application area for which Ada was designed?
39. What are the concurrent program units of Ada called?
40. What Ada construct provides support for abstract data types?
41. What populates the Smalltalk world?
42. What three concepts are the basis for object-oriented programming?
43. Why does C++ include the features of C that are known to be unsafe?
44. What do the Ada and COBOL languages have in common?
45. What was the first application for Java?
46. What characteristic of Java is most evident in JavaScript?
47. How does the typing system of PHP and JavaScript differ from that of Java?
48. What array structure is included in C#, but not in C, C++, or Java?
49. What feature of Delphi's classes is included in C#?
50. What deficiency of the **switch** statement of C is addressed with the changes made by C# to that statement?
51. What are the inputs to an XSLT processor?
52. What is the output of an XSLT processor?
53. What element of the JSTL is related to a subprogram?
54. To what is a JSP document converted by a JSP processor?
55. Where are servlets executed?

PROBLEM SET

1. What features of Plankalkül do you think would have had the greatest influence on Fortran 0 if the Fortran designers had been familiar with Plankalkül?

2. Determine the capabilities of Backus's 701 Speedcoding system, and compare them with those of a contemporary programmable hand calculator.

3. Write a short history of the A-0, A-1, and A-2 systems designed by Grace Hopper and her associates.

4. As a research project, compare the facilities of Fortran 0 with those of the Laning and Zierler system.

5. Which of the three original goals of the ALGOL design committee, in your opinion, was most difficult to achieve at that time?

6. Make an educated guess as to the most common syntax error in LISP programs.

7. LISP began as a pure functional language but gradually acquired more and more imperative features. Why?

8. Describe in detail the three most important reasons, in your opinion, why ALGOL 60 did not become a very widely used language.

9. Why, in your opinion, did COBOL allow long identifiers when Fortran and ALGOL did not?

10. Outline the major motivation of IBM in developing PL/I.

11. Was IBM's major motivation for developing PL/I correct, given the history of computers and language developments since 1964?

12. Describe, in your own words, the concept of orthogonality in programming language design.

13. What is the primary reason why PL/I became more widely used than ALGOL 68?

14. What are the arguments both for and against the idea of a typeless language?

15. Are there any logic programming languages, other than Prolog?

16. What is your opinion of the argument that languages that are too complex are too dangerous to use and we should therefore keep all languages small and simple?

17. Do you think language design by committee is a good idea? Support your opinion.

18. Languages continually evolve. What sort of restrictions do you think are appropriate for changes in programming languages? Compare your answers with the evolution of Fortran.

19. Build a table identifying all of the major language developments, together with when they occurred, in what language they first appeared, and the identities of the developers.

20. There have been some public interchanges between Microsoft and Sun concerning the design of Microsoft's J++ and C# and Sun's Java. Read some of these documents, which are available on their respective Web sites, and write an analysis of the disagreements concerning delegates.

21. Give a brief general description of a markup/programming hybrid language.

PROGRAMMING EXERCISES

1. To understand the value of records in a programming language, write a small program in a C-based language that uses an array of structs that store student information, including name, age, GPA as a float, and grade level as a string (e.g., "freshmen", etc.). Also write the same program in the same language without using structs.

2. To understand the value of recursion in a programming language, write a program that implements quicksort, first using recursion, and then without recursion.

3. To understand the value of counting loops, write a program that implements matrix multiplication using counting loop constructs. Then write the same program using only logical loops, for example, `while` loops.

3

Describing Syntax and Semantics

This chapter covers the following topics. First, the terms *syntax* and *semantics* are defined. Then a detailed discussion of the most common method of describing syntax, context-free grammars (also known as Backus–Naur Form), is presented. Included in this discussion are derivations, parse trees, ambiguity, describing operator precedence and associativity, and extended Backus–Naur Form. Attribute grammars, which can be used to describe both the syntax and static semantics of programming languages, are discussed next. Finally, three formal methods of describing semantics—operational, axiomatic, and denotational semantics—are introduced. Because of the inherent complexity of the semantics description methods, our discussion of them will be brief. One could easily write an entire book on just one of the three (as several authors have).

3.1 Introduction

The task of providing a concise yet understandable description of a programming language is difficult but essential to the language's success. ALGOL 60 and ALGOL 68 were first presented using concise formal descriptions; in both cases, however, the descriptions were not easily understandable, partly because each used a new notation. The levels of acceptance of both languages suffered as a result. On the other hand, some languages have suffered the problem of having many slightly different dialects, a result of a simple but informal and imprecise definition.

One of the problems in describing a language is the diversity of the people who must understand the description. Among these are initial evaluators, implementors, and production users. Most new programming languages are subjected to a period of scrutiny by potential users, often within the organization that employs the language's designer, before their designs are completed. These are the initial evaluators. The success of this feedback cycle depends heavily on the clarity of the description.

Programming language implementors obviously must be able to determine how the expressions, statements, and program units of a language are formed, and also their intended effect when executed. The difficulty of the job of implementors is in part determined by the completeness and precision of the language description.

Finally, language users must be able to determine how to encode software systems by referring to a language reference manual. Textbooks and courses enter into this process, but language manuals are usually the only authoritative printed information source about a language.

The study of programming languages, like the study of natural languages, can be divided into examinations of syntax and semantics. The **syntax** of a programming language is the form of its expressions, statements, and program units. Its **semantics** is the meaning of those expressions, statements, and program units. For example, the syntax of a Java **while** statement is

```
while (<boolean_expr>) <statement>
```

The semantics of this statement form is that when the current value of the Boolean expression is true, the embedded statement is executed. Otherwise, control continues after the **while** construct. Then control implicitly returns to the Boolean expression to repeat the process.

Although they are often separated for discussion purposes, syntax and semantics are closely related. In a well-designed programming language, semantics should follow directly from syntax; that is, the appearance of a statement should strongly suggest what the statement is meant to accomplish.

Describing syntax is easier than describing semantics, partly because a concise and universally accepted notation is available for syntax description, but none has yet been developed for semantics.

3.2 The General Problem of Describing Syntax

A language, whether natural (such as English) or artificial (such as Java), is a set of strings of characters from some alphabet. The strings of a language are called **sentences** or statements. The syntax rules of a language specify which strings of characters from the language's alphabet are in the language. English, for example, has a large and complex collection of rules for specifying the syntax of its sentences. By comparison, even the largest and most complex programming languages are syntactically very simple.

Formal descriptions of the syntax of programming languages, for simplicity's sake, often do not include descriptions of the lowest-level syntactic units. These small units are called **lexemes**. The description of lexemes can be given by a lexical specification, which is usually separate from the syntactic description of the language. The lexemes of a programming language include its numeric literals, operators, and special words, among others. One can think of programs as strings of lexemes rather than of characters.

Lexemes are partitioned into groups, for example, the names of variables, methods, classes, and so forth, in a programming language form a group called *identifiers*. Each of these groups is represented by a name, or token. So, a **token** of a language is a category of its lexemes. For example, identifier is a token that can have lexemes, or instances, such as sum and total. In some cases, a token has only a single possible lexeme. For example, the token for the arithmetic operator symbol +, which may have the name plus_op, has just one possible lexeme. Consider the following Java statement:

```
index = 2 * count + 17;
```

The lexemes and tokens of this statement are

Lexemes	Tokens
index	identifier
=	equal_sign
2	int_literal

*	mult_op
count	identifier
+	plus_op
17	int_ literal
;	semicolon

The example language descriptions in this chapter are very simple, and most include lexeme descriptions.

3.2.1 Language Recognizers

In general, languages can be formally defined in two distinct ways: by **recognition** and by **generation** (although neither provides a definition that is practical by itself for people trying to learn or even use a programming language). Suppose we have a language L that uses an alphabet Σ of characters. To formally define L using the recognition method, we would need to construct a mechanism R, called a recognition device, capable of reading strings of characters from the alphabet Σ. R would need to be designed so that it indicated whether a given input string was or was not in L. In effect, R would either accept or reject the given string. Such devices are like filters, separating correct sentences from those that are incorrectly formed. If R, when fed any string of characters over Σ, accepts it only if it is in L, then R is a description of L. Because most useful languages are, for all practical purposes, infinite, this might seem like a lengthy and ineffective process. Recognition devices, however, are not used to enumerate all of the sentences of a language.

The syntax analysis part of a compiler is a recognizer for the language the compiler translates. In this role, the recognizer need not test all possible strings of characters from some set to determine whether each is in the language. Rather, it need only determine whether given programs are in the language. In effect then, the syntax analyzer determines whether the given programs are syntactically correct. The structure of syntax analyzers, also known as parsers, is discussed in Chapter 4.

3.2.2 Language Generators

A language generator is a device that can be used to generate the sentences of a language. We can think of the generator as having a button that produces a sentence of the language every time it is pushed. Because the particular sentence that is produced by a generator when its button is pushed is unpredictable, a generator seems to be a device of limited usefulness as a language descriptor. However, people prefer certain forms of generators over recognizers because they can more easily read and understand them. By contrast, the syntax-checking portion of a compiler (a language recognizer) is not as useful a language description for a programmer because it can be used only in trial-and-error mode. For example, to determine the correct syntax of a particular statement using a compiler, the programmer can only submit a guessed-at version and see whether the compiler accepts it. On the other hand, it is often possible to determine whether the syntax of a particular statement is correct by comparing it with the structure of the generator.

There is a close connection between formal generation and recognition devices for the same language. This was one of the seminal discoveries in computer science, and it led to much of what is now known about formal languages and compiler design theory. We return to the relationship of generators and recognizers in the next section.

3.3 Formal Methods of Describing Syntax

This section discusses the formal language generation mechanisms, usually called **grammars,** that are commonly used to describe the syntax of programming languages.

3.3.1 Backus–Naur Form and Context-Free Grammars

In the middle to late 1950s, two men, Noam Chomsky and John Backus, in unrelated research efforts, developed the same syntax description formalism, which subsequently became the most widely used method for programming language syntax.

3.3.1.1 Context-free Grammars

In the mid-1950s, Chomsky, a noted linguist, described four classes of generative devices or grammars that define four classes of languages (Chomsky, 1956, 1959). Two of these grammar classes, named *context-free* and *regular*, turned out to be useful for describing the syntax of programming languages. The forms of the tokens of programming languages can be described by regular grammars. The syntax of whole programming languages, with minor exceptions, can be described by context-free grammars. Because Chomsky was a linguist, his primary interest was the theoretical nature of natural languages. He had no interest at the time in the artificial languages used to communicate with computers. So it was not until later that his work was applied to programming languages.

3.3.1.2 Origins of Backus–Naur Form

Shortly after Chomsky's work on language classes, the ACM-GAMM group began designing ALGOL 58. A landmark paper describing ALGOL 58 was presented by John Backus, a prominent member of the ACM-GAMM group, at an international conference in 1959 (Backus, 1959). This paper introduced a new formal notation for specifying programming language syntax. The new notation was later modified slightly by Peter Naur for the description of

ALGOL 60 (Naur, 1960). This revised method of syntax description became known as **Backus–Naur form,** or simply **BNF.**

BNF is a natural notation for describing syntax. In fact, something similar to BNF was used by Panini to describe the syntax of Sanskrit several hundred years before Christ (Ingerman, 1967).

Although the use of BNF in the ALGOL 60 report was not immediately accepted by computer users, it soon became and is still the most popular method of concisely describing programming language syntax.

It is remarkable that BNF is nearly identical to Chomsky's generative devices for context-free languages, called **context-free grammars.** In the remainder of the chapter, we refer to context-free grammars simply as grammars. Furthermore, the terms BNF and grammar are used interchangeably.

3.3.1.3 Fundamentals

A **metalanguage** is a language that is used to describe another language. BNF is a metalanguage for programming languages.

BNF uses abstractions for syntactic structures. A simple Java assignment statement, for example, might be represented by the abstraction <assign> (pointed brackets are often used to delimit names of abstractions). The actual definition of <assign> can be given by

<assign> $\rightarrow$ <var> = <expression>

The symbol on the left side of the arrow, which is aptly called the left-hand side (LHS), is the abstraction being defined. The text to the right of the arrow is the definition of the LHS. It is called the right-hand side (RHS) and consists of some mixture of tokens, lexemes, and references to other abstractions. (Actually, tokens are also abstractions.) Altogether, the definition is called a rule, or production. In the example rule just given, the abstractions <var> and <expression> obviously must be defined for the <assign> definition to be useful.

This particular rule specifies that the abstraction <assign> is defined as an instance of the abstraction <var>, followed by the lexeme =, followed by an instance of the abstraction <expression>. One example sentence whose syntactic structure is described by the rule is

```
total = subtotal1 + subtotal2
```

The abstractions in a BNF description, or grammar, are often called **nonterminal symbols,** or simply **nonterminals,** and the lexemes and tokens of the rules are called **terminal symbols,** or simply **terminals.** A BNF description, or **grammar,** is simply a collection of rules.

Nonterminal symbols can have two or more distinct definitions, representing two or more possible syntactic forms in the language. Multiple definitions can be written as a single rule, with the different definitions separated by the symbol | , meaning logical OR. For example, an Ada **if** statement can be described with the rules

<if_stmt> → **if** <logic_expr> **then** <stmt>
<if_stmt> → **if** <logic_expr> **then** <stmt> **else** <stmt>

or with the rule

<if_stmt> → **if** <logic_expr> **then** <stmt>
        | **if** <logic_expr> **then** <stmt> **else** <stmt>

Although BNF is simple, it is sufficiently powerful to describe nearly all of the syntax of programming languages. In particular, it can describe lists of similar constructs, the order in which different constructs must appear, and nested structures to any depth, and even imply operator precedence and operator associativity.

3.3.1.4 Describing Lists

Variable-length lists in mathematics are often written using an ellipsis (...); 1, 2, ... is an example. BNF does not include the ellipsis, so an alternative method is required for describing lists of syntactic elements in programming languages (for example, a list of identifiers appearing on a data declaration statement). The most common alternative is recursion. A rule is **recursive** if its LHS appears in its RHS. The following rules illustrate how recursion is used to describe lists:

<ident_list> → identifier
        | identifier , <ident_list>

This defines <ident_list> as either a single token (identifier) or an identifier followed by a comma followed by another instance of <ident_list>. Recursion is used to describe lists in many of the example grammars in the remainder of this chapter.

3.3.1.5 Grammars and Derivations

A grammar is a generative device for defining languages. The sentences of the language are generated through a sequence of applications of the rules, beginning with a special nonterminal of the grammar called the **start symbol.** A sentence generation is called a **derivation.** In a grammar for a complete programming language, the start symbol represents a complete program and is usually named <program>. The simple grammar shown in Example 3.1 is used to illustrate derivations.

EXAMPLE 3.1	A Grammar for a Small Language

<program> → **begin** <stmt_list> **end**
<stmt_list> → <stmt>
           | <stmt> ; <stmt_list>
<stmt> → <var> = <expression>
<var> → A | B | C
<expression> → <var> + <var>
           | <var> – <var>
           | <var>

The language in Example 3.1 has only one statement form: assignment. A program consists of the special word **begin,** followed by a list of statements separated by semicolons, followed by the special word **end.** An expression is either a single variable, or two variables separated by either a + or – operator. The only variable names in this language are A, B, and C.

A derivation of a program in this language follows:

<program> => **begin** <stmt_list> **end**
      => **begin** <stmt> ; <stmt_list> **end**
      => **begin** <var> = <expression> ; <stmt_list> **end**
      => **begin** A = <expression> ; <stmt_list> **end**
      => **begin** A = <var> + <var> ; <stmt_list> **end**
      => **begin** A = B + <var> ; <stmt_list> **end**
      => **begin** A = B + C ; <stmt_list> **end**
      => **begin** A = B + C ; <stmt> **end**
      => **begin** A = B + C ; <var> = <expression> **end**
      => **begin** A = B + C ; B = <expression> **end**
      => **begin** A = B + C ; B = <var> **end**
      => **begin** A = B + C ; B = C **end**

This derivation, like all derivations, begins with the start symbol, in this case <program>. The symbol => is read "derives." Each successive string in the sequence is derived from the previous string by replacing one of the nonterminals with one of that nonterminal's definitions. Each of the strings in the derivation, including <program>, is called a **sentential form.**

In this derivation, the replaced nonterminal is always the leftmost nonterminal in the previous sentential form. Derivations that use this order of replacement are called **leftmost derivations.** The derivation continues until the sentential form contains no nonterminals. That sentential form, consisting of only terminals, or lexemes, is the generated sentence.

In addition to leftmost, a derivation may be rightmost or in an order that is neither leftmost nor rightmost. Derivation order has no effect on the language generated by a grammar.

By choosing alternative RHSs of rules with which to replace nonterminals in the derivation, different sentences in the language can be generated. By exhaustively choosing all combinations of choices, the entire language can be generated. This language, like most others, is infinite, so one cannot generate *all* the sentences in the language in finite time.

Example 3.2 is another example of a grammar for part of a typical programming language.

EXAMPLE 3.2	A Grammar for Simple Assignment Statements

<assign> → <id> = <expr>
<id> → A | B | C
<expr> → <id> + <expr>
     | <id> * <expr>
     | (<expr>)
     | <id>

The grammar of Example 3.2 describes assignment statements whose right sides are arithmetic expressions with multiplication and addition operators and parentheses. For example, the statement

```
A = B * ( A + C )
```

is generated by the leftmost derivation:

```
<assign> => <id> = <expr>
         => A = <expr>
         => A = <id> * <expr>
         => A = B * <expr>
         => A = B * ( <expr> )
         => A = B * ( <id> + <expr> )
         => A = B * ( A + <expr> )
         => A = B * ( A + <id> )
         => A = B * ( A + C )
```

3.3.1.6 Parse Trees

One of the most attractive features of grammars is that they naturally describe the hierarchical syntactic structure of the sentences of the languages they define. These hierarchical structures are called **parse trees.** For example, the parse tree in Figure 3.1 shows the structure of the assignment statement derived previously.

Figure 3.1

A parse tree for the
simple statement
`A = B * (A + C)`

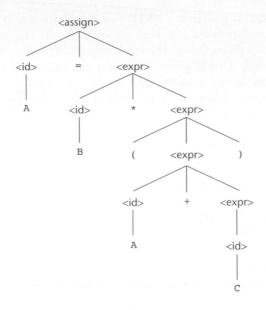

Every internal node of a parse tree is labeled with a nonterminal symbol;
every leaf is labeled with a terminal symbol. Every subtree of a parse tree
describes one instance of an abstraction in the sentence.

3.3.1.7 Ambiguity

A grammar that generates a sentential form for which there are two or more
distinct parse trees is said to be **ambiguous.** Consider the grammar shown in
Example 3.3, which is a minor variation of the grammar in Example 3.2.

EXAMPLE 3.3   An Ambiguous Grammar for Simple Assignment Statements

<assign> → <id> = <expr>
<id> → A | B | C
<expr> → <expr> + <expr>
          | <expr> * <expr>
          | (<expr>)
          | <id>

The grammar of Example 3.3 is ambiguous because the sentence

`A = B + C * A`

has two distinct parse trees, as shown in Figure 3.2. The ambiguity occurs because
the grammar specifies slightly less syntactic structure than does the grammar of
Example 3.2. Rather than allowing the parse tree of an expression to grow only on
the right, this grammar allows growth on both the left and the right.

Figure 3.2

Two distinct parse
trees for the same
sentence,
A = B + C * A

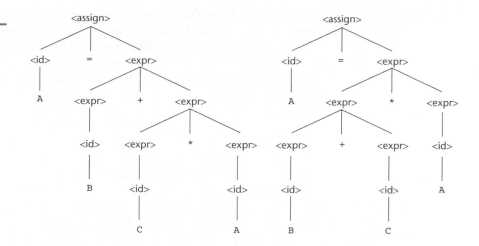

Syntactic ambiguity of language structures is a problem because compilers often base the semantics of those structures on their syntactic form. Specifically, the compiler chooses the code to be generated for a statement by examining its parse tree. If a language structure has more than one parse tree, then the meaning of the structure cannot be determined uniquely. This problem is discussed in two specific examples in the following subsections.

There are several other characteristics of a grammar that are sometimes useful in determining whether a grammar is ambiguous.[1] Among these are: (1) if the grammar generates a sentence with more than one leftmost derivation and (2) if the grammar generates a sentence with more than one rightmost derivation.

Some parsing algorithms can be based on ambiguous grammars. When such a parser encounters an ambiguous construct, it uses nongrammatical information provided by the designer to construct the correct parse tree. In many cases, an ambiguous grammar can be rewritten to be unambiguous, but still generate the desired language.

3.3.1.8 Operator Precedence

When an expression includes two different operators, for example, x + y * z, one obvious semantic issue is the order of evaluation of the two operators (is it add and then multiply, or vice versa in the expression above). This semantic question can be answered by assigning different precedence levels to operators. For example, if * has been assigned higher precedence than + (by the language designer), multiplication will be done first, regardless of the order of appearance of the two operators in the expression.

As stated earlier, a grammar can describe a certain syntactic structure so that part of the meaning of the structure can be determined from its parse

---

1. Note that it is mathematically not possible to determine whether an arbitrary grammar is ambiguous.

tree. In particular, the fact that an operator in an arithmetic expression is generated lower in the parse tree (and therefore must be evaluated first) can be used to indicate that it has precedence over an operator produced higher up in the tree. In the first parse tree of Figure 3.2, for example, the multiplication operator is generated lower in the tree, which could indicate that it has precedence over the addition operator in the expression. The second parse tree, however, indicates just the opposite. It appears, therefore, that the two parse trees indicate conflicting precedence information.

Notice that although the grammar of Example 3.2 is not ambiguous, the precedence order of its operators is not the usual one. In this grammar, a parse tree of a sentence with multiple operators, regardless of the particular operators involved, has the rightmost operator in the expression at the lowest point in the parse tree, with the other operators in the tree moving progressively higher as one moves to the left in the expression. For example, in the expression A + B * C, * will be lowest in the tree, indicating it is to be done first. However, in the expression A * B + C, + will be lowest, indicating it is to be done first.

A grammar for the simple expressions we have been discussing can be written that is both unambiguous and specifies a consistent precedence of the + and * operators, regardless of the order in which the operators appear in an expression. The correct ordering is specified by using separate nonterminal symbols to represent the operands of the operators that have different precedence. This requires additional nonterminals and some new rules. Instead of using <expr> for both operands of both + and *, we could use three nonterminals to represent operands, which allows the grammar to force different operators to different levels in the parse tree. If <expr> is the root symbol for expressions, + can be forced to the top of the parse tree by having <expr> directly generate only + operators, using the new nonterminal, <term>, as the right operand of +. Next, we can define <term> to generate * operators, using <term> as the left operand and a new nonterminal, <factor> as its right operand. Now, * will always be lower in the parse tree, simply because it is farther from the start symbol than + in every derivation. The grammar of Example 3.4 is such a grammar.

EXAMPLE 3.4	An Unambiguous Grammar for Expressions

<assign> → <id> = <expr>
<id> → A | B | C
<expr> → <expr> + <term>
      | <term>
<term> → <term> * <factor>
      | <factor>
<factor> → (<expr>)
      | <id>

The grammar in Example 3.4 generates the same language as the grammars of Examples 3.2 and 3.3, but it is unambiguous and it specifies the usual precedence order of multiplication and addition operators. The following derivation of the sentence A = B + C * A uses the grammar of Example 3.4:

```
<assign> => <id> = <expr>
          => A = <expr>
          => A = <expr> + <term>
          => A = <term> + <term>
          => A = <factor> + <term>
          => A = <id> + <term>
          => A = B + <term>
          => A = B + <term> * <factor>
          => A = B + <factor> * <factor>
          => A = B + <id> * <factor>
          => A = B + C * <factor>
          => A = B + C * <id>
          => A = B + C * A
```

The unique parse tree for this sentence, using the grammar of Example 3.4, is shown in Figure 3.3.

The connection between parse trees and derivations is very close: Either can easily be constructed from the other. Every derivation with an unambiguous grammar has a unique parse tree, although that tree can be represented by different derivations. For example, the following derivation of the sentence A = B + C * A is different from the derivation of the same sentence given previously. This is a rightmost derivation, whereas the previous one is leftmost. Both of these derivations, however, are represented by the same parse tree.

```
<assign> => <id> = <expr>
          => <id> = <expr> + <term>
          => <id> = <expr> + <term> * <factor>
          => <id> = <expr> + <term> * <id>
          => <id> = <expr> + <term> * A
          => <id> = <expr> + <factor> * A
          => <id> = <expr> + <id> * A
          => <id> = <expr> + C * A
          => <id> = <term> + C * A
          => <id> = <factor> + C * A
          => <id> = <id> + C * A
          => <id> = B + C * A
          => A = B + C * A
```

Figure 3.3

The unique parse
tree for A = B +
C * A using an
unambiguous grammar

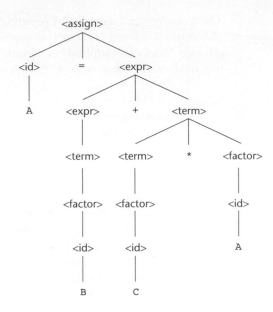

3.3.1.9 Associativity of Operators

When an expression includes two operators that have the same precedence (as
* and / usually have), for example A / B* C, a semantic rule is required to specify which should have precedence.[2] This rule is named *associativity*.

As was the case with precedence, a grammar for expressions may correctly
imply operator associativity. Consider the following example of an assignment statement:

A = B + C + A

The parse tree for this sentence, as defined with the grammar of Example 3.4,
is shown in Figure 3.4.

The parse tree of Figure 3.4 shows the left addition operator lower than
the right addition operator. This is the correct order if addition is meant to
be left associative, which is typical. In most cases, the associativity of addition
in a computer is irrelevant. In mathematics, addition is associative, which
means that left and right associative orders of evaluation mean the same
thing. That is, (A + B) + C = A + (B + C). Floating-point addition in
a computer, however, is not necessarily associative. For example, suppose
floating-point values store seven digits of accuracy. Consider the problem of
adding 11 numbers together, where one of the numbers is 10^7 and the other

---

2. An expression with two occurrences of the same operator has the same issue, for example,
A / B / C.

Figure 3.4

A parse tree for **A** = **B** + **C** + **A** illustrating the associativity of addition

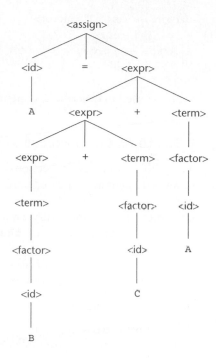

ten are 1. If the small numbers (the 1s) are each added to the large number, one at a time, there is no effect on that number, because the small numbers occur in the eighth digit of the large number. However, if the small numbers are first added together and the result is added to the large number, the result in seven-digit accuracy is $1.000001 * 10^7$. Subtraction and division are not associative, whether in mathematics or in a computer. Therefore, correct associativity may be essential for an expression that contains either of them.

When a grammar rule has its LHS also appearing at the beginning of its RHS, the rule is said to be **left recursive.** This left recursion specifies left associativity. For example, the left recursion of the rules of the grammar of Example 3.4 causes it to make both addition and multiplication left associative. Unfortunately, left recursion disallows the use of some important syntax analysis algorithms. When such algorithms are to be used, the grammar must be modified to remove the left recursion. This, in turn, disallows the grammar from precisely specifying that certain operators are left associative. Fortunately, left associativity can be enforced by the compiler, even though the grammar does not dictate it.

In most languages that provide it, the exponentiation operator is right associative. To indicate right associativity, right recursion can be used. A grammar rule is **right recursive** if the LHS appears at the right end of the RHS. Rules such as

```
<factor> → <exp> ** <factor>
        | <exp>
  <exp> → ( <expr> )
        | id
```

could be used to describe exponentiation as a right-associative operator.

3.3.1.10 An Unambiguous Grammar for `if-then-else`

The BNF rules given in Section 3.3.1.3 for one particular form of **if-then-else** statement are repeated here:

```
<if_stmt> → if <logic_expr> then <stmt>
          | if <logic_expr> then <stmt> else <stmt>
```

If we also have <stmt> → <if_stmt>, this grammar is ambiguous. The simplest sentential form that illustrates this ambiguity is

if <logic_expr> **then if** <logic_expr> **then** <stmt> **else** <stmt>

The two parse trees in Figure 3.5 show the ambiguity of this sentential form. Consider the following example of this construct:

```
if (done == true)
  then if (denom == 0)
    then quotient = 0;
    else quotient = num / denom;
```

The problem is that if the upper parse tree in Figure 3.5 is used as the basis for translation, the else clause would be executed when done is not true, which probably is not what was intended by the author of the construct. We will examine the practical problems associated with this else-association problem in Chapter 8.

We will now develop an unambiguous grammar that describes this **if** statement. The rule for **if** constructs in many languages is that an else clause, when present, is matched with the nearest previous unmatched **then.** Therefore, there cannot be an **if** statement without an **else** between a **then** and its matching **else.** So, for this situation, statements must be distinguished between those that are matched and those that are unmatched, where unmatched statements are **else**-less **if**s and all other statements are matched. The problem with the earlier grammar is that it treats all statements as if they had equal syntactic significance, that is, as if they were all matched.

To reflect the different categories of statements, different abstractions, or nonterminals, must be used. The unambiguous grammar based on these ideas follows:

Figure 3.5

Two distinct parse
trees for the same
sentential form

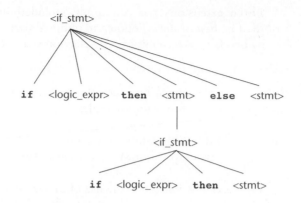

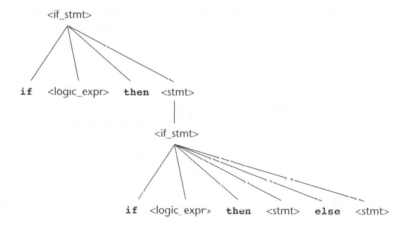

<stmt> → <matched> | <unmatched>
<matched> → **if** <logic_expr> **then** <matched> **else** <matched>
          | any non-if statement
<unmatched> → **if** <logic_expr> **then** <stmt>
            | **if** <logic_expr> **then** <matched> **else** <unmatched>

There is just one possible parse tree, using this grammar, for the following
sentential form:

if <logic_expr> **then if** <logic_expr> **then** <stmt> **else** <stmt>

3.3.2 Extended BNF

Because of a few minor inconveniences in BNF, it has been extended in several ways. Most extended versions are called Extended BNF, or simply EBNF,
even though they are not all exactly the same. The extensions do not enhance
the descriptive power of BNF; they only increase its readability and
writability.

Three extensions are commonly included in the various versions of EBNF. The first of these denotes an optional part of an RHS, which is delimited by brackets. For example, a C selection statement can be described as

<selection> → **if** (<expression>) <statement> [**else** <statement>]

Without the use of the brackets, the syntactic description of this statement would require the following two rules:

<selection → **if** (<expression>) <statement>
      | **if** (<expression>) <statement> **else** <statement>

The second extension is the use of braces in an RHS to indicate that the enclosed part can be repeated indefinitely or left out altogether. This extension allows lists to be built with a single rule, instead of using recursion and two rules. For example, lists of identifiers separated by commas can be described by the following rule:

<ident_list> → <identifier> {, <identifier>}

This is a replacement of the recursion by a form of implied iteration; the part enclosed within braces can be iterated any number of times.

The third common extension deals with multiple-choice options. When a single element must be chosen from a group, the options are placed in parentheses and separated by the OR operator, | . For example,

<term> → <term> (* | / | %) <factor>

In BNF, a description of this <term> would require the following three rules:

<term> → <term> * <factor>
      | <term> / <factor>
      | <term> % <factor>

The brackets, braces, and parentheses in the EBNF extensions are **metasymbols,** which means they are notational tools and not terminal symbols in the syntactic entities they help describe. In cases where these metasymbols are also terminal symbols in the language being described, the instances that are terminal symbols can be underlined or quoted.

The BNF rule

<expr> → <expr> + <term>

clearly specifies—in fact forces—the + operator to be left associative. However, the EBNF version,

<expr> → <term> { + <term>}

does not imply the direction of associativity. This problem is overcome in a syntax analyzer based on an EBNF grammar for expressions by designing the

EXAMPLE 3.5	BNF and EBNF Versions of an Expression Grammar

BNF:

    <expr> → <expr> + <term>
           | <expr> - <term>
           | <term>
    <term> → <term> * <factor>
           | <term> / <factor>
           | <factor>
    <factor> → <exp> ** <factor>
           | <exp>
    <exp> → (<expr>)
        | id

EBNF:

    <expr> → <term> {(+ | -) <term>}
    <term> → <factor> {(* | /) <factor>}
    <factor> → <exp> { ** <exp>}
    <exp> → (<expr>)
        | id

syntax analysis process to enforce the correct associativity. This is further discussed in Chapter 4.

Some versions of EBNF allow a numeric superscript to be attached to the right brace to indicate an upper limit to the number of times the enclosed part can be repeated. Also, some versions use a plus (+) superscript to indicate one or more repetitions. For example,

<compound> → **begin** <stmt> {<stmt>} end

and

<compound> → **begin** {<stmt>}⁺ end

are equivalent.

In recent years, some variations on BNF and EBNF have appeared. Among these are the following:

- In place of the arrow, a colon is used and the RHS is placed on the next line.

- Instead of a vertical bar to separate alternative RHSs, they are simply placed on separate lines.

- In place of square brackets to indicate something being optional, the subscript $_{opt}$ is used. For example,

  Constructor Declarator → SimpleName (FormalParameterList$_{opt}$)

- Rather than using the | symbol in a parenthesized list of elements to indicate a choice, the words "one of" are used. For example,

$$\text{AssignmentOperator} \rightarrow \text{one of} \quad = \quad *= \quad /= \quad \%= \quad += \quad -= \quad <<= \quad >>=$$
$$\&= \quad \textasciicircum= \quad |=$$

There is a standard for EBNF, ISO/IEC 14977:1996(1996), but it is rarely used. The standard uses the equal sign (=) instead of an arrow in rules, terminates each RHS with a semicolon, and requires quotes on all terminal symbols; it also specifies a host of other notational rules.

3.3.3 Grammars and Recognizers

Earlier in this chapter, we suggested that there was a close relationship between generation and recognition devices for a given language. In fact, given a context-free grammar, a recognizer for the language generated by the grammar can be algorithmically constructed. A number of software systems have been developed that perform this construction. Such systems allow the quick creation of the syntax analysis part of a compiler for a new language and are therefore quite valuable. One of the first of these syntax analyzer generators is named yacc (yet another compiler-compiler; Johnson, 1975). There are now many such systems available.

3.4 Attribute Grammars

An **attribute grammar** is a device used to describe more of the structure of a programming language than can be described with a context-free grammar. An attribute grammar is an extension to a context-free grammar. The extension allows certain language rules to be conveniently described, such as type compatibility. Before we formally define the form of attribute grammars, we must clarify the concept of static semantics.

3.4.1 Static Semantics

There are some characteristics of the structure of programming languages that are difficult to describe with BNF, and some that are impossible. As an example of a language rule that is difficult to specify with BNF, consider type compatibility rules. In Java, for example, a floating-point value cannot be assigned to an integer type variable, although the opposite is legal. Although this restriction can be specified in BNF, it requires additional nonterminal symbols and rules. If all of the typing rules of Java were specified in BNF, the grammar would become too large to be useful, because the size of the grammar determines the size of the parser.

As an example of a language rule that cannot be specified in BNF, consider the common rule that all variables must be declared before they are referenced. It has been proven that this rule cannot be specified in BNF.

This problem exemplifies the categories of language rules called static semantics rules. The **static semantics** of a language is only indirectly related to the meaning of programs during execution; rather, it has to do with the legal forms of programs (syntax rather than semantics). Many static semantic rules of a language state its type constraints. Static semantics is so named because the analysis required to check these specifications can be done at compile time.

Because of the problems of describing static semantics with BNF, a variety of more powerful mechanisms has been devised for that task. One such mechanism, attribute grammars, was designed by Knuth (1968a) to describe both the syntax and the static semantics of programs.

Attribute grammars are a formal approach to both describing and checking the correctness of the static semantics rules of a program. Although they are not always used in a formal way in compiler design, the basic concepts of attribute grammars are at least informally used in every compiler (see Aho et al., 1986, Chapter 5).

Dynamic semantics, which is the meaning of expressions, statements, and program units, is discussed in Section 3.5.

3.4.2 Basic Concepts

Attribute grammars are context-free grammars to which have been added attributes, attribute computation functions, and predicate functions. **Attributes,** which are associated with grammar symbols (the terminal and nonterminal symbols), are similar to variables in the sense that they can have values assigned to them. **Attribute computation functions,** sometimes called semantic functions, are associated with grammar rules. They are used to specify how attribute values are computed. **Predicate functions,** which state the static semantic rules of the language, are associated with grammar rules.

These concepts will become clearer after we formally define attribute grammars and provide an example.

3.4.3 Attribute Grammars Defined

An attribute grammar is a grammar with the following additional features:

- Associated with each grammar symbol X is a set of attributes A(X). The set A(X) consists of two disjoint sets S(X) and I(X), called synthesized and inherited attributes, respectively. **Synthesized attributes** are used to pass semantic information up a parse tree, while **inherited attributes** pass semantic information down and across a tree.

- Associated with each grammar rule is a set of semantic functions and a possibly empty set of predicate functions over the attributes of the symbols in the grammar rule. For a rule $X_0 \rightarrow X_1 \ldots X_n$, the synthesized attributes of X_0 are computed with semantic functions of the form $S(X_0) = f(A(X_1), \ldots, A(X_n))$. So the value of a synthesized attribute on a parse tree node depends only on the values of the attributes on that node's children nodes. Inherited attributes of symbols X_j, $1 \leq j \leq n$ (in the rule above), are computed with a semantic function of the form $I(X_j) = f(A(X_0), ..., A(X_n))$. So the value of an inherited attribute on a parse tree node depends on the attribute values of that node's parent node and those of its sibling nodes. Note that, to avoid circularity, inherited attributes are often restricted to functions of the form $I(X_j) = f(A(X_0), ..., A(X_{(j-1)}))$. This form prevents an inherited attribute from depending on itself or on attributes to the right in the parse tree.

- A predicate function has the form of a Boolean expression on the union of the attribute set $\{A(X_0), ... ,A(X_n)\}$ and a set of literal attribute values. The only derivations allowed with an attribute grammar are those in which every predicate associated with every nonterminal is true. A false predicate function value indicates a violation of the syntax or static semantics rules of the language.

A parse tree of an attribute grammar is the parse tree based on its underlying BNF grammar, with a possibly empty set of attribute values attached to each node. If all the attribute values in a parse tree have been computed, the tree is said to be **fully attributed.** Although in practice it is not always done this way, it is convenient to think of attribute values as being computed after the complete unattributed parse tree has been constructed by the compiler.

3.4.4 Intrinsic Attributes

Intrinsic attributes are synthesized attributes of leaf nodes whose values are determined outside the parse tree. For example, the type of an instance of a variable in a program could come from the symbol table, which is used to store variable names and their types. The contents of the symbol table are determined from earlier declaration statements. Initially, assuming that an unattributed parse tree has been constructed and that attribute values are desired, the only attributes with values are the intrinsic attributes of the leaf nodes. Given the intrinsic attribute values on a parse tree, the semantic functions can be used to compute the remaining attribute values.

3.4.5 Examples of Attribute Grammars

As a very simple example of how attribute grammars can be used to describe static semantics, consider the following fragment of an attribute grammar that describes the rule that the name on the **end** of an Ada procedure must match the procedure's name. The string attribute of <proc_name>, denoted by <proc_name>.string, is the actual string of characters that were found immediately following the reserved word **procedure** by the compiler. Notice that when there is more than one occurrence of a nonterminal in a syntax rule in an attribute grammar, the nonterminals are subscripted with brackets to distinguish them. Neither the subscripts nor the brackets are part of the described language.

Syntax rule: <proc_def> → **procedure** <proc_name>[1]
<proc_body> **end** <proc_name>[2];
Predicate: <proc_name>[1].string == <proc_name>[2].string

In this example, the predicate rule states that the name string attribute of the <proc_name> nonterminal in the subprogram header must match the name string attribute of the <proc_name> nonterminal following the end of the subprogram.

Next, we consider a larger example of an attribute grammar. In this case, the example illustrates how an attribute grammar can be used to check the type rules of a simple assignment statement. The syntax and static semantics of this assignment statement are as follows: The only variable names are A, B, and C. The right side of the assignments can be either a variable or an expression in the form of a variable added to another variable. The variables can be one of two types: int or real. When there are two variables on the right side of an assignment, they need not be the same type. The type of the expression when the operand types are not the same is always real. When they are the same, the expression type is that of the operands. The type of the left side of the assignment must match the type of the right side. So the types of operands in the right side can be mixed, but the assignment is valid only if the LHS and the value resulting from evaluating the RHS have the same type. The attribute grammar specifies these static semantic rules.

The syntax portion of our example attribute grammar is

<assign> → <var> = <expr>
<expr> → <var> + <var>
        | <var>
<var> → A | B | C

The attributes for the nonterminals in the example attribute grammar are described in the following paragraphs:

- *actual_type*—A synthesized attribute associated with the nonterminals <var> and <expr>. It is used to store the actual type, int or real, of a variable or expression. In the case of a variable, the actual type is intrinsic. In the case of an expression, it is determined from the actual types of the child node or children nodes of the <expr> nonterminal.

- *expected_type*—An inherited attribute associated with the nonterminal <expr>. It is used to store the type, either int or real, that is expected for the expression, as determined by the type of the variable on the left side of the assignment statement.

The complete attribute grammar follows in Example 3.6.

EXAMPLE 3.6   An Attribute Grammar for Simple Assignment Statements

1. Syntax rule: <assign> → <var> = <expr>
   Semantic rule: <expr>.expected_type ← <var>.actual_type

2. Syntax rule: <expr> → <var>[2] + <var>[3]
   Semantic rule: <expr>.actual_type ←
   $\quad$ if (<var>[2].actual_type = int) and
   $\quad\quad$ (<var>[3].actual_type = int)
   $\quad$ then int
   $\quad$ else real
   $\quad$ end if
   Predicate: <expr>.actual_type == <expr>.expected_type

3. Syntax rule: <expr> → <var>
   Semantic rule: <expr>.actual_type ← <var>.actual_type
   Predicate: <expr>.actual_type == <expr>.expected_type

4. Syntax rule: <var> → A | B | C
   Semantic rule: <var>.actual_type ← look-up(<var>.string)

The look-up function looks up a given variable name in the symbol table and returns the variable's type.

An example of a parse tree of the sentence A = A + B generated by the grammar in Example 3.6 is shown in Figure 3.6. As in the grammar, bracketed numbers are added after the repeated node labels in the tree so they can be referenced unambiguously.

Figure 3.6

A parse tree for
A = A + B

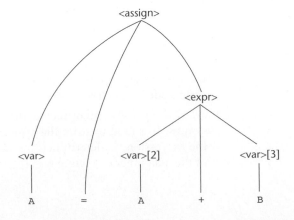

3.4.6 Computing Attribute Values

Now, consider the process of computing the attribute values of a parse tree, which is sometimes called **decorating** the parse tree. This could proceed in a completely top-down order, from the root to the leaves, if all attributes were inherited. Alternatively, it could proceed in a completely bottom-up order, from the leaves to the root, if all the attributes were synthesized. Because our grammar has both synthesized and inherited attributes, the evaluation process cannot be in any single direction. The following is an evaluation of the attributes, in an order in which it is possible to compute them:

1. <var>.actual_type ← look-up(A) (Rule 4)
2. <expr>.expected_type ← <var>.actual_type (Rule 1)
3. <var>[2].actual_type ← look-up(A) (Rule 4)
   <var>[3].actual_type ← look-up(B) (Rule 4)
4. <expr>.actual_type ← either int or real (Rule 2)
5. <expr>.expected_type == <expr>.actual_type is either
   TRUE or FALSE (Rule 2)

The tree in Figure 3.7 shows the flow of attribute values in the example of Figure 3.6. Solid lines are used for the parse tree; dashed lines show attribute flow in the tree.

The tree in Figure 3.8 shows the final attribute values on the nodes. In this example, A is defined as a real and B is defined as an int.

Determining attribute evaluation order for the general case of an attribute grammar is a complex problem, requiring the construction of a dependency graph to show all attribute dependencies.

Figure 3.7

The flow of attributes in the tree

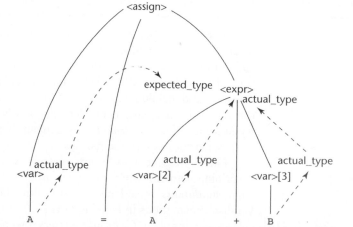

Figure 3.8

A fully attributed
parse tree

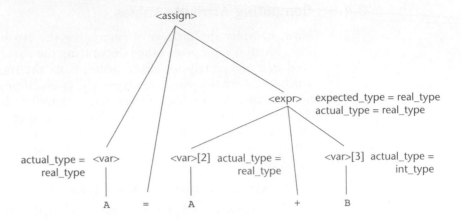

3.4.7 Evaluation

Checking the static semantic rules of a language is an essential part of all compilers. Even if a compiler writer has never heard of an attribute grammar, he or she would need to use the fundamental ideas of them to design the checks of static semantics rules for his or her compiler.

One of the main difficulties in using an attribute grammar to describe all of the syntax and static semantics of a real contemporary programming language is its size and complexity. The large number of attributes and semantic rules required for a complete programming language make such grammars difficult to write and read. Furthermore, the attribute values on a large parse tree are costly to evaluate. On the other hand, less formal attribute grammars are a powerful and commonly used tool for compiler writers, who are more interested in the process of producing a compiler than they are in formalism.

3.5 Describing the Meanings of Programs: Dynamic Semantics

We now turn to the difficult task of describing the **dynamic semantics**, or meaning, of expressions, statements, and program units. Because of the power and naturalness of the available notation, describing syntax is a relatively simple matter. On the other hand, no universally accepted notation has been devised for dynamic semantics. In this section, we briefly describe several of the methods that have been developed. For the remainder of this section, when we use the term *semantics*, we mean dynamic semantics; we will refer to static semantics as static semantics.

There are several different reasons why one might be concerned with describing semantics. First, programmers obviously need to know precisely what statements of a language do. But they usually find out by reading English explanations in language manuals. Such explanations are often imprecise and incomplete. Compiler writers also typically determine the semantics of the languages for which they are writing compilers from English descriptions. These informal descriptions are used because of the complexity of formal semantic descriptions. It is an obvious research goal to find a semantics formalism that could be used by programmers and compiler writers.

Scheme, a functional language described in Chapter 15, is one of only a few programming languages whose definition includes a formal semantics description. However, the method used is not one described in this chapter, as this chapter is focused on approaches that are suitable for imperative languages.

3.5.1   Operational Semantics

The idea behind **operational semantics** is to describe the meaning of a statement or program by translating it into a more easily understood language.

There are different levels of the use of operational semantics. At the highest level, the interest is in the final result of the execution of a complete program. This is sometimes called **natural operational semantics.** At the lowest level, operational semantics can be used to determine the precise meaning of a single statement, often by examination of the translated version of the statement. This use is sometimes called **structural operational semantics.**

3.5.1.1 The Basic Process

The first step in creating an operational semantics description of a language is to design an appropriate intermediate language, where the primary characteristic of the language is clarity. Every construct of the intermediate language must have an obvious and unambiguous meaning. This language is at the intermediate level, because machine language is too low-level to be easily understood and another high-level language is obviously not suitable. If the semantics description is to be used for natural operational semantics, a virtual machine (an interpreter) must be constructed for the intermediate language. The virtual machine can be used to execute either single statements, code segments, or whole programs. If the semantics description is to be used for structural operational semantics, the virtual machine is not necessary.

The basic process of operational semantics is not unusual. In fact, the concept is frequently used in programming textbooks and programming language reference manuals. For example, the semantics of the C **for** construct can be described in terms of very simple statements, as in

C Statement	*Operational Semantics*
`for (expr1; expr2; expr3) {`	`expr1;`
`. . .`	`loop:` **if** `expr2` $== 0$ **goto** out
`}`	`. . .`
	`expr3;`
	goto loop
	`out: . . .`

The human reader of such a description is the virtual computer and is assumed to be able to correctly "execute" the instructions in the definition and recognize the effects of the "execution."

As an example of a low-level language that could be used for operational semantics, consider the following list of statements, which would be adequate for the simple control statements of a typical programming language:

```
ident = var
ident = ident + 1
ident = ident – 1
goto label
if var relop var goto label
```

In this list, relop is one of the relational operators from the set {=, <>, >, <, >=, <=}, ident is an identifier, and var is either an identifier or a constant. These statements are all simple and therefore easy to understand and implement.

A slight generalization of these three assignment statements allows more general arithmetic expressions and assignment statements to be described. The new statements are

```
ident = var bin_op var
ident = un_op var
```

where bin_op is a binary arithmetic operator and un_op is a unary operator. Multiple arithmetic data types and automatic type conversions, of course, complicate this generalization. Adding just a few more relatively simple instructions would allow the semantics of arrays, records, pointers, and subprograms to be described.

In Chapter 8, the semantics of various control statements are described using operational semantics.

3.5.1.2 Evaluation

The first and most significant use of formal operational semantics was to describe the semantics of PL/I (Wegner, 1972). That particular abstract machine and the translation rules for PL/I were together named the Vienna Definition Language (VDL), after the city where IBM devised it.

Operational semantics provides an effective means of describing semantics for language users and language implementors, as long as the descriptions are kept simple and informal. The VDL description of PL/I, unfortunately, is so complex that it serves no practical purpose.

Operational semantics depends on programming languages of lower levels, not mathematics. The statements of one programming language are described in terms of the statements of a lower-level programming language. This approach can lead to circularities, in which concepts are indirectly defined in terms of themselves. The methods described in the following two sections are much more formal, in the sense that they are based on logic and mathematics, not programming languages.

3.5.2 Axiomatic Semantics

Axiomatic semantics was defined in conjunction with the development of a method to prove the correctness of programs. Such correctness proofs, when they can be constructed, show that a program performs the computation described by its specification. In a proof, each statement of a program is both preceded and followed by a logical expression that specifies constraints on program variables. These, rather than the entire state of an abstract machine (as with operational semantics), are used to specify the meaning of the statement. The notation used to describe constraints—indeed, the language of axiomatic semantics—is predicate calculus. Although simple Boolean expressions are often adequate to express constraints, in some cases they are not.

When axiomatic semantics is used to specify formally the semantics of a statement, the meaning is defined by the statement's effect on assertions about the data being processed by the statement.

3.5.2.1 Assertions

Axiomatic semantics is based on mathematical logic. The logical expressions are called predicates, or **assertions.** An assertion immediately preceding a program statement describes the constraints on the program variables at that point in the program. An assertion immediately following a statement describes the new constraints on those variables (and possibly others) after execution of the statement. These assertions are called the **precondition** and **postcondition,** respectively, of the statement. For two adjacent statements, the postcondition of the first serves as the precondition of the second. Developing an axiomatic description or proof of a given program requires that every statement in the program have both a precondition and a postcondition.

In the following sections, we examine assertions from the point of view that preconditions for statements are computed from given postconditions, although it is possible to consider these in the opposite sense. We assume all variables are integer type. As a simple example, consider the following assignment statement and postcondition:

```
sum = 2 * x + 1 {sum > 1}
```

Precondition and postcondition assertions are presented in braces to distinguish them from program statements. One possible precondition for this statement is {x > 10}.

In axiomatic semantics, the meaning of a specific kind of statement is defined by the process of computing a precondition from a statement of that kind, along with its postcondition. In effect, such a process specifies precisely the effect of executing the statement, in terms of logic expressions.

In the following subsections, we focus on correctness proofs of statements and programs, which is a common use of axiomatic semantics. The more general concept of axiomatic semantics is to state precisely the meaning of statements and programs in terms of logic expressions. Program verification is one application of axiomatic descriptions of languages.

3.5.2.2 Weakest Preconditions

The **weakest precondition** is the least restrictive precondition that will guarantee the validity of the associated postcondition. For example, in the above statement and postcondition, {x > 10}, {x > 50}, and {x > 1000} are all valid preconditions. The weakest of all preconditions in this case is {x > 0}.

If the weakest precondition can be computed from the most general postcondition for each of the statement types of a language, then the processes used to compute these preconditions provide a concise description of the semantics of that language. Furthermore, correctness proofs can be constructed for programs in that language. A program proof is begun by using the desired results of the program's execution as the postcondition of the last statement of the program. This postcondition, along with the last statement, is used to compute the weakest precondition for the last statement. This precondition is then used as the postcondition for the second last statement. This process continues until the beginning of the program is reached. At that point, the precondition of the first statement states the conditions under which the program will compute the desired results. If these conditions are implied by the input specification of the program, the program has been verified to be correct.

An **inference rule** is a method of inferring the truth of one assertion on the basis of the values of other assertions. The general form of an inference rule is

$$\frac{S1, S2, \ldots, Sn}{S}$$

which states that if S1, S2, ..., and Sn are true, then the truth of S can be inferred. The top part of an inference rule is called its *antecedent*; the bottom part is called its *consequent*.

An **axiom** is a logical statement that is assumed to be true. Therefore, an axiom is an inference rule without an antecedent.

For some program statements, the computation of a weakest precondition from the statement and a postcondition is simple and can be specified by an axiom. In most cases, however, the weakest precondition can be computed only by an inference rule.

To use axiomatic semantics with a given programming language, whether for correctness proofs or for formal semantics specifications, either an axiom or an inference rule must be available for each kind of statement in the language. In the following subsections, we present an axiom for assignment statements and inference rules for statement sequences, selection statements, and logical pretest loops. Note that we assume that neither arithmetic nor Boolean expressions have side effects.

3.5.2.3 Assignment Statements

The precondition and postcondition of an assignment statement together define precisely the meaning of the assignment statement. So, to define the meaning of an assignment statement, we need to be able to compute its precondition.

Let x = E be a general assignment statement and Q be its postcondition. Then its precondition, P, is defined by the axiom

$$P = Q_{x \rightarrow E}$$

which means that P is computed as Q with all instances of x replaced by E. For example, if we have the assignment statement and postcondition

```
a = b / 2 - 1 {a < 10}
```

the weakest precondition is computed by substituting b / 2 - 1 in the postcondition {a < 10}, as follows:

```
b / 2 - 1 < 10
b < 22
```

Thus the weakest precondition for the given assignment and postcondition is {b < 22}. Recall that the assignment axiom is guaranteed to be correct only in the absence of side effects. An assignment statement has a side effect if it changes some variable other than its left side.

The usual notation for specifying the axiomatic semantics of a given statement form is

{P} S {Q}

where P is the precondition, Q is the postcondition, and S is the statement form. In the case of the assignment statement, the notation is

$\{Q_{x \rightarrow E}\}$ x = E {Q}

As another example of computing a precondition for an assignment statement, consider the following:

```
x = 2 * y - 3 {x > 25}
```

The precondition is computed as follows:

```
2 * y - 3 > 25
y > 14
```

So {y > 14} is the weakest precondition for this assignment statement and postcondition.

Note that the appearance of the left side of the assignment statement in its right side does not affect the process of computing the weakest precondition. For example, for

```
x = x + y - 3 {x > 10}
```

the weakest precondition is

```
x + y - 3 > 10
y > 13 - x
```

At the beginning of our discussion of axiomatic semantics, we stated that axiomatic semantics was developed to prove the correctness of programs. In light of that, it is natural at this point to wonder how the axiom for assignment statements can be used to prove anything. Here is how: A given assignment statement with both a precondition and a postcondition can be considered a theorem. If the assignment axiom, when applied to the postcondition and the assignment statement, produces the given precondition, the theorem is proved. For example, consider the logical statement

```
{x > 3} x = x - 3 {x > 0}
```

Using the assignment axiom on

```
x = x - 3 {x > 0}
```

produces {x > 3}, which is the given precondition. Therefore, we have proven the example logical statement.

Next, consider the logical statement

```
{x > 5} x = x - 3 {x > 0}
```

In this case, the given precondition, {x > 5}, is not the same as the assertion produced by the axiom. However, it is obvious that {x > 5} implies {x > 3}. To use this in a proof, we need an inference rule, named the **rule of consequence.** The form of the rule of consequence is

$$\frac{\{P\} \ S \ \{Q\}, \ P'=>P, \ Q=>Q'}{\{P'\} \ S \ \{Q'\}}$$

The => symbol means "implies," and S can be any program statement. The rule can be stated as follows: If the logical statement {P} S {Q} is true, the assertion P' implies the assertion P, and the assertion Q implies the assertion Q', then it can be inferred that {P'} S {Q'}. In other words, the rule of consequence says that a postcondition can always be weakened and a precondition can always be strengthened. This is quite useful in program proofs. For example, it allows the completion of the proof of the last logical statement example above. If we let P be {x > 3}, Q and Q′ be {x > 0}, P′ be {x > 5}, we have

$$\frac{\{x > 3\}\ x\ =\ x\ -\ 3\ \{x > 0\},\ (x > 5)=>\{x > 3\},\ (x > 0)=>(x > 0)}{\{x > 5\}\ x\ =\ x\ -\ 3\ \{x > 0\}}$$

The first term of the antecedent ({x > 3} x = x − 3 {x > 0}) was proven with the assignment axiom. The second and third terms are obvious. Therefore, by the rule of consequence, the consequent is true.

3.5.2.4 Sequences

The weakest precondition for a sequence of statements cannot be described by an axiom, because the precondition depends on the particular kinds of statements in the sequence. In this case, the precondition can only be described with an inference rule. Let S1 and S2 be adjacent program statements. If S1 and S2 have the following pre- and postconditions

{P1} S1 {P2}
{P2} S2 {P3}

the inference rule for such a two-statement sequence is

$$\frac{\{P1\}\ S1\ \{P2\},\ \{P2\}\ S2\ \{P3\}}{\{P1\}\ S1;\ S2\ \{P3\}}$$

So, for the above example, {P1} S1; S2 {P3} describes the axiomatic semantics of the sequence S1; S2. The inference rule states that to get the sequence precondition, the precondition of the second statement is computed. This new assertion is then used as the postcondition of the first statement, which can then be used as the precondition of both the first statement and the whole sequence. If S1 and S2 are the assignment statements

x1 = E1

and

x2 = E2

then we have

{P3$_{x2 \rightarrow E2}$} x2 = E2 {P3}
{(P3$_{x2 \rightarrow E2}$)$_{x1 \rightarrow E1}$} x1 = E1 {P3$_{x2 \rightarrow E2}$}

Therefore, the weakest precondition for the sequence x1 = E1; x2 = E2 with postcondition P3 is {(P3$_{x2 \rightarrow E2}$)$_{x1 \rightarrow E1}$}.

For example, consider the following sequence and postcondition:

```
y = 3 * x + 1;
x = y + 3;
{x < 10}
```

The precondition for the last assignment statement is

```
y < 7
```

which is used as the postcondition for the first statement. The precondition for the first assignment statement can now be computed:

```
3 * x + 1 < 7
x < 2
```

3.5.2.5 Selection

We next consider the inference rule for selection statements, the general form of which is

```
if B then S1 else S2
```

We consider only selections that include **else** clauses. The inference rule is

$$\frac{\{B \text{ and } P\}\ S1\ \{Q\},\ \{(\text{not } B) \text{ and } P\}\ S2\ \{Q\}}{\{P\}\ \text{if } B \text{ then } S1 \text{ else } S2\ \{Q\}}$$

This rule indicates that selection statements must be proven for both when the Boolean control expression is true and when it is false. The first logical statement above the line represents the **then** clause; the second represents the **else** clause. According to the inference rule, we need a precondition P that can be used in the precondition of both the **then** and **else** clauses.

Consider the following example of the computation of the precondition using the selection inference rule. The example selection statement is

```
if (x > 0)
    y = y - 1
else y = y + 1
```

Suppose the postcondition, Q, for this selection statement is {y > 0}. We can use the axiom for assignment on the **then** clause

```
y = y - 1 {y > 0}
```

This produces {y - 1 > 0} or {y > 1}. It can be used as the P part of the precondition for the **then** clause. Now we apply the same axiom to the **else** clause

```
y = y + 1 {y > 0}
```

which produces the precondition {y + 1 > 0} or {y > -1}. Because {y > 1} => {y > -1}, the rule of consequence allows us to use {y > 1} for the precondition of the whole selection statement.

3.5.2.6 Logical Pretest Loops

Another essential construct of an imperative programming language is the logical pretest, or **while** loop. Computing the weakest precondition for a **while** loop is inherently more difficult than for a sequence, because the number of iterations cannot always be predetermined. In a case where the number of iterations is known, the loop can be unrolled and treated as a sequence.

The problem of computing the weakest precondition for loops is similar to the problem of proving a theorem about all positive integers. In the latter case, induction is normally used, and the same inductive method can be used for some loops. The principal step in induction is finding an inductive hypothesis. The corresponding step in the axiomatic semantics of a **while** loop is finding an assertion called a **loop invariant**, which is crucial to finding the weakest precondition.

The inference rule for computing the precondition for a **while** loop is

$$\frac{\text{(I and B) S \{I\}}}{\text{\{I\} while B do S end \{I and (not B)\}}}$$

where I is the loop invariant. This seems simple, but it is not. The complexity lies in finding an appropriate loop invariant.

The axiomatic description of a **while** loop is written as

{P} **while** B **do** S **end** {Q}

The loop invariant must satisfy a number of requirements to be useful. First, the weakest precondition for the **while** must guarantee the truth of the loop invariant. In turn, the loop invariant must guarantee the truth of the postcondition upon loop termination. These constraints move us from the inference rule to the axiomatic description. During execution of the loop, the truth of the loop invariant must be unaffected by the evaluation of the loop-controlling Boolean expression and the loop body statements. Hence the name *invariant*.

Another complicating factor for **while** loops is the question of loop termination. If Q is the postcondition that holds immediately after loop exit, then a precondition P for the loop is one that guarantees Q at loop exit and also guarantees that the loop terminates.

The complete axiomatic description of a **while** construct requires all of the following to be true, in which I is the loop invariant:

P => I
{I and B} S {I}
(I and (not B)) => Q
the loop terminates

If a loop computes a sequence of numeric values, we may be able to find a loop invariant using an approach that is used for determining the inductive hypothesis when mathematical induction is used to prove a statement about a mathematical sequence. The relationship between the number of iterations and the precondition for the loop body is computed for a few cases, with the hope that a pattern emerges that will apply to the general case. It is helpful to treat the process of producing a weakest precondition as a function, wp. In general

wp(statement, postcondition) = precondition

To find I, we use the loop postcondition Q to compute preconditions for several different numbers of iterations of the loop body, starting with none. If the loop body contains a single assignment statement, the axiom for assignment statements can be used to compute these cases. Consider the example loop

```
while y <> x do y = y + 1 end {y = x}
```

Remember that the equal sign is being used for two different purposes here. In assertions, it means mathematical equality; outside assertions, it means the assignment operator.

For zero iterations, the weakest precondition is, obviously,

```
{y = x}
```

For one iteration, it is

wp (y = y + 1, {y = x}) = {y + 1 = x}, or {y = x - 1}

For two iterations, it is

wp (y = y + 1, {y = x - 1}) = {y + 1 = x - 1}, or {y = x - 2}

For three iterations, it is

wp (y = y + 1, {y = x - 2}) = {y + 1 = x - 2}, or {y = x - 3}

It is now obvious that {y < x} will suffice for cases of one or more iterations. Combining this with {y = x} for the zero iterations case, we get {y <= x}, which can be used for the loop invariant. A precondition for the **while** statement can be determined from the loop invariant. In fact, I can be used as the precondition, P.

We must ensure that our choice satisfies the four criteria for I for our example loop. First, because P = I, P => I. The second requirement is that it must be true that

{I and B} S {I}

In our example, we have

{y <= x and y <> x} y = y + 1 {y <= x}

Applying the assignment axiom to

y = y + 1 {y <= x}

we get {y + 1 <= x}, which is equivalent to {y < x}, which is implied by {y <= x and y <> x}. So, the earlier statement is proven.

Next, we must have

{I and (not B)} => Q

In our example, we have

```
{(y <= x) and not (y <> x)} => {y = x}
{(y <= x) and (y = x)} => {y = x}
{y = x} => {y = x}
```

So this is obviously true. Next, loop termination must be considered. In this example, the question is whether the loop

{y <= x} **while** y <> x **do** y = y + 1 **end** {y = x}

terminates. Recalling that x and y are assumed to be integer variables, we can easily see that this loop does terminate. The precondition guarantees that y initially is not larger than x. The loop body increases y with each iteration, until y is equal to x. No matter how much smaller y is than x initially, it will eventually become equal to x. So the loop will terminate. Because our choice of I satisfies all four criteria, it is adequate for the loop invariant and the loop precondition.

The previous process used to compute the invariant for a loop does not always produce an assertion that is the weakest precondition (although it does in the earlier example).

As another example of finding a loop invariant using the approach used in mathematical induction, consider the following loop statement:

while s > 1 **do** s = s / 2 **end** {s = 1}

As before, we use the assignment axiom to try to find a loop invariant and a precondition for the loop. For zero iterations, the weakest precondition is {s = 1}. For one iteration, it is

wp(s = s / 2, {s = 1}) = {s / 2 = 1}, or {s = 2}

For two iterations, it is

wp(s = s / 2, {s = 2}) = {s / 2 = 2}, or {s = 4}

For three iterations, it is

wp(s = s / 2, {s = 4}) = {s / 2 = 4}, or {s = 8}

From these cases, we can see clearly that the invariant is

{s is a nonnegative power of 2}

Once again, the computed I can serve as P, and I passes the four requirements. Unlike our earlier example of finding a loop precondition, this one clearly is not a weakest precondition. Consider using the precondition {s > 1}. The logical statement

{s > 1} **while** s > 1 **do** s = s / 2 **end** {s = 1}

can easily be proven, and this precondition is significantly broader than the one computed earlier. The loop and precondition are satisfied for any positive value for s, not just powers of 2, as the process indicates. Because of the rule of consequence, using a precondition that is stronger than the weakest precondition does not invalidate a proof.

Finding loop invariants is not always easy. It is helpful to understand the nature of these invariants. First, a loop invariant is a weakened version of the loop postcondition and also a precondition for the loop. So I must be weak enough to be satisfied prior to the beginning of loop execution, but when combined with the loop exit condition, it must be strong enough to force the truth of the postcondition.

Because of the difficulty of proving loop termination, that requirement is often ignored. If loop termination can be shown, the axiomatic description of the loop is called **total correctness.** If the other conditions can be met but termination is not guaranteed, it is called **partial correctness.**

In more complex loops, finding a suitable loop invariant, even for partial correctness, requires a good deal of ingenuity. Because computing the precondition for a **while** loop depends on finding a loop invariant, proving the correctness of programs with **while** loops using axiomatic semantics can be difficult.

3.5.2.7 Program Proofs

This section provides validations for two simple programs. The first example of a correctness proof is for a very short program, consisting of a sequence of three assignment statements that interchange the values of two variables.

```
{x = A AND y = B}
t = x;
x = y;
y = t;
{x = B AND y = A}
```

Because the program consists entirely of assignment statements in a sequence, the assignment axiom and the inference rule for sequences can be used to prove its correctness. The first step is to use the assignment axiom on the last statement and the postcondition for the whole program. This yields the precondition

```
{x = B AND t = A}
```

Next, we use this new precondition as a postcondition on the middle statement and compute its precondition, which is

```
{y = B AND t = A}
```

Next, we use this new assertion as the postcondition on the first statement and apply the assignment axiom, which yields

```
{y = B AND x = A}
```

which is the same as the precondition on the program, except for the order of operands on the and operator. Because and is a symmetric operator, our proof is complete.

The following example is a proof of correctness of a pseudocode program that computes the factorial function.

```
{n >= 0}
count = n;
fact = 1;
while count <> 0 do
    fact = fact * count;
    count = count - 1;
end
{fact = n!}
```

The method described earlier for finding the loop invariant does not work for the loop in this example. Some ingenuity is required here, which can be aided by a brief study of the code. The loop computes the factorial function in order of the last multiplication first; that is, $(n - 1) * n$ is done first, assuming n is greater than 1. So, part of the invariant can be

```
fact = (count + 1) * (count + 2) * . . . * (n - 1) * n
```

But we must also ensure that `count` is always nonnegative, which we can do by adding that to the part above, to get

```
I = (fact = (count + 1) * . . . * n) AND (count >= 0)
```

Next, we must confirm that this I meets the requirements for invariants. We once again let I also be used for P, so P clearly implies I. The next question is

{I and B} S {I}

I and B is

```
((fact = (count + 1) * . . . * n) AND (count >= 0)) AND
    (count <> 0)
```

which reduces to

```
(fact = (count + 1) * . . . * n) AND (count > 0)
```

In our case, we must compute the precondition of the body of the loop, using the invariant for the postcondition. For

{P} count = count - 1 {I}

we compute P to be

```
{(fact = count * (count + 1) * . . . * n)    AND
    (count >= 1)}
```

Using this as the postcondition for the first assignment in the loop body,

```
{P} fact = fact * count {(fact = count * (count + 1)
                              * . . . * n) AND (count >= 1)}
```

In this case, P is

```
{(fact = (count + 1) * . . . * n) AND (count >= 1)}
```

It is clear that I and B implies this P, so by the rule of consequence,

{I AND B} S {I}

is true. Finally, the last test of I is

I AND (NOT B) => Q

For our example, this is

```
((fact = (count + 1) * . . . * n) AND (count >= 0)) AND
    (count = 0)) => fact = n!
```

This is clearly true, for when count = 0, the first part is precisely the definition of factorial. So, our choice of I meets the requirements for a loop invariant. Now we can use our P (which is the same as I) from the **while** as the postcondition on the second assignment of the program

```
{P} fact = 1 {(fact = (count + 1) * . . . * n) AND
     (count >= 0)}
```

which yields for P

```
(1 = (count + 1) * . . . * n) AND (count >= 0))
```

Using this as the postcondition for the first assignment in the code

```
{P} count = n {(1 = (count + 1) * . . . * n) AND
     (count >= 0))}
```

produces for P

```
{(n + 1) * . . . * n = 1) AND (n >= 0)}
```

The left operand of the AND operator is true (because 1 = 1) and the right operand is exactly the precondition of the whole code segment, {n >= 0}. Therefore, the program has been proven to be correct.

3.5.2.8 Evaluation

To define the semantics of a complete programming language using the axiomatic method, there must be an axiom or an inference rule for each statement type in the language. Defining axioms or inference rules for some of the statements of programming languages has proven to be a difficult task. An obvious solution to this problem is to design the language with the axiomatic method in mind, so that only statements for which axioms or inference rules can be written are included. Unfortunately, such a language would be quite small and simple, given the state of the science of axiomatic semantics.

Axiomatic semantics is a powerful tool for research into program correctness proofs, and it provides an excellent framework in which to reason about programs, both during their construction and later. Its usefulness in describing the meaning of programming languages to either language users or compiler writers is, however, highly limited.

3.5.3 Denotational Semantics

Denotational semantics is the most rigorous, widely known method for describing the meaning of programs. It is solidly based on recursive function theory. A thorough discussion of the use of denotational semantics to describe the semantics of programming languages is necessarily long and complex. It is our intent to introduce just enough to make the reader aware of how denotational semantics works.

The fundamental concept of denotational semantics is to define for each language entity both a mathematical object and a function that maps instances of that entity onto instances of the mathematical object. Because the objects are rigorously defined, they represent the exact meaning of their corresponding entities. The idea is based on the fact that there are rigorous ways of manipulating mathematical objects but not programming language constructs. The difficulty with this method lies in creating the objects and the mapping functions. The method is named *denotational* because the mathematical objects denote the meaning of their corresponding syntactic entities.

3.5.3.1 Two Simple Examples

We use a very simple language construct, binary numbers, to introduce the denotational method. The syntax of binary numbers can be described by the following grammar rules:

```
<bin_num> → '0'
          | '1'
          | <bin_num> '0'
          | <bin_num> '1'
```

A parse tree for the example binary number, 110, is shown in Figure 3.9.

To describe the meaning of binary numbers using denotational semantics and the example grammar rules, we associate the actual meaning with each rule that has a single terminal symbol as its RHS. The objects in this case are simple decimal numbers. So, in this example the meaning of a binary number will be its decimal equivalent.

In our example, meaningful objects must be associated with the first two grammar rules. The other two grammar rules are, in a sense, computational rules, because they combine a terminal symbol, to which an object can be associated, with a nonterminal, which can be expected to represent some construct. Presuming an evaluation that progresses upward in the parse tree, the nonterminal in the right side would already have its meaning attached. Then such a syntax rule would require a function that computed the meaning of the LHS, which must then represent the meaning of the complete RHS.

history note

A significant amount of work has been done on the possibility of using denotational language descriptions to generate compilers automatically (Jones, 1980; Milos et al., 1984; Bodwin et al., 1982). These efforts have shown that the method is feasible, but the work has never progressed to the point where it can be used to generate useful compilers.

Figure 3.9

A parse tree of the binary number 110

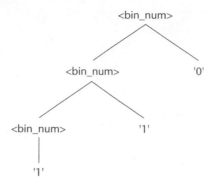

Let the domain of semantic values of the objects be N, the set of nonnegative decimal integer values. It is these objects that we wish to associate with binary numbers. The semantic function, named M_{bin}, maps the syntactic objects, as described in the previous grammar rules, to the objects in N. The function M_{bin} is defined as follows:

$M_{bin}('0') = 0$
$M_{bin}('1') = 1$
$M_{bin}(<bin\_num> '0') = 2 * M_{bin}(<bin\_num>)$
$M_{bin}(<bin\_num> '1') = 2 * M_{bin}(<bin\_num>) + 1$

Notice that we put apostrophes around the syntactic digits to show they are not mathematical digits. This is similar to the relationship between ASCII coded digits and mathematical digits. When a program reads a number as a string, it must be converted to a mathematical number before it can be used as a number in the program.

The meanings, or denoted objects (which in this case are decimal numbers), can be attached to the nodes of the parse tree above, yielding the tree in Figure 3.10. This is syntax-directed semantics. Syntactic entities are mapped to mathematical objects with concrete meaning.

In part because we need it later, we now show a similar example for describing the meaning of syntactic decimal literals.

$<dec\_num> \rightarrow$ '0' | '1' | '2' | '3' | '4' | '5' | '6' | '7' | '8' | '9'
         | $<dec\_num>$ ('0' | '1' | '2' | '3' | '4' | '5' | '6' | '7'
| '8' | '9')

The denotational mappings for these syntax rules are

$M_{dec}('0') = 0, M_{dec}('1') = 1, M_{dec}('2') = 2, ..., M_{dec}('9') = 9$
$M_{dec}(<dec\_num> '0') = 10 * M_{dec}(<dec\_num>)$
$M_{dec}(<dec\_num> '1') = 10 * M_{dec}(<dec\_num>) + 1$
...
$M_{dec}(<dec\_num> '9') = 10 * M_{dec}(<dec\_num>) + 9$

Figure 3.10

A parse tree with denoted objects for 110

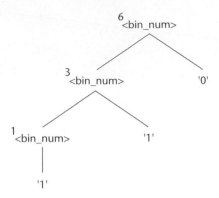

In the following sections, we present the denotational semantics of a few simple constructs. The most important simplifying assumption made here is that both the syntax and static semantics of the constructs are correct. In addition, we assume that only two scalar types are included, integer and Boolean.

3.5.3.2 The State of a Program

The denotational semantics of a program could be defined in terms of state changes in an ideal computer. Operational semantics are defined in this way, and denotational semantics are defined in nearly the same way, too. In a further simplification, however, they are defined in terms of only the values of all of the program's variables. The key difference between operational semantics and denotational semantics is that state changes in operational semantics are defined by coded algorithms, written in some programming language, whereas in denotational semantics, state changes are defined by rigorous mathematical functions.

Let the state s of a program be represented as a set of ordered pairs, as follows:

$$\{<i_1, v_1>, <i_2, v_2>, \ldots, <i_n, v_n>\}$$

Each i is the name of a variable, and the associated v's are the current values of those variables. Any of the v's can have the special value **undef,** which indicates that its associated variable is currently undefined. Let VARMAP be a function of two parameters, a variable name and the program state. The value of VARMAP(i_j, s) is v_j (the value paired with i_j in state s). Most semantics mapping functions for programs and program constructs map states to states. These state changes are used to define the meanings of programs and program constructs. Some language constructs, for example, expressions, are mapped to values, not states.

3.5.3.3 Expressions

Expressions are fundamental to most programming languages. We assume here that expressions have no side effects. Furthermore, we deal with only very simple expressions: The only operators are + and *, and an expression can have at most one operator; the only operands are scalar variables and integer literals; there are no parentheses; and the value of an expression is an integer. Following is the BNF description of these expressions:

<expr> → <dec_num> | <var> | <binary_expr>
<binary_expr> → <left_expr> <operator> <right_expr>
<left_expr> → <dec_num> | <var>
<right_expr> → <dec_num> | <var>
<operator> → + | *

The only error we consider in expressions is that a variable has an undefined value. Obviously other errors can occur, but most of them are machine-dependent. Let Z be the set of integers, and let **error** be the error value. Then Z ∪ {**error**} is the set of values to which an expression can evaluate.

The required mapping function for a given expression E and state s follows. To distinguish between mathematical function definitions and the assignment statements of programming languages, we use the symbol Δ = to define mathematical functions. The implication symbol, ->, used in this definition connects the form of an operand with its associated case (or switch) construct. Dot notation is used to refer to the child nodes of a node. For example, <binary_expr>.<left_expr> refers to the left child node of <binary_expr>.

M_e(<expr>, s) Δ=
  case <expr> of
    <dec_num> => M_{dec}(<dec_num>, s)
    <var> => if VARMAP(<var>, s) == **undef**
              then **error**
              else VARMAP(<var>, s)
    <binary_expr> =>
        if (M_e(<binary_expr>.<left_expr>, s) == **undef** OR
          M_e(<binary_expr>.<right_expr>, s) == **undef**)
        then **error**
        else if (<binary_expr>.<operator> == '+') then
              M_e(<binary_expr>.<left_expr>, s) +
                              M_e(<binary_expr>.<right_expr>, s)
            else M_e(<binary_expr>.<left_expr>, s) *
                              M_e(<binary_expr>.<right_expr>, s)

3.5.3.4 Assignment Statements

An assignment statement is an expression evaluation plus the setting of the left-side variable to the expression's value. In this case, the meaning function maps a state to a state. This function can be described with the following:

$$M_a(x = E, s) \triangleq \text{if } M_e(E, s) == \textbf{error}$$
$$\text{then } \textbf{error}$$
$$\text{else } s' = \{<i_1', v_1'>, <i_2', v_2'>, \ldots, <i_n', v_n'>\}, \text{ where}$$
$$\text{for } j = 1, 2, \ldots, n$$
$$\text{if } i_j == x$$
$$\text{then } v_j' = M_e(E, s)$$
$$\text{else } v_j' = \text{VARMAP}(i_j, s)$$

Note that the comparison in the third last line above, $i_j == x$, is of names, not values.

3.5.3.5 Logical Pretest Loops

The denotational semantics of a simple logical loop is deceptively simple. To expedite the discussion, we assume that there are two other existing mapping functions, M_{sl} and M_b, that map statement lists to states and Boolean expressions to Boolean values (or **error**), respectively. The function is

$$M_l(\textbf{while } B \textbf{ do } L, s) \triangleq \text{if } M_b(B, s) == \textbf{undef}$$
$$\text{then } \textbf{error}$$
$$\text{else if } M_b(B, s) == \text{false}$$
$$\text{then } s$$
$$\text{else if } M_{sl}(L, s) == \textbf{error}$$
$$\text{then } \textbf{error}$$
$$\text{else } M_l(\textbf{while } B \textbf{ do } L, M_{sl}(L, s))$$

The meaning of the loop is simply the value of the program variables after the statements in the loop have been executed the prescribed number of times, assuming there have been no errors. In essence, the loop has been converted from iteration to recursion, where the recursion control is mathematically defined by other recursive state mapping functions. Recursion is easier to describe with mathematical rigor than iteration.

One significant observation at this point is that this definition, like actual program loops, may compute nothing because of nontermination.

3.5.3.6 Evaluation

Objects and functions, such as those used in the earlier statements, can be defined for the other syntactic entities of programming languages. When a complete system has been defined for a given language, it can be used to determine the meaning of complete programs in that language. This provides a framework for thinking about programming in a highly rigorous way.

Denotational semantics can be used as an aid to language design. For example, statements for which the denotational semantic description is complex and difficult may indicate to the designer that such statements may also be difficult for language users to understand and that an alternative design may be in order.

Because of the complexity of denotational descriptions, they are of little use to language users. On the other hand, they provide an excellent way to describe a language concisely.

Although the use of denotational semantics is normally attributed to Scott and Strachey (1971), the general denotational approach to language description can be traced back to the nineteenth century (Frege, 1892).

SUMMARY

Backus–Naur Form and context-free grammars are equivalent metalanguages that are well suited for the task of describing the syntax of programming languages. Not only are they concise descriptive methods, but the parse trees that can be associated with their generative actions give graphical evidence of the underlying syntactic structures. Furthermore, they are naturally related to recognition devices for the languages they generate, which leads to the relatively easy construction of syntax analyzers for compilers for these languages.

An attribute grammar is a descriptive formalism that can describe both the syntax and static semantics of a language. Attribute grammars are extensions to context-free grammars. An attribute grammar consists of a grammar, a set of attributes, a set of attribute computation functions, and a set of predicates, which describe static semantics rules

There are three primary methods of semantic description: operational, axiomatic, and denotational. Operational semantics is a method of describing the meaning of language constructs in terms of their effects on an ideal machine. Axiomatic semantics, which is based on formal logic, was devised as a tool for proving the correctness of programs. In denotational semantics, mathematical objects are used to represent the meanings of language constructs. Language entities are converted to these mathematical objects with recursive functions.

BIBLIOGRAPHIC NOTES

Syntax description using context-free grammars and BNF are thoroughly discussed in Cleaveland and Uzgalis (1976).

Research in axiomatic semantics was begun by Floyd (1967) and further developed by Hoare (1969). The semantics of a large part of Pascal was described by Hoare and Wirth (1973) using this method. The parts they did not complete involved functional side effects and goto statements. These were found to be the most difficult to describe.

The technique of using preconditions and postconditions during the development of programs is described (and advocated) by Dijkstra (1976) and also discussed in detail in Gries (1981).

Good introductions to denotational semantics can be found in Gordon (1979) and Stoy (1977). Introductions to all three semantics description methods discussed in this chapter can be found in Marcotty et al. (1976). Another good reference for much of the material of this chapter is Pagan (1981). The form of the denotational semantic functions in this chapter is similar to that in Meyer (1990).

REVIEW QUESTIONS

1. Define *syntax* and *semantics*.
2. Who are language descriptions for?
3. Describe the operation of a general language generator.
4. Describe the operation of a general language recognizer.
5. What is the difference between a sentence and a sentential form?
6. Define a left-recursive grammar rule.
7. What three extensions are common to most EBNFs?
8. Distinguish between static and dynamic semantics.
9. What purpose do predicates serve in an attribute grammar?
10. What is the difference between a synthesized and an inherited attribute?
11. How is the order of evaluation of attributes determined for the trees of a given attribute grammar?
12. What is the primary use of attribute grammars?
13. What is the problem with using a software pure interpreter for operational semantics?
14. Explain what the preconditions and postconditions of a given statement mean in axiomatic semantics.
15. Describe the approach of using axiomatic semantics to prove the correctness of a given program.
16. Describe the basic concept of denotational semantics.
17. In what fundamental way do operational semantics and denotational semantics differ?

PROBLEM SET

1. The two mathematical models of language description are generation and recognition. Describe how each can define the syntax of a programming language.

2. Write EBNF descriptions for the following:

   a. A Java class definition header statement

   b. A Java method call statement

   c. A C **switch** statement

   d. A C **union** definition

   e. C **float** literals

3. Rewrite the BNF of Example 3.4 to give + precedence over * and force + to be right associative.

4. Rewrite the BNF of Example 3.4 to add the ++ and -- unary operators of Java.

5. Write a BNF description of the Boolean expressions of Java, including the three operators &&, ||, and !, and the relational expressions.

6. Using the grammar in Example 3.2, show a parse tree and a leftmost derivation for each of the following statements:

   ```
   a. A = A * (B + (C * A))
   b. B = C * (A * C + B)
   c. A = A * (B + (C))
   ```

7. Using the grammar in Example 3.4, show a parse tree and a leftmost derivation for each of the following statements:

   ```
   a. A = ( A + B ) * C
   b. A = B + C + A
   c. A = A * (B + C)
   d. A = B * (C * (A + B))
   ```

8. Prove that the following grammar is ambiguous:

   <S> → <A>

   <A> → <A> + <A> | <id>

   <id> → a | b | c

9. Modify the grammar of Example 3.4 to add a unary minus operator that has higher precedence than either + or *.

10. Describe, in English, the language defined by the following grammar:

<S> → <A> <B> <C>

<A> → a <A> | a

<B> → b <B> | b

<C> → c <C> | c

11. Consider the following grammar:

<S> → <A> a <B> b

<A> → <A> b | b

<B> → a <B> | a

Which of the following sentences are in the language generated by this grammar?

a. baab

b. bbbab

c. bbaaaaa

d. bbaab

12. Consider the following grammar:

<S> → a <S> c <B> | <A> | b

<A> → c <A> | c

<B> → d | <A>

Which of the following sentences are in the language generated by this grammar?

a. abcd

b. acccbd

c. acccbcc

d. acd

e. accc

13. Write a grammar for the language consisting of strings that have n copies of the letter a followed by the same number of copies of the letter b, where $n > 0$. For example, the strings ab, aaaabbbb, and aaaaaaaabbbbbbbb are in the language but a, abb, ba, and aaabb are not.

14. Draw parse trees for the sentences aabb and aaaabbbb, as derived from the grammar of Problem 13.

15. Convert the BNF of Example 3.1 to EBNF.

16. Convert the BNF of Example 3.3 to EBNF.

17. Convert the following EBNF to BNF:

$S → A \{ bA \}$

$A → a [b]A$

18. Using the virtual machine instructions given in Section 3.5.1.1, give an operational semantic definition of the following:

    a. Java **do-while**

    b. Ada **for**

    c. Fortran Do of the form: Do label K = start, end, step

    d. Pascal **if-then-else**

    e. C **for**

    f. C **switch**

19. Compute the weakest precondition for each of the following assignment statements and postconditions:

    a. a = 2 * (b - 1) - 1 {a > 0}

    b. b = (c + 10) / 3 {b > 6}

    c. a = a + 2 * b - 1 {a > 1}

    d. x = 2 * y + x - 1 {x > 11}

20. Compute the weakest precondition for each of the following sequences of assignment statements and their postconditions:

    a. a = 2 * b + 1;
       b = a - 3
       {b < 0}

    b. a = 3 * (2 * b + a);
       b = 2 * a - 1
       {b > 5}

21. Write a denotational semantics mapping function for the following statements:

    a. Ada **for**

    b. Java **do-while**

    c. Java Boolean expressions

    d. Java **for**

    e. C **switch**

22. What is the difference between an intrinsic attribute and a nonintrinsic synthesized attribute?

23. Write an attribute grammar whose BNF basis is that of Example 3.6 in Section 3.4.5, but whose language rules are as follows: Data types cannot be mixed in expressions, but assignment statements need not have the same types on both sides of the assignment operator.

24. Write an attribute grammar whose base BNF is that of Example 3.2 and whose type rules are the same as for the assignment statement example of Section 3.4.5.

25. Prove the following program is correct:

```
{n > 0}
count = n;
sum = 0;
while count <> 0 do
   sum = sum + count;
   count = count - 1;
end
{sum = 1 + 2 + … + n}
```

4

Lexical and Syntax Analysis

A serious investigation of compiler design requires at least a semester of intensive study, including the design and implementation of a compiler for a small but realistic programming language. The first part of such a course is devoted to lexical and syntax analysis. The syntax analyzer is the heart of a compiler, because several other important components, including the semantic analyzer and the intermediate code generator, are driven by the actions of the syntax analyzer.

Some readers may wonder why a chapter on any part of a compiler would be included in a book on programming languages. There are at least two reasons to include a discussion of lexical and syntax analysis in this book: First, syntax analyzers are based directly on the grammars discussed in Chapter 3, so it is natural to discuss them as an application of grammars. Second, lexical and syntax analyzers are needed in numerous situations outside compiler design. Many applications, among them program listing formatters, programs that compute the complexity of programs, and programs that must analyze and react to the contents of a configuration file, all need to do both lexical and syntax analysis. Therefore, lexical and syntax analysis are important topics for software developers, even if they never need to write a compiler. Furthermore, some computer science programs no longer require students to take a compiler design course, which leaves students with no instruction in lexical or syntax analysis. In those cases, this chapter can be covered in the programming language course. In degree programs that require a compiler design course, this chapter can be skipped.

This chapter begins with an introduction to lexical analysis, along with a simple example. Then the general parsing problem is discussed, including the two primary approaches to parsing and the complexity of parsing. Next, we introduce the recursive-descent implementation technique for top-down parsers, including examples of parts of a recursive-descent parser and a trace of a parse using one. The last section discusses bottom-up parsing and the LR parsing algorithm. This section includes an example of a small LR parsing table and the parse of a string using the LR parsing process.

4.1 Introduction

Three different approaches to implementing programming languages are introduced in Chapter 1: compilation, pure interpretation, and hybrid implementation. The compilation approach uses a program called a compiler, which translates programs written in a high-level programming language into machine code. Compilation is typically used to implement programming languages that are used for large applications, often written in languages such as C++ and COBOL. Pure interpretation systems perform no translation; rather, programs are interpreted in their original form by a software interpreter. Pure interpretation is usually used for smaller systems in which execution efficiency is not critical, such as scripts embedded in HTML documents, written in languages such as JavaScript. Hybrid implementation systems translate programs written in high-level languages into intermediate forms, which are interpreted. These systems are now more widely used than ever, thanks in large part to the popularity of Java and Perl. Traditionally, hybrid systems have resulted in much slower program execution than compiler systems. However, in recent years the use of just-in-time (JIT) compilers has become widespread, particularly for Java programs and programs written for the .NET system. The JIT compiler, which translates intermediate code to machine code, is used on methods at the time they are first called. In effect, a JIT compiler transforms a hybrid system to a delayed compiler system.

Syntax analyzers, or parsers, are nearly always based on a formal description of the syntax of programs. The most commonly used syntax-description formalism is context-free grammars, or BNF, which are introduced in Chapter 3. Using BNF, as opposed to using some informal syntax description, has at least three compelling advantages. First, BNF descriptions of the syntax of programs are clear and concise, both for humans and for software systems that use them. Second, the BNF description can be used as the direct basis for the syntax analyzer. Third, implementations based on BNF are relatively easy to maintain because of their modularity.

Nearly all compilers separate the task of analyzing syntax into two distinct parts, lexical analysis and syntax analysis, although this terminology is confusing. The lexical analyzer deals with small-scale language constructs, such as names and numeric literals. The syntax analyzer deals with the large-scale constructs, such as expressions, statements, and program units. Section 4.2 introduces lexical analyzers. Sections 4.3, 4.4, and 4.5 discuss syntax analyzers.

There are several reasons why lexical analysis is separated from syntax analysis:

1. Simplicity—Techniques for lexical analysis are less complex than those required for syntax analysis, so the lexical-analysis process can be simpler if it is separate. Also, removing the low-level details of lexical analysis from the syntax analyzer makes the syntax analyzer both smaller and cleaner.

2. Efficiency—Although it pays to optimize the lexical analyzer, because lexical analysis requires a significant portion of total compilation time, it is not fruitful to optimize the syntax analyzer. Separation facilitates this selective optimization.

3. Portability—Because the lexical analyzer reads input program files and often includes buffering of that input, it is somewhat platform-dependent. However, the syntax analyzer can be platform-independent. It is always good to isolate machine-dependent parts of any software system.

4.2 Lexical Analysis

A lexical analyzer is essentially a pattern matcher. A pattern matcher attempts to find a substring of a given string of characters that matches a given character pattern. Pattern matching is a traditional part of computing. One of the earliest uses of pattern matching was with text editors, such as the `ed` line editor, which was introduced in an early version of UNIX. Since then, pattern matching has found its way into some programming languages, for example, Perl and JavaScript. It is also available through the standard class libraries of Java, C++, and C#.

A lexical analyzer serves as the front end of a syntax analyzer. Technically, lexical analysis is a part of syntax analysis. A lexical analyzer performs syntax analysis at the lowest level of program structure. An input program appears to a compiler as a single string of characters. The lexical analyzer collects characters into logical groupings and assigns internal codes to the groupings according to their structure. In Chapter 3, these logical groupings are named *lexemes*, and the internal codes for categories of these groupings are named *tokens*. Lexemes are recognized by matching the input character string against character string patterns. Although tokens are usually represented as integer values, for the sake of readability of lexical and syntax analyzers, they are often referenced through named constants.

Consider the following example of an assignment statement:

```
result = oldsum - value / 100;
```

Following are the tokens and lexemes of this statement:

Token	*Lexeme*
IDENT	result
ASSIGN_OP	=
IDENT	oldsum
SUBTRACT_OP	-
IDENT	value
DIVISION_OP	/
INT_LIT	100
SEMICOLON	;

Lexical analyzers extract lexemes from a given input string and produce the corresponding tokens. In the early days of compilers, lexical analyzers often processed an entire source program file and produced a file of tokens and lexemes. Now, however, most lexical analyzers are subprograms that locate the next lexeme in the input, determine its associated token code, and return them to the caller, which is the syntax analyzer. The only view of the input program seen by the syntax analyzer is the output of the lexical analyzer, one token at a time.

The lexical-analysis process includes skipping comments and blanks outside lexemes, as they are not relevant to the meaning of the program. Also, the lexical analyzer inserts lexemes for user-defined names into the symbol table, which is used by later phases of the compiler. Finally, lexical analyzers detect syntactic errors in tokens, such as ill-formed floating-point literals, and report such errors to the user.

There are three approaches to building a lexical analyzer:

1. Write a formal description of the token patterns of the language using a descriptive language related to regular expressions.[1] These descriptions are used as input to a software tool that automatically generates a lexical analyzer. There are many such tools available for this. The oldest and most accessible of these, named lex, is commonly included as part of UNIX systems.

2. Design a state transition diagram that describes the token patterns of the language and write a program that implements the diagram.

3. Design a state transition diagram that describes the token patterns of the language and hand-construct a table-driven implementation of the state diagram.

A state transition diagram, or just **state diagram,** is a directed graph. The nodes of a state diagram are labeled with state names. The arcs are labeled with the input characters that cause the transitions. An arc may also include actions the lexical analyzer must perform when the transition is taken.

State diagrams of the form used for lexical analyzers are representations of a class of mathematical machines called **finite automata.** Finite automata can be designed to recognize a class of languages called **regular languages.** Regular grammars are generative devices for regular languages. The tokens of a programming language are a regular language, and a lexical analyzer is a finite automaton.

We now illustrate lexical-analyzer construction with a state diagram and the code that implements it. The state diagram could simply include states and transitions for each and every token pattern. However, that approach results in a very large and complex diagram, because every node in the state diagram would need a transition for every character in the character set of the language being analyzed. We therefore consider ways to simplify it.

Suppose we need a lexical analyzer that recognizes only program names, reserved words, and integer literals. The names consist of strings of uppercase letters, lowercase letters, and digits, but must begin with a letter. Names have no length limitation. The first thing to observe is that there are 52 different characters (any uppercase or lowercase letter) that can begin a name, which would require 52 transitions from the transition diagram's initial state. However, a lexical analyzer is interested only in determining that it is a name and is not concerned with which specific name it happens to be. Therefore, we define a character class named LETTER for all 52 letters and use a single transition on the first character of any name.

Next, we observe that names and reserved words have similar patterns. Although it is possible to build a state diagram to recognize every specific reserved word of a programming language, that would result in a

---

1. These regular expressions are the basis for the pattern-matching facilities now part of many programming languages, either directly or through a class library.

prohibitively large state diagram. It is much simpler and faster to have the lexical analyzer recognize names and reserved words with the same pattern and use a lookup in a table of reserved words to determine which names are reserved words. Using this approach considers reserved words to be exceptions in the names token category.

Another opportunity for simplifying the transition diagram is with the integer literal tokens. There are 10 different characters that could begin an integer literal lexeme. This would require 10 transitions from the start state of the state diagram. Because specific digits are not a concern of the lexical analyzer, we can build a much more compact state diagram if we define a character class named DIGIT for digits and use a single transition on any character in this character class to a state that collects integer literals.

Observe that most programming languages allow digits in program names, after the initial letter. For the transition from the node following the first character of a name, we can use a single transition on LETTER or DIGIT to continue collecting the characters of a name.

Next, we define some utility subprograms for the common tasks inside the lexical analyzer. First, we need a subprogram, which we can name `get-Char`, that has several duties. When called, `getChar` gets the next character of input from the input program and puts it in the global variable `nextChar`. This may require reading the next line or buffer of input. `getChar` must also determine the character class of the input character and put it in the global variable `charClass`. The lexeme being built by the lexical analyzer, which could be implemented as a character string or an array, will be named `lexeme`.

We implement the process of putting the character in `nextChar` into the string variable `lexeme` in a subprogram named `addChar`. This subprogram must be explicitly called because programs include some characters that need not be put in `lexeme`, just white-space characters between lexemes in our language.

When the lexical analyzer is called, it is convenient if the next character of input is the first character of the next lexeme. For this, a function named `getNonBlank` is used to skip white space.

Finally, we need a subprogram named `lookup` to determine whether the current contents of `lexeme` is a reserved word or a name. This subprogram will return zero if the lexeme is not a reserved word, but will return the token code for any reserved word. This assumes the token code for names is zero. Token codes are numbers arbitrarily assigned to tokens by the compiler writer.

The state diagram in Figure 4.1 describes the patterns for our tokens. It includes the actions required on each transition of the state diagram.

Implementing this state diagram in code is relatively easy. The following C code is an example of a lexical analyzer for the state diagram of Figure 4.1:

```
/* Global variables   */
    int charClass;
```

```
          char lexeme [100];
          char nextChar;
          int lexLen;
          int LETTER = 0;
          int DIGIT = 1;
          int UNKNOWN = -1;

/* addChar - a function to add nextChar to lexeme */

          void addChar() {
            if(lexLen <= 99)
              lexeme[lexLen++] = nextChar;
            else printf("Error - lexeme is too long \n");
          }

/* getChar - a function to get the next character of input
          and determine its character class */

        void getChar() {
          /* do whatever is required to get the next
              character from input and put it in nextChar */
          if(isalpha(nextChar))
            charClass = LETTER;
            else if (isdigit(nextChar))
                  charClass = DIGIT;
                else charClass = UNKNOWN;
        }

/* getNonBlank - calls getChar until it returns
                    a non-whitespace character */

          void getNonBlank() {
            while(isspace(nextChar))
              getChar();
          }

/* lex - a simple lexical analyzer */

          int lex() {
            lexLen = 0;
            static int first = 1;

/* If it is the first call to lex, initialize by calling
getChar */

            if(first) {
```

```
              getChar();
              first = 0;
        }
        getNonBlank();
        switch (charClass) {

/* Parse identifiers and reserved words */

            case LETTER:
              addChar();
              getChar();
              while (charClass == LETTER ||
                     charClass == DIGIT) {
                addChar();
                getChar();
              }
              return lookup(lexeme);
              break;

/* Parse integer literals */

            case DIGIT:
              addChar();
              getChar();
              while (charClass == DIGIT) {
                addChar();
                getChar();
              }
              return INT_LIT;
              break;
        }   /* End of switch */
    }   /* End of function lex */
```

This code illustrates the relative simplicity of lexical analyzers. Of course, we have left out the lookup functions and input buffering, as well as some other important details. Furthermore, we have dealt with a very small and simple token set.

A lexical analyzer often is responsible for the initial construction of the symbol table, which acts as a database of names for the compiler. The entries in the symbol table store information about user-defined names, as well as the attributes of the names. For example, if the name is that of a variable, the variable's type is one of it attributes that will be stored in the symbol table. Names are usually placed in the symbol table by the lexical analyzer. The attributes of a name are usually put in the symbol table by some part of the compiler that is subsequent to the actions of the lexical analyzer.

Figure 4.1

A state diagram to recognize names, reserved words, and integer literals

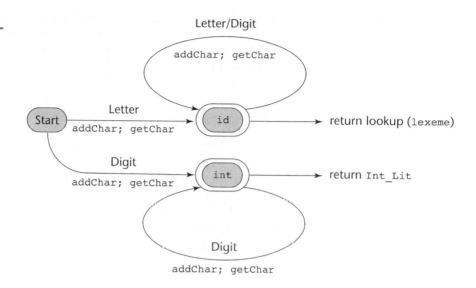

4.3 The Parsing Problem

The part of the process of analyzing syntax that is referred to as *syntax analysis* is often called *parsing*. We will use these two interchangeably.

This section discusses the general parsing problem and introduces the two main categories of parsing algorithms, top-down and bottom-up, as well as the complexity of the parsing process.

4.3.1 Introduction to Parsing

Parsers for programming languages construct parse trees for given programs. In some cases, the parse tree is only implicitly constructed, meaning that perhaps only a traversal of the tree is generated. But in all cases, the information required to build the parse tree is created during the parse. Both parse trees and derivations include all of the syntactic information needed by a language processor.

There are two distinct goals of syntax analysis: First, the syntax analyzer must check the input program to determine whether it is syntactically correct. When an error is found, the analyzer must produce a diagnostic message and recover. Recovery here means it must get back to a normal state and continue its analysis of the input program. This step is required so that the compiler finds as many errors as possible during a single analysis of the input program. If it is not done well, error recovery may create more errors, or at least more error messages. The second goal of syntax analysis is to produce either a complete parse tree, or at least trace the structure of the complete parse tree, for syntactically correct input. The parse tree (or its trace) is used as the basis for translation.

Parsers are categorized according to the direction in which they build parse trees. The two broad classes of parsers are **top-down,** in which the tree is built from the root downward to the leaves, and **bottom-up,** in which the parse tree is built from the leaves upward to the root.

In this chapter, we will use a small set of notational conventions for grammar symbols and strings to make the discussion less cluttered. For formal languages, these are as follows:

1. Terminal symbols—lowercase letters at the beginning of the alphabet (a, b, …)
2. Nonterminal symbols—uppercase letters at the beginning of the alphabet (A, B, …)
3. Terminals or nonterminals—uppercase letters at the end of the alphabet (W, X, Y, Z)
4. Strings of terminals—lowercase letters at the end of the alphabet (w, x, y, z)
5. Mixed strings (terminals and/or nonterminals)—lowercase Greek letters (α, β, δ, γ)

For programming languages, terminal symbols are the small-scale syntactic constructs of the language, or tokens. The nonterminal symbols of programming languages are usually connotative names or abbreviations, surrounded by pointed brackets—for example, <while_statement>, <expr>, and <function_def>. The sentences of a language (programs, in the case of a programming language) are strings of terminals. Mixed strings describe right-hand sides (RHSs) of grammar rules and are used in parsing algorithms.

4.3.2 Top-Down Parsers

A top-down parser traces or builds the parse tree in preorder. This corresponds to a leftmost derivation. A preorder traversal of a parse tree begins with the root. Each node is visited before its branches are followed. Branches from a particular node are followed in left-to-right order.

In terms of the derivation, a top-down parser can be described as follows: Given a sentential form that is part of a leftmost derivation, the parser's task is to find the next sentential form in that leftmost derivation. The general form of a left sentential form is $xA\alpha$, whereby our notational conventions x is a string of terminal symbols, A is a nonterminal, and α is a mixed string. Because x contains only terminals, A is the leftmost nonterminal in the sentential form, so it is the one that must be expanded to get the next sentential form in a leftmost derivation. Determining the next sentential form is a matter of choosing the correct grammar rule that has A as its LHS. For example, if the current sentential form is

$xA\alpha$

and the A-rules are A → bB, A → cBb, and A → a, a top-down parser must choose among these three rules to get the next sentential form, which could be xbBα, xcBbα, or xaα. This is the parsing decision problem for top-down parsers.

Different top-down parsing algorithms use different information to make parsing decisions. The most common top-down parsers choose the correct RHS for the leftmost nonterminal in the current sentential form by comparing the next token of input with the first symbols that can be generated by the RHSs of those rules. Whichever RHS has that token at the left end of the string it generates is the correct one. So, in the sentential form xAα, the parser would use whatever token followed the last lexeme in the string, x, to determine which A-rule should be used to get the next sentential form. In the example above, the **three RHSs of the A-rules** all begin with different terminal symbols. The parser can easily choose the correct RHS based on the next token of input, which must be a, b, or c in this example. In general, choosing the correct RHS is not so straightforward, because some of the RHSs of the leftmost nonterminal in the current sentential form may begin with a nonterminal.

The most common top-down parsing algorithms are closely related. A **recursive-descent parser** is a coded version of a syntax analyzer based directly on the BNF description of the syntax of language. The most common alternative to recursive descent is to use a parsing table, rather than code, to implement the BNF rules. Both of these, which are called **LL algorithms,** are equally powerful, meaning they work on the same subset of grammars. The first L in LL specifies a left-to-right scan of the input; the second L specifies that a leftmost derivation is generated. Section 4.4 introduces the recursive-descent approach to implementing an LL parser.

4.3.3 Bottom-Up Parsers

A bottom-up parser constructs a parse tree by beginning at the leaves and progressing toward the root. This parse order corresponds to the reverse of a rightmost derivation. In terms of the derivation, a bottom-up parser can be described as follows: Given a right sentential form α,[2] the parser must determine what substring of α is the RHS of the rule in the grammar that must be reduced to its LHS to produce the previous sentential form in the rightmost derivation. For example, the first step for a bottom-up parser is to determine which substring of the initial given sentence is the RHS to be reduced to its corresponding LHS to get the second last sentential form in the derivation. The process of finding the correct RHS to reduce is complicated by the fact that a given right sentential form may include more than one RHS from the grammar of the language being parsed. The correct RHS is called the **handle.**

Consider the following grammar and derivation:

---

2. A right sentential form is a sentential form that appears in a rightmost derivation.

$$S \rightarrow aAc$$
$$A \rightarrow aA \mid b$$

$$S \Rightarrow aAc \Rightarrow aaAc \Rightarrow aabc$$

A bottom-up parser of this sentence, aabc, starts with the sentence and must find the handle in it. In this example, this is an easy task, for the string contains only one RHS, b. When the parser replaces b with its LHS, A, it gets the second last sentential form in the derivation, aaAc. In the general case, as stated previously, finding the handle is much more difficult, because a sentential form may include many different RHSs.

A bottom-up parser finds the handle of a given right sentential form by examining the symbols on one or both sides of a possible handle. Symbols to the right of the possible handle are usually tokens in the input that have not yet been analyzed.

The most common bottom-up parsing algorithms are in the LR family, where the L specifies a left-to-right scan of the input and the R specifies that a rightmost derivation is generated.

4.3.4   The Complexity of Parsing

Parsing algorithms that work for any unambiguous grammar are complex and inefficient. In fact, the complexity of such algorithms is $O(n^3)$, which means the amount of time they take is on the order of the cube of the length of the string to be parsed. This relatively large amount of time is required because these algorithms frequently must back up and reparse part of the sentence being analyzed. Reparsing is required when the parser has made a mistake in the parsing process. Backing up the parser also requires that part of the parse tree being constructed (or its trace) must be dismantled and rebuilt. $O(n^3)$ algorithms are normally not useful for practical processes, such as syntax analysis for a compiler, because they are too slow. In this kind of situation, computer scientists often search for algorithms that are faster, though not as general. Generality is traded for efficiency. In terms of parsing, faster algorithms have been found that work for only a subset of the set of all possible grammars. These algorithms are acceptable as long as the subset includes grammars that describe programming languages. (Actually, as discussed in Chapter 3, the whole class of grammars is not adequate to describe all of the syntax of most programming languages.)

All algorithms used for the syntax analyzers of compilers have complexity $O(n)$, which means the time they take is linearly related to the length of the string to be parsed. This is vastly more efficient than $O(n^3)$ algorithms.

4.4 Recursive-Descent Parsing

This section introduces the top-down parser implementation process, recursive-descent.

4.4.1 The Recursive-Descent Parsing Process

A recursive-descent parser is so named because it consists of a collection of subprograms, many of which are recursive, and it produces a parse tree in top-down order. This recursion is a reflection of the nature of programming languages, which include several different kinds of nested structures. For example, statements are often nested in other statements. Also, parentheses in expressions must be properly nested. The syntax of these structures is naturally described with recursive grammar rules.

EBNF is ideally suited for recursive-descent parsers. Recall from Chapter 3 that the primary EBNF extensions are braces, which specify that what they enclose can appear zero or more times, and brackets, which specify that what they enclose can appear once or not at all. Note that in both cases, the enclosed symbols are optional. For example:

<if_statement> → **if** <logic_expr> <statement> [**else** <statement>]
<ident_list> → ident {, ident}

In the first rule, the **else** clause of an **if** statement is optional. In the second, an <ident_list> is an identifier, followed by zero or more repetitions of a comma and an identifier.

A recursive-descent parser has a subprogram for each nonterminal in the grammar. The responsibility of the subprogram associated with a particular nonterminal is as follows: When given an input string, it traces out the parse tree that can be rooted at that nonterminal and whose leaves match the input string. In effect, a recursive-descent parsing subprogram is a parser for the language (set of strings) that can be generated by its associated nonterminal.

Consider the following EBNF description of simple arithmetic expressions:

<expr> → <term> {(+ | −) <term>}
<term> → <factor> {(* | /) <factor>}
<factor> → id | (<expr>)

Recall from Chapter 3 that an EBNF grammar for arithmetic expressions, such as this one, does not force any associativity rule. Therefore, when using such a grammar as the basis for a compiler, one must take care to ensure that the code generation process, which is normally driven by syntax analysis, produces code that adheres to the associativity rules of the language. This can easily be done when recursive-descent parsing is used.

In the following example recursive-descent function, `expr`, the lexical analyzer is a function that is appropriately named `lex`. It gets the next lexeme and puts its token code in the global variable `nextToken`. The token codes are defined as named constants. For example, `PLUS_CODE` is a named constant for the token code for plus symbols.

A recursive-descent subprogram for a rule with a single RHS is relatively simple. For each terminal symbol in the RHS, that terminal symbol is compared with `nextToken`. If they do not match, it is a syntax error. If they match, the lexical analyzer is called to get the next input token. For each nonterminal, the parsing subprogram for that nonterminal is called.

The recursive-descent subprogram for the first rule in the previous example grammar, written in C, is

```c
/* Function expr
   Parses strings in the language generated by the rule:
   <expr> -> <term> {(+ | -) <term>}
   */
void expr() {

/* Parse the first term */

   term();

/* As long as the next token is + or -, call lex to get
the next token, and parse the next term */

  while (nextToken == PLUS_CODE ||
         nextToken == MINUS_CODE){
    lex();
    term();
  }
}
```

Recursive-descent parsing subprograms are written with the convention that each one leaves the next token of input in `nextToken`. So, whenever a parsing function begins, it is assured that `nextToken` has the code for the leftmost token of the input that has not yet been used in the parsing process.

The part of the language that the `expr` function parses consists of one or more terms, separated by either plus or minus operators. This is the language generated by the nonterminal `<expr>`. Therefore, it first calls the function that parses terms (`term`). Then it continues to call that function as long as it finds `PLUS_CODE` or `MINUS_CODE` tokens (which it passes over by calling `lex`). This recursive-descent function is simpler than most, because its rule has only one RHS. Furthermore, it does not include any code for syntax error detection or recovery, because there are no detectable errors associated with the grammar rule.

A recursive-descent parsing subprogram for a nonterminal whose rule has more than one RHS begins with code to determine which RHS is to be parsed. Each RHS is examined (at compiler construction time) to determine the set of terminal symbols that can appear at the beginning of sentences it can generate. By matching these sets against the next token of input, the parser can choose the correct RHS.

The parsing subprogram for <term> is similar to that for <expr>:

```
/* Function term
   Parses strings in the language generated by the rule:
   <term> -> <factor> {(* | /) <factor>}
   */
void term() {

/* Parse the first factor */

   factor();

/* As long as the next token is * or /, call lex to get
   the next token, and parse the next factor */

  while (nextToken == AST_CODE ||
         nextToken == SLASH_CODE){
    lex();
    factor();
  }
}
```

The function for the <factor> nonterminal of our arithmetic expression grammar must choose between its two RHSs. It also includes error detection. In the function for <factor>, the reaction to detecting a syntax error is simply to call the error function. In a real parser, a diagnostic message must be produced when an error is detected. Furthermore, parsers must recover from the error so that the parsing process can continue.

```
/* Function factor
   Parses strings in the language generated by the rule:
      <factor> -> id  |  (<expr>)
   */

void factor() {

/* Determine which RHS */

  if (nextToken == ID_CODE)
```

```
/* Get the next token */

    lex();

/* If the RHS is (<expr>), call lex to pass over the left
   parenthesis, call expr, and check for the right
   parenthesis */

  else if (nextToken == LEFT_PAREN_CODE) {
    lex();
    expr();
    if (nextToken == RIGHT_PAREN_CODE)
      lex();
    else
      error();
  }  /* End of else if (nextToken == ...  */

/* It was neither an id nor a left parenthesis */

  else error();

}
```

To get a parse trace, code could be added at the beginning and end of each parsing routine. Also, each call to `lex` could be added to the trace, including the token that was returned. For example, at the beginning of the `expr` function, there would be

```
printf("Enter <expr> \n");
```

and at its end

```
printf("Exit <expr> \n");
```

Following is a trace of the parse of a + b using the parsing functions `expr`, `term`, and `factor`, and the function `lex`. Note that the parse begins by calling `lex` and the start symbol routine, in this case, `expr`.

```
Call lex  /* returns a */
Enter <expr>
Enter <term>
Enter <factor>
Call lex  /* returns + */
Exit <factor>
Exit <term>
Call lex  /* returns b */
```

```
Enter <term>
Enter <factor>
Call lex  /* returns end-of-input */
Exit <factor>
Exit <term>
Exit <expr>
```

The parse tree traced by this parser is shown in Figure 4.2.

Following is a grammatical description of the Java **if** statement:

<ifstmt> → **if** (<boolexpr>) <statement> [**else** <statement>]

The recursive-descent subprogram for this rule follows:

```
/* Function ifstmt
     Parses strings in the language generated by the rule:
     <ifstmt> -> if (<boolexpr>) <statement>
                    [else <statement>]
     */
void ifstmt() {
/* Be sure the first token is 'if' */
  if (nextToken != IF_CODE)
    error();
  else {
/* Call lex to get to the next token */
    lex();
/* Check for the left parenthesis */
    if (nextToken != LEFT_PAREN_CODE)
      error();
    else {
/* Call boolexpr to parse the Boolean expression */
      boolexpr();
/* Check for the right parenthesis */
      if (nextToken != RIGHT_PAREN_CODE)
        error();
      else {
```

Figure 4.2

Parse tree for a + b

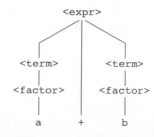

```
/* Call statement to parse the then clause */
      statement();
/* If an else is next, parse the else clause */
      if (nextToken == ELSE_CODE) {
/* Call lex to get over the else */
        lex();
        statement();
      } /* end of if (nextToken == ELSE_CODE ... */
    } /* end of else of if (nextToken != RIGHT ... */
  } /* end of else of if (nextToken != LEFT ... */
 } /* end of else of if (nextToken != IF_CODE ... */
} /* end of ifstmt */
```

The objective of these examples is to convince you that a recursive-descent parser can be easily written if an appropriate grammar is available for the language. The characteristics of a grammar that allows a recursive-descent parser to be built are discusssed in the following subsection.

4.4.2   The LL Grammar Class

Before choosing to use recursive descent as a parsing strategy for a compiler or other program analysis tool, one must consider the limitations of the approach, in terms of grammar restrictions. This section discusses these restrictions and possible solutions to them.

One simple grammar characteristic that causes a catastrophic problem for LL parsers is left recursion. For example, consider the following rule:

$A \rightarrow A + B$

A recursive-descent parser subprogram for A immediately calls itself to parse the first symbol in its RHS. That activation of the A parser subprogram then immediately calls itself again, and again, and so forth. It is easy to see that this gets nowhere.

The left recursion in the rule $A \rightarrow A + B$ is called **direct left recursion**, because it occurs in one rule. Direct left recursion can be eliminated from a grammar by the following process:

For each nonterminal, A,
1. Group the A-rules as $A \rightarrow A\alpha_1, | ... | A\alpha_m | \beta_1 | \beta_2 | ... | \beta_n$
   where none of the β's begins with A
2. Replace the original A-rules with

$$A \rightarrow \beta_1 A' | \beta_2 A' | ... | \beta_n A'$$
$$A' \rightarrow \alpha_1 A' | \alpha_2 A' | ... | \alpha_m A' | \varepsilon$$

Note that ε specifies the empty string. A rule that has ε as its RHS is called an *erasure rule*, because its use in a derivation effectively erases its LHS from the sentential form.

Consider the following example grammar and the application of the above process:

$$E \rightarrow E + T \mid T$$
$$T \rightarrow T * F \mid F$$
$$F \rightarrow (E) \mid id$$

For the E-rules, we have $\alpha_1 = + T$ and $\beta = T$, so we replace the E-rules with

$$E \rightarrow T E'$$
$$E' \rightarrow + T E' \mid \varepsilon$$

For the T-rules, we have $\alpha_1 = * F$ and $\beta = F$, so we replace the T-rules with

$$T \rightarrow F T'$$
$$T' \rightarrow * F T' \mid \varepsilon$$

Because there is no left recursion in the F-rules, they remain the same, so the complete replacement grammar is

$$E \rightarrow T E'$$
$$E' \rightarrow + T E' \mid \varepsilon$$
$$T \rightarrow F T'$$
$$T' \rightarrow * F T' \mid \varepsilon$$
$$F \rightarrow (E) \mid id$$

This grammar generates the same language as the original grammar, but is not left recursive.

As was the case with the expression grammar written using EBNF in Section 4.1.1, this grammar does not specify left associativity of operators. However, it is relatively easy to design the code generation based on this grammar so that the addition and mulitplication operators will have left associativity.

Indirect left recursion poses the same problem as direct left recursion. For example, suppose we have

$$A \rightarrow B a A$$
$$B \rightarrow A b$$

A recursive-descent parser for these rules would have the A subprogram immediately call the subprogram for B, which immediately calls the A subprogram. So, the problem is the same as for direct left recursion. The problem of left recursion is not confined to the recursive-descent approach to building top-down parsers. It is a problem for all top-down parsing algorithms. Fortunately, left recursion is not a problem for bottom-up parsing algorithms.

There is an algorithm to modify a given grammar to remove indirect left recursion (Aho et al., 1986), but it is not covered here. When writing a grammar for a programming language, one can usually avoid including left recursion, both direct and indirect.

Left recursion is not the only grammar trait that disallows top-down parsing. Another is whether the parser can always choose the correct RHS on the basis of the next token of input, using only the first token generated by the leftmost nonterminal in the current sentential form. There is a relatively simple test of a non–left recursive grammar that indicates whether this can be done, called the **pairwise disjointness test.** This test requires the ability to compute a set based on the RHSs of a given nonterminal symbol in a grammar. These sets, which are called FIRST, are defined as

$$\text{FIRST}(\alpha) = \{a \mid \alpha =>^* a\beta\} \text{ (If } \alpha =>^* \varepsilon, \varepsilon \text{ is in FIRST}(\alpha))$$

in which $=>^*$ means 0 or more derivation steps.

An algorithm to compute FIRST for any mixed string α can be found in Aho et al. (1986). For our purposes, FIRST can usually be computed by inspection of the grammar.

The pairwise disjointness test is

For each nonterminal, A, in the grammar that has more than one RHS, for each pair of rules, $A \rightarrow \alpha_i$ and $A \rightarrow \alpha_j$, it must be true that

$$\text{FIRST}(\alpha_i) \cap \text{FIRST}(\alpha_j) = \phi$$

(The intersection of the two sets, $\text{FIRST}(\alpha_i)$ and $\text{FIRST}(\alpha_j)$, must be empty.)

In other words, if a nonterminal A has more than one RHS, the first terminal symbol that can be generated in a derivation for each of them must be unique to that RHS. Consider the following rules:

```
A → aB | bAb | Bb
B → cB | d
```

The FIRST sets for the RHSs of the A-rules are {a}, {b}, and {c, d}, which are clearly disjoint. Therefore, these rules pass the pairwise disjointness test. What this means, in terms of a recursive-descent parser, is that the code of the subprogram for parsing the nonterminal A can choose which RHS it is dealing with by seeing only the first terminal symbol of input (token) that is generated by the nonterminal. Now consider the rules

```
A → aB | BAb
B → aB | b
```

The FIRST sets for the RHSs in the A-rules are {a} and {a, b}, which are clearly not disjoint. So, these rules fail the pairwise disjointness test. In terms of the parser, the subprogram for A could not determine which RHS was being parsed by looking at the next symbol of input, because if it were an a, it could be either RHS. This issue is of course more complex if one or more of the RHSs begin with nonterminals.

In many cases, a grammar that fails the pairwise disjointness test can be modified so that it will pass the test. For example, consider the rule

<variable> → identifier | identifier [<expression>]

This states that a <variable> is either an identifier or an identifier followed by an expression in brackets (a subscript). These rules clearly do not pass the pairwise disjointness test, because both RHSs begin with the same terminal, identifier. This problem can be alleviated through a process called **left factoring.**

We now take an informal look at left factoring. Consider the earlier rules for <variable>. Both RHSs begin with identifier. The parts that follow identifier in the two RHSs are ε (the empty string) and [<expression>]. The two rules can be replaced by

<variable> → identifier <new>

where <new> is defined as

<new> → ε | [<expression>]

It is not difficult to see that together, these two rules generate the same language as the two rules with which we began. However, these two pass the pairwise disjointness test.

If the grammar is being used as the basis for a recursive-descent parser, an alternative to left factoring is available. With an EBNF extension, the problem disappears in a way that is very similar to the left factoring-solution. Consider the first rules above for <variable>. The subscript can be made optional by placing it in square brackets, as in

<variable> → identifier [[<expression>]]

In this rule, the outer brackets are metasymbols that indicate that what is inside is optional. The inner brackets are terminal symbols of the programming language being described. The point is that we replaced two rules with a single rule that generates the same language but passes the pairwise disjointness test.

A formal algorithm for left factoring can be found in Aho et al. (1986). Left factoring cannot solve all pairwise disjointness problems of grammars. In some cases, rules must be rewritten in other ways to eliminate the problem.

4.5 Bottom-Up Parsing

This section introduces the general process of bottom-up parsing and includes a description of the LR parsing algorithm.

4.5.1 The Parsing Problem for Bottom-Up Parsers

Consider the following grammar, which generates arithmetic expressions with addition and multiplication operators, parentheses, and the operand id.

$$E \rightarrow E + T \mid T$$
$$T \rightarrow T * F \mid F$$
$$F \rightarrow (E) \mid id$$

Notice that this grammar generates the same arithmetic expressions as the example in Section 4.4. The difference is that this grammar is left recursive, which is acceptable to bottom-up parsers. Also note that grammars for bottom-up parsers normally do not include metasymbols such as those used to specify extensions to BNF. The following rightmost derivation illustrates this grammar:

$$
\begin{aligned}
E \quad &\Rightarrow \underline{E + T} \\
&\Rightarrow E + \underline{T * F} \\
&\Rightarrow E + T * \underline{id} \\
&\Rightarrow E + \underline{F} * id \\
&\Rightarrow E + \underline{id} * id \\
&\Rightarrow \underline{T} + id * id \\
&\Rightarrow \underline{F} + id * id \\
&\Rightarrow \underline{id} + id * id
\end{aligned}
$$

The underlined part of each sentential form in this derivation is the RHS that is rewritten as its corresponding LHS to get the previous sentential form. The process of bottom-up parsing produces the reverse of a rightmost derivation. So, in the example derivation, a bottom-up parser starts with the last sentential form (the input sentence) and produces the sequence of sentential forms from there until all that remains is the start symbol, which in this grammar is E. In each step, the task of the bottom-up parser is to find the specific RHS, the handle, in the sentential form that must be rewritten to get the next (previous) sentential form. As mentioned earlier, a right sentential form may include more than one RHS. For example, the right sentential form

$$E + T * id$$

includes three RHSs, E + T, T, and id. Only one of these is the handle. For example, if the RHS E + T were chosen to be rewritten in this sentential form, the resulting sentential form would be E * id, but E * id is not a legal right sentential form for the given grammar.

The handle of a right sentential form is unique. The task of a bottom-up parser is to find the handle of any given right sentential form that can be generated by its associated grammar. Formally, handle is defined as follows:

Definition: β is the **handle** of the right sentential form $\gamma = \alpha\beta w$ if and only if $S =>^*_{rm} \alpha A w =>_{rm} \alpha\beta w$

In this definition, $=>_{rm}$ specifies a rightmost derivation step, and $=>^*_{rm}$ specifies zero or more rightmost derivation steps. Although the definition of a handle is mathematically concise, it provides little help in finding the handle of a given right sentential form. In the following, we provide the definitions of several substrings of sentential forms that are related to handles. The purpose of these is to provide some intuition about handles.

Definition: β is a **phrase** of the right sentential form γ if and only if $S =>^* \gamma = \alpha_1 A \alpha_2 =>+ \alpha_1 \beta \alpha_2$

In this definition, $=>+$ means one or more derivation steps.

Definition: β is a **simple phrase** of the right sentential form γ if and only if $S =>^* \gamma = \alpha_1 A \alpha_2 => \alpha_1 \beta \alpha_2$

If you compare these two definitions carefully, you will discover that they differ only in the last derivation specification. The definition of phrase uses one or more steps, while the definition of simple phrase uses exactly one step.

The definitions of phrase and simple phrase may appear to have the same lack of practical value as that of a handle, but that is not true. Consider what a phrase is relative to a parse tree. It is the string consisting of all of the leaves of the partial parse tree that is rooted at one particular internal node of the whole parse tree. A simple phrase is just a phrase that takes a single derivation step from its root nonterminal node. In terms of a parse tree, a phrase can be derived from a single nonterminal in one or more tree levels, but a simple phrase can be derived in just a single tree level. Consider the parse tree shown in Figure 4.3.

Figure 4.3

A parse tree for E + T * id

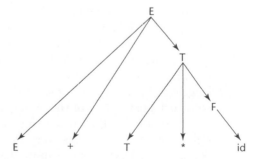

The leaves of the parse tree in Figure 4.3 comprise the sentential form E + T * id. Because there are three internal nodes, there are three phrases. Each internal node is the root of a subtree, whose leaves are a phrase. The root node of the whole parse tree, E, generates all of the resulting sentential form, E + T * id, which is a phrase. The internal node, T, generates the leaves T * id, which is another phrase. Finally, the internal node, F, generates id, which is also a phrase. So the phrases of the sentential form E + T * id are E + T * id, T * id, and id. Notice that phrases are not necessarily RHSs in the underlying grammar.

The simple phrases are a subset of the phrases. In the previous example, the only simple phrase is id. A simple phrase is always an RHS in the grammar.

The reason for discussing phrases and simple phrases is this: The handle of any rightmost sentential form is its leftmost simple phrase. So now we have a highly intuitive way to find the handle of any right sentential form, assuming we have the grammar and can draw a parse tree. This approach to finding handles is of course not practical for a parser. (If you already have a parse tree, why do you need a parser?) Its only purpose is to provide the reader with some intuitive feel for what a handle is, relative to a parse tree, which is easier than trying to think about handles in terms of sentential forms.

We can now consider bottom-up parsing in terms of parse trees, although the purpose of a parser is to produce a parse tree. Given the parse tree for an entire sentence, you easily can find the handle, which is the first thing to rewrite in the sentence to get the previous sentential form. Then the handle can be pruned from the parse tree and the process repeated. Continuing to the root of the parse tree, the entire rightmost derivation can be constructed.

4.5.2 Shift-Reduce Algorithms

Bottom-up parsers are often called **shift-reduce algorithms,** because shift and reduce are the two most common actions they specify. An integral part of every bottom-up parser is a stack. The shift action moves the next input token onto the parser's stack. A reduce action replaces a RHS (the handle) on top of the parser's stack by its corresponding LHS. Every parser for a programming language is a **pushdown automaton** (PDA). You need not be intimate with PDAs to understand how a bottom-up parser works, although it helps. A PDA is a very simple mathematical machine that scans strings of symbols from left to right. A PDA is so named because it uses a pushdown stack as its memory. PDAs can be used as recognizers for context-free languages. Given a string of symbols over the alphabet of a context-free language, a PDA that is designed for the purpose can determine whether the string is or is not a sentence in the language. In the process, the PDA can produce the information needed to construct a parse tree for the sentence.

With a PDA, the input string is examined, one symbol at a time, left to right. The input is treated very much as if it were stored in another stack, because the PDA never sees more than the leftmost symbol of the input.

Note that a recursive-descent parser is also a PDA. In this case, the stack is that of the runtime system, which records subprogram calls (among other things), which correspond to the nonterminals of the grammar.

4.5.3   LR Parsers

Many different bottom-up parsing algorithms have been devised. Most of these are variations of a process called LR. LR parsers use a relatively small program and a parsing table. The original LR algorithm was designed by Donald Knuth (Knuth, 1965). This algorithm, which is sometimes called **canonical LR,** was not used in the years immediately following its publication because producing the required parsing table required large amounts of computer time and memory. Subsequently, several variations on the canonical LR table constuction process were developed (DeRemer, 1971; DeRemer & Pennello, 1982). These are characterized by two properties: (1) They require much less computer resources to produce the required parsing table than the canonical LR algorithm, and (2) they work on smaller classes of grammars than the canonical LR algorithm.

There are several advantages to LR parsers:

1. They can be built for all programming languages.
2. They can detect syntax errors as soon as it is possible in a left-to-right scan.
3. The LR class of grammars is a proper superset of the class parsable by LL parsers (for example, many left recursive grammars are LR, but none are LL).

The only disadvantage of LR parsing is that it is difficult to produce by hand the parsing table for a given grammar for a complete programming language. This is not a serious disadvantage, however, for there are several programs available that take a grammar as input and produce the parsing table, as discussed later in this section.

Prior to the appearance of the LR parsing algorithm, there were a number of parsing algorithms that found handles of right sentential forms by looking both to the left and to the right of the substring of the sentential form that was suspected of being the handle. Knuth's insight was that one could effectively look to the left of the suspected handle all the way to the bottom of the parse stack to determine whether it was the handle. But all of the information in the parse stack that was relevant to the parsing process could be represented by a single state, which could be stored on the top of the stack. In other words, Knuth discovered that regardless of the length of the input string, the length of the sentential form, or the depth of the parse stack, there were only a relatively small number of different situations, as far as the parsing process is concerned. Each situation could be represented by a state and stored in the parse stack, one state symbol for each grammar symbol on the stack. At the top of the stack would always be a state symbol, which represented the relevant information from the entire history of the parse, up to the current time. We will use subscripted uppercase Ss to represent the parser states.

Figure 4.4 shows the structure of an LR parser.

Figure 4.4

The structure of an LR parser

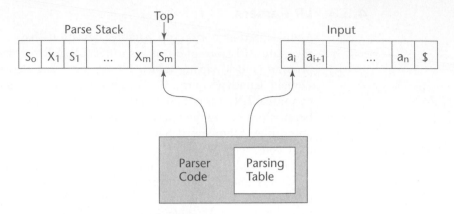

The contents of the parse stack for an LR parser has the following form:

$$S_0X_1S_1X_2 \ldots X_mS_m \text{ (top)}$$

where the Ss are state symbols and the Xs are grammar symbols. An LR parser configuration is a pair of strings (stack, input), with the detailed form

$$(S_0X_1S_1X_2S_2 \ldots X_mS_m, a_ia_{i+1} \ldots a_n\$)$$

Notice that the input string has a dollar sign at its right end. This sign is put there during initialization of the parser. It is used for normal termination of the parser. Using this parser configuration, we can formally define the LR parser process, which is based on the parsing table.

An LR parsing table has two parts, named ACTION and GOTO. The ACTION part of the table specifies most of what the parser does. It has state symbols as its row labels and the terminal symbols of the grammar as its column labels. Given a current parser state, which is represented by the state symbol on top of the parse stack, and the next symbol (token) of input, the parse table specifies what the parser should do. The two primary parser actions are shift and reduce. Either the parser shifts the next input symbol onto the parse stack or it already has the handle on top of the stack, which it reduces to the LHS of the rule whose RHS is the same as the handle. Two other actions are possible: accept, which means the parser has successfully completed the parse of the input; and error, which means the parser has detected a syntax error.

The rows of the GOTO part of the LR parsing table have state symbols as labels. This part of the table has nonterminals as column labels. The values in the GOTO part of the table indicate which state symbol should be pushed onto the parse stack after a reduction has been completed, which means the handle has been removed from the parse stack and the new nonterminal has been pushed onto the parse stack. The specific symbol is found at the row whose label is the state symbol on top of the parse stack after the handle and its associated state symbols have been removed. The column of the GOTO table that is used is the one with the label that is the LHS of the rule used in the reduction.

Consider the traditional grammar for arithmetic expressions that follows:

1. $E \rightarrow E + T$
2. $E \rightarrow T$
3. $T \rightarrow T * F$
4. $T \rightarrow F$
5. $F \rightarrow (E)$
6. $F \rightarrow id$

The rules of this grammar are numbered to provide a simple way to reference them in a parsing table.

Figure 4.5 shows the LR parsing table for this grammar. Abbreviations are used for the actions, R for reduce and S for shift. R4 means reduce using rule 4; S6 means shift the next symbol of input onto the stack and push state S_6 onto the stack. Empty positions in the ACTION table indicate syntax errors. In a complete parser, these could have calls to error-handling routines.

LR parsing tables can easily be constructed using a software tool, such as yacc[3] (Johnson, 1975), which takes the grammar as input. Although LR parsing tables can be produced by hand, for a grammar of a real programming language, the task would be lengthy, tedious, and error-prone. For real compilers, LR parsing tables are always generated with software tools.

The initial configuration of an LR parser is

$(S_0, a_1 \ldots a_n \$)$

The parser actions are formally defined as follows:

1. If ACTION$[S_m, a_i]$ = Shift S, the next configuration is

   $(S_0 X_1 S_1 X_2 S_2 \ldots X_m S_m a_i S, a_{i+1} \ldots a_n \$)$

   The Shift process is simple: The next symbol of input is pushed onto the stack, along with the state symbol that is part of the Shift specification in the ACTION table.

   For example, suppose the configuration is $(S_0 E S_1, +id \ldots \$)$. The ACTION table specifies S6 as the action in its [1, +] position. This results in the configuration $(S_0 E S_1 + S_6, id \ldots \$)$.

2. If ACTION$[S_m, a_i]$ = Reduce $A \rightarrow \beta$ and S = GOTO$[S_{m-r}, A]$, where r = the length of β, the next configuration is

   $(S_0 X_1 S_1 X_2 S_2 \ldots X_{m-r} S_{m-r} A S, a_i a_{i+1} \ldots a_n \$)$

   This is a much more complicated action. For a reduce action, the handle must be removed from the stack. Because for every grammar symbol on the stack there is a state symbol, the number of symbols removed from the stack is twice the number of symbols in the handle. After removing the handle and its associated state symbols, the LHS of

---

3. The term yacc is an acronym for "yet another compiler compiler."

Figure 4.5

The LR parsing table
for an arithmetic
expression grammar

State	Action						Goto		
	id	+	*	(	)	$	E	T	F
0	S5			S4			1	2	3
1		S6				accept			
2		R2	S7		R2	R2			
3		R4	R4		R4	R4			
4	S5			S4			8	2	3
5		R6	R6		R6	R6			
6	S5			S4				9	3
7	S5			S4					10
8		S6			S11				
9		R1	S7		R1	R1			
10		R3	R3		R3	R3			
11		R5	R5		R5	R5			

the rule is pushed onto the stack. Finally, the GOTO table is used, with the row label being the symbol that was exposed when the handle and its state symbols were removed from the stack, and the column label being the nonterminal that is the LHS of the rule used in the reduction. So in the new configuration, the top symbol comes from the GOTO part of the table, and the topmost grammar symbol is the LHS of the rule used in the reduction.

For example, suppose the configuration is $(S_0 id S_5, +id ... \$)$. The ACTION table specifies R6 in its [5, +] position. This indicates a reduction using rule 6, which is $F \rightarrow id$. The RHS of this rule has length 1, so two symbols must be popped off the stack. This exposes S_0 at the top of the stack, so we look at the 0 row F column of the GOTO table (because F is the LHS of the rule used in the reduction). At that position of the GOTO table we find 3, so S_3 is pushed on to the stack after F has been pushed.

3. If $ACTION[S_m, a_i]$ = Accept, the parse is complete and no errors were found.

4. If $ACTION[S_m, a_i]$ = Error, the parser calls an error-handling routine.

Although there are many parsing algorithms based on the LR concept, they differ only in the construction of the parsing table. All LR parsers use this same parsing algorithm.

Perhaps the best way to become familiar with the LR parsing process is through an example. Initially, the parse stack has the single symbol 0, which represents state 0 of the parser. The input contains the input string with an end marker, in this case a dollar sign, attached to its right end. At each step, the parser actions are dictated by the top (rightmost in Figure 4.4) symbol of the parse stack and the next (leftmost in Figure 4.4) token of input. The correct action is chosen from the corresponding cell of the ACTION part of the parse table. The GOTO part of the parse table is used after a reduction action. Recall that GOTO is used to determine which state symbol is placed on the parse stack after a reduction.

Following is a trace of a parse of the string id + id * id, using the LR parsing algorithm and the parsing table shown in Figure 4.5.

Stack	Input	Action
0	id + id * id $	Shift 5
0id5	+ id * id $	Reduce 6 (use GOTO[0, F])
0F3	+ id * id $	Reduce 4 (use GOTO[0, T])
0T2	+ id * id $	Reduce 2 (use GOTO[0, E])
0E1	+ id * id $	Shift 6
0E1+6	id * id $	Shift 5
0E1+6id5	* id $	Reduce 6 (use GOTO[6, F])
0E1+6F3	* id $	Reduce 4 (use GOTO[6, T])
0E1+6T9	* id $	Shift 7
0E1+6T9*7	id $	Shift 5
0E1+6T9*7id5	$	Reduce 6 (use GOTO[7, F])
0E1+6T9*7F10	$	Reduce 3 (use GOTO[6, T])
0E1+6T9	$	Reduce 1 (use GOTO[0, E])
0E1	$	Accept

The algorithms to generate LR parsing tables from given grammars, which are described in Aho et al. (1986), are not overly complex, but are beyond the scope of a book on programming languages. As stated previously, there are a number of different software systems available to generate LR parsing tables.

SUMMARY

Syntax analysis is a common part of language implementation, regardless of the implementation approach used. Syntax analysis is normally based on a formal syntax description of the language being implemented. A context-free grammar, which is also called BNF, is the most common approach for describing syntax. The task of syntax analysis is usually divided into two parts, lexical analysis and syntax analysis. There are several reasons for separating lexical analysis, namely, simplicity, efficiency, and portability.

A lexical analyzer is a pattern matcher that isolates the small-scale parts of a program, which are called lexemes. Lexemes occur in categories, such as integer literals and names. These categories are called tokens. Each token is assigned a numeric code, which along with the lexeme is what the lexical analyzer produces. There are three distinct approaches to constructing a lexical analyzer: using a software tool to generate a table for a table-driven analyzer, building such a table by hand, and writing code to implement a state diagram description of the tokens of the language being implemented. The state diagram for tokens can be reasonably small if character classes are used for transitions, rather than having transitions for every possible character from every state node. Also, the state diagram can be simplified by using a table lookup to recognize reserved words.

Syntax analyzers have two goals: to detect syntax errors in a given program and to produce a parse tree, or possibly only the information required to build such a tree, for a given program. Syntax analyzers are either top-down, meaning they construct leftmost derivations and a parse tree in top-down order, or bottom-up, in which case they construct the reverse of a rightmost derivation and a parse tree in bottom-up order. Parsers that work for all unambiguous grammars have complexity $O(n^3)$. However, parsers used for implementing syntax analyzers for programming languages work on subclasses of unambiguous grammars and have complexity $O(n)$.

A recursive-descent parser is an LL parser that is implemented by writing code directly from the grammar of the source language. EBNF is ideal as the basis for recursive-descent parsers. A recursive-descent parser has a subprogram for each nonterminal in the grammar. The code for a given grammar rule is simple if the rule has a single RHS. The RHS is examined left to right. For each nonterminal, the code calls the associated subprogram for that nonterminal, which parses whatever the nonterminal generates. For each terminal, the code compares the terminal with the next token of input. If they match, the code simply calls the lexical analyzer to get the next token. If they do not, the subprogram reports a syntax error. If a rule has more than one RHS, the subprogram must first determine which RHS it should parse. It must be possible to make this determination on the basis of the next token of input.

Two distinct grammar characteristics prevent the construction of a recursive-descent parser based on the grammar. One of these is left recursion. The process of eliminating direct left recursion from a grammar is relatively simple. Although we do not cover it, an algorithm exists to remove both direct and indirect left recursion from a grammar. The other problem is detected with the pairwise disjointness test, which tests whether a parsing subprogram can determine which RHS is being parsed on the basis of the next token of input. Some grammars that fail the pairwise disjointness test often can be modified to pass it, using left factoring.

The parsing problem for bottom-up parsers is to find the substring of the current sentential form that must be reduced to its associated LHS to get the next (previous) sentential form in the rightmost derivation. This substring is called the handle of the sentential form. A parse tree can provide an intuitive basis for recognizing a handle. A bottom-up parser is a shift-reduce algorithm, because in most cases it either shifts the next lexeme of input onto the parse stack or reduces the handle that is on top of the stack.

The LR family of shift-reduce parsers is the most commonly used bottom-up parsing approach for programming languages, because parsers in this family have several advantages over alternatives. An LR parser uses a parse stack, which contains grammar symbols and state symbols to maintain the state of the parser. The top symbol on the parse stack is always a state symbol that represents all of the information in the parse stack that is relevant to the parsing process. LR parsers use two parsing tables, ACTION and GOTO. The ACTION part specifies what the parser should do, given the state symbol on top of the parse stack and the next token of input. The GOTO table is used to determine which state symbol should be placed on the parse stack after a reduction has been done.

REVIEW QUESTIONS

1. What are three reasons why syntax analyzers are based on grammars?
2. Explain the three reasons why lexical analysis is separated from syntax analysis.
3. Define *lexeme* and *token*.
4. What are the primary tasks of a lexical analyzer?
5. Describe briefly the three approaches to building a lexical analyzer.
6. What is a state transition diagram?
7. Why are character classes used, rather than individual characters, for the transitions of a state diagram for a lexical analyzer?
8. What are the two distinct goals of syntax analysis?
9. Describe the differences between top-down and bottom-up parsers.
10. Describe the parsing problem for a top-down parser.
11. Describe the parsing problem for a bottom-up parser.
12. Explain why compilers use parsing algorithms that work on only a subset of all grammars.
13. Why are named constants used, rather than numbers, for token codes?
14. Describe how a recursive-descent parsing subprogram is written for a rule with a single RHS.
15. Explain the two grammar characteristics that prohibit them from being used as the basis for a top-down parser.
16. What is the FIRST set for a given grammar and sentential form?
17. Describe the pairwise disjointness test.
18. What is left factoring?

19. What is a phrase of a sentential form?

20. What is a simple phrase of a sentential form?

21. What is the handle of a sentential form?

22. What is the mathematical machine on which both top-down and bottom-up parsers are based?

23. Describe three advantages of LR parsers.

24. What was Knuth's insight in developing the LR parsing technique?

25. Describe the purpose of the ACTION table of an LR parser.

26. Describe the purpose of the GOTO table of an LR parser.

27. Is left recursion a problem for LR parsers?

PROBLEM SET

1. Perform the pairwise disjointness test for the following grammar rules.
   a. A → aB | b | cBB
   b. B → aB | bA | aBb
   c. C → aaA | b | caB

2. Perform the pairwise disjointness test for the following grammar rules.
   a. S → aSb | bAA
   b. A → b{aB} | a
   c. B → aB | a

3. Show a trace of the recursive descent parser given in Section 4.4.1 for the string a + b * c.

4. Show a trace of the recursive descent parser given in Section 4.4.1 for the string a * (b + c).

5. Given the following grammar and the right sentential form, draw a parse tree and show the phrases and simple phrases, as well as the handle.

   S → aAb | bBA   A → ab | aAB   B → aB | b
   a. aaAbb
   b. bBab
   c. aaAbBb

6. Given the following grammar and the right sentential form, draw a parse tree and show the phrases and simple phrases, as well as the handle.

   S → AbB | bAc   A → Ab | aBB   B → Ac | cBb | c
   a. aAcccbbc
   b. AbcaBccb
   c. baBcBbbc

7. Show a complete parse, including the parse stack contents, input string, and action for the string id * (id + id), using the grammar and parse table in Section 4.5.3.

8. Show a complete parse, including the parse stack contents, input string, and action for the string (id + id) * id, using the grammar and parse table in Section 4.5.3.

9. Write an EBNF rule that describes the **while** statement of Java or C++. Write the recursive-descent subprogram in Java or C++ for this rule.

10. Write an EBNF rule that describes the **for** statement of Java or C++. Write the recursive-descent subprogram in Java or C++ for this rule.

PROGRAMMING EXERCISES

1. Design a state diagram to recognize one form of the comments of the C-based programming languages, those that begin with /* and end with */.

2. Design a state diagram to recognize the floating-point literals of your favorite programming language.

3. Write and test the code to implement the state diagram of Problem 1.

4. Write and test the code to implement the state diagram of Problem 2.

5. Convert the lexical analyzer (which is written in C) given in Section 4.2 to Java.

6. For those rules that pass the test in Problem 1, write a recursive-descent parsing subprogram that parses the language generated by the rules. Assume you have a lexical analyzer named `lex` and an error-handling subprogram named `error`, which is called whenever a syntax error is detected.

7. For those rules that pass the test in Problem 2, write a recursive-descent parsing subprogram that parses the language generated by the rules. Assume you have a lexical analyzer named `lex` and an error-handling subprogram named `error`, which is called whenever a syntax error is detected.

8. Implement and test the LR parsing algorithm given in Section 4.5.3.

5

Names, Bindings, Type Checking, and Scopes

This chapter introduces the fundamental semantic issues of variables. The most basic of these topics is covered first: the nature of names and special words in programming languages. The attributes of variables, including type, address, and value, are then discussed. The issue of aliases is included in that discussion. The important concepts of binding and binding times are then introduced. The different possible binding times for variable attributes define four different categories of variables. Their descriptions are followed by a thorough investigation of type checking, strong typing, and type equivalence rules. The two very different scoping rules for names, static and dynamic, are then described, along with the concept of a referencing environment of a statement. Finally, named constants and variable initialization are discussed.

5.1 Introduction

Imperative programming languages are, to varying degrees, abstractions of the underlying von Neumann computer architecture. The architecture's two primary components are its memory, which stores both instructions and data, and its processor, which provides operations for modifying the contents of the memory. The abstractions in a language for the memory cells of the machine are variables. In some cases, the characteristics of the abstractions are very close to the characteristics of the cells; an example of this is an integer variable, which is usually represented directly in one or more bytes of memory. In other cases, the abstractions are far removed from the organization of the hardware memory, as with a three-dimensional array, which requires a software mapping function to support the abstraction.

A variable can be characterized by a collection of properties, or attributes, the most important of which is type, a fundamental concept in programming languages. The design of the data types of a language requires that a variety of issues be considered. (Data types are discussed in Chapter 6.) Among the most important of these issues are the scope and lifetime of variables. Related to these are the issues of type checking and initialization. Type equivalence is another important part of the data type design of a language. A knowledge of all these concepts is requisite to understanding the imperative languages.

In the remainder of this book, we will often refer to families of languages as if they were a single language. For example, when we refer to Fortran, we mean all of the versions of Fortran. This is also the case for Ada. References to C include the original version of C, as well as C89 and C99. We use the phrase **C-based languages** to refer to C, C++, Java, and C#.[1] When we refer to a specific version of a language, it is because it is different from the other family members within the topic being discussed.

---

1. We were tempted to include the scripting languages JavaScript and PHP as C-based languages, but decided they were just a bit too different from their ancestors.

5.2 Names

Before we can begin our discussion of variables, we must discuss one of the fundamental attributes of variables: names, which have broader use than simply for variables. Names are also associated with subprograms, formal parameters, and other program constructs. The term *identifier* is often used interchangeably with *name*.

5.2.1 Design Issues

The following are the primary design issues for names:

- Are names case-sensitive?
- Are the special words of the language reserved words or keywords?

These issues are discussed in the following two subsections, which also include examples of several design choices.

5.2.2 Name Forms

A **name** is a string of characters used to identify some entity in a program.

history note

The earliest programming languages used single-character names. This notation was natural because early programming was primarily mathematical, and mathematicians have long used single-character names for unknowns in their formal notations.

Fortran I broke with the tradition of the single-character name, allowing up to six characters in its names. Fortran 77 still restricted names to six characters.

Fortran 95 allows up to 31 characters in its names. C89 had no length limitation on its internal names, but only the first 31 were significant. C99 is like C89, except the first 63 characters are significant. External names (those defined outside functions, which must be handled by the linker) in C89 were restricted to six characters; in C99, this was increased to 31. Names in Java, C#, and Ada have no length limit, and all characters in them are significant. However, Ada implementations are allowed to impose a length limitation, though it must be at least 200 characters—obviously not an annoying restriction. C++ does not specify a length limit on names, although implementors sometimes do. They do this so that the symbol table in which identifiers are stored during compilation need not be too large, and also to simplify the maintenance of that table.

Names in most programming languages have the same form: a letter followed by a string consisting of letters, digits, and underscore characters (_). Although the use of underscore characters to form names was widely used in the 1970s and 1980s, that practice is now far less popular. In the C-based languages, it has to a large extent been replaced by the so-called "camel" notation, in which all of the words of a multiple-word name except the first are capitalized, as in myStack.[2] Note that the use of underscores and mixed case in names is a programming style issue, not a language design issue.

---

2. It is called "camel" because words written in it often have embedded uppercase letters, which look like a camel's humps.

history note

In versions of Fortran prior to 90, only uppercase letters could be used in names—a needless restriction. The origin of this restriction was the fact that card punches had only uppercase letters. Like Fortran 90, many implementations of Fortran 77 allow lowercase letters; they simply translate them to uppercase for internal use during compilation.

In versions of Fortran prior to Fortran 90, names could have embedded spaces, which were ignored. For example, the following two names were equivalent:

```
Sum Of Salaries
SumOfSalaries
```

In many languages, notably the C-based languages, uppercase and lowercase letters in names are distinct; that is, names in these languages are **case-sensitive.** For example, the following three names are distinct in C++: rose, ROSE, and Rose. To some people, this is a serious detriment to readability, because names that look very similar in fact denote different entities. In that sense, case sensitivity violates the design principle that language constructs that look similar should have similar meanings. But in languages whose variable names are case-sensitive, although Rose and rose look similar, there is no connection between them.

Obviously, not everyone agrees that case sensitivity is bad for names. In C, the problems of case sensitivity are avoided by the convention that variable names do not include uppercase letters. In Java and C#, however, the problem cannot be escaped because many of the predefined names include both uppercase and lowercase letters. For example, the Java method for converting a string to an integer value is parseInt, and spellings such as ParseInt and parseint are not recognized. This is a problem of writability rather than readability, because the need to remember specific case usage makes it more difficult to write correct programs. It is a kind of intolerance on the part of the language designer, which is enforced by the compiler.

5.2.3 Special Words

Special words in programming languages are used to make programs more readable by naming actions to be performed. They also are used to separate the syntactic entities of programs. In program code examples in this book, special words are presented in boldface. In most languages, special words are classified as reserved words, but in some they are only keywords.

A **keyword** is a word of a programming language that is special only in certain contexts. Fortran is one of the languages whose special words are keywords. In Fortran, the word Real, when found at the beginning of a statement and followed by a name, is considered a keyword that indicates the statement is a declarative statement. However, if the word Real is followed by the assignment operator, it is considered a variable name. These two uses are illustrated in the following:

```
Real Apple
Real = 3.4
```

Fortran compilers and people reading Fortran programs must distinguish between names and special words by context.

A **reserved word** is a special word of a programming language that cannot be used as a name. As a language design choice, reserved words are better than keywords because the ability to redefine keywords can be confusing. For example, in Fortran, one could have the statements

```
Integer Real
Real Integer
```

which declare the program variable Real to be of Integer type and the variable Integer to be of Real type.[3] In addition to the strange appearance of these declaration statements, the appearance of Real and Integer as variable names elsewhere in the program could be misleading to program readers.

There is one potential problem with reserved words: If the language includes a large number of reserved words, the user has difficulty making up names that are not reserved. The best example of this is COBOL, which has 300 reserved words. Unfortunately, some of the most commonly chosen names by programmers are in the list of reserved words, for example, LENGTH, BOTTOM, DESTINATION, and COUNT.

Some languages include predefined names, which are in a sense between special words and user defined names. They have predefined meanings but can be redefined by the user. For example, the built-in data type names in Ada, such as Integer and Float, are predefined. These names are not reserved; they can be redefined by any Ada program.

In most languages, names that are defined in other program units, such as Ada and Java packages and C and C++ libraries, can be made visible to a program. These names are predefined, but visible only if explicitly imported. Once imported, they cannot be redefined.

5.3 Variables

A program variable is an abstraction of a computer memory cell or collection of cells. Programmers often think of variables as names for memory locations, but there is much more to a variable than just a name. The move from machine languages to assembly languages was largely one of replacing absolute numeric memory addresses for data with names, making programs far more readable and therefore easier to write and maintain. That step also provided an escape from the problem of manual absolute addressing, because the

---

3. Of course, any professional programmer who wrote such code should not expect job security.

translator that converted the names to actual addresses also chose those addresses.

A variable can be characterized as a sextuple of attributes: (name, address, value, type, lifetime, scope). Although this may seem too complicated for such an apparently simple concept, it provides the clearest way to explain the various aspects of variables.

Our discussion of variable attributes will lead to examinations of the important related concepts of aliases, binding, binding times, declarations, type checking, strong typing, scoping rules, and referencing environments.

The name, address, type, and value attributes of variables are discussed in the following subsections. The lifetime and scope attributes are discussed in Sections 5.4.3 and 5.8, respectively.

5.3.1 Name

Variable names are the most common names in programs. They were discussed at length in Section 5.2 in the general context of entity names in programs. Most variables have names. The ones that do not are discussed in Section 5.4.3.3.

5.3.2 Address

The **address** of a variable is the machine memory address with which it is associated. This association is not as simple as it may at first appear. In many languages, it is possible for the same variable to be associated with different addresses at different times in the program. For example, if a subprogram has a local variable that is allocated from the run-time stack when the subprogram is called, different calls may result in that variable having different addresses. These are in a sense different instantiations of the same variable.

The process of associating variables with addresses is further discussed in Section 5.4.3. An implementation model for subprograms and their activations is discussed in Chapter 10.

The address of a variable is sometimes called its **l-value,** because the address is what is required when a variable appears in the left side of an assignment.

It is possible to have multiple variables that have the same address. When more than one variable can be used to access the same memory location, they are called **aliases.** Aliasing is a hindrance to readability because it allows a variable to have its value changed by an assignment to a different variable. For example, if variables `total` and `sum` are aliases, any change to `total` also changes `sum` and vice versa. A reader of the program must always remember that `total` and `sum` are different names for the same memory cell. Because there can be any number of aliases in a program, this is very difficult in practice. Aliasing also makes program verification more difficult.

Aliases can be created in programs in several different ways. One common way in C and C++ is with their union types. Unions are discussed at length in Chapter 6.

Two pointer variables are aliases when they point to the same memory location. The same is true for reference variables. This kind of aliasing is simply a side effect of the nature of pointers and references. When a C++ pointer is set to point at a named variable, the pointer, when dereferenced, and the variable's name are aliases.

Aliasing can be created in many languages through subprogram parameters. These kinds of aliases are discussed in Chapter 9.

The time when a variable becomes associated with an address is very important to an understanding of programming languages. This subject is discussed in Section 5.4.3.

5.3.3 Type

The **type** of a variable determines the range of values the variable can store and the set of operations that are defined for values of the type. For example, the **int** type in Java specifies a value range of -2147483648 to 2147483647 and arithmetic operations for addition, subtraction, multiplication, division, and modulus.

5.3.4 Value

The value of a variable is the contents of the memory cell or cells associated with the variable. It is convenient to think of computer memory in terms of *abstract* cells, rather than physical cells. The physical cells, or individually addressable units, of most contemporary computer memories are byte-size, with a byte usually being 8 bits in length. This size is too small for most program variables. We define an abstract memory cell to have the size required by the variable with which it is associated. For example, although floating-point values may occupy four physical bytes in a particular implementation of a particular language, we think of a floating-point value as occupying a single abstract memory cell. We consider the value of each simple nonstructured type to occupy a single abstract cell. Henceforth, when we use the term *memory cell*, we mean abstract memory cell.

A variable's value is sometimes called its **r-value** because it is what is required when the variable is used on the right side of an assignment statement. To access the *r*-value, the *l*-value must be determined first. Such determinations are not always simple. For example, scoping rules can greatly complicate matters, as is discussed in Section 5.8.

5.4 The Concept of Binding

In a general sense, a **binding** is an association, such as between an attribute and an entity or between an operation and a symbol. The time at which a binding takes place is called **binding time.** Binding and binding times are prominent concepts in the semantics of programming languages. Bindings can take place at language design time, language implementation time, compile time, load time, link time, or run time. For example, the asterisk symbol (*) is usually bound to the multiplication operation at language design time. A data type, such as **int** in C, is bound to a range of possible values at language implementation time. At compile time, a variable in a Java program is bound to a particular data type. A variable may be bound to a storage cell when the program is loaded into memory. That same binding does not happen until run time in some cases, as with variables declared in Java methods. A call to a library subprogram is bound to the subprogram code at link time.

Consider the following C assignment statement:

```
count = count + 5;
```

Some of the bindings and their binding times for the parts of this assignment statement are as follows:

- The type of count is bound at compile time.
- The set of possible values of count is bound at compiler design time.
- The meaning of the operator symbol + is bound at compile time, when the types of its operands have been determined.
- The internal representation of the literal 5 is bound at compiler design time.
- The value of count is bound at execution time with this statement.

A complete understanding of the binding times for the attributes of program entities is a prerequisite for understanding the semantics of a programming language. For example, to understand what a subprogram does, one must understand how the actual parameters in a call are bound to the formal parameters in its definition. To determine the current value of a variable, you may need to know when the variable was bound to storage.

5.4.1 Binding of Attributes to Variables

A binding is **static** if it first occurs before run time and remains unchanged throughout program execution. If the binding first occurs during run time or can change in the course of program execution, it is called **dynamic.** The physical binding of a variable to a storage cell in a virtual memory environment is complex, because the page or segment of the address space in which the cell resides may be moved in and out of memory many times during program execution. In a sense, such variables are bound and unbound repeatedly. These bindings, however, are maintained by computer hardware, and the changes are invisible to the program and the user. Because they are not important to the discussion, we are not concerned with these hardware bindings. The essential point is to distinguish between static and dynamic bindings.

5.4.2 Type Bindings

Before a variable can be referenced in a program, it must be bound to a data type. The two important aspects of this binding are how the type is specified and when the binding takes place. Types can be specified statically through some form of explicit or implicit declaration.

5.4.2.1 Static Type Binding

An **explicit declaration** is a statement in a program that lists variable names and specifies that they are a particular type. An **implicit declaration** is a means of associating variables with types through default conventions, rather than declaration statements. In this case, the first appearance of a variable name in a program constitutes its implicit declaration. Both explicit and implicit declarations create static bindings to types.

Most programming languages designed since the mid-1960s require explicit declarations of all variables (Perl, JavaScript, Ruby, and ML are some exceptions). Several widely used languages whose initial designs were done before the late 1960s—notably Fortran, PL/I, and BASIC—have implicit declarations. For example, in Fortran, an identifier that appears in a program that is not explicitly declared is implicitly declared according to the following convention: If the identifier begins with one of the letters I, J, K, L, M, or N, or their lowercase versions, it is implicitly declared to be Integer type; otherwise, it is implicitly declared to be Real type.

Although they are a minor convenience to programmers, implicit declarations can be detrimental to reliability because they prevent the compilation process from detecting some typographical and programmer errors. In Fortran, variables that are accidentally left undeclared by the programmer are given default types and unexpected attributes, which could cause subtle errors that are difficult to diagnose. Many Fortran programmers now include the declaration—Implicit none—in their programs. This declaration instructs the compiler to not implicitly declare any variables, thereby avoiding the potential problems of accidentally undeclared variables.

Some of the problems with implicit declarations can be avoided by requiring names for specific types to begin with particular special characters. For example, in Perl any name that begins with $ is a scalar, which can store either a string or a numeric value. If a name begins with @, it is an array; if it begins with a %, it is a hash structure. This creates different namespaces for different type variables. In this scenario, the names @apple and %apple are unrelated, because each is from a different namespace. Furthermore, a program reader always knows the type of a variable when reading its name. Note that this design is different from Fortran, because Fortran has both implicit and explicit declarations, so the type of a variable cannot necessarily be determined from the spelling of its name.

Section 5.4.2.3 discusses another kind of implicit type binding, type inference.

C and C++ have both declarations and definitions of data. Declarations specify types and other attributes but do not cause allocation of storage. Definitions specify attributes *and* cause storage allocation. For a specific name, a C program can have any number of compatible declarations, but only a single definition. One purpose of variable declarations in C is to provide the type of a variable defined external to a function but used in the function. This idea of declarations and definitions carries over to the functions of C and C++, where prototypes declare names and interfaces of functions, but do not provide their code. Function definitions, on the other hand, are complete.

5.4.2.2 Dynamic Type Binding

With dynamic type binding, the type of a variable is not specified by a declaration statement, nor can it be determined by the spelling of its name. Instead, the variable is bound to a type when it is assigned a value in an assignment statement. When the assignment statement is executed, the variable being assigned is bound to the type of the value of the expression on the right side of the assignment.

Languages in which types are dynamically bound are dramatically different from those in which types are statically bound. The primary advantage of dynamic binding of variables to types is that it provides more programming flexibility. For example, a program to process numeric data in a language that uses dynamic type binding can be written as a generic program, meaning that it is capable of dealing with data of any numeric type. Whatever type data is input will be acceptable, because the variables in which the data is to be stored can be bound to the correct type when the data is assigned to the variables after input. By contrast, because of static binding of types, one cannot write a Java program to process data without knowing the type of that data.

In JavaScript and PHP, the binding of a variable to a type is dynamic. For example, a JavaScript script may contain the following statement:

```
list = [10.2, 3.5];
```

Regardless of the previous type of the variable named `list`, this assignment causes it to become a single-dimensioned array of length 2. If the statement

```
list = 47;
```

followed the example assignment, `list` would become a scalar variable.

There are two disadvantages to dynamic type binding. First, it causes programs to be less reliable, because the error detection capability of the compiler is diminished relative to a compiler for a language with static type bindings. Dynamic type binding allows any variable to be assigned a value of any type. Incorrect types of right sides of assignments are not detected as errors; rather, the type of the left side is simply changed to the incorrect type. For example, suppose that in a particular JavaScript program, `i` and `x` are currently storing scalar numeric values, and y is currently storing an array. Further suppose that the program needs the assignment statement

```
i = x;
```

but because of a keying error, it has the assignment statement

```
i = y;
```

In JavaScript (or any other language that uses dynamic type binding), no error is detected in this statement by the interpreter—i is simply changed to an array. But later uses of i will expect it to be a scalar, and correct results will be impossible. In a language with static type binding, such as Java, the compiler would detect the error in the assignment i = y, and the program would not get to execution.

Note that this disadvantage is also present to some extent in some languages that use static type binding, such as Fortran, C, and C++, which in many cases automatically convert the type of the RHS of an assignment to the type of the LHS.

Perhaps the greatest disadvantage of dynamic type binding is cost. The cost of implementing dynamic attribute binding is considerable, particularly in execution time. Type checking must be done at run time. Furthermore, every variable must have a run time descriptor associated with it to maintain the current type. The storage used for the value of a variable must be of varying size, because different type values require different amounts of storage.

Finally, languages that have dynamic type binding for variables are usually implemented using pure interpreters rather than compilers. Computers do not have instructions whose operand types are not known at compile time. Therefore, a compiler cannot build machine instructions for the expression A + B if the types of A and B are not known at compile time. Pure interpretation typically takes at least 10 times as long as to execute equivalent machine code. Of course, if a language is implemented with a pure interpreter, the time to do dynamic type binding is hidden by the overall time of interpretation, so it seems less costly in that environment. On the other hand, languages with static type bindings are seldom implemented by pure interpretation, because programs in these languages can be easily translated to very efficient machine code versions.

5.4.2.3 Type Inference

ML is a programming language that supports both functional and imperative programming (Ullman, 1998). ML employs an interesting type inference mechanism, in which the types of most expressions can be determined without requiring the programmer to specify the types of the variables.

Before investigating type inference through ML functions, let us look at the general syntax of an ML function:

Scripting Languages and Other Examples of Slick Solutions

RASMUS LERDORF

Rasmus Lerdorf was born on Disko Island, off the coast of Greenland, in 1968. After graduating with a degree in engineering, Lerdorf held a number of consulting jobs. Then, in an effort to track those viewing his online resume, he created the first iteration of PHP. These days he is an advocate for the open-source movement and an employee at Yahoo! in Sunnyvale, California.

SOME BACKGROUND

What was your earliest experience with computing? My father and I built a "pong" game together from a kit he ordered from the United States, circa 1976. I also remember getting a Texas Instruments "Speak & Spell" thing around 1978 that had the first-ever single-chip speech synthesizer in it. My first computer I got in 1983 or so. It was a Commodore Vic20 with 5k of RAM and a 1MHz 6502 CPU. I spent hours typing in code snippets from magazines. In high school, I played with Commodore PET and UNISYS 80186 boxes running QNX. QNX was by far the coolest operating system I had ever seen and it was somewhat anticlimactic when I later got an MS-DOS box. I think that early experience biased me toward UNIX and UNIX-like operating systems.

Do you have a favorite past job? I really enjoyed my time in Brazil, and they also gave me my first introduction to Silicon Valley when they opened an office in Mountain View and I moved there in 1993. I also really liked working at the University of Toronto after that, helping them build a dial-up system. A big chunk of PHP was created during that job.

> **My official title is 'Technical Yahoo!' and I am on the infrastructure team that maintains and supports the various tools used across all of Yahoo! My particular focus is PHP and Apache.**

ON SCRIPTING LANGUAGES

What's your definition of a scripting language? A higher-level language that hides the tedium and complexity of whatever traditional programming technique was used to solve a particular class of problem.

When you were working on your personal home page, then later on the system for the University of Toronto, and wanted to track the visitors to your site, then to track students, what available tools did you consider using? I don't recall really considering any existing solutions for this. Back then you would normally just read the raw access logs from your Web server. There were of course some log analysis tools mostly written in Perl that would summarize things, but I wanted to get an e-mail every time someone read my resume, and I wanted to know where that person came from. There were no tools that specifically did that.

How did you come to decide that spending the time to devise your own solution was better than using the tools out there? The main alternative was always Perl. And despite what some have attributed to me over the years, I don't actually hate Perl. I like it and use it quite a bit, but back then my needs were simple. I was running my home page on a shared server that did not have very much RAM or CPU and forking and execing a Perl CGI for every request was too resource-intensive. I needed a simple parser I could embed directly into my Web server, and Perl was way too hard and way too big to embed, and I didn't need any of the power of Perl for what I was doing back then. So I wrote a simple little parser that I understood and could easily embed. Then, of course, it started to grow, and once you start to add any sort of logical flow, it is a slippery slope toward a full programming language. The original intent was never to write a full language.

> *Coming up with solutions to problems is all about being able to approach them from many angles. Sometimes formal training and conventional wisdom can get in the way and limit what people will try. You also have to be prepared to fail repeatedly.*

What does PHP offer today that other scripting languages (Perl, Tcl, Python, Ruby) do not? PHP is targeted specifically at the Web problem. Everything you read about PHP is geared toward the Web, so if you are trying to solve the Web problem it is very obvious how you apply PHP. This is not as clear with other, more general-purpose languages. You first pick the language, and then you have to scramble around looking for the best way to apply that particular language.

The future of PHP: What's the next kink in the code, or the next functionality you would like to see worked out or added? We need a quality repository of PHP code and extensions because our previous trend of bundling everything with PHP itself just doesn't scale very well.

ON SLICK SOLUTIONS

Here's something you said in a previous interview: "I definitely appreciate and respect a slick solution to a tough problem." What thought process, what activities, lead to finding that slick solution? Coming up with solutions to problems is all about being able to approach them from many angles.

Sometimes formal training and conventional wisdom can get in the way and limit what people will try. You also have to be prepared to fail repeatedly.

A problem is tough only because you haven't found the slick solution yet. It is a bit like those scrambled word puzzles you see in the newspaper. You look at the jumbled word and it makes no sense. You try and you try to come up with the right combination of letters but you can't see it. Then someone whispers the word to you and suddenly it is obvious. Now when you look at the letters the word is right there and you can't figure out why you didn't see it right away. That's exactly the same feeling I get when I come up with, or see someone else's slick solution to a problem.

What are some of your favorite slick solutions? The world is full of slick solutions. Paperclips, Velcro, the ballpoint pen. But I guess you are asking for things within PHP. I think one of the slick solutions was tying HTML get, post, and cookie data directly to PHP variables. It seems like an obvious thing, but at the time nobody was doing that and it made PHP a very approachable solution to Web problems. The feature has since taken some criticism because of how it might be used improperly, but I still stand by it and deem it to be slick.

fun function_name(formal parameters) = expression;

The value of the expression is returned by the function.[4]

Now we can discuss type inference. Consider the ML function declaration

```
fun circumf(r) = 3.14159 * r * r;
```

This specifies a function named `circumf` that takes a floating-point (**real** in ML) argument and produces a floating-point result. The types are inferred from the type of the constant in the expression. Likewise, in the function

```
fun times10(x) = 10 * x;
```

the argument and functional value are inferred to be of type **int**.

Consider the following ML function:

```
fun square(x) = x * x;
```

ML determines the type of both the parameter and the return value from the * operator in the function definition. Because this is an arithmetic operator, the type of the parameter and the function are assumed to be numeric. In ML, the default numeric type to be **int**. So, it is inferred that the type of the parameter and the return value of square is **int**.

If square were called with a floating-point value, as in

```
square(2.75);
```

it would cause an error, because ML does not coerce **real** values to **int** type. If we wanted square to accept **real** parameters, it could be rewritten as

```
fun square(x) : real = x * x;
```

Because ML does not allow overloaded functions, this version could not coexist with the earlier **int** version.

The fact that the functional value is typed **real** is sufficient to infer that the parameter is also **real** type. Each of the following definitions is also legal:

```
fun square(x : real) = x * x;
fun square(x) = (x : real) * x;
fun square(x) = x * (x : real);
```

Type inference is also used in the purely functional languages Miranda and Haskell.

---

4. The expression can be a list of expressions, separated by semicolons and surrounded by parentheses. The return value in this case is that of the last expression.

5.4.3   Storage Bindings and Lifetime

The fundamental character of an imperative programming language is in large part determined by the design of the storage bindings for its variables. It is therefore important to have a clear understanding of these bindings.

The memory cell to which a variable is bound somehow must be taken from a pool of available memory. This process is called **allocation. Deallocation** is the process of placing a memory cell that has been unbound from a variable back into the pool of available memory.

The **lifetime** of a variable is the time during which the variable is bound to a specific memory location. So the lifetime of a variable begins when it is bound to a specific cell and ends when it is unbound from that cell. To investigate storage bindings of variables, it is convenient to separate scalar (unstructured) variables into four categories, according to their lifetimes. We call these categories static, stack-dynamic, explicit heap-dynamic, and implicit heap-dynamic. In the following sections, we discuss the meanings of these four categories, along with their purposes, advantages, and disadvantages.

5.4.3.1 Static Variables

Static variables are those that are bound to memory cells before program execution begins and remain bound to those same memory cells until program execution terminates. Variables that are statically bound to storage have several valuable applications in programming. Obviously, globally accessible variables are often used throughout the execution of a program, thus making it necessary to have them bound to the same storage during that execution. Sometimes it is convenient to have variables that are declared in subprograms be **history-sensitive,** that is, have them retain values between separate executions of the subprogram. This is a characteristic of a variable that is statically bound to storage.

Another advantage of static variables is efficiency. All addressing of static variables can be direct;[5] other kinds of variables often require indirect addressing, which is slower. Furthermore, no run-time overhead is incurred for allocation and deallocation of static variables, although this time is often negligible.

One disadvantage of static binding to storage is reduced flexibility; in particular, in a language that has only variables that are statically bound to storage, recursive subprograms cannot be supported. Another disadvantage is that storage cannot be shared among variables. For example, suppose a program has two subprograms, both of which require large arrays. Further suppose that the two subprograms are never active at the same time. If the arrays are static, they cannot share the same storage for their arrays.

---

5. In some implementations, static variables are addressed through a base register, making accesses to them cost the same as for stack-allocated variables.

C and C++ allow programmers to include the **static** specifier on a variable definition in a function, making the variables it defines static. Note that when the **static** modifier appears in the declaration of a variable in a class definition in C++, Java, and C#, its meaning has only an indirect connection to the concept of the lifetime of the variable. In that context, it means the variable is a class variable, rather than an instance variable. Class variables are created some time before the class is first instantiated. This multiple use of a reserved word can be confusing, particularly to those learning the language.

5.4.3.2 Stack-Dynamic Variables

Stack-dynamic variables are those whose storage bindings are created when their declaration statements are elaborated, but whose types are statically bound. **Elaboration** of such a declaration refers to the storage allocation and binding process indicated by the declaration, which takes place when execution reaches the code to which the declaration is attached. Therefore, elaboration occurs during run time. For example, the variable declarations that appear at the beginning of a Java method are elaborated when the method is called and the variables defined by those declarations are deallocated when the method completes its execution.

As their name indicates, stack-dynamic variables are allocated from the run-time stack.

Some languages—for example, C++ and Java—allow variable declarations to occur anywhere a statement can appear. In some implementations of these languages, all of the stack-dynamic variables declared in a function or method (not including those declared in nested blocks) may be bound to storage at the beginning of execution of the function or method, even though the declarations of some of these variables do not appear at the beginning. In such cases, the variable becomes visible at the declaration, but the storage binding (and initialization, if it is specified in the declaration) occurs when the function or method begins execution. The fact that storage binding of a variable takes place before it becomes visible does not affect the semantics of the language.

To be useful, at least in most cases, recursive subprograms require some form of dynamic local storage so that each active copy of the recursive subprogram has its own version of the local variables. These needs are conveniently met by stack-dynamic variables. Even in the absence of recursion, having stack-dynamic local storage for subprograms is not without merit, because all subprograms share the same memory space for their locals. The disadvantages, relative to static variables, are the run-time overhead of allocation and deallocation, slower accesses because indirect addressing is required, and the fact that subprograms cannot be history-sensitive. The time required to allocate and deallocate stack-dynamic variables is not significant, because all of the stack-dynamic variables that are declared at the beginning of a subprogram are allocated and deallocated together, rather than by separate operations.

Fortran 95 allows implementors to use stack-dynamic variables for locals, but includes a statement

Save list

that allows the programmer to specify that some or all of the variables (those in list) in the subprogram in which Save is placed will be static.

In Java, C++, and C#, variables defined in methods are by default stack-dynamic. In Ada, all non-heap variables defined in subprograms are stack-dynamic.

All attributes other than storage are statically bound to stack-dynamic scalar variables. That is not the case for some structured types, as is discussed in Chapter 6. Implementation of allocation/deallocation processes for stack-dynamic variables is discussed in Chapter 10.

5.4.3.3 Explicit Heap-Dynamic Variables

Explicit heap-dynamic variables are nameless (abstract) memory cells that are allocated and deallocated by explicit run-time instructions specified by the programmer. These variables, which are allocated from and deallocated to the heap, can only be referenced through pointer or reference variables. The heap is a collection of storage cells whose organization is highly disorganized because of the unpredictability of its use. The pointer or reference variable that is used to access an explicit heap-dynamic variable is created as any other scalar variable. An explicit heap-dynamic variable is created by either an operator (for example, in Ada and C++) or a call to a system subprogram provided for that purpose (for example, in C).

In C++, the allocation operator, named **new**, uses a type name as its operand. When executed, an explicit heap-dynamic variable of the operand type is created and a pointer to it is returned. Because an explicit heap-dynamic variable is bound to a type at compile time, that binding is static. However, such variables are bound to storage at the time they are created, which is during run time.

In addition to a subprogram or operator for creating explicit heap-dynamic variables, some languages include a subprogram or operator for explicitly destroying them.

As an example of explicit heap-dynamic variables, consider the following C++ code segment:

```
int *intnode;      // Create a pointer
...
intnode = new int; // Create the heap-dynamic variable
...
delete intnode;    // Deallocate the heap-dynamic variable
                   // to which intnode points
```

In this example, an explicit heap-dynamic variable of **int** type is created by the **new** operator. This variable can then be referenced through the pointer, intnode. Later, the variable is deallocated by the **delete** operator. C++ requires the explicit deallocation operator, **delete**, because it does not use implicit storage reclamation, such as garbage collection.

In Java, all data except the primitive scalars are objects. Java objects are explicitly heap-dynamic and are accessed through reference variables. Java has no way of explicitly destroying a heap-dynamic variable; rather, implicit garbage collection is used.

C# has both explicit heap-dynamic and stack-dynamic objects, all of which are implicitly deallocated. Beyond this, C# also supports C++-style pointers. Such pointers are used to reference heap, stack, and even static variables and objects. These pointers have the same dangers as those of C++, and the objects they reference on the heap are not implicitly deallocated. Pointers are included in C# to allow C# components to interoperate with C and C++ components. To discourage their use, the header of any method that defines a pointer must include the reserved word, **unsafe.**

Explicit heap-dynamic variables are often used to construct dynamic structures, such as linked lists and trees, that need to grow and/or shrink during execution. Such structures can be built conveniently using pointers or references and explicit heap-dynamic variables.

The disadvantages of explicit heap-dynamic variables are the difficulty of using pointer and reference variables correctly, the cost of references to the variables, and the complexity of storage management implementation. This is essentially the problem of heap management, which is costly and complicated. Implementation methods for explicit heap-dynamic variables are discussed at length in Chapter 6.

5.4.3.4 Implicit Heap-Dynamic Variables

Implicit heap-dynamic variables are bound to heap storage only when they are assigned values. In fact, all their attributes are bound every time they are assigned. In a sense, they are just names that adapt to whatever use they are asked to serve. For example, consider the following JavaScript assignment statement:

```
highs = [74, 84, 86, 90, 71];
```

Regardless of whether the variable highs was previously used in the program or what it was used for, it is now an array of five numeric values.

The advantage of such variables is that they have the highest degree of flexibility, allowing highly generic code to be written. One disadvantage of implicit heap-dynamic variables is the run-time overhead of maintaining all the dynamic attributes, which could include array subscript types and ranges, among others. Another disadvantage is the loss of some error detection by the compiler, as discussed in Section 5.4.2.2. Examples of implicit heap-dynamic variables in JavaScript appear in Section 5.4.2.2.

5.5 Type Checking

For our discussion of type checking, we generalize the concept of operands and operators to include subprograms and assignment statements. We will think of subprograms as operators whose operands are their parameters. The assignment symbol will be thought of as a binary operator, with its target variable and its expression being the operands.

Type checking is the activity of ensuring that the operands of an operator are of compatible types. A **compatible** type is one that either is legal for the operator or is allowed under language rules to be implicitly converted by compiler-generated code (or the interpreter) to a legal type. This automatic conversion is called a **coercion.** For example, if an **int** variable and a **float** variable are added in Java, the value of the **int** variable is coerced to **float** and a floating-point add is done.

A **type error** is the application of an operator to an operand of an inappropriate type. For example, in the original version of C, if an **int** value was passed to a function that expected a **float** value, a type error would occur (because compilers for that language did not check the types of parameters).

If all bindings of variables to types are static in a language, then type checking can nearly always be done statically. Dynamic type binding requires type checking at run time, which is called **dynamic type checking.**

Some languages, such as JavaScript and PHP, because of their dynamic type binding, allow only dynamic type checking. It is better to detect errors at compile time than at run time, because the earlier correction is usually less costly. The penalty for static checking is reduced programmer flexibility. Fewer shortcuts and tricks are possible. Such techniques, though, are now generally held in low esteem.

Type checking is complicated when a language allows a memory cell to store values of different types at different times during execution. Such memory cells can be created with Ada variant records, Fortran `Equivalence`, and C and C++ unions. In these cases, type checking, if done, must be dynamic and requires the run-time system to maintain the type of the current value of such memory cells. So even though all variables are statically bound to types in languages such as C++, not all type errors can be detected by static type checking.

5.6 Strong Typing

One of the new ideas in language design that became prominent in the so-called structured-programming revolution of the 1970s is **strong typing.** Strong typing is widely acknowledged as being a highly valuable language characteristic. Unfortunately, it is often loosely defined, and it is sometimes used in computing literature without being defined at all.

A programming language is **strongly typed** if type errors are always detected. This requires that the types of all operands can be determined, either at compile time or at run time. The importance of strong typing lies in its ability to detect all misuses of variables that result in type errors. A strongly typed language also allows the detection, at run time, of uses of the incorrect type values in variables that can store values of more than one type.

Fortran 95 is not strongly typed because the use of `Equivalence` between variables of different types allows a variable of one type to refer to a value of a different type, without the system being able to check the type of the value when one of the `Equivalenced` variables is referenced or assigned. In fact, type checking of `Equivalenced` variables would eliminate most of their usefulness.

Ada is nearly strongly typed. It is only *nearly* strongly typed because it allows programmers to breach the type-checking rules by specifically requesting that type checking be suspended for a particular type conversion. This temporary suspension of type checking can be done only when an instantation of the generic function `Unchecked_Conversion` is called. Such functions can be instantiated for any pair of subtypes.[6] One takes a value of its parameter type and returns the bit string that is the parameter's current value. No actual conversion takes place; it is merely a means of extracting the value of a variable of one type and using it as if it were of a different type. This approach can be useful for user-defined storage allocation and deallocation operations, in which addresses are manipulated as integers but must be used as pointers. Because no checking is done in `Unchecked_Conversion`, it is the programmer's responsibility to ensure that the use of a value gotten from it is meaningful.

C and C++ are not strongly typed languages because both include union types, which are not type checked.

ML is strongly typed, even though the types of some function parameters may not be known at compile time.

Java and C#, although they are based on C++, are strongly typed in the same sense as Ada. Types can be explicitly cast, which could result in a type error. However, there are no implicit ways type errors can go undetected.

The coercion rules of a language have an important effect on the value of type checking. For example, expressions are strongly typed in Java. However, an arithmetic operator with one floating-point operand and one integer operand is legal. The value of the integer operand is coerced to floating-point, and a floating-point operation takes place. This is what is usually intended by the programmer. However, the coercion also results in a loss of part of the reason for strong typing—error detection. For example, suppose a program had the **int** variables a and b and the **float** variable d. Now, if a programmer meant

---

6. Normally, the two subtypes must have the same length. However, an implementation can provide a generic Unchecked_Conversion for different length subtypes and furnish rules for how the differences are implemented.

to type a + b, but mistakenly typed a + d, the error would not be detected by the compiler. The value of a would simply be coerced to **float.** So, the value of strong typing is weakened by coercion. Languages with a great deal of coercion, like Fortran, C, and C++, are less reliable than those with little coercion, such as Ada. Java and C# have half as many assignment type coercions as C++, so their error detection is better than that of C++, but still not nearly as effective as that of Ada. The issue of coercion is examined in detail in Chapter 7.

5.7 Type Equivalence

The idea of type compatibility was defined when the issue of type checking was introduced. The compatibility rules dictate the types of operands that are acceptable for each of the operators and thereby specify the possible type errors of the language.[7] The rules are called compatibility because in some cases the type of an operand can be implicitly converted by the compiler or run-time system to make it acceptable to the operator.

The type compatibility rules are simple and rigid for the predefined scalar types. However, in the cases of structured types, such as arrays and records, and user-defined types, the rules are more complex. Coercion of these types is rare, so the issue is not type compatibility, but type equivalence. That is, two types are equivalent if an operand of one type in an expression is substituted for one of the other type, without coercion. Type equivalence is a strict form of type compatibility — compatibility without coercion. The central issue here is how type equivalence is defined.

history note

The original definition of Pascal (Wirth, 1971) does not specify clearly when name or structure type compatibility is to be used. This is highly detrimental to portability, because a program that is correct in one implementation could be illegal in another. The ISO Standard Pascal (ISO, 1982) clearly states the type compatibility rules of the language, which are neither completely by name nor completely by structure. Structure is used in most cases, while name is used for formal parameters and a few other situations.

The design of the type equivalence rules of a language is important, because it influences the design of the data types and the operations provided for values of those types. With the types discussed here, there are very few predefined operations. Perhaps the most important result of two variables being of equivalent types is that either one can have its value assigned to the other.

There are two approaches to defining type equivalence: name type equivalence and structure type equivalence. **Name type equivalence** means that two variables have equivalent types if they are defined either in the same declaration or in declarations that use the same type name. **Structure type equivalence** means that two variables have equivalent types if their types have identical structures. There are some variations of these two approaches, and many languages use combinations of them.

---

7. Type campatibility is also an issue in the relationship bewteen the actual parameters in a subprogram call and the formal parameters of the subprogram definition. This issue is discussed in Chapter 9.

Name type equivalence is easy to implement but is more restrictive. Under a strict interpretation, a variable whose type is a subrange of the integers would not be equivalent to an integer type variable. For example, supposing Ada used strict name type equivalence, consider the following Ada code:

```
type Indextype is 1..100;
count : Integer;
index : Indextype;
```

The types of the variables `count` and `index` would not be equivalent; `count` could not be assigned to `index` or vice versa.

Another problem with name type equivalence arises when a structured type is passed among subprograms through parameters. Such a type must be defined only once, globally. A subprogram cannot state the type of such formal parameters in local terms. This was the case with the original version of Pascal.

Note that to use name type equivalence, all types must have names. Most languages allow users to define types that are anonymous—they do not have names. For a language to use name type equivalence, such types must implicitly be given internal names by the compiler.

Structure type equivalence is more flexible than name type equivalence, but it is more difficult to implement. Under name type equivalence, only the two type names must be compared to determine equivalence. Under structure type equivalence, however, the entire structures of the two types must be compared. This comparison is not always simple. (Consider a data structure that refers to its own type, such as a linked list.) Other questions can also arise. For example, are two record (or **struct**) types equivalent if they have the same structure but different field names? Are two single-dimensioned array types in an Ada program equivalent if they have the same element type but have subscript ranges of `0..10` and `1..11`? Are two enumeration types equivalent if they have the same number of components but spell the literals differently?

Another difficulty with structure type equivalence is that it disallows differentiating between types with the same structure. For example, consider the following Pascal-like declarations:

```
type celsius = float;
     fahrenheit = float;
```

The types of variables of these two types are considered equivalent under structure type equivalence, allowing them to be mixed in expressions, which is surely undesirable in this case. In general, types with different names are likely to be abstractions of different categories of problem values and should not be considered equivalent.

Ada uses a restrictive form of name type equivalence but provides two type constructs, subtypes and derived types, that avoid the problems associated with name type equivalence. A **derived type** is a new type that is based on some previously defined type with which it is not equivalent, although it may have identical structure. Derived types inherit all the properties of their parent types. Consider the following example:

```
type celsius is new Float;
type fahrenheit is new Float;
```

The types of variables of these two derived types are not equivalent, although their structures are identical. Furthermore, variables of both types are not type equivalent with any other floating-point type. Literals are exempt from the rule. A literal such as 3.0 has the type universal real and is type equivalent to any floating-point type. Derived types can also include range constraints on the parent type, while still inheriting all of the parent's operations.

An Ada **subtype** is a possibly range-constrained version of an existing type. A subtype is type equivalent with its parent type. For example, consider the following declaration:

```
subtype Small_type is Integer range 0..99;
```

The type Small_type is equivalent to the type Integer.

For variables of an Ada unconstrained array type, structure type equivalence is used. For example, consider the following type declaration and two object declarations:

```
type Vector is array (Integer range <>) of Integer;
Vector_1: Vector (1..10);
Vector_2: Vector (11..20);
```

The types of these two objects are equivalent, even though they have different names and different subscript ranges, because for objects of unconstrained array types, structure type equivalence rather than name type equivalence is used. Because both types have 10 elements and the elements of both are of type Integer, they are type equivalent.

For constrained anonymous types, Ada uses a highly restrictive form of name type equivalence. Consider the following Ada declarations of constrained anonymous types:

```
A : array (1..10) of Integer;
```

In this case, A has an anonymous but unique type assigned by the compiler and unavailable to the program. If we also had

```
B : array (1..10) of Integer;
```

A and B would be of anonymous but distinct and not equivalent types, though they are structurally identical. The multiple declaration

```
C, D : array (1..10) of Integer;
```

creates two anonymous types, one for C and one for D, which are not equivalent. This declaration is actually treated as if it were the following two declarations:

```
C : array (1..10) of Integer;
D : array (1..10) of Integer;
```

Note that Ada's form of name type equivalence is more restrictive than the name type equivalence that is defined at the beginning of this section. If we had written instead

```
type List_10 is array (1..10) of Integer;
C, D : List_10;
```

then the types of C and D would be equivalent.

Name type equivalence works well for Ada, in part because all types, except anonymous arrays, are required to have type names (and anonymous types are given internal names by the compiler).

Type equivalence rules for Ada are more rigid than those for languages that have many coercions among types. For example, the two operands of an addition operator in Java can have virtually any combination of numeric types in the language. One of the operands will simply be coerced to the type of the other. But in Ada, there are no coercions of the operands of an arithmetic operator.

C uses both name and structure type equivalence. Every **struct, enum,** and **union** declaration creates a new type that is not equivalent to any other type. So, name type equivalence is used for structure, enumeration, and union types. Other nonscalar types use structure type equivalence. Array types are equivalent if they have the same type components. Also, if an array type has a constant size, it is equivalent either to other arrays with the same constant size or to with those without a constant size. Note that **typedef** in C and C++ does not introduce a new type; it simply defines a new name for an existing type. So, any type defined with **typedef** is type equivalent to its parent type. One exception to C using name type equivalence for structures, enumerations, and unions is if two structures, enumerations, or unions are defined in different files, in which case structural type equivalence is used. This is a loophole in the name type equivalence rule to allow equivalence of structures, enumerations, and unions that are defined in different files.

C++ is like C except there is no exception for structures and unions defined in different files.

In languages that do not allow users to define and name types, such as Fortran and COBOL, name equivalence obviously cannot be used.

Object-oriented languages such as Java and C++ bring another kind of type compatibility issue with them. The issue is object compatibility and its relationship to the inheritance hierarchy, which is discussed in Chapter 12.

Type compatibility in expressions is discussed in Chapter 7; type compatibility for subprogram parameters is discussed in Chapter 9.

5.8 Scope

One of the most important factors in gaining an understanding of variables is scope. The **scope** of a variable is the range of statements in which the variable is visible. A variable is **visible** in a statement if it can be referenced in that statement.

The scope rules of a language determine how a particular occurrence of a name is associated with a variable. In particular, scope rules determine how references to variables declared outside the currently executing subprogram or block are associated with their declarations and thus their attributes (blocks are discussed in Section 5.8.2). A complete knowledge of these rules for a language is therefore essential to the ability to write or read programs in that language.

As defined in Section 5.4.3.2, a variable is local in a program unit or block if it is declared there. The **nonlocal** variables of a program unit or block are those that are visible within the program unit or block but are not declared there.

Scoping issues of classes, packages, and namespaces are discussed in Chapter 11.

5.8.1 Static Scope

ALGOL 60 introduced the method of binding names to nonlocal variables, called **static scoping,** which has been copied by many subsequent imperative languages, and many nonimperative languages as well. Static scoping is so named because the scope of a variable can be statically determined, that is, prior to execution. This permits a human program reader to determine the type of every variable in the program.

There are two categories of static-scoped languages: those in which subprograms can be nested, which creates nested static scopes, and those in which subprograms cannot be nested. In this latter category, static scopes are also created by subprograms but nested scopes are created only by nested class definitions and blocks (see Section 5.8.2).

Ada, JavaScript, and PHP allow nested subprograms, but the C-based languages do not.

Our discussion of static scoping in this chapter focuses on those languages that allow nested subprograms. So, for now we assume that *all* scopes are associated with program units. In this chapter, we also assume that scoping is the only method of accessing nonlocal variables in the languages under discussion. This is not true for all languages. It is not even true for all languages that use static scoping, but the assumption simplifies the discussion here.

When the reader of a program written in a static-scoped language finds a reference to a variable, the attributes of the variable can be determined by finding the statement in which it is declared. In static-scoped languages with nested subprograms, this process can be thought of in the following way. Suppose a reference is made to a variable x in subprogram Sub1. The correct declaration is found by first searching the declarations of subprogram Sub1. If no declaration is found for the variable there, the search continues in the declarations of the subprogram that declared subprogram Sub1, which is called its **static parent.** If a declaration of x is not found there, the search continues to the next-larger enclosing unit (the unit that declared Sub1's parent), and so forth, until a declaration for x is found or the largest unit's declarations have been searched without success. In that case, an undeclared variable error has been detected. The static parent of subprogram Sub1, and its static parent, and so forth up to and including the largest enclosing subprogram, are called the **static ancestors** of Sub1. Note that implementation techniques for static scoping, which are discussed in Chapter 10, are much more efficient than the process just described.

Consider the following Ada procedure:

```
procedure Big is
  X : Integer;
  procedure Sub1 is
    X : Integer;
    begin  -- of Sub1
    ...
    end;  -- of Sub1
  procedure Sub2 is
    begin  -- of Sub2
    ...X...
    end;  -- of Sub2
  begin  -- of Big
  ...
  end;  -- of Big
```

Under static scoping, the reference to the variable X in Sub2 is to the X declared in the procedure Big. This is true because the search for X begins in the procedure in which the reference occurs, Sub2, but no declaration for X is found there. The search thus continues in the static parent of Sub2, Big, where the declaration of X is found. The X declared in Sub1 is ignored, because it is not in the static ancestry of Sub2.

The presence of predefined names, which are discussed in Section 5.2.3, complicates this process somewhat. In some cases, a predefined name is like a keyword in that it can be redefined by the user. In such cases, a predefined name is used only if the user program does not contain a redefinition. In other cases, a predefined name may be reserved, which means the search for the meaning of a given name begins with the list of predefined names, even before the local scope declarations are checked.

In some languages that use static scoping, regardless of whether nested subprograms are allowed, some variable declarations can be hidden from some other code segments. For example, consider the following skeletal C++ method:

```cpp
void sub() {
  int count;
  ...
  while ( ... ) {
    int count;
    count++;
    ...
  }
  ...
}
```

The reference to count in the **while** loop is to that loop's local count. In this case, the count of sub is hidden from the code inside the **while** loop. In general, a declaration for a variable effectively hides any declaration of a variable with the same name in a larger enclosing scope. Note that this code is legal in C and C++, but illegal in Java and C#. The designers of Java and C# believed that the reuse of names in nested blocks was too error-prone to be allowed.

In Ada, hidden variables from ancestor scopes can be accessed with selective references, which include the ancestor scope's name. For example, in the preceding procedure, Big, the X declared in Big can be accessed in Sub2 by the reference Big.X.

Although the C-based languages do not allow subprograms to be nested inside other subprogram definitions, they do have global variables. These variables are declared outside any subprogram definition. Local variables can hide these globals, as in Ada. In C++, such hidden globals can be accessed using the scope operator (::). For example, if x is a global that is hidden in a subprogram by a local named x, the global could be referenced as ::x.

5.8.2 Blocks

Many languages allow new static scopes to be defined in the midst of executable code. This powerful concept, introduced in ALGOL 60, allows a section of code to have its own local variables whose scope is minimized. Such variables are typically stack dynamic, so they have their storage allocated when the section is entered and deallocated when the section is exited. Such a section of code is called a **block.**

In Ada, blocks are specified with **declare** clauses, as in

```
...
declare Temp : Integer;
  begin
  Temp := First;
  First := Second;
  Second := Temp;
  end;
...
```

Note that if an Ada compound statement (delimited by **begin** and **end**) does not include declarations, the **declare** clause is not included. Blocks provide the origin of the phrase **block-structured language**.

The C-based languages allow any compound statement (a statement sequence surrounded by matched braces) to have declarations and thus define a new scope. Such compound statements are blocks. For example, if list were an integer array, one could write

```
if (list[i] < list[j]) {
  int temp;
  temp = list[i];
  list[i] = list[j];
  list[j] = temp;
}
```

The scopes created by blocks are treated exactly like those created by subprograms. References to variables in a block that are not declared there are connected to declarations by searching enclosing scopes in order of increasing size.

C++ allows variable definitions to appear anywhere in functions. When a definition appears at a position other than at the beginning of a function, but not within a block, that variable's scope is from its definition statement to the end of the function. Note that in C, all data declarations in a function but not in blocks within the function must appear at the beginning of the function.

The **for** statements of C++, Java, and C# allow variable definitions in their initialization expressions. In early versions of C++, the scope of such a variable was from its definition to the end of the smallest enclosing block. In the standard version, however, the scope is restricted to the **for** construct, as is the case with Java and C#. Consider the following skeletal method:

```
void fun() {
  ...
  for (int count = 0; count < 10; count++){
    ...
  }
```

```
        . . .
}
```

In early versions of C++, the scope of count would be from the **for** statement to the end of the method. In later versions, as well as in Java and C#, the scope of count would be from the **for** statement to the end of its body.

The classes of C++, Java, and C# treat their instance and class variables differently from the variables defined in their methods. The scope of a variable defined in a method starts at the definition. However, regardless of where an instance or class variable is defined in a class, its scope is the whole class.

The class and method definitions in object-oriented languages also create nested static scopes. This is discussed in Chapter 12. In Ruby, the forms of the names of variables indicate their scope. Because Ruby is a pure object-oriented language and because its scopes are all related to object-oriented constructs, this is also discussed in Chapter 12.

5.8.3 Evaluation of Static Scoping

Static scoping provides a method of nonlocal access that works well in many situations. However, it is not without its problems. Consider the program whose skeletal structure is shown in Figure 5.1. For this example, assume that all scopes are created by the definitions of the main program and the procedures.

Figure 5.1

The structure of a program

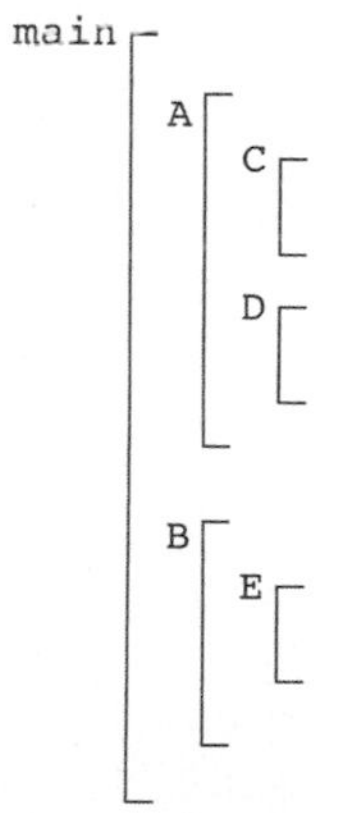

This program contains an overall scope for main, with two procedures that define scopes inside main, A and B. Inside A are scopes for the procedures C and D. Inside B is the scope of procedure E. We assume that the necessary data and procedure access determined the structure of this program. The required procedure access is as follows: main can call A and B, A can call C and D, and B can call A and E.

It is convenient to view the structure of the program as a tree in which each node represents a procedure and thus a scope. A tree representation of the program of Figure 5.1 is shown in Figure 5.2. The structure of this program might appear to be a very natural program organization that clearly reflects the design needs. However, a graph of the potential procedure calls of this system, shown in Figure 5.3, shows that a great deal of calling opportunity beyond that required is possible.

Figure 5.4 shows the desired calls of the example program. The difference between Figures 5.3 and 5.4 illustrates the number of possible calls that are not necessary in this specific application.

A programmer could mistakenly call a subprogram that should not have been callable, which would not be detected as an error by the compiler. That delays detection of the error until run time, which may make its correction more costly. Therefore, access to procedures should be restricted to those that are necessary.

Too much data access is a closely related problem. For example, all variables declared in the main program are visible to all of the procedures, whether or not that is desired, and there is no way to avoid it.

Figure 5.2

The tree structure of the program in Figure 5.1

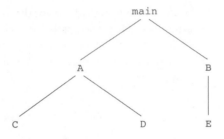

Figure 5.3

The potential call graph of the program in Figure 5.1

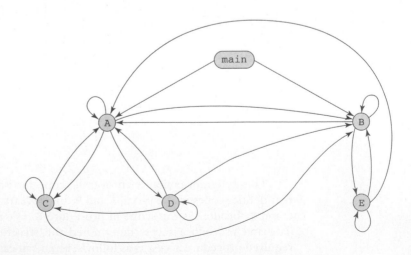

Figure 5.4

The graph of the
desirable calls in the
program in Figure 5.1

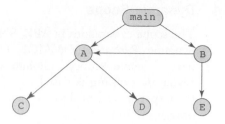

To illustrate another kind of problem with static scoping, consider the following scenario. Suppose that after the program has been developed and tested, a modification of its specification is required. In particular, suppose that procedure E must now gain access to some variables of the scope of D. One way to provide that access is to move E inside the scope of D. But then E can no longer access the scope of B, which it presumably needs. Another solution is to move the variables defined in D that are needed by E into main. This would allow access by all the procedures, which would be more than is needed and thus would create the possibility of incorrect accesses. For example, a misspelled identifier in a procedure can be taken as a reference to an identifier in some enclosing scope, instead of being detected as an error. Furthermore, suppose the variable that is moved to main is named x, and x is needed by D and E. But suppose that there is a variable named x declared in A. That would hide the correct x from its original owner, D. One final problem with moving the declaration of x to main is that it is harmful to readability to have the declaration of variables so far from their uses.

The problems associated with variable visibility with static scoping are also present for subprogram access. In the tree of Figure 5.2, suppose that due to some specification change, procedure E needed to call procedure D. This could be accomplished only by moving D to nest directly in main, assuming that it was also needed by either A or C. It would then also lose access to the variables defined in A. This solution, when used repeatedly, results in programs that begin with long lists of low-level utility procedures.

Thus, getting around the restrictions of static scoping can lead to program designs that bear little resemblance to the original, even in areas of the program in which changes have not been made. Designers are encouraged to use far more globals than are necessary. All procedures can end up being nested at the same level, in the main program, using globals instead of deeper levels of nesting.[8] Moreover, the final design may be awkward and contrived, and it may not reflect the underlying conceptual design. These and other defects of static scoping are discussed in detail in Clarke, Wileden, and Wolf (1980). One solution to the problems of static scoping is an encapsulation construct, discussed in Chapter 11, which is included in many newer languages.

---

8. Sounds like the structure of a C program, doesn't it?

5.8.4 Dynamic Scope

The scope of variables in APL, SNOBOL4, and the early versions of LISP is dynamic. Perl and COMMON LISP also allow variables to be declared to have dynamic scope, although these languages also use static scoping. **Dynamic scoping** is based on the calling sequence of subprograms, not on their spatial relationship to each other. Thus the scope can be determined only at run time.

Consider again the procedure `Big` from Section 5.8.1, which is reproduced here:

```
procedure Big is
  X : Integer;
  procedure Sub1 is
    X : Integer;
    begin  -- of Sub1
    ...
    end;  -- of Sub1
  procedure Sub2 is
    begin  -- of Sub2
    ...X...
    end;  -- of Sub2
  begin  -- of Big
  ...
  end;  -- of Big
```

Assume that dynamic-scoping rules apply to nonlocal references. The meaning of the identifier `X` referenced in `Sub2` is dynamic—it cannot be determined at compile time. It may reference the variable from either declaration of `X`, depending on the calling sequence.

One way the correct meaning of `X` can be determined at run time is to begin the search with the local declarations. This is also the way the process begins with static scoping, but that is where the similarity between the two techniques ends. When the search of local declarations fails, the declarations of the dynamic parent, or calling procedure, are searched. If a declaration for `X` is not found there, the search continues in that procedure's dynamic parent, and so forth, until a declaration for `X` is found. If none is found in any dynamic ancestor, it is a run-time error.

Consider the two different call sequences for `Sub2` in the earlier example. First, `Big` calls `Sub1`, which calls `Sub2`. In this case, the search proceeds from the local procedure, `Sub2`, to its caller, `Sub1`, where a declaration for `X` is found. So the reference to `X` in `Sub2` in this case is to the `X` declared in `Sub1`. Next, `Sub2` is called directly from `Big`. In this case, the dynamic parent of `Sub2` is `Big`, and the reference is to the `X` declared in `Big`.

Note that if static scoping were used, in either calling sequence discussed, the reference to X in Sub2 would be to Big's X.

Perl's dynamic scoping is unusual—in fact it is not exactly like that discussed in this section, although the semantics are often that of traditional dynamic scoping (see Programming Exercise 1).

5.8.5 Evaluation of Dynamic Scoping

The effect of dynamic scoping on programming is profound. The correct attributes of nonlocal variables visible to a program statement cannot be determined statically. Furthermore, such variables are not always the same. A statement in a subprogram that contains a reference to a nonlocal variable can refer to different nonlocal variables during different executions of the subprogram. Several kinds of programming problems follow directly from dynamic scoping.

First, during the time span beginning when a subprogram begins its execution and ending when that execution ends, the local variables of the subprogram are all visible to any other executing subprogram, regardless of its textual proximity or how execution got to the currently executing subprogram. There is no way to protect local variables from this accessibility. Subprograms are *always* executed in the environment of all previously called subprograms that have not yet completed their executions. As a result, dynamic scoping results in less reliable programs than static scoping.

A second problem with dynamic scoping is the inability to statically type check references to nonlocals. This problem results from the inability to statically determine the declaration for a variable referenced as a nonlocal.

Dynamic scoping also makes programs much more difficult to read, because the calling sequence of subprograms must be known to determine the meaning of references to nonlocal variables. This task can be virtually impossible for a human reader.

Finally, accesses to nonlocal variables in dynamic-scoped languages take far longer than accesses to nonlocals when static scoping is used. The reason for this is explained in Chapter 10.

On the other hand, dynamic scoping is not without merit. In some cases, the parameters passed from one subprogram to another are variables that are defined in the caller. None of these need to be passed in a dynamically scoped language, because they are implicitly visible in the called subprogram.

It is not difficult to understand why dynamic scoping is not as widely used as static scoping. Programs in static-scoped languages are easier to read, are more reliable, and execute faster than equivalent programs in dynamic-scoped languages. It was precisely for these reasons that dynamic scoping was replaced by static scoping in most current dialects of LISP. Implementation methods for both static and dynamic scoping are discussed in Chapter 10.

5.9 Scope and Lifetime

Sometimes the scope and lifetime of a variable appear to be related. For example, consider a variable that is declared in a Java method that contains no method calls. The scope of such a variable is from its declaration to the end of the method. The lifetime of that variable is the period of time beginning when the method is entered and ending when execution of the method terminates. Although the scope and lifetime of the variable are clearly not the same, because static scope is a textual, or spatial, concept whereas lifetime is a temporal concept, they at least appear to be related in this case.

This apparent relationship between scope and lifetime does not hold in other situations. In C and C++, for example, a variable that is declared in a function using the specifier **static** is statically bound to the scope of that function and is also statically bound to storage. So its scope is static and local to the function, but its lifetime extends over the entire execution of the program of which it is a part.

Scope and lifetime are also unrelated when subprogram calls are involved. Consider the following C++ functions:

```
void printheader() {
  ...
  }  /* end of printheader */
void compute() {
  int sum;
  ...
  printheader();
  }  /* end of compute */
```

The scope of the variable sum is completely contained within the compute function. It does not extend to the body of the function printheader, although printheader executes in the midst of the execution of compute. However, the lifetime of sum extends over the time during which printheader executes. Whatever storage location sum is bound to before the call to printheader, that binding will continue during and after the execution of printheader.

5.10 Referencing Environments

The **referencing environment** of a statement is the collection of all variables that are visible in the statement. The referencing environment of a statement in a static-scoped language is the variables declared in its local scope plus the collection of all variables of its ancestor scopes that are visible. In such a language, the referencing environment of a statement is needed while that statement is being compiled, so code and data structures can be created to allow references to variables from other scopes during run time. Techniques for implementing references to nonlocal variables in both static- and dynamic-scoped languages are discussed in Chapter 10.

In Ada, scopes can be created by procedure definitions. The referencing environment of a statement includes the local variables, plus all of the variables declared in the procedures in which the statement is nested (excluding variables in nonlocal scopes that are hidden by declarations in nearer procedures). Each procedure definition creates a new scope and thus a new environment. Consider the following Ada skeletal program:

```
procedure Example is
  A, B : Integer;
  ...
  procedure Sub1 is
    X, Y : Integer;
    begin  -- of Sub1
    ...    <--------------- 1
    end;   -- of Sub1
  procedure Sub2 is
    X : Integer;
    ...
    procedure Sub3 is
      X : Integer;
      begin  -- of Sub3
      ...    <------------- 2
      end;   -- of Sub3
    begin  -- of Sub2
    ...    <--------------- 3
    end;   -- of Sub2
  begin  -- of Example
  ...    <----------------- 4
  end.   -- of Example
```

The referencing environments of the indicated program points are as follows:

Point	Referencing Environment
1	X and Y of Sub1, A and B of Example
2	X of Sub3, (X of Sub2 is hidden), A and B of Example
3	X of Sub2, A and B of Example

Now consider the variable declarations of this skeletal program. First note that, although the scope of Sub1 is at a higher level (it is less deeply nested) than Sub3, the scope of Sub1 is not a static ancestor of Sub3, so Sub3 does not have access to the variables declared in Sub1. There is a good reason for this. The variables declared in Sub1 are stack dynamic, so they are not bound to storage if Sub1 is not in execution. Because Sub3 can be in execution when Sub1 is not, it cannot be allowed to access variables in Sub1, which would not necessarily be bound to storage during the execution of Sub3.

A subprogram is **active** if its execution has begun but has not yet terminated. The referencing environment of a statement in a dynamically scoped language is the locally declared variables, plus the variables of all other subprograms that are currently active. Once again, some variables in active subprograms can be hidden from the referencing environment. Recent subprogram activations can have declarations for variables that hide variables with the same names in previous subprogram activations.

Consider the following example program. Assume that the only function calls are the following: main calls sub2, which calls sub1.

```
void sub1() {
  int a, b;
  ...   <--------------- 1
}  /* end of sub1 */
void sub2() {
  int b, c;
  ...   <--------------- 2
  sub1;
}  /* end of sub2 */
void main() {
  int c, d;
  ...   <--------------- 3
  sub2();
}  /* end of main */
```

The referencing environments of the indicated program points are as follows:

Point	Referencing Environment
1	a and b of sub1, c of sub2, d of main, , (c of main and b of sub2 are hidden)
2	b and c of sub2, d of main, (c of main is hidden)
3	c and d of main

5.11 Named Constants

A **named constant** is a variable that is bound to a value only once. Named constants are useful as aids to readability and program reliability. Readability can be improved, for example, by using the name pi instead of the constant 3.14159.

Another important use of named constants is to parameterize a program. For example, consider a program that processes a fixed number of data values, say 100. Such a program usually uses the constant 100 in a number of locations for declaring array subscript ranges and for loop control limits. Consider the following skeletal Java program segment:

```java
void example() {
  int[] intList = new int[100];
  String[] strList = new String[100];
  ...
  for (index = 0; index < 100; index++) {
    ...
  }
  ...
  for (index = 0; index < 100; index++) {
    ...
  }
  ...
  average = sum / 100;
  ...
}
```

When this program must be modified to deal with a different number of data values, all occurrences of 100 must be found and changed. On a large program, this can be tedious and error-prone. An easier and more reliable method is to use a named constant as a program parameter, as in:

```java
void example() {
  final int len = 100;
  int[] intList = new int[len];
  String[] strList = new String[len];
  ...
  for (index = 0; index < len; index++) {
    ...
  }
  ...
  for (index = 0; index < len; index++) {
    ...
  }
  ...
  average = sum / len;
  ...
}
```

Now when the length must be changed, only one line must be changed (the variable len), regardless of the number of times it is used in the program. This is another example of the benefits of abstraction. The name len is an abstraction for the number of elements in some arrays and the number of iterations in some loops. This illustrates how named constants can aid modifiability.

Fortran 95 allows only constant expressions to be used as the values of its named constants. These constant expressions can contain previously declared named constants, constant values, and operators. The reason for the restriction to constants and constant expressions in Fortran 95 is that it uses static binding of values to named constants. Named constants in languages that use static binding of values are sometimes called **manifest constants.**

Ada and C++ allow dynamic binding of values to named constants. This allows expressions containing variables to be assigned to constants in the declarations. For example, the C++ statement

```
const int result = 2 * width + 1;
```

declares `result` to be an integer type named constant whose value is set to the value of the expression `2 * width + 1`, where the value of the variable `width` must be visible when `result` is allocated and bound to its value.

Java also allows dynamic binding of values to named constants. In Java, named constants are defined with the **final** reserved word (as in the earlier example). The initial value can be given in the declaration statement or in a subsequent assignment statement. The assigned value can be specified with any expression.

C# has two kinds of named constants: those defined with **const** and those defined with **readonly.** The **const** named constants, which are implicitly **static,** are statically bound to values; that is, they are bound to values at compile time, which means those values can be specified only with literals or other **const** members. The **readonly** named constants, which are dynamically bound to values, can be assigned in the declaration or with a static constructor.[9] So, if a program needs a constant-valued object whose value is the same on every use of the program, a **const** constant is used. However, if a program needs a constant-valued object whose value is determined only when the object is created and can be different for different executions of the program, then a **readonly** constant is used.

Ada allows named constants of enumeration and structured types, which are discussed in Chapter 6.

The discussion of binding values to named constants naturally leads to the topic of initialization, because binding a value to a named constant is the same process, except it is permanent.

In many instances, it is convenient for variables to have values before the code of the program or subprogram in which they are declared begins executing. The binding of a variable to a value at the time it is bound to storage is called **initialization.** If the variable is statically bound to storage, binding and initialization occur before run time. In these cases, the initial value must be specified as a literal or an expression whose only nonliteral operands are named constants that have already been defined. If the storage binding is dynamic, initialization is also dynamic and the initial values can be any expression.

---

9. Static constructors in C# run at some indeterminant time before the class is instantiated.

In most languages, initialization is specified on the declaration that creates the variable. For example, in C++, we could have

```
int sum = 0;
int* ptrSum = &sum;
char name[] = "George Washington Carver";
```

SUMMARY

Case sensitivity and the relationship of names to special words, which are either reserved words or keywords, are the design issues for names.

Variables can be characterized by the sextuple of attributes: name, address, value, type, lifetime, scope.

Aliases are two or more variables bound to the same storage address. They are regarded as detrimental to reliability, but are difficult to eliminate entirely from a language.

Binding is the association of attributes with program entities. Knowledge of the binding times of attributes to entities is essential to understanding the semantics of programming languages. Binding can be static or dynamic. Declarations, either explicit or implicit, provide a means of specifying the static binding of variables to types. In general, dynamic binding allows greater flexibility but at the expense of readability, efficiency, and reliability.

Scalar variables can be separated into four categories by considering their lifetimes: static, stack dynamic, explicit heap dynamic, and implicit heap dynamic.

Strong typing is the concept of requiring that all type errors be detected. The value of strong typing is increased reliability.

The type equivalence rules of a language determine what operations are legal among the structured types of a language. Name type equivalence and structure type equivalence are the two fundamental approaches to defining type equivalence.

Static scoping is a central feature of ALGOL 60 and some of its descendants. It provides a simple, reliable, and efficient method of allowing visibility of nonlocal variables in subprograms. Dynamic scoping provides more flexibility than static scoping but, again, at the expense of readability, reliability, and efficiency.

The referencing environment of a statement is the collection of all of the variables that are visible to that statement.

Named constants are simply variables that are bound to values only once.

REVIEW QUESTIONS

1. What are the design issues for names?
2. What is the potential danger of case-sensitive names?

3. In what way are reserved words better than keywords?

4. What is an alias?

5. Which category of C++ reference variables are always aliases?

6. What is the *l*-value of a variable? What is the *r*-value?

7. Define *binding* and *binding time*.

8. After language design and implementation, what are the four times bindings can take place in a program?

9. Define *static binding* and *dynamic binding*.

10. What are the advantages and disadvantages of implicit declarations?

11. What are the advantages and disadvantages of dynamic type binding?

12. Define *static*, *stack-dynamic*, *explicit heap-dynamic*, and *implicit heap-dynamic variables*. What are the advantages and disadvantages of these?

13. Define *coercion*, *type error*, *type checking*, and *strong typing*.

14. Define *name type compatibility* and *structure type compatibility*. What are the relative merits of these two?

15. What is the difference between an Ada derived type and an Ada subtype?

16. Define *lifetime*, *scope*, *static scope*, and *dynamic scope*.

17. How is a reference to a nonlocal variable in a static-scoped program connected to its definition?

18. What is the general problem with static scoping?

19. What is the referencing environment of a statement?

20. What is a static ancestor of a subprogram? What is a dynamic ancestor of a subprogram?

21. What is a block?

22. What are the advantages and disadvantages of dynamic scoping?

23. What are the advantages of named constants?

PROBLEM SET

1. Decide which of the following identifier forms is most readable, and then support that decision.

   ```
   SumOfSales
   sum_of_sales
   SUMOFSALES
   ```

2. Some programming languages are typeless. What are the obvious advantages and disadvantages of having no types in a language?

3. One common use of Fortran's `Equivalence` is the following: A large array of numeric values is made available to a subprogram as a parameter.

The array contains many different unrelated variables, rather than a collection of repetitions of the same variable. It is represented as an array to reduce the number of names that need to be passed as parameters. Within the subprogram, a lengthy `Equivalence` statement is used to create connotative names as aliases to the various array elements, which increases the readability of the code of the subprogram. Is this a good idea or not? What alternatives to aliasing are available?

4. Write a simple assignment statement with one arithmetic operator in some language you know. For each component of the statement, list the various bindings that are required to determine the semantics when the statement is executed. For each binding, indicate the binding time used for the language.

5. Dynamic type binding is closely related to implicit heap-dynamic variables. Explain this relationship.

6. Describe a situation when a history-sensitive variable in a subprogram is useful.

7. Look up the definition of *strongly typed* as given in Gehani (1983) and compare it with the definition given in this chapter. How do they differ?

8. Consider the following Ada skeletal program:

```
procedure Main is
  X : Integer;
  procedure Sub3;  -- This is a declaration of Sub3
                   -- It allows Sub1 to call it
  procedure Sub1 is
    X : Integer;
    procedure Sub2 is
      begin  -- of Sub2
      ...
      end;  -- of Sub2
    begin  -- of Sub1
    ...
    end;  -- of Sub1
  procedure Sub3 is
    begin  -- of Sub3
    ...
    end;  -- of Sub3
  begin  -- of Main
  ...
  end;  -- of Main
```

Assume that the execution of this program is in the following unit order:

```
Main calls Sub1
Sub1 calls Sub2
Sub2 calls Sub3
```

a. Assuming static scoping, in the following which declaration of X is the correct one for a reference to X?

    i. Sub1

    ii. Sub2

    iii. Sub3

b. Repeat part a, but assume dynamic scoping.

9. Assume the following Ada program was compiled and executed using
static-scoping rules. What value of X is printed in procedure Sub1?
Under dynamic-scoping rules, what value of X is printed in procedure
Sub1?

```
procedure Main is
  X : Integer;
  procedure Sub1 is
    begin  -- of Sub1
    Put(X);
    end;  -- of Sub1
  procedure Sub2 is
    X : Integer;
    begin  -- of Sub2
    X := 10;
    Sub1
    end;  -- of Sub2
  begin  -- of Main
  X := 5;
  Sub2
  end;  -- of Main
```

10. Consider the following program:

```
procedure Main is
  X, Y, Z : Integer;
  procedure Sub1 is
    A, Y, Z : Integer;
    procedure Sub2 is
    A, B, Z : Integer;
    begin  -- of Sub2
    ...
    end;  -- of Sub2
    begin  -- of Sub1
    ...
    end;  -- of Sub1
  procedure Sub3 is
    A, X, W : Integer;
    begin  -- of Sub3
    ...
```

```
    end;  -- of Sub3
  begin  -- of Main
  ...
  end;  -- of Main
```

List all the variables, along with the program units where they are declared, that are visible in the bodies of Sub1, Sub2, and Sub3, assuming static scoping is used.

11. Consider the following program:

```
procedure Main is
   X, Y, Z : Integer;
   procedure Sub1 is
     A, Y, Z : Integer;
     begin  -- of Sub1
     ...
     end;  -- of Sub1
   procedure Sub2 is
     A, X, W : Integer;
     procedure Sub3 is
       A, D, Z : Integer;
       begin  -- of Sub3
       ...
       end;  -- of Sub3
     begin  -- of Sub2
     ...
     end;  -- of Sub2
   begin  -- of Main
   ...
   end;  -- of Main
```

List all the variables, along with the program units where they are declared, that are visible in the bodies of Sub1, Sub2, and Sub3, assuming static scoping is used.

12. Consider the following C program:

```
void fun(void) {
  int a, b, c; /* definition 1 */
  ...
  while (...) {
    int b, c, d; /*definition 2 */
    ... <-------------- 1
    while (...) {
    int c, d, e; /* definition 3 */
    ... <------------- 2
    }
    ... <-------------- 3
```

```
        }
        ...  <---------------- 4
        }
```

For each of the four marked points in this function, list each visible variable, along with the number of the definition statement that defines it.

13. Consider the following skeletal C program:

```
void fun1(void);    /* prototype */
void fun2(void);    /* prototype */
void fun3(void);    /* prototype */
void main() {
  int a, b, c;
  ...
  }
void fun1(void) {
  int b, c, d;
  ...
  }
void fun2(void) {
  int c, d, e;
  ...
  }
void fun3(void) {
  int d, e, f;
  ...
  }
```

Given the following calling sequences and assuming that dynamic scoping is used, what variables are visible during execution of the last function called? Include with each visible variable the name of the function in which it was defined.

a. main calls fun1; fun1 calls fun2; fun2 calls fun3.

b. main calls fun1; fun1 calls fun3.

c. main calls fun2; fun2 calls fun3; fun3 calls fun1.

d. main calls fun3; fun3 calls fun1.

e. main calls fun1; fun1 calls fun3; fun3 calls fun2.

f. main calls fun3; fun3 calls fun2; fun2 calls fun1.

14. Consider the following program:

```
procedure Main is
  X, Y, Z : Integer;
  procedure Sub1 is
    A, Y, Z : Integer;
    begin  -- of Sub1
    ...
```

```
      end;  -- of Sub1
   procedure Sub2 is
     A, B, Z : Integer;
     begin  -- of Sub2
     ...
     end;  -- of Sub2
   procedure Sub3 is
     A, X, W : Integer;
     begin  -- of Sub3
     ...
     end;  -- of Sub3
   begin  -- of Main
   ...
   end;  -- of Main
```

Given the following calling sequences and assuming that dynamic scoping is used, what variables are visible during execution of the last subprogram activated? Include with each visible variable the name of the unit where it is declared.

a. Main calls Sub1; Sub1 calls Sub2; Sub2 calls Sub3.

b. Main calls Sub1; Sub1 calls Sub3.

c. Main calls Sub2; Sub2 calls Sub3; Sub3 calls Sub1.

d. Main calls Sub3; Sub3 calls Sub1.

e. Main calls Sub1; Sub1 calls Sub3; Sub3 calls Sub2.

f. Main calls Sub3; Sub3 calls Sub2; Sub2 calls Sub1.

PROGRAMMING EXERCISES

1. Perl allows both static and a kind of dynamic scoping. Write a Perl program that uses both and clearly shows the difference in effect of the two. Explain clearly the difference between the dynamic scoping described in this chapter and that implemented in Perl.

2. Write a COMMON LISP program that clearly shows the difference between static and dynamic scoping.

3. Write a JavaScript script that has subprograms nested three deep and in which each nested subprogram references variables defined in all of its enclosing subprograms.

4. Write a C function that includes the following sequence of statements:

```
x = 21;
int x;
x = 42;
```

Run the program and explain the results. Rewrite the same code in C++ and Java and compare the results.

5. Write test programs in C++, Java, and C# to determine the scope of a variable declared in a `for` statement. Specifically, the code must determine whether such a variable is visible after the body of the `for` statement.

6. Write three functions in C or C++: one that declares a large array statically, one that declares the same large array on the stack, and one that creates a the same large array from the heap. Call each of the subprograms a large number of times (at least 100,000) and output the time required by each. Explain the results.

7. Write a program in the language of your choice that behaves differently if the language used name equivalence than if it used structural equivalence.

8. For what types of A and B is the simple assignment statement A = B legal in C++ but not Java?

9. For what types of A and B is the simple assignment statement A = B legal in Java but not in Ada?

Data Types

T his chapter first introduces the concept of a data type and the characteristics of the common primitive data types. Then the designs of enumeration and subrange types are discussed. Next, the details of structured data types—specifically arrays, records, and unions—are investigated. This section is followed by an in-depth look at pointers and references.

For each of the various categories of data types, the design issues are stated and the design choices made by the designers of some common languages are described. These designs are then evaluated.

Implementation methods for data types sometimes have a significant impact on their design. Therefore, implementation of the various data types is another important part of this chapter, especially for the implementation of arrays.

6.1 Introduction

A **data type** defines a collection of data values and a set of predefined operations on those values. Computer programs produce results by manipulating data. An important factor in determining the ease with which they can perform this task is how well the data types available in the language being used match the objects in the real-world problem space. It is therefore crucial that a language support an appropriate collection of data types and structures.

The contemporary concepts of data typing have evolved over the last 50 years. In the earliest languages, all problem space data structures had to be modeled with only a few basic language-supported data structures. For example, in pre-90 Fortrans, linked lists and binary trees were commonly implemented with arrays.

The data structures of COBOL took the first step away from the Fortran I model by allowing programmers to specify the accuracy of decimal data values, and also by providing a structured data type for records of information. PL/I extended the capability of accuracy specification to integer and floating-point types. This has since been incorporated in Ada and Fortran. The designers of PL/I included many data types, with the intent of supporting a large range of applications. A better approach, introduced in ALGOL 68, is to provide a few basic types and a few flexible structure-defining operators that allow a programmer to design a data structure for each need. This was clearly one of the most important advances in the evolution of data type design. User-defined types also provide improved readability through the use of meaningful names for types. They allow type checking of the variables of a special category of use, which would otherwise not be possible. User-defined types also aid modifiability: A programmer can change the type of a category of variables in a program by changing only a type declaration statement.

Taking the concept of a user-defined type a step further, we arrive at abstract data types, which can be simulated in Ada 83 and are part of most subsequent programming languages. The fundamental idea of an abstract data type is that the interface of a type, which is visible to the user, is separated from the representation and set of operations on values of that type, which are hidden from the user. All of the types provided by a high-level programming language are abstract data types. User-defined abstract data types are discussed in detail in Chapter 11.

The two most common structured (nonscalar) data types are arrays and records, although the popularity of associative arrays has increased significantly. These and a few other data types are specified by type operators, or constructors, which are used to form type expressions. For example, C uses brackets and asterisks as type operators to specify arrays and pointers.

It is convenient, both logically and concretely, to think of variables in terms of descriptors. A **descriptor** is the collection of the attributes of a variable. In an implementation, a descriptor is an area of memory that stores the attributes of a variable. If the attributes are all static, descriptors are required only at compile time. These descriptors are built by the compiler, usually as a part of the symbol table, and are used during compilation. For dynamic attributes, however, part or all of the descriptor must be maintained during execution. In this case, the descriptor is used by the run-time system. In all cases, descriptors are used for type checking and to build the code for the allocation and deallocation operations.

The word *object* is often associated with the value of a variable and the space it occupies. In this book, however, we reserve *object* exclusively for instances of user-defined abstract data types, rather than also using it for the values of variables of predefined types. In object-oriented languages, every instance of every class, whether predefined or user-defined, is called an object. Objects are discussed in detail in Chapters 11 and 12.

In the following sections, all common data types are discussed. For most, design issues particular to the type are stated. For all, one or more example designs are described. One design issue is fundamental to all data types: What operations are provided for variables of the type and how are they specified?

6.2 Primitive Data Types

Data types that are not defined in terms of other types are called **primitive data types.** Nearly all programming languages provide a set of primitive data types. Some of the primitive types are merely reflections of the hardware—for example, most integer types. Others require only a little nonhardware support for their implementation.

The primitive data types of a language are used, along with one or more type constructors, to provide the structured types.

6.2.1 Numeric Types

Many early programming languages had only numeric primitive types. Numeric types still play a central role among the collections of types supported by contemporary languages.

6.2.1.1 Integer

The most common primitive numeric data type is **integer.** Many computers now support several sizes of integers. These sizes of integers, and often a few others, are supported by some programming languages. For example, Java includes four signed integer sizes: **byte, short, int,** and **long.** Some languages, such as C++ and C#, include unsigned integer types, which are simply types for integer values without signs. Unsigned types are often used for binary data.

A signed integer value is represented in a computer by a string of bits, with one of the bits (typically the leftmost) representing the sign. Most integer types are supported directly by the hardware. One example of an integer type that is not supported directly by the hardware is the long integer type of Python. Values of this type can have unlimited length. Long integer values can be specified as literals, as in

```
243725839182756281923L
```

Also, integer arithmetic operations that produce values too large to be represented with **int** type are stored as long integer type values.

A negative integer could be stored in sign-magnitude notation, in which the sign bit is set to indicate negative and the remainder of the bit string represents the absolute value of the number. Sign-magnitude notation, however, does not lend itself to computer arithmetic. Most computers now use a notation called **twos complement** to store negative integers, which is convenient for addition and subtraction. In twos-complement notation, the representation of a negative integer is formed by taking the logical complement of the positive version of the number and adding one. Ones-complement notation is still used by some computers. In ones-complement notation, the negative of an integer is stored as the logical complement of its absolute value. Ones-complement notation has the disadvantage that it has two representations of zero. See any book on assembly language programming for details of integer representations.

6.2.1.2 Floating-Point

Floating-point data types model real numbers, but the representations are only approximations for most real values. For example, neither of the fundamental numbers π or e (the base for the natural logarithms) can be correctly represented in floating-point notation. Of course, neither of these numbers can be accurately represented in any finite space. On most computers, floating-point numbers are stored in binary, which exacerbates the problem. For example, even the value 0.1 in decimal cannot be represented by a finite number of binary digits.[1] Another problem with floating-point types is the

---

1. 0.1 in decimal is 0.0001100110011... in binary.

loss of accuracy through arithmetic operations. For more information on the problems of floating-point notation, see any book on numerical analysis.

Floating-point values are represented as fractions and exponents, a form that is borrowed from scientific notation. Older computers used a variety of different representations for floating-point values. However, most newer machines use the IEEE Floating-Point Standard 754 format. Language implementers use whatever representation is supported by the hardware. Most languages include two floating-point types, often called **float** and **double.** The float type is the standard size, usually being stored in four bytes of memory. The double type is provided for situations where larger fractional parts are needed. Double-precision variables usually occupy twice as much storage as float variables and provide at least twice the number of bits of fraction.

The collection of values that can be represented by a floating-point type is defined in terms of precision and range. **Precision** is the accuracy of the fractional part of a value, measured as the number of bits. **Range** is a combination of the range of fractions, and, more important, the range of exponents.

Figure 6.1 shows the IEEE Floating-Point Standard 754 format for single- and double-precision representation (IEEE, 1985). Details of the IEEE formats can be found in Tanenbaum (2005).

6.2.1.3 Complex

Some programming languages support a complex data type, for example, Fortran and Python. Complex values are represented as ordered pairs of floating-point values. In Python, the imaginary part of a complex literal is specified by following it with a j or J, for example,

```
(7 + 3j)
```

Languages that support a complex type include operations for arithmetic on complex values.

Figure 6.1

IEEE floating-point formats: (a) single precision, (b) double precision

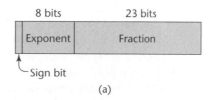

(a)

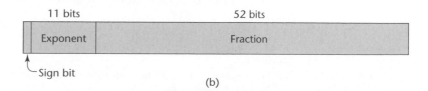

(b)

6.2.1.4 Decimal

Most larger computers that are designed to support business systems applications have hardware support for **decimal** data types. Decimal data types store a fixed number of decimal digits, with the decimal point at a fixed position in the value. These are the primary data types for business data processing and are therefore essential to COBOL. C# also has a decimal data type.

Decimal types have the advantage of being able to precisely store decimal values, at least those within a restricted range, which cannot be done with floating-point. For example, the number 0.1 (in decimal) can be exactly represented in a decimal type, but not in a floating-point type, as we saw in Section 6.2.1.2. The disadvantages of decimal types are that the range of values is restricted because no exponents are allowed, and their representation in memory is wasteful, for reasons discussed in the following paragraph.

Decimal types are stored very much like character strings, using binary codes for the decimal digits. These representations are called **binary coded decimal** (BCD). In some cases, they are stored one digit per byte, but in others they are packed two digits per byte. Either way, they take more storage than binary representations. It takes at least four bits to code a decimal digit. Therefore, to store a six-digit coded decimal number requires 24 bits of memory. However, it takes only 20 bits to store the same number in binary.[2] The operations on decimal values are done in hardware on machines that have such capabilities; otherwise, they are simulated in software.

6.2.2   Boolean Types

Boolean types are perhaps the simplest of all types. Their range of values has only two elements: one for true and one for false. They were introduced in ALGOL 60 and have been included in most general-purpose languages designed since 1960. One popular exception is C89, in which numeric expressions are used as conditionals. In such expressions, all operands with nonzero values are considered true, and zero is considered false. Although C99 and C++ have a Boolean type, they also allow numeric expressions to be used as if they were Boolean. This is not the case in the subsequent languages, Java and C#.

Boolean types are often used to represent switches or flags in programs. Although other types, such as integers, can be used for these purposes, the use of Boolean types is more readable.

A Boolean value could be represented by a single bit, but because a single bit of memory cannot be accessed efficiently on many machines, they are often stored in the smallest efficiently addressable cell of memory, typically a byte.

---

2. Of course, unless a program needs to maintain a large number of large decimal values, the difference is insignificant.

6.2.3 Character Types

Character data are stored in computers as numeric codings. Traditionally, the most commonly used coding was the eight-bit code ASCII (American Standard Code for Information Interchange), which uses the values 0 to 127 to code 128 different characters. ISO 8859-1 is another eight-bit character code, but it allows 256 different characters. Ada 95 uses ISO 8859-1.

Because of the globalization of business and the need for computers to communicate with other computers around the world, the ASCII character set is becoming inadequate. A 16-bit character set named Unicode has been developed as an alternative. Unicode includes the characters from most of the world's natural languages. For example, Unicode includes the Cyrillic alphabet, as used in Serbia, and the Thai digits. The first 128 characters of Unicode are identical to those of ASCII. Java was the first widely used language to use the Unicode character set. Since then, it has found its way into JavaScript, Python, Perl, and C#.

To provide the means of processing codings of single characters, most programming languages include a primitive type for them. However, Python supports single characters only as character strings of length 1.

6.3 Character String Types

A **character string type** is one in which the values consist of sequences of characters. Character string constants are used to label output, and the input and output of all kinds of data are often done in terms of strings. Of course, character strings also are an essential type for all programs that do character manipulation.

6.3.1 Design Issues

The two most important design issues that are specific to character string types are the following:

- Should strings be simply a special kind of character array or a primitive type?
- Should strings have static or dynamic length?

6.3.2 Strings and Their Operations

The common string operations are assignment, catenation, substring reference, comparison, and pattern matching.

A **substring reference** is a reference to a substring of a given string. Substring references are discussed in the more general context of arrays, where the substring references are called **slices.**

In general, both assignment and comparison operations on character strings are complicated by the possibility of assigning and comparing operands of different lengths. For example, what happens when a longer string is assigned to a shorter string, or vice versa? Usually, simple and sensible choices are made for these situations, although users often have trouble remembering them.

Pattern matching is another fundamental character string operation. In some languages, pattern matching is supported directly in the language. In others, it is provided by a function or class library.

If strings are not defined as a primitive type, string data is usually stored in arrays of single characters and referenced as such in the language. This is the approach taken by C and C++.

C and C++ use **char** arrays to store character strings. These languages provide a collection of string operations through a standard library whose header file is `string.h`. Most uses of strings and most of the library functions use the convention that character strings are terminated with a special character, null, which is represented with zero. This is an alternative to maintaining the length of string variables. The library operations simply carry out their operations until the null character appears in the string being operated on. Library functions that produce strings often supply the null character. The character string literals that are built by the compiler also have the null character. For example, consider the following declaration:

```
char str[] = "apples";
```

In this example, `str` is an array of **char** elements, specifically apples0, where 0 is the null character.

Some of the most commonly used library functions for character strings in C and C++ are `strcpy`, which moves strings; `strcat`, which catenates one given string onto another; `strcmp`, which lexicographically compares (by the order of their character codes) two given strings; and `strlen`, which returns the number of characters, not counting the null, in the given string. The parameters and return values for most of the string manipulation functions are **char** pointers that point to arrays of **char**. Parameters can also be string literals.

The string manipulation functions of the C standard library, which are also available in C++, are inherently unsafe and have led to numerous programming errors. The problem is that the functions in this library that move string data do not guard against overflowing the destination. For example, consider the following call to `strcpy`:

```
strcpy(src, dest);
```

If the length of `dest` is 20 and the length of `src` is 50, `strcpy` will write over the 30 bytes that follow `dest`. The point is that `strcpy` does not know the length of `dest`, so it cannot ensure that the memory following it will not be overwritten. The same problem can occur with several of the other functions in the C string library. In addition to C-style strings, C++ also supports strings through its standard class library, which is also similar to that of Java. Because of the insecurities of the C string library, C++ programmers should use the `string` class from the standard library, rather than **char** arrays and the C string library.

Fortran 95 treats strings as a primitive type and provides assignment, relational operators, catenation, and substring reference operations for them.

In Java, strings are supported as a primitive type by the `String` class, whose values are constant strings, and the `StringBuffer` class, whose values are changeable and are more like arrays of single characters. Subscripting is allowed on `StringBuffer` variables. C# and Ruby include string classes that are similar to those of Java.

Python also has strings as a primitive type and has operations for substring reference, catenation, indexing to access individual characters, as well as methods for searching and replacement. There is also an operation for character membership in a string. So, even though Python's strings are primitive types, for character and substring references they act very much like arrays of characters. However, Python strings are immutable, similar to the `String` class objects of Java.

Perl, JavaScript, Ruby, and PHP include built-in pattern-matching operations. In these languages, the pattern-matching expressions are somewhat loosely based on mathematical regular expressions. In fact, they are often called **regular expressions.** They evolved from the early UNIX line editor, `ed`, to become part of the UNIX shell languages. Eventually, they grew to their current complex form. There is at least one complete book on this kind of pattern-matching expressions (Friedl, 2006). In this section, we provide only a brief look at the style of these expressions through two relatively simple examples.

Consider the following pattern expression:

```
/[A-Za-z][A-Za-z\d]+/
```

This pattern matches (or describes) the typical name form in programming languages. The brackets enclose character classes. The first character class specifies all letters; the second specifies all letters and digits (a digit is specified with the abbreviation \d). If only the second character class were included, we could not prevent a name from beginning with a digit. The plus operator following the second category specifies that there must be one or more of what is in the category. So, the whole pattern matches strings that begin with a letter, followed by one or more letters or digits.

Next, consider the following pattern expression:

```
/\d+\.?\d*|\.\d+/
```

This pattern matches numeric literals. The `\.` specifies a literal decimal point.[3] The question mark quantifies what it follows to have zero or one appearance. The vertical bar (|) separates two alternatives in the whole pattern. The first alternative matches strings of one or more digits, possibly followed by a decimal point, followed by zero or more digits; the second alternative matches strings that begin with a decimal point, followed by one or more digits.

Pattern-matching capabilities are included in the class libraries of C++, Java, Python, and C#.

6.3.3   String Length Options

There are several design choices regarding the length of string values. First, the length can be static and set when the string is created. Such a string is called a **static length string.** This is the choice for the strings of Python, the immutable objects of Java's `String` class, as well as similar classes in the C++ standard class library, Ruby's built-in `String` class, and the .NET class library available to C#.

The second option is to allow strings to have varying length up to a declared and fixed maximum set by the variable's definition, as exemplified by the strings in C and the C-style strings of C++. These are called **limited dynamic length strings.** Such string variables can store any number of characters between zero and the maximum. Recall that strings in C use a special character to indicate the end of the string's characters, rather than maintaining the string length.

The third option is to allow strings to have varying length with no maximum, as in JavaScript and Perl. These are called **dynamic length strings.** This option requires the overhead of dynamic storage allocation and deallocation but provides maximum flexibility.

Ada 95 supports all three string length options. Type `String` from the `Standard` package provides static length strings. Type `Bounded_String`, from the `Ada.Strings.Bounded` package, supports limited dynamic length strings. Type `Unbounded_String`, from the `Ada.Strings.Unbounded` package, supports dynamic length strings.

6.3.4   Evaluation

String types are important to the writability of a language. Dealing with strings as arrays can be more cumbersome than dealing with a primitive string type. For example, consider a language that treats strings as arrays of characters and does not have a predefined function that does what `strcpy` in C does. Then a simple assignment of one string to another would require a loop.

---

3. The period must be "escaped" with the backslash because period has special meaning in a regular expression.

The addition of strings as a primitive type to a language is not costly in terms of either language or compiler complexity. Therefore, it is difficult to justify the omission of primitive string types in some contemporary languages. Of course, providing strings through a standard library is nearly as convenient as having them as a primitive type.

String operations such as simple pattern matching and catenation are essential and should be included for string type values. Although dynamic-length strings are obviously the most flexible, the overhead of their implementation must be weighed against that additional flexibility.

6.3.5 Implementation of Character String Types

Character string types could be supported directly in hardware, but in most cases software is used to implement string storage, retrieval, and manipulation. When character string types are represented as character arrays, the language often supplies few operations.

A descriptor for a static character string type, which is required only during compilation, has three fields. The first field of every descriptor is the name of the type. In the case of static character strings, the second field is the type's length (in characters). The third field is the address of the first character. This descriptor is shown in Figure 6.2. Limited dynamic strings require a run-time descriptor to store both the fixed maximum length and the current length, as shown in Figure 6.3. Dynamic length strings require a simpler run-time descriptor because only the current length needs to be stored. Although we depict descriptors as independent blocks of storage, in most cases they are stored in the symbol table.

The limited dynamic strings of C and C++ do not require run-time descriptors, because the end of a string is marked with the null character. They do not need the maximum length, because index values in array references are not range-checked in these languages.

Figure 6.2

Compile-time descriptor for static strings

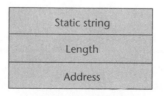

Figure 6.3

Run-time descriptor for limited dynamic strings

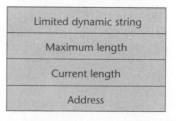

Static length and limited dynamic length strings require no special dynamic storage allocation. In the case of limited dynamic length strings, sufficient storage for the maximum length is allocated when the string variable is bound to storage, so only a single allocation process is involved.

Dynamic length strings require more complex storage management. The length of a string, and therefore the storage to which it is bound, must grow and shrink dynamically.

There are three approaches to supporting the dynamic allocation and deallocation that is required for dynamic length strings. First, strings can be stored in a linked list, so that when a string grows, the newly required cells can come from anywhere in the heap. The drawbacks to this method are the extra storage occupied by the links in the list representation and the necessary complexity of string operations.

The second approach is to store strings as arrays of pointers to individual characters allocated in the heap. This method still uses extra memory, but string processing can be faster than with the linked-list approach.

The third alternative is to store complete strings in adjacent storage cells. The problem with this method arises when a string grows: How can storage that is adjacent to the existing cells continue to be allocated for the string variable? Frequently, such storage is not available. Instead, a new area of memory is found that can store the complete new string, and the old part is moved to this area. Then the memory cells used for the old string are deallocated. This latter approach is the one typically used. The general problem of managing allocation and deallocation of variable-size segments is discussed in Section 6.9.9.3.

Although the linked-list method requires more storage, the associated allocation and deallocation processes are simple. However, some string operations are slowed by the required pointer chasing. On the other hand, using adjacent memory for complete strings results in faster string operations and requires significantly less storage, but the allocation and deallocation processes are slower.

6.4 User-Defined Ordinal Types

An **ordinal type** is one in which the range of possible values can be easily associated with the set of positive integers. In Java, for example, the primitive ordinal types are **integer, char,** and **boolean.** There are two user-defined ordinal types that have been supported by programming languages: enumeration and subrange.

6.4.1 Enumeration Types

An **enumeration type** is one in which all of the possible values, which are named constants, are provided, or enumerated, in the definition. Enumeration types provide a way of defining and grouping collections of named constants, which are called **enumeration constants.** The definition of a typical enumeration type is shown in the following C# example:

```
enum days {Mon, Tue, Wed, Thu, Fri, Sat, Sun};
```

The enumeration constants are typically implicitly assigned the integer values, 0, 1, . . . , but can be explicitly assigned any integer literal in the type's definition.

The design issues for enumeration types are:

- Is an enumeration constant allowed to appear in more than one type definition, and if so, how is the type of an occurrence of that constant in the program checked?
- Are enumeration values coerced to integer?
- Are any other types coerced to an enumeration type?

All of these design issues are related to type checking. If an enumeration variable is coerced to a numeric type, there is little control over its range of legal operations or its range of values. If an **int** type value is coerced to an enumeration type, an enumeration type variable could be assigned any integer value, whether it represented an enumeration constant or not.

6.4.1.1 Designs

In languages that do not have enumeration types, programmers usually simulate them with integer values. For example, suppose we needed to represent colors in a C program and C did not have an enumeration type. We might use 0 to represent blue, 1 to represent red, and so forth. These values could be defined, as in

```
int red = 0, blue = 1;
```

Now, in the program we could use `red` and `blue` as if they were of a color type. The problem with this approach is that because we have not defined a type for our colors, there is no type checking when they are used. For example, it would be legal to add the two together, although that would rarely be an intended operation. They could also be combined with any other numeric type operand using any arithmetic operator, which would also rarely be useful. Furthermore, because they are just variables, they could be assigned any integer value, thereby destroying the relationship with the colors. This latter problem could be prevented by making them named constants.

C and Pascal were the first widely used languages to include an enumeration data type. C++ includes C's enumeration types. In C++, we could have

```
enum colors {red, blue, green, yellow, black};
colors myColor = blue, yourColor = red;
```

The `colors` type uses the default internal values for the enumeration constants, 0, 1, . . . , although the constants could have been assigned any integer literal (or any constant-valued expression). The enumeration values are coerced to **int** when they are put in integer context. This allows their use in any numeric expression. For example, if the current value of `myColor` is `blue`, the expression

```
myColor++
```

would assign `green` to `myColor`.

C++ also allows enumeration constants to be assigned to variables of any numeric type, though that would likely be an error. However, no other type value is coerced to an enumeration type in C++. For example,

```
myColor = 4;
```

is illegal in C++. This assignment would be legal if the right side had been cast to `colors` type. This prevents some potential errors.

C++ enumeration constants can appear in only one enumeration type in the same referencing environment.

In Ada, enumeration literals are allowed to appear in more than one declaration in the same referencing environment. These are called **overloaded literals.** The rule for resolving the overloading—that is, deciding the type of an occurrence of such a literal—is that it must be determinable from the context of its appearance. For example, if an overloaded literal and an enumeration variable are compared, the literal's type is resolved to be that of the variable. In some cases, the programmer must indicate some type specification for an occurrence of an overloaded literal to avoid a compilation error.

Because neither the enumeration literals nor the enumeration variables in Ada are coerced to integers, both the range of operations and the range of values of enumeration types are restricted, allowing many programmer errors to be compiler detected.

An enumeration type was added to Java in Java 5.0 in 2004. All enumeration types in Java are implicitly subclasses of the predefined class `Enum`. Because enumeration types are classes, they can have instance data fields, constructors, and methods. Syntactically, Java enumeration type definitions appear like those of C++, except that they can include fields, constructors, and methods. The possible values of an enumeration are the only possible intances of the class. All enumeration types inherit `toString`, as well as a few other methods. An array of the instances of an enumeration type can be fetched with the static method `values`. The internal numeric value of an enumeration variable can be fetched with the `ordinal` method. No expression of any other type can be assigned to an enumeration variable. Also, an enumeration variable is never coerced to any other type.

C# enumeration types are like those of C++, except that they are never coerced to integer. So, operations on enumeration types are restricted to those that make sense. Also, the range of values is restricted to that of the particular enumeration type.

Interestingly, none of the relatively recent scripting kinds of languages include enumeration types. These include Perl, JavaScript, PHP, Python, and Ruby. Even Java was a decade old before enumeration types were added.

6.4.1.2 Evaluation

Enumeration types can provide advantages in both readability and reliability. Readability is enhanced in a very direct way: Named values are easily recognized, whereas coded values are not.

In the area of reliability, the enumeration types of Ada, C#, and Java 5.0 provide two advantages. First, no arithmetic operations are legal on enumeration types. This prevents adding days of the week, for example. Second, no enumeration variable can be assigned a value outside its defined range. If the `colors` enumeration type has 10 enumeration constants and uses 0..9 as its internal values, no number greater than 9 can be assigned to a `colors` type variable.

Because C treats enumeration variables like integer variables, it does not provide either of the two advantages.

C++ is a little better. Numeric values can be assigned to enumeration type variables only if they are cast to the type of the assigned variable. Numeric values assigned to enumeration type variables are checked to determine whether they are in the range of the internal values of the enumeration type. Unfortunately, if the user uses a wide range of explicitly assigned values, this checking is not effective. For example,

```
enum colors {red = 1, blue = 1000, green = 100000}
```

In this example, a value assigned to a variable of `colors` type will only be checked to determine whether it is in the range of 1..100000.

The enumeration types in Ada, C#, and Java 5.0 are better than those of C++, because enumeration type variables are never coerced to integer types.

6.4.2   Subrange Types

A **subrange type** is a contiguous subsequence of an ordinal type. For example, `12..14` is a subrange of integer type. Subrange types were introduced by Pascal and are included in Ada. There are no design issues that are specific to subrange types.

6.4.2.1 Ada's Design

In Ada, subranges are included in the category of types called subtypes. As was stated in Chapter 5, subtypes are not new types; rather, they are new names for possibly restricted, or constrained, versions of existing types. For example, consider the following declarations:

```
type Days is (Mon, Tue, Wed, Thu, Fri, Sat, Sun);
subtype Weekdays is Days range Mon..Fri;
subtype Index is Integer range 1..100;
```

In these examples, the restriction on the existing types is in the range of possible values. All of the operations defined for the parent type are also defined for the subtype, except assignment of values outside the specified range. For example, in the following

```
Day1 : Days;
Day2 : Weekdays;
...
Day2 := Day1;
```

the assignment is legal unless the value of Day1 is Sat or Sun.

The compiler must generate range-checking code for every assignment to a subrange variable. While types are checked for compatibility at compile time, subranges require run-time range checking.

One of the most common uses of user-defined ordinal types is for the indices of arrays, as will be discussed in Section 6.5. They can also be used for loop variables. In fact, subranges of ordinal types are the only way the range of Ada **for** loop variables can be specified.

Note that subrange types are very different from Ada's derived types, which were discussed in Chapter 5. For example, consider the following type declarations:

```
type Derived_Small_Int is new Integer range 1..100;
subtype Subrange_Small_Int is Integer range 1..100;
```

Variables of both types, Derived_Small_Int and Subrange_Small_Int, have the same range of legal values and both inherit the operations of Integer. However, variables of type Derived_Small_Int are not compatible with any Integer type. On the other hand, variables of type Subrange_Small_Int are compatible with variables and constants of Integer type and any subtype of Integer.

6.4.2.2 Evaluation

Subrange types enhance readability by making it clear to readers that variables of subtypes can store only certain ranges of values. Reliability is increased with subrange types, because assigning a value to a subrange variable that is outside the specified range is detected as an error, either by the compiler (in the case of the assigned value being a literal value) or by the run-time system (in the case of a variable or expression). It is odd that no contemporary language except Ada 95 has subrange types.

6.4.3 Implementation of User-Defined Ordinal Types

As discussed earlier, enumeration types are usually implemented as integers. Without restrictions on ranges of values and operations, this provides no increase in reliability.

Subrange types are implemented in exactly the same way as their parent types, except that range checks must be implicitly included by the compiler in every assignment of a variable or expression to a subrange variable. This step increases code size and execution time but is usually considered well worth the cost. Also, a good optimizing compiler can optimize away some of the checking.

6.5 Array Types

An **array** is a homogeneous aggregate of data elements in which an individual element is identified by its position in the aggregate, relative to the first element. A reference to an array element in a program often includes one or more nonconstant subscripts. Such references require additional run-time calculation to determine the memory location being referenced. The individual data elements of an array are of some previously defined type, either primitive or otherwise. A majority of computer programs need to model collections of values in which the values are of the same type and must be processed in the same way. Thus, the universal need for arrays is obvious.

6.5.1 Design Issues

The primary design issues specific to arrays are the following:

- What types are legal for subscripts?
- Are subscripting expressions in element references range-checked?
- When are subscript ranges bound?
- When does array allocation take place?
- Are ragged or rectangular multidimensioned arrays allowed, or both?
- Can arrays be initialized when they have their storage allocated?
- What kinds of slices are allowed, if any?

In the following sections, examples of the design choices made for the arrays of the most common programming languages are discussed.

6.5.2 Arrays and Indices

Specific elements of an array are referenced by means of a two-level syntactic mechanism, where the first part is the aggregate name, and the second part is a possibly dynamic selector consisting of one or more items known as **subscripts** or **indices.** If all of the subscripts in a reference are constants, the selector is static; otherwise, it is dynamic. The selection operation can be thought of as a mapping from the array name and the set of subscript values to an element in the aggregate. Indeed, arrays are sometimes called **finite mappings.** Symbolically, this mapping can be shown as

array_name(subscript_value_list) → element

The syntax of array references is fairly universal: The array name is followed by the list of subscripts, which is surrounded by either parentheses or brackets. In most languages that provide multidimensioned arrays as arrays of arrays, each subscript appears in its own brackets. A problem with using parentheses to enclose subscript expressions is that they often are also used to enclose the parameters in subprogram calls; this use makes references to arrays appear exactly like those calls. For example, consider the following Ada assignment statement:

```
Sum := Sum + B(I);
```

Because parentheses are used for both subprogram parameters and array subscripts in Ada, both program readers and compilers are forced to use other information to determine whether B(I) in this assignment is a function call or a reference to an array element. This results in reduced readability.

The designers of Ada specifically chose parentheses to enclose subscripts so there would be uniformity between array references and function calls in expressions, in spite of potential readability problems. They made this choice in part because both array element references and function calls are mappings. Array element references map the subscripts to a particular element of the array. Function calls map the actual parameters to the function definition and, eventually, a functional value.

The C-based languages use brackets to delimit their array indices.

Two distinct types are involved in an array type: the element type and the type of the subscripts. The type of the subscripts is often a subrange of integers, but Ada allows any ordinal type to be used as subscripts, such as Boolean, character, and enumeration. For example, in Ada one could have:

```
type Week_Day_Type is (Monday, Tuesday, Wednesday, Thursday, Friday);
type Sales is array (Week_Day_Type) of Float;
```

> **history note**
>
> The designers of pre-90 Fortrans and PL/I chose parentheses for array subscripts because no other suitable characters were available at the time. Card punches did not include bracket characters.

An Ada **for** loop can use any ordinal type variable for its counter, as we will see in Chapter 8. This allows arrays with ordinal type subscripts to be conveniently processed.

Early programming languages did not specify that subscript ranges must be implicitly checked. Range errors in subscripts are common in programs, so requiring range checking is an important factor in the reliability of languages. Among contemporary languages, C, C++, Perl, and Fortran do not specify range checking of subscripts, but Java, ML, and C# do. By default, Ada checks the range of all subscripts, but this feature can be disabled by the programmer.

Subscripting in Perl is a bit unusual in that although the names of all arrays begin with at signs (@), because array elements are always scalars and the names of scalars always begin with dollar signs ($), references to array elements use dollar signs rather than at signs in their names. For example, for the array @list, the second element is referenced with $list[1].

One can reference an array element in Perl with a negative subscript, in which case the subscript value is an offset from the end of the array. For example, if the array @list has five elements with the subscripts 0..4, $list[-2] references the element with the subscript 3. A reference to a nonexistent element in Perl yields **undef**, but no error is reported.

6.5.3 Subscript Bindings and Array Categories

The binding of the subscript type to an array variable is usually static, but the subscript value ranges are sometimes dynamically bound.

In some languages, the lower bound of the subscript range is implicit. For example, in the C-based languages, the lower bound of all subscript ranges is fixed at zero; in Fortran 95, it defaults to one. In some other languages, subscript ranges must be completely specified by the programmer.

There are five categories of arrays. The category definitions are based on the binding to subscript ranges, the binding to storage, and from where the storage is allocated. The category names indicate the design choices of these three. In the first four of these categories, once the subscript ranges are bound and the storage is allocated, they remain fixed for the lifetime of the variable. Keep in mind that when the subscript ranges are fixed, the array cannot change size.

A **static array** is one in which the subscript ranges are statically bound and storage allocation is static (done before run time). The advantage of static arrays is efficiency: No dynamic allocation or deallocation is required.

A **fixed stack-dynamic array** is one in which the subscript ranges are statically bound, but the allocation is done at declaration elaboration time during execution. The advantage of fixed stack-dynamic arrays over static arrays is space efficiency. A large array in one subprogram can use the same space as a large array in a different subprogram, as long as both subprograms are not active at the same time.

A **stack-dynamic array** is one in which both the subscript ranges and the storage allocation are dynamically bound at elaboration time. Once the subscript ranges are bound and the storage is allocated, however, they remain fixed during the lifetime of the variable. The advantage of stack-dynamic arrays over static and fixed stack-dynamic arrays is flexibility. The size of an array need not be known until the array is about to be used.

A **fixed heap-dynamic array** is similar to a fixed stack-dynamic array, in that the subscript ranges and the storage binding are both fixed after storage is allocated. The differences are that both the subscript ranges and storage bindings are done when the user program requests them during execution, and the storage is allocated from the heap, rather than the stack.

A **heap-dynamic array** is one in which the binding of subscript ranges and storage allocation is dynamic and can change any number of times during the array's lifetime. The advantage of heap-dynamic arrays over the others is flexibility: Arrays can grow and shrink during program execution as the need for space changes. Examples of the five categories are given in the following paragraphs.

Arrays declared in C and C++ functions that include the `static` modifier are static.

Arrays that are declared in C and C++ functions (without the `static` specifier) are examples of fixed stack-dynamic arrays.

Ada arrays can be stack-dynamic, as in the following:

```
Get(List_Len);
declare
  List : array (1..List_Len) of Integer;
  begin
  ...
  end;
```

In this example, the user inputs the number of desired elements for the array `List`. The elements are then dynamically allocated when execution reaches the `declare` block. When execution reaches the end of the block, the `List` array is deallocated.

C and C++ also provide fixed heap-dynamic arrays. The standard library functions `malloc` and `free`, which are general heap allocation and deallocation operations, respectively, can be used for C arrays. C++ uses the operators **new** and **delete** to manage heap storage. An array is treated as a pointer to a collection of storage cells, where the pointer can be indexed, as discussed in Section 6.9.5.

Fortran 95 also supports fixed heap-dynamic arrays.

In Java, all arrays are fixed heap-dynamic arrays. Once created, these arrays keep the same subscript ranges and storage. C# also provides fixed heap-dynamic arrays.

history note

Fortran I limited the number of array subscripts to three, because at the time of the design, execution efficiency was a primary concern. Fortran I designers had developed a very fast method for accessing the elements of arrays of up to three dimensions, using the three index registers of the IBM 704. Fortran IV was first implemented on an IBM 7094, which had seven index registers. This allowed Fortran IV's designers to allow arrays with up to seven subscripts. Most other contemporary languages enforce no such limits.

C# includes a second array class, `ArrayList`, that provides heap-dynamic arrays. Objects of this class are created without any elements, as in

```
ArrayList intList = new ArrayList();
```

Elements are added to this object with the `Add` method, as in

```
ArrayList.Add(nextOne);
```

Java includes a structure similar to C#'s `ArrayList`, except subscripting is not supported—`get` and `set` methods must be used to access the elements.

A Perl array can be made to grow by using the `push` (puts one or more new elements on the end of the array) and `unshift` (puts one or more new elements on the beginning of the array), or by assigning a value to the array specifying a subscript beyond the highest current subscript of the array. An array can be made to shrink to no elements by assigning it the empty list, `()`. The length of an array is defined to be the largest subscript plus one.

Like Perl, JavaScript allows arrays to grow with the `push` and `unshift` methods and shrink by setting them to the empty list. However, negative subscripts are not supported.

JavaScript arrays can be sparse, meaning the subscript values need not be contiguous. For example, suppose we have an array named `list` that has 10 elements with the subscripts `0..9`.[4] Consider the assignment statement

```
list[50] = 42;
```

Now, list has 11 elements and length 51. The elements with subscripts `11..49` are not defined and therefore do not require storage. A reference to a nonexistent element in a JavaScript array yields **undefined.**

Arrays in Python and Ruby can be made to grow only through methods to add elements or catenate other arrays. Ruby supports negative subscripts, but Python does not. In both Python and Ruby, an element or slice of an array can be deleted. A reference to a nonexistent element in Python results in a run-time error, whereas a similar reference in Ruby yields **nil** and no error is reported.

6.5.4 Heterogeneous Arrays

A heterogeneous array is one in which the elements need not be of the same type. Such arrays are supported by Perl, Python, JavaScript, and Ruby. In all of these languages, arrays are heap dynamic.

---

4. The subscript range could just as easily have been 1000..1009.

In Perl, the elements of an array can be any mixture of the scalar types, which includes numbers, strings, and references. JavaScript is a dynamically typed language. Any array element can be any type. In Python and Ruby, array elements are references to objects of any type.

For the remainder of this chapter, when we discuss arrays, heterogeneous arrays will be considered part of the discussion.

6.5.5 Array Initialization

Some languages provide the means to initialize arrays at the time their storage is allocated. In Fortran 95, an array can be initialized by assigning it an array aggregate in its declaration. A Fortran 95 array aggregate for a single-dimensional array is a list of literals delimited by parentheses and slashes. For example, we could have

```
Integer, Dimension (3) :: List = (/0, 5, 5/)
```

C, C++, Java, and C# also allow initialization of their arrays, but with one new twist: In the C declaration

```
int list [] = {4, 5, 7, 83};
```

the compiler sets the length of the array. This is meant to be a convenience but is not without cost. It effectively removes the possibility that the system could detect some kinds of programmer errors, such as mistakenly leaving a value out of the list.

As discussed in Section 6.3.2, character strings in C and C++ are implemented as arrays of **char.** These arrays can be initialized to string constants, as in

```
char name [] = "freddie";
```

The array name will have eight elements, because all strings are terminated with a null character (zero), which is implicitly supplied by the system for string constants.

Arrays of strings in C and C++ can also be initialized with string literals. In this case, the array is one of pointers to characters. For example,

```
char *names [] = {"Bob", "Jake", "Darcie"};
```

This example illustrates the nature of character literals in C and C++. In the previous example of a string literal being used to initialize the **char** array name, the literal is taken to be a **char** array. But in the latter example (names), the literals are taken to be pointers to characters, so the array is an array of pointers to characters. For example, names[0] is a pointer to the letter 'B' in the literal character array that contains the characters 'B', 'o', 'b', and the null character.

In Java, similar syntax is used to define and initialize an array of references to String objects. For example,

```
String[] names = ["Bob", "Jake", "Darcie"];
```

Ada provides two mechanisms for initializing arrays in the declaration statement: by listing them in the order in which they are to be stored, or by directly assigning them to an index position using the => operator, which in Ada is called an **arrow**. For example, consider the following:

```
List : array (1..5) of Integer := (1, 3, 5, 7, 9);
Bunch : array (1..5) of Integer := (1 => 17, 3 => 34,
                                    others => 0);
```

In the first statement, all the elements of the array List have initializing values, which are assigned to the array element locations in the order in which they appear. In the second, the first and third array elements are initialized using direct assignment, and the **others** clause is used to initialize the remaining elements. As with Fortran, these parenthesized lists of values are called **aggregate values.**

6.5.6   Array Operations

An array operation is one that operates on an array as a unit. The most common array operations are assignment, catenation, comparison for equality and inequality, and slices, which are discussed separately in Section 6.5.8.

The C-based languages do not provide any array operations, except through the methods of Java, C++, and C#. Perl supports array assignments, but does not support comparisons.

Ada allows array assignments, including those where the right side is an aggregate value rather than an array name. Ada also provides catenation, specified by the ampersand (&). Catenation is defined between two single-dimensioned arrays and between a single-dimensioned array and a scalar. Nearly all types in Ada have the built-in relational operators for equality and inequality.

The elements of Python's arrays are references to objects. Python provides array assignment, although it is only a reference change. Python also has operations for array catenation (+) and element membership (**in**). It includes two different comparison operators, one that determines whether the two variables reference the same object (**is**) and one that compares all corresponding objects in the referenced objects, regardless of how deeply they are nested, for equality (==).

Like Python, the elements of Ruby's arrays are references to objects. And like Python, when a Ruby==operator is used between two arrays, the result is true only if the two arrays have the same length and the corresponding elements are equal. Ruby's arrays can be catenated with an `Array` method.

Fortran 95 includes a number of array operations that are called **elemental** because they are operations between pairs of array elements. For example, the add operator (+) between two arrays results in an array of the sums of the element pairs of the two arrays. The assignment, arithmetic, relational, and logical operators are all overloaded for arrays of any size or shape. Fortran 95 also includes intrinsic, or library, functions for matrix multiplication, matrix transpose, and vector dot product.

Arrays and their operations are the heart of APL; it is the most powerful array-processing language ever devised. Because of its relative obscurity and its lack of effect on subsequent languages, however, we present here only a glimpse into its array operations.

In APL, the four basic arithmetic operations are defined for vectors (single-dimensioned arrays) and matrices, as well as scalar operands. For example,

```
A + B
```

is a valid expression, whether A and B are scalar variables, vectors, or matrices.

APL includes a collection of unary operators for vectors and matrices, some of which are as follows (where V is a vector and M is a matrix):

ϕV reverses the elements of V
ϕM reverses the columns of M
θM reverses the rows of M
⍉M transposes M (its rows become its columns and vice versa)
÷M inverts M

APL also includes several special operators that take other operators as operands. One of these is the inner product operator, which is specified with a period (`.`). It takes two operands, which are binary operators. For example,

```
+.×
```

is a new operator that takes two arguments, either vectors or matrices. It first multiplies the corresponding elements of two arguments, and then it sums the results. For example, if A and B are vectors,

```
A × B
```

is the mathematical inner product of A and B (a vector of the products of the corresponding elements of A and B). The statement

```
A +.× B
```

is the sum of the inner product of A and B. If A and B are matrices, this expression specifies the matrix multiplication of A and B.

The special operators of APL are actually functional forms, which are described in Chapter 15.

6.5.7   Rectangular and Jagged Arrays

A **rectangular array** is a multidimensioned array in which all of the rows have the same number of elements, all of the columns have the same number of elements, and so forth. Rectangular arrays model tables exactly.

A **jagged array** is one in which the lengths of the rows need not be the same. For example, a jagged matrix may consist of three rows, one with 5 elements, one with 7 elements, and one with 12 elements. This also applies to the columns and higher dimensions. So, if there is a third dimension (layers), each layer can have a different number of elements. Jagged arrays are made possible when multidimensioned arrays are actually arrays of arrays. For example, a matrix would appear as an array of arrays.

C, C++, and Java support jagged arrays but not rectangular arrays. In those languages, a reference to an element of a multidimensioned array uses a separate pair of brackets for each dimension. For example,

```
myArray[3][7]
```

Fortran, Ada, and C# support rectangular arrays. (C# also supports jagged arrays.) In these cases, all subscript expressions in references to elements are placed in a single pair of brackets. For example,

```
myArray[3, 7]
```

6.5.8   Slices

A **slice** of an array is some substructure of that array. For example, if A is a matrix, the first row of A is one possible slice, as are the last row and the first column. It is important to realize that a slice is not a new data type. Rather, it is a mechanism for referencing part of an array as a unit. If arrays cannot be manipulated as units in a language, that language has no use for slices.

Consider the following Fortran 95 declarations:

```
Integer, Dimension (10) :: Vector
Integer, Dimension (3, 3) :: Mat
Integer, Dimension (3, 3, 4) :: Cube
```

Recall that the default lower bound for Fortran arrays is 1. Vector(3:6) is a four-element array with the third through sixth elements of Vector; Mat(:, 2) refers to the second column of Mat; Mat(3, :) refers to the third row of Mat. All of these references can be used as single-dimensioned arrays. References to all array slices are treated as if they were arrays of the remaining dimensionality. Thus a slice reference such as Cube(:, :, 2) could be legally assigned to Mat. Slices can also appear as the destinations of assignment statements. For example, a single-dimensioned array could be assigned to a slice of a matrix. Figure 6.4 shows several slices of Mat and Cube.

More complex slices can also be specified in Fortran 95. For example, Vector(2:10:2) is a five-element array consisting of the second, fourth, sixth, eighth, and tenth elements of Vector. Slices can also have nonregular arrangements of elements of an existing array. For example, Vector((/3, 2, 1, 8/)) is an array of the third, second, first, and eighth elements of Vector.

Perl supports slices of two forms, a list of specific subscripts or a range of subscripts. For example,

```
@list[1..5] = @list2[3, 5, 7, 9, 13];
```

Notice that slice references use array names, not scalar names, because slices are arrays (not scalars).

Python also supports both simple and complex slices of arrays. For example, list[1:20:2] references every other element of list, starting with the subscript 1; list[10:] references all of the elements after the one with subscript 10, including that element; list[:5] references all elements before the one with the subscript 5, excluding that element.

Figure 6.4

Example slices in
Fortran 95

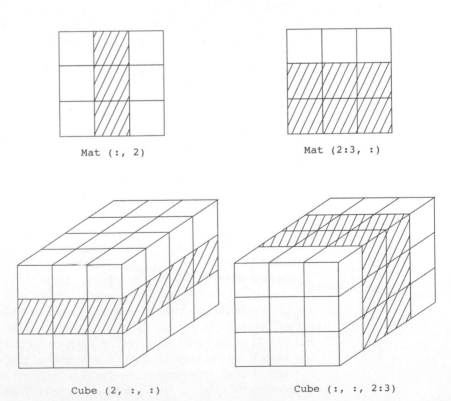

Mat (:, 2)

Mat (2:3, :)

Cube (2, :, :)

Cube (:, :, 2:3)

Ruby supports two kinds of slices, one in which the elements are specified by a starting subscript and an ending subscript, not including the last, and one in which the first given subscript specifies the first element and the second specifies the number of elements in the slice.

In Ada, only highly restricted slices are allowed: those that consist of consecutive elements of a single-dimensioned array. For example, if `List` is an array with index range `(1..100)`, `List(5..10)` is a slice of `List` consisting of the six elements indexed from 5 to 10. As discussed in Section 6.3.2, a slice of a `String` type is a substring reference.

6.5.9   Evaluation

Arrays have been included in virtually all languages. They are simple and have been well developed. The primary advances since their introduction in Fortran I have been the inclusion of all ordinal types as possible subscript types, slices, and, of course, dynamic arrays. Although arrays are essential and fundamental, there is little controversy involved in their design.

6.5.10   Implementation of Array Types

Implementing arrays requires considerably more compile-time effort than does implementing simple types, such as integer. The code to allow accessing of array elements must be generated at compile time. At run time, this code must be executed to produce element addresses. There is no way to precompute the address to be accessed by a reference such as

```
list[k]
```

A single-dimensioned array is a list of adjacent memory cells. Suppose the array `list` is defined to have a subscript range lower bound of 1. The access function for `list` is often of the form

$$\text{address}(\texttt{list[k]}) = \text{address}(\texttt{list[1]}) + (k-1) * \text{element\_size}$$

This simplifies to

$$\text{address}(\texttt{list[k]}) = (\text{address}(\texttt{list[1]}) - \text{element\_size}) + \\ (k * \text{element\_size})$$

where the first operand of the addition is the constant part of the access function, and the second is the variable part.

If the element type is statically bound and the array is statically bound to storage, then the value of the constant part can be computed before run time. Only the addition and multiplication operations remain to be done at run time. If the *base*, or beginning address, of the array is not known until run time, the subtraction must be done when the array is allocated.

The generalization of this access function for an arbitrary lower bound is

$$\text{address}(\texttt{list[k]}) = \text{address}(\texttt{list}[\text{lower\_bound}]) +$$
$$((k - \text{lower\_bound}) * \text{element\_size})$$

The compile-time descriptor for single-dimensioned arrays can have the form shown in Figure 6.5. The descriptor includes information required to construct the access function. If run-time checking of index ranges is not done and the attributes are all static, then only the access function is required during execution; no descriptor is needed. If run-time checking of index ranges is done, then those index ranges may need to be stored in a run-time descriptor. If the subscript ranges of a particular array type are static, the ranges may be incorporated into the code that does the checking, thus eliminating the need for the run-time descriptor. If any of the descriptor entries are dynamically bound, then those parts of the descriptor must be maintained at run time.

Multidimensional arrays are more complex to implement than single-dimensioned arrays, although the extension to more dimensions is straightforward. Hardware memory is linear—it is usually a simple sequence of bytes. So values of data types that have two or more dimensions must be mapped onto the single-dimensioned memory. There are two common ways in which multidimensional arrays can be mapped to one dimension: row major order and column major order. In **row major order**, the elements of the array that have as their first subscript the lower bound value of that subscript are stored first, followed by the elements of the second value of the first subscript, and so forth. If the array is a matrix, it is stored by rows. For example, if the matrix had the values

```
3   4   7
6   2   5
1   3   8
```

it would be stored in row major order as

3, 4, 7, 6, 2, 5, 1, 3, 8

In **column major order**, the elements of an array that have as their last subscript the lower bound value of that subscript are stored first, followed by the

Figure 6.5

Compile-time descriptor for single-dimensioned arrays

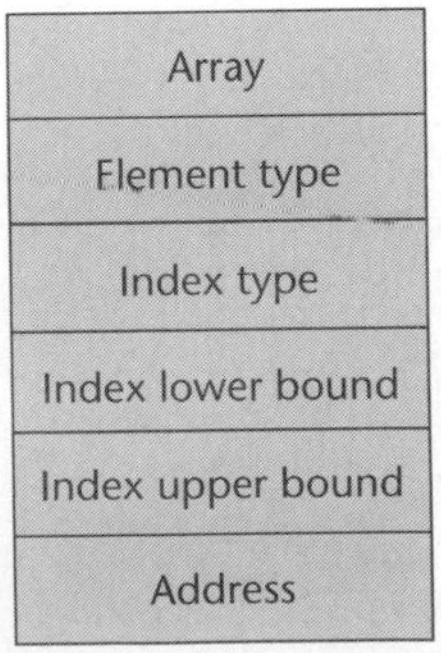

elements of the second value of the last subscript, and so forth. If the array is a matrix, it is stored by columns. If the example matrix were stored in column major order, it would have the following order in memory:

3, 6, 1, 4, 2, 3, 7, 5, 8

Column major order is used in Fortran, but the other languages use row major order.

It is sometimes essential to know the storage order of multidimensional arrays, for example, when such arrays are processed using pointers in C programs. In all cases, sequential access to matrix elements will be faster if they are accessed in the order in which they are stored, because that will result in better memory locality.[5]

We will now discuss the access functions used for languages that have true multidimensional arrays.[6] The access function for a multidimensional array is the mapping of its base address and a set of index values to the address in memory of the element specified by the index values. The access function for two-dimensional arrays stored in row major order can be developed as follows. In general, the address of an element is the base address of the structure plus the element size times the number of elements that precede it in the structure. For a matrix in row major order, the number of elements that precedes an element is the number of rows above the element times the size of a row, plus the number of elements to the left of the element. This is illustrated in Figure 6.6, in which we make the simplifying assumption that subscript lower bounds are all one.

Figure 6.6

The location of the [i,j] element in a matrix

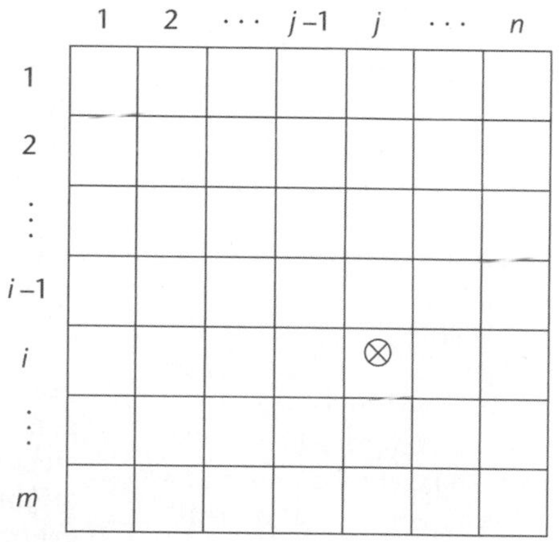

5. Better memory locality means that fewer cache reloads will be required.

6. The C-based languages support multidimensional arrays as arrays of arrays, rather than as true multidimesional arrays.

The Open-Source Movement and Work Life

RASMUS LERDORF

After graduating with a degree in engineering, Rasmus Lerdorf held a number of consulting jobs. Then, in an effort to track those viewing his online resume, he created the first iteration of PHP. These days he is an advocate for the open-source movement and an employee at Yahoo! in Sunnyvale, California.

What are some of your thoughts on the open-source community versus the commercial community? Consider your PHP solution to database connectivity to Web pages versus the corporate options: ASP, Cold Fusion, etc. What about a solution derived by way of open source versus the ideas derived from corporate-led initiatives. What do you get with one that you don't with the other? Whenever you are dealing with a commercial solution you always have to worry about the fact that you are now completely dependent on that particular commercial company. You rarely have much say in which features will be in the next version, or even, sometimes, whether there will be a next version. They also tend to like to tie you completely to their technology, depriving you of the flexibility to switch solutions or easily integrate one solution with another. An obvious benefit of at least some commercial products is that you can buy guaranteed technical support, and there will be someone on the other end of the phone helping you out if you get stuck.

In the open-source world, at least when it comes to PHP, there is a big focus on the community. I didn't write PHP—hundreds of people wrote PHP. We formed a big community of people who all share a common problem. We created a tool to help us solve that problem and we all feel a sense of ownership in it. This is also why you will often see a fanatical devotion to a certain technology in the open-source world, whereas that is somewhat rare when it comes to commercial technologies. It is very easy to join this community and help, in whatever small way, with the development of PHP. People who do this get a very good sense of the technology. They can feel confident that the technology isn't going to disappear on them, that it will solve their current and likely their future problems, and that through this community they can get the technical support they need.

Think of it as going to the store to buy a shrink-wrapped solution to your problem and hoping that it is able to solve most of the problem or sitting down with a thousand of your closest friends, who all have the same problem, and comparing notes and tools. The commercial solution may at times be the better solution, but that strong peer group that inevitably builds itself up around most open-source projects is a very attractive alternative. Commercial companies try to create these communities around their solutions as well and some have done it quite well, but in the end the atmosphere is completely different from a healthy open-source community, and you really can't compare the two. As the tools that the community builds mature, they start to rival or surpass any already existing commercial tool. In the case of PHP, we actually preceded both ASP and Cold Fusion, so in the early days we weren't really chasing any particular commercial tool; we were simply trying to figure out how to solve the Web problem.

Can you share some thoughts on working alone to develop the solutions that you needed for your personal home page back in 1995 versus working on some sort of distributed team to take your original idea and make it into something used by over a million Web sites? I wanted to get away from having to write the same CGI code in C over and over again. Collecting common functionality in a C library and putting a simple macro-replacement parser on top of it so I could put special tags in my HTML to trigger my various routines written in C seemed like an obvious solution. So my main early requirement was speed of development and deployment of dynamic Web pages, and to get that I needed a simple framework from creating the business logic in C and accessing it from HTML.

> **❝ The [open-source] community has contributed everything to PHP. Without it there would be no PHP. ❞**

I probably spent a good 18 months on the initial code before it caught anybody's attention. This was around 1994, so it was quite a bit before there was any sort of buzz around open-source or free-software development. I also think the barrier of entry was quite a bit lower back then. There weren't a lot of free tools that addressed the Web problem, but I still had to get PHP to the point where someone would look at it and determine that it solved enough of their problem that it was easier to use it and perhaps extend it a little bit than it was for them to start from scratch and solve the problem themselves. That is the barrier any successful open-source project has had to clear at some point In its history. Taking someone else's solution, understanding it, and applying it to your own problem is a big investment in terms of time and energy, and you are never sure whether it is going to work. Before an open-source project has proven itself, that barrier is a tough one, and if you ask anybody who has started a successful open-source project, you are likely to find that they had a period of their lives where they devoted absolutely every spare second of free time to it. That was true for me in 1994–1995 with PHP.

Do you remember the first addition you received from someone else? What was the need or requirement? I got a number of small bug fixes, but the first early large contributions were database extensions for Sybase and Oracle. I had written the original database connectivity code against a free database out of Australia called mSQL. I didn't use Sybase or Oracle, but someone out there needed to talk to those databases so they wrote the code and contributed it back.

Share what PHP looked like and what it did when you first posted it. It was a set of CGI programs loosely related that solved common problems for people's personal home pages. It had a hit counter, which also showed the IP or hostname of the person who last browsed the page. It could also log hits to an SQL database and included some tools to create pretty reports of this traffic. So the early focus was on the tools, not on the framework/language these tools were written in.

What has the open-source movement contributed? What does PHP look like today in comparison? The community has contributed everything to PHP. Without it there would be no PHP. PHP has grown to be a general-purpose Web scripting language that can talk to just about anything you can imagine and is in use on about 30 percent of all the domains on the Web. It is powering the tiniest family Web page that gets hit maybe twice a month, to some of the busiest sites in the world.

ON WORKING AND YEARS IN THE BUSINESS

You've had a varied career, from big companies to dot-coms and personal consulting: How do you decide what you are going to do next? I look for fun and challenging projects and people I think I will enjoy working with. Sometimes you just have to take a leap of faith as well. I went to Brazil initially purely because I was working in Calgary in the winter and it was too cold. I saw some Mickey Rourke movie set in Rio and wondered what I was doing in the frozen Arctic when surely they must have computers in Brazil that needed programming.

How do you decide when to move on? When things stop being fun, I quit. If I wake up every morning dreading going to work, or if I sit each and every day watching the clock, wondering when I have put in enough hours to go home, I know it is time to quit. There will always be short periods where you would rather be elsewhere than at work, but if that feeling persists, life is too short to spend it in frustration or boredom. If you ever find yourself calculating what you

(continued)

277

make per second, or how much the company paid you to walk to the washroom and back, quit!

Do you have some sort of criteria or rules for picking your next assignment? None whatsoever. I have jumped around quite a bit, but I never have any sort of preconceived notion that I will only stay at a company for X months or years. Most often the job itself dictates how long I stay. With some jobs I was brought in to solve a particular problem. After solving the problem, they would probably have preferred it if I had stuck around to help them maintain and support the solution, but by then the challenge was gone and I needed something new. Of course, now that I have a small baby at home, this may change the priorities a bit. Perhaps a cozy job without the stress that goes along with the challenges isn't such a bad idea. I'll let you know in a couple of years.

To get an actual address value, the number of elements that precede the desired element must be multiplied by the element size. Now, the access function can be written as

location(a[i,j]) = address of a[1, 1] +
$\qquad$ ((((number of rows above the *ith* row) * (size of a row))
$\qquad$ + (number of elements left of the *jth* column)) *
$\qquad$ element size)

Because the number of rows above the *ith* row is (i - 1) and the number of elements to the left of the *jth* column is (j - 1), we have

location(a[i, j]) = address of a[1, 1] + ((((i - 1) * n) + (j - 1)) *
$\qquad$ element_size)

where *n* is the number of elements per row. This can be rearranged to the form

location(a[i, j]) = address of a[1, 1] – ((n + 1) * element_size) +
$\qquad$ ((i * n + j) * element_size)

where the first two terms are the constant part and the last is the variable part.

$\qquad$ The generalization to arbitrary lower bounds results in the following access function:

location(a[i, j]) = address of a[row_lb, col_lb] +
$\qquad$ (((i – row_lb) * n) + (j – col_lb)) * element_size

where row_lb is the lower bound of the rows and col_lb is the lower bound of the columns. This can be rearranged to the form

location(a[i, j]) = address of a[row_lb, col_lb] –
$\qquad$ (((row_lb * n) + col_lb) * element_size) +
$\qquad$ (((i * n) + j) * element_size)

where the first two terms are the constant part and the last is the variable part. This can be generalized relatively easily to an arbitrary number of dimensions.

$\qquad$ For each dimension of an array, one add and one multiply instruction are required for the access function. Therefore, accesses to elements of arrays with several subscripts are costly. The compile-time descriptor for a multidimensional array is shown in Figure 6.7.

$\qquad$ Slices add another layer of complexity to storage-mapping functions. To illustrate, consider a program in which there is a matrix and an array, and a column of the matrix is assigned to the array, as in

Figure 6.7

A compile-time
descriptor for a
multidimensional array

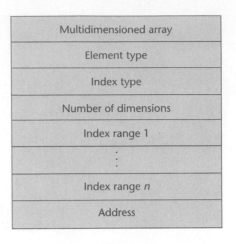

| Multidimensioned array |
| Element type |
| Index type |
| Number of dimensions |
| Index range 1 |
| ⋮ |
| Index range *n* |
| Address |

```
Integer, Dimension (10, 5) :: Mat
Integer, Dimension (10) :: List
...
List = Mat (1:3, 3)
```

The storage-mapping function for the matrix, `Mat`, assuming row major order and an element size of 1, is

$$\text{location}(\texttt{Mat[i, j]}) = \text{address of } \texttt{Mat[1,1]} + ((i-1) * 5 + (j-1)) * 1$$
$$= (\text{address of } \texttt{Mat[1,1]} - 6) + ((5 * i) + j)$$

The storage-mapping function for the slice reference `Mat[1:3, 3]` is

$$\text{location}(\texttt{Mat[i, 3]}) = \text{address of } \texttt{Mat[1,1]} + ((i-1) * 5 + (3-1)) * 1$$
$$= (\text{address of } \texttt{Mat[1,1]} - 3) + (5 * i)$$

Notice that this mapping has exactly the same form as any other one-dimensional array access function, although the form of the constant part is different because the basic array is two-dimensional.

The elements of `Mat` that are to be assigned to `List` are found by letting `i` take on the values in the specified subscript range (`1:3`) of the first dimension of `Mat`.

6.6 Associative Arrays

An **associative array** is an unordered collection of data elements that are indexed by an equal number of values called **keys.** In the case of non-associative arrays, the indices never need to be stored (because of their regularity). In an associative array, however, the user-defined keys must be stored in the structure. So each element of an associative array is in fact a pair of entities, a key and a value. We use Perl's design of associative arrays to illustrate this data structure. Associative arrays are also supported directly by Python and Ruby, and by the standard class libraries of Java, C++, and C#.

The only design issue that is specific for associative arrays is the form of references to their elements.

6.6.1 Structure and Operations

In Perl, associative arrays are often called **hashes,** because in the implementation their elements are stored and retrieved with hash functions. The namespace for Perl hashes is distinct: Every hash variable must begin with a percent sign (%). Hashes can be set to literal values with the assignment statement, as in

```
%salaries = ("Gary" => 75000, "Perry" => 57000,
             "Mary" => 55750, "Cedric" => 47850);
```

Individual element values are referenced using notation that is unique to Perl. The key value is placed in braces and the hash name is replaced by a scalar variable name that is the same except for the first character. As is the case with Perl arrays, although hashes are not scalars, the value parts of hash elements are scalars, so references to hash element values use scalar names. Recall that scalar variable names begin with dollar signs ($). For example,

```
$salaries{"Perry"} = 58850;
```

A new element is added using the same statement form. An element can be removed from the hash with the **delete** operator, as in

```
delete $salaries{"Gary"};
```

The entire hash can be emptied by assigning the empty literal to it, as in

```
@salaries = ();
```

The size of a Perl hash is dynamic: It grows when a new element is added and shrinks when an element is deleted, and also when it is emptied by assignment of the empty literal. The `exists` operator returns true or false, depending on whether its operand key is an element in the hash. For example,

```
if (exists $salaries{"Shelly"}) . . .
```

The `keys` operator, when applied to a hash, returns an array of the keys of the hash. The `values` operator does the same for the values of the hash. The `each` operator iterates over the element pairs of a hash.

Python's associative arrays, which are called dictionaries, are similar to those of Perl, except the values are references to objects. The associative arrays supported by Ruby are similar to those of Python, except that the keys can be any object, rather than just strings.

PHP's arrays are both normal arrays and associative arrays. They can be treated as either. The language provides functions that allow both indexed and hashed access to elements. An array can have elements that are created with simple numeric indices and elements that are created with string hash keys.

A hash is much better than an array if searches of the elements are required, because the implicit hashing operation used to access hash elements is very efficient. Furthermore, hashes are ideal when the data to be stored is paired, as with employee names and their salaries. On the other hand, if every element of a list must be processed, it is more efficient to use an array.

6.6.2 Implementing Associative Arrays

The implementation of Perl's associative arrays is optimized for fast lookups, but it also provides relatively fast reorganization when array growth requires it. A 32-bit hash value is computed for each entry and is stored with the entry, although an associative array initially uses only a small part of the hash value. When an associative array must be expanded beyond its initial size, the hash function need not be changed; rather, more bits of the hash value are used. Only half of the entries must be moved when this happens. So, although expansion of an associative array is not free, it is not as costly as might be expected.

The elements in PHP's arrays are stored in a linked list, in which the nodes appear in the order in which they were created. The links are used to support iterative access to elements through the `current` and `next` functions. A hash function is used to provide access to all elements through their keys.

6.7 Record Types

A **record** is a possibly heterogeneous aggregate of data elements in which the individual elements are identified by names.

There is frequently a need in programs to model collections of data that are not homogeneous. For example, information about a college student might include name, student number, grade point average, and so forth. A data type for such a collection might use a character string for the name, an integer for the student number, a floating-point for the grade point average, and so forth. Records are designed for this kind of need.

Records have been part of all of the most popular programming languages, except pre-90 versions of Fortran, since the early 1960s, when they were introduced by COBOL.

In C, C++, and C#, records are supported with the **struct** data type. In C++, structures are a minor variation on classes. In C#, structures are also related to classes, but are also quite different. C# structures are stack-allocated value types, as opposed to class objects, which are heap-allocated reference types. Structures in C++ and C# are normally used as encapsulation structures, rather than data structures. They are further discussed in this capacity in Chapter 11.

In Python and Ruby, records can be implemented as hashes, which themselves can be elements of arrays.

The following sections describe how records are declared or defined, how references to fields within records are made, and the common record operations.

The design issues that are specific to records are:

- What is the syntactic form of references to fields?
- Are elliptical references allowed?

6.7.1 Definitions of Records

The fundamental difference between a record and an array is the homogeneity of elements in arrays versus the possible heterogeneity of elements in records. One result of this difference is that record elements, or **fields,** are not usually referenced by indices. Instead, the fields are named with identifiers, and references to the fields are made using these identifiers. One more important difference between arrays and records is that records in some languages are allowed to include unions, which are discussed in Section 6.8.

The COBOL form of a record declaration, which is part of the data division of a COBOL program, is illustrated in the following example:

```
01   EMPLOYEE-RECORD.
     02   EMPLOYEE-NAME.
          05   FIRST    PICTURE IS X(20).
          05   MIDDLE   PICTURE IS X(10).
          05   LAST     PICTURE IS X(20).
     02   HOURLY-RATE PICTURE IS 99V99.
```

The EMPLOYEE-RECORD record consists of the EMPLOYEE-NAME record and the HOURLY-RATE field. The numerals 01, 02, and 05 that begin the lines of the record declaration are **level numbers,** which indicate by their relative values the hierarchical structure of the record. Any line that is followed by a line with a higher-level number is itself a record. The PICTURE clauses show the formats of the field storage locations, with X(20) specifying 20 alphanumeric characters and 99V99 specifying four decimal digits with the decimal point in the middle.

Ada uses a different syntax for records; rather than using the level numbers of COBOL, record structures are indicated in an orthogonal way by simply nesting record declarations inside record declarations. In Ada, records cannot be anonymous—they must be named types. Consider the following Ada declaration:

```
type Employee_Name_Type is record
   First : String (1..20);
   Middle : String (1..10);
   Last : String (1..20);
end record;
type Employee_Record_Type is record
   Employee_Name: Employee_Name_Type;
   Hourly_Rate: Float;
end record;
Employee_Record: Employee_Record_Type;
```

Fortran 95 record declarations require that any nested records be previously defined as types. So, for the example employee record, the employee name record would need to be defined first, and then the employee record would simply name it as the type of its first field.

In Java and C#, records can be defined as data classes, with nested records defined as nested classes. Data members of such classes serve as the record fields.

6.7.2   References to Record Fields

References to the individual fields of records are syntactically specified by several different methods, two of which name the desired field and its enclosing records. COBOL field references have the form

field_name OF record_name_1 OF ... OF record_name_n

where the first record named is the smallest or innermost record that contains the field. The next record name in the sequence is that of the record that contains the previous record, and so forth. For example, the MIDDLE field in the COBOL record example above can be referenced with

MIDDLE OF EMPLOYEE-NAME OF EMPLOYEE-RECORD

Most of the other languages use **dot notation** for field references, where the components of the reference are connected with periods. Names in dot notation have the opposite order of COBOL references: They use the name of the largest enclosing record first and the field name last. For example, the following is a reference to the field Middle in the earlier Ada record example:

Employee_Record.Employee_Name.Middle

C and C++ use this same syntax for referencing the members of their structures. Fortran 95 field references also have this form, except that percent signs (%) are used instead of periods.

A **fully qualified reference** to a record field is one in which all intermediate record names, from the largest enclosing record to the specific field, are named in the reference. Both the COBOL and the Ada example field references above are fully qualified. As an alternative to fully qualified references, COBOL allows **elliptical references** to record fields. In an elliptical reference, the field is named, but any or all of the enclosing record names can be omitted, as long as the resulting reference is unambiguous in the referencing environment. For example, FIRST, FIRST OF EMPLOYEE-NAME, and FIRST OF EMPLOYEE-RECORD are elliptical references to the employee's first name in the COBOL record declared above. Although elliptical references are a programmer convenience, they require a compiler to have elaborate data structures and procedures in order to correctly identify the referenced field. They are also somewhat detrimental to readability.

6.7.3 Operations on Records

Assignment is a common record operation. In most cases, the types of the two sides must be identical. Ada allows record comparisons for equality and inequality. Also, Ada records can be initialized with aggregate literals.

COBOL provides the MOVE CORRESPONDING statement for moving records. This statement copies a field of the specified source record to the destination record only if the destination record has a field with the same name. This is frequently a useful operation in data-processing applications, where input records are moved to output files after some modifications. Because input records often have many fields that have the same names and purposes as fields in output records, but not necessarily in the same order, the MOVE CORRESPONDING operation can save many statements. For example, consider the following COBOL structures:

```
01   INPUT-RECORD.
     02   NAME.
          05   LAST        PICTURE IS X(20).
          05   MIDDLE      PICTURE IS X(15).
          05   FIRST       PICTURE IS X(20).
     02 EMPLOYEE-NUMBER    PICTURE IS 9(10).
     02 HOURS-WORKED       PICTURE IS 99.

01   OUTPUT-RECORD.
     02   NAME.
          05   FIRST       PICTURE IS X(20).
          05   MIDDLE      PICTURE IS X(15).
          05   LAST        PICTURE IS X(20).
```

```
02   EMPLOYEE-NUMBER PICTURE IS 9(10).
02   GROSS-PAY       PICTURE IS 999V99.
02   NET-PAY         PICTURE IS 999V99.
```

The statement

```
MOVE CORRESPONDING INPUT-RECORD TO OUTPUT-RECORD.
```

copies the FIRST, MIDDLE, LAST, and EMPLOYEE-NUMBER fields from the input record to the output record.

6.7.4 Evaluation

Records are frequently valuable data types in programming languages. The design of record types is straightforward, and their use is safe. The only aspect of records that is not clearly readable is the elliptical references allowed by COBOL.

Records and arrays are closely related structural forms, and it is therefore interesting to compare them. Arrays are used when all the data values have the same type and are processed in the same way. This processing is easily done when there is a systematic way of sequencing through the structure. Such processing is well supported by using dynamic subscripting as the addressing method.

Records are used when the collection of data values is heterogeneous and the different fields are not processed in the same way. Also, the fields of a record often need not be processed in a particular order. Field names are like literal, or constant, subscripts. Because they are static, they provide very efficient access to the fields. Dynamic subscripts could be used to access record fields, but it would disallow type checking and would also be slower.

Records and arrays represent thoughtful and efficient methods of fulfilling two separate but related applications of data structures.

6.7.5 Implementation of Record Types

The fields of records are stored in adjacent memory locations. But because the sizes of the fields are not necessarily the same, the access method used for arrays is not used for records. Instead, the offset address, relative to the beginning of the record, is associated with each field. Field accesses are all handled using these offsets. The compile-time descriptor for a record has the general form shown in Figure 6.8. Run-time descriptors for records are unnecessary.

6.8 Union Types

A **union** is a type that may store different type values at different times during program execution. As an example of the need for a union type, consider a

Figure 6.8

A compile-time
descriptor for a record

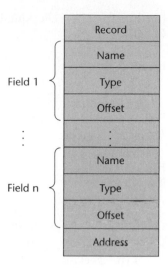

table of constants for a compiler, which is used to store the constants found in a program being compiled. One field of each table entry is for the value of the constant. Suppose that for a particular language being compiled, the types of constants were integer, floating point, and Boolean. In terms of table management, it would be convenient if the same location, a table field, could store a value of any of these three types. Then all constant values could be addressed in the same way. The type of such a location is, in a sense, the union of the three value types it can store.

6.8.1 Design Issues

The problem of type checking union types, which was discussed in Chapter 5, leads to one major design issue. The other fundamental question is how to syntactically represent a union. In some designs, unions are confined to be parts of record structures, but in others they are not. So the primary design issues that are particular to union types are the following:

- Should type checking be required? Note that any such type checking must be dynamic.
- Should unions be embedded in records?

6.8.2 Discriminated versus Free Unions

Fortran, C, and C++ provide union constructs in which there is no language support for type checking. In Fortran, the `Equivalence` statement is used to specify unions; in C and C++, it is the **union** construct. The unions in these languages are called **free unions,** because programmers are allowed complete freedom from type checking in their use. For example, consider the following C union:

```
union flexType {
   int intEl;
   float floatEl;
union flexType el1;
float x ;
...
el1.intEl = 27;
x = el1.floatEl;
```

This last assignment is not type checked, because the system cannot determine the current type of the current value of el1, so it assigns the bit string representation of 27 to the **float** variable x, which of course is nonsense.

Type checking of unions requires that each union construct include a type indicator. Such an indicator is called a **tag,** or **discriminant,** and a union with a discriminant is called a **discriminated union.** The first language to provide discriminated unions was ALGOL 68. They are now supported by Ada.

6.8.3   Ada Union Types

The Ada design for discriminated unions, which is based on that of its predecessor language, Pascal, allows the user to specify variables of a variant record type that will store only one of the possible type values in the variant. In this way, the user can tell the system when the type checking can be static. Such a restricted variable is called a **constrained variant variable.**

The tag of a constrained variant variable is treated like a named constant. Unconstrained variant records in Ada allow the values of their variants to change types during execution. However, the type of the variant can be changed only by assigning the entire record, including the discriminant. This disallows inconsistent records because if the newly assigned record is a constant data aggregate, the value of the tag and the type of the variant can be statically checked for consistency.[7] If the assigned value is a variable, its consistency was guaranteed when it was assigned, so the new value of the variable now being assigned is sure to be consistent.

The following example shows an Ada variant record:

```
type Shape is (Circle, Triangle, Rectangle);
type Colors is (Red, Green, Blue);
type Figure (Form : Shape) is
  record
```

---

7. Consistency here means that if the tag indicates the current type of the union is Integer, the current value of the union is in fact Integer.

```
      Filled : Boolean;
      Color : Colors;
      case Form is
        when Circle =>
          Diameter : Float;
        when Triangle =>
          Left_Side : Integer;
          Right_Side : Integer;
          Angle : Float;
        when Rectangle =>
          Side_1 : Integer;
          Side_2 : Integer;
      end case;
  end record;
```

The structure of this variant record is shown in Figure 6.9. The following two statements declare variables of type Figure:

```
Figure_1 : Figure;
Figure_2 : Figure(Form => Triangle);
```

Figure_1 is declared to be an unconstrained variant record that has no initial value. Its type can change by assignment of a whole record, including the discriminant, as in the following:

```
Figure_1 := (Filled => True,
             Color => Blue,
             Form => Rectangle,
             Side_1 => 12,
             Side_2 => 3);
```

The right side of this assignment is a data aggregate.

The variable Figure_2 declared is constrained to be a triangle and cannot be changed to another variant.

This form of discriminated union is safe, because it always allows type checking, although the references to fields in unconstrained variants must be dynamically checked. For example, suppose we have the following statement:

```
if(Figure_1.Diameter > 3.0) ...
```

The run-time system would need to check Figure_1 to determine whether its Form tag was Circle. If it was not, it would be a type error to reference its Diameter.

Figure 6.9

A discriminated union of three shape variables (assume all variables are the same size)

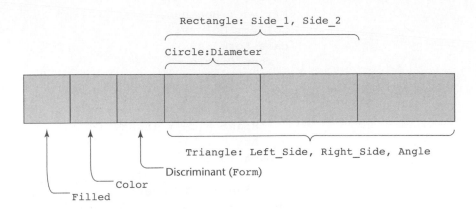

6.8.4 Evaluation

Unions are potentially unsafe constructs in some languages. They are one of the reasons why Fortran, C, and C++ are not strongly typed: These languages do not allow type checking of references to their unions. On the other hand, unions can be safely used, as in their design in Ada. In most other languages, unions must be used with care.

Neither Java nor C# include unions, which may be reflective of the growing concern for safety in programming languages.

6.8.5 Implementation of Union Types

Unions are implemented by simply using the same address for every possible variant. Sufficient storage for the largest variant is allocated. In the case of constrained variants in the Ada language, the exact amount of storage can be used because there is no variation. The tag of a discriminated union is stored with the variant in a recordlike structure.

At compile time, the complete description of each variant must be stored. This can be done by associating a case table with the tag entry in the descriptor. The case table has an entry for each variant, which points to a descriptor for that particular variant. To illustrate this arrangement, consider the following Ada example:

```
type Node (Tag : Boolean) is
  record
  case Tag is
      when True => Count : Integer;
      when False => Sum : Float;
  end case;
end record;
```

The descriptor for this type could have the form shown in Figure 6.10.

Figure 6.10

A compile-time descriptor for a discriminated union

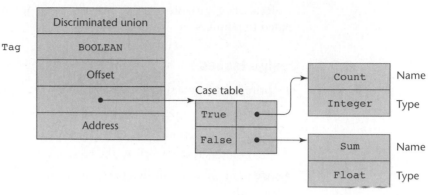

6.9 Pointer and Reference Types

A **pointer** type is one in which the variables have a range of values that consists of memory addresses and a special value, **nil.** The value nil is not a valid address and is used to indicate that a pointer cannot currently be used to reference a memory cell.

Pointers have been designed for two distinct kinds of uses. First, pointers provide some of the power of indirect addressing, which is heavily used in assembly language programming. Second, pointers provide a way to manage dynamic storage. A pointer can be used to access a location in the area where storage is dynamically allocated, which is usually called a **heap.**

Variables that are dynamically allocated from the heap are called **heap-dynamic variables.** They often do not have identifiers associated with them and thus can be referenced only by pointer or reference type variables. Variables without names are called **anonymous variables.** It is in this latter application area of pointers that the most important design issues arise.

Pointers, unlike arrays and records, are not structured types, although they are defined using a type operator (* in C and C++, and **access** in Ada). Furthermore, they are also different from scalar variables because they are most often used to reference some other variable, rather than being used to store data of some sort. These two categories of variables are called **reference types** and **value types,** respectively.

Both kinds of uses of pointers add writability to a language. For example, suppose it is necessary to implement a dynamic structure like a binary tree in a language like Fortran 77, which does not have pointers. This would require the programmer to provide and maintain a pool of available tree nodes, which would probably be implemented in parallel arrays. Also, because of the lack of dynamic storage in Fortran 77, it would be necessary for the programmer to guess the maximum number of required nodes. This is clearly an awkward and error-prone way to deal with binary trees.

Reference variables, which are discussed in Section 6.9.7, are closely related to pointers.

6.9.1 Design Issues

The primary design issues particular to pointers are the following:

- What are the scope and lifetime of a pointer variable?
- What is the lifetime of a heap-dynamic variable?
- Are pointers restricted as to the type of value to which they can point?
- Are pointers used for dynamic storage management, indirect addressing, or both?
- Should the language support pointer types, reference types, or both?

6.9.2 Pointer Operations

Languages that provide a pointer type usually include two fundamental pointer operations: assignment and dereferencing. The first operation sets a pointer variable's value to some useful address. If pointer variables are used only to manage dynamic storage, the allocation mechanism, whether by operator or built-in subprogram, serves to initialize the pointer variable. If pointers are used for indirect addressing to variables that are not heap-dynamic, then there must be an explicit operator or built-in subprogram for fetching the address of a variable, which can then be assigned to the pointer variable.

An occurrence of a pointer variable in an expression can be interpreted in two distinct ways. First, it could be interpreted as a reference to the contents of the memory cell to which it is bound, which in the case of a pointer is an address. This is exactly how a nonpointer variable in an expression would be interpreted, although in that case its value likely would not be an address. However, the pointer could also be interpreted as a reference to the value in the memory cell pointed to by the memory cell to which the pointer variable is bound. In this case, the pointer is interpreted as an indirect reference. The former case is a normal pointer reference; the latter is the result of **dereferencing** the pointer. Dereferencing, which takes a reference through one level of indirection, is the second fundamental pointer operation.

Dereferencing of pointers can be either explicit or implicit. In Fortran 95 it is implicit, but in many other contemporary languages, it occurs only when explicitly specified. In C++, it is explicitly specified with the asterisk (*) as a prefix unary operator. Consider the following example of dereferencing: If `ptr` is a pointer variable with the value 7080 and the cell whose address is 7080 has the value 206, then the assignment

```
j = *ptr
```

sets j to 206. This process is shown in Figure 6.11.

Figure 6.11

The assignment
operation j = *ptr

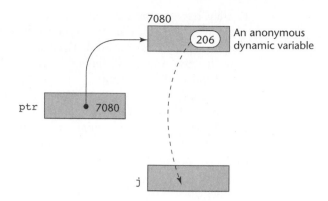

When pointers point to records, the syntax of the references to the fields of these records varies among languages. In C and C++, there are two ways a pointer to a record can be used to reference a field in that record. If a pointer variable p points to a record with a field named age, (*p).age can be used to refer to that field. The operator ->, when used between a pointer to a record and a field of that record, combines dereferencing and field reference. For example, the expression p -> age is equivalent to (*p).age. In Ada, p.age can be used, because such uses of pointers are implicitly dereferenced.

Languages that provide pointers for the management of a heap must include an explicit allocation operation. Allocation is sometimes specified with a subprogram, such as malloc in C. In languages that support object-oriented programming, allocation of heap objects is often specified with the **new** operator. C++, which does not provide implicit deallocation, uses **delete** as its deallocation operator.

6.9.3   Pointer Problems

The first high-level programming language to include pointer variables was PL/I, in which pointers could be used to refer to both heap-dynamic variables and other program variables. The pointers of PL/I were highly flexible, but their use could lead to several kinds of programming errors. Some of the problems of PL/I pointers are also present in the pointers of subsequent languages. Some recent languages, such as Java, have replaced pointers completely with reference types, which, along with implicit deallocation, minimize the primary problems with pointers. A reference type is really only a pointer with restricted operations. Reference types are discussed in Section 6.9.7.

6.9.3.1 Dangling Pointers

A **dangling pointer,** or **dangling reference,** is a pointer that contains the address of a heap-dynamic variable that has been deallocated. Dangling pointers are dangerous for several reasons. First, the location being pointed to may have been reallocated to some new heap-dynamic variable. If the new variable is not the same type as the old one, type checks of uses of the dangling pointer are invalid. Even if the new dynamic variable is the same type, its new value will have no relationship to the old pointer's dereferenced value. Furthermore, if the dangling pointer is used to change the heap-dynamic variable, the value of the new heap-dynamic variable will be destroyed. Finally, it is possible that the location now is being temporarily used by the storage management system, possibly as a pointer in a chain of available blocks of storage, thereby allowing a change to the location to cause the storage manager to fail.

The following sequence of operations creates a dangling pointer in many languages:

1. Pointer p1 is set to point at a new heap-dynamic variable.

2. Pointer p2 is assigned p1's value.

3. The heap-dynamic variable pointed to by p1 is explicitly deallocated (possibly setting p1 to nil), but p2 is not changed by the operation. p2 is now a dangling pointer. If the deallocation operation did not change p1, both p1 and p2 would be dangling.

For example, in C++ we could have

```
int * arrayPtr1;
int * arrayPtr2 = new int[100];
arrayPtr1 = arrayPtr2;
delete [] arrayPtr2;
// Now, arrayPtr1 is dangling, because the heap storage
// to which it was pointing has been deallocated.
```

In C++, both arrayPtr1 and arrayPtr2 are now dangling pointers, because the C++ **delete** operator has no effect on the value of its operand pointer. In C++, it is common (and safe) to follow a **delete** operator with an assignment of zero, which represents null, to the pointer whose pointed-to value has been deallocated.

Notice that the explicit deallocation of dynamic variables is the cause of dangling pointers.

6.9.3.2 Lost Heap-Dynamic Variables

A **lost heap-dynamic variable** is an allocated heap-dynamic variable that is no longer accessible to the user program. Such variables are often called **garbage,** because they are not useful for their original purpose, and they also cannot be reallocated for some new use in the program. Lost heap-dynamic variables are most often created by the following sequence of operations:

1. Pointer p1 is set to point to a newly created heap-dynamic variable.

2. p1 is later set to point to another newly created heap-dynamic variable.

The first heap-dynamic variable is now inaccessible, or lost. Sometimes this is called **memory leakage.** Memory leakage is a problem, regardless of whether the language uses implicit or explicit deallocation. In the following sections, we investigate how language designers have dealt with the problems of dangling pointers and lost heap-dynamic variables.

6.9.4   Pointers in Ada

Ada's pointers are called **access** types. The dangling-pointer problem is partially alleviated by Ada's design, at least in theory. A heap-dynamic variable may be (at the implementor's option) implicitly deallocated at the end of the scope of its pointer type, thus dramatically lessening the need for explicit deallocation. However, few if any Ada compilers implement this form of garbage collection, so the advantage is nearly always in theory only. Because heap-dynamic variables can be accessed by variables of only one type, when the end of the scope of that type declaration is reached, no pointers can be left pointing at the dynamic variable. This diminishes the problem, because improperly implemented explicit deallocation is the major source of dangling pointers. Unfortunately, the Ada language also has an explicit deallocator, `Unchecked_Deallocation`. Its name is meant to discourage its use, or at least warn the user of its potential problems. When used, `Unchecked_Deallocation`, can cause dangling pointers.

The lost heap-dynamic variable problem is not eliminated by Ada's design of pointers.

6.9.5   Pointers in C and C++

history note

Pascal included an explicit deallocate operator: `dispose`. Because of the problem of dangling pointers caused by dispose, some Pascal implementations simply ignored dispose when it appeared in a program. Although this effectively prevents dangling pointers, it also disallows the reuse of heap storage that the program no longer needs. Recall that Pascal was designed as a teaching language, rather than an industrial tool.

In C and C++, pointers can be used in the same ways as addresses are used in assembly languages. This means they are extremely flexible but must be used with great care. This design offers no solutions to the dangling pointer or lost heap-dynamic variable problems. However, the fact that pointer arithmetic is possible in C and C++ makes their pointers more interesting than those of the other programming languages.

Unlike the pointers of Ada, which can point only into the heap, C and C++ pointers can point at any variable, regardless of where it is allocated. In fact, they can point anywhere in memory, whether there is a variable there or not, which is one of the dangers of such pointers.

In C and C++, the asterisk (*) denotes the dereferencing operation, and the ampersand (&) denotes the operator for producing the address of a variable. For example, consider the following code:

```
int *ptr;
int count, init;
```

```
...
ptr = &init;
count = *ptr;
```

The assignment to the variable `ptr` sets it to the address of `init`. The first assignment to `count` dereferences `ptr` to produce the value at `init`, which is then assigned to `count`. So the effect of the first two assignment statements is to assign the value of `init` to `count`. Notice that the declaration of a pointer specifies its domain type.

Notice that the two assignment statements above are equivalent in their effect on `count` to the single assignment

```
count = init;
```

Pointers can be assigned the address value of any variable of the correct domain type, or they can be assigned the constant zero, which is used for nil.

Pointer arithmetic is also possible in some restricted forms. For example, if `ptr` is a pointer variable that is declared to point at some variable of some data type, then

```
ptr + index
```

is a legal expression. The semantics of such an expression is as follows. Instead of simply adding the value of `index` to `ptr`, the value of `index` is first scaled by the size of the memory cell (in memory units) to which `ptr` is pointing (its base type). For example, if `ptr` points to a memory cell for a type that is four memory units in size, then `index` is multiplied by 4, and the result is added to `ptr`. The primary purpose of this sort of address arithmetic is array manipulation. The following discussion is related to single-dimensioned arrays only.

In C and C++, all arrays use zero as the lower bound of their subscript ranges, and array names without subscripts always refer to the address of the first element. In fact, an array name without a subscript is treated exactly like a pointer, except that it is a constant and therefore cannot be assigned. Consider the following declarations:

```
int list [10];
int *ptr;
```

Consider the assignment

```
ptr = list;
```

which assigns the address of `list[0]` to `ptr`, because an array name without a subscript is interpreted as the base address of the array. Given this assignment, the following are true:

- `*(ptr + 1)` is equivalent to `list[1]`

- *(ptr + index) is equivalent to list[index]
- ptr[index] is equivalent to list[index]

It is clear from these statements that the pointer operations include the same scaling that is used in indexing operations. Furthermore, pointers to arrays can be indexed as if they were array names.

Pointers in C and C++ can point to functions. This feature is used to pass functions as parameters to other functions. Pointers are also used for parameter passing, as discussed in Chapter 9.

C and C++ include pointers of type **void** *, which can point at values of any type. They are in effect generic pointers. However, type checking is not a problem with **void** * pointers, because they cannot be dereferenced. One common use of **void** * pointers is as the types of parameters of functions that operate on memory. For example, suppose we wanted a function to move a sequence of bytes of data from one place in memory to another. It would be most general if it could be passed two pointers of any type. This would be legal if the corresponding formal parameters in the function were **void** * type. The function could then convert them to **char** * type and do the operation, regardless of what type pointers were sent as actual parameters.

6.9.6 Reference Types

A **reference type** variable is similar to a pointer, with one important and fundamental difference: A pointer refers to an address in memory, while a reference refers to an object or a value in memory. As a result, although it is natural to perform arithmetic on addresses, it is not sensible to do arithmetic on references.

C++ includes a special kind of reference type that is used primarily for the formal parameters in function definitions. A C++ reference type variable is a constant pointer that is always implicitly dereferenced. Because a C++ reference type variable is a constant, it must be initialized with the address of some variable in its definition, and after initialization a reference type variable can never be set to reference any other variable. The implicit dereference of course prevents assignment to the address value of a reference variable.

Reference type variables are specified in definitions by preceding their names with ampersands (&). For example,

```
int result = 0;
int &ref_result = result;
...
ref_result = 100;
```

In this code segment, result and ref_result are aliases.

When used as formal parameters in function definitions, C++ reference types provide for two-way communication between the caller function and the called function. This is not possible with nonpointer primitive parameter types, because C++ parameters are passed by value. Passing a pointer as a parameter accomplishes the same two-way communication, but pointer formal parameters require explicit dereferencing, making the code less readable and less safe. Reference parameters are referenced in the called function exactly as are other parameters. The calling function need not specify that a parameter whose corresponding formal parameter is a reference type is anything unusual. The compiler passes addresses, rather than values, to reference parameters.

In Java, reference variables are extended from their C++ form to one that allows them to replace pointers entirely. In their quest for increased safety over C++, the designers of Java removed C++-style pointers altogether. Unlike C++ reference variables, Java reference variables can be assigned to refer to different class instances; that is, they are not constants. All Java class instances are referenced by reference variables. That is, in fact, the only use of reference variables in Java. These issues are further discussed in Chapter 12.

In the following, `String` is a standard Java class:

```
String str1;
. . .
str1 = "This is a Java literal string";
```

In this code, `str1` is defined to be a reference to a `String` class instance or object, but is initially set to null. The subsequent assignment sets `str1` to reference the `String` object, `"This is a Java literal string"`.

Because Java class instances are implicitly deallocated (there is no explicit deallocation operator), there cannot be a dangling reference.

C# includes both the references of Java and the pointers of C++. However, the use of pointers is strongly discouraged. In fact, any subprogram that uses pointers must include the **unsafe** modifier. Note that although objects pointed to by references are implicitly deallocated, that is not true for objects pointed to by pointers. Pointers were included in C# primarily to allow C# programs to interoperate with C and C++ code.

All variables in the pure object-oriented languages Smalltalk, Python, and Ruby are references. They are always implicitly dereferenced. Furthermore, the direct values of these variables cannot be accessed.

6.9.7   Evaluation

The problems of dangling pointers and garbage have already been discussed at length. The problems of heap management are discussed in Section 6.9.9.3.

Pointers have been compared with the goto. The goto statement widens the range of statements that can be executed next. Pointer variables widen the range of memory cells that can be referenced by a variable. Perhaps the most damning statement about pointers was made by Hoare (1973): "Their introduction into high-level languages has been a step backward from which we may never recover."

On the other hand, pointers are essential in some kinds of programming applications. For example, pointers are necessary to write device drivers, in which specific absolute addresses must be accessed.

The references of Java and C# provide some of the flexibility and the capabilities of pointers, without the hazards. It remains to be seen whether programmers will be willing to trade the full power of C and C++ pointers for the greater safety of references. The extent to which C# programs use pointers will be one measure of this.

6.9.8 Implementation of Pointer and Reference Types

In most languages, pointers are used in heap management. The same is true for Java and C# references, as well as the variables in Smalltalk, Python, and Ruby, so we cannot treat pointers and references separately. First, we briefly describe how pointers and references are represented internally. We then discuss two possible solutions to the dangling pointer problem. Finally, we describe the major problems with heap management techniques.

6.9.8.1 Representations of Pointers and References

In most larger computers, pointers and references are single values stored in memory cells. However, most microcomputers are based on Intel microprocessors, which use addresses with two parts, a segment and an offset. So pointers and references are implemented in these systems as pairs of 16-bit cells, one for each of the two parts of an address.

6.9.8.2 Solutions to the Dangling-Pointer Problem

There have been several proposed solutions to the dangling-pointer problem. Among these are **tombstones** (Lomet, 1975), in which every heap-dynamic variable includes a special cell, called a tombstone, that is itself a pointer to the heap-dynamic variable. The actual pointer variable points only at tombstones and never to heap-dynamic variables. When a heap-dynamic variable is deallocated, the tombstone remains but is set to nil, indicating that the heap-dynamic variable no longer exists. This approach prevents a pointer from ever pointing to a deallocated variable. Any reference to any pointer that points to a nil tombstone can be detected as an error.

Tombstones are costly in both time and space. Because tombstones are never deallocated, their storage is never reclaimed. Every access to a heap-dynamic variable through a tombstone requires one more level of indirection, which requires an additional machine cycle on most computers. Apparently none of the designers of the more popular languages have found the additional safety to be worth this additional cost, because no widely used language uses tombstones.

An alternative to tombstones is the **locks-and-keys approach** used in the implementation of UW-Pascal (Fischer and LeBlanc, 1977, 1980). In this compiler, pointer values are represented as ordered pairs (key, address), where the key is an integer value. Heap-dynamic variables are represented as the storage for the variable plus a header cell that stores an integer lock value. When a heap-dynamic variable is allocated, a lock value is created and placed both in the lock cell of the heap-dynamic variable and in the key cell of the pointer that is specified in the call to **new.** Every access to the dereferenced pointer compares the key value of the pointer to the lock value in the heap-dynamic variable. If they match, the access is legal; otherwise the access is treated as a run-time error. Any copies of the pointer value to other pointers must copy the key value. Therefore, any number of pointers can reference a given heap-dynamic variable. When a heap-dynamic variable is deallocated with **dispose,** its lock value is cleared to an illegal lock value. Then, if a pointer other than the one specified in the **dispose** is dereferenced, its address value will still be intact, but its key value will no longer match the lock, so the access will not be allowed.

Of course, the best solution to the dangling-pointer problem is to take deallocation of heap-dynamic variables out of the hands of programmers. If programs cannot explicitly deallocate heap-dynamic variables, there will be no dangling pointers. To do this, the run-time system must implicitly deallocate heap-dynamic variables when they are no longer useful. LISP systems have always done this. Both Java and C# also use this approach for their reference variables. Recall that C#'s pointers do not include implicit deallocation.

6.9.8.3 Heap Management

Heap management can be a very complex run-time process. We examine the process in two separate situations: one in which all heap storage is allocated and deallocated in units of a single size, and one in which variable-size segments are allocated and deallocated. Note that for deallocation, we discuss only implicit approaches. Our discussion will be brief and far from comprehensive, since a thorough analysis of these processes and their associated problems is not so much a language design issue as it is an implementation issue.

Single-Size Cells   The simplest situation is when all allocation and deallocation is of a single-size cell. It is further simplified when every cell already contains a pointer. This is the scenario of many implementations of LISP, where the problems of dynamic storage allocation were first encountered on a large scale. All LISP programs and most LISP data consist of cells connected into linked lists.

In a single-size allocation heap, all available cells are linked together using the pointers in the cells, forming a list of available space. Allocation is a simple matter of taking the required number of cells from this list when they are needed. Deallocation is a much more complex process. A heap-dynamic variable can be pointed to by more than one pointer, making it difficult to determine when the variable is no longer useful to the program. Simply because one pointer is disconnected from a cell obviously does not make it garbage; there could be several other pointers still pointing to the cell.

In LISP, several of the most frequent operations in programs create collections of cells that are no longer accessible to the program and therefore should be deallocated (put back on the list of available space). One of the fundamental design goals of LISP was to ensure that reclamation of unused cells would not be the task of the programmer but rather that of the run-time system. This goal left LISP implementors with the fundamental design question: When should deallocation be performed?

There are several different approaches to garbage collection. The two most common traditional techniques are in some ways opposite processes. These are named **reference counters,** in which reclamation is incremental and is done when inaccessible cells are created; and **mark-sweep,** in which reclamation occurs only when the list of available space becomes empty. These two methods are sometimes called the **eager approach** and the **lazy approach,** respectively. Many variations of these two approaches have been developed. In this section, however, we discuss only the basic processes.

The reference counter method of storage reclamation accomplishes its goal by maintaining in every cell a counter that stores the number of pointers that are currently pointing at the cell. Embedded in the decrement operation for the reference counters, which occurs when a pointer is disconnected from the cell, is a check for a zero value. If the reference counter reaches zero, it means that no program pointers are pointing at the cell, and it has thus become garbage and can be returned to the list of available space.

There are three distinct problems with the reference counter method. First, if storage cells are relatively small, the space required for the counters is significant. Second, some execution time is obviously required to maintain the counter values. Every time a pointer value is changed, the cell to which it was pointing must have its counter decremented, and the cell to which it is now pointing must have its counter incremented. In a language like LISP, in which nearly every action involves changing pointers, that can be a significant portion of the total execution time of a program. Of course, if pointer changes are not too frequent, this is not a problem. Some of the inefficiency of reference counters can be eliminated by an approach named **deferred reference counting,** which avoids reference counters for some pointers. Third, complications arise when a collection of cells is connected circularly. The problem here is that each cell in the circular list has a reference counter value of at least 1, which prevents it from being collected and placed back on the list of available space. A solution to this problem can be found in Friedman and Wise (1979).

The advantage of the reference counter approach is that it is intrinsically incremental. Its actions are interleaved with those of the application, so it never causes significant delays in the execution of the application.

The original mark-sweep process of garbage collection operates as follows: The run-time system allocates storage cells as requested and disconnects pointers from cells as necessary, without regard for storage reclamation (allowing garbage to accumulate), until it has allocated all available cells. At this point, a mark-sweep process is begun to gather all the garbage left floating around in the heap. To facilitate the process, every heap cell has an extra indicator bit or field that is used by the collection algorithm.

The mark-sweep process consists of three distinct phases. First, all cells in the heap have their indicators set to indicate they are garbage. This is, of course, a correct assumption for only some of the cells. The second part, called the marking phase, is the most difficult. Every pointer in the program is traced into the heap, and all reachable cells are marked as not being garbage. After this, the third phase, called the sweep phase, is executed: All cells in the heap that have not been specifically marked as still being used are returned to the list of available space.

To illustrate the flavor of algorithms used to mark the cells that are currently in use, we provide the following simple version of a marking algorithm. We assume that all heap-dynamic variables, or heap cells, consist of an information part; a part for the mark, named `marker`; and two pointers named `llink` and `rlink`. These cells are used to build directed graphs with at most two edges leading from any node. The marking algorithm traverses all spanning trees of the graphs, marking all cells that are found. Like other graph traversals, the marking algorithm uses recursion.

```
for every pointer r do
    mark(r)

void mark(void * ptr) {
    if (ptr != 0)
      if (*ptr.marker is not marked) {
         set *ptr.marker
         mark(*ptr.llink)
         mark(*ptr.rlink)
      }
}
```

An example of the actions of this procedure on a given graph is shown in Figure 6.12. This simple marking algorithm requires a great deal of storage (for stack space to support recursion). A marking process that does not require additional stack space was developed by Schorr and Waite (1967). Their method reverses pointers as it traces out linked structures. Then, when the end of a list is reached, the process can follow the pointers back out of the structure.

The most serious problem with the original version of mark-sweep was that it was done too infrequently—only when a program had used all or nearly all of the heap storage. Mark-sweep in that situation takes a good deal of time, because most of the cells must be traced and marked as being currently used. This causes a significant delay in the progress of the application. Furthermore, the process may yield only a small number of cells that can be placed on

Figure 6.12

An example of the actions of the marking algorithm

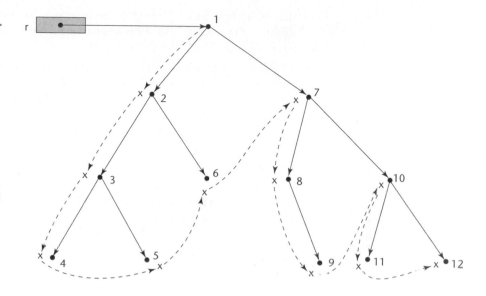

Dashed lines show the order of node_marking

the list of available space. This problem has been addressed in a variety of improvements. For example, **incremental mark-sweep** garbage collection occurs more frequently, long before memory is exhausted, making the process more effective in terms of the amount of storage that is reclaimed. The time required for each run of the process is obviously shorter, thus reducing the delay in application execution. Another alternative is to perform the mark-sweep process on parts, rather than all of the memory associated with the application, at different times. This provides the same kinds of improvements as incremental mark-sweep.

Both the marking algorithms for the mark-sweep method and the processes required by the reference counter method can be made more efficient by use of the pointer rotation and slide operations that are described by Suzuki (1982).

Variable-Size Cells Managing a heap from which variable-size cells are allocated has all the difficulties of managing one for single-size cells, but also has additional problems. Unfortunately, variable-size cells are required by most programming languages. The additional problems posed by variable-size cell management depend on the method used. If mark-sweep is used, the following additional problems occur:

- The initial setting of the indicators of all cells in the heap to indicate that they are garbage is difficult. Because the cells are different sizes, scanning them is a problem. One solution is to require each cell to have the cell size as its first field. Then the scanning can be done, although it takes slightly more space and somewhat more time than its counterpart for fixed-size cells.

- The marking process is nontrivial. How can a chain be followed from a pointer if there is no predefined location for the pointer in the pointed-to cell? Cells that do not contain pointers at all are also a problem. Adding an internal pointer to each cell, which is maintained in the background by the run-time system, will work. However, this background maintenance processing adds both space and execution time overhead to the cost of running the program.

- Maintaining the list of available space is another source of overhead. The list can begin with a single cell consisting of all available space. Requests for segments simply reduce the size of this block. Reclaimed cells are added to the list. The problem is that before long, the list becomes a long list of various-size segments, or blocks. This slows allocation because requests cause the list to be searched for sufficiently large blocks. Eventually, the list may consist of a large number of very small blocks, which are not large enough for most requests. At this point, adjacent blocks may need to be collapsed into larger blocks. Alternatives to using the first sufficiently large block on the list can shorten the search but require the list to be ordered by block size. In either case, maintaining the list is additional overhead.

If reference counters are used, the first two problems are avoided, but the available-space list-maintenance problem remains.

For a comprehensive study of memory management problems, see Wilson (2005).

SUMMARY

The data types of a language are a large part of what determines that language's style and usefulness. Along with control structures, they form the heart of a language.

The primitive data types of most imperative languages include numeric, character, and Boolean types. The numeric types are often directly supported by hardware.

The user-defined enumeration and subrange types are convenient and add to the readability and reliability of programs.

Arrays are part of most programming languages. The relationship between a reference to an array element and the address of that element is given in an access function, which is an implementation of a mapping. Arrays can be either static, as in C++ arrays whose definition includes the **static** specifier; fixed stack-dynamic, as in C functions (without the **static** specifier); stack-dynamic, as in Ada blocks; fixed heap-dynamic, as with Java's objects; or heap-dynamic, as in Perl's arrays. Most languages allow only a few operations on complete arrays.

A heterogeneous array is one whose elements can be of different types. Heterogeneous arrays are supported by Perl, JavaScript, Python, and Ruby.

Records are now included in most languages. Fields of records are specified in a variety of ways. In the case of COBOL, they can be referenced without naming all of the enclosing records, although this is messy to implement and harmful to readability. In Java, records are supported in the class construct.

Unions are locations that can store different type values at different times. Discriminated unions include a tag to record the current type value. A free union is one without the tag. Most languages with unions do not have safe designs for them, the exception being Ada.

Pointers are used for addressing flexibility and to control dynamic storage management. Pointers have some inherent dangers: Dangling pointers are difficult to avoid, and memory leakage can occur.

Reference types, such as those in Java, provide heap management without the dangers of pointers.

The level of difficulty in implementing a data type has a strong influence on whether the type will be included in a language. Enumeration types, subrange types, and record types are all relatively easy to implement. Arrays are also straightforward, although array element access is an expensive process when the array has several subscripts. The access function requires one addition and one multiplication for each subscript.

Pointers are relatively easy to implement, if heap management is not considered. Heap management is relatively easy if all cells have the same size, but is complicated for variable-size cell allocation and deallocation.

BIBLIOGRAPHIC NOTES

A wealth of literature exists that is concerned with data type design, use, and implementation. Hoare gives one of the earliest systematic definitions of structured types in Dahl et al. (1972). A general discussion of a wide variety of data types is given in Cleaveland (1986).

Implementing run-time checks on the possible insecurities of Pascal data types is discussed in Fischer and LeBlanc (1980). Most compiler design books, such as Fischer and LeBlanc (1991) and Aho et al. (1986), describe implementation methods for data types, as do the other programming language texts, such as Pratt and Zelkowitz (2001) and Scott (2000). A detailed discussion of the problems of heap management can be found in Tenenbaum et al. (1990). Garbage collection methods are developed by Schorr and Waite (1967) and Deutsch and Bobrow (1976). A comprehensive discussion of garbage collection algorithms can be found in Cohen (1981) and Wilson (2005).

REVIEW QUESTIONS

1. What is a descriptor?

2. What are the advantages and disadvantages of decimal data types?

3. What are the design issues for character string types?

4. Describe the three string length options.

5. Define *ordinal, enumeration,* and *subrange types.*

6. What are the advantages of user-defined enumeration types?

7. In what ways are the user-defined enumeration types of C# more reliable than those of C++?

8. What are the design issues for arrays?

9. Define *static, fixed stack-dynamic, stack-dynamic, fixed heap-dynamic,* and *heap-dynamic arrays.* What are the advantages of each?

10. What is a heterogeneous array?

11. What happens when a nonexistent element of an array is referenced in Perl?

12. How does JavaScript support sparse arrays?

13. What languages support negative subscripts?

14. What languages support array slices with stepsizes?

15. What array initialization feature is available in Ada that is not available in other common imperative languages?

16. What is an aggregate constant?

17. What array operations are provided specifically for single-dimensioned arrays in Ada?

18. What are the differences between the slices of Fortran 95 and those of Ada?

19. Define *row major order* and *column major order.*

20. What is an access function for an array?

21. What are the required entries in a Java array descriptor, and when must they be stored (at compile time or run time)?

22. What is the purpose of level numbers in COBOL records?

23. Define *fully qualified* and *elliptical references* to fields in records.

24. Define *union, free union,* and *discriminated union.*

25. What are the design issues for unions?

26. Are the unions of Ada always type checked?

27. What are the design issues for pointer types?

28. What are the two common problems with pointers?

29. Why are the pointers of most languages restricted to pointing at a single type variable?

30. What is a C++ reference type and what is its common use?

31. Why are reference variables in C++ better than pointers for formal parameters?

32. What advantages do Java and C# reference type variables have over the pointers in other languages?

33. Describe the lazy and eager approaches to reclaiming garbage.

34. Why wouldn't arithmetic on Java and C# references make sense?

PROBLEM SET

1. What are the arguments for and against representing Boolean values as single bits in memory?

2. How does a decimal value waste memory space?

3. VAX minicomputers use a format for floating-point numbers that is not the same as the IEEE standard. What is this format, and why was it chosen by the designers of the VAX computers? A reference for VAX floating-point representations is Sebesta (1991).

4. Compare the tombstone and lock-and-key methods of avoiding dangling pointers, from the points of view of safety and implementation cost.

5. What disadvantages are there in implicit dereferencing of pointers, but only in certain contexts? For example, consider the implicit dereference of a pointer to a record in Ada when it is used to reference a record field.

6. Explain all of the differences between subtypes and derived types.

7. What significant justification is there for the -> operator in C and C++?

8. What are all of the differences between the enumeration types of C++ and those of Java?

9. The unions in C and C++ are separate from the records of those languages, rather than combined as they are in Ada. What are the advantages and disadvantages to these two choices?

10. Multidimensional arrays can be stored in row major order, as in C++, or in column major order, as in Fortran. Develop the access functions for both of these arrangements for three-dimensional arrays.

11. In the Burroughs Extended ALGOL language, matrices are stored as a single-dimensioned array of pointers to the rows of the matrix, which are treated as single-dimensioned arrays of values. What are the advantages and disadvantages of such a scheme?

12. Analyze and write a comparison of C's `malloc` and `free` functions with C++'s **new** and **delete** operators. Use safety as the primary consideration in the comparison.

13. Analyze and write a comparison of using C++ pointers and Java reference variables to refer to fixed heap-dynamic variables. Use safety and convenience as the primary considerations in the comparison.

14. Write a short discussion of what was lost and what was gained in Java's designers' decision to not include the pointers of C++.

15. What are the arguments for and against Java's implicit heap storage recovery, when compared with the explicit heap storage recovery required in C++? Consider real-time systems.

16. What are the arguments for the inclusion of enumeration types in C#, although they are not in the first few versions of Java?

17. What would you expect to be the level of use of pointers in C#? How often will they be used when it is not absolutely necessary?

18. Make two lists of applications of matrices, one for those that require jagged matrices and one for those that require rectangular matrices. Now, argue whether just jagged, just rectangular, or both should be included in a programming language.

19. Compare the string manipulation capabilities of the class libraries of C++, Java, and C#.

PROGRAMMING EXERCISES

1. Design a set of simple test programs to determine the type compatibility rules of a C compiler to which you have access. Write a report of your findings.

2. Determine whether some C compiler to which you have access implements the `free` function.

3. Write a program that does matrix multiplication in some language that does subscript range checking and for which you can obtain an assembly language or machine language version from the compiler. Determine the number of instructions required for the subscript range checking and compare it with the total number of instructions for the matrix multiplication process.

4. If you have access to a compiler in which the user can specify whether subscript range checking is desired, write a program that does a large number of matrix accesses and times their execution. Run the program with subscript range checking and without it, and compare the times.

5. Write a simple program in C++ to investigate the safety of its enumeration types. Include at least 10 different operations on enumeration types

to determine what incorrect or just silly things are legal. Now, write a C# program that does the same things and run it to determine how many of the incorrect or silly things are legal. Compare your results.

6. Write a program in C++ or C# that includes two different enumeration types and has a significant number of operations using the enumeration types. Also write the same program using only integer variables. Compare the readability and predict the reliability differences between the two programs.

7. Write a C program that does a large number of references to elements of two-dimensional arrays, using only subscripting. Write a second program that does the same operations but uses pointers and pointer arithmetic for the storage-mapping function to do the array references. Compare the time efficiency of the two programs. Which of the two programs is likely to be more reliable? Why?

8. Write a Perl program that uses a hash and a large number of operations on the hash. For example, the hash could store people's names and their ages. A random-number generator could be used to create three-character names and ages, which could be added to the hash. When a duplicate name was generated, it would cause an access to the hash, but not add a new element. Rewrite the same program without using hashes. Compare the execution efficiency of the two. Compare the ease of programming and readability of the two.

7

Expressions and Assignment Statements

As the title indicates, the topic of this chapter is expressions and assignment statements. The semantics rules that determine the order of evaluation of operators in expressions are discussed first. This is followed by a discussion of the potential problems of operand evaluation order when functions can have side effects. Overloaded operators, both predefined and user defined, are then discussed, along with their effects on the expressions in programs. Next, mixed-mode expressions are discussed and evaluated. This leads to the definition and evaluation of widening and narrowing type conversions, both implicit and explicit. Relational and Boolean expressions are then discussed, including the process of short-circuit evaluation. Finally, the assignment statement, from its simplest form to all of its variations, is covered, including assignments as expressions and mixed-mode assignments.

The chapter is focused on the expressions and assignment statements of the imperative languages. Issues of expression specification and evaluation in functional and logic languages are discussed in Chapters 15 and 16, respectively.

Character string pattern-matching expressions were discussed as a part of the material on character strings in Chapter 6, so they are not mentioned in this chapter.

7.1 Introduction

Expressions are the fundamental means of specifying computations in a programming language. It is crucial for a programmer to understand both the syntax and semantics of expressions of the language being used. A formal mechanism (BNF) for describing the syntax of expressions was introduced in Chapter 3. In this chapter, we discuss the semantics of expressions—that is, what they mean—which is governed by how they are evaluated.

To understand expression evaluation, it is necessary to be familiar with the orders of operator and operand evaluation. The operator evaluation order of expressions is dictated by the associativity and precedence rules of the language. Although the value of an expression sometimes depends on it, the order of operand evaluation in expressions is often unstated by language designers. This allows implementors to choose the order, which leads to the possibility of programs producing different results in different implementations. Other issues in expression semantics are type mismatches, coercions, and short-circuit evaluation.

The essence of the imperative programming languages is the dominant role of assignment statements. The purpose of an assignment statement is to change the value of a variable. So an integral part of all imperative languages is the concept of variables whose values change during program execution. (Nonimperative languages sometimes include variables of a different sort, such as the parameters of functions in functional languages.)

Simple assignment statements specify an expression to be evaluated and a target location in which to place the result of the expression evaluation. As we shall see in this chapter, there are a number of variations on the basic form.

7.2 Arithmetic Expressions

Automatic evaluation of arithmetic expressions similar to those found in mathematics, science, and engineering was one of the primary goals of the first high-level programming languages. Most of the characteristics of arithmetic expressions in programming languages were inherited from conventions that had evolved in mathematics. In programming languages, arithmetic expressions consist of operators, operands, parentheses, and function calls. An operator can be **unary,** meaning it has a single operand, **binary,** meaning it has two operands, or **ternary,** meaning it has three operands.

In most imperative programming languages, binary operators are **infix,** which means they appear between their operands. One exception is Perl, which has some operators that are prefix, which means they precede their operands.

The purpose of an arithmetic expression is to specify an arithmetic computation. An implementation of such a computation must cause two actions: fetching the operands, usually from memory, and executing the arithmetic operations on those operands. In the following sections, we investigate the common design details of arithmetic expressions in the imperative languages.

Following are the primary design issues for arithmetic expressions, all of which are discussed in this section:

- What are the operator precedence rules?
- What are the operator associativity rules?
- What is the order of operand evaluation?
- Are there restrictions on operand evaluation side effects?
- Does the language allow user-defined operator overloading?
- What type mixing is allowed in expressions?

7.2.1 Operator Evaluation Order

We first investigate the language rules that specify the order of evaluation of operators.

7.2.1.1 Precedence

The value of an expression depends at least in part on the order of evaluation of the operators in the expression. Consider the following expression:

```
a + b * c
```

Suppose the variables a, b, and c have the values 3, 4, and 5, respectively. If evaluated left to right (the addition first and then the multiplication), the result is 35. If evaluated right to left, the result is 23.

Instead of simply evaluating the operators in an expression from left to right or right to left, mathematicians long ago developed the concept of placing operators in a hierarchy of evaluation priorities and basing the evaluation order of expressions partly on this hierarchy. For example, in mathematics, multiplication is considered to be of higher priority than addition, perhaps due to its higher level of complexity. If we apply that convention in our example expression, as most programming languages do, the multiplication would be done first.

The **operator precedence rules** for expression evaluation define the order in which the operators of different precedence levels are evaluated. The operator precedence rules for expressions are based on the hierarchy of operator priorities, as seen by the language designer. The operator precedence rules of the common imperative languages are nearly all the same, because they are all based on those of mathematics. In these languages, exponentiation has the highest precedence (when it is provided by the language), followed by multiplication and division on the same level, followed by binary addition and subtraction on the same level.

Many languages also include unary versions of addition and subtraction. Unary addition is called the **identity operator** because it usually has no associated operation and thus has no effect on its operand. Ellis and Stroustrup, speaking about C++, call it a historical accident and correctly label it useless (1990, p. 56). In Java and C#, unary plus actually does have an effect when its operand is **short** or **byte** and C it causes an implicit conversion of that operand to **int** type. Unary minus, of course, always changes the sign of its operand. In Java and C#, unary minus also causes the implicit conversion of **short** and **byte** operands to **int** type.

In all of the common imperative languages, the unary minus operator can appear in an expression either at the beginning or anywhere inside the expression, as long as it is parenthesized to prevent it from being next to another operator. For example,

```
A + (- B) * C
```

is legal, but

```
A + - B * C
```

usually is not.

Next, consider the following expressions:

```
- A / B
- A * B
- A ** B
```

In the first two cases, the relative precedence of the unary minus operator and the binary operator is irrelevant—the order of evaluation of the two operators has no effect on the value of the expression. In the last case, however, it does matter. Of the common programming languages, only Fortran, Ruby, Visual Basic, and Ada have the exponentiation operator. In all four, exponentiation has higher precedence than unary minus, so

```
- A ** B
```

is equivalent to

```
-(A ** B)
```

There is one situation where the precedence of a unary operator can be confusing. In Ada, the precedence of unary minus is lower than that of **mod,** so the expression

```
- 17 mod 5
```

is equivalent to

```
- (17 mod 5)
```

which evaluates to –2, rather than 3, which would be the result if unary minus had higher precedence than **mod,** as it does in the C-based languages.

The precedences of the arithmetic operators of a few common programming languages are as follows:

	Ruby	*C-based Languages*	*Ada*
Highest	**	postfix ++, --	**, **abs**
	unary +, –	prefix ++, --, unary +, –	*, /, **mod**, **rem**
	*, /, %	*, /, %	unary +, –
Lowest	binary +, –		binary +,–

The ** operator is exponentiation. The % operator of the C-based languages and Ruby is exactly like the **rem** operator of Ada: It takes two integer operands and yields the remainder of the first after division by the second.[1] The Ada **mod** operator is identical to **rem** when both operands are positive, but can be different when one or both are negative. The ++ and -- operators of the C-based languages are described in Section 7.7.4. The **abs** operator of Ada is a unary operator that yields the absolute value of its operand.

APL is odd among languages because it has a single level of precedence, as illustrated in the next section.

Precedence accounts for only some of the rules for the order of operator evaluation; associativity rules also affect it.

---

1. In versions of C before C99, the % operator was implementation-dependent in some situations, because division was also implementation-dependent.

7.2.1.2 Associativity

Consider the following expression:

```
a - b + c - d
```

If the addition and subtraction operators have the same level of precedence, as they do in programming languages, the precedence rules say nothing about the order of evaluation of the operators in this expression.

When an expression contains two adjacent[2] occurrences of operators with the same level of precedence, the question of which operator is evaluated first is answered by the **associativity** rules of the language. An operator can have either left or right associativity, meaning that the leftmost occurrence is evaluated first or the rightmost occurrence is evaluated first, respectively.

Associativity in common imperative languages is left to right, except that the exponentiation operator (when provided) associates right to left. In the Java expression

```
a - b + c
```

the left operator is evaluated first. But exponentiation in Fortran and Ruby is right associative, so in the expression

```
A ** B ** C
```

the right operator is evaluated first.

In Ada, exponentiation is nonassociative, which means that the expression

```
A ** B ** C
```

is illegal. Such an expression must be parenthesized to show the desired order, as in either

```
(A ** B) ** C
```

or

```
A ** (B ** C)
```

In Visual Basic, the exponentiation operator, ^, is left associative.

The associativity rules for a few common imperative languages are given here:

Language	Associativity Rule
Ruby	Left: *, /, +, –

---

2. We call operators "adjacent" if they are separated by a single operand.

Right: **
C-based languages   Left: *, /, %, binary +, binary –
Right: ++, --, unary –, unary +
Ada   Left: all except **
Nonassociative: **

As stated in Section 7.2.1.1, in APL, all operators have the same level of precedence. Thus the order of evaluation of operators in APL expressions is determined entirely by the associativity rule, which is right to left for all operators. For example, in the expression

A × B + C

the addition operator is evaluated first, followed by the multiplication operator (× is the APL multiplication operator). If A were 3, B were 4, and C were 5, the value of this APL expression would be 27.

Many compilers for the common imperative languages make use of the fact that some arithmetic operators are mathematically associative, meaning that the associativity rules have no impact on the value of an expression containing only those operators. For example, addition is mathematically associative, so in mathematics the value of the expression

A + B + C

does not depend on the order of operator evaluation. If floating-point operations for mathematically associative operations were also associative, the compiler could use this fact to perform some simple optimizations. Specifically, if the compiler is allowed to reorder the evaluation of operators, it may be able to produce slightly faster code for expression evaluation. Compilers actually do these kinds of optimizations.

Unfortunately, in a computer both floating-point representations and floating-point arithmetic operations are only approximations of their mathematical counterparts (because of size limitations). The fact that a mathematical operator is associative does not necessarily imply that the corresponding floating-point operation is associative. In fact, only if all the operands and intermediate results can be exactly represented in floating-point notation will the process be precisely associative. For example, there are pathological situations in which integer addition on a computer is *not* associative. For example, suppose that a program must evaluate the expression

A + B + C + D

and that A and C are very large positive numbers, and B and D are negative numbers with very large absolute values. In this situation, adding B to A does not cause an overflow, but adding C to A does. Likewise, adding C to B does not cause overflow, but adding D to B does. Because of the limitations of computer arithmetic, addition is catastrophically nonassociative in this case. Therefore, if the compiler reorders these addition operations, it affects the value of the expression. This problem, of course, can be avoided by the programmer, assuming the approximate values of the variables are known. The programmer can specify the expression in two parts (in two assignment statements), ensuring that overflow is avoided. However, this situation can arise in far more subtle ways, in which the programmer is less likely to notice the order dependence.

7.2.1.3 Parentheses

Programmers can alter the precedence and associativity rules by placing parentheses in expressions. A parenthesized part of an expression has precedence over its adjacent unparenthesized parts. For example, although multiplication has precedence over addition, in the expression

```
(A + B) * C
```

the addition will be evaluated first. Mathematically, this is perfectly natural. In this expression, the first operand of the multiplication operator is not available until the addition in the parenthesized subexpression is evaluated. Also, the expression from Section 7.2.1.2 could be specified as

```
(A + B) + (C + D)
```

to avoid overflow.

Languages that allow parentheses in arithmetic expressions could dispense with all precedence rules and simply associate all operators left to right or right to left. The programmer would specify the desired order of evaluation with parentheses. This approach would be simple because neither the author nor the readers of programs would need to remember any precedence or associativity rules. The disadvantage of this scheme is that it makes writing expressions more tedious, and it also seriously compromises the readability of the code. Yet this was the choice made by Ken Iverson, the designer of APL.

7.2.1.4 Ruby Expressions

Recall that Ruby is a pure object-oriented language, which means, among other things, that every data value, including literals, is an object. Ruby supports the collection of arithmetic and logic operations that are included in the C-based languages. What sets Ruby apart from the C-based languages in the area of expressions is that all of the arithmetic, relational, and assignment operators, as well as array indexing, shifts, and bit-wise logic operators, are implemented as methods. For example, the expression a + b is a call to the + method of the object referenced by a, passing the object referenced by b as a parameter.

One interesting result of the implementation of operators as methods is that they can be overriden by application programs. Therefore, these operators can be redefined. While it is often not useful to redefine operators for predefined types, it is useful, as we will see in Section 7.3, to define predefined operators for user-defined types, which can be done with operator overloading in some languages.

7.2.1.5 Conditional Expressions

We now look at the ternary operator, `?:`, which is included in the C-based languages. This operator is used to form conditional expressions.

Sometimes **if-then-else** statements are used to perform a conditional expression assignment. For example, consider

```
if (count == 0)
  average = 0;
else
  average = sum / count;
```

In the C-based languages, this code can be specified more conveniently in an assignment statement using a conditional expression, which has the form

expression_1 ? expression_2 : expression_3

where expression_1 is interpreted as a Boolean expression. If expression_1 evaluates to true, the value of the whole expression is the value of expression_2; otherwise, it is the value of expression_3. For example, the effect of the example **if-then-else** can be achieved with the following assignment statement, using a conditional expression:

```
average = (count == 0) ? 0 : sum / count;
```

In effect, the question mark denotes the beginning of the **then** clause, and the colon marks the beginning of the **else** clause. Both clauses are mandatory. Note that **?** is used in conditional expressions as a ternary operator.

Conditional expressions can be used anywhere in a program (in a C-based language) where any other expression can be used. In addition to the C-based languages, conditional expressions are provided in Perl, JavaScript, and Ruby.

7.2.2   Operand Evaluation Order

A less commonly discussed design characteristic of expressions is the order of evaluation of operands. Variables in expressions are evaluated by fetching their values from memory. Constants are sometimes evaluated the same way. In other cases, a constant may be part of the machine language instruction and not require a memory fetch. If an operand is a parenthesized expression, then all operators it contains must be evaluated before its value can be used as an operand.

If neither of the operands of an operator has side effects, then operand evaluation order is irrelevant. Therefore, the only interesting case arises when the evaluation of an operand does have side effects.

7.2.2.1 Side Effects

A **side effect** of a function, called a functional side effect, occurs when the function changes one of its parameters or a global variable. (A global variable is declared outside the function but is accessible in the function.)

Consider the expression

```
a + fun(a)
```

If fun does not have the side effect of changing a, then the order of evaluation of the two operands, a and fun(a), has no effect on the value of the expression. However, if fun changes a, there is an effect. Consider the following situation: fun returns 10 and changes the value of its parameter to 20. Suppose we have the following:

```
a = 10;
b = a + fun(a);
```

Then, if the value of a is fetched first (in the expression evaluation process), its value is 10 and the value of the expression is 20. But if the second operand is evaluated first, then the value of the first operand is 20 and the value of the expression is 30.

The following C program illustrates the same problem when a function changes a global variable that appears in an expression:

```
int a = 5;
int fun1() {
  a = 17;
  return 3;
}  /* of fun1 */
void main() {
  a = a + fun1();
}  /* of main */
```

The value computed for a in main depends on the order of evaluation of the operands in the expression a + fun1(). The value of a will be either 8 (if a is evaluated first) or 20 (if the function call is evaluated first).

Note that functions in mathematics do not have side effects, because there is no notion of variables in mathematics. The same

history note

The designers of Fortran 77 envisioned a third solution to the problem of operand evaluation order. The Fortran 77 definition states that expressions that have function calls are legal only if the functions do not change the values of other operands in the expression. Unfortunately, it is not easy for the compiler to determine the exact effect a function can have on variables outside the function, especially in the presence of global variables provided by Common and the aliasing provided by Equivalence. This is a case where the language definition specifies the conditions under which a construct is legal but leaves it to the programmer to ensure that such constructs are legally specified in programs.

is true for pure functional-programming languages. In both mathematics and pure functional-programming languages, functions are much eaiser to reason about and understand than those in imperative languages, because their context is irrelevant to their meaning.

There are two possible solutions to the problem of operand evaluation order and side effects. First, the language designer could disallow function evaluation from affecting the value of expressions by simply disallowing functional side effects. The second method of avoiding the problem is to state in the language definition that operands in expressions are to be evaluated in a particular order and demand that implementors guarantee that order.

Disallowing functional side effects is difficult, and it eliminates some flexibility for the programmer. Consider the case of C and C++, which have only functions, meaning that all subprograms return one value. To eliminate the side effects of two-way parameters and still provide subprograms that return more than one value, a new subprogram type that is similar to the procedures of some other imperative languages would be required. Access to globals in functions would also have to be disallowed. However, when efficiency is important, using access to global variables to avoid parameter passing is an important method of increasing execution speed. In compilers, for example, global access to data such as the symbol table is commonplace.

The problem with having a strict evaluation order is that some code optimization techniques used by compilers involve reordering operand evaluations. A guaranteed order disallows those optimization methods when function calls are involved. There is, therefore, no perfect solution, as is borne out by actual language designs.

The Java language definition guarantees that operands appear to be evaluated in left-to-right order, eliminating the problem discussed in this section.

7.2.2.2 Referential Transparency and Side Effects

The concept of referential transparency is related to and affected by functional side effects. A program has the property of **referential transparency** if any two expressions in the program that have the same value can be substituted for one another anywhere in the program, without affecting the action of the program. The value of a referentially transparent function depends entirely on its parameters.[3] The connection of referential transparency and functional side effects is illustrated by the following example:

```
result1 = (fun(a) + b) / (fun(a) - c);
temp = fun(a);
result2 = (temp + b) / (temp - c);
```

---

3. Furthermore, the value of the function cannot depend on the order in which its parameters are evaluated.

If the function `fun` has no side effects, `result1` and `result2` will be equal, because the expressions assigned to them are equivalent. However, suppose `fun` has the side effect of adding 1 to either `b` or `c`. Then `result1` would not be equal to `result2`. So, that side effect violates the referential transparency of the program in which the code appears.

There are several advantages to referentially transparent programs. The most important of these is that the semantics of such programs is much easier to understand than the semantics of programs that are not referentially transparent. Being referentially transparent makes a function equivalent to a mathematical function, in terms of ease of understanding.

Because they do not have variables, programs written in pure functional languages are referentially transparent. Functions in a pure functional language cannot have state, which would be stored in local variables. If such a function uses a value from outside the function, that value must be a constant, since there are no variables. Therefore, the value of the function depends on the values of its parameters and possible one or more global constants.

Referential transparency will be further discussed in Chapter 15, "Functional Programming Languages."

7.3 Overloaded Operators

Arithmetic operators are often used for more than one purpose. For example, in the imperative programming languages + is used to specify integer addition and floating-point addition. Some languages, Java, for example, also use it for string catenation. This multiple use of an operator is called **operator overloading** and is generally thought to be acceptable, as long as readability and/or reliability do not suffer.

As an example of the possible dangers of overloading, consider the use of the ampersand (`&`) in C. As a binary operator, it specifies a bitwise logical AND operation. As a unary operator, however, its meaning is totally different. As a unary operator with a variable as its operand, the expression value is the address of that variable. In this case, the ampersand is called the address-of operator. For example, the execution of

```
x = &y;
```

causes the address of `y` to be placed in `x`. There are two problems with this multiple use of the ampersand. First, using the same symbol for two completely unrelated operations is detrimental to readability. Second, the simple keying error of leaving out the first operand for a bitwise AND operation can go undetected by the compiler, because it is interpreted as an address-of operator. Such an error may be difficult to diagnose.

Virtually all programming languages have a less serious but similar problem, which is often due to the overloading of the minus operator. The problem is only that the compiler cannot tell if the operator is meant to be binary or unary. So once again, failure to include the first operand when the operator is meant to be binary cannot be detected as an error by the compiler. However, the meanings of the two operations, unary and binary, are at least closely related, so readability is not adversely affected.

Distinct operator symbols not only increase readability, but they are sometimes convenient to use for common operations as well. The division operator is an example. Consider the problem of finding the floating-point average of a list of integers. Normally the sum of those integers is computed as an integer. Suppose this computation has been done and the result has been placed in the variable sum and the number of values is in count. Now, if the the floating-point average is to be computed and placed in the floating-point variable avg, this computation could be specified in C++ as

```
avg = sum / count;
```

But this assignment produces an incorrect result in most cases. Because both operands of the division operator are integer type, an integer division operation takes place in which the result is truncated to an integer. Then, in spite of the fact that the destination (avg) is floating-point type, its value from this assignment cannot have a fractional part. The integer result of division is converted to floating-point for the assignment *after* the truncation from the integer division.

One solution to the problem is to include two different division operators, one for integer division and one for floating-point division. This solution is employed in Pascal, in which **div** specifies integer division and / specifies floating-point division. So, the following assignment can be used to get the correct floating-point quotient of the two integer values in **sum** and **count:**

```
avg := sum / count
```

where avg is floating-point type. Both operands of the division operator will be implicitly converted to floating-point, and a floating-point division operation is used. This kind of implicit conversion operation is further discussed in Section 7.4.1.

JavaScript avoids this problem by not having any integer arithmetic.

Another alternative solution is included in PHP. In PHP, if two integers are divided and the result is not an integer (a number with no fractional part), a floating-point value is produced.

Outside of JavaScript and PHP, explicit conversions must be used on the integer operands. Such conversions are discussed in Section 7.4.2.

Some languages that support abstract data types (see Chapter 11), for example, Ada, C++, Fortran 95, and C#, allow the programmer to further overload operator symbols. For instance, suppose a user wants to define the * operator between a scalar integer and an integer array to mean that each element of the array is to be multiplied by the scalar. Such an operator could be defined by writing a function subprogram named * that performs this new operation. The compiler will choose the correct meaning when an overloaded operator is specified, based on the types of the operands, as with language-defined overloaded operators. For example, if this new definition for * is defined in a C# program, a C# compiler will use the new definition for * whenever the * operator appears with a simple integer as the left operand and an integer array as the right operand.

When sensibly used, user-defined operator overloading can aid readability. For example, if + and * are overloaded for a matrix abstract data type and A, B, C, and D are variables of that type, then

```
A * B + C * D
```

can be used instead of

```
MatrixAdd(MatrixMult(A, B), MatrixMult(C, D))
```

On the other hand, user-defined overloading can be harmful to readability. For one thing, nothing prevents a user from defining + to mean multiplication. Furthermore, seeing an * operator in a program, the reader must find both the types of the operands and the definition of the operator to determine its meaning. Any or all of these definitions could be in other files.

C++ has a few operators that cannot be overloaded. Among these are the class or structure member operator (.) and the scope resolution operator (::). Interestingly, operator overloading was one of the C++ features that was not copied into Java. However, it did reappear in C#.

The implementation of user-defined operator overloading is discussed in Chapter 9.

7.4 Type Conversions

Type conversions are either narrowing or widening. A **narrowing conversion** converts a value to a type that cannot store even approximations of all of the values of the original type, for example, converting a **double** to a **float** in Java (the range of **double** is much larger than that of **float**). A widening conversion converts a value to a type that can include at least approximations of all of the values of the original type, for example, converting an **int** to a **float** in Java. Widening conversions are nearly always safe, meaning that the magnitude of the converted value is maintained. Narrowing conversions are not always safe—sometimes the magnitude of the converted value is changed in the process. For example, if the floating-point value 1.3E25 is converted to an integer in a Java program, the result will be only distantly related to the original value.

The issue of widening and narrowing conversions is relatively simple for the primitive numeric types. For example, in Java the following are the widening conversions for the primitive numeric types:

byte to **short, int, long, float,** or **double**
short to **int, long, float,** or **double**
char to **int, long, float,** or **double**
int to **long, float** or **double**
long to **float** or **double**
float to **double**

The narrowing conversions are:

short to **byte** or **char**
char to **byte** or **short**
int to **byte, short,** or **char**
long to **byte, short, char,** or **int**
float to **byte, short, char, int,** or **long**
double to **byte, short, char, int, long,** or **float**

Although widening conversions are usually safe, they can result in reduced accuracy. In many language implementations, although integer-to-floating-point conversions are widening conversions, some precision may be lost. For example, in many cases, integers are stored in 32 bits, which allows at least nine decimal digits of precision. But floating-point values are also stored in 32 bits, with only about seven decimal digits of precision (because of the space used for the exponent). So, integer-to-floating-point widening can result in the loss of two digits of precision.

Coercions of nonprimitive types are, of course, more complex. In Chapter 5, the complications of assignment compatibility of array and record types were discussed. There is also the question of what parameter types and return types of a method allow it to override a method in a superclass—only when the types are the same, or also some other situations. That issue, as well as the concept of subclasses as subtypes, are discussed in Chapter 12.

Type conversions can be either explicit or implicit. The following two subsections discuss these two kinds of type conversions.

7.4.1 Coercion in Expressions

One of the design decisions concerning arithmetic expressions is whether an operator can have operands of different types. Languages that do allow such expressions, which are called **mixed-mode expressions,** must define conventions for implicit operand type conversions because computers usually do not have binary operations that take operands of different types. Recall that in Chapter 5 we defined coercion as an implicit type conversion that is initiated by the compiler. We refer to type conversions explicitly requested by the programmer as explicit conversions, or casts, not coercions.

Although some operator symbols may be overloaded, we assume that a computer system, either in hardware or in some level of software simulation, has an operation for each operand type and operator defined in the language.[4] For overloaded operators in a language that uses static type binding, the compiler chooses the correct type of operation on the basis of the types of the operands. When the two operands of an operator are not of the same type and that is legal in the language, the compiler must choose one of them to be coerced and supply the code for that coercion. In the following discussion, we examine the coercion design choices of several common languages.

Language designers are not in agreement on the issue of coercions in arithmetic expressions. Those against a broad range of coercions are concerned with the reliability problems that can result from such coercions, because they reduce the benefits of type checking. Those who would rather include a wide range of coercions are more concerned with the loss in flexibility that results from restrictions. The issue is whether programmers should be concerned with this category of errors or whether the compiler should detect them.

As a simple illustration of the problem, consider the following Java code:

```
int a;
float b, c, d;
...
d = b * a;
```

Assume that the second operand of the multiplication operator was supposed to be c, but because of a keying error it was typed as a. Because mixed-mode expressions are legal in Java, the compiler would not detect this as an error. It would simply insert code to coerce the value of the **int** operand, a, to **float.** If mixed-mode expressions were not legal in Java, this keying error would have been detected by the compiler as a type error.

Because error detection is reduced when mixed-mode expressions are allowed, Ada allows very few mixed type operands in expressions. It does not allow mixing of integer and floating-point operands in an expression, with one exception: The exponentiation operator, ******, can take either a floating-point or an integer type for the first operand and an integer type for the second operand. Ada allows a few other kinds of operand type mixing, usually related to subrange types. If the Java code example were written in Ada, as in

```
A : Integer;
B, C, D : Float;
...
C := B * A;
```

4. This assumption is not true for many languages. An example is given later in this section.

the Ada compiler would find the expression erroneous, because `Float` and `Integer` operands cannot be mixed for the `*` operator.

In most of the other common languages, there are no restrictions on mixed-mode arithmetic expressions.

The C-based languages have integer types that are smaller than the **int** type. In Java, they are **byte** and **short**. Operands of all of these types are coerced to **int** whenever virtually any operator is applied to them. So while data can be stored in variables of these types, it cannot be manipulated before conversion to a larger type. For example, consider the following Java code:

```
byte a, b, c;
...
a = b + c;
```

The values of b and c are coerced to **int** and an **int** addition is performed. Then the sum is converted to **byte** and put in a. Given the large size of the memories of contemporary computers, there seems to be little incentive to use **byte** and **short**, unless a large number of them must be stored.

7.4.2 Explicit Type Conversion

Most languages provide some capability for doing explicit conversions, both widening and narrowing. In some cases, warning messages are produced when an explicit narrowing conversion results in a significant change to the value of the object being converted.

In the C-based languages, explicit type conversions are called **casts.** To specify a cast, the desired type is placed in parentheses just before the expression to be converted, as in

```
(int) angle
```

One of the reasons for the parentheses around the type name in these conversions is that the first of these languages, C, has several two-word type names, such as **long int.**

In Ada, the casts have the syntax of function calls. For example,

```
Float(Sum)
```

Recall (from Chapter 5) that Ada also has a generic type conversion function, `Unchecked_Conversion`, that does not change the representation of the value—it merely changes its type.

7.4.3 Errors in Expressions

A number of errors can occur in expression evaluation. If the language requires type checking, either static or dynamic, then operand type errors cannot occur. We already discussed the errors that can occur because of coercions of operands in expressions. The other kinds of errors are due to the limitations of computer arithmetic and the inherent limitations of arithmetic. The most common error occurs when the result of an operation cannot be represented in the memory cell where it must be stored. This is called **overflow** or **underflow,** depending on whether the result was too large or too small. One limitation of arithmetic is that division by zero is disallowed. Of course, the fact that it is not mathematically allowed does not prevent a program from attempting to do it.

Floating-point overflow, underflow, and division by zero are examples of run-time errors, which are sometimes called **exceptions.** Language facilities that allow programs to detect and deal with exceptions are discussed in Chapter 14.

7.5 Relational and Boolean Expressions

In addition to arithmetic expressions, programming languages include relational and Boolean expressions.

7.5.1 Relational Expressions

history note

The Fortran I designers used English abbreviations because the symbols > and < were not on the card punches at the time of Fortran I's design.

A **relational operator** is an operator that compares the values of its two operands. A relational expression has two operands and one relational operator. The value of a relational expression is Boolean, except when Boolean is not a type included in the language. The relational operators are often overloaded for a variety of types. The operation that determines the truth or falsehood of a relational expression depends on the operand types. It can be simple, as for integer operands, or complex, as for character string operands. Typically, the types of the operands that can be used for relational operators are numeric types, strings, and ordinal types.

The syntax of the relational operators available in some common languages is as follows:

Operation	Ada	C-based Languages	Fortran 95
Equal	=	==	.EQ. or ==
Not equal	/=	!=	.NE. or <>
Greater than	>	>	.GT. or >
Less than	<	<	.LT. or <
Greater than or equal	>=	>=	.GE. or >=
Less than or equal	<=	<=	.LE. or >=

JavaScript and PHP have two additional relational operators, === and !==. These are similar to their relatives, == and !=, but prevent their operands from being conerced. For example, the expression

```
"7" == 7
```

is true in JavaScript, because when a string and a number are the operands of a relational operator, the string is coerced to a number. However,

```
"7" === 7
```

is false, because no coercion is done on the operands of this operator.

Ruby uses == for the equality relational operator that uses coercions, and eql? for equality with no coercions (thus requiring that the types and values of the operands be equal). Ruby uses === only in the **when** clause of its **case** statement, as discussed in Chapter 8.

The relational operators always have lower precedence than the arithmetic operators, so that in expressions such as

```
a + 1 > 2 * b
```

the arithmetic expressions are evaluated first.

7.5.2 Boolean Expressions

Boolean expressions consist of Boolean variables, Boolean constants, relational expressions, and Boolean operators. The operators usually include those for the AND, OR, and NOT operations, and sometimes for exclusive OR and equivalence. Boolean operators usually take only Boolean operands (Boolean variables, Boolean literals, or relational expressions) and produce Boolean values.

In the mathematics of Boolean algebras, the OR and AND operators must have equal precedence. In accordance with this, Ada's AND and OR operators have equal precedence. However, the C-based languages assign a higher precedence to AND than OR. Perhaps this resulted from the baseless correlation of multiplication with AND and of addition with OR, which would naturally assign higher precedence to AND.

Because arithmetic expressions can be the operands of relational expressions, and relational expressions can be the operands of Boolean expressions, the three categories of operators must be placed in different precedence levels, relative to each other.

The precedence of the arithmetic, relational, and Boolean operators in the C-based languages is

Highest	*postfix* ++, --
	unary +, -, prefix ++, --, !
	*, /, %

binary +, –

<, >, <=, >=

=, !=

&&

Lowest ||

Versions of C prior to C99 are odd among the popular imperative languages in that they have no Boolean type and thus no Boolean values. Instead, numeric values are used to represent Boolean values. In place of Boolean operands, scalar variables (numeric or character) and constants are used, with zero considered false and all nonzero values considered true. If such an expression has only one relational operator and no Boolean operands, its appearance is conventional. For example

```
x > 17
```

Expressions with Boolean operators have a less conventional appearance, illustrated with

```
ptr && count
```

in which `ptr` is a pointer and `count` is an **int.** The result of evaluating such an expression is an integer, with the value 0 if false and 1 if true. Arithmetic expressions can also be used for Boolean expressions in C99 and C++.

One odd result of C's design is that the expression

```
a > b > c
```

is legal. The leftmost relational operator is evaluated first because the relational operators of C are left associative, producing either 0 or 1. Then this result is compared with the variable `c`. There is never a comparison between `b` and `c` in this expression.

Some languages, including Perl and Ruby, provide two sets of the binary logic operators, `&&` and **and** for AND and `||` and **or** for OR. One difference between `&&` and **and** (and `||` and **or**) is that the spelled versions have lower precedence. Also, **and** and **or** have equal precedence, but `&&` has higher precedence than `||`.

When the nonarithmetic operators of the C-based languages are included, there are more than 40 operators and at least 14 different levels of precedence. This is clear evidence of the richness of the collections of operators and the complexity of expressions possible in these languages.

Readability dictates that a language should include a Boolean type, as we stated in Chapter 6, rather than simply using numeric types in Boolean expressions. Some error detection is lost in the use of numeric types for Boolean operands, because any numeric expression, whether intended or not, is a legal operand to a Boolean operator. In the other imperative languages, any non-Boolean expression used as an operand of a Boolean operator is detected as an error.

7.6 Short-Circuit Evaluation

A **short-circuit evaluation** of an expression is one in which the result is determined without evaluating all of the operands and/or operators. For example, the value of the arithmetic expression

```
(13 * a) * (b / 13 - 1)
```

is independent of the value of (b / 13 - 1) if a is 0, because 0 * x = 0 for any x. So when a is 0, there is no need to evaluate (b / 13 - 1) or perform the second multiplication. However, in arithmetic expressions this shortcut is not easily detected during execution, so it is never taken.

The value of the Boolean expression

```
(a >= 0) && (b < 10)
```

is independent of the second relational expression if a < 0, because the expression (FALSE && (b < 10)) is FALSE for all values of b. So when a < 0, there is no need to evaluate b, the constant 10, the second relational expression, or the && operation. Unlike the case of arithmetic expressions, this shortcut can be easily discovered during execution.

To illustrate a potential problem with non-short-circuit evaluation of Boolean expressions, suppose Java did not use short-circuit evaluation. Now suppose we write a table lookup loop using the **while** statement. One simple version of Java code for such a lookup, assuming that list, which has listlen elements, is the array to be searched and key is the searched-for value, is

```
index = 0;
while ((index < listlen) && (list[index] != key))
  index = index + 1;
```

If evaluation is not short-circuit, both relational expressions in the Boolean expression of the **while** statement are evaluated, regardless of the value of the first. Thus, if key is not in list, the program will terminate with a subscript out-of-range exception. The same iteration that has index == listlen will reference list[listlen], which causes the indexing error because list is declared to have listlen-1 as an upper-bound subscript value.

If a language provides short-circuit evaluation of Boolean expressions and it is used, this is not a problem. In the preceding example, a short-circuit evaluation scheme would evaluate the first operand of the AND operator, but it would skip the second operand if the first operand is false.

A language that provides short-circuit evaluations of Boolean expressions and also has side effects in expressions allows subtle errors to occur. Suppose that short-circuit evaluation is used on an expression and part of the expression that contains a side effect is not evaluated; then the side effect will occur only in complete evaluations of the whole expression. If program correctness depends on the side effect, short-circuit evaluation can result in a serious error. For example, consider the Java expression

```
(a > b) || ((b++) / 3)
```

In this expression, b is changed (in the second arithmetic expression) only when a <= b. If the programmer assumed b would be changed every time this expression is evaluated during execution (and the program's correctness depends on it), the program will fail.

Ada allows the programmer to specify short-circuit evaluation of the Boolean operators AND and OR by using the two-word operators **and then** and **or else.** For example, again assuming that List is declared to have a subscript range of 1..Listlen, the Ada code

```
Index := 1;
while (Index <= Listlen) and then (List (Index) /= Key)
  loop
  Index := Index + 1;
  end loop;
```

will not cause an error when Key is not in List and Index becomes larger than Listlen.

In the C-based languages, the usual AND and OR operators, && and ||, respectively, are short-circuit. However, these languages also have bitwise AND and OR operators, & and |, respectively, that can be used on Boolean-valued operands and are not short-circuit. Of course, the bitwise operators are only equivalent to the usual Boolean operators if all operands are restricted to being either 0 (for true) or 1 (for false).

All of the logical operators of Ruby, Perl, and Python are short-circuit evaluated.

The inclusion of both short-circuit and ordinary operators in Ada is clearly the best design, because it provides the programmer the flexibility of choosing short-circuit evaluation for any Boolean expression for which it is appropriate.

7.7 Assignment Statements

As we have previously stated, the assignment statement is one of the central constructs in imperative languages. It provides the mechanism by which the user can dynamically change the bindings of values to variables. In the following section, the simplest form of assignment is discussed. Subsequent sections describe a variety of alternatives.

7.7.1   Simple Assignments

The general syntax of the simple assignment statement is

<target_variable> <assignment_operator> <expression>

Nearly all programming languages currently being used use the equal sign for the assignment operator. All of these must use something different from an equal sign for the equality relational operator to avoid confusion with their assignment operator.

ALGOL 60 pioneered the use of := as the assignment operator, which avoids the confusion of assignment with equality. Ada also uses this assignment operator.

The assignment operator in the C-based languages is treated much like a binary operator, and as such it can appear embedded in expressions. This operator is discussed in Section 7.7.5.

The design choices of how assignments are used in a language have varied widely. In some languages, such as Fortran and Ada, an assignment can appear only as a stand-alone statement, and the destination is restricted to a single variable. There are, however, many alternatives.

7.7.2   Conditional Targets

C++ allows conditional targets on assignment statements. For example, consider

```
flag ? count1 : count2 = 0;
```

which is equivalent to

```
if (flag)
  count1 = 0;
else
  count2 = 0;
```

7.7.3   Compound Assignment Operators

A **compound assignment operator** is a shorthand method of specifying a commonly needed form of assignment. The form of assignment that can be abbreviated with this technique has the destination variable also appearing as the first operand in the expression on the right side, as in

```
a = a + b
```

Compound assignment operators were introduced by ALGOL 68, were later adopted in a slightly different form by C, and are part of the other C-based languages, as well as Perl, JavaScript, Python, and Ruby. The syntax of these assignment operators is the catenation of the desired binary operator to the = operator. For example,

```
sum += value;
```

is equivalent to

```
sum = sum + value;
```

The languages that support compound assignment operators have versions for most of their binary operators.

7.7.4 Unary Assignment Operators

The C-based languages, Perl, and JavaScript include two special unary arithmetic operators that are actually abbreviated assignments. They combine increment and decrement operations with assignment. The operators ++ for increment, and -- for decrement, can be used either in expressions or to form stand-alone single-operator assignment statements. They can appear either as prefix operators, meaning that they precede the operands, or as postfix operators, meaning that they follow the operands. In the assignment statement

```
sum = ++ count;
```

the value of count is incremented by 1 and then assigned to sum. This operation could also be stated as

```
count = count + 1;
sum = count;
```

If the same operator is used as a postfix operator, as in

```
sum = count ++;
```

the assignment of the value of count to sum occurs first; then count is incremented. The effect is the same as that of the two statements

```
sum = count;
count = count + 1;
```

An example of the use of the unary increment operator to form a complete assignment statement is

```
count ++;
```

history note

The PDP-11 computer, on which C was first implemented, has autoincrement and autodecrement addressing modes, which are hardware versions of the increment and decrement operators of C when they are used as array indices. One might guess from this that the design of these C operators was based on the design of the PDP-11 architecture. That guess would be wrong, however, because the C operators were inherited from the B language, which was designed before the first PDP-11.

which simply increments `count`. It does not look like an assignment, but it certainly is one. It is equivalent to the statement

```
count = count + 1;
```

When two unary operators apply to the same operand, the association is right to left. For example, in

```
- count ++
```

`count` is first incremented and then negated. So it is equivalent to

```
- (count ++)
```

rather than

```
(- count) ++
```

7.7.5   Assignment as an Expression

In the C-based languages, Perl, and JavaScript, the assignment statement produces a result, which is the same as the value assigned to the target. It can therefore be used as an expression and as an operand in other expressions. This design treats the assignment operator much like any other binary operator, except that it has the side effect of changing its left operand. For example, in C, it is common to write statements such as

```
while ((ch = getchar()) != EOF) { ... }
```

In this statement, the next character from the standard input file, usually the keyboard, is gotten with `getchar` and assigned to the variable `ch`. The result, or value assigned, is then compared with the constant `EOF`. If `ch` is not equal to `EOF`, the compound statement `{ ... }` is executed. Note that the assignment must be parenthesized—in the languages that support assignment as an expression, the precedence of the assignment operator is lower than that of the relational operators. Without the parentheses, the new character would be compared with `EOF` first. Then the result of that comparison, either 0 or 1, would be assigned to `ch`.

The disadvantage of allowing assignment statements to be operands in expressions is that it provides yet another kind of expression side effect. This type of side effect can lead to expressions that are difficult to read and understand. An expression with any kind of side effect has this disadvantage. Such an expression cannot be read as an expression, which in mathematics is a denotation of a value, but only as a list of instructions with an odd order of execution. For example, the expression

```
a = b + (c = d / b++) - 1
```

denotes the instructions

Assign b to `temp`
Assign b + 1 to b
Assign d / `temp` to c
Assign b + c to `temp`
Assign `temp` - 1 to a

Note that the treatment of the assignment operator as any other binary operator allows the effect of multiple-target assignments, such as

```
sum = count = 0;
```

in which `count` is first assigned the zero, and then `count`'s value is assigned to `sum`. This form of multiple-target assignments is also legal in Python.

There is a loss of error detection in the C design of the assignment operation that frequently leads to program errors. In particular, if we type

```
if (x = y) ...
```

instead of

```
if (x == y) ...
```

which is an easily made mistake, it is not detectable as an error by the compiler. Rather than testing a relational expression, the value that is assigned to x is tested (in this case, it is the value of y that reaches this statement). This is actually a result of three design decisions: allowing assignment to behave like an ordinary binary operator, using arithmetic expressions as Boolean operands, and using two very similar operators, = and ==, to have completely different meanings. This is another example of the safety deficiencies of C and C++ programs. Note that Java and C# allow only **boolean** expressions in their **if** statements, disallowing this problem.

7.7.6   List Assignments

Several recent programming languages, including Perl and Ruby, provide multiple-target, multiple-source assignment statements. For example, in Perl one can write

```
($first, $second, $third) = (20, 40, 60);
```

The semantics is that 20 is assigned to `$first`, 40 is assigned to `$second`, and 60 is assigned to `$third`. If the values of two variables must be interchanged, this can be done with a single assignment, as with

```
($first, $second) = ($second, $first);
```

This correctly interchanges the values of `$first` and `$second`, without the use of a temporary variable (at least one created and managed by the programmer).

In Perl, if there are more values on the right side than variables on the left side, the excess values are ignored. If there are more variables on the left side than values on the right side, they are set to **undef**. If the left side includes an array name, that array gets all of the remaining values in the right side. If any variables follow an array name in a left side, they are all set to **undef**.

The syntax of the simplest form of Ruby's list assignment is similar to that of Perl, except the left and right sides are not parenthesized. Also, Ruby includes a few more elaborate versions of list assignment, which are not discussed here.

7.8 Mixed-mode Assignment

We discussed mixed-mode expressions in Section 7.4.1. Frequently, assignment statements also are mixed-mode. The design question is: Does the type of the expression have to be the same as the type of the variable being assigned, or can coercion be used in some cases of type mismatch?

Fortran, C, C++, and Perl use coercion rules for mixed-mode assignment that are similar to those they use for mixed-mode expressions; that is, many of the possible type mixes are legal, with coercion freely applied.[5] Ada does not allow mixed-mode assignment.

In a clear departure from C++, Java and C# allow mixed-mode assignment only if the required coercion is widening.[6] So, an **int** value can be assigned to a **float** variable, but not vice versa. Disallowing half of the possible mixed-mode assignments is a simple but effective way to increase the reliability of Java and C#, relative to C and C++.

In all languages that allow mixed-mode assignment, the coercion takes place only after the right-side expression has been evaluated. One alternative would be to coerce all operands in the right side to the type of the target before evaluation. For example, consider the following code:

```
int a, b;
float c;
...
c = a / b;
```

---

5. Note that in Python and Ruby, types are associated with objects, not variables, so there is no such thing as mixed-mode assignment in those languages.

6. Not quite true: If an integer literal, which the compiler by default assigns the type **int**, is assigned to a **char, byte,** or **short** variable and the literal is in the range of the type of the variable, the **int** value is coerced to the type of the variable in a narrowing conversion. This narrowing conversion cannot result in an error.

Because c is **float,** the values of a and b could be coerced to **float** before the division, which could produce a different value for c than if the coercion were delayed (for example, if a were 2 and b were 3).

SUMMARY

Expressions consist of constants, variables, parentheses, function calls, and operators. Assignment statements include target variables, assignment operators, and expressions.

The semantics of an expression is determined in large part by the order of evaluation of operators. The associativity and precedence rules for operators in the expressions of a language determine the order of operator evaluation in those expressions. Operand evaluation order is important if functional side effects are possible. Type conversions can be widening or narrowing. Some narrowing conversions produce erroneous values. Implicit type conversions, or coercions, in expressions are common, although they eliminate the error-detection benefit of type checking, thus lowering reliability.

Assignment statements have appeared in a wide variety of forms, including conditional targets, assigning operators, and list assignments.

REVIEW QUESTIONS

1. Define *operator precedence* and *operator associativity.*

2. Define *functional side effect.*

3. What is a coercion?

4. What is a conditional expression?

5. What is an overloaded operator?

6. Define *narrowing* and *widening conversions.*

7. What is a mixed-mode expression?

8. How does operand evaluation order interact with functional side effects?

9. What is short-circuit evaluation?

10. Name a language that always does short-circuit evaluation of Boolean expressions. Name one that never does it. Name one in which the programmer is allowed to choose.

11. How does C support relational and Boolean expressions?

12. What is the purpose of a compound assignment operator?

13. What is the associativity of C's unary arithmetic operators?

14. What is one possible disadvantage of treating the assignment operator as if it were an arithmetic operator?

15. What two languages include list assignments?

16. What mixed-mode assignments are allowed in Ada?

17. What mixed-mode assignments are allowed in Java?

PROBLEM SET

1. When might you want the compiler to ignore type differences in an expression?

2. State your own arguments for and against allowing mixed-mode arithmetic expressions.

3. Do you think the elimination of overloaded operators in your favorite language would be beneficial? Why or why not?

4. Would it be a good idea to eliminate all operator precedence rules and require parentheses to show the desired precedence in expressions? Why or why not?

5. Should C's assigning operations (for example, +=) be included in other languages? Why or why not?

6. Should C's single-operand assignment forms (for example, ++count) be included in other languages? Why or why not?

7. Describe a situation in which the add operator in a programming language would not be commutative.

8. Describe a situation in which the add operator in a programming language would not be associative.

9. Assume the following rules of associativity and precedence for expressions:

Precedence:	Highest	$*$, $/$, **not**
		$+$, $-$, $\&$, **mod**
		$-$ (unary)
		$=$, $/=$, $<$, $<=$, $>=$, $>$
		and
	Lowest	**or, xor**
Associativity:	Left to right	

Show the order of evaluation of the following expressions by parenthesizing all subexpressions and placing a superscript on the right parenthesis to indicate order. For example, for the expression

```
a + b * c + d
```

the order of evaluation would be represented as

$$((a + (b * c)^1)^2 + d)^3$$

a. a * b - 1 + c

b. a * (b - 1) / c **mod** d

c. (a - b) / c & (d * e / a - 3)

d. -a **or** c = d **and** e

e. a > b **xor** c **or** d <= 17

f. -a + b

10. Show the order of evaluation of the expressions of Problem 9, assuming that there are no precedence rules and all operators associate right to left.

11. Write a BNF description of the precedence and associativity rules defined for the expressions in Problem 9. Assume the only operands are the names a, b, c, d, and e.

12. Using the grammar of Problem 11, draw parse trees for the expressions of Problem 9.

13. Let the function fun be defined as

```
int fun(int *k) {
  *k += 4;
  return 3 * (*k) - 1;
 }
```

Suppose fun is used in a program as follows:

```
void main() {
  int i = 10, j = 10, sum1, sum2;
  sum1 = (i / 2) + fun(&i);
  sum2 = fun(&j) + (j / 2);
 }
```

What are the values of sum1 and sum2

a. if the operands in the expressions are evaluated left to right?

b. if the operands in the expressions are evaluated right to left?

14. What is your primary argument against (or for) the operator precedence rules of APL?

15. For some language of your choice, make up a list of operator symbols that could be used to eliminate all operator overloading.

16. Determine whether the narrowing explicit type conversions in two languages you know provide error messages when a converted value loses its usefulness.

17. Should an optimizing compiler for C or C++ be allowed to change the order of subexpressions in a Boolean expression? Why or why not?

18. Answer the question in Problem 17 for Ada.

19. Consider the following C program:

```c
int fun(int *i) {
  *i += 5;
  return 4;
 }
void main() {
  int x = 3;
  x = x + fun(&x);
 }
```

What is the value of x after the assignment statement in main, assuming

a. operands are evaluated left to right.

b. operands are evaluated right to left.

20. Why does Java specify that operands in expressions are all evaluated in left-to-right order?

PROGRAMMING EXERCISES

1. Run the code given in Problem 13 (in the Problem Set) on some system that supports C to determine the values of sum1 and sum2. Explain the results.

2. Rewrite the program of Exercise 1 in C++, Java, and C#, run them, and compare the results.

3. Write a test program in your favorite language that determines and outputs the precedence and associativity of its arithmetic and Boolean operators.

4. Write an Ada program that illustrates the difference between **mod** and **rem** using a variety of positive and negative integer operands.

5. Write a Java program that exposes Java's rule for operand evaluation order when one of the operands is a method call.

6. Repeat Exercise 5 with C++.

7. Repeat Exercise 6 with C#.

8. Write a program in either C++, Java, or C# that illustrates the order of evaluation of expressions used as actual parameters to a method.

9. Write a C program that has the following statements:

```c
int a, b;
a = 10;
b = a + fun();
```

```
printf("With the function call on the right, ");
printf(" b is: %d\n", b);
a = 10;
b = fun() + a;
printf("With the function call on the left, ");
printf(" b is: %d\n", b);
```

and define fun to add 10 to a. Explain the results.

10. Write a C# program to determine whether C# uses Java's rule on operand evaluation order.

Statement-Level Control Structures

The flow of control, or execution sequence, in a program can be examined at several levels. In Chapter 7, we discussed the flow of control within expressions, which is governed by operator associativity and precedence rules. At the highest level is the flow of control among program units, which is discussed in Chapters 9 and 13. Between these two extremes is the important issue of the flow of control among statements, which is the subject of this chapter.

We begin by giving an overview of the evolution of control statements in the imperative programming languages. This topic is followed by a thorough examination of selection constructs, both those for two-way and those for multiple selection. We then discuss the variety of looping constructs that have been developed and used in programming languages. Then we take a brief look at the problems associated with unconditional branch statements. Finally, we describe the guarded command control constructs.

8.1 Introduction

Computations in imperative-language programs are accomplished by evaluating expressions and assigning the resulting values to variables. There are, however, few useful programs that consist entirely of assignment statements. At least two additional linguistic mechanisms are necessary to make the computations in programs flexible and powerful: some means of selecting among alternative control flow paths (of statement execution) and some means of causing the repeated execution of sequences of statements. Statements that provide these kinds of capabilities are called **control statements.**

The control statements of the first successful programming language, Fortran, were, in effect, designed by the architects of the IBM 704. All were directly related to machine language instructions, so their capabilities were more the result of instruction design than language design. At the time, little was known about the difficulty of programming, and, as a result, the control statements of Fortran in the middle 1950s were thought to be entirely acceptable. By today's standards, however, they would be considered wholly inadequate.

A great deal of research and discussion was devoted to control statements in the 10 years between the mid-1960s and the mid-1970s. One of the primary conclusions of these efforts was that, although a single control statement (a selectable goto) is minimally sufficient, a language that is designed *not* to include a goto needs only a small number of different control statements. In fact, it was proven that all algorithms that can be expressed by flowcharts can be coded in a programming language with only two control statements: one for choosing between two control flow paths and one for logically controlled iterations (Böhm and Jacopini, 1966). An important result of this is that the unconditional branch statement is superfluous—potentially useful but nonessential. This fact, combined with the practical problems of using unconditional branches, or gotos, led to a great deal of debate about the goto, as will be discussed in Section 8.4.1.

Programmers care less about the results of theoretical research on control statements than they do about writability and readability. All languages that have become widely used include more control statements than the two that are minimally required, because writability is enhanced by a larger number and wider variety of control statements. For example, rather than requiring the use of a logically conrolled loop statement for all loops, it is easier to write programs when a counter-controlled loop statement can be used to build loops that are naturally controlled by a counter. The primary factor that restricts the number of control statements in a language is readability, because the presence of a large number of statement forms demands that program readers learn a larger language. Recall that few people learn all of the constructs of a relatively large language; instead, they learn the subset they choose to use, which is often a different subset from that used by the programmer who wrote the program they are trying to read. On the other hand, too few control statements can require the use of lower-level statements, such as the goto, which also makes programs less readable.

The question as to the best collection of control statements to provide the required capabilities and the desired writability has been widely debated. It is essentially a question of how much a language should be expanded to increase its writability at the expense of its simplicity, size, and readability.

A **control structure** is a control statement and the collection of statements whose execution it controls.

There is only one design issue that is relevant to all of the selection and iteration control statements: Should the control structure have multiple entries? All selection and iteration statements control the execution of code segments, and the question is whether the execution of those code segments always begins with the first statement in the segment. It is now generally believed that multiple entries add little to the flexibility of a control construct, relative to the decrease in readability caused by the increased complexity. Note that multiple entries are possible only in languages that include gotos and statement labels.

At this point, the reader might wonder why we do not consider multiple exits from control structures to be a design issue. The reason is that all programming languages allow some form of multiple exits from control structures, the rationale being as follows: If all exits from a control structure are restricted to transferring control to the first statement following the structure, where control would flow if the control structure had no explicit exit, there is no harm to readability and also no danger. However, if an exit can have an unrestricted target and therefore can result in a transfer of control to anywhere in the program unit that contains the control structure, the harm to readability is the same as for a goto statement anywhere else in a program. Languages that have a goto statement allow it to appear anywhere, including in a control structure. Therefore, the issue is the inclusion of a goto, not whether multiple exits from control expressions are allowed.

8.2 Selection Statements

A **selection statement** provides the means of choosing between two or more execution paths in a program. Such statements are fundamental and essential parts of all programming languages, as was proven by Böhm and Jacopini.

Selection statements fall into two general categories, two-way and *n*-way, or multiple selection. Two-way selectors are discussed in Section 8.2.1; multiple-way selectors are covered in Section 8.2.2.

8.2.1 Two-Way Selection Statements

Although the two-way selection statements of contemporary imperative languages are quite similar, there are some variations in their designs. The general form of a two-way selector is as follows:

```
if control_expression
    then clause
    else clause
```

8.2.1.1 Design Issues

The design issues for two-way selectors can be summarized as follows:

- What is the form and type of the expression that controls the selection?
- How are the then and else clauses specified?
- How should the meaning of nested selectors be specified?

history note

Fortran includes a three-way selector named "the arithmetic If" that uses an arithmetic expression for control. It causes control to go to one of three different labeled statements, depending on whether the value of its control expression is negative, zero, or greater than zero. This statement is on the obsolescent feature list of Fortran 95.

8.2.1.2 The Control Expression

Control expressions are specified in parentheses if the **then** reserved word (or some other syntactic marker) is not used to introduce the then clause. In those cases where the **then** reserved word (or alternative marker) is used, there is less need for the parentheses, so they are often omitted, as in Ruby.

In C89, which did not have a Boolean data type, arithmetic expressions were used as control expressions. This can also be done in Python, C99, and C++. However, in those languages either arithmetic or Boolean expressions can be used. In other contemporary languages, such as Ada, Java, Ruby, and C#, only Boolean expressions can be used for control expressions.

8.2.1.3 Clause Form

In many contemporary languages, the then and else clauses appear as either single statements or compound statements. One variation of this is Perl, in which all then and else clauses must be compound statements, even if they contain single statements. The C-based languages, as well as Perl, JavaScript, and PHP, use braces to form compound statements, which serve as the bodies of then and else clauses. In Fortran 95, Ada, Python, and Ruby, the then and else clauses are statement sequences. The complete selection construct is terminated in Fortran 95, Ada, and Ruby with a reserved word.[1]

Python uses indentation to specify compound statements. For example,

```
if x > y :
  x = y
  print "case 1"
```

All statements equally indented are included in the compound statement.[2] Notice that rather than **then,** a colon is used to introduce the then clause in Python.

The variations in clause form have implications for the specification of the meaning of nested selectors, as is discussed in the next subsection.

8.2.1.4 Nesting Selectors

Recall that in Chapter 3 the problem of syntactic ambiguity of a straightforward grammar for a two-way selector construct was discussed. That grammar was as follows:

```
<if_stmt> → if <logic_expr> then <stmt>
          | if <logic_expr> then <stmt> else <stmt>
```

The issue was that when a selection construct is nested in the then clause of a selection construct, it is not clear to which if an else clause should be associated. This problem is reflected in the semantics of selection statements. Consider the following Java-like code:

```
if (sum == 0)
  if (count == 0)
    result = 0;
else
    result = 1;
```

This construct can be interpreted in two different ways, depending on whether the else clause is matched with the first then clause or the second. Notice that the indentation seems to indicate that the else clause belongs with the first then clause. However, with the exception of Python, indentation has no effect on semantics in contemporary languages and is therefore ignored by their compilers.

---

1. Actually, in Ada and Fortran it is two reserved words, **end if** (Ada) or End If (Fortran).

2. The statement following the compound statement must have the same indentation as the if.

history note

The designers of ALGOL 60 chose to use syntax, rather than a rule, to connect else clauses to then clauses. Specifically, an if statement is not allowed to be nested directly in a then clause. If an if must be nested in a then clause, it must be placed in a compound statement, as in the latter Java example.

The difference between the two designs is that the Java version allows one to write the nested selector that looks like it pairs the else clause with the first then clause but does not, whereas this same form is syntactically illegal in ALGOL 60, thereby disallowing Java's subtle problem.

The crux of the problem in this example is that the else clause follows two then clauses with no intervening else clause, and there is no syntactic indicator to specify a matching of the else clause to one of the then clauses. In Java, as in many other imperative languages, the static semantics of the language specify that the else clause is always paired with the nearest previous unpaired then clause. A static semantics rule, rather than a syntactic entity, is used to provide the disambiguation. So, in the example, the else clause would be the alternative to the second then clause. The disadvantage of using a rule rather than some syntactic entity is that although the programmer may have meant the else clause to be the alternative to the first then clause and the compiler found the structure syntactically correct, its semantics is the opposite. To force the alternative semantics in Java, a different syntactic form is required, in which the inner **if** is put in a compound, as in

```
if (sum == 0) {
  if (count == 0)
    result = 0;
}
else
  result = 1;
```

C, C++, and C# have the same problem as Java with selection statement nesting. Because Perl requires that all then and else clauses be compound, it does not have the problem. In Perl, the previous code would be written as

```
if (sum == 0) {
  if (count == 0) {
    result = 0;
  }
} else {
  result = 1;
}
```

If the alternative semantics were needed, it would be

```
if (sum == 0) {
  if (count == 0) {
    result = 0;
  }
  else {
    result = 1;
  }
}
```

Another way to avoid the issue of nested selection statements is to use an alternative means of forming compound statements. Consider the syntactic structure of the Java **if** statement. The then clause follows the control expression and the else clause is introduced by the reserved word **else.** When the then clause is a single statement and the else clause is present, although there is no need to mark the end, the **else** reserved word in fact marks the end of the then clause. When the then clause is a compound, it is terminated by a right brace. However, if the last clause in an **if,** whether then or else, is not a compound, there is no syntactic entity to mark the end of the whole selection construct. The use of a special word for this purpose resolves the question of the semantics of nested selectors and also adds to the readability of the construct. This is the design of the selection construct in Fortran 95, Ada, and Ruby. For example, consider the following Ruby construct:

```
if a > b then
  sum = sum + a
  acount = acount + 1
else
  sum = sum + b
  bcount = bcount + 1
end
```

The design of this construct is more regular than that of the selection constructs of the C-based languages, because the form is the same regardless of the number of statements in the then and else clauses. (This is also true for Perl.) Recall that in Ruby, the then and else clauses consist of statement sequences rather than compound statements. The first interpretation of the selector example at the beginning of Section 8.2.1.4, in which the else clause is matched to the nested if, can be written in Ruby as follows:

```
if sum == 0 then
  if count == 0 then
    result = 0
  else
    result = 1
  end
end
```

Because the **end** reserved word closes the nested **if,** it is clear that the else clause is matched to the inner then clause.

The second interpretation of the selection construct in Section 8.2.1.4, in which the else clause is matched to the outer if, can be written in Ruby as follows:

```
if sum == 0 then
  if count == 0 then
```

```
      result = 0
   end
else
  result = 1
end
```

The following construct, written in Python, is semantically equivalent to the last Ruby construct above:

```
if sum == 0 :
  if count == 0 :
    result = 0
else:
  result = 1
```

If the line **else:** were indented to begin in the same column as the nested if, the else clause would be matched with the inner if.

8.2.2   Multiple-Selection Constructs

The **multiple-selection** construct allows the selection of one of any number of statements or statement groups. It is, therefore, a generalization of a selector. In fact, two-way selectors can be built with a multiple selector.

The need to choose from among more than two control paths in a program is common. Although a multiple selector can be built from two-way selectors and gotos, the resulting structures are cumbersome, difficult to write and read, and unreliable. Therefore, the need for a special structure is clear.

8.2.2.1 Design Issues

Some of the design issues for multiple selectors are similar to some of those for two-way selectors. For example, one issue is the question of the type of expression on which the selector is based. In this case, the range of possibilities is larger, in part because the number of possible selections is larger. A two-way selector needs an expression with only two possible values. Another issue is whether single statements, compound statements, or statement sequences may be selected. Next, there is the question of whether only a single selectable segment can be executed when the construct is executed. This is not an issue for two-way selectors, because they allow only one of the clauses to be on a control path during one execution. As we shall see, the resolution of this issue for multiple selectors is a trade-off between reliability and flexibility. Another issue is the form of the case value specifications. Finally, there is the issue of what should result from the selector expression evaluating to a value that does not select one of the segments. (Such a value would be unrepresented among the selectable segments.) The choice here is between simply disallowing the situation from arising and having the construct do nothing at all when it does arise.

The following is a summary of these design issues:

- What is the form and type of the expression that controls the selection?
- How are the selectable segments specified?
- Is execution flow through the structure restricted to include just a single selectable segment?
- How are the case values specified?
- How should unrepresented selector expression values be handled, if at all?

8.2.2.2 Examples of Multiple Selectors

The C multiple-selector construct, **switch,** which is also part of C++, Java, and JavaScript, is a relatively primitive design. Its general form is

```
switch (expression) {
  case constant_expression_1: statement_1;
  . . .
  case constant_expression_n: statement_n;
  [default: statement_n+1]
}
```

where the control expression and the constant expressions are some integer type. The selectable statements can be statement sequences, compound statements, or blocks. The optional **default** segment is for unrepresented values of the control expression. If the value of the control expression is not represented and no default segment is present, the construct does nothing.

The **switch** construct does not provide implicit branches at the end of its code segments. This allows control to flow through more than one selectable code segment on a single execution. Consider the following example:

```
switch (index) {
  case 1:
  case 3: odd += 1;
          sumodd += index;
  case 2:
  case 4: even += 1;
          sumeven += index;
  default: printf("Error in switch, index = %d\n", index);
}
```

This code prints the error message on every execution. Likewise, the code for the 2 and 4 constants is executed every time the code at the 1 or 3 constants is executed. To logically separate these segments, an explicit branch must be included. The **break** statement, which is actually a restricted goto, is normally used for exiting **switch** constructs.

The following **switch** construct uses **break** to restrict each execution to a single selectable segment:

```
switch (index) {
  case 1:
  case 3: odd += 1;
          sumodd += index;
          break;
  case 2:
  case 4: even += 1;
          sumeven += index;
          break;
  default: printf("Error in switch, index = %d\n", index);
}
```

Occasionally, it is convenient to allow control to flow from one selectable code segment to another. This is obviously the reason why there are no implicit branches in the **switch** construct. The reliability problem with this design arises when the mistaken absence of a **break** statement in a segment allows control to incorrectly flow to the next segment. The designers of C's **switch** traded a decrease in reliability for an increase in flexibility. Studies have shown, however, that the ability to have control flow from one selectable segment to another is rarely used. C's **switch** is modeled on the multiple-selection statement in ALGOL 68, which also does not have implicit branches from selectable segments.

The C# switch statement differs from that of its C-based predecessors in that a static semantics rule disallows the implicit execution of more than one segment. The rule is that every selectable segment must end with an explicit unconditional branch statement: either a **break,** which transfers control out of the **switch** construct, or a **goto,** which can transfer control to one of the selectable segments (or virtually anywhere else). For example,

```
switch (value) {
  case -1:
    Negatives++;
    break;
  case 0:
    Zeros++;
    goto case 1;
  case 1:
    Positives++;
```

```
      default:
        Console.WriteLine("Error in switch \n");
  }
```

Note that `Console.WriteLine` is the method for displaying strings in C#.

The Ada **case** statement is a descendant of the multiple-selector state-ment that appeared in ALGOL W in 1966. The general form of this con-struct is as follows:

```
case expression is
  when choice list => statement_sequence;
  . . .
    when choice list => statement_sequence;
    [when others => statement_sequence;]
end case;
```

where the expression is of ordinal type (integer, Boolean, character, or enu-meration type) and the **when others** clause is optional.

The choice lists of Ada **case** statements are often single literals, but they can also be subranges, such as `10..15`. They can also use OR operators, spec-ified by the symbol |, to create lists of literals. For example, the following could appear as a choice list: `10|15|20`. The **when others** clause is used for unrepresented values. Ada requires the choice lists to be exhaustive, which provides a bit more reliability because it disallows the error of inadvertent omission of one or more choice values. Most Ada **case** statements include a **when others** clause to ensure that the choice list is exhaustive. Because the choice lists must be exhaustive, there is never a question of what happens when the control expression has an unrepresented value.

The values in the choice lists must be mutually exclusive; that is, a con-stant may not appear in more than one choice list. Also, the literals (they can also be named constants) in the choice lists must be of the same type as the expression.

The semantics of the Ada **case** is as follows: The expression is evalu-ated, and the value is compared with the literals in the choice lists. If a match is found, control transfers to the statement attached to the matched constant. When statement execution is completed, control trans-fers to the first statement following the whole **case** construct. So, the Ada **case** statement is more reliable than the **switch** statements of the C-based languages, which do not have implicit exits after the select-able segments.

PHP's **switch** uses the syntax of C's **switch**, but allows more type flex-ibility. The case values can be any of the PHP scalar types—string, integer, or double precision. As with C, if there is no **break** at the end of the selected segment, execution contiues into the next segment.

Ruby has two forms of multiple-selection contructs, both of which are called *case expressions* and both of which yield the value of the last expression evaluated. One of Ruby's case expressions is semantically similar to a list of nested if statements:

```
case
when Boolean_expression then expression
...
when Boolean_expression then expression
[else expression]
end
```

The semantics of this case expression is that the Boolean expressions are evaluated one at a time, top to bottom. The value of the case expression is the value of the first then expression whose Boolean expression is true. The else represents true in this construct, and the else clause is optional. For example,[3]

```
leap = case
       when year % 400 == 0 then true
       when year % 100 == 0 then false
       else year % 4 == 0
       end
```

This case expression evaluates to true if year is a leap year.

The other case expression form, which is more like a switch, has the form:

```
case expression
when value then
  - statement sequence
when value then
  - statement sequence
[else
  - statement sequence]
end
```

The case values are compared with the case expressions, one at a time from top to bottom until a match is found. The comparison is done using the === relational operator, which is defined for all built-in classes. If the case value is a range, such as (1..100), === is defined as an inclusive test, yielding true if the value of the case expression is in the given range. If the case value is a class name, === is defined to yield true if the case value is an object of the case expression class or one of its superclasses. If the case value is a regular expression, === is defined to be a simple pattern match.

Consider the following example:

---

3. This example is from Thomas et. al (2005).

```
century = case year
            when (1700..1799) then "Eighteenth"
            when (1800..1899) then "Nineteenth"
            when (1900..1999) then "Twentieth"
            else "other"
            end
```

Neither Perl nor Python has a multiple-selection construct.

8.2.2.3 Multiple Selection Using `if`

In many situations, a **switch** or **case** construct (Ruby's **case** is an exception) is inadequate for multiple selection. For example, when selections must be made on the basis of a Boolean expression rather than some ordinal type, nested two-way selectors can be used to simulate a multiple selector. To alleviate the poor readability of deeply nested two-way selectors, some languages, such as Perl and Python, have been extended specifically for this use. The extension allows some of the special words to be left out. In particular, **else-if** sequences are replaced with a single special word, and the closing special word on the nested **if** is dropped. The nested selector is then called an **else-if clause**. Consider the following Python selector construct (Note that the logical else if is spelled **elif** in Python):

```
if count < 10 :
  bag1 = True
elif count < 100  :
  bag2 = True
elif count < 1000 :
  bag3 = True
```

which is equivalent to the following:

```
if count < 10 :
  bag1 = True
else :
  if count < 100 :
    bag2 = True
  else :
    if count < 1000 :
      bag3 = True
    else :
      bag4 = True
```

The else-if version (the first) is the more readable of the two. Notice that this example is not easily simulated with a **switch** statement, because each selectable statement is chosen on the basis of a Boolean expression. Therefore, the else-if construct is not a redundant form of **switch.** In fact, none of the multiple selectors in contemporary languages are as general as the if-then-else-if construct. An operational semantics description of a general selector statement with else-if clauses, in which the E's are logic expressions and the S's are statements, is given here:

```
if E1 goto 1
if E2 goto 2
...
1: S1
   goto out
2: S2
   goto out
...
out: ...
```

From this description, we can see the difference between multiple selection structures and else-if constructs: In a multiple selection construct, all the E's would be restricted to comparisons between the value of a single expression and some other values.

Languages that do not include the else-if construct can use the same control structure, with only slightly more typing.

The Python example if-then-else-if construct above can be written as the Ruby **case** statement:

```
case
when count < 10 then bag1 = True
when count < 100 then bag2 = True
when count < 1000 then bag3 = True
end
```

Else-if constructs are based on the common mathematics construct of the conditional expression. Functional programming languages, which will be discussed in Chapter 15, often use conditional expressions as one of their basic control constructs.

8.3 Iterative Statements

An **iterative statement** is one that causes a statement or collection of statements to be executed zero, one, or more times. An iterative construct is often called a **loop.** Every programming language from Plankalkül on has included some method of repeating the execution of segments of code. Iteration is the very essence of the power of the computer. If iteration were not possible, programmers would be required to state every action in sequence; useful programs would be huge and inflexible, and take unacceptably large amounts of time to write and mammoth amounts of memory to store.

The repeated execution of a statement is often accomplished in a functional language by recursion rather than by iterative constructs. Recursion in functional languages will be discussed in Chapter 15.

The first iterative constructs in programming languages were directly related to arrays. This resulted from the fact that in the earliest years of the computer era, computing was largely numerical in nature, frequently using loops to process data in arrays.

Several categories of iteration control statements have been developed. The primary categories are defined by how designers answered two basic design questions:

- How is the iteration controlled?
- Where should the control mechanism appear in the loop construct?

The primary possibilities for iteration control are logical, counting, or a combination of the two. The main choices for the location of the control mechanism are the top of the loop or the bottom of the loop. Top and bottom here are logical, rather than physical, denotations. The issue is not the physical placement of the control mechanism; rather, it is whether the mechanism is executed and affects control before or after execution of the construct's body. A third option, which allows the user to decide where to put the control, is discussed in Section 8.3.3.

The **body** of an iterative construct is the collection of statements whose execution is controlled by the iteration statement. We use the term **pretest** to mean that the test for loop completion occurs before the loop body is executed and **posttest** to mean that it occurs after the loop body is executed. The iteration statement and the associated loop body together form an **iteration construct.**

In addition to the primary iteration statements, we discuss an alternative form that is in a class by itself: user-defined iteration control.

8.3.1 Counter-Controlled Loops

A counting iterative control statement has a variable, called the **loop variable,** in which the count value is maintained. It also includes some means of specifying the **initial** and **terminal** values of the loop variable, and the difference between sequential loop variable values, often called the **stepsize.** The initial, terminal, and stepsize specifications of a loop are called the **loop parameters.**

Although logically controlled loops are more general than counter-controlled loops, they are not necessarily more commonly used. Because counter-controlled loops are more complex, their design is more demanding.

Counter-controlled loops are sometimes supported by machine instructions designed for that purpose. Unfortunately, machine architecture might outlive the prevailing approaches to programming at the time of the architecture design. For example, VAX computers have an instruction that is very convenient for the implementation of posttest counter-controlled loops, which Fortran had at the time of the design of the VAX (mid-1970s). But Fortran no longer had such a loop by the time VAX computers became widely used.

It is, of course, also true that language constructs outlive machine architecture. For example, the author knows of no contemporary machine that has a three-way branch instruction to implement Fortran's arithmetic If statement, although that statement initially was included in Fortran because the IBM 704 had such an instruction a half century ago.

8.3.1.1 Design Issues

There are many design issues for iterative counter-controlled statements. The nature of the loop variable and the loop parameters provide a number of design issues. The type of the loop variable and that of the loop parameters obviously should be the same or at least compatible, but what types should be allowed? One apparent choice is integer, but what about enumeration, character, and floating-point types? Another question is whether the loop variable is a normal variable, in terms of scope, or whether it should have some special scope. Related to the scope issue is the question of the value of the loop variable after loop termination. Allowing the user to change the loop variable or the loop parameters within the loop can lead to code that is very difficult to understand, so another question is whether the additional flexibility that might be gained by allowing such changes is worth that additional complexity. A similar question arises about the number of times and the specific time when the loop parameters are evaluated: If they are evaluated just once, it results in simple but less flexible loops.

The following is a summary of these design issues:

- What are the type and scope of the loop variable?
- What value does the loop variable have at loop termination?
- Should it be legal for the loop variable or loop parameters to be changed in the loop, and if so, does the change affect loop control?
- Should the loop parameters be evaluated only once, or once for every iteration?

8.3.1.2 The Do Statements of Fortran 95

Fortran 95 has two different counting loop statements, both of which use the Do keyword. The general form of one of the Do statements is

Do label variable = initial, terminal [, stepsize]

where the label is that of the last statement in the loop body, and the stepsize, when absent, defaults to 1. The loop variable must be Integer type; the loop parameters are allowed to be expressions and can have positive or negative values. The stepsize, when present, is not allowed to have the value zero. The

history note

Fortran I included a Do counting iterative control statement,
which remained the same in
Fortran II, IV, and 66. The distinctive feature of this statement was that it was posttest,
making it different from the
counting iterative statements of
all other programming languages. (Actually, the Fortran
66 specification did not dictate
that its Do statement must be a
posttest loop. However, most
implementations of Fortran 66
did implement it as one.)

loop parameters are evaluated at the beginning of the execution of the Do statement, and the values are used to compute an **iteration count,** which then has the number of times the loop is to be executed. The loop is controlled by the iteration count, not the loop parameters, so even if the parameters are changed in the loop, which is legal, those changes cannot affect loop control. The iteration count is an internal variable that is inaccessible to the user code.

Do constructs can be entered only through the Do statement, thereby making the statement a single-entry structure. When a Do terminates—regardless of how it terminates—the loop variable has its most recently assigned value. Thus the usefulness of the loop variable is independent of the method by which the loop terminates. Consider the construct

```
Do 10 Index = 1, 10
    ...
10 Continue
```

The value of Index just after normal termination of the loop is 11.

An operational semantics description of the Fortran 95 Do statement follows:[4]

```
init_value = init_expression
terminal_value = terminal_expression
step_value = step_expression
do_var = init_value
iteration_count =
   max(int((terminal_value - init_value + step_value) / step_value) , 0)
loop:
   if iteration_count ≤ 0 goto out
   [loop body]
   do_var = do_var + step_value
   iteration_count = iteration_count - 1
   goto loop
out: ...
```

Fortran 95 also has a second form of Do:

```
[name:]Do variable = initial, terminal [, stepsize]
    ...
End Do [name]
```

---

4. Note that this description fails if init_value is 0 and terminal_value is the largest legal integer value for the implementation, because these values cause an integer overflow in the computation of iteration_count.

This Do uses a specific closing special word (or phrase), End Do, instead of a labeled statement. Following is an example of a skeletal Do construct of this second form:

```
Do Count = 1, 10
    ...
End Do
```

8.3.1.3 The Ada for Statement

The Ada **for** statement has the following form:

```
for variable in [reverse] discrete_range loop
    ...
end loop;
```

A discrete range is a subrange of an integer or enumeration type, such as 1..10 or Monday..Friday. The **reverse** reserved word, when present, indicates that the values of the discrete range are assigned to the loop variable in reverse order. Note that Ada's **for** is simpler than Fortran's Do, because the stepsize is always one (or the next element of the discrete range).

The most interesting new feature of the Ada **for** statement is the scope of the loop variable, which is the range of the loop. The variable is implicitly declared at the **for** statement and implicitly undeclared after loop termination. For example, in

```
Count : Float := 1.35;
for Count in 1..10 loop
   Sum := Sum + Count;
end loop;
```

the Float variable Count is unaffected by the **for** loop. Upon loop termination, the variable Count is still Float type with the value of 1.35. Also, the Float-type variable Count is hidden from the code in the body of the loop, being masked by the loop counter Count, which is implicitly declared to be the type of the discrete range, Integer.

The Ada loop variable cannot be assigned a value in the loop body. Variables used to specify the discrete range can be changed in the loop, but because the range is evaluated only once, these changes do not affect loop control. It is not legal to branch into the Ada **for** loop body. Following is an operational semantics description of the Ada **for** loop:

> [define for_var (its type is that of the discrete range)]
> [evaluate discrete range]
> loop:
>   **if** [there are no elements left in the discrete range] **goto** out

```
    for_var = [next element of discrete range]
    [loop body]
    goto loop
out:
    [undefine for_var]
```

Because the scope of the loop variable is the loop body, loop variables are not defined after loop termination, so their values there are not relevant.

8.3.1.4 The for Statement of the C-Based Languages

The general form of C's **for** statement is

for (expression_1; expression_2; expression_3)
　loop body

The loop body can be a single statement, a compound statement, or a null statement.

Because statements in C produce results and thus can be considered expressions, the expressions in a **for** statement are often statements. The first expression is for initialization and is evaluated only once, when the **for** statement execution begins. The second expression is the loop control and is evaluated before each execution of the loop body. As is usual in C, a zero value means false and all nonzero values mean true. Therefore, if the value of the second expression is zero, the **for** is terminated; otherwise, the loop body statements are executed. In C99, the expression could be a Boolean type. A C99 Boolean type stores only the values 0 or 1. The last expression in the **for** is executed after each execution of the loop body. It is often used to increment the loop counter. An operational semantics description of the C **for** statement is shown next. Because C expressions are also statements, we show expression evaluations as statements.

```
    expression_1
loop:
    if expression_2 = 0 goto out
    [loop body]
    expression_3
    goto loop
out: . . .
```

Following is an example of a skeletal C for construct:

```
for (count = 1; count <= 10; count++)
  . . .
}
```

All of the expressions of C's **for** are optional. An absent second expression is considered true, so a **for** without one is potentially an infinite loop. If the first and/or third expressions are absent, no assumptions are made. For example, if the first expression is absent, it simply means that no initialization takes place.

Note that C's **for** need not count. It can easily model counting *and* logical loop structures, as demonstrated in the next section.

The C **for** design choices are the following: There are no explicit loop variables or loop parameters. All involved variables can be changed in the loop body. The expressions are evaluated in the order stated previously. Although it can create havoc, it is legal to branch into a C **for** loop body.

C's **for** is more flexible than the counting loop statements of Fortran and Ada, because each of the expressions can comprise multiple statements, which in turn allow multiple loop variables that can be of any type. When multiple statements are used in a single expression of a **for** statement, they are separated by commas. All C statements have values, and this form of multiple statement is no exception. The value of such a multiple statement is the value of the last component.

Consider the following **for** statement:

```
for (count1 = 0, count2 = 1.0;
     count1 <= 10 && count2 <= 100.0;
     sum = ++count1 + count2, count2 *= 2.5);
```

The operational semantics description of this is

```
        count1 = 0
        count2 = 1.0
loop:
        if count1 > 10 goto out
        if count2 > 100.0 goto out
        count1 = count1 + 1
        sum = count1 + count2
        count2 = count2 * 2.5
        goto loop
out: ...
```

The example C **for** statement does not need and thus does not have a loop body. All the desired actions happen to be part of the **for** statement itself, rather than in its body. The first and third expressions are multiple statements. In both of these cases, the whole expression is evaluated, but the resulting value is not used in the loop control.

The **for** statement of C99 and C++ differs from that of earlier versions of C in two ways. First, in addition to an arithmetic expression, it can use a Boolean expression for loop control. Second, the first expression can include variable definitions. For example,

```
for (int count = 0; count < len; count++) { ... }
```

The scope of a variable defined in the **for** statement is from its definition to the end of the loop body.

The **for** statement of Java and C# is like that of C++, except that the loop control expression is restricted to **boolean.**

In all of the C-based languages, the loop parameters are evaluated with every iteration. Furthermore, variables that appear in the loop parameter expression can be changed in the loop body. Therefore, these loops can be far more complex and are often less reliable than the counting loops of Fortran and Ada.

8.3.1.5 The for Statement of Python

The general form of Python's **for** is

```
for loop_variable in object:
 - loop body
else:
 - else clause
```

The loop variable is assigned the value in the object, which is often a range, one for each execution of the loop body. The else clause, when present, is executed if the loop terminates normally.

Consider the following example:

```
for count in [2, 4, 6]:
    print count
```

produces

```
2
4
6
```

For most simple counting loops in Python, the **range** function is used. **range** takes one, two, or three parameters. The following examples demonstrate the actions of **range:**

```
range(5) returns [0, 1, 2, 3, 4]
range(2, 7) returns [2, 3, 4, 5, 6]
range(0, 8, 2) returns [0, 2, 4, 6]
```

Note that **range** never returns the highest value in a given parameter range. For example,

```
for count in range(5, 11, 2):
    print count
```

Part 1: Linguistics and the Birth of Perl

LARRY WALL

Larry Wall wears many hats—he is involved in book publishing, language publishing, software publishing, and child rearing (he has four kids). He has spent time studying at Seattle Pacific University, at Berkeley, and at UCLA. He has also worked at Unisys, Jet Propulsion Laboratories, and Seagate. Language publishing has brought him the most fame ("and the least money" he adds): Larry is the author of the Perl scripting language.

FIRST, A BIT ABOUT YOUR PROFESSIONAL BACKGROUND

What was your best job? Working at JPL [Jet Propulsion Laboratories] was a lot of fun. I did both system administration and software development there. The sysadmin job was particularly nice because it was one of those 90 percent boredom, 10 percent panic jobs, so I had plenty of time to work on Perl.

What was your weirdest job? That's a hard one. Most of my jobs turn out weird, one way or another, so it's hard to pick. Let's see . . . I've been a camp counselor called "Crazy Horse." I've written business software in BASIC on a Wang system that could be manipulated only via menus. I was the concertmaster for several years at MusiComedy Northwest. Perhaps my weirdest gig is the recording session at which I was the only one who could play the violin part, so they recorded me eight or ten times so I'd sound like the whole violin section.

What's your current job? My current job is to design Perl 6. Unfortunately nobody is paying me for that at the moment. Of course, nobody was officially paying me for the first five versions either. But it would be nice if someone were at least unofficially paying me for it this time. Perhaps by the time you read this someone will have hired me to be a waiter/actor in Hollywood.

LINGUISTICS AND COMPUTING LANGUAGES

You studied linguistics. At the time you were engaged in these studies, what career paths were you considering? My wife and I were going to be field linguists in Africa and were for a time associated with

Wycliffe Bible Translators, until my (newly developed) food allergies put the kibosh on that. In any event, I don't know that I'd have made a very good field linguist—I've probably done linguists more good by staying out of the field and writing Perl. Nevertheless, I still love linguistics and have been teaching myself Japanese for the last few years just to keep the synapses from coagulating, or curdling, or whatever it is they most naturally do.

How did your interest in spoken languages translate to program languages? [Before] I wrote Perl, I have to admit that my linguistics and my computer science were pretty much compartmentalized. On the computer side, I wrote several compilers without asking myself why most computer languages seem so unnatural. On the linguistics side, I wrote a few natural-language programs in Lisp, but generally didn't consider natural languages amenable to analysis by computer. (Anyone who has used Babblefish will discover this is still the case.) But it wasn't until I started working on Perl that I realized there are many principles that make a natural language feel natural, and some of those principles can be taught to computers without driving them nuts.

THE BIRTH OF PERL

What were you working on at Unisys in the days leading up to the creation of Perl? I was a system administrator and systems programmer in support of a secret project for the NSA [National Security Agency]. If I told you about it, you'd have to kill me. Er, that seems wrong. . . . Anyway, I spent a lot of time locked in "copper rooms," as they call them, playing with computers that didn't officially exist.

How did the idea for a new language come about? We were trying to do configuration management across the country over a low-speed encrypted link. This was producing mounds of textual data but little useful information. So Perl was initially designed to sift through scattered files containing text, find the important bits, and print out reports. Both of the official glosses for Perl reflect this: "Practical Extraction and Report Language" and "Pathologically Eclectic Rubbish Lister."

What business need was not being met? Essentially, the need for flexibility. We were using UNIX for its flexibility, but the toolkit UNIX provided for shell scripting was too unwieldy to navigate around inside text files the way we needed. The awk programming language was a step in the right direction, but just didn't do it for me. And I figured I could do better. The UNIX tools were all really good at what they were good at, and made it next to impossible to do the things they weren't good at. The problem was . . . that the basic toolbox approach was trying to act like an extensible language without actually succeeding. I thought if I could distill the good bits of UNIX into a real language with fine enough granularity to get at the fiddly bits when you needed to, people might find it useful. And that's why Perl 1 was born.

Which is your first love: designing a language or designing a program? Did one lead to the other? To answer the second part first, I don't think anyone

> **" It wasn't until I started working on Perl that I realized there are many principles that make a natural language feel natural, and some of those principles can be taught to computers without driving them nuts. "**

can design a language without first using language. We naturally learn languages [from the] bottom up, first imitating the various pieces of language, and only later abstracting out the principles that hold the language together. Computer scientists like to think that they can design things [from the] top down, but that only works when you already know what kind of answer you're looking for. In general, languages designed to solve particular kinds of problems aren't terribly interesting—at least not to me.

So I had to learn to program first. That being said, I don't think you could call it a "first love." It's more like a "first love/hate." People who truly love programming don't design new computer languages. They aren't motivated. You only design a new language when you find your current language frustrating to you in some way. So it follows that if you want to pursue a career in computer language design, you'd better be prepared for a life of continual frustration. That just goes with the territory. If you ever find yourself satisfied with your new language, you're an arrogant idiot. Not that that precludes being a good language designer. Of course, you can be an arrogant idiot like me and still be properly frustrated. So there's certainly some hope for you.

produces

```
5
7
9
```

8.3.2   Logically Controlled Loops

In many cases, collections of statements must be repeatedly executed, but the repetition control is based on a Boolean expression rather than a counter. For these situations, a logically controlled loop is convenient. Actually, logically controlled loops are more general than counter-controlled loops. Every counting loop can be built with a logical loop, but the reverse is not true. Also, recall that only selection and logical loops are essential to express the control structure of any flowchart.

8.3.2.1 Design Issues

Because they are much simpler than counter-controlled loops, logically controlled loops have fewer design issues.

- Should the control be pretest or posttest?
- Should the logically controlled loop be a special form of a counting loop or a separate statement?

8.3.2.2 Examples

The C-based programming languages include both pretest and posttest logically controlled loops that are not special forms of their counter-controlled iterative statements. The pretest and posttest logical loops have the following forms:

```
while (control_expression)
    loop body
```

and

```
do
    loop body
while (control_expression)
```

These two statement forms are exemplified by the following C# code segments:

```
sum = 0;
indat = Int32.Parse(Console.ReadLine());
while (indat >= 0) {
```

```
    sum += indat;
    indat = Int32.Parse(Console.ReadLine());
}

value = Int32.Parse(Console.ReadLine());
do {
  value /= 10;
  digits ++;
} while (value > 0);
```

Note that all variables in these examples are integer type. The `ReadLine` method of the `Console` object gets a line of text from the keyboard. `Int32.Parse` finds the number in its string parameter, converts it to **int** type, and returns it.

In the pretest version (**while**), the statement is executed as long as the expression evaluates to true. In the C, C++, and Java posttest statement (**do**), the loop body is executed until the expression evaluates to false. The only real difference between the **do** and the **while** is that the **do** always causes the loop body to be executed at least once. In both cases, the statement can be compound. The operational semantics descriptions of those two statements are:

```
while
```

loop:
  if control_expression is false **goto** out
  [loop body]
  goto loop
out: ...

```
do-while
```

loop:
  [loop body]
  if control_expression is true **goto** loop

It is legal in both C and C++ to branch into both **while** and **do** loop bodies. The C89 version uses an arithmetic expression for control; in C99 and C++, it may be either arithmetic or Boolean.

Java's **while** and **do** statements are similar to those of C and C++, except the control expression must be **boolean** type, and because Java does not have a goto, the loop bodies cannot be entered anywhere but at their beginnings.

Fortran 95 has neither a pretest nor a posttest logical loop. Ada has a pretest logical loop but no posttest version of the logical loop.

Perl and Ruby have two pretest logical loops, **while** and **until**. The **until** is similar to **while**, but uses the inverse of the value of the control expression. Perl also has two posttest loops, which use **while** and **until** as statement modifiers on **do** blocks.

Posttest loops are infrequently useful and also can be somewhat dangerous, in the sense that programmers sometimes forget that the loop body will always be executed at least once. The syntactic design of placing a posttest control after the loop body, where it has its semantic effect, helps avoid such problems by making the logic clear.

8.3.3 User-Located Loop Control Mechanisms

In some situations, it is convenient for a programmer to choose a location for loop control other than the top or bottom of the loop. As a result, some languages provide this capability. A syntactic mechanism for user-located loop control, or exit, can be relatively simple, so its design is not difficult. Perhaps the most interesting question is whether a single loop or several nested loops can be exited. The design issues for such a mechanism are the following:

- Should the conditional mechanism be an integral part of the exit?
- Should only one loop body be exited, or can enclosing loops also be exited?

C, C++, Python, Ruby, and C# have unconditional unlabeled exits (**break**). Java and Perl have unconditional labeled exits (**break** in Java, **last** in Perl).

Following is an example of nested loops in Java, in which there is a break out of the outer loop from the nested loop:

```
outerLoop:
  for (row = 0; row < numRows; row++)
    for (col = 0; col < numCols; col++) {
      sum += mat[row][col];
      if (sum > 1000.0)
        break outerLoop;
    }
```

C, C++, and Python include an unlabeled control statement, **continue**, that transfers control to the control mechanism of the smallest enclosing loop. This is not an exit but rather a way to skip the rest of the loop statements on the current iteration without terminating the loop structure. For example, consider the following:

```
while (sum < 1000) {
  getnext(value);
  if (value < 0) continue;
  sum += value;
}
```

A negative value causes the assignment statement to be skipped, and control is transferred instead to the conditional at the top of the loop. On the other hand, in

```
while (sum < 1000) {
  getnext(value);
  if (value < 0) break;
  sum += value;
}
```

a negative value terminates the loop.

Java and Perl have statements similar to **continue,** except that they can include labels that specify which loop is to be continued.

Both **last** and **break** provide for multiple exits from loops, which may seem to be somewhat of a hindrance to readability. However, unusual conditions that require loop termination are so common that such a construct is justified. Furthermore, readability is not seriously harmed, because the target of all such loop exits is the first statement after the loop (or an enclosing loop) rather than just anywhere in the program. Finally, the alternative of using multiple breaks to leave more than one level of loops is much worse for readability.

The motivation for user-located loop exits is simple: They fulfill a common need for goto statements through a highly restricted branch statement. The target of a goto can be many places in the program, both above and below the goto itself. However, the targets of user-located loop exits must be below the exit and can only follow immediately the end of a compound statement.

8.3.4 Iteration Based on Data Structures

Only one additional kind of looping structure remains to be considered here: iteration that is controlled by a data structure. Rather than have a counter or Boolean expression control the iterations, these loops are controlled by the number of elements in a data structure. Perl, JavaScript, PHP, Java, and C# have such statements.

A general data-based iteration statement uses a user-defined data structure and a user-defined function to go through the structure's elements. This function is called an **iterator.** The iterator is called at the beginning of each iteration, and each time it is called, the iterator returns an element from a particular data structure in some specific order. For example, suppose a program has a user-defined binary tree of data nodes, and the data in each node must be processed in some particular order. A user-defined iteration statement for the tree would successively set the loop variable to point to the nodes in the tree, one for each iteration. The initial execution of the user-defined iteration statement needs to issue a special call to the iterator to get the first tree element. The iterator must always remember which node it presented last so that it visits all nodes without visiting any node more than once. So an iterator must be history-sensitive. A user-defined iteration statement terminates when the iterator fails to find more elements.

The **for** construct of the C-based languages, because of its great flexibility, can be used to simulate a user-defined iteration statement. Once again, suppose the nodes of a binary tree are to be processed. If the tree root is pointed to by a variable named `root`, and if `traverse` is a function that sets its parameter to point to the next element of a tree in the desired order, the following could be used:

```
for (ptr = root; ptr == null; ptr = traverse(ptr)) {
  ...
}
```

In this statement, `traverse` is the iterator.

Predefined iterators are used to provide iterative access to PHP's unique arrays. The **current** pointer points at the element last accessed through iteration. The **next** iterator moves **current** to the next element in the array. The **prev** iterator moves **current** to the previous element. **current** can be set or reset to the array's first element with the **reset** operator. The following code displays all of the elements of an array of numbers `$list`:

```
reset $list;
print ("First number: " + current($list) + "<br />");
while ($current_value = next($list))
  print ("Next number: " + $current_value + "<br \>");
```

User-defined iteration statements are more important in object-oriented programming than they were in earlier software development paradigms, because users now routinely construct abstract data types for data structures, especially collections. In such cases, a user-defined iteration statement and its iterator must be provided by the author of the data abstraction because the representation of the objects of the type is not known to the user.

In C++, iterators for user-defined types, or classes, are often implemented either as friend functions to the class or as separate iterator classes.

In Java, the elements of a user-defined collection that implements the `Collection` interface can be iteratively visited with an implementation of the `Iterator` interface. The `Iterator` interface has three fundamental methods: `next`, `hasNext`, and `remove`. The `next` method is the actual iterator. It throws the `NoSuchElementException` when there are no more elements in the collection being iterated. The `hasNext` method, which is often called before `next` is called, returns **true** if there is at least one more element.

An enhanced version of the **for** statement was added to Java in Java 5.0. This statement simplifies iterating through the values in an array or objects in a collection that implements the `Iterable` interface. For example, if we had an `ArrayList`[5] collection named `myList` of strings, the following statement would iterate through all of its elements, setting each to `myElement`:

for (String myElement : myList) { ... }

This new statement is referred to as "foreach," although its reserved word is **for.**

C#'s `foreach` statement iterates on the elements of arrays and other collections. For example,

```
String[] strList = {"Bob", "Carol", "Ted", "Beelzebub"};
...
foreach (String name in strList)
  Console.WriteLine("Name: {0}", name);
```

The notation `{0}` in the parameter to `Console.WriteLine` above indicates the position in the string to be displayed where the value of the first named variable, `name` in this example, is to be placed.

Ruby includes iterators for each of its predefined container classes. Because these are associated with blocks, which are actually subprograms in Ruby, they are discussed in Chapter 9.

8.4 Unconditional Branching

An **unconditional branch statement** transfers execution control to a specified location in the program. The most heated debate in language design of the late 1960s was over the issue of whether unconditional branching should be part of any high-level language, and if so, whether its use should be restricted.

The unconditional branch, or goto, is the most powerful statement for controlling the flow of execution of a program's statements. However, using the goto carelessly can lead to serious problems. The goto has stunning power and great flexibility (all other control structures can be built with goto and a selector), but it is this power that makes its use dangerous. Without restrictions on use, imposed by either language design or programming standards, goto statements can make programs very difficult to read, and as a result, highly unreliable and costly to maintain.

These problems follow directly from a goto's capability of forcing any program statement to follow any other in execution sequence, regardless of whether that statement precedes or follows the previously executed statement in textual order. Readability is best when the execution order of statements is

---

5. An `ArrayList` is a predefined collection that is actually a dynamic array of objects that can be of any type—that is, it is a collection of references to obejcts of any class. It implements the Iterable interface.

history note

Although several thoughtful people had suggested them earlier, it was Edsger Dijkstra who gave the computing world the first widely read exposé on the dangers of the goto. In his letter he noted, "The goto statement as it stands is just too primitive; it is too much an invitation to make a mess of one's program" (Dijkstra, 1968a). During the first few years after publication of Dijkstra's views on the goto, a large number of people argued publicly for either outright banishment or at least restrictions on the use of the goto. Among those who did not favor complete elimination was Donald Knuth, who argued that there were occasions when the efficiency of the goto outweighed its harm to readability (Knuth, 1974).

nearly the same as the order in which they appear—in our case, this would mean top to bottom, which is the order with which we are accustomed. Thus, restricting gotos so they can transfer control only downward in a program partially alleviates the problem. It allows gotos to transfer control around code sections in response to errors or unusual conditions, but disallows their use to build any sort of loop.

A few languages have been designed without a goto—for example, Java, Python, and Ruby. However, most currently popular languages include a goto statement. Kernighan and Ritchie (1978) call the goto infinitely abusable, but it is nevertheless included in Ritchie's language, C. The languages that have eliminated the goto have provided additional control statements, usually in the form of loop exits, to replace one of the justifiable applications of the goto.

The relatively new language, C#, includes a goto, even though one of the languages on which it is based, Java, does not. One legitimate use of C#'s goto is in the **switch** statement, as discussed in Section 8.2.2.2.

All of the loop exit statements discussed in Section 8.3.3 are actually camouflaged goto statements. They are, however, severely restricted gotos and are not harmful to readability. In fact, it can be argued that they improve readability, because to avoid their use results in convoluted and unnatural code that would be much harder to understand.

8.5 Guarded Commands

New and quite different forms of selection and loop structures were suggested by Dijkstra (1975). His primary motivation was to provide control statements that would support a program design methodology that ensured correctness during development rather than relying on verification or testing of completed programs to ensure their correctness. This methodology is described in Dijkstra (1976). Another motivation for developing guarded commands is that nondeterminism is sometimes needed in concurrent programs, as will be discussed in Chapter 13. Yet another motivation is the increased clarity in reasoning that is possible with guarded commands. Simply put, a selectable segment of a selection construct in a guarded-command construct can be considered independently of any other part of the construct, which is not true for the selection constructs of the common programming languages.

Guarded commands are covered in this chapter because they are the basis for two linguistic mechanisms developed later for concurrent programming in two languages, CSP (Hoare, 1978) and Ada. Concurrency in Ada is discussed in Chapter 13. They are also used to define functions in Haskell, as discussed in Chapter 15.

Dijkstra's selection construct has the form

```
if <Boolean expression> -> <statement>
[] <Boolean expression> -> <statement>
[] ...
[] <Boolean expression> -> <statement>
fi
```

The closing reserved word, **fi,** is the opening reserved word spelled backward. This form of closing reserved word is taken from ALGOL 68. The small blocks, called *fatbars*, are used to separate the guarded clauses and allow the clauses to be statement sequences. Each line in the selection construct, consisting of a Boolean expression (a guard) and a statement or statement sequence, is called a **guarded command.**

This selection construct has the appearance of a multiple selection, but its semantics is different. All of the Boolean expressions are evaluated each time the construct is reached during execution. If more than one expression is true, one of the corresponding statements can be nondeterministically chosen for execution. An implementation may always choose the statement associated with the first Boolean expression that evaluates to true. But it may choose any statement associated with a true Boolean expression. So, the correctness of the program cannot depend on which statement is chosen (among those associated with true Boolean expressions). If none of the Boolean expressions is true, a run-time error occurs that causes program termination. This forces the programmer to consider and list all possibilities, as with Ada's **case** statement. Consider the following example:

```
if i = 0 -> sum := sum + i
[] i > j -> sum := sum + j
[] j > i -> sum := sum + i
fi
```

If i = 0 and j > i, this construct chooses nondeterministically between the first and third assignment statements. If i is equal to j and is not zero, a run-time error occurs because none of the conditions is true.

This construct can be an elegant way of allowing the programmer to state that the order of execution, in some cases, is irrelevant. For example, to find the largest of two numbers, we can use

```
if x >= y -> max := x
[] y >= x -> max := y
fi
```

This computes the desired result without overspecifying the solution. In particular, if x and y are equal, it does not matter which we assign to max. This is a form of abstraction provided by the nondeterministic semantics of the statement.

Now, consider this same process coded in a traditional programming language selector:

```
if (x >= y)
  max = x;
else
  max = y;
```

This could also be coded as:

```
if (x > y)
  max = x;
else
  max = y;
```

There is no practical difference between these two constructs. The first assigns x to max when x and y are equal; the second assigns y to max in the same circumstance. This choice between the two constructs complicates the formal analysis of the code and the correctness proof of it. This is one of the reasons why guarded commands were developed by Dijkstra.

The semantics of the guarded commands is difficult to describe precisely. Although flow diagrams are not good tools for program design, they are sometimes useful for semantics descriptions. Figure 8.1 is a flowgraph describing the approach used by Dijkstra's selector statement. Note that this flowgraph is relatively imprecise, reflecting the difficulty in capturing the semantics of the guarded commands.

The loop structure proposed by Dijkstra has the form

```
do <Boolean expression> -> <statement>
[] <Boolean expression> -> <statement>
[] ...
[] <Boolean expression> -> <statement>
od
```

The semantics of this construct is that all Boolean expressions are evaluated on each iteration. If more than one are true, one of the associated statements is nondeterministically (perhaps randomly) chosen for execution, after which the expressions are again evaluated. When all expressions are simultaneously false, the loop terminates.

Consider the following problem: Given four integer variables, q1, q2, q3, and q4, rearrange the values of the four so that $q1 \leq q2 \leq q3 \leq q4$. Without guarded commands, one straightforward solution is to put the four values into an array, sort the array, and then assign the values from the array back into the scalar variables q1, q2, q3, and q4. While this solution is not difficult, it requires a good deal of code, especially if the sort process must be included.

Figure 8.1

Flowgraph of the approach used with Dijkstra's selector statement

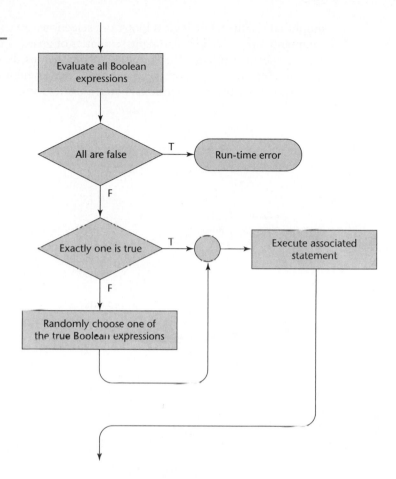

Now, consider the following code, which uses guarded commands to solve the same problem but in a more concise and elegant way.[6]

```
do q1 > q2 -> temp := q1; q1 := q2; q2 := temp;
[] q2 > q3 -> temp := q2; q2 := q3; q3 := temp;
[] q3 > q4 -> temp := q3; q3 := q4; q4 := temp;
od
```

A flowgraph describing the approach used by Dijkstra's loop statement is shown in Figure 8.2. Once again, note that the control-flow semantics of this construct cannot be completely depicted in a flowgraph.

Dijkstra's guarded command control constructs are interesting, in part because they illustrate how the syntax and semantics of statements can have an impact on program verification and vice versa. Program verification is virtually impossible when goto statements are used. Verification is greatly

---

6. This code appears in slightly different form in Dijkstra (1975).

simplified if either only logical loops and selections are used, or only guarded commands are used. The axiomatic semantics of guarded commands is conveniently specified (Gries, 1981). It should be obvious, however, that there is considerably increased complexity in the implementation of the guarded commands over their conventional deterministic counterparts.

Figure 8.2

Flowgraph of the approach used with Dijkstra's loop statement

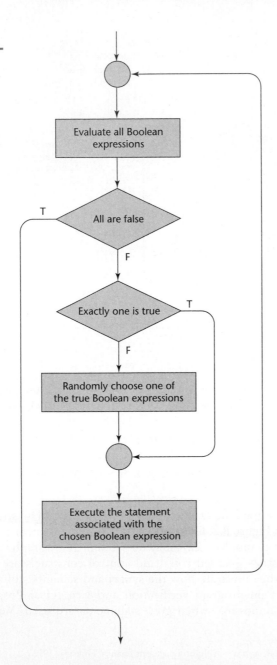

8.6 Conclusions

We have described and discussed a variety of statement-level control structures. A brief evaluation now seems to be in order.

First, we have the theoretical result that only sequence, selection, and pretest logical loops are absolutely required to express computations (Böhm and Jacopini, 1966). This result has been used by those who wish to ban unconditional branching altogether. Of course, there are already sufficient practical problems with the goto to condemn it without also using a theoretical reason. One of the main legitimate needs for gotos—premature exits from loops—can be met with highly restricted branch statements, such as **break.**

One obvious misuse of the Böhm and Jacopini result is to argue against the inclusion of *any* control structures beyond selection and pretest logical loops. No widely used language has yet taken that step; further, we doubt that any ever will, because of the negative effect on writability and readability. Programs written with only selection and pretest logical loops are generally less natural in structure, more complex, and therefore harder to write and more difficult to read. For example, the C# multiple selection structure is a great boost to C# writability, with no obvious negatives. Another example is the counting loop structure of many languages, especially when the statement is simple, as in Ada.

It is not so clear that the utility of many of the other control structures that have been proposed is worth their inclusion in languages (Ledgard and Marcotty, 1975). This question rests to a large degree on the fundamental question of whether the size of languages must be minimized. Both Wirth (1975) and Hoare (1973) strongly endorse simplicity in language design. In the case of control structures, simplicity means that only a few control statements should be in a language, and they should all be simple.

The rich variety of statement-level control structures that have been invented shows the diversity of opinion among language designers. After all the invention, discussion, and evaluation, there is still no unanimity of opinion on the precise set of control statements that should be in a language. Most contemporary languages do, of course, have similar control statements, but there is still some variation in the details of their syntax and semantics. Furthermore, there is still disagreement on whether a language should include a goto; C++ and C# do, but Java and Ruby do not.

One final note: The control structures of functional and logic programming languages are all quite different from those described in this chapter. These mechanisms are discussed in some detail in Chapters 15 and 16, respectively.

SUMMARY

The control statements of the imperative languages occur in several categories: selection, multiple selection, iterative, and unconditional branching

The **switch** statement of the C-based languages is representative of multiple-selection statements. The C# version eliminates the reliability problem of its predecessors by disallowing the implicit fall through from a selected segment to the following selectable segment.

A large number of different loop statements have been invented for high-level languages, starting with Fortran's counting Do. Ada's **for** statement is, in terms of complexity, the opposite. It elegantly implements only the most commonly needed counting loop forms. C's **for** statement is the most flexible iteration construct, although its flexibility leads to some reliability problems.

The C-based languages have exit statements for their loops; these statements take the place of one of the most common uses of goto statements.

Data-based iterators are loop constructs for processing data structures, such as linked lists, hashes, and trees. The **for** statement of the C-based languages allows the user to create iterators for user-defined data. The **foreach** statement of Perl and C# is a predefined iterator for standard data structures. In the contemporary object-oriented languages, iterators for collections are specified with standard interfaces, which are implemented by the designers of the collections.

The unconditional branch, or goto, has been part of most imperative languages. Its problems have been widely discussed and debated. The current consensus is that it should remain in most languages but that its dangers should be minimized through programming discipline.

Dijkstra's guarded commands are alternative control constructs with positive theoretical characteristics. Although they have not been adopted as the control constructs of a language, part of the semantics appear in the concurrency mechanisms of CSP and Ada and the function definitions of Haskell.

REVIEW QUESTIONS

1. What is the definition of *control structure*?
2. What is the definition of *block*?
3. What are the design issues for selection structures?
4. What is unusual about Python's design of compound statements?
5. What are the common solutions to the nesting problem for two-way selectors?
6. What are the design issues for multiple-selection statements?
7. What is unusual about C's multiple-selection statement? What design trade-off was made in this design?
8. Explain how C#'s switch statement is safer than that of Java.
9. What are the design issues for counter-controlled loop statements?
10. What is a pretest loop statement? What is a posttest loop statement?

11. What is the difference between the **for** statement of C++ and that of Java?

12. What are the design issues for logically controlled loop statements?

13. What is the main reason user-located loop control statements were invented?

14. What advantage does Java's **break** statement have over C's **break** statement?

15. What are the differences between the **break** statement of C++ and that of Java?

16. What is a user-defined iteration control?

17. What common programming language borrows part of its design from Dijkstra's guarded commands?

PROBLEM SET

1. Describe three situations where a combined counting and logical looping construct is needed.

2. Study the iterator feature of CLU in Liskov et al. (1981) and determine its advantages and disadvantages.

3. Compare the set of Ada control statements with those of C# and decide which are better and why.

4. What are the pros and cons of using unique closing reserved words on compound statements?

5. What are the arguments, pro and con, for Python's use of indentation to specify compound statements in control constructs?

6. Analyze the potential readability problems with using closure reserved words for control statements that are the reverse of the corresponding initial reserved words, such as the **case-esac** reserved words of ALGOL 68. For example, consider common typing errors such as the reversal of two adjacent characters.

7. Use the *Science Citation Index* to find an article that refers to Knuth (1974). Read the article and Knuth's paper and write a paper that summarizes both sides of the goto issue.

8. In his paper on the goto issue, Knuth (1974) suggests a loop control construct that allows multiple exits. Read the paper and write an operational semantics description of the construct.

9. What are the arguments both for and against the exclusive use of Boolean expressions in the control statements in Java (as opposed to also allowing arithmetic expressions, as in C and C++)?

10. In Ada, the choice lists of the **case** construct must be exhaustive, so that there can be no unrepresented values in the control expression. In C++, unrepresented values can be caught at run time with the **default** selector. If there is no **default,** an unrepresented value causes the whole construct to be skipped. What are the pros and cons of these two designs (Ada and C++)?

11. Explain the advantages and disadvantages of the Java **for** statement, compared to Ada's **for.**

12. Describe a programming situation in which the else clause in Python's **for** statement would be convenient.

PROGRAMMING EXERCISES

1. Rewrite the following pseudocode segment using a loop structure in the specified languages:

```
k = (j + 13) / 27
loop:
  if k > 10 then goto out
  k = k + 1
  i = 3 * k - 1
  goto loop
out: ...
```

   a. Fortran 95
   b. Ada
   c. C, C++, Java, or C#
   d. Python
   e. Ruby

   Assume all variables are integer type. Discuss which language, for this code, has the best writability, the best readability, and the best combination of the two.

2. Redo Problem 1, except this time make all the variables and constants floating-point type, and change the statement

```
k = k + 1
```

   to

```
k = k + 1.2
```

3. Rewrite the following code segment using a multiple-selection statement in the following languages:

```
if ((k == 1) || (k == 2)) j = 2 * k - 1
```

```
if ((k == 3) || (k == 5)) j = 3 * k + 1
if (k == 4)  j = 4 * k - 1
if ((k == 6) || (k == 7) || (k == 8))  j = k - 2
```

a. Fortran 95 (you'll have to look this one up)

b. Ada

c. C, C++, Java, or C#

d. Python

e. Ruby

Assume all variables are integer type. Discuss the relative merits of the use of these languages for this particular code.

4. Consider the following C program segment. Rewrite it using no gotos or **breaks**.

```
j = -3;
for (i = 0; i < 3; i++) {
  switch (j + 2) {
    case 3:
    case 2: j--; break;
    case 0: j += 2; break;
    default: j = 0;
  }
  if (j > 0) break;
  j = 3 - i
}
```

5. In a letter to the editor of *CACM*, Rubin (1987) uses the following code segment as evidence that the readability of some code with gotos is better than the equivalent code without gotos. This code finds the first row of an *n* by *n* integer matrix named x that has nothing but zero values.

```
for (i = 1; i <= n; i++) {
  for (j = 1; j <= n; j++)
    if (x[i][j] != 0)
      goto reject;
  println ('First all-zero row is:', i);
  break;
reject:
}
```

Rewrite this code without gotos in one of the following languages: C, C++, Java, C#, or Ada. Compare the readability of your code to that of the example code.

6. Consider the following programming problem: The values of three integer variables—first, second, and third—must be placed in the three variables max, mid, and min, with the obvious meanings, without using arrays or user-defined or predefined subprograms. Write two solutions to

this problem, one that uses nested selections and one that does not. Compare the complexity and expected reliability of the two.

7. Write the following Java **for** construct in Ada:

```
int i, j, n = 100;
for (i = 0, j = 17; i < n; i++, j--)
    sum += i * j + 3;
```

8. Rewrite the C program segment of Programming Exercise 4 using **if** and **goto** statements in C.

9. Rewrite the C program segment of Programming Exercise 4 in Java without using a **switch** construct.

Subprograms

Subprograms are the fundamental building blocks of programs and are therefore among the most important concepts in programming language design. We now explore the design of subprograms, including parameter-passing methods, local referencing environments, overloaded subprograms, generic subprograms, and the aliasing and side-effects problems that are associated with subprograms. We also include a brief discussion of coroutines, which provide symmetric unit control. Implementation methods for subprograms are discussed in Chapter 10.

9.1 Introduction

Two fundamental abstraction facilities can be included in a programming language: process abstraction and data abstraction. In the early history of high-level programming languages, only process abstraction was included. Process abstraction has been a central concept in all programming languages. In the 1980s, however, many people began to believe that data abstraction was equally important. Data abstraction is discussed in detail in Chapter 11.

The first programmable computer, Babbage's Analytical Engine, built in the 1840s, had the capability of reusing collections of instruction cards at several different places in a program. In a modern programming language, such a collection of statements is written as a subprogram. This reuse results in several different kinds of savings, including memory space and coding time. Such reuse is also an abstraction, for the details of the subprogram's computation are replaced in a program by a statement that calls the subprogram. Instead of explaining how some computation is to be done in a program, that explanation (the collection of statements in the subprogram) is enacted by a call statement, effectively abstracting away the details. This increases the readability of a program by exposing its logical structure while hiding the low-level details.

The methods of object-oriented languages are closely related to the subprograms discussed in this chapter. The primary ways methods differ from subprograms is the way they are called and their associations with classes and objects. Although these special characteristics of methods are discussed in Chapter 12, the features they share with subprograms, such as parameters and local variables, are discussed in this chapter.

9.2 Fundamentals of Subprograms

9.2.1 General Subprogram Characteristics

All subprograms discussed in this chapter, except the coroutines described in Section 9.11, have the following characteristics:

- Each subprogram has a single entry point.

- The calling program unit is suspended during the execution of the called subprogram, which implies that there is only one subprogram in execution at any given time.

- Control always returns to the caller when the subprogram execution terminates.

Alternatives to these result in coroutines (Section 9.11) and concurrent units (Chapter 13).

Although Fortran subprograms can have multiple entries, that particular kind of entry is relatively unimportant because it does not provide any fundamentally different capabilities. Therefore, in this chapter, we will ignore the possibility of multiple entries in Fortran subprograms.

9.2.2 Basic Definitions

A **subprogram definition** describes the interface to and the actions of the subprogram abstraction. A **subprogram call** is the explicit request that the called subprogram be executed. A subprogram is said to be **active** if, after having been called, it has begun execution but has not yet completed that execution. The two fundamental kinds of subprograms, procedures and functions, are defined and discussed in Section 9.2.4.

A **subprogram header,** which is the first part of the definition, serves several purposes. First, it specifies that the following syntactic unit is a subprogram definition of some particular kind.[1] The kind of the subprogram is often specified with a special word. Second, the header provides a name for the subprogram. Third, it may optionally specify a list of parameters.

Consider the following header examples:

```
Subroutine Adder(parameters)
```

This is the header of a Fortran subroutine subprogram named `Adder`. In Ada, the header for this subprogram would be

```
procedure Adder(parameters)
```

In Python, the header of a subprogram has the following form:

```
def adder(parameters):
```

No special word appears in the header of a subprogram in languages other than Fortran and Ada to specify its kind. These languages have only one kind of subprogram, functions (and/or methods), and the header of a function is recognized by context rather than by a special word. For example, in C

```
void adder(parameters)
```

----

1. Some programming languages include two different kinds of subprograms, specifically, procedures and functions.

would serve as the header of a function named adder, where **void** indicates that it does not return a value.

As with compound statements, the statements in the body of a Python function must be indented and the end of the body is indicated by the first statement that is not indented (which is the first statement following the function definition). One characteristic of Python functions that sets them apart from the functions of other common programming languages is that function **def** statements are executable. When a **def** statement is executed, it assigns the given name to the given function body. Until a function's **def** has been executed, the function cannot be called. Consider the following skeletal example:

```
if ...
  def fun(...):
    ...
else
  def fun(...):
    ...
```

If the then clause of this selection construct is executed, that version of the function fun can be called, but not the version in the else clause. Likewise, if the else clause is chosen, its version of the function can be called but the one in the then clause cannot.

Ruby methods differ from the subprograms of other programming languages in several interesting ways. Ruby methods are often defined in class definitions, but can also be defined outside class definitions, in which case they are considered methods of the root object, Object. Such methods can be called without an object receiver, as if they were functions in C or C++. If a **return** statement in a Ruby method is not followed by an expression, **nil** is returned. If followed by one expression, the value of the expression is returned. If followed by more than one expression, an array of the values of all of the expressions is returned. If a Ruby method is called without a receiver, **self** is assumed. If there is no method by that name in the class, enclosing classes are searched, up to Object, if necessary.

The **parameter profile** of a subprogram contains the number, order, and types of its formal parameters. The **protocol** of a subprogram is its parameter profile plus, if it is a function, its return type. In languages in which subprograms have types, those types are defined by the subprogram's protocol.

Subprograms can have declarations as well as definitions. This form parallels the variable declarations and definitions in C, in which the declarations can be used to provide type information but not to define variables. A variable declaration in C, which uses the **extern** specifier, is used to specify in a function that a variable that is used there is defined elsewhere. Subprogram declarations provide the subprogram's protocol, but do not include their bodies. They are necessary in languages that do not allow forward references to subprograms. In both the cases of variables and subprograms, declarations are needed for static type checking. In the case of subprograms, it is the type of the parameters that must be checked. Function declarations are common in C and C++ programs, where they are called **prototypes.** Such declarations are often placed in header files.

In most other languages (other than C and C++), subprograms do not need declarations, because there is no requirement that subprograms be defined before they are called.

9.2.3   Parameters

Subprograms typically describe computations. There are two ways that a non-method subprogram can gain access to the data that it is to process: through direct access to nonlocal variables (declared elsewhere but visible in the subprogram) or through parameter passing. Data passed through parameters are accessed through names that are local to the subprogram. Parameter passing is more flexible than direct access to nonlocal variables. In essence, a subprogram with parameter access to the data that it is to process is a parameterized computation. It can perform its computation on whatever data it receives through its parameters (presuming the types of the parameters are as expected by the subprogram). If data access is through nonlocal variables, the only way the computation can proceed on different data is to assign new values to those nonlocal variables between calls to the subprogram. Extensive access to nonlocals can reduce reliability. Variables that are visible to the subprogram where access is desired often end up also being visible where access to them is not needed. This problem was discussed in Chapter 5.

Although methods also access external data through nonlocal references and parameters, the primary data to be processed by a method is the object through which the method is called. However, when a method does access nonlocal data, the reliability problems are the same as with non-method subprograms. Also, in an object-oriented language, method access to class variables (those associated with the class, rather than an object) is related to the concept of nonlocal data and should be avoided whenever possible. In this case, as well as the case of a C function accessing nonlocal data, the method can have the side effect of changing something other than its parameters or local data. Such changes complicate the semantics of the method and make it less reliable.

In some situations, it is convenient to be able to transmit computations, rather than data, as parameters to subprograms. In these cases, the name of the subprogram that implements that computation may be used as a parameter. This form of parameter is discussed in Section 9.6. Data parameters are discussed in Section 9.5.

The parameters in the subprogram header are called **formal parameters.** They are sometimes thought of as dummy variables because they are not variables in the usual sense: In most cases, they are bound to storage only when the subprogram is called, and that binding is often through some other program variables.

Subprogram call statements must include the name of the subprogram and a list of parameters to be bound to the formal parameters of the subprogram. These parameters are called **actual parameters.** They must be distinguished from formal parameters, because the two can have different restrictions on their forms, and of course their uses are quite different.

In nearly all programming languages, the correspondence between actual and formal parameters—or the binding of actual parameters to formal parameters—is done by position: The first actual parameter is bound to the first formal parameter and so forth. Such parameters are called **positional parameters.** This is an effective and safe method of relating actual parameters to their corresponding formal parameters, as long as the parameter lists are relatively short.

When lists are long, however, it is easy for a programmer to make mistakes in the order of actual parameters in the list. One solution to this problem is to provide **keyword parameters,** in which the name of the formal parameter to which an actual parameter is to be bound is specified with the actual parameter. The advantage of keyword parameters is that they can appear in any order in the actual parameter list. Python functions can be called using this technique, as in

```
sumer(length = my_length,
      list = my_array,
      sum = my_sum)
```

where the definition of `sumer` has the formal parameters `length`, `list`, and `sum`.

The disadvantage to keyword parameters is that the user of the subprogram must know the names of formal parameters.

In addition to keyword parameters, Ada, Fortran 95, and Python allow positional parameters. The two can be mixed in a call, as in

```
sumer(my_length,
      sum = my_sum,
      list = my_array)
```

The only restriction with this approach is that after a keyword parameter appears in the list, all remaining parameters must be keyworded. This restriction is necessary because a position may no longer be well defined after a keyword parameter has appeared.

In Python, Ruby, C++, Fortran 95, Ada, and PHP, formal parameters can have default values. A default value is used if no actual parameter is passed to the formal parameter in the subprogram header. Consider the following Python function header:

```
def compute_pay(income, exemptions = 1, tax_rate)
```

The `exemptions` formal parameter can be absent in a call to `compute_pay`; when it is, the value 1 is used. No comma is included for an absent actual parameter in a Python call, because the only value of such a comma would be to indicate the position of the next parameter, which in this case is not necessary because all actual parameters after an absent actual parameter must be keyworded. For example, consider the following call:

```
pay = compute_pay(20000.0, tax_rate = 0.15)
```

In C++, which does not support keyword parameters, the rules for default parameters are necessarily different. The default parameters must appear last, because parameters are positionally associated. Once a default parameter is omitted in a call, all remaining formal parameters must have default values. A C++ function header for the compute_pay function can be written as follows:

```
float compute_pay(float income, float tax_rate,
                  int exemptions = 1)
```

Notice that the parameters are rearranged so that the one with the default value is last. An example call to the C++ compute_pay function is

```
pay = compute_pay(20000.0, 0.15);
```

In most languages that do not have default values for formal parameters, the number of actual parameters in a call must match the number of formal parameters in the subprogram definition header. However, in C, C++, Perl, and JavaScript this is not required. When there are fewer actual parameters in a call than formal parameters in a function definition, it is the programmer's responsibility to ensure that the parameter correspondence, which is always positional, and the subprogram execution are sensible.

Although this design, which allows a variable number of parameters, is clearly prone to error, it is also sometimes convenient. For example, the `printf` function of C can print any number of items (data values and/or literal strings).

C# allows methods to accept a variable number of parameters, as long as they are of the same type. The method specifies its formal parameter with the **params** modifier. The call can send either an array or a list of expressions, whose values are placed in an array by the compiler and provided to the called method. For example, consider the following method:

```
public void DisplayList(params int[] list) {
   foreach (int next in list) {
      Console.WriteLine("Next value {0}", next);
   }
}
```

If `DisplayList` is defined for the class `MyClass` and we have the following declarations,

```
Myclass myObject = new Myclass;
int[] myList = new int[6] {2, 4, 6, 8, 10, 12};
```

`DisplayList` could be called with both of the following:

```
myObject.DisplayList(myList);
myObject.DisplayList(2, 4, 3 * x - 1, 17);
```

Ruby supports a complicated but highly flexible actual parameter configuration. The initial parameters are expressions, whose value objects are passed to the corresponding formal parameters. The initial parameters can be following by a list of key => value pairs, which are placed in an anonymous hash and a reference to that hash is passed to the next formal parameter. These are used as a substitute for keyword parameters, which Ruby does not support. The hash item can be followed by a single parameter preceded by an asterisk. This parameter is called the *array formal parameter*. When the method is called, the array formal parameter is set to reference a new `Array` object. All remaining actual parameters are assigned to the elements of the new `Array` object. If the actual parameter that corresponds to the array formal parameter is an array, it must also be preceded by an asterisk, and it must the be the last actual parameter.[2] So, Ruby allows a variable number of parameters in a way similar to that of C#. Because Ruby arrays can store different types, there is no requirement that the actual parameters passed to the array have the same type.

The following example skeletal function definition and call illustrate the parameter structure of Ruby:

```
list = [2, 4, 6, 8]
def tester(p1, p2, p3, *p4)
  ...
end
...
tester('first', mon => 72, tue => 68, wed => 59, *list)
```

Inside `tester`, the values of its formal parameters are:

```
p1 is 'first'
p2 is {mon => 72, tue => 68, wed => 59}
p3 is 2
p4 is [4, 6, 8]
```

---

2. Not quite true, becauase the array formal parameter can be followed by a method or function reference, which is preceded by an ampersand (&).

Python supports parameters that are similar to those of Ruby. The initial formal parameters are like those in most common languages. These can be followed by a constant array (called a *tuple* in Python), which is specified by preceding the formal parameter with an asterisk. This parameter, which becomes an array when the subprogram is called, receives all nonkeyword actual parameters beyond those corresponding to the initial parameters. Finally, the last formal parameter, which is specified by preceding the formal parameter with two asterisks, becomes a hash (called a *dictionary* in Python). The actual parameters that correspond to this parameter are key = value pairs, which are placed in the hash formal parameter. Consider the following skeletal example function and the call to it:

```
def fun1(p1, p2, *p3, **p4):
  ...
...
fun1(2, 4, 6, 8, mon=68, tue=72, wed=77)
```

In fun1, the formal parameters have the following values:

```
p1 is 2
p2 is 4
p3 is [6, 8]
p4 is {'mon': 68, 'tue': 72, 'wed': 77}
```

9.2.4   Ruby Blocks

In most other programming languages, processing the data in an array or other collection is done by iterating over the data structure with a loop, processing each data element in the loop. Recall that Ruby includes iterator methods for its data structures. For example, the Array structure has the iterator method, each, which can be used to process any array. This is done in Ruby by specifying a block of code on the call to the iterator. Such a block, which is a sequence of statements that must be delimited by braces or a **do-end** pair, can appear only following a method call. Furthermore, it must begin on the same line as at least the last part of the call. Blocks can have formal parameters, which are specified between vertical bars. The block that is passed to the called subprogram is itself called with a **yield** statement, which consists of the **yield** reserved word followed by the actual parameters. The **yield** cannot include more actual parameters than the block has formal parameters. The value returned from a block (to the **yield** that called it) is the value of the last expression evaluted in the block.

Iterators are usually used to process data in an existing data structure. However, they can also be used when the data to be processed is being computed in the iterator method. Consider the following simple example of a method and two calls to it, both including a block:

```
# A method to compute and yield Fibonacci numbers up to a
# limit
def fibonacci(last)
  first, second = 1, 1
  while first <= last
    yield first
    first, second = second, first + second
  end
end

# Call fibonacci with a block to display the numbers
puts "Fibonacci numbers less than 100 are:"
fibonacci(100) {|num| print num, " "}
puts  # Output a newline

# Call it again to sum the numbers and display the sum
sum = 0
fibonacci(100) {|num| sum += num}
puts "Sum of the Fibonacci numbers less than 100  is: #{sum}"
```

Note the use of parallel assignments, similar to those in Perl, in the method. Also, note that the notation #{...} in the parameter string to puts is used to specify that the value of the enclosed expression is to be converted to a string and inserted into the character string. The output of this code is as follows:

```
Fibonacci numbers less than 100 are:
1 1 2 3 5 8 13 21 34 55 89
Sum of the Fibonacci numbers less than 100 is: 232
```

Blocks are closures, which means that they retain the environment of the place where they are defined, including the local variables and the current object, regardless of where they are called.

9.2.5 Procedures and Functions

There are two distinct categories of subprograms—procedures and functions—both of which can be viewed as approaches to extending the language. Procedures are collections of statements that define parameterized computations. These computations are enacted by single call statements. In effect, procedures define new statements. For example, because Ada does not have a sort statement, a user can build a procedure to sort arrays of data and use a call to that procedure in place of the unavailable sort statement. In Ada, procedures are called just that; in Fortran, they are called subroutines.

Procedures can produce results in the calling program unit by two methods. First, if there are variables that are not formal parameters but are still visible in both the procedure and the calling program unit, the procedure can change them. Second, if the subprogram has formal parameters that allow the transfer of data to the caller, those parameters can be changed.

Functions structurally resemble procedures but are semantically modeled on mathematical functions. If a function is a faithful model, it produces no side effects; that is, it modifies neither its parameters nor any variables defined outside the function. Such a pure function returns a value—that is its only desired effect. In practice, many functions in programs have side effects.

Functions are called by appearances of their names in expressions, along with the required actual parameters. The value produced by a function's execution is returned to the calling code, effectively replacing the call itself. For example, the value of the expression f(x) is whatever value f produces when called with the parameter x. For a function that does not produce side effects, the returned value is its only effect.

Functions define new user-defined operators. For example, if a language does not have an exponentiation operator, a function can be written that returns the value of one of its parameters raised to the power of another parameter. Its header in C++ could be

```
float power(float base, float exp)
```

which could be called with

```
result = 3.4 * power(10.0, x)
```

The standard C++ library already includes a similar function named pow. Compare this with the same operation in Perl, in which exponentiation is a built-in operation:

```
result = 3.4 * 10.0 ** x
```

In Ada, Python, Ruby, C++, and C#, users are permitted to overload operators by defining new functions. In these languages, the user could define an exponentiation operator that could be used much like the built-in exponentiation operator in Perl. User-defined operator overloading is discussed in Section 9.10.

Some programming languages, for example, Fortran and Ada, provide both functions and procedures. The C-based languages have only functions (and/or methods). However, these functions can behave like procedures. They can be defined to return no value if their return type is **void**. Because expressions in these languages can be used as statements, a stand-alone call to a **void** function is legal. For example, consider the following function header and call:

```
void sort(int list[], int listlen);
...
sort(scores, 100);
```

The methods of Java, C++, and C# are syntactically similar to the functions of C.

9.3 Design Issues for Subprograms

Subprograms are complex structures in programming languages, and it follows from this that a lengthy list of issues is involved in their design. One obvious issue is the choice of one or more parameter-passing methods that will be used. The wide variety of approaches that have been used in various languages is a reflection of the diversity of opinion on the subject. A closely related issue is whether the types of actual parameters will be type checked against the types of the corresponding formal parameters.

The nature of the local environment of a subprogram dictates to some degree the nature of the subprogram. The most important question here is whether local variables are statically or dynamically allocated.

Next, there is the question of whether subprogram definitions can be nested. Another issue is whether subprogram names can be passed as parameters. If subprogram names can be passed as parameters and the language allows subprograms to be nested, there is the question of the correct referencing environment of a subprogram that has been passed as a parameter.

Finally, there are the questions of whether subprograms can be overloaded or generic. An **overloaded subprogram** is one that has the same name as another subprogram in the same referencing environment. A **generic subprogram** is one whose computation can be done on data of different types in different calls.

The following is a summary of these design issues for subprograms in general. Additional issues that are specifically associated with functions are discussed in Section 9.9.

- Are local variables statically or dynamically allocated?
- Can subprogram definitions appear in other subprogram definitions?
- What parameter-passing method or methods are used?
- Are the types of the actual parameters checked against the types of the formal parameters?
- If subprograms can be passed as parameters and subprograms can be nested, what is the referencing environment of a passed subprogram?
- Can subprograms be overloaded?
- Can subprograms be generic?

These issues and example designs are discussed in the following sections.

9.4 Local Referencing Environments

This section discusses the issues related to variables that are defined within subprograms. The issue of nested subprogram definitions is also briefly covered.

9.4.1 Local Variables

Subprograms can define their own variables, thereby defining local referencing environments. Variables that are defined inside subprograms are called **local variables,** because their scope is usually the body of the subprogram in which they are defined.

In the terminology of Chapter 5, local variables can be either static or stack-dynamic. If local variables are stack-dynamic, they are bound to storage when the subprogram begins execution and are unbound from storage when that execution terminates. There are several advantages of stack-dynamic local variables, the primary one being the flexibility they provide the subprogram. It is essential that recursive subprograms have stack-dynamic local variables. Another advantage of stack-dynamic locals is that the storage for local variables in an active subprogram can be shared with the local variables in all inactive subprograms. This is not as great an advantage as it was when computers had smaller memories.

The main disadvantages of stack-dynamic local variables are the following: First there is the cost of the time required to allocate, initialize (when necessary), and deallocate such variables for each call to the subprogram. Second, accesses to stack-dynamic local variables must be indirect, whereas accesses to static variables can be direct.[1] This indirectness is required because the place in the stack where a particular local variable will reside can be determined only during execution (see Chapter 10). Finally, when all local variables are stack-dynamic, subprograms cannot be history-sensitive; that is, they cannot retain data values of local variables between calls. It is sometimes convenient to be able to write history-sensitive subprograms. A common example of a need for a history-sensitive subprogram is one whose task is to generate pseudorandom numbers. Each call to such a subprogram computes one pseudorandom number, using the last one it computed. It must, therefore, store the last one in a static local variable. Coroutines and the subprograms used in iterator loop constructs (discussed in Chapter 8) are other examples of subprograms that need to be history-sensitive.

The primary advantage of static local variables over stack-dynamic local variables is that they are slightly more efficient—they require no run-time overhead for allocation and deallocation. Also, if accessed directly, these accesses are obviously more efficient. And, of course, they allow subprograms

---

1. In some implementations, static variables are also accessed indirectly, thereby eliminating this disadvantage.

to be history-sensitive. The greatest disadvantage of static local variables is their inability to support recursion. Also, their storage cannot be shared with the local variables of other inactive subprograms.

In most comtemporary languages, local variables in a subprogram are by default stack-dynamic. In C and C++ functions, locals are stack-dynamic unless specifically declared to be **static**. For example, in the following C (or C++) function, the variable sum is static and count is stack-dynamic.

```c
int adder(int list[], int listlen) {
  static int sum = 0;
  int count;
  for (count = 0; count < listlen; count ++)
    sum += list [count];
  return sum;
}
```

Ada subprograms and the methods of C++, Java, and C# have only stack-dynamic local variables.

As discussed in Chapter 5, Fortran 95 implementors can choose whether local variables are to be static or stack-dynamic. Actually, because pre-90 Fortrans do not allow recursion, there is really no compelling reason to make them stack-dynamic. The savings in storage is not usually thought to be worth the loss in efficiency. Fortran 95 users can force one or more local variables to be static regardless of the implementation by listing their names on a Save statement.

In Fortran 95, a subprogram can be explicitly specified to be recursive, in which case its local variables are stack-dynamic by default. The idea of specifying that a particular subprogram can be recursively called originated with PL/I. The purpose of this explicit specification is to allow nonrecursive subprograms to be implemented in a more efficient way. Following is a skeletal example of a recursive subroutine:

```
Recursive Subroutine Sub ()
   Integer :: Count
   Save, Real :: Sum
   ...
End Subroutine Sub
```

In this subroutine, Count is stack-dynamic, because the subprogram is defined to be recursive. Sum is static because it is marked Save.

In Python, the only declarations used in method definitions are for globals. Any variable declared to be global in a method must be a variable defined outside the method. A variable defined outside the method can be referenced in the method without declaring it to be global, but such a variable cannot be assigned in the method. If the name of a global variable is assigned in a method, it is implicitly declared to be a local and the assignment does not disturb the global. All local variables in Python methods are stack-dynamic.

9.4.2 Nested Subprograms

The idea of nesting subprograms originated with Algol 60. The motivation was to be able to create a hierarchy of both logic and scopes. If a subprogram is needed only within another subprogram, why not place it there and hide it from the rest of the program. Because static scoping is usually used in languages that allow subprograms to be nested, this also provides a highly structured way to grant access to nonlocal variables in enclosing subprograms. Recall that in Chapter 5 the problems introduced by this were discussed. For a long time, the only languages that allowed nested subprograms were those directly descending from Algol 60, which were Algol 68, Pascal, and Ada. Many other languages, including all of the direct descendants of C, do not allow subprogram nesting. Recently, some new langauges again allow it. Among these are JavaScript, Python, and Ruby.

9.5 Parameter-Passing Methods

Parameter-passing methods are the ways in which parameters are transmitted to and/or from called subprograms. We first focus on the different semantics models of parameter-passing methods. Then we discuss the various implementation models invented by language designers for these semantics models. Next we survey the design choices of the various imperative languages and discuss the actual methods used to implement the implementation models. Finally, we consider the design considerations that face a language designer in choosing among the methods.

9.5.1 Semantics Models of Parameter Passing

Formal parameters are characterized by one of three distinct semantics models: (1) They can receive data from the corresponding actual parameter; (2) they can transmit data to the actual parameter; or (3) they can do both. These three semantics models are called **in mode, out mode,** and **inout mode,** respectively. For example, consider a subprogram that takes two arrays of int values as parameters—list1 and list2. The subprogram must add list1 to list2 and return the result as a revised version of list2. Furthermore, the subprogram must create a new array from the two given arrays and return it. For this subprogram, list1 should be in mode, because it is not to be changed by the subprogram. list2 must be inout mode, because the subprogram needs the given value of the array and must return its new value. The third array should be out mode, because there is no initial value for this array and its computed value must be returned to the caller.

Part 2: Scripting Languages in General and Perl in Particular

LARRY WALL

Larry Wall wears many hats—he is involved in book publishing, language publishing, software publishing, child rearing (he has four kids). He has spent time studying at Seattle Pacific University, at Berkeley, and at UCLA. He has also worked at Unisys, Jet Propulsion Laboratories, and Seagate. Language publishing has brought him the most fame ("and the least money," he adds): Larry is the author of the Perl scripting language.

SOME SPECIFICS ON SCRIPTING LANGUAGES
Can you share your definition of a scripting language? People often argue over the difference between a scripting language and a programming language. If you ask me, I'll tell you that a script is what you hand the actors, and a program is what you hand the audience, the idea being that a script is something that is being molded into shape by the writer, the director, and the actors, while a program denotes a relatively fixed sequence of predetermined events.

There's no hards-and-fast distinction between scripting and programming, and scripts have a way of turning into programs over time. But to run with our metaphor, while you're writing your program, it's behaving more like a script, and when you're finished developing your script, it's acting more like a program.

Certain kinds of language make it a little easier to whip things up on the spur of the moment, so those languages tend to be classified as "scripting" languages. Other languages try to make it easier to manipulate complex data precisely and efficiently, at the expense of having to specify a lot of things in advance before you can say what you really want to say. These languages tend to be called "programming" languages. Perl is generally presented to people as a scripting language, but that's an oversimplification, or maybe an undercomplexification. . . .

What should the reader understand about a scripting language? The most important thing to understand is that while people usually plan to throw away the prototype, they rarely in fact do. What you intended to be one-shot code often turns out to be "good enough" to stay in production far longer than you might have guessed. So it's generally better to plan for

that in the first place, with the expectation that your quick-and-dirty prototype will in fact grow into a clean, modular design over time. That's all assuming your language will let you evolve your program, of course. Not all languages will.

MORE ON PERL AND HOW IT CAME TO BE
What distinguishes Perl from the other scripting languages? I think a good scripting language should support the evolution of your script into a "Real Program." To that end, Perl gives you complete multiparadigm programming support to back up its scripting support. In other words, Perl acts like a grown-up computer language when you're ready for it to.

Scripts are like on-ramps to a freeway. Most programming languages try to provide either the on-ramps without the freeway or the freeway without the on-ramps. Perl tries to give you both, because Perl is an eat-your-cake-and-have-it-too language. That's why the Perl slogan is "There's More Than One Way To Do It." Perl doesn't try to enforce a particular style; some problems might be better solved by pipes and pattern matching, while others might be better solved by functional programming, or by event-driven programming, or by object-oriented programming.

In contrast, other languages often try to lock you into a particular way of thinking, or make it difficult to interface to the outside world. Perl isn't trying to be a perfect language, but a useful language, which often involves cooperating with other languages and systems in a humble sort of way. Natural languages are not utopias, nor do they try to lock you into a monastery. Computer languages shouldn't either.

When you created Perl, did you think it would be what it is now? What is it about Perl that makes it so useful for the Internet? And, because marketing is so important, what was going on in industry or the computing realm that helped Perl take off, in your opinion? Hmm. Well, I knew Perl would be big, but I didn't know it would be this big. I figured from the start that Perl would make awk and sed obsolete for text processing, and (to a lesser extent) shell programming obsolete for gluing random interfaces together. Once I added in all the system administration operations, I was not at all surprised that it became the language of choice for most UNIX system administrators.

What I did not anticipate was the Web, nor that much of the Web would be prototyped in Perl. Given that the HTTP is a text-based protocol, however, and given that Web servers needed glue code to translate between that text and backend database servers, Perl was in the right place at the right time with the right capabilities.

But this is just another example of how a good tool is used for purposes not envisioned by its creator. But that's not entirely an accident; a good creator will try

> *People often argue over the difference between a scripting language and a programming language. If you ask me, I'll tell you that a script is what you hand the actors, and a program is what you hand the audience.*

to build in capabilities that could be used serendipitously when the opportunity arises.

What part of the language do you like the most? The part I like the best is that I'm allowed to change the parts I like the least. Seriously, the parts I like the best are the ones that are being conserved in the design of Perl 6. For instance, Perl has always been pretty good at evolving, and at cooperating humbly with other programs and languages in its environment. This should only continue to get better. Perl will remain good at rapid prototyping and text processing. It will get even better at pattern matching. (All assuming we ever finish Perl 6. . . .)

On a closing note, if you weren't doing all this, how would you be spending your days? Probably driving the people around me crazy. Oh, wait . . .

There are two conceptual models of how data transfers take place in parameter transmission: Either an actual value is copied (to the caller, to the callee, or both ways), or an access path is transmitted. Most commonly, the access path is a simple pointer or reference. Figure 9.1 illustrates the three semantics models of parameter passing when values are copied.

9.5.2 Implementation Models of Parameter Passing

A variety of models have been developed by language designers to guide the implementation of the three basic parameter transmission modes. In the following sections, we discuss several of these, along with their relative strengths and weaknesses.

9.5.2.1 Pass-by-Value

When a parameter is **passed by value,** the value of the actual parameter is used to initialize the corresponding formal parameter, which then acts as a local variable in the subprogram, thus implementing in-mode semantics.

Pass-by-value is normally implemented by copy, because accesses often are more efficient with this approach. It could be implemented by transmitting an access path to the value of the actual parameter in the caller, but that would require that the value be in a write-protected cell (one that can only be read). Enforcing the write protection is not always a simple matter. For example, suppose the subprogram to which the parameter was passed passes it in turn to another subprogram. This is another reason to use copy transfer. As

Figure 9.1

The three semantics models of parameter passing when physical moves are used

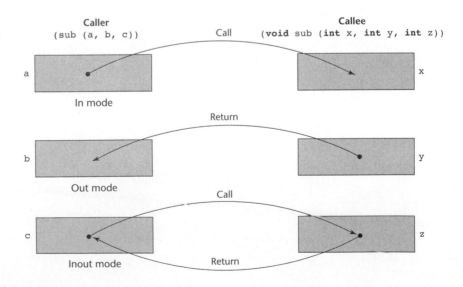

we will see in Section 9.5.4, C++ provides a convenient and effective method for enforcing write protection on pass-by-value parameters that are transmitted by access path.

The advantage of pass-by-value is that for scalars it is fast, in both linkage cost and access time.

The main disadvantage of the pass-by-value method if copies are used is that additional storage is required for the formal parameter, either in the called subprogram or in some area outside both the caller and the called subprogram. In addition, the actual parameter must be copied to the storage area for the corresponding formal parameter. The storage and the copy operations can be costly if the parameter is large, such as an array with many elements.

9.5.2.2 Pass-by-Result

Pass-by-result is an implementation model for out-mode parameters. When a parameter is passed by result, no value is transmitted to the subprogram. The corresponding formal parameter acts as a local variable, but just before control is transferred back to the caller, its value is transmitted back to the caller's actual parameter, which obviously must be a variable. (How would the caller reference the computed result if it were a literal or an expression?)

The pass-by-result method has the advantages and disadvantages of pass-by-value, plus some additional disadvantages. If values are returned by copy (as opposed to access paths), as they typically are, pass-by-result also requires the extra storage and the copy operations that are required by pass-by-value. As with pass-by-value, the difficulty of implementing pass-by-result by transmitting an access path usually results in it being implemented by data copy. In this case, the problem is in ensuring that the initial value of the actual parameter is not used in the called subprogram.

One additional problem with the pass-by-result model is that there can be an actual parameter collision, such as the one created with the call

```
sub(p1, p1)
```

In sub, assuming the two formal parameters have different names, the two can obviously be assigned different values. Then whichever of the two is copied to their corresponding actual parameter last becomes the value of p1. Thus the order in which the actual parameters are copied determines their value. For example, consider the following C# method, which specifies the pass-by-result method with the out specifier on its formal parameter.[3]

```
void Fixer(out int x, out int y) {
  x = 17;
  y = 35;
```

---

3. The out specifier must also be specified on the corresponding actual parameter.

```
}
...
f.Fixer(out a, out a);
```

If at the end of the execution of `Fixer` the formal parameter x is assigned to its corresponding actual parameter first, the value of the actual parameter a in the caller will be 35. If y is assigned first, the value of the actual parameter a in the caller will be 17.

Because the order, is sometimes implementation-dependent for some languages, different implementations can produce different results.

Calling a procedure with two identical actual parameters can also lead to different kinds of problems when other parameter-passing methods are used, as discussed in Section 9.5.2.4.

Yet another problem that can occur with pass-by-result is that the implementor may be able to choose between two different times to evaluate the addresses of the actual parameters: at the time of the call or at the time of the return. For example, consider the following C# method and following code:

```
void DoIt(out int x, int index){
  x = 17;
  index = 42;
}
...
sub = 21;
f.DoIt(list[sub], sub);
```

The address of `list[sub]` changes between the beginning and end of the method. The implementor must choose the time at which the address to which to return the value will be determined, at the time of the call or at the time of the return. If the address is computed on entry to the method, the value 17 will be returned to `list[21]`; if computed just before return, 17 will be returned to `list[42]`. This makes programs unportable between an implementation that chooses to evaluate the addresses for out-mode parameters at the beginning of a subprogram and one that chooses to do that evaluation at the end.

9.5.2.3 Pass-by-Value-Result

Pass-by-value-result is an implementation model for inout-mode parameters in which actual values are copied. It is in effect a combination of pass-by-value and pass-by-result. The value of the actual parameter is used to initialize the corresponding formal parameter, which then acts as a local variable. In fact, pass-by-value-result formal parameters must have local storage associated with the called subprogram. At subprogram termination, the value of the formal parameter is transmitted back to the actual parameter.

Pass-by-value-result is sometimes called **pass-by-copy,** because the actual parameter is copied to the formal parameter at subprogram entry and then copied back at subprogram termination.

Pass-by-value-result shares with pass-by-value and pass-by-result the disadvantages of requiring multiple storage for parameters and time for copying values. It shares with pass-by-result the problems associated with the order in which actual parameters are assigned.

The advantages of pass-by-value-result are relative to pass-by-reference, so they are discussed in Section 9.5.2.4.

9.5.2.4 Pass-by-Reference

Pass-by-reference is a second implementation model for inout-mode parameters. Rather than copying data values back and forth, however, as in pass-by-value-result, the pass-by-reference method transmits an access path, usually just an address, to the called subprogram. This provides the access path to the cell storing the actual parameter. Thus the called subprogram is allowed to access the actual parameter in the calling program unit. In effect, the actual parameter is shared with the called subprogram.

The advantage of pass-by-reference is that the passing process itself is efficient, in terms of both time and space. Duplicate space is not required, nor is any copying required.

There are, however, several disadvantages to the pass-by-reference method. First, access to the formal parameters will be slower than pass-by-value parameters, because of the additional level of indirect addressing that is required.[4] Second, if only one-way communication to the called subprogram is required, inadvertent and erroneous changes may be made to the actual parameter.

Another serious problem of pass-by-reference is that aliases can be created. This problem should be expected, because pass-by-reference makes access paths available to the called subprograms, thereby broadening their access to nonlocal variables. There are several different ways aliases can be created when parameters are passed by reference. The problem with these kinds of aliasing is the same as in other circumstances: It is harmful to readability and thus to reliability. It also makes program verification extremely difficult.

We now discuss some ways pass-by-reference parameters can create aliases. First, collisions can occur between actual parameters. Consider a C++ function that has two parameters that are to be passed by reference (see Section 9.5.3), as in

```
void fun(int &first, int &second)
```

---

4. This is further explained in Section 9.5.3.

If the call to `fun` happens to pass the same variable twice, as in

```
fun(total, total)
```

then `first` and `second` in `fun` will be aliases.

Second, collisions between array elements can also cause aliases. For example, suppose the function `fun` is called with two array elements that are specified with variable subscripts, as in

```
fun(list[i], list[j])
```

If these two parameters are passed by reference and `i` happens to be equal to `j`, then `first` and `second` are again aliases.

Third, if two of the formal parameters of a subprogram are an element of an array and the other is the whole array, and both are passed by reference, then a call such as

```
fun1(list[i], list)
```

could result in aliasing in `fun1`, because `fun1` can access all elements of `list` through the second parameter and access a single element through its first parameter.

Still another way to get aliasing with pass-by-reference parameters is through collisions between formal parameters and nonlocal variables that are visible. For example, consider the following C code:

```
int * global;
void main() {
   ...
   sub(global);
   ...
}
void sub(int * param) {
   ...
}
```

Inside `sub`, `param`, and `global` are aliases.

All these possible aliasing situations are eliminated if pass-by-value-result is used instead of pass-by-reference. However, in place of aliasing, other problems sometimes arise, as discussed in Section 9.5.2.3.

9.5.2.5 Pass-by-Name

Pass-by-name is an inout-mode parameter transmission method that does not correspond to a single implementation model. When parameters are passed by name, the actual parameter is, in effect, textually substituted for the corresponding formal parameter in all its occurrences in the subprogram. This method is quite different from those discussed thus far, in which cases formal parameters are bound to actual values or addresses at the time of the subprogram call. A pass-by-name formal parameter is bound to an access method at the time of the subprogram call, but the actual binding to a value or an address is delayed until the formal parameter is assigned or referenced.

Because pass-by-name is not part of any widely used language, it is not discussed further here. However, it is used at compile time by the macros in assembly languages and for the generic parameters of the generic subprograms in C++ and Ada, as discussed in Section 9.8.

9.5.3 Implementing Parameter-Passing Methods

We now address the question of how the various implementation models of parameter passing are actually implemented.

In most contemporary languages, parameter communication takes place through the run-time stack. The run-time stack is initialized and maintained by the run-time system, which is a system program that manages the execution of programs. The run-time stack is used extensively for subprogram control linkage and parameter passing, as discussed in Chapter 10. In the following discussion, we assume that the stack is used for all parameter transmission.

Pass-by-value parameters have their values copied into stack locations. The stack locations then serve as storage for the corresponding formal parameters. Pass-by-result parameters are implemented as the opposite of pass-by-value. The values assigned to the pass-by-result actual parameters are placed in the stack, where they can be retrieved by the calling program unit upon termination of the called subprogram. Pass-by-value-result parameters can be implemented directly from their semantics as a combination of pass-by-value and pass-by-result. The stack location for the parameters is initialized by the call and is then used like a local variable in the called subprogram.

Pass-by-reference parameters are perhaps the simplest to implement. Regardless of the type of the actual parameter, only its address must be placed in the stack. In the case of literals, the address of the literal is put in the stack. In the case of an expression, the compiler must build code to evaluate the expression just before the transfer of control to the called subprogram. The address of the memory cell in which the code places the result of its evaluation is then put in the stack. The compiler must be sure to prevent the called subprogram from changing parameters that are literals or expressions, as discussed later in this chapter. Access to the formal parameters in the called subprogram is by indirect addressing from the stack location of the address. The implementation of pass-by-value, -result, -value-result, and -reference, where the run-time stack is used, is shown in Figure 9.2. Subprogram `sub` is called from `main` with the call `sub(w, x, y, z)`, where w is passed by value, x is passed by result, y is passed by value-result, and z is passed by reference.

A subtle but fatal error can occur with pass-by-reference and pass-by-value-result parameters if care is not taken in their implementation. Suppose a

Figure 9.2

One possible stack implementation of the common parameter-passing methods

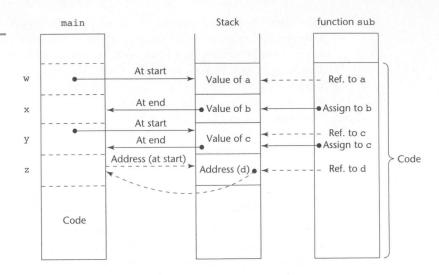

Function header: **void** sub (**int** a, **int** b, **int** c, **int** d)
Function call in main: sub (w,x,y,z)
(pass w by value, x by result, y by value-result, z by reference)

program contains two references to the constant 10, the first as an actual parameter in a call to a subprogram. Further suppose that the subprogram mistakenly changes the formal parameter that corresponds to the 10 to the value 5. The compiler for this program may have built a single location for the value 10 during compilation, as compilers often do, and uses that location for all references to the constant 10 in the program. But after the return from the subprogram, all subsequent occurrences of 10 will actually be references to the value 5. If this is allowed to happen, it creates a programming problem that is very difficult to diagnose. This did in fact happen with many implementations of Fortran IV.

9.5.4   Parameter-Passing Methods of Some Common Languages

C uses pass-by-value. Pass-by-reference (inout mode) semantics is achieved by using pointers as parameters. The value of the pointer is made available to the called function and nothing is copied back. However, because what was passed is an access path to the data of the caller, the called function can change the caller's data. C copied this use of the pass-by-value method from ALGOL 68. In both C and C++, formal parameters can be typed as pointers to constants. The corresponding actual parameters need not be constants, for in such cases they are coerced to constants. This allows pointer parameters to provide the efficiency of pass-by-reference with the one-way semantics of pass-by-value. Write protection of those parameters in the called function is implicit.

C++ includes a special pointer type, called a *reference type*, as discussed in Chapter 6, that is often used for parameters. Reference parameters are implicitly dereferenced in the function or method, and their semantics is pass-by-reference. C++ also allows reference parameters to be defined to be constants. For example, we could have

```
void fun(const int &p1, int p2, int &p3) { ... }
```

history note

ALGOL 60 introduced the pass-by-name method. It also allows pass-by-value as an option. Primarily because of the difficulty in implementing them, pass-by-name parameters were not carried from ALGOL 60 to any subsequent languages that became popular (other than SIMULA 67).

where p1 is pass-by-reference but cannot be changed in the function fun, p2 is pass-by-value, and p3 is pass-by-reference. Neither p1 nor p3 need be explicitly dereferenced in fun.

Constant parameters and in-mode parameters are not exactly alike. Constant parameters clearly implement in mode. However, in all of the common imperative languages except Ada, in mode parameters can be assigned in the subprogram even though those changes are never reflected in the values of the corresponding actual parameters. Constant parameters can never be assigned.

As with C and C++, all Java parameters are passed by value. However, because objects can be accessed only through reference variables, object parameters are in effect passed by reference. Although an object reference passed as a parameter cannot itself be changed in the called subprogram, the referenced object can be changed if a method is available to cause the change. Because reference variables cannot point to scalar variables directly and Java does not have pointers, scalars cannot be passed by reference in Java (although a reference to an object that contains a scalar can).

history note

ALGOL W (Wirth and Hoare, 1966) introduced the pass-by-value-result method of parameter passing as an alternative to the inefficiency of pass-by-name and the problems of pass-by-reference.

The designers of Ada defined versions of the three semantics modes of parameter transmission: in, out, and inout. The three modes are appropriately named with the reserved words **in**, **out**, and **in out**, where **in** is the default method. For example, consider the following Ada subprogram header:

```
procedure Adder(A : in out Integer;
                B : in Integer;
                C : out Float)
```

Ada formal parameters declared to be **out** mode can be assigned but not referenced. Parameters that are **in** mode can be referenced but not assigned. Quite naturally, **in out** mode parameters can be both referenced and assigned.

In Ada 95, all scalars are passed by copy and all structured parameters are passed by reference.

Fortran 95 is similar to Ada in that its formal parameters can be declared to be in, out, or inout mode, using the Intent attribute. For example, consider the following beginning of a Fortran 95 subprogram:

```
Subroutine Adder(A, B, C)
   Integer, Intent(Inout) :: A
```

```
Integer, Intent(In) :: B
Integer, Intent(Out) :: C
```

The semantics modes of the parameters of this subprogram are the same as the previous Ada example.

The default parameter-passing method of C# is pass-by-value. Pass-by-reference can be specified by preceding both a formal parameter and its corresponding actual parameter with **ref**. For example, consider the following C# skeletal method and call:

```
void sumer(ref int oldSum, int newOne) { ... }
...
sumer(ref sum, newValue);
```

The first parameter to sumer is passed by reference; the second is passed by value.

C# supports out-mode parameters, which are pass-by-reference parameters that do not need initial values. Such parameters are specified in the formal parameter list with the **out** modifier.

A C# method can take a variable number of parameters, as long as all are of the same type. The method defines just one parameter, an array with the params qualifier. For example,

```
void SumInts(params int [] intValues) { ... }
```

This method can be called with an array or a list of integer expressions. For example,

```
int [] myIntArray = new int[6] {2, 4, 6, 8, 10, 12};
sum1 = SumInts(myIntArray);
sum2 = SumInts(10, i, 17, k);
```

PHP's parameter passing is similar to that of C#, except that either the actual parameter or the formal parameter can specify pass-by-reference. Pass-by-reference is specified by preceding one or both of the parameters with an ampersand.

Perl employs a primitive means of passing parameters. All actual parameters are implicitly placed in a predefined array named @_ (of all things!). The subprogram retrieves the actual parameter values (or addresses) from this array. The most peculiar thing about this array is its magical nature, exposed by the fact that its elements are in effect aliases for the actual parameters. Therefore, if an element of @_ is changed in the called subprogram, that change is reflected in the corresponding actual parameter in the call, assuming there is a corresponding actual parameter (the number of actual parameters need not be the same as the number of formal parameters) and it is a variable.

The parameter-passing method of Python and Ruby is called *pass-by-assignment*. Because all data values are objects, every variable is a reference to an object. In pass-by-assignment, the actual parameter value is assigned to the formal parameter. Therefore, pass-by-assignment is in effect pass-by-reference, because the value of all actual parameters are references. However, only in certain cases does this result in pass-by-reference parameter-passing semantics. For example, many objects are essentially immutable. In a pure object-oriented language, the process of changing the value of a variable with an assignment statement, as in

```
x = x + 1
```

does not change the object referenced by x. Rather, it takes the object referenced by x, increments it by 1, thereby creating a new object (with the value x + 1), and then changes x to reference the new object. So, when a reference to a scalar object is passed to a subprogram, the object being referenced cannot be changed in place. Because the reference is passed by value, even though the formal parameter is changed in the subprogram, that change has no effect on the actual parameter in the caller.

Now, suppose a reference to an array is passed as a parameter. If the corresponding formal parameter is assigned a new array object, there is no effect on the caller. However, if the formal parameter is used to assign a value to an element of the array, as in

```
list[3] = 47
```

the actual parameter is affected. So, changing the reference of the formal parmeter has no effect on the caller, but changing an element of the array that is passed as a parameter does.

9.5.5   Type Checking Parameters

It is now widely accepted that software reliability demands that the types of actual parameters be checked for consistency with the types of the corresponding formal parameters. Without such type checking, small typographical errors can lead to program errors that may be difficult to diagnose because they are not detected by the compiler or the run-time system. For example, in the function call

```
result = sub1(1)
```

the actual parameter is an integer constant. If the formal parameter of sub1 is a floating-point type, no error will be detected without parameter type checking. Although an integer 1 and a floating-point 1 have the same value, the representations of these two are very different. sub1 cannot produce a correct result given an integer actual parameter value when it expects a floating-point value.

Early programming languages, such as Fortran 77 and the original version of C, did not require parameter type checking; most later languages require it. However, the relatively recent languages Perl, JavaScript, and PHP do not.

C and C++ require some special discussion in the matter of parameter type checking. In the original C, neither the number of parameters nor their types were checked. In C89, the formal parameters of functions can be defined in two ways. First, they can be as in the original C; that is, the names of the parameters are listed in parentheses and the type declarations for them follow, as in

```
double sin(x)
  double x;
  { ... }
```

Using this method avoids type checking, thereby allowing calls such as

```
double value;
int count;
...
value = sin(count);
```

to be legal, although they are never correct.

The alternative is called the **prototype** method, in which the formal parameter types are included in the list, as in

```
double sin(double x)
  { ... }
```

If this version of `sin` is called with the same call; that is,

```
value = sin(count);
```

it is also legal. The type of the actual parameter (**int**) is checked against that of the formal parameter (**double**). Although they do not match, **int** is coercible to **double** (it is a widening coercion), so the conversion is done. If the conversion is not possible (for example, if the actual parameter had been an array) or if the number of parameters is wrong, then a syntax error is detected. So in C89, the user chooses whether parameters are to be type checked.

In C99 and C++, all functions must have their formal parameters in prototype form. However, type checking can be avoided for some of the parameters by replacing the last part of the parameter list with an ellipsis, as in

```
int printf(const char* format_string, ...);
```

history note

The Ada 83 language definition specifies that scalar (nonstructured) parameters are to be passed by copy; that is, in- and inout-mode parameters are to be local variables that are initialized by copying the value of the corresponding actual parameter. Simple parameters that are out or inout mode are to have their values copied back to the corresponding actual parameter at subprogram termination. The order of these copies, when there are more than one, is not defined by the language definition. The evaluation of out- and inout-mode parameters is done before the transfer of control to the called subprogram occurs. For example, suppose an outmode actual parameter has the form

`List(Index)`

The address value of this parameter is computed at the time of the call. If Index happened to be visible in the called subprogram and the subprogram changed it, the parameter address would not be affected.

In the case of formal parameters that are arrays or records, Ada 83 implementors were given the choice between pass-by-value-result and pass-by-reference. By failing to specify the implementation method for passing structured parameters, the Ada 83 designers left open the possibility of a subtle problem. The problem is that the two implementation methods can

(continues)

A call to `printf` must include at least one parameter, a pointer to a constant character string. Beyond that, anything (including nothing) is legal. The way `printf` determines whether there are additional parameters is by the presence of special symbols in the string parameter. For example, the format code for integer output is `%d`. This appears as part of the string, as in

```
printf("The sum is %d\n", sum);
```

The `%` tells the `printf` function that there is one more parameter.

There is one more interesting issue with actual to formal parameter coercions when primitives can be passed by reference, as in C#. Suppose a call to a method passes a **float** value to a **double** formal parameter. If this parameter is passed by value, the **float** value is coerced to **double** and there is no problem. This particular coercion is very useful, for it allows a library to provide double versions of subprograms that can be used for both **float** and **double** values. However, suppose the parameter is passsed by reference. When the value of the **double** formal parameter is returned to the **float** actual parameter in the caller, the value will overflow its location. To avoid this problem, C# requires the type of a **ref** actual parameter to match exactly the type of its corresponding formal parameter (no coercion is allowed).

In Python and Ruby, there is no type checking of parameters, because typing in these languages is a different concept. Objects have types, but variables do not, so formal parameters are typeless. This disallows the very idea of type checking parameters.

9.5.6 Multidimensional Arrays as Parameters

The storage-mapping functions that are used to map the index values of references to elements of multidimensional arrays to addresses in memory were discussed at length in Chapter 6. In some languages, such as C and C++, when a multidimensional array is passed as a parameter to a subprogram, the compiler must be able to build the mapping function for that array while seeing only the text of the subprogram (not the calling subprogram). This is true because the subprograms can be compiled separately from the programs that call them. Consider the problem of passing a matrix to a function in C. Multidimensional arrays in C are really arrays of arrays, and they are stored in row major order. Following is a storage-mapping function for row major order for matrices when the lower bound of all indices is zero and the element size is 1:

$$\text{address}(\text{mat}[i, j]) = \text{address}(\text{mat}[0,0]) + i * \text{number\_of\_columns} + j$$

history note

(continued)

lead to different program results for certain programs. This difference can occur because the pass-by-reference method provides access to a location in the calling program that can also be provided if the actual parameter is also visible as a global, or if the same actual parameter is passed to two formal parameters, in either case creating an alias. If pass-by-value-result is used in place of pass-by-reference, this dual access to the actual parameter is not possible.

An additional problem is the following: Suppose the subprogram terminates abnormally (via an exception); the actual parameter in the pass-by-value-result implementation will be unchanged, whereas the pass-by-reference implementation may have changed the corresponding actual parameter before the error occurred. Once again, there can be a difference between the two implementation methods.

Ada 83 programs that produce different results depending on how the inout method is implemented are termed erroneous. Despite this label, however, there is no way that the compiler can detect the erroneous condition. So the error is usually detected only when the user moves the program from one implementation to another and realizes that it no longer behaves the same way. The Ada 83 design philosophy in this situation is that programmers must guard against aliasing: If they create aliases, they must contend with the potential problems.

Notice that this mapping function needs the number of columns but not the number of rows. Therefore, in C and C++, when a matrix is passed as a parameter, the formal parameter must include the number of columns in the second pair of brackets. This is illustrated in the following skeletal C program:

```c
void fun(int matrix[][10]) {
 ... }
void main() {
  int mat[5][10];
  ...
  fun(mat);
  ...
}
```

The problem with this method of passing matrixes as parameters is that it does not allow a programmer to write a function that can accept matrixes with different numbers of columns; a new function must be written for every matrix with a different number of columns. This, in effect, disallows writing flexible functions that may be effectively reusable if the functions deal with multidimensional arrays. In C and C++, there is a way around the problem because of their inclusion of pointer arithmetic. The matrix can be passed as a pointer, and the actual dimensions of the matrix can be included as parameters. Then the function can evaluate the user-written storage-mapping function using pointer arithmetic each time an element of the matrix must be referenced. For example, consider the following function prototype:

```c
void fun(float *mat_ptr,
         int num_rows,
         int num_cols);
```

The following statement can be used to move the value of the variable x to the [row][col] element of the parameter matrix in fun:

```c
*(mat_ptr + (row * num_cols) + col) = x;
```

Although this works, it is obviously difficult to read, and because of its complexity it is error-prone. The difficulty with reading this can be alleviated by using a macro to define the storage-mapping function, such as

```c
#define mat_ptr(r,c)  (*mat_ptr + ((r) *
                       (num_cols) + (c)))
```

With this, the assignment can be written as

```
mat_ptr(row,col) = x;
```

Other languages use different approaches to dealing with the problem of passing multiimensional arrays. Ada compilers are able to determine the defined size of the dimensions of all arrays that are used as parameters at the time subprograms are compiled. In Ada, unconstrained array types can be formal parameters. An unconstrained array type is one in which the index ranges are not given in the array type definition. Definitions of variables of unconstrained array types must include index ranges. The code in a subprogram that is passed an unconstrained array can obtain the index range information of the actual parameter associated with such parameters. For example, consider the following definitions:

```
type Mat_Type is array (Integer range <>, Integer range <>)
   of Float;
Mat_1 : Mat_Type(1..100, 1..20);
```

A function that returns the sum of the elements of arrays of Mat_Type type follows:

```
function Sumer(Mat : in Mat_Type) return Float is
  Sum : Float := 0.0;
  begin
  for Row in Mat'range(1) loop
    for Col in Mat'range(2) loop
      Sum := Sum + Mat(Row, Col);
    end loop;  -- for Col ...
  end loop;  -- for Row ...
  return Sum;
  end Sumer;
```

The **range** attribute returns the subscript range of the named subscript of the actual parameter array, so this works regardless of the size or index ranges of the parameter.

In Fortran, the problem is addressed in the following way. Formal parameters that are arrays must have a declaration after the header. For single-dimensioned arrays, the subscripts in such declarations are irrelevant. But for multidimensional arrays, the subscripts in such declarations allow the compiler to build the storage-mapping function. Consider the following example skeletal Fortran subroutine:

```
Subroutine Sub(Matrix, Rows, Cols, Result)
  Integer, Intent(In) :: Rows, Cols
  Real, Dimension(Rows, Cols), Intent(In) :: Matrix
```

```
Real, Intent(In) :: Result
...
End Subroutine Sub
```

This works perfectly as long as the `Rows` actual parameter has the value used for the number of rows in the definition of the passed matrix. The number of rows is needed because Fortran stores arrays in column major order. If the array to be passed is not currently filled with useful data to the defined size, then both the defined index sizes and the filled index sizes can be passed to the subprogram. Then the defined sizes are used in the local declaration of the array, and the filled index sizes are used to control the computation in which the array elements are referenced. For example, consider the following Fortran subprogram:

```
Subroutine Matsum(Matrix, Rows, Cols, Filled_Rows,
    Filled_Cols, Sum)
  Real, Dimension(Rows, Cols), Intent(In) :: Matrix
  Integer, Intent(In) :: Rows, Cols, Filled_Rows,
                            Filled_Cols
  Real, Intent(Out) :: Sum
  Integer :: Row_Index, Col_Index
  Sum = 0.0
  Do Row_Index = 1, Filled_Rows
    Do Col_Index = 1, Filled_Cols
      Sum = Sum + Matrix(Row_Index, Col_Index)
    End Do
  End Do
End Subroutine Matsum
```

Java and C# use a technique for passing multidimensional arrays as parameters that is similar to that of Ada. In Java and C#, arrays are objects. They are all single-dimensioned, but the elements can be arrays. Each array inherits a named constant (`length` in Java and `Length` in C#) that is set to the length of the array when the array object is created. The formal parameter for a matrix appears with two sets of empty brackets, as in the following Java method that does what the Ada example function `Sumer` does:

```
float sumer(float mat[][]) {
  float sum = 0.0f;
  for (int row = 0; row < mat.length; row++) {
    for (int col = 0; col < mat[row].length; col++) {
      sum += mat[row][col];
    } //** for (int row ...
  } //** for (int col ...
  return sum;
}
```

Because each array has its own length value, in a matrix the rows can have different lengths.

9.5.7 Design Considerations

Two important considerations are involved in choosing parameter-passing methods: efficiency and whether one-way or two-way data transfer is needed.

Contemporary software-engineering principles dictate that access by subprogram code to data outside the subprogram should be minimized. With this goal in mind, in-mode parameters should be used whenever no data are to be returned through parameters to the caller. Out-mode parameters should be used when no data are transferred to the called subprogram but the subprogram must transmit data back to the caller. Finally, inout-mode parameters should be used only when data must move in both directions between the caller and the called subprogram.

There is a practical consideration that is in conflict with this principle. Sometimes it is justifiable to pass access paths for one-way parameter transmission. For example, when a large array is to be passed to a subprogram that does not modify it, a one-way method may be preferred. However, pass-by-value would require that the entire array be moved to a local storage area of the subprogram. This would be costly in both time and space. Because of this, large arrays are often passed by reference. This is precisely the reason why the Ada 83 definition allowed implementors to choose between the two methods for structured parameters. C++ constant reference parameters offer another solution. Another alternative approach would be to allow the user to choose between the methods.

The choice of a parameter-passing method for functions is related to another design issue: functional side effects. This issue is discussed in Section 9.9.

9.5.8 Examples of Parameter Passing

Consider the following C function:

```
void swap1(int a, int b) {
  int temp = a;
  a = b;
  b = temp;
}
```

Suppose this function is called with

```
swap1(c, d);
```

Recall that C uses pass-by-value. The actions of swap1 can be described by the following pseudocode:

```
a = c          — Move first parameter value in
b = d          — Move second parameter value in
temp = a
a = b
b = temp
```

Although a ends up with d's value and b ends up with c's value, the values of c and d are unchanged because nothing is transmitted back to the caller.

We can modify the C swap function to deal with pointer parameters to achieve the effect of pass-by-reference:

```
void swap2(int *a, int *b) {
  int temp = *a;
  *a = *b;
  *b = temp;
}
```

swap2 can be called with

```
swap2(&c, &d);
```

The actions of swap2 can be described with

```
a = &c  — Move first parameter address in
b = &d  — Move second parameter address in
temp = *a
*a = *b
*b = temp
```

In this case, the swap operation is successful: The values of c and d are in fact interchanged. swap2 can be written in C++ using reference parameters as follows:

```
void swap2(int &a, int &b) {
  int temp = a;
  a = b;
  b = temp;
}
```

This simple swap operation is not possible in Java, because it has neither pointers nor C++'s kind of references. In Java, a reference variable can point to only an object, not a scalar value.

The semantics of pass-by-value-result is identical to those of pass-by-reference, except when aliasing is involved. Recall that Ada uses pass-by-value-result for inout-mode scalar parameters. To explore pass-by-value-result, consider the following function, swap3, which we assume uses pass by-value-result parameters. It is written in a syntax similar to that of Ada.

```
procedure swap3(a : in out Integer, b : in out Integer) is
  temp : Integer;
  begin
  temp := a;
  a := b;
  b := temp;
  end swap3;
```

Suppose swap3 is called with

```
swap3(c, d);
```

The actions of swap3 with this call are

```
addr_c = &c         — Move first parameter address in
addr_d = &d         — Move second parameter address in
a = *addr_c         — Move first parameter value in
b = *addr_d         — Move second parameter value in
temp = a
a = b
b = temp
*addr_c = a         — Move first parameter value out
*addr_d = b         — Move second parameter value out
```

So once again, this swap subprogram operates correctly. Next, consider the call

```
swap3(i, list[i]);
```

In this case, the actions are

```
addr_i = &i           — Move first parameter address in
addr_listi = &list[i] — Move second parameter address in
a = *addr_i           — Move first parameter value in
b = *addr_listi       — Move second parameter value in
temp = a
a = b
b = temp
*addr_i = a           — Move first parameter value out
*addr_listi = b       — Move second parameter value out
```

Again, the subprogram operates correctly, in this case because the addresses to which to return the values of the parameters are computed at the time of the call rather than at the time of the return. If the addresses of the actual parameters were computed at the time of the return, the results would be wrong.

Finally, we must explore what happens when aliasing is involved with pass-by-value-result and pass-by-reference. Consider the following skeletal program written in C-like syntax:

```
int i = 3;  /* i is a global variable */
void fun(int a, int b) {
  i = b;
}
void main() {
  int list[10];
  list[i] = 5;
  fun(i, list[i]);
}
```

In fun, if pass-by-reference is used, i and a are aliases. If pass-by-value-result is used, i and a are not aliases. The actions of fun, assuming pass-by-value-result, are

```
addr_i = &i              — Move first parameter address in
addr_listi = &list[i]    — Move second parameter address in
a = *addr_i              — Move first parameter value in
b = *addr_listi          — Move second parameter value in
i = b                    — Sets i to 5
*addr_i = a              — Move first parameter value out
*addr_listi = b          — Move second parameter value out
```

In this case, the assignment to the global i in fun changes its value from 3 to 5, but the copy back of the first formal parameter (the second to last line in the example) sets it back to 3. The important observation here is that if pass-by-reference is used, the result is that the copy back is not part of the semantics, and i remains 5. Also note that because the address of the second parameter is computed at the beginning of fun, any change to the global i has no effect on the address used at the end to return the value of list[i].

9.6 Parameters That Are Subprograms

A number of situations occur in programming that are most conveniently handled if subprogram names can be sent as parameters to other subprograms. One of the more common of these occurs when a subprogram must sample some mathematical function. For example, a subprogram that does numerical integration estimates the area under the graph of a function by sampling the function at a number of different points. When such a subprogram is written, it should be usable for any given function; it should not need to be rewritten for every function that must be integrated. It is therefore natural that the name of a program function that evaluates the mathematical function to be integrated be sent to the integrating subprogram as a parameter.

Although the idea is natural and seemingly simple, the details of how it works can be confusing. If only the transmission of the subprogram code was necessary, it could be done by passing a single pointer. However, two complications arise.

First, there is the matter of type checking the parameters of the activations of the subprogram that was passed as a parameter. In C and C++, functions cannot be passed as parameters, but pointers to functions can. The type of a pointer to a function is the function's protocol. Because the protocol includes all parameter types, such parameters can be completely type checked. Fortran 95 has a mechanism for providing types of parameters for subprograms that are passed as parameters, and they must be checked. Ada does not allow subprograms to be passed as parameters. The functionality of passing subprograms as parameters is instead provided by Ada's generic facility, which is discussed in Section 9.8.

The second complication with parameters that are subprograms appears only with languages that allow nested subprograms. The issue is what referencing environment for executing the passed subprogram should be used. The three choices are:

1. The environment of the call statement that enacts the passed subprogram (**shallow binding**)

2. The environment of the definition of the passed subprogram (**deep binding**)

3. The environment of the call statement that passed the subprogram as an actual parameter (**ad hoc binding**)

The following example program, written with the syntax of JavaScript, illustrates these choices:

```
function sub1() {
  var x;
  function sub2() {
    alert(x);  // Creates a dialog box with the value of x
    };
  function sub3() {
    var x;
    x = 3;
    sub4(sub2);
    };
  function sub4(subx) {
```

history note

The original definition of Pascal (Jensen and Wirth, 1974) allowed subprograms to be passed as parameters without including their parameter type information. If independent compilation is possible (which it was not in the original Pascal), the compiler is not even allowed to check for the correct number of parameters. In the absence of independent compilation, checking for parameter consistency is possible but is a very complex task, and it usually is not done. Fortran 77 suffered the same problem, but because parameter type consistency is never checked in Fortran 77, it was not an additional problem.

```
    var x;
    x = 4;
    subx();
    };
  x = 1;
  sub3();
  };
```

Consider the execution of sub2 when it is called in sub4. For shallow binding, the referencing environment of that execution is that of sub4, so the reference to x in sub2 is bound to the local x in sub4, and the output of the program is 4. For deep binding, the referencing environment of sub2's execution is that of sub1, so the reference to x in sub2 is bound to the local x in sub1, and the output is 1. For ad hoc binding, the binding is to the local x in sub3, and the output is 3.

In some cases, the subprogram that declares a subprogram also passes that subprogram as a parameter. In those cases, deep binding and ad hoc binding are the same. Ad hoc binding has never been used because, one might surmise, the environment in which the procedure appears as a parameter has no natural connection to the passed subprogram.

Shallow binding is not appropriate for static-scoped languages with nested subprograms. For example, suppose the procedure Sender passes the procedure Sent as a parameter to the procedure Receiver. The problem is that Receiver may not be in the static environment of Sent, thereby making it very unnatural for Sent to have access to Receiver's variables. On the other hand, it is perfectly normal in such a language for any subprogram, including one sent as a parameter, to have its referencing environment determined by the lexical position of its definition. It is therefore more logical for these languages to use deep binding. Some dynamic-scoped languages use shallow binding.

9.7 Overloaded Subprograms

An overloaded operator is one that has multiple meanings. The meaning of a particular instance of an overloaded operator is determined by the types of its operands. For example, if the * operator has two floating-point operands in a Java program, it specifies floating-point multiplication. But if the same operator has two integer operands, it specifies integer multiplication.

An **overloaded subprogram** is a subprogram that has the same name as another subprogram in the same referencing environment. Every version of an overloaded subprogram must have a unique protocol; that is, it must be different from the others in the number, order, or types of its parameters, or in its return type if it is a function. The meaning of a call to an overloaded subprogram is determined by the actual parameter list (and/or possibly the type of the returned value, in the case of a function). Although it is not necessary, overloaded subprograms usually implement the same process.

C++, Java, Ada, and C# include predefined overloaded subprograms. For example, many classes in C++, Java, and C# have overloaded constructors. Because each version of an overloaded subprogram has a unique parameter profile, the compiler can disambiguate occurrences of calls to them by the different type parameters. Unfortunately, it is not that simple. Parameter coercions, when allowed, complicate the disambiguation process enormously. Simply stated, the issue is that if no method's parameter profile matches the number and types of the actual parameters in a method call, but two or more methods have parameter profiles that can be matched through coercions, which method should be called. For a language designer to answer this question, he or she must decide how to rank all of the different coercions, so that the compiler can choose the method that "best" matches the call. This can be a horrendously complex task. To see the high level of complexity of this situation, we suggest the reader refer to the rules for disambiguation of method calls used in C++ (Stroustrup, 1997).

In Ada, the return type of an overloaded function can used to disambiguate calls. Therefore, two overloaded functions can have the same parameter profile and differ only in their return types. This works because Ada does not allow mixed-mode expressions, so the context of a function call can specify the type that is returned from the function. For example, if an Ada program has two functions named Fun, both of which take an Integer parameter, but one returns an Integer and one returns a Float, the following call would be legal:

```
A, B : Integer;
...
A := B + Fun(7);
```

In this code, the call to Fun is bound to the version of Fun that returns an Integer, because choosing the version that returns a Float would cause a type error.

Because C++, Java, and C# allow mixed-mode expressions, the return type is irrelevant to disambiguation of overloaded functions (or methods). The context of the call does not allow the determination of the return type. For example, if a C++ program has two functions named fun and both take an int parameter but one returns an int and one returns a float, the program would not compile, because the compiler could not determine which version of fun should be used.

Users are also allowed to write multiple versions of subprograms with the same name in Ada, Java, C++, and C#. Once again, in C++, Java, and C# the most common user-defined overloaded methods are constructors.

Overloaded subprograms that have default parameters can lead to ambiguous subprogram calls. For example, consider the following C++ code:

```
void fun(float b = 0.0);
void fun();
...
fun();
```

The call is ambiguous and will cause a compilation error.

9.8 Generic Subprograms

Software reuse can be an important contributor to software productivity increases. One way to increase the reusability of software is to lessen the need to create different subprograms that implement the same algorithm on different types of data. For example, a programmer should not need to write four different sort subprograms to sort four arrays that differ only in element type.

A **polymorphic** subprogram takes parameters of different types on different activations. Overloaded subprograms provide a particular kind of polymorphism called **ad hoc polymorphism.** Overloaded subprograms need not behave similarly.

A more general kind of polymorphism is provided by the methods of Python and Ruby. Recall that variables in these languages do not have types, so formal parmeters do not have types. Therefore, a method will work for any type of actual parameter, as long as the operators used on the formal parameters in the method are defined.

Parametric polymorphism is provided by a subprogram that takes generic parameters that are used in type expressions that describe the types of the parameters of the subprogram. Different instantiations of such subprograms can be given different generic parameters, producing subprograms that take different types of parameters. Parametric definitions of subprograms all behave the same. Parametrically polymorphic subprograms are often called **generic** subprograms. Both Ada and C++ provide a kind of compile-time parametric polymorphism. Java 5.0 also supports parametric polymorphism, but that support is quite different from the way it is supported by C++ and Ada.

9.8.1 Generic Subprograms in Ada

Ada provides parametric polymorphism through a construct that supports the construction of multiple versions of program units to accept parameters of different data types. The different versions of the subprogram are instantiated, or constructed, by the compiler on request from the user program. Because the versions of the subprogram all have the same name, this provides the illusion that a single subprogram can process data of different types on different calls. Because program units of this sort are generic in nature, they are sometimes called **generic units.**

The same mechanism can be used to allow different executions of a subprogram to call different instantiations of a generic subprogram. This is useful in providing the functionality of subprograms passed as parameters.

The following example illustrates a procedure that has three generic parameters, allowing the subprogram to take as a parameter a generic array. It is an exchange sort procedure that is designed to work on any array with elementary numeric type elements, using any ordinal type subscript range:

```
generic
  type Index_Type is (<>);
  type Element_Type is private;
  type Vector is array (Integer range <>) of
       Element_Type;
  procedure Generic_Sort(List : in out Vector);
  procedure Generic_Sort(List : in out Vector) is
    Temp : Element_Type;
    begin
    for Top in List'First..Index_Type'Pred(List'Last) loop
      for Bottom in Index_Type'Succ(Top)..List'Last loop
        if List(Top) > List(Bottom) then
          Temp := List(Top);
          List(Top) := List(Bottom);
          List(Bottom) := Temp;
        end if;
      end loop; - for Bottom ...
    end loop; - for Top ...
  end Generic_Sort;
```

Parts of this generic procedure may appear rather odd if you are not familiar with Ada. However, it is not important to understand all the details of the syntax. The array type and the type of its elements are the two generic parameters of this procedure. The array is declared to have any type subscript (that is, any type that is legal as a subscript) with any range.

This generic sort is nothing more than a template for a procedure; no code is generated for it by the compiler, and it has no effect on a program unless it is instantiated for some type. Instantiation is accomplished with a declaration statement such as the following:

```
procedure Integer_Sort is new Generic_Sort(
                        Index_Type => Integer;
                        Element_Type => Integer;
                        Vector => Int_Array);
```

The compiler reacts to this statement by building a version of `Generic_Sort` named `Integer_Sort` that sorts arrays of type `Int_Array` with `Integer` type elements and `Integer` type subscripts.

Generic_Sort, as written, assumes that the operator > is defined for the elements of the array to be sorted. The genericity of Generic_Sort can be increased by including a comparison function among its generic parameters.

Recall that Ada does not allow subprograms to be passed as parameters to other subprograms. To provide that functionality, Ada uses generic formal subprograms. In a language such as Fortran, subprograms are passed as parameters so that a particular call of a subprogram can execute using the specific passed subprogram to compute its result. In Ada, the same result is achieved by allowing the user to instantiate a generic subprogram any number of times, each with a different subprogram that can be used. For example, consider the following Ada generic procedure:

```
generic
  with function Fun(X : Float) return Float;
  procedure Integrate (Lowerbd : in Float;
                       Upperbd : in Float;
                       Result : out Float);
  procedure Integrate (Lowerbd : in Float;
                       Upperbd : in Float;
                       Result : out Float) is
    Funval : Float;
    begin
    ...
    Funval := Fun(Lowerbd);
    ...
    end Integrate;
```

This code procedure could be instantiated for a user-defined function Fun1 with

```
procedure Integrate_Fun1 is new Integrate(Fun => Fun1);
```

Now, Integrate_Fun1 is a procedure for integrating the function Fun1.

9.8.2 Generic Functions in C++

Generic functions in C++ have the descriptive name of template functions. The definition of a template function has the general form

template <template parameters>
— a function definition that may include the template parameters

A template parameter (there must be at least one) has one of the forms

```
class identifier
typename identifier
```

The class form is used for type names. The typename form is used for passing a value to the template function. For example, it is sometimes convenient to pass an integer value for the size of an array in the template function.

A template can take another template, in practice often a template class that defines a user-defined generic type, as a parameter, but we do not consider that option here. [5]

As an example of a template function, consider the following:

```
template <class Type>
Type max(Type first, Type second) {
  return first > second ? first : second;
}
```

where `Type` is the parameter that specifies the type of data on which the function will operate. This template function can be instantiated for any type for which the operator > is defined. For example, if it were instantiated with **int** as the parameter, it would be

```
int max(int first, int second) {
  return first > second ? first : second;
}
```

Although this process could be defined as a macro, a macro would have the disadvantage of not operating correctly if the parameters were expressions with side effects. For example, suppose the macro were defined as

```
#define max(a, b) ((a) > (b)) ? (a) : (b)
```

This definition is generic in the sense that it works for any numeric type. However, it does not always work correctly if called with a parameter that has a side effect, such as

```
max(x++, y)
```

which produces

```
((x++) > (y) ? (x++) : (y))
```

Whenever the value of x is greater than that of y, x will be incremented twice.

C++ template functions are instantiated implicitly either when the function is named in a call or when its address is taken with the & operator. For example, the example template function defined would be instantiated twice

---

5. Template classes are discusssed in Chapter 11.

by the following code segment, once for **int** type parameters and once for
char type parameters:

```
int a, b, c;
char d, e, f;
...
c = max(a, b);
f = max(d, e);
```

The following is the C++ version of the generic sort subprogram given in
Section 9.8.1. It is somewhat different because C++ array subscripts are
restricted to being integers with the lower bound fixed at zero.

```
template <class Type>
void generic_sort(Type list[], int len) {
  int top, bottom;
  Type temp;
  for (top = 0; top < len - 2; top++)
    for (bottom = top + 1; bottom < len - 1; bottom++)
      if (list[top] > list[bottom]) {
        temp = list[top];
        list[top] = list[bottom];
        list[bottom] = temp;
      } //** end of if (list[top] ...
} //** end of generic_sort
```

An example instantiation of this template function is

```
float flt_list[100];
...
generic_sort(flt_list, 100);
```

The generic subprograms of Ada and the templated functions of C++ are
a kind of poor cousin to a subprogram in which the types of the formal
parameters are dynamically bound to the types of the actual parameters in a
call. In this case, only a single copy of the code is needed, whereas with the
Ada and C++ approaches, a copy must be created at compile time for each different type that is required and the binding of subprogram calls to subprograms is static.

9.8.3   Generic Methods in Java 5.0

Support for generic types and methods was added to Java in Java 5.0. The
name of a generic class in Jave 5.0 is specified by a name followed by one or
more type variables delimited by pointed brackets. For example,

```
GenType<T>
```

where `T` is the type variable. Generic types are discussed in more detail in Chapter 11.

Java's generic methods differ from the generic subprograms of Ada and C++ in several important ways. First, generic parameters must be classes—they cannot be primitive types. This requirement disallows a generic method that mimics our examples in Ada and C++, in which the component types of arrays are generic and can be primitives. In Java, the components of arrays (as opposed to containers) cannot be generic. Second, although Java generic methods can be instantiated any number of times, only one copy of the code is built. The internal version of a generic method, which is called a *raw* method, operates on `Object` class objects. At the point where the generic value of a generic method is returned, the compiler inserts a cast to the proper type. Third, in Java, restrictions can be specified on the range of classes that can be passed to the generic method as generic parameters. Such restrictions are called **bounds**.

As an example of a generic Java 5.0 method, consider the following skeletal method definition:

```
public static <T> T DoIt(T[] list) {
  . . .
}
```

This defines a method named `DoIt` that takes an array of elements of a generic type. The name of the generic type is `T` and it must be an array. Following is an example call to `DoIt`:

```
DoIt<int>(myList);
```

Now, consider the following version of `doIt`, which has a bound on its generic parameter:

```
public static <T extends Comparable> T doIt(T[] list) {
  . . .
}
```

This defines a method that takes a generic array parameter whose elements are of a class that implements the `Comparable` interface. That is the restriction, or bound, on the generic parameter. The reserved word **extends** seems to imply that the generic class subclasses the following class. In this context, however, **extends** has a different meaning. The expression `<T extends BoundingType>` specifies that `T` should be a "subtype" of the bounding type. So, **extends** in this context means the generic class (or interface) either extends the bounding class (the bound if it is a class) or implements the bounding interface (if the bound is an interface). The bound ensures that the elements of any instantiation of the generic can be compared with the Comparable method, compareTo.

If a generic method has two or more restrictions on its generic type, they are added to the **extends** clause, separated by ampersands (&). Also, generic methods can have more than one generic parameter.

Java 5.0 supports *wildcard types*. For example, Collection<?> is a wildcard type for collection classes. This type can be used for any collection type of any class components. For example, consider the following generic method:

```
void printCollection(Collection<?> c) {
  for (Object e: c) {
    System.out.println(e);
  }
}
```

This method prints the elements of any Collection class, regardless of the class of its components. Some care must be taken with objects of the wildcard type. For example, because the components of a particular object of this type have a type, other type objects cannot be added to the collection. For example, consider:

```
Collection<?> c = new ArrayList<String>();
```

It would be illegal to use the add method to put something into this collection unless its type were String.

Wildcard types can restricted, as is the case with nonwildcard types. Such types are called *bounded wildcard types*. For example, consider the following method header:

```
public void drawAll(ArrayList<? extends Shape> things)
```

The generic type here is a wildcard type that is a subclass of the Shape class. This method could be written to draw any object whose type is a subclass of Shape.

9.8.4   Generic Methods in C# 2005

The generic methods of C# 2005 are similar in capability to those of Java 5.0, except there is no support for wildcard types. One unique feature of C# 2005 generic methods is that the actual type parameters in a call can be omitted if the compiler can infer the unspecified type. For example, consider the following skeletal class definition:

```
class MyClass {
  public static T doIt<T>(T p1) {
```

```
        . . .
    }
}
```

The method `DoIt` can be called without specifying the generic parameter if the compiler can infer the generic type from the actual parameter in the call. For example, both of the following calls are legal:

```
int myInt = MyClass.DoIt(17);  // Calls DoIt<int>
string myStr = MyClass.DoIt('apples');  // Calls
DoIt<string>
```

9.9 Design Issues for Functions

The following two design issues are specific to functions:

- Are side effects allowed?
- What types of values can be returned?

9.9.1 Functional Side Effects

Because of the problems of side effects of functions that are called in expressions, as described in Chapter 5, parameters to functions should always be in-mode parameters. Some languages, in fact, require this; for example, Ada functions can have only in-mode formal parameters. This requirement effectively prevents a function from causing side effects through its parameters or through aliasing of parameters and globals. In most other languages, however, functions can have either pass-by-value or pass-by-reference parameters, thus allowing functions that cause side effects and aliasing.

9.9.2 Types of Returned Values

Most imperative-programming languages restrict the types that can be returned by their functions. C allows any type to be returned by its functions except arrays and functions. Both of these can be handled by pointer type return values. C++ is like C but also allows user-defined types, or classes, to be returned from its functions. Ada, Python, and Ruby are the only languages among current imperative languages whose functions (and/or methods) can return values of any type. In the case of Ada, however, because functions are not types in Ada, they cannot be returned from functions. Of course, pointers to functions can be returned by functions.

In some programming languages, subprograms are first-class objects, which means that they can be treated much like data objects. In JavaScript, for example, functions can be passed as parameters and returned from functions. In Python and Ruby, methods are objects that can be treated as any other object. The same is true for many functional languages (see Chapter 15).

Neither Java nor C# can have functions, although their methods are similar to functions. In both, any type or class can be returned by methods. Because methods are not types, they cannot be returned.

9.10 User-Defined Overloaded Operators

Operators can be overloaded by the user in Ada, C++, Python, and Ruby. As an example of this, consider the following Ada function that overloads the multiplication operator (*) to compute the dot product of two arrays. The dot product of two arrays of equal length is the sum of the products of each of the corresponding pairs of elements of the two arrays. Suppose Vector_Type has been defined as an array type with Integer elements:

```
function "*"(A, B : in Vector_Type) return Integer is
  Sum : Integer := 0;
  begin
  for Index in A'range loop
    Sum := Sum + A(Index) * B(Index);
  end loop;  -- for Index ...
  return Sum;
  end "*";
```

The dot product, as specified in this function definition, is computed whenever the asterisk appears with two operands of Vector_Type type. The asterisk can be further overloaded any number of times, as long as the defining functions have unique protocols.

The example dot product function could also be written in C++. The prototype of such a function could be:

```
int operator *(const vector &a, const vector &b, int len);
```

The question naturally arises: How much operator overloading is good, or can you have too much? The answer is, to a large degree, a matter of taste. The argument against too much operator overloading is mainly one of readability. In many cases, it is more readable to call a function to carry out an operation than to use an operator that is more frequently used for other type operands. Even in the case of the dot product, it can be too easy to forget what is involved when a simple assignment statement, such as

```
c = a * b
```

is found in a program. It is easy to assume a, b, and c are numeric scalars.

Another consideration is the process of building a software system from modules created by different groups. If the different groups overloaded the same operators in different ways, these differences would obviously need to be eliminated before putting the system together.

9.11 Coroutines

A **coroutine** is a special kind of subprogram. Rather than the master–slave relationship between a caller and a called subprogram that exists with conventional subprograms, caller and called coroutines are on a more equal basis. In fact, the coroutine control mechanism is often called the symmetric unit control model.

Coroutines can have multiple entry points, which are controlled by the coroutines themselves. They also have the means to maintain their status between activations. This means that coroutines must be history-sensitive and thus have static local variables. Secondary executions of a coroutine often begin at points other than its beginning. Because of this, the invocation of a coroutine is called a **resume** rather than a call.

For example, consider the following skeletal coroutine:

```
sub co1(){
  ...
  resume co2();
  ...
  resume co3();
  ...
}
```

The first time co1 is resumed, its execution begins at the first statement and executes down to and including the resume of co2, which transfers control to co2. The next time co1 is resumed, its execution begins at the first statement after its call to co2. When co1 is resumed the third time, its execution begins at the first statement after the resume of co3.

One of the usual characteristics of subprograms is maintained in coroutines: Only one coroutine is actually in execution at a given time.

As we saw in the example above, rather than executing to their ends, coroutines often partially execute and then transfer control to some other coroutine, and when restarted, a coroutine resumes execution just after the statement it used to transfer control elsewhere. This sort of interleaved execution sequence is related to the way multiprogramming operating systems work. Although there may be only one processor, all of the executing programs in such a system appear to run concurrently while sharing the processor. In the case of coroutines, this is sometimes called **quasi-concurrency**.

history note

The actual origin of the concept of symmetric unit control is difficult to determine. One of the earliest published applications of coroutines was in the area of syntax analysis (Conway, 1963). The first high-level programming language to include facilities for coroutines was SIMULA 67. Recall that the original purpose of SIMULA was system simulation, which often requires the modeling of independent processes. This need was the motivation for the development of SIMULA 67's coroutines. Other languages that support coroutines are BLISS (Wulf et al., 1971), INTERLISP (Teitelman, 1975), and Modula-2 (Wirth, 1985).

Typically, coroutines are created in an application by a program unit called the master unit, which is not a coroutine. When created, coroutines execute their initialization code and then return control to that master unit. When all of a family of coroutines are constructed, the master program resumes one of the coroutines, and the members of the family of coroutines then resume each other in some order until their work is completed, if in fact it can be completed. If the execution of a coroutine reaches the end of its code section, control is transferred to the master unit that created it. This is the mechanism for ending execution of the collection of coroutines, when that is desirable. In some programs, the coroutines run whenever the computer is running.

One example of a problem that can be solved with this sort of collection of coroutines is the simulation of a card game. Suppose the game has four players who all use the same strategy for playing. Such a game can be simulated by having a master program unit create a family of coroutines, each with a collection, or hand, of cards. The master program could then start the simulation by resuming one of the player coroutines, which, after it had played its turn, could resume the next player coroutine, and so forth until the game ended.

The same form of resume statement can be used both to start and to restart the execution of a coroutine.

Figure 9.3

Two possible execution control sequences for two coroutines without loops

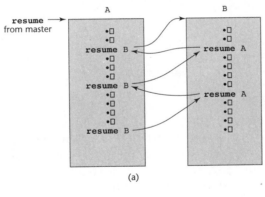

(a)

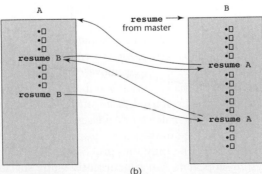

(b)

Suppose program units A and B are coroutines. Figure 9.3 shows two ways an execution sequence involving A and B might proceed.

In Figure 9.3a, the execution of coroutine A is started by the master unit. After some execution, A starts B. When coroutine B in Figure 9.3a first causes control to return to coroutine A, the semantics is that A continues from where it ended its last execution. In particular, its local variables have the values left them by the previous activation. Figure 9.3b shows an alternative execution sequence of coroutines A and B. In this case, B is started by the master unit.

Rather than have the patterns shown in Figure 9.3, a coroutine often has a loop containing a resume. Figure 9.4 shows the execution sequence of this scenario. In this case, A is started by the master unit. Inside its main loop, A resumes B, which in turn resumes A in its main loop.

Figure 9.4

Coroutine execution sequence with loops

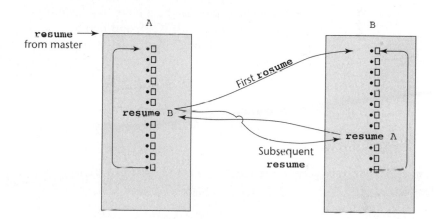

SUMMARY

Process abstractions are represented in programming languages by subprograms. A subprogram definition describes the actions represented by the subprogram. A subprogram call enacts those actions.

Formal parameters are the names that subprograms use to refer to the actual parameters given in subprogram calls. In Python and Ruby, array and hash formal parameters are used to support variable numbers of parameters.

Ruby allows blocks to be attached to method calls. Such blocks can have parameters. They are called with a **yield** statement in the called method.

Subprograms can be either functions, which model mathematical functions and are used to define new operations, or procedures, which define new statements.

Local variables in subprograms can be stack-dynamic, providing support for recursion, or static, providing efficiency and history-sensitive local variables.

There are three fundamental semantics models of parameter passing—in mode, out mode, and inout mode—and a number of approaches to implementing them.

Aliasing can occur when pass-by-reference parameters are used, both among two or more parameters and between a parameter and an accessible nonlocal variable.

Parameters that are subprogram names provide a necessary service but are sometimes difficult to understand. The opacity lies in the referencing environment that is available when a subprogram that has been passed as a parameter is executing.

Ada, C++, C#, Ruby, and Python allow both subprogram and operator overloading. Subprograms can be overloaded as long as the various versions can be disambiguated by the types of their parameters or returned values. Function definitions can be used to build additional meanings for operators.

Subprograms in Ada, C++, and Java 5.0 can be generic, using parametric polymorphism, so the desired types of their data objects can be passed to the compiler, which then can construct units for the requested types. Methods in Java 5.0 can also be generic, a more restrictive but more memory-efficient way.

A coroutine is a special subprogram that has multiple entries. They can be used to provide interleaved execution of subprograms.

REVIEW QUESTIONS

1. What are the three general characteristics of subprograms?

2. What does it mean for a subprogram to be active?

3. What is a parameter profile? What is a subprogram protocol?

4. What are formal parameters? What are actual parameters?

5. What are the advantages and disadvantages of keyword parameters?

6. What are the design issues for subprograms?

7. What are the advantages and disadvantages of dynamic local variables?

8. What are the three semantic models of parameter passing?

9. What are the modes, the conceptual models of transfer, the advantages, and the disadvantages of pass-by-value, pass-by-result, pass-by-value-result, and pass-by-reference parameter-passing methods?

10. In what ways can aliases occur with pass-by-reference parameters?

11. What is the difference between the way original C and C89 deal with an actual parameter whose type is not identical to that of the corresponding formal parameter?

12. What is the problem with Ada's policy of allowing implementors to decide which parameters to pass by reference and which to pass by value-result?

13. What are two fundamental design considerations for parameter-passing methods?

14. What are the two issues that arise when subprogram names are parameters?

15. Define *shallow* and *deep binding* for referencing environments of subprograms that have been passed as parameters.

16. What is an overloaded subprogram?

17. What is parametric polymorphism?

18. What causes a C++ template function to be instantiated?

19. In what fundamental ways do the generic parameters to a Java 5.0 generic method differ from those of C++ methods?

20. If a Java 5.0 method returns a generic type, what type of object is actually returned?

21. If a Java 5.0 generic method is called with three different generic parameters, how many versions of the method will be generated by the compiler?

22. What are the design issues for functions?

23. In what ways are coroutines different from conventional subprograms?

PROBLEM SET

1. What are arguments for and against a user program building additional definitions for existing operators, as can be done in Ada and C++? Do you believe such user-defined operator overloading is good or bad? Support your answer.

2. In most Fortran IV implementations, parameters were passed by reference, using access path transmission only. State both the advantages and disadvantages of this design choice.

3. Argue in support of the Ada 83 designers' decision to allow the implementor to choose between implementing **in out** mode parameters by copy or by reference.

4. Suppose you wish to write a method that prints a heading on a new output page, along with a page number that is 1 in the first activation and that increases by 1 with each subsequent activation. Can this be done without parameters and without reference to nonlocal variables in Java? Can it be done in C#?

5. Consider the following program written in C syntax:

```
void swap(int a, int b) {
  int temp;
```

```
      temp = a;
      a = b;
      b = temp;
  }
  void main() {
    int value = 2, list[5] = {1, 3, 5, 7, 9};
    swap(value, list[0]);
    swap(list[0], list[1]);
    swap(value, list[value]);
  }
```

For each of the following parameter-passing methods, what are all of the values of the variables `value` and `list` after each of the three calls to swap?

a. Passed by value

b. Passed by reference

c. Passed by value-result

6. Present one argument against providing both static and dynamic local variables in subprograms.

7. Consider the following program written in C syntax:

```
void fun (int first, int second) {
  first += first;
  second += second;
}
void main() {
  int list[2] = {1, 3};
  fun(list[0], list[1]);
}
```

For each of the following parameter-passing methods, what are the values of the `list` array after execution?

a. Passed by value

b. Passed by reference

c. Passed by value-result

8. Argue against the C design of providing only function subprograms.

9. From a textbook on Fortran, learn the syntax and semantics of statement functions. Justify their existence in Fortran.

10. Study the methods of user-defined operator overloading in C++ and Ada, and write a report comparing the two using our criteria for evaluating languages.

11. C# supports out-mode parameters, but neither Java nor C++ does. Give an explanation of this difference.

12. Research Jensen's Device, which was a widely known use of pass-by-name parameters, and write a short description of what it is and how it can be used.

PROGRAMMING EXERCISES

1. Write a Fortran program that determines whether a Fortran compiler to which you have access implements local variables as static or stack dynamic. *Hint:* The easiest way to check this is to have your program test the history sensitivity of a subprogram.

2. Write a program in a language that you know to determine the ratio of the time required to pass a large array by reference and the time required to pass the same array by value. Make the array as large as possible on the machine and implementation you use. Pass the array as many times as necessary to get reasonably accurate timings of the passing operations.

3. Write a C# or Ada program that determines when the address of an out-mode parameter is computed (at the time of the call or at the time execution of the subprogram finishes).

4. Write a Perl program that passes by reference a literal to a subprogram, which attempts to change the parameter. Given the overall design philosopy of Perl, explain the results.

5. Repeat Programming Exercise 4 in C#.

6. Write a program in some language that has both static and stack-dynamic local variables in subprograms. Create six large (at least 100×100) matrices in the subprogram—three static and three stack-dynamic. Fill two of the static matrices and two of the stack-dynamic matrices with random numbers in the range of 1 to 100. The code in the subprogram must perform a large number of matrix multiplication operations on the static matrices and time the process. Then it must repeat this with the stack-dynamic matrices. Compare and explain the results.

7. Write a C# program that includes two methods that are called a large number of times. Both methods are passed a large array, one by value and one by reference. Compare the times required to call these two methods and explain the difference. Be sure to call them a sufficient number of times to illustrate a difference in the required time.

8. Write an Ada program that determines whether it is legal to call a function that has been passed by passing a pointer to it to another function.

9. Write a program, using the syntax of whatever language you like, that produces different behavior depending on whether pass-by-reference or pass-by-value-result is used in its parameter passing.

10. Write a generic Ada function that takes an array of generic elements and a scalar of the same type as the array elements. The type of the array elements and the scalar is the generic parameter. The subscripts of the array

are positive integers. The function must search the given array for the given scalar and return the subscript of the scalar in the array. If the scalar is not in the array, the function must return −1. Instantiate the function for `Integer` and `Float` types and test both.

11. Write a generic C++ function that takes an array of generic elements and a scalar of the same type as the array elements. The type of the array elements and the scalar is the generic parameter. The function must search the given array for the given scalar and return the subscript of the scalar in the array. If the scalar is not in the array, the function must return −1. Test the function for `int` and `float` types.

12. Devise a subprogram and calling code in which pass-by-reference and pass-by-value-result of one or more parameters produces different results.

Implementing Subprograms

T he purpose of this chapter is to explore the implementation of subprograms. The discussion will provide the reader with some insight into how subprogram linkage works, and also why ALGOL 60 was a challenge to the unsuspecting compiler writers of the early 1960s. We begin with the simplest situation, non-nestable subprograms with static local variables, and advance to more complicated subprograms with stack-dynamic local variables, and finally to nested subprograms with stack-dynamic local variables and static scoping. The increased difficulty of implementing subprograms in languages with nested subprograms is caused by the need to include mechanisms to access nonlocal variables.

The static chain method of accessing nonlocals in static-scoped languages is discussed in detail. Techniques for implementing blocks are covered briefly. Several methods of implementing nonlocal variable access in a dynamic-scoped language are discussed.

Sections 10.1 to 10.5 deal exclusively with static-scoped languages; Section 10.6 discusses the implementation of subprograms in dynamic-scoped languages.

10.1 The General Semantics of Calls and Returns

The subprogram call and return operations are together called **subprogram linkage.** The implementation of subprograms must be based on the semantics of the subprogram linkage of the language being implemented.

A subprogram call in a typical language has numerous actions associated with it. The call process must include the implementation of whatever parameter-passing method is used. If local variables are not static, the call process must cause storage to be allocated for the locals declared in the called subprogram and bind those variables to that storage. It must save the execution status of the calling program unit. The execution status is everything needed to resume execution of the calling program unit. This includes register values, CPU status bits, and the environment pointer (EP). The EP, which is further discussed in Section 10.3.2, is used to access parameters and local variables during the execution of a subprogram. The calling process also must arrange to transfer control to the code of the subprogram and ensure that control can return to the proper place when the subprogram execution is completed. Finally, if the language supports nested subprograms, the call process must cause some mechanism to be created to provide access to nonlocal variables that are visible to the called subprogram.

The required actions of a subprogram return are also complicated. If the subprogram has parameters that are out mode or inout mode and are implemented by copy, the first action of the return process is to move the local values of the associated formal parameters to the actual parameters. Next, it must deallocate the storage used for local variables and restore the execution status of the calling program unit. Finally, control must be returned to the calling program unit.

10.2 Implementing "Simple" Subprograms

We begin with the task of implementing simple subprograms; by "simple" we mean that subprograms cannot be nested and all local variables are static. Early versions of Fortran were examples of languages that had this kind of subprograms.

The semantics of a call to a "simple" subprogram requires the following actions:

1. Save the execution status of the current program unit.
2. Pass the parameters.
3. Pass the return address to the callee.
4. Transfer control to the callee.

The semantics of a return from a simple subprogram requires the following actions:

1. If there are pass-by-value-result or out-mode parameters, the current values of those parameters are moved to the corresponding actual parameters.
2. If the subprogram is a function, the functional value is moved to a place accessible to the caller.
3. The execution status of the caller is restored.
4. Control is transferred back to the caller.

The call and return actions require storage for the following:

- Status information about the caller
- Parameters
- Return address
- Return value for functions

These, along with the local variables and the subprogram code, form the complete collection of information a subprogram needs to execute and then return control to the caller.

A simple subprogram consists of two separate parts: the actual code of the subprogram, which is constant, and the local variables and data listed previously, which can change when the subprogram is executed. In the case of simple subprograms, both of these parts have fixed sizes.

The format, or layout, of the noncode part of a subprogram is called an **activation record,** because the data it describes are relevant only during the activation, or execution of the subprogram. The form of an activation record is static. An **activation record instance** is a concrete example of an activation record, a collection of data in the form of an activation record.

Because languages with simple subprograms do not support recursion, there can be only one active version of a given subprogram at a time. Therefore, there can be only a single instance of the activation record for a subprogram.

One possible layout for activation records is shown in Figure 10.1. The saved execution status of the caller is omitted here and in the remainder of this chapter because it is simple and not relevant to the discussion.

Because an activation record instance for a "simple" subprogram has fixed size, it can be statically allocated. In fact, it could be attached to the code part of the subprogram.

Figure 10.2 shows a program consisting of a main program and three subprograms: A, B, and C. Although the figure shows all the code segments separated from all the activation record instances, in some cases the activation record instances are attached to their associated code segments.

Figure 10.1

An activation record for simple subprograms

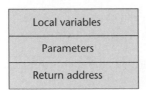

Figure 10.2

The code and activation records of a program with simple subprograms

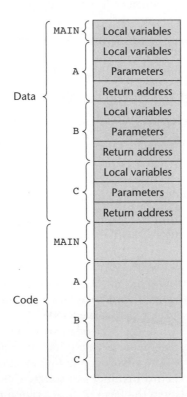

The construction of the complete program shown in Figure 10.2 is not done entirely by the compiler. In fact, because of independent compilation, the four program units—MAIN, A, B, and C—may have been compiled on different days, or even in different years. At the time each unit is compiled, the machine code for it, along with a list of references to external subprograms is written to a file. The executable program shown in Figure 10.2 is put together by the **linker,** which is part of the operating system. (Sometimes linkers are called *loaders, linker/loaders,* or *link editors.*) When the linker is called for a main program, its first task is to find the files that contain the translated subprograms referenced in that program, along with their activation record instances, and load them into memory. Then the linker must set the target addresses of all calls to those subprograms in the main program to the entry addresses of those subprograms. The same must be done for all calls to subprograms in the loaded subprograms and all calls to library subprograms. In the previous example, the linker was called for MAIN. The linker had to find the machine code programs for A, B, and C, along with their activation record instances, and load them into memory with the code for MAIN. Then it had to patch in the target addresses for all calls to A, B, C, and any library subprograms in A, B, C, and MAIN.

10.3 Implementing Subprograms with Stack-Dynamic Local Variables

We now examine the implementation of the subprogram linkage in languages in which locals are stack-dynamic, again focusing on the call and return operations.

One of the most important advantages of stack-dynamic local variables is support for recursion. Therefore, languages that use stack-dynamic local variables also support recursion.

We postpone discussing the additional complexity required when subprograms can be nested until Section 10.4.

10.3.1 More Complex Activation Records

Subprogram linkage in languages that use stack-dynamic local variables are more complex than the linkage of simple subprograms for the following reasons:

- The compiler must generate code to cause the implicit allocation and deallocation of local variables.

- Recursion adds the possibility of multiple simultaneous activations of a subprogram, which means that there can be more than one instance (incomplete execution) of a subprogram at a given time, with at least one call from outside the subprogram and one or more recursive calls. Recursion, therefore, requires multiple instances of activation records, one for each subprogram activation that can exist at the same time. The number of activations is limited only by the memory size of the machine. Each activation requires its own copy of the formal parameters and the dynamically allocated local variables, along with the return address.

The format of an activation record for a given subprogram in most languages is known at compile time. In many cases, the size is also known for activation records because all local data are of fixed size. That is not the case in some other languages, such as Ada, in which the size of a local array can depend on the value of an actual parameter. In those cases, the format is static, but the size can be dynamic. In languages with stack-dynamic local variables, activation record instances must be created dynamically. The typical activation record for such a language is shown in Figure 10.3.

Because the return address, dynamic link, and parameters are placed in the activation record instance by the caller, these entries must appear first.

The return address usually consists of a pointer to the instruction following the call in the code segment of the calling program unit. The **dynamic link** is a pointer to the top of the activation record instance of the caller. In static-scoped languages, this link is used in the destruction of the current activation record instance when the procedure completes its execution. The stack top is set to the value of the old dynamic link. The dynamic link is required because in some cases there are other allocations from the stack by a subprogram beyond its activation record. For example, temporaries needed by the machine language version of the subprogram may be allocated there. So, although the size of the activation record may be known, the size cannot simply be subtracted from the stack top pointer to remove the activation record. The actual parameters in the activation record are the values or addresses provided by the caller.

Local scalar variables are bound to storage within an activation record instance. Local variables that are structures are sometimes allocated elsewhere, and only their descriptors and a pointer to that storage are part of the activation record. Local variables are allocated and possibly initialized in the called subprogram, so they appear last.

Consider the following skeletal C function:

```c
void sub(float total, int part) {
  int list[5];
  float sum;
  ...
}
```

Figure 10.3

A typical activation record for a language with stack-dynamic local variables

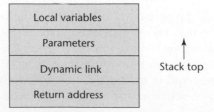

| Local variables |
| Parameters |
| Dynamic link |
| Return address |

↑ Stack top

The activation record for sub is shown in Figure 10.4.

Activating a subprogram requires the dynamic creation of an instance of the activation record for the subprogram. As stated earlier, the format of the activation record is fixed at compile time, although its size may depend on the call in some languages. Because the call and return semantics specify that the subprogram last called is the first to complete, it is reasonable to create instances of these activation records on a stack. This stack is part of the run-time system, and therefore is called the **run-time stack,** although we will usually just refer to it as the stack. Every subprogram activation, whether recursive or nonrecursive, creates a new instance of an activation record on the stack. This provides the required separate copies of the parameters, local variables, and return address.

One more thing is required to control the execution of a subprogram, the EP. Initially, the EP points at the base, or first address of the activation record instance of the main program. Subsequently, the run-time system must ensure that it always points at the base of the activation record instance of the currently executing program unit. When a subprogram is called, the current EP is saved in the new activation record instance along with the other execution status information. The EP is then set to point at the base of the new activation record instance. Upon return from the subprogram, the EP is restored from the activation record instance of the subprogram that has completed its execution.

Note that the EP currently being used is not stored in the run-time stack. Only saved versions are stored in the activation record instances. Because such saved versions are stored with the other execution status information, the stored EPs are not shown in the figures of the run-time stack.

Figure 10.4

The activation record for function **sub**

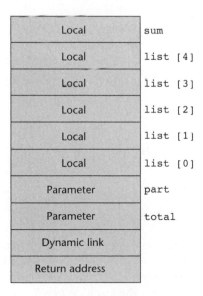

Local	sum
Local	list [4]
Local	list [3]
Local	list [2]
Local	list [1]
Local	list [0]
Parameter	part
Parameter	total
Dynamic link	
Return address	

Recall from Chapter 9 that a subprogram is **active** from the time it is called until the time that execution is completed. At the time it becomes inactive, its local scope ceases to exist and its referencing environment is no longer meaningful. So at that time, its activation record instance can be destroyed.

10.3.2 An Example Without Recursion

Consider the following skeletal C program:

```
void fun1(float r) {
  int s, t;
  ...          <—————————1
  fun2(s);
  ...
}

void fun2(int x) {
  int y;
  ...          <—————————2
  fun3(y);
  ...
}

void fun3(int q) {
  ...          <—————————3
}

void main() {
  float p;
  ...
  fun1(p);
  ...
}
```

The sequence of procedure calls in this program is

```
main calls fun1
fun1 calls fun2
fun2 calls fun3
```

The stack contents for the points labeled 1, 2, and 3 are shown in Figure 10.5.

At point 1, only the activation record instances for function `main` and function `fun1` are on the stack. When `fun1` calls `fun2`, an instance of `fun2`'s activation record is created on the stack. When `fun2` calls `fun3`, an instance of `fun3`'s activation record is created on the stack. When `fun3`'s execution ends, the instance of its activation record is removed from the stack, and the

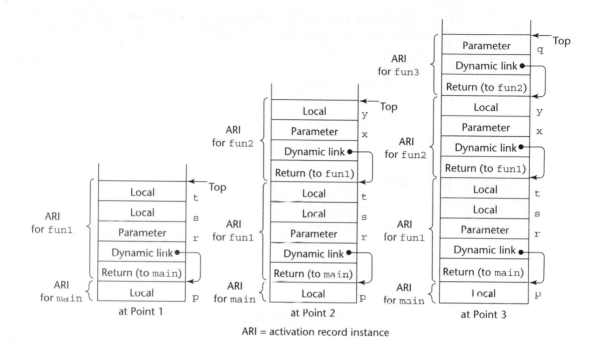

ARI = activation record instance

Figure 10.5

Stack contents for three points in a program

dynamic link is used to reset the stack top pointer. A similar process takes place when functions fun2 and fun1 terminate. After the return from the call to fun1 from main, the stack has only the instance of the activation record of main. Note that some implementations do not actually use an activation record instance on the stack for main functions, such as the one shown in the figure. However, it can be done this way, and it simplifies both the implementation and our discussion. In this example and in all others in this chapter, we assume that the stack grows from lower addresses to higher addresses, although in a particular implementation, the stack may grow in the opposite direction.

The collection of dynamic links present in the stack at a given time is called the **dynamic chain,** or **call chain.** It represents the dynamic history of how execution got to its current position, which is always in the subprogram code whose activation record instance is on top of the stack. References to local variables can be represented in the code as offsets from the beginning of the activation record of the local scope. Such an offset is called a **local_offset.**

The local_offset of a variable in an activation record can be determined at compile time, using the order, types, and sizes of variables declared in the subprogram associated with the activation record. To simplify the discussion, we assume that all variables take one position in the activation record. The first local variable declared in a subprogram would be allocated in the activation record two positions plus the number of parameters from the bottom (the first two positions are for the return address and the dynamic link). The second local variable declared would be one position nearer the stack top and so forth. For example, consider the preceding example program. In fun1, the local_offset of s is 3; for t it is 4. Likewise, in fun2, the local_offset of y is 3. To get the address of any local variable, the local_offset of the variable is added to the EP.

10.3.3   Recursion

Consider the following example C program, which uses recursion to compute the factorial function:

```
int factorial(int n) {
    <———————————1
  if (n <= 1)
    return 1;
  else return (n * factorial(n - 1));
      <———————————2
  }
void main() {
  int value;
  value = factorial(3);
      <———————————3
  }
```

The activation record format for the function factorial is shown in Figure 10.6. Notice that it has an additional entry for the return value of the function.

Figure 10.7 shows the contents of the stack for the three times execution reaches position 1 in the function factorial. Each shows one more activation of the function, with its functional value undefined. The first activation record instance has the return address to the calling function, main. The others have a return address to the function itself; these are for the recursive calls.

Figure 10.6

The activation record for factorial

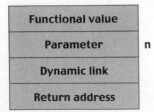

Functional value	
Parameter	n
Dynamic link	
Return address	

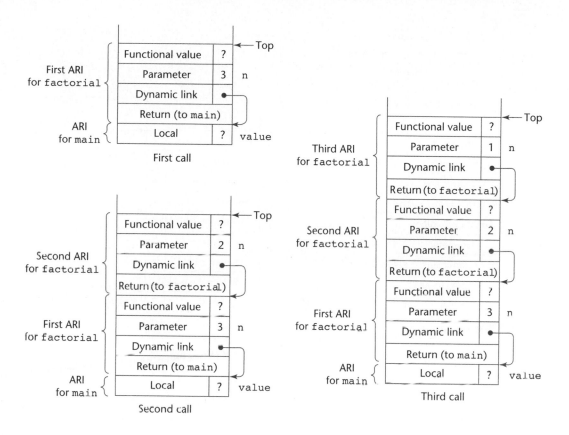

ARI = activation record instance

Figure 10.7

Stack contents at position 1 in factorial

Figure 10.8 shows the stack contents for the three times that execution reaches position 2 in the function factorial. Position 2 is meant to be the time after the **return** is executed but before the activation record has been removed from the stack. Recall that the code for the function multiplies the current value of the parameter n by the value returned by the recursive call to the function. The first return from factorial returns the value 1. The activation record instance for that activation has a value of 1 for its version of the parameter n. The result from that multiplication, 1, is returned to the second activation of factorial to be multiplied by its parameter value for n, which is 2. This step returns the value 2 to the first activation of factorial to be multiplied by its parameter value for n, which is 3, yielding the final functional value of 6, which is then returned to the first call to factorial in main.

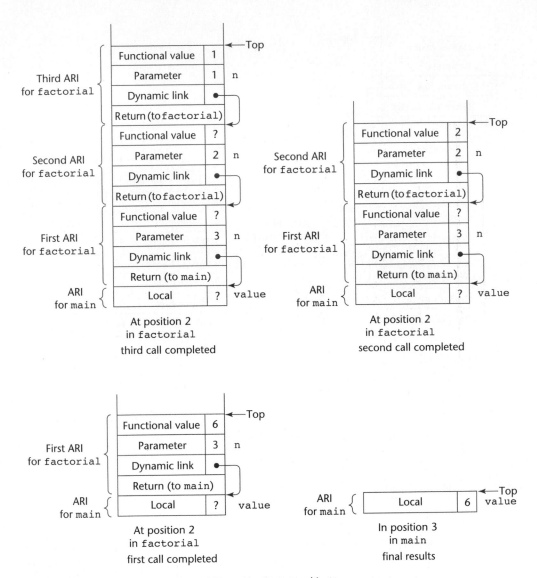

Figure 10.8

Stack contents during execution of main and factorial

10.4 Nested Subprograms

Some of the non-C-based static-scoped programming languages use stack-dynamic local variables and allow subprograms to be nested. Among these are Fortran 95, Ada, Python, and JavaScript. In this section, we examine the most commonly used approach to implementing subprograms in this environment.

10.4.1 The Basics

A reference to a nonlocal variable in a static-scoped language with nested subprograms requires a two-step access process. All nonstatic variables that can be nonlocally accessed are in existing activation record instances and therefore are somewhere in the stack. The first step of the access process is to find the instance of the activation record in the stack in which the variable was allocated. The second part is to use the local_offset of the variable (within the activation record instance) to access it.

Finding the correct activation record instance is the more interesting and more difficult of the two steps. First, note that in a given subprogram, only variables that are declared in static ancestor scopes are visible and can be accessed. Also, activation record instances of all of the static ancestors are always on the stack when variables in them are referenced by a nested subprogram. This is guaranteed by the static semantic rules of the static-scoped languages: A subprogram is callable only when all of its static ancestor subprograms are active. If a particular static ancestor were not active, its local variables would not be bound to storage, so it would be nonsense to allow access to them.

The semantics of nonlocal references dictates that the correct declaration is the first one found when looking through the enclosing scopes, most closely nested first. So to support nonlocal references, it must be possible to find all of the instances of activation records in the stack that correspond to those static ancestors. This observation leads to the implementation approach described in the following subsection.

We do not address the issue of blocks until Section 10.5, so in the remainder of this section, all scopes are defined by subprograms. Because functions cannot be nested in the C-based languages (the only static scopes in those languages are those created with blocks), the discussions of this section do not apply to those languages directly.

10.4.2 Static Chains

The most common way to implement static scoping in languages that allow nested subprograms is static chaining. In this approach, a new pointer, called a static link, is added to the activation record. The **static link,** which is sometimes called a *static scope pointer*, points to the bottom of the activation record instance of an activation of the static parent. It is used for accesses to nonlocal variables. Typically, the static link appears in the activation record below the

Keeping It Simple

Niklaus Wirth

Niklaus Wirth began his career in engineering at the Swiss Federal Institute of Technology (ETH) in Zurich. He then studied in Canada and went on to receive a Ph.D. from the University of California at Berkeley in 1963. Throughout his career he has held positions such as assistant professor of computer science (at Stanford University and then at the University of Zürich), professor of informatics at ETH Zürich, and researcher at Xerox PARC in California. Professor Wirth won a Computer Pioneer award from the IEEE and received ACM's Turing Award "for developing a sequence of innovative computer languages: EULER, ALGOL-W, PASCAL and MODULA."

ON DESIGNS AND SOLUTIONS

The clear and uniform structure of Pascal set a new standard. What was it about Pascal that improved so significantly on these tools? Mainly the fact that Pascal expresses the most basic elements of programming and lets them be composed and combined in a free and general way. It is a structured language both for statements and data.

You've spent a lot of time thinking about solutions that marry hardware and software: The Lilith Computer and Oberon and Modula. What about considering programming tool solutions within the larger framework of the hardware draws you to considering both when designing solutions? If computer architecture and software are built properly and fit together harmoniously, both parts become simpler and more economical. Most importantly, they become easier to understand.

I read this quote in an interview you gave: "A good designer must rely on experience, on precise, logical thinking, and on pedantic exactness. No magic will do." How is one able to distinguish between the magic and the best solution, and dismiss the former for the latter? I guess mostly through experience. Good teachers who have this ability to distinguish help enormously.

In another interview you mentioned the state of design today and what drove it: "The wishes of the users count more than their needs, and people are more easily sold by cool features—even if rarely used—than by the goal of reliable and transparent programs." If the opposite had been true, what do you think today's operating system or today's Web interfaces would look like to the average user? How would they be better? Very often, clients specifying a software system do not know exactly what they require. Hence their "wishes" may not truly reflect their actual needs. The results are specifications with many items that on closer inspection are quite superfluous, or at least unimportant. Concentrating on the essentials and leaving off bells and whistles would lead to simpler systems that would be more economical, simpler to understand and operate, and might therefore be less susceptible to mistakes.

You've expressed this idea that what technology makes possible is most commonly exaggerated—for example, leading artificial intelligence on a mission to try and create machines that "think." Can you elaborate some on why you think this exaggerated belief in technology leads scientists down a fruitless path? The hype about many items of modern IT—not only artificial intelligence—misleads not so much scientists, but rather customers (and funding agencies). It is one thing to support long-term research with calculated risk, and another to sell products with exaggerated promises that cannot be substantiated.

ABOUT THE STATE OF THE ART AND ITS TOOLS

Thinking about the past 10 years, what are a couple of advancements in language features that have most contributed to better programming? Program and data structures, and the associated idea of assertions and loop invariants. Modular design and separate compilation of modules. Hierarchies of data types (in OOP called subclasses with inheritance).

In this comparative-languages course, students study functional languages, logic languages, procedural languages, and OOP. How should students consider procedural programming in their studies and work? Is it a historical style? One soon to become a niche style? It is important that CS students know the various programming paradigms: procedural, functional, logic, and object-oriented. But obviously the procedural style remains closest to the

" Concentrating on the essentials and leaving off bells and whistles would lead to simpler systems that would be more economical, simpler to understand and operate, and might therefore be less susceptible to mistakes. "

computer on which programs are interpreted ("run"). The computer's characteristic feature is memory with individually updated cells. Their correspondence in programming languages is the variable. The object-oriented style is based on the procedural style; it is a variant of it, not really different, even if procedures are now called "methods," and calling a procedure is termed "sending a message." I consider functional and logic programming "niche styles" much rather than procedural programming.

parameters. The addition of the static link to the activation record requires that local offsets be different from when the static link is not included. Instead of having two activation record elements before the parameters, there are now three: the return address, the static link, and the dynamic link.

A **static chain** is a chain of static links that connect certain activation record instances in the stack. During the execution of a procedure P, the static link of its activation record instance points to an activation record instance of P's static parent program unit. That instance's static link points in turn to P's static grandparent program unit's activation record instance, if there is one. So the static chain connects all the static ancestors of an executing subprogram, in order of static parent first. This chain can obviously be used to implement the accesses to nonlocal variables in static-scoped languages.

Finding the correct activation record instance of a nonlocal variable using static links is relatively straightforward. When a reference is made to a nonlocal variable, the activation record instance containing the variable can be found by searching the static chain until a static ancestor activation record instance is found that contains the variable. However, it can be much easier than that. Because the nesting of scopes is known at compile time, the compiler can determine not only that a reference is nonlocal but also the length of the static chain that must be followed to reach the activation record instance that contains the nonlocal object.

Let **static_depth** be an integer associated with a static scope that indicates how deeply it is nested in the outermost scope. An Ada main procedure has a static_depth of 0. If procedure A is defined in a main procedure, its static_depth is 1. If procedure A contains the definition of a nested procedure B, then B's static_depth is 2.

The length of the static chain needed to reach the correct activation record instance for a nonlocal reference to a variable X is exactly the difference between the static_depth of the procedure containing the reference to X and the static_depth of the procedure containing the declaration for X. This difference is called the **nesting_depth,** or **chain_offset,** of the reference. The actual reference can be represented by an ordered pair of integers (chain_offset, local_offset), where chain_offset is the number of links to the correct activation record instance (local_offset is described in Section 10.3.2). For example, consider the following skeletal program:

```
procedure A is
  procedure B is
    procedure C is
      ...
    end;  -- of C
    ...
  end;  -- of B
  ...
end;  -- of A
```

The static_depths of A, B, and C are 0, 1, and 2, respectively. If procedure C references a variable declared in A, the chain_offset of that reference would be 2 (static_depth of C minus the static_depth of A). If procedure C references a variable declared in B, the chain_offset of that reference would be 1. References to locals can be handled using the same mechanism, with a chain_offset of 0, but instead of using the static pointer to the activation record instance of the subprogram where the variable was declared as the base address, the EP is used.

To illustrate the complete process of nonlocal accesses, consider the following skeletal Ada program:

```
procedure Main_2 is
  X : Integer;
  procedure Bigsub is
    A, B, C : Integer;
    procedure Sub1 is
      A, D : Integer;
      begin  -- of Sub1
      A := B + C;    <——————— 1
      ...
    end;  -- of Sub1
    procedure Sub2(X : Integer) is
      B, E : Integer;
      procedure Sub3 is
        C, E : Integer;
        begin  -- of Sub3
        ...
        Sub1;
        ...
        E := B + A;  <———————— 2
      end;  -- of Sub3
      begin  -- of Sub2
      ...
      Sub3;
      ...
      A := D + E;  <——————— 3
    end;  -- of Sub2
    begin  -- of Bigsub
    ...
    Sub2(7);
    ...
  end;  -- of Bigsub
  begin  -- of Main_2
  ...
  Bigsub;
  ...
end;  -- of Main_2
```

The sequence of procedure calls is

```
Main_2 calls Bigsub
Bigsub calls Sub2
Sub2 calls Sub3
Sub3 calls Sub1
```

The stack situation when execution first arrives at point 1 in this program is shown in Figure 10.9.

Figure 10.9

Stack contents at position 1 in the program Main_2

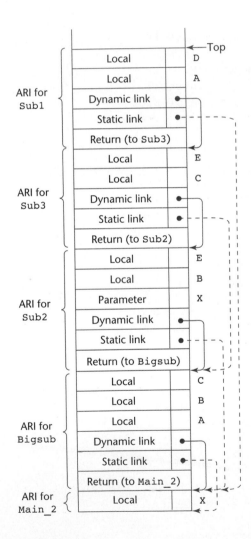

ARI = activation record instance

At position 1 in procedure Sub1, the reference is to the local variable, A, not to the nonlocal variable A from Bigsub. This reference to A has the chain_offset/local_offset pair (0, 3). The reference to B is to the nonlocal B from Bigsub. It can be represented by the pair (1, 4). The local_offset is 4, because a 3 offset would be the first local variable (Bigsub has no parameters). Notice that if the dynamic link were used to do a simple search for an activation record instance with a declaration for the variable B, it would find the variable B declared in Sub2, which would be incorrect. If the (1, 4) pair were used with the dynamic chain, the variable E from Sub3 would be used. The static link, however, points to the activation record for Bigsub, which has the correct version of B. The variable B in Sub2 is not in the referencing environment at this point and is (correctly) not accessible. The reference to C at point 1 is to the C defined in Bigsub, which is represented by the pair (1, 5).

After Sub1 completes its execution, the activation record instance for Sub1 is removed from the stack, and control returns to Sub3. The reference to the variable E at position 2 in Sub3 is local and uses the pair (0, 4) for access. The reference to the variable B is to the one declared in Sub2, because that is the nearest static ancestor that contains such a declaration. It is accessed with the pair (1, 4). The local_offset is 4 because B is the first variable declared in Sub1, and Sub2 has one parameter. The reference to the variable A is to the A declared in Bigsub, because neither Sub3 nor its static parent Sub2 has a declaration for a variable named A. It is referenced with the pair (2, 3).

After Sub3 completes its execution, the activation record instance for Sub3 is removed from the stack, leaving only the activation record instances for Main_2, Bigsub, and Sub2. At position 3 in Sub2, the reference to the variable A is to the A in Bigsub, which has the only declaration of A among the active routines. This access is made with the pair (1, 3). At this position, there is no visible scope containing a declaration for the variable D, so this reference to D is a static semantics error. The error would be detected when the compiler attempted to compute the chain_offset/local_offset pair. The reference to E is to the local E in Sub2, which can be accessed with the pair (0, 5).

In summary, the references to the variable A at points 1, 2, and 3 would be represented by the following points:

- (0, 3) (local)
- (2, 3) (two levels away)
- (1, 3) (one level away)

It is reasonable at this point to ask how the static chain is maintained during program execution. If its maintenance is too complex, the fact that it is simple and effective will be unimportant. We assume here that parameters that are subprograms are not implemented.

The static chain must be modified for each subprogram call and return. The return part is trivial: When the subprogram terminates, its activation record instance is removed from the stack. After this removal, the new top activation record instance is that of the unit that called the subprogram whose execution just terminated. Because the static chain from this activation record instance was never changed, it works correctly just as it did before the call to the other subprogram. Therefore, no other action is required.

The action required at a subprogram call is more complex. Although the correct parent scope is easily determined at compile time, the most recent activation record instance of the parent scope must be found at the time of the call. This can be done by looking at activation record instances on the dynamic chain until the first one of the parent scope is found. However, this search can be avoided by treating procedure declarations and references exactly like variable declarations and references. When the compiler encounters a subprogram call, among other things, it determines the subprogram that declared the called subprogram, which must be a static ancestor of the calling routine. It then computes the nesting_depth, or number of enclosing scopes between the caller and the subprogram that declared the called subprogram. This information is stored and can be accessed by the subprogram call during execution. At the time of the call, the static link of the called subprogram's activation record instance is determined by moving down the static chain of the caller the number of links equal to the nesting_depth computed at compile time.

Consider again the program Main_2 and the stack situation shown in Figure 10.9. At the call to Sub1 in Sub3, the compiler determines the nesting_depth of Sub3 (the caller) to be two levels inside the procedure that declared the called procedure Sub1, which is Bigsub. When the call to Sub1 in Sub3 is executed, this information is used to set the static link of the activation record instance for Sub1. This static link is set to point to the activation record instance that is pointed to by the second static link in the static chain from the caller's activation record instance. In this case, the caller is Sub3, whose static link points to its parent's activation record instance (that of Sub2). The static link of the activation record instance for Sub2 points to the activation record instance for Bigsub. So the static link for the new activation record instance for Sub1 is set to point to the activation record instance for Bigsub.

This method works for all subprogram linkage, except when parameters that are subprograms are involved.

One criticism of using the static chain to access nonlocal variables is that references to variables in scopes beyond the static parent cost more than references to locals. The static chain must be followed, one link per enclosing scope from the reference to the declaration. Fortunately, in practice references to distant nonlocal variables are rare, so this is not a serious problem. Another criticism of the static-chain approach is that it is difficult for a programmer working on a time-critical program to estimate the costs of nonlocal references, because the cost of each reference depends on the depth of nesting between the reference and the scope of declaration. Further complicating this problem is that subsequent code modifications may change nesting depths, thereby changing the timing of some references, both in the changed code and possibly in code far from the changes.

Some alternatives to static chains have been developed, most notably an approach that uses an auxiliary data structure called a display. However, none of the alternatives has been found to be superior to the static-chain method, which is still the most widely used approach. Therefore, none of the alternatives is discussed here.

10.5 Blocks

Recall from Chapter 5 that a number of languages, including the C-based languages, provide for user-specified local scopes for variables called **blocks**. As an example of a block, consider the following code segment:

```
{ int temp;
  temp = list[upper];
  list[upper] = list[lower];
  list[lower] = temp;
}
```

A block is specified in the C-based languages as a compound statement that begins with one or more data definitions. The lifetime of the variable temp in the preceding block begins when control enters the block and ends when control exits the block. The advantage of using such a local is that it cannot interfere with any other variable with the same name that is declared elsewhere in the program.

Blocks can be implemented by using the static-chain process we described for implementing nested subprograms. Blocks are treated as parameterless subprograms that are always called from the same place in the program. Therefore, every block has an activation record. An instance of its activation record is created every time the block is executed.

Blocks can also be implemented in a different and somewhat simpler and more efficient way. The maximum amount of storage required for block variables at any time during the execution of a program can be statically determined, because blocks are entered and exited in strictly textual order. This amount of space can be allocated after the local variables in the activation record. Offsets for all block variables can be statically computed, so block variables can be addressed exactly as if they were local variables.

For example, consider the following skeletal program:

```
void main() {
  int x, y, z;
  while ( ... ) {
    int a, b, c;
    ...
    while ( ... ) {
      int d, e;
      ...
    }
```

```
    }
    while ( ... ) {
      int f, g;
      ...
    }
    ...
}
```

For this program, the static-memory layout shown in Figure 10.10 could be used. Note that f and g occupy the same memory locations as a and b, because a and b are popped off the stack when their block is exited (before f and g are allocated).

Figure 10.10

Block variable storage when blocks are not treated as parameterless procedures

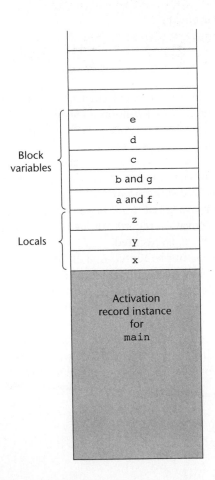

10.6 Implementing Dynamic Scoping

There are at least two distinct ways in which local variables and nonlocal references to them can be implemented in a dynamic-scoped language: deep access and shallow access. Note that deep access and shallow access are not concepts related to deep and shallow binding. An important difference between binding and access is that deep and shallow bindings result in different semantics; deep and shallow accesses do not.

10.6.1   Deep Access

If local variables are stack-dynamic and are part of the activation records in a dynamic-scoped language, references to nonlocal variables can be resolved by searching through the activation record instances of the other subprograms that are currently active, beginning with the one most recently activated. This concept is similar to that of accessing nonlocal variables in a static-scoped language with nested subprograms, except that the dynamic—rather than the static—chain is followed. The dynamic chain links together all subprogram activation record instances in the reverse of the order in which they were activated. Therefore, the dynamic chain is exactly what is needed to reference nonlocal variables in a dynamic-scoped language. This method is called **deep access,** because access may require searches deep in the stack.

Consider the following example program:

```
void sub3() {
  int x, z;
  x = u + v;
  ...
}

void sub2() {
  int w, x;
  ...
}

void sub1() {
  int v, w;
  ...
}

void main() {
  int v, u;
  ...
}
```

This program is written in a syntax that gives it the appearance of a program in a C-based language, but it is not meant to be in any particular language. Suppose the following sequence of function calls occurs:

main calls sub1
sub1 calls sub1
sub1 calls sub2
sub2 calls sub3

Figure 10.11 shows the stack during the execution of function sub3 after this calling sequence. Notice that the activation record instances do not have static links, which would serve no purpose in a dynamic-scoped language.

Consider the references to the variables x, u, and v in function sub3. The reference to x is found in the activation record instance for sub3. The reference to u is found by searching *all* of the activation record instances on the stack, because the only existing variable with that name is in main. This

Figure 10.11

Stack contents for a dynamic-scoped program

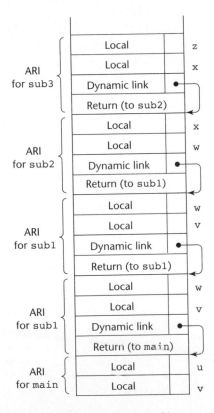

ARI = activation record instance

search involves following four dynamic links and examining 10 variable names. The reference to v is found in the most recent (nearest on the dynamic chain) activation record instance for the procedure sub1.

There are two important differences between the deep-access method for nonlocal access in a dynamic-scoped language and the static-chain method for static-scoped languages. First, in a dynamic-scoped language, there is no way to determine at compile time the length of the chain that must be searched. Every activation record instance in the chain must be searched until the first instance of the variable is found. This is one reason why dynamic-scoped languages typically have slower execution speeds than static-scoped languages. Second, activation records must store the names of variables for the search process, whereas in static-scoped language implementations only the values are required. (Names are not required for static scoping, because all variables are represented by the chain_offset/local_offset pairs.)

10.6.2 Shallow Access

Shallow access is an alternative implementation method, not an alternative semantics. As stated previously, the semantics of deep access and shallow access are identical. In the shallow-access method, variables declared in subprograms are not stored in the activation records of those subprograms. Because with dynamic scoping there is at most one visible version of a variable of any specific name at a given time, a very different approach can be taken. One variation of shallow access is to have a separate stack for each variable name in a complete program. Every time a new variable with a particular name is created by a declaration at the beginning of a subprogram that has been called, the variable is given a cell at the top of the stack for its name. Every reference to the name is to the variable on top of the stack associated with that name, because the top one is the most recently created. When a subprogram terminates, the lifetime of its local variables ends, and the stacks for those variable names are popped. This method allows very fast references to variables, but maintaining the stacks at the entrances and exits of subprograms is costly.

Figure 10.12 shows the variable stacks for the earlier example program in the same situation as shown with the stack in Figure 10.11.

Another option for implementing shallow access is to use a central table that has a location for each different variable name in a program. Along with each entry, a bit called **active** is maintained that indicates whether the name has a current binding or variable association. Any access to any variable can then be to an offset into the central table. The offset is static, so the access can be fast. SNOBOL implementations use the central table implementation technique.

Maintenance of a central table is straightforward. A subprogram call requires that all of its local variables be logically placed in the central table. If the position of the new variable in the central table is already active—that is, if it contains a variable whose lifetime has not yet ended (which is indicated by the active bit)—that value must be saved somewhere during the lifetime of the

Figure 10.12

One method of using
shallow access to
implement dynamic
scoping

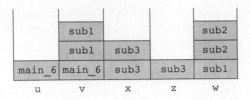

(The names in the stack cells indicate the
program units of the variable declaration.)

new variable. Whenever a variable begins its lifetime, the active bit in its central table position must be set.

There have been several variations in the design of the central table and in the way values are stored when they are temporarily replaced. One variation is to have a "hidden" stack on which all saved objects are stored. Because subprogram calls and returns, and thus the lifetimes of local variables, are nested, this works well.

The second variation is perhaps the cleanest and least expensive to implement. A central table of single cells is used, storing only the current version of each variable name. Replaced variables are stored in the activation record of the subprogram that created the replacement variable. This is a stack mechanism, but it uses the stack that already exists, so the new overhead is minimal.

The choice between shallow and deep access to nonlocal variables depends on the relative frequencies of subprogram calls and nonlocal references. The deep-access method provides fast subprogram linkage, but references to nonlocals, especially references to distant nonlocals (in terms of the call chain), are costly. The shallow-access method provides much faster references to nonlocals, especially distant nonlocals, but is more costly in terms of subprogram linkage.

SUMMARY

Subprogram linkage semantics requires many actions by the implementation. In the case of "simple" subprograms, these actions are relatively basic. In languages with stack-dynamic local variables and nested subprograms, subprogram linkage is more complex.

Subprograms in languages with stack-dynamic local variables and nested subprograms have two components: the actual code, which is static, and the activation record, which is stack-dynamic. Activation record instances contain the formal parameters and local variables, among other things.

Static chains are the primary method of implementing accesses to nonlocal variables in static-scoped languages with nested subprograms.

Access to nonlocal variables in a dynamic-scoped language can be implemented by use of the dynamic chain or through some central variable table method. Dynamic chains provide slow accesses but fast calls and returns. The central table methods provide fast accesses but slow calls and returns.

REVIEW QUESTIONS

1. What are the two reasons why implementing subprograms with stack-dynamic local variables is more difficult than implementing simple subprograms?

2. What is the difference between an activation record and an activation record instance?

3. Why are the return address, dynamic link, and parameters placed in the bottom of the activation record?

4. What are the two steps in locating a nonlocal variable in a static-scoped language with stack-dynamic local variables and nested subprograms?

5. Define *static chain*, *static_depth*, *nesting_depth*, and *chain_offset*.

6. What are the two potential problems with the static-chain method?

7. What is an EP and what is its purpose?

8. How are references to variables represented in the static-chain method?

9. Explain the two methods of implementing blocks.

10. Describe the deep-access method of implementing dynamic scoping.

11. Describe the shallow-access method of implementing dynamic scoping.

12. What are the two differences between the deep-access method for non-local access in dynamic-scoped languages and the static-chain method for static-scoped languages?

13. Compare the efficiency of the deep-access method to that of the shallow-access method, in terms of both calls and nonlocal accesses.

PROBLEM SET

1. Show the stack with all activation record instances, including static and dynamic chains, when execution reaches position 1 in the following skeletal program. Assume Bigsub is at level 1.

```
procedure Bigsub is
  procedure A is
    procedure B is
      begin  -- of B
      ...  <——————1
      end;  -- of B
```

```
      procedure C is
        begin   -- of C
        ...
        B;
        ...
        end;   -- of C
      begin   -- of A
      ...
      C;
      ...
      end;   -- of A
    begin   -- of Bigsub
    ...
    A;
    ...
    end;   -- of Bigsub
```

2. Show the stack with all activation record instances, including static and dynamic chains, when execution reaches position 1 in the following skeletal program. Assume Bigsub is at level 1.

```
procedure Bigsub is
  MySum : Float;
  procedure A is
    X : Integer;
    procedure B(Sum : Float) is
      Y, Z : Float;
      begin   -- of B
      ...
      C(Z)
      ...
      end;   -- of B
    begin   -- of A
    ...
    B(X);
    ...
    end;   -- of A
  procedure C(Plums : Float) is
    begin   -- of C
    ...<————————1
    end;   -- of C
  L : Float;
  begin   -- of Bigsub
  ...
  A;
  ...
  end;   -- of Bigsub
```

3. Show the stack with all activation record instances, including static and dynamic chains, when execution reaches position 1 in the following skeletal program. Assume `Bigsub` is at level 1.

```
procedure Bigsub is
  procedure A(Flag : Boolean) is
    procedure B is
      ...
      A(false);
      end;  -- of B
    begin  -- of A
    if flag
      then B;
      else C;
    ...
    end;  -- of A
  procedure C is
    procedure D is
      ... <——————1
      end;  -- of D
    ...
    D;
    end;  -- of C
  begin  -- of Bigsub
  ...
  A(true);
  ...
  end;  -- of Bigsub
```

The calling sequence for this program for execution to reach D is

```
Bigsub calls A
A calls B
B calls A
A calls C
C calls D
```

4. Show the stack with all activation record instances, including the dynamic chain, when execution reaches position 1 in the following skeletal program. This program uses the deep-access method to implement dynamic scoping.

```
void fun1() {
  float a;
  ...
}

void fun2() {
```

```
      int b, c;
      ...
  }

  void fun3() {
    float d;
    ... <————————1
  }

  void main() {
    char e, f, g;
  ...
  }
```

The calling sequence for this program for execution to reach fun3 is

```
main calls fun2
fun2 calls fun1
fun1 calls fun1
fun1 calls fun3
```

5. Assume the program of Problem 4 is implemented using the shallow-access method using a stack for each variable name. Show the stacks for the time of the execution of fun3, assuming execution found its way to that point through the sequence of calls shown in Problem 4.

6. Although local variables in Java methods are dynamically allocated at the beginning of each activation, under what circumstances could the value of a local in a particular activation retain the value of the previous activation?

7. It is stated in this chapter that when nonlocal variables are accessed in a dynamic-scoped language using the dynamic chain, variable names must be stored in the activation records with the values. If this were actually done, every nonlocal access would require a sequence of costly string comparisons on names. Design an alternative to these string comparisons that would be faster.

8. Pascal allows gotos with nonlocal targets. How could such statements be handled if static chains were used for nonlocal variable access? *Hint:* Consider the way the correct activation record instance of the static parent of a newly enacted procedure is found (see Section 10.4.2).

9. The static-chain method could be expanded slightly by using two static links in each activation record instance where the second points to the static grandparent activation record instance. How would this approach affect the time required for subprogram linkage and nonlocal references?

10. Design a skeletal program and a calling sequence that results in an activation record instance in which the static and dynamic links point to different activation-recorded instances in the run-time stack.

11

Abstract Data Types and Encapsulation Constructs

I n this chapter, we explore programming language constructs that support data abstraction. Among the new ideas of the last 50 years in programming methodologies and programming language design, data abstraction is one of the most profound.

We begin by discussing the general concept of abstraction in programming and programming languages. Data abstraction is then defined and illustrated with an example. This topic is followed by descriptions of the support for data abstraction in Ada, C++, Java, C#, and Ruby. Implementations of the same example data abstraction are given in Ada, C++, Java, and Ruby to illuminate the similarities and differences in the design of the language facilities that support data abstraction. Next, the capabilities of Ada, C++ , Java 5.0, and C# 2005 to build parameterized abstract data types are discussed.

Constructs that support abstract data types are encapsulations of the data and operations on objects of the type. Encapsulations that contain multiple types are required for the construction of larger programs. These encapsulations and the associated namespace issues are also discussed in this chapter.

11.1 The Concept of Abstraction

An **abstraction** is a view or representation of an entity that includes only the most significant attributes. In a general sense, abstraction allows one to collect instances of entities into groups in which their common attributes need not be considered. For example, suppose we define birds to be creatures with the following attributes: two wings, two legs, a tail, and the ability to fly. Then if we say a crow is a bird, a description of a crow need not include those attributes. The same is true for robins, sparrows, and yellow-bellied sap suckers. These common attributes in the descriptions of specific species of birds can be abstracted away. Within a particular species, only the attributes that distinguish that species need be considered. This results in significant simplification of the descriptions of members of the species. A less abstract view of a species, that of a bird, may be considered when it is necessary to see a higher level of detail.

In the world of programming languages, abstraction is a weapon against the complexity of programming; its purpose is to simplify the programming process. It is an effective weapon because it allows programmers to focus on essential attributes, while ignoring subordinate attributes.

The two fundamental kinds of abstraction in contemporary programming languages are process abstraction and data abstraction.

The concept of **process abstraction** is among the oldest in programming language design. Even Plankalkül supported process abstraction. All subprograms are process abstractions because they provide a way for a program to specify that some process is to be done, without providing the details of how it is to be done (at least in the calling program). For example, when a program needs to sort an array of numeric data objects of some type, it usually uses a subprogram for the sorting process. At the point where the sorting process is required, a statement such as

```
sortInt(list, listLen)
```

is placed in the program. This call is an abstraction of the actual sorting process, whose algorithm is not specified. The call is independent of the algorithm implemented in the called subprogram.

In the case of the subprogram `sortInt`, the only essential attributes are the name of the array to be sorted, the type of its elements, the array's length, and the fact that the call to `sortInt` will result in the array being sorted. The particular algorithm that `sortInt` implements is an attribute that is not essential to the user. The user needs to see only the name and protocol of the sorting subprogram to be able to use it.

The evolution of data abstraction necessarily followed that of process abstraction because an integral and central part of every data abstraction is its operations, which are defined as process abstractions.

11.2 Introduction to Data Abstraction

Syntactically, an abstract data type is an enclosure that includes only the data representation of one specific data type and the subprograms that provide the operations for that type. Through access controls, unnecessary details of the type can be hidden from units outside the enclosure that use the type. Program units that use an abstract data type can declare variables of that type, even though the actual representation is hidden from them. An instance of an abstract data type is called an **object.**

One of the motivations for data abstraction is similar to that of process abstraction. It is a weapon against complexity; a means of making large and/or complicated programs more manageable. Other motivations for and advantages of abstract data types are discussed later in this section.

Object-oriented programming, which is described in Chapter 12, is an outgrowth of the use of data abstraction in software development, and data abstraction is one of its most important components.

11.2.1 Floating-Point as an Abstract Data Type

The concept of an abstract data type, at least in terms of built-in types, is not a recent development. All built-in data types, even those of Fortran I, are abstract data types, although they are rarely called that. For example, consider a floating-point data type. Most languages include at least one of these. A floating-point type provides a way of creating variables for floating-point data, and also provides a set of arithmetic operations for manipulating objects of the type.

Floating-point types in high-level languages employ a key concept in data abstraction: information hiding. The actual format of the data value in a floating-point memory cell is hidden from the user, and the only operations available are those provided by the language. The user is not allowed to create new operations on data of the type, except those that can be constructed using the built-in operations. The user cannot directly manipulate the parts of the actual representation of objects because that representation is hidden. It is this feature that allows program portability between implementations of a particular language, even though the implementations may use different representations for particular data types. For example, before the IEEE 754 standard floating-point representations appeared in the mid-1980s, there were several different representations being used by different computer architectures. However, this variation did not prevent programs that used floating-point types from being portable to the various architectures.

11.2.2 User-Defined Abstract Data Types

A user-defined abstract data type should provide the same characteristics provided by language-defined types, such as a floating-point type: (1) a type definition that allows program units to declare variables of the type but hides the representation of objects of the type; and (2) a set of operations for manipulating objects of the type.

We now formally define an abstract data type in the context of user-defined types. An **abstract data type** is a data type that satisfies the following two conditions:

- The declarations of the type and the protocols of the operations on objects of the type, which provide the type's interface, are contained in a single syntactic unit. The type's interface does not depend on the representation of the objects or the implementation of the operations. The implementation of the type and its operations may be in the same syntactic unit, or may be given in a separate unit. Also, other program units are allowed to create variables of the defined type.

- The representation of objects of the type is hidden from the program units that use the type, so the only direct operations possible on those objects are those provided in the type's definition.

The primary advantage of packaging the declarations of the type and its operations in a single syntactic unit is it provides a method of organizing a program into logical units that can be compiled separately. The advantage of having the implementation of the type and its operations in a different syntactic unit is that it is good to keep specifications and their implementations separate. Program units that use a specific abstract data type, which are called **clients** of that type, need to see the specification, but cannot be allowed to see the implementation. If both the declarations and the definitions of types and operations are in the same syntactic unit, there must be some means of hiding from clients the parts of the unit that specify the definitions.

The advantage of having the interface not depend on object representation or implementation of operations is that it allows them to be changed without requiring changes to clients of the type.

An important benefit of information hiding is increased reliability. Clients cannot manipulate the underlying representations of objects directly, either intentionally or by accident, thus increasing the integrity of such objects. Objects can be changed only through the provided operations.

11.2.3   An Example

Suppose an abstract data type is to be constructed for a stack that has the following abstract operations:

create(stack)	Creates and possibly initializes a stack object
destroy(stack)	Deallocates the storage for the stack
empty(stack)	A predicate (or Boolean) function that returns true if the specified stack is empty and false otherwise
push(stack, element)	Pushes the specified element on the specified stack
pop(stack)	Removes the top element from the specified stack
top(stack)	Returns a copy of the top element from the specified stack

Note that some implementations of abstract data types do not require the create and destroy operations. For example, simply defining a variable to be of an abstract data type may implicitly create the underlying data structure and initialize it. The storage for such a variable may be implicitly deallocated at the end of the variable's scope.

A client of the stack type could have a code sequence such as the following:

```
...
create(stk1);
push(stk1, color1);
push(stk1, color2);
if(! empty(stk1))
  temp = top(stk1);
...
```

Suppose that the original implementation of the stack abstraction uses an adjacency representation (one that implements a stack in an array). At a later time, because of memory management problems with the adjacency representation, it is changed to a linked list representation. Because data abstraction was used, this change can be made in the code that defines the stack type, but no changes will be required in any of the clients of the stack abstraction. In particular, the example code sequence need not be changed. Of course, a change in protocol of any of the operations would require changes in the clients.

11.3 Design Issues for Abstract Data Types

A facility for defining abstract data types in a language must provide a syntactic unit that encloses the type definition and subprogram definitions of the abstraction operations. It must be possible to make the type name and subprogram headers visible to clients of the abstraction. This allows clients to declare variables of the abstract type and manipulate their values. Although the type name must have external visibility, the type representation must be hidden.

Few, if any, general built-in operations should be provided for objects of abstract data types, other than those provided with the type definition. There simply are not many operations that apply to a broad range of abstract data types. Among these are assignment and comparisons for equality and inequality. If the language does not allow users to overload assignment, it must be built in. Comparisons for equality and inequality should be predefined in some cases but not in others. For example, if the type is implemented as a pointer, equality may mean pointer equality, but the user may want it to mean equality of the structures referenced by the pointers.

Some operations are required by many abstract data types, but because they are not universal, they must be provided by the designer of the type. Among these are iterators, accessors, constructors, and destructors. Iterators were discussed in Chapter 8. Accessors provide a form of access to data that is hidden from direct access by clients. Constructors are used to initialize parts of newly created objects. Destructors are often used to reclaim heap storage that may be used by parts of abstract data type objects.

As stated earlier, the enclosure for an abstract data type defines a single data type and its operations. Many contemporary languages, including C++, Java, and C#, directly support abstract data types. The alternative method is to provide a more generalized encapsulation construct that can define any number of entities, any of which can be selectively specified to be visible outside the enclosing unit. Ada uses this approach. These enclosures are not abstract data types, but rather are generalizations of abstract data types. As such, they can be used to define abstract data types. Although we discuss Ada's encapsulation construct in this section, we treat it as a minimal encapsulation for single data types. Generalized encapsulations are the topic of Section 11.6.

The first design issue for abstract data types is whether they can be parameterized. For example, if the language supports parameterized abstract data types, one could design an abstract data type for queues that could store elements of any type. Parameterized abstract data types are discussed in Section 11.5. Another design issue is what access controls are provided and how such controls are specified.

11.4 Language Examples

The concept of data abstraction had its origins in SIMULA 67, although that language provided only partial support for abstract data types. In this section, we describe the support for data abstraction provided by Ada, C++, Java, C#, and Ruby.

11.4.1 Abstract Data Types in Ada

Ada provides an encapsulation construct that can be used to define a single abstract data type, including the ability to hide its representation. Ada was one of the first languages to offer full support for abstract data types.

11.4.1.1 Encapsulation

The encapsulating constructs in Ada are called **packages.** A package can have two parts, each of which is also a package. These are called the **specification package,** which provides the interface of the encapsulation (and perhaps more), and the **body package,** which provides the implementation of most, if not all, of the entities named in the associated specification package. Not all packages have a body part (packages that encapsulate only types and constants do not have or need bodies).

A specification package and its associated body package share the same name. The reserved word **body** in a package header identifies it as being a body package. Specification and body packages may be compiled separately, provided the specification package is compiled first.

11.4.1.2 Information Hiding

The designer of an Ada package that defines a data type can choose to make the type entirely visible to clients or provide only the interface information. Of course, if the representation is not hidden, then the defined type is not an abstract data type. There are two approaches to hiding the representation from clients in the specification package. One is to include two sections in the specification package—one in which entities are visible to clients and one that hides its contents. For an abstract data type, an abbreviated declaration appears in the visible part of the specification, providing only the name of the type and the fact that its representation is hidden. The representation of the type appears in a part of the specification called the **private** part, which is introduced by the reserved word **private.** The private clause is always at the end of the specification package.

The second way to hide the representation is to define the abstract data type as a pointer and provide the pointed-to structure's definition in the body package, whose entire contents are hidden from clients.

Following is an example of the former approach to hiding a type's representation from clients. Suppose an abstract data type named Node_Type is to be defined in a package. Node_Type is declared in the visible part of the specification package without its representation details, as in

```
type Node_Type is private;
```

Types that are declared to be private are called **private types.** Private data types have built-in operations for assignment and comparisons for equality and inequality. Any other operation must be declared in the specification package that defined the type.

Notice that in the private clause of the following example, the declaration of Node_Type is repeated, but this time with the complete type definition:

```
package Linked_List_Type is
  type Node_Type is private;
  ...
  private
    type Node_Type;
    type Ptr is access Node_Type;
    type Node_Type is
      record
      Info : Integer;
      Link : Ptr;
      end record;
  end Linked_List_Type;
```

The private clause of this package has both a declaration and a definition of Node_Type. The declaration is necessary because of the reference to Node_Type in the definition of Ptr, which must precede the definition of Node_Type. Because they are defined in the private clause, neither Info nor Link are visible to clients of Linked_List_Type.

If none of the entities in a package are to be hidden, there is no purpose or need for the private part of the specification. Of course, such a package could not define an abstract data type.

The reason why a type's representation appears in the specification package at all has to do with compilation issues. A client can see only the specification package (not the body package), but the compiler must be able to allocate objects of the exported type when compiling the client. Furthermore, the client is compilable when only the specification package for the abstract data type has been compiled and is present. Therefore, the compiler must be able to determine the size of an object from the specification package. So the representation of the type must be visible to the compiler but not to the client code. This is exactly the situation specified by the private clause in a specification package.

It is somewhat troubling that the specification package provides part of the implementation details (the definition of the data) above, while the remaining implementation details (the definitions of the operations) are in the body package. It would be much cleaner if the specification provided only the interface and the body provided all of the implementation details. This problem can be alleviated by making the abstract data type a pointer, as in

```
package Linked_List_Type is
  type Node is private;
  function Create_Node() return Node;
  private
    type Node_Record;
    type Node is access Node_Record;
end Linked_list_Type;
```

Now, all of the details of the implementation can be given in the body package, as in

```
package body Linked_List_Type is
  type Node_Record is
    record
      Info : Integer;
      Link : Ptr;
    end record;
    ...
end Linked_List_Type;
```

There are several problems with this somewhat cleaner version. First, there are the inherent difficulties of dealing with pointers. Second, comparisons between two objects of the new abstract data type will be between pointers, which do not produce expected results, because the pointers are compared, rather than the objects to which they point. Another problem of defining an abstract data type as a pointer is the inability of the type to control allocation and deallocation of objects of the type. For example, a client can create a pointer to an object (with a variable declaration) and use it without creating an object.

An alternative to private types is a more restricted form: **limited private types.** Nonpointer limited private types are described in the private section of a specification package, as are nonpointer private types. The only syntactic difference is that limited private types are declared to be **limited private** in the visible part of the package specification. The semantic difference is that objects of a type that is declared limited private have no built-in operations. Such a type is useful when the usual predefined operations of assignment and comparison are not meaningful or useful. For example, assignment and comparison are rarely used for stacks. If assignment or equality comparisons are required but the built-in versions are not useful, these operations must be provided by the specification package. This is one way to avoid the comparison problems when the abstract data type is a pointer. The assignment operation must be in the form of a normal procedure, whereas the equal and not-equal operators can be provided by overloading those operators for the new type.

C++: Its Birth, Its Ubiquitousness, and Common Criticisms

BJARNE STROUSTRUP

Bjarne Stroustrup is the designer and original implementer of C++ and the author of *The C++ Programming Language* and *The Design and Evolution of C++.* His research interests include distributed systems, simulation, design, programming, and programming languages. Dr. Stroustrup is the College of Engineering Professor in Computer Science at Texas A&M University. He is actively involved in the ANSI/ISO standardization of C++. After more than two decades at AT&T, he retains a link with AT&T Labs, doing research as a member of the Information and Software Systems Research Lab. He is an ACM Fellow, an AT&T Bell Laboratories Fellow, and an AT&T Fellow. In 1993, Stroustrup received the ACM Grace Murray Hopper award "for his early work laying the foundations for the C++ programming language. Based on the foundations and Dr. Stroustrup's continuing efforts, C++ has become one of the most influential programming languages in the history of computing."

I. A BRIEF HISTORY OF YOU AND COMPUTING

What were you working on, and where, before you joined Bell Labs in the early 1980s? At Bell Labs, I was doing research in the general area of distributed systems. I joined in 1979. Before that, I was finishing my Ph.D. in that field in Cambridge University.

Did you immediately start on "with Classes" (which would later become C++)? I worked on a few projects related to distributed computing before starting on C with Classes and during the development of that and of C++. For example, I was trying to find a way to distribute the UNIX kernel across several computers and helped a lot of projects build simulators.

Was it an interest in mathematics that got you into this profession? I signed up for a degree in "mathematics with computer science" and my master's degree is officially a math degree. I—wrongly—thought that computing was some kind of applied math. I did a couple of years of math and rate myself a poor mathematician, but that's still much better than not knowing math. At the time I signed up, I had never even seen a computer. What I love about computing is the programming rather than the more mathematical fields.

II. DISSECTING A SUCCESSFUL LANGUAGE

I'd like to work backward, listing some items I think make C++ ubiquitous, and get your reaction. It's "open source," nonproprietary, and standardized by ANSI/ ISO. The ISO C++ standard is important. There are many independently developed and evolving C++ implementations. Without a standard for them to adhere to and a standards process to help coordinate the evolution of C++, a chaos of dialects would erupt.

It is also important that there are both open-source and commercial implementations available. In addition, for many users, it is crucial that the standard provides a measure of protection from manipulation by implementation providers.

The ISO standards process is open and democratic. The C++ committee rarely meets with fewer than 50 people present and typically more than eight nations are represented at each meeting. It is not just a vendors' forum.

It's ideal for systems programming (which, at the time C++ was born, was the largest sector of the market developing code).

Yes, C++ is a strong contender for any systems-programming project. It is also effective for embedded systems programming, which is currently the fastest-growing sector. Yet another growth area for C++ is high-performance numeric/engineering/scientific programming.

Its object-oriented nature and inclusion of classes/libraries make programming more efficient and transparent. C++ is a multiparadigm programming language. That is, it supports several fundamental styles of programming (including object-oriented programming) and combinations of those styles. When used well, this leads to cleaner, more flexible, and more efficient libraries than can be provided using just one paradigm. The C++ standard library containers and algorithms, which is basically a generic programming framework, is an example. When used together with (object-oriented) class hierarchies, the result is an unsurpassed combination of type safety, efficiency, and flexibility.

Its incubation in the AT&T development environment. AT&T Bell Labs provided an environment that was crucial for C++'s development. The labs were an exceptionally rich source of challenging problems and a uniquely supportive environment for practical research. C++ emerged from the same research lab as C did and benefited from the same intellectual tradition, experience, and exceptional people. Throughout, AT&T supported the standardization of C++. However, C++ was not the beneficiary of a massive marketing campaign, like many modern languages. That's simply not the way the labs work.

Did I miss anything on your top list? Undoubtedly.

Now, let me paraphrase from the C++ critiques and get your reactions: It's huge/unwieldy. The "hello world" problem is 10 times larger in C++ than in C. C++ is certainly not a small language, but then few modern languages are. If a language is small, you tend to need huge libraries to get work done and often have to rely on conventions and extensions. I prefer to have key parts of the inevitable complexity in the language where it can be seen, taught, and effectively standardized rather than hidden elsewhere in a system. For most purposes, I don't consider C++ unwieldy. The C++ "hello world" program isn't larger than its C equivalent on my machine, and it shouldn't be on yours. In fact, the object code for the C++ version of the "hello world" program is smaller than the C version on my machine. There is no language reason why the one version should be larger than the other. It is all an issue of how the implementor organized the libraries. If one version is significantly larger than the other, report the problem to the implementor of the larger version.

It's tougher to program in C++ (compared with C). (Something the critics say.) Even you once admitted it, saying something about shooting yourself in the foot with C versus C++. Yes, I did say something along the lines of "C makes it easy to shoot yourself in the foot; C++ makes it harder, but when you do, C++ blows your whole leg off." What people tend to miss is that what I said about C++ is to a varying extent true for all powerful languages. As you protect people from simple dangers, they get themselves into new and less obvious problems. Someone who avoids the simple problems may simply be heading for a not-so-simple one. One problem with very supporting and protective environments is that the hard problems may be discovered too late or be too hard to remedy once discovered. Also, a rare problem is harder to find than a frequent one because you don't suspect it.

It's appropriate for embedded systems of today but not for the Internet software of today. C++ is suitable for embedded systems today. It is also suitable—and widely used—for "Internet software" today. For example, have a look at my "C++ applications" Web page. You'll notice that some of the major Web service providers, such as Amazon, Adobe, Google, Quicken, and Microsoft, critically rely on C++. Gaming is a related area in which you find heavy C++ use.

Did I miss another one that you get a lot? Sure.

11.4.1.3 An Example

The following is the specification package for a stack abstract data type:

```
package Stack_Pack is
-- The visible entities, or public interface
  type Stack_Type is limited private;
  Max_Size : constant := 100;
  function Empty(Stk : in Stack_Type) return Boolean;
  procedure Push(Stk : in out Stack_Type;
                 Element : in Integer);
  procedure Pop(Stk : in out Stack_Type);
  function Top(Stk : in Stack_Type) return Integer;
-- The part that is hidden from clients
  private
    type List_Type is array (1..Max_Size) of Integer;
    type Stack_Type is
      record
      List : List_Type;
      Topsub : Integer range 0..Max_Size := 0;
      end record;
  end Stack_Pack;
```

Notice that no create or destroy operations are included, because they are not necessary.

The body package for Stack_Pack is

```
with Ada.Text_IO; use Ada.Text_IO;
package body Stack_Pack is
  function Empty(Stk: in Stack_Type) return Boolean is
    begin
    return Stk.Topsub = 0;
    end Empty;

  procedure Push(Stk : in out Stack_Type;
     Element : in Integer) is
    begin
    if Stk.Topsub >= Max_Size then
      Put_Line("ERROR - Stack overflow");
    else
      Stk.Topsub := Stk.Topsub + 1;
      Stk.List(Topsub) := Element;
    end if;
  end Push;
```

```ada
   procedure Pop(Stk : in out Stack_Type) is
     begin
     if Stk.Topsub = 0
       then Put_Line("ERROR - Stack underflow");
       else Stk.Topsub := Stk.Topsub - 1;
     end if;
     end Pop;

   function Top(Stk : in Stack_Type) return Integer is
     begin
     if Stk.Topsub = 0
       then Put_Line("ERROR - Stack is empty");
       else return Stk.List(Stk.Topsub);
     end if;
     end Top;
   end Stack_Pack;
```

The first line of the code of this body package contains two clauses: a **with** and a **use**. The **with** clause makes the names defined in external packages visible; in this case Ada.Text_IO, which provides functions for input and output of text. The **use** clause eliminates the need for explicit qualification of the references to entities from the named package. The issues of access to external encapsulations and name qualifications are further discussed in Section 11.6.

The body package must have subprogram definitions with headings that match the subprogram headings in the associated specification package. The specification package promises that these subprograms will be defined in the associated body package.

The following procedure, Use_Stacks, is a client of package Stack_Pack. It illustrates how the package might be used.

```ada
with Stack_Pack;
use Stack_Pack;
procedure Use_Stacks is
  Topone : Integer;
  Stack : Stack_Type;    -- Creates a Stack_Type object
  begin
  Push(Stack, 42);
  Push(Stack, 17);
  Topone := Top(Stack);
  Pop(Stack);
  ...
  end Use_Stacks;
```

A stack is a silly example for most contemporary languages, because support for stacks is included in their standard class libraries. However, stacks provide a simple example we can use to allow comparisons of the languages discussed in this section.

11.4.2 Abstract Data Types in C++

C++ was created by adding features to C. The first important additions were those to support object-oriented programming. Because one of the primary components of object-oriented programming is abstract data types, C++ obviously must support them.

While Ada provides an encapsulation that can be used to simulate abstract data types, C++ provides two constructs that are very similar to each other, the class and the struct, which more directly support abstract data types. Because structs are most commonly used when only data is included, we do not discuss them further here.

C++ classes are types; as stated previously, Ada packages are more generalized encapsulations that can define any number of abstract data types. A program unit that gains visibility to an Ada package can access any of its public entities directly by their names. A C++ program unit that declares an instance of a class can also access any of the public entities in that class, but only through an instance of the class. This is a cleaner and more direct way to provide abstract data types.

11.4.2.1 Encapsulation

The data defined in a C++ class are called **data members;** the functions (methods) defined in a class are called **member functions.** Data members and member functions appear in two categories, class and instance. Class members are associated with the class; instance members are associated with the instances of the class. In this chapter, we discuss only the instance members of a class. All of the instances of a class share a single set of member functions, but each instance gets its own set of the class's data members. Class instances can be either stack-dynamic or heap-dynamic. If stack-dynamic, they are referenced directly with value variables. If heap-dynamic, they are referenced through pointers. Stack-dynamic instances of classes are always created by the elaboration of an object declaration. Furthermore, the lifetime of such a class instance ends when the end of the scope of its declaration is reached. Heap-dynamic class objects are created with the **new** operator and destroyed with the **delete** operator. Both stack- and heap-dynamic classes can have pointer data members that reference heap-dynamic data, so that even though a class instance is stack-dynamic, it can include data members that reference heap-dynamic data.

A member function of a class can be defined in two distinct ways: The complete definition can appear in the class, or only its header. When both the header and the body of a member function appear in the class definition, the member function is implicitly inlined. Recall that this means that its code is placed in the caller's code, rather than requiring the usual call and return linkage process. If only the header of a member function appears in the class definition, its complete definition appears outside the class and is separately compiled. The rationale for allowing member functions to be inlined was to save linkage time in real-time applications, in which run-time efficiency is of utmost importance. The downside of inlining member functions is that it clutters the class definition interface, resulting in a reduction in readability.

11.4.2.2 Information Hiding

A C++ class can contain both hidden and visible entities (meaning they are either hidden from or visible to clients of the class). Entities that are to be hidden are placed in a **private** clause, and visible, or public, entities appear in a **public** clause. The **public** clause therefore describes the interface to class objects. There is also a third category of visibility, **protected**, which is discussed in the context of inheritance in Chapter 12.

C++ allows the user to include **constructor** functions in class definitions, which are used to initialize the data members of newly created objects. A constructor may also allocate the heap-dynamic data that are referenced by the pointer members of the new object. Constructors are implicitly called when an object of the class type is created. A constructor has the same name as the class whose objects it initializes. Constructors can be overloaded, but of course each constructor of a class must have a unique parameter profile.

A C++ class can also include a function called a **destructor,** which is implicitly called when the lifetime of an instance of the class ends. As stated earlier, stack-dynamic class instances can contain pointer members that reference heap-dynamic data. The destructor function for such an instance can include a **delete** operator on the pointer members to deallocate the heap space they reference. Destructors are often used as a debugging aid, in which case they simply display or print the values of some or all of the object's data members before those members are deallocated. The name of a destructor is the class's name, preceded by a tilde (~).

Neither constructors nor destructors have return types, and neither use **return** statements. Both constructors and destructors can be explicitly called.

11.4.2.3 An Example

Our example of a C++ abstract data type is, once again, a stack:

```
#include <iostream.h>
class stack {
  private:  //** These members are visible only to other
            //** members and friends (see Section 11.6.4)
    int *stackPtr;
    int maxLen;
    int topPtr;
  public:   //** These members are visible to clients
    stack() {   //** A constructor
      stackPtr = new int [100];
```

```
      maxLen = 99;
      topPtr = -1;
    }
    ~stack() {delete [] stackPtr;};  //** A destructor
    void push(int number) {
      if (topPtr == maxLen)
        cerr << "Error in push--stack is full\n";
      else stackPtr[++topPtr] = number;
    }
    void pop() {
      if (topPtr == -1)
        cerr << "Error in pop--stack is empty\n";
      else topPtr--;
    }
    int top() {return (stackPtr[topPtr]);}
    int empty() {return (topPtr == -1);}
}
```

We discuss only a few aspects of this class definition, because it is not necessary to understand all of the details of the code. Objects of the stack class are stack-dynamic but include a pointer that references heap-dynamic data. The stack class has three data members—stackPtr, maxLen, and topPtr—all of which are private. stackPtr is used to reference the heap-dynamic data, which is the array that implements the stack. The class also has four public member functions—push, pop, top, and empty—as well as a constructor and a destructor. The constructor uses the **new** operator to allocate an array of 100 **int** elements from the heap. It also initializes maxLen and topPtr. The purpose of the destructor function is to deallocate the storage for the array used to implement the stack when the lifetime of a stack object ends. This array was allocated by the constructor. Because the bodies of the member functions are included, they are all implicitly inlined.

An example program that uses the stack abstract data type is

```
void main() {
  int topOne;
  stack stk;  //** Creates an instance of the stack class
  stk.push(42);
  stk.push(17);
  topOne = stk.top();
  stk.pop();
  ...
}
```

11.4.2.4 Evaluation

C++ support for abstract data types, through its class construct, is similar in expressive power to that of Ada, through its packages. Both provide effective mechanisms for encapsulation and information hiding of abstract data types. The primary difference is that classes are types, whereas Ada packages are more general encapsulations. Furthermore, the class construct was designed for more than data abstraction, as discussed in Chapter 12.

11.4.3   Abstract Data Types in Java

Java support for abstract data types is similar to that of C++. There are, however, a few important differences. All user-defined data types in Java are classes (Java does not include structs), and all objects are allocated from the heap and accessed through reference variables. Another difference is that methods in Java must be defined completely in a class. A method body must appear with its corresponding method header. Therefore, a Java abstract data type is both declared and defined in a single syntactic unit. A Java compiler can inline any method that is not overriden. Definitions are hidden from clients by making them private.

Rather than having private and public clauses in its class definitions, in Java access modifiers can be attached to method and variable definitions.

The following is a Java class definition for our stack example:

```java
import java.io.*;
class StackClass {
  private int [] stackRef;
  private int maxLen,
             topIndex;
  public StackClass() {  // A constructor
    stackRef = new int [100];
    maxLen = 99;
    topIndex = -1;
  }
  public void push(int number) {
    if (topIndex == maxLen)
      System.out.println("Error in push—stack is full");
    else stackRef[++topIndex] = number;
  }
  public void pop() {
    if (topIndex == -1)
      System.out.println("Error in pop—stack is empty");
    else --topIndex;
  }
  public int top() {return (stackRef[topIndex]);}
  public boolean empty() {return (topIndex == -1);}
}
```

An example class that uses `StackClass` follows:

```java
public class TstStack {
  public static void main(String[] args) {
    StackClass myStack = new StackClass();
    myStack.push(42);
    myStack.push(29);
    System.out.println("29 is: " + myStack.top());
    myStack.pop();
    System.out.println("42 is: " + myStack.top());
    myStack.pop();
    myStack.pop();  // Produces an error message
  }
}
```

One obvious difference is the lack of a destructor in the Java version, obviated by Java's implicit garbage collection.

Our example does not illustrate many of the important differences between the support for abstract data types of C++ and that of Java. However, as will be discussed in Section 11.6, there are more differences between the multiple type encapsulations of C++ and those of Java. Furthermore, when considering the other aspects of object-oriented programming, as is done in Chapter 12, many more differences between Java's classes and those of C++ will be discussed.

11.4.4 Abstract Data Types in C#

Recall that C# is based on both C++ and Java, and that it also includes some new constructs.

C# uses the **private, public,** and **protected**[1] access modifiers exactly as they are used in Java. However, it includes two modifiers that Java does not have, **internal** and **protected internal.** The **internal** modifier is described in Section 11.6, where generalized encapsulations are discussed.

Also like Java, all C# class instances are heap-dynamic. Default constructors, which provide initial values for instance data, are predefined for all classes. These constructors provide typical initial values, such as 0 for **int** types and **false** for **boolean** type. A user can furnish a constructor for any class he or she defines. Such a constructor can assign initial values to some or all of the instance data of the class. Any instance variable that is not initialized in a user-defined constructor is assigned a value by the default constructor.

Because C# uses garbage collection for most of its heap objects, destructors are rarely used.

---

1. The **protected** access modifier is discussed in Chapter 12.

Although the principles of abstract data types dictate that data members of objects should be hidden from clients, many situations arise in which clients must access these data members. The common solution is to provide accessor methods, getters and setters, that allow clients indirect access to the so-called hidden data—a better solution than simply making the data public, which would provide direct access. The reasons accessors are better are as follows:

1. Read-only access can be provided, by having a getter method but no corresponding setter method.

2. Constraints can be included in setters. For example, if the data value should be restricted to a particular range, the setter can enforce that.

3. The actual implementation of the data member can be changed without affecting the clients if getters and setters are the only access.

C# provides properties, which it inherited from Delphi, as a way of implementing getters and setters without requiring explicit method calls. Properties provide implicit access to specific private instance data. For example, consider the following simple class and client code:

```csharp
public class Weather {
  public int DegreeDays {  //** DegreeDays is a property
    get {
      return degreeDays;
    }
    set {
      if(value < 0 || value > 30)
        Console.WriteLine(
            "Value is out of range: {0}", value);
      else
        degreeDays = value;
    }
  }
  private int degreeDays;
  ...
  }
...
Weather w = new Weather();
int degreeDaysToday, oldDegreeDays;
...
w.DegreeDays = degreeDaysToday;
...
oldDegreeDays = w.DegreeDays;
```

In the class Weather, the property DegreeDays is defined. This property provides a getter method and a setter method for access to the private data member, degreeDays. In the client code following the class definition, degreeDays is treated as if it were a public-member variable, although access to it is available only through the property. Notice the use of the implicit variable **value** in the setter method. This is the mechanism by which the new value of the property is referenced.

As mentioned in Section 11.4.2, C++ includes both classes and structs, which are nearly identical constructs. The only difference is that the default access modifier for class is **private**, whereas for structs it is **public**. C# also has structs, but they are very different from those of C++. In C#, structs are in a sense lightweight classes. They can have constructors, properties, methods, and data fields, and can implement interfaces, but do not support inheritance. One other fundamental difference between structs and classes in C# is that structs are value types, as opposed to reference types. They are allocated on the run-time stack, rather than the heap. If they are passed as parameters, they are passed by value. All C# value types, including all of its primitive types, are actually structs. Although it seems odd, struct objects are created with the same **new** operator used to create class objects.

Structs are used in C# primarily to implement relatively small simple types that need never be base types for inheritance. They are also used when it is convenient for the objects of the type to be stack- as opposed to heap-allocated.

11.4.5 Abstract Data Types in Ruby

Ruby provides complete support for abstract data types through its classes. In terms of capabilities, Ruby classes are similar to those in C++ and Java.

In Ruby, a class is defined in a compound statement opened with the **class** reserved word. Local variables have names that have the form of the names of variables in other programming languages. The names of instance variables begin with at signs (@). Classes can have class variables (those associated with the class, rather than its instances), whose names must begin with two at signs (@@). Instance methods have the same syntax as functions in Ruby: They begin with the **def** reserved word and are closed with **end.** Class methods are distinguished from instance methods by having the class name appended to the beginning of their names with a period separator. For example, in a class named Stack, a class method's name would begin with Stack. Constructors in Ruby are named initialize. They can be overloaded by defining multiple copies that have different numbers of parameters.

Members of a class can be marked as being private or public, with public being the default.[2] Private and public access in Ruby have the same meanings as they do in Java. All data members must be private to support information hiding.

Classes in Ruby are dynamic in the sense that members can be added at any time. This is done by simply including additional class definitions that specify the new members. Methods can also be removed from a class. This is done by providing another class definition in which the method to be

---

2. Ruby also supports the protected-access mode, as discussed in Chapter 12.

removed is sent to the method `remove_method` as a parameter. The dynamic classes of Ruby are another example of a language designer trading readability (and as a consequence, reliability) for flexibility. Allowing dynamic changes to classes clearly adds flexibility to the language, while harming readability. To determine the current definition of a class, one must find all of its definitions in the program and consider all of them.

Following is the stack example written in Ruby:

```ruby
# Stack.rb - defines and tests a stack of maximum length
#            100, implemented in an array

class StackClass

# Constructor

  def initialize
    @stackRef = Array.new
    @maxLen = 100
    @topIndex = -1
  end

# push method

  def push(number)
    if @topIndex =- @maxLen
      puts "Error in push - stack is full"
    else
      @topIndex = @topIndex + 1
      @stackRef[@topIndex] = number
    end
  end

# pop method

  def pop
    if @topIndex == -1
      puts "Error in pop - stack is empty"
    else
      @topIndex = @topIndex - 1
    end
  end

# top method

  def top
    @stackRef[@topIndex]
```

```ruby
    end
# empty method
  def empty
    @topIndex == -1
  end
end   # of Stack class

# Test code for StackClass

myStack = StackClass.new
myStack.push(42)
myStack.push(29)
puts "Top element is (should be 29): #{myStack.top}"
myStack.pop
puts "Top element is (should be 42): #{mystack.top}"
myStack.pop

# The following pop should produce an
#  error message - stack is empty

myStack.pop
```

Recall that the notation #{variable} converts the value of the variable to a string, which is then inserted into the string in which it appears. This class defines a stack structure that can store objects of any type. Recall that in Ruby everything is an object and arrays are actually arrays of references to objects. That clearly makes this stack more flexible than the similar examples in Ada, C++, and Java. Furthermore, simply by passing the desired maximum length to the constructor, objects of this class could have any given maximum length. Of course, because arrays in Ruby have dynamic length, the class could be modified to implement stack objects that are not restricted to any length, except that imposed by the machine's memory capacity.

11.5 Parameterized Abstract Data Types

It is often convenient to be able to parameterize abstract data types. For example, we should be able to design a stack abstract data type that can store any scalar type elements rather than be required to write a separate stack abstraction for every different scalar type. In the following four subsections, the capabilities of Ada, C++, Java 5.0, and C# 2005 to construct parameterized abstract data types are discussed.

11.5.1 Ada

Generic procedures in Ada were discussed and illustrated in Chapter 9. Packages can also be generic, so we can construct generic, or parameterized, abstract data types.

The Ada stack abstract data type example shown in Section 11.4.1 suffers two restrictions: (1) Stacks of its type can store only integer type elements, and (2) the stacks can have only up to 100 elements. Both of these restrictions can be eliminated by using a generic package, which can be instantiated for other element types and any desirable size. (This is a generic instantiation, which is very different from the instantiation of a class to create an object.) The following specification package describes the interface of a generic stack abstract data type with these features:

```ada
generic
   Max_Size : Positive;   -- A generic parameter for stack
                          -- size
   type Element_Type is private;   -- A generic parameter
                                   -- for element type
package Generic_Stack is
-- The visible entities, or public interface
   type Stack_Type is limited private;
   function Empty(Stk : in Stack_Type) return Boolean;
   procedure Push(Stk : in out Stack_Type;
                  Element : in Element_Type);
   procedure Pop(Stk : in out Stack_Type);
   function Top(Stk : in Stack_Type) return Element_Type;
-- The hidden part
private
   type List_Type is array (1..Max_Size) of Element_Type;
   type Stack_Type is
     record
     List : List_Type;
     Topsub : Integer range 0..Max_Size := 0;
     end record;
   end Generic_Stack;
```

The body package for `Generic_Stack` is the same as the body package for `Stack_Pack` in the previous section except that the type of the `Element` formal parameter in `Push` and `Top` is `Element_Type` instead of `Integer`.

The following statement instantiates `Generic_Stack` for a stack of 100 elements of `Integer` type:

```ada
package Integer_Stack is new Generic_Stack(100, Integer);
```

One could also build an abstract data type for a stack of length 500 for `Float` elements, as in

```
package Float_Stack is new Generic_Stack(500, Float);
```

These instantiations build two different source code versions of `Generic_Stack` at compile time.

11.5.2 C++

C++ also supports parameterized, or generic, abstract data types. To make the example C++ stack class of Section 11.4.2 generic in the stack size, only the constructor function needs to be changed, as in

```
stack(int size) {
  stkPtr = new int [size];
  maxLen = size - 1;
  top = -1;
}
```

The declaration for a stack object now may appear as

```
stack stk(150);
```

The class definition for `stack` can include both constructors, so users can use the default-size stack or specify some other size.

The element type of the stack can be made generic by making the class a templated class. Then the element type can be a template parameter. The definition of the templated class for a stack type is

```
#include <iostream.h>
template <class Type>  // Type is the template parameter
class stack {
  private:
    Type *stackPtr;
    int maxLen;
    int topPtr;
  public:
// A constructor for 100 element stacks
    stack() {
      stackPtr = new Type [100];
      maxLen = 99;
      topPtr = -1;
    }
// A constructor for a given number of elements
    stack(int size) {
```

```
      stackPtr = new Type [size];
      maxLen = size - 1;
      topPtr = -1;
    }
    ~stack() {delete stackPtr;};   // A destructor
    void push(Type number) {
      if (topPtr == maxLen)
        cout << "Error in push—stack is full\n";
      else stackPtr[++ topPtr] = number;
    }
    void pop() {
      if (topPtr == -1)
        cout << "Error in pop—stack is empty\n";
      else topPtr --;
    }
    Type top() {return (stackPtr[topPtr]);}
    int empty() {return (topPtr == -1);}
}
```

As in Ada, C++ templated classes are instantiated at compile time. The difference is that in C++ the instantiations are implicit: A new instantiation is created whenever an object is created that requires a version of the templated class that does not yet exist.

11.5.3 Java 5.0

Java 5.0 supports a form of parameterized abstract data types in which the generic parameters must be classes. Recall that these are briefly discussed in Chapter 9.

The most common generic types are collection types, such as LinkedList and ArrayList, which were in the Java class library before support for generics appeared. The collection types store Object class objects, so they can store any objects (but not primitive types). Therefore, the collection types have always been able to store multiple types (as long as they are classes). There were three issues with this: First, every time an object is removed from the collection, it must be cast to the appropriate type. Second, there is no error checking when elements are added to the collection. This means that once the collection is created, objects of any class can be added to the collection. Third, the collection types cannot store primitive types. So, to store **int** values in an ArrayList, the value first must be put in an Integer class object. For example, consider the following code:

```
ArrayList myArray = new ArrayList(); //* Create an ArrayList
myArray.add(0, new Integer(47));       //* Create an element
Integer myInt = (Integer)myArray.get(0); //* Get first object
```

In Java 5.0, the collection classes, the most commonly used of which are `List`, `ArrayList,` and `Queue`, became generic classes. Such classes are instantiated by calling **new** on the class constructor and passing it the generic parameter in pointed brackets. For example, the `ArrayList` class can be instantiated to store `Integer` objects with the following statement:

```
ArrayList <Integer> myArray = new ArrayList <Integer>();
```

This new class overcomes two of the problems with pre–Java 5.0 collections. Only `Integer` objects can be put into the `myArray` collection. Furthermore, there is no need to cast an object being removed from the collection. However, it is still not possible to instantiate a generic collection that stores primitive values.

Recall from Chapter 9 that Java 5.0 supports wildcard classes. For example, `Collection <?>` is a wildcard class for all collection classes. This allows method to be written that can accept any collection type as a parameter. Because a collection can itself be generic, the `Collection <?>` class is in a sense a generic of a generic class.

Some care must be taken with objects of the wildcard type. For example, because the components of a particular object of this type have a type, other type objects cannot be added to the collection. For example, consider

```
Collection<?> c = new ArrayList<String>();
```

It would be illegal to use the `add` method to put something into this collection unless its type were `String`.

Users can define generic classes in Java 5.0. This is a straightforward process and the resulting classes behave exactly like the predefined generic classes.

11.5.4   C# 2005

As was the case with Java, the first version of C# defined collection classes that stored objects of any class. These were `ArrayList`, `Stack`, and `Queue`. These classes had the same problems as the collection classes of pre-5.0 Java.

Generic classes were added to C# in its 2005 version. The five predefined generic collections are `Array`, `List`, `Stack`, `Queue`, and `Dictionary` (the `Dictionary` class implements hashes). Exactly as in Java 5.0, these classes eliminate the problems of allowing mixed types in collections and requiring casts when objects are removed from the collections.

As with Java 5.0, users can define generic classes in C# 2005. One capability of the user-defined C# generic collections is that any of them can be defined to allow their elements to be indexed (accessed through subscripting). Although the indexes are usually integers, an alternative is to use strings as indexes.

One capability that Java 5.0 provides that C# 2005 does not is wildcard classes.

11.6 Encapsulation Constructs

The first five sections of this chapter discuss abstract data types, which are minimal encapsulations.[3] This section describes the multiple-type encapsulations that are needed for larger programs.

11.6.1 Introduction

When the size of a program reaches beyond a few thousand lines, two practical problems become evident. From the programmer's point of view, having such a program appear as a single collection of subprograms or abstract data type definitions does not impose an adequate level of organization on the program to keep it intellectually manageable. The second practical problem for larger programs is recompilation. For relatively small programs, recompiling the whole program after each modification is not costly. But for large programs, the cost of recompilation is significant. So there is an obvious need to find ways to avoid recompilation of the parts of a program that are not affected by a change. The obvious solution to both of these problems is to organize programs into collections of logically related code and data, each of which can be compiled without recompilation of the rest of the program. An **encapsulation** is such a collection.

Encapsulations are often placed in libraries and made available for reuse in programs other than those for which they were written. People have been writing programs with more than a few thousand lines for at least the last 40 years, so techniques for providing encapsulations have been evolving for some time.

11.6.2 Nested Subprograms

In languages that allow nested subprograms, programs can be organized by nesting subprogram definitions inside the logically larger subprograms that use them. This can be done in Ada, Fortran 95, Python, and Ruby. As discussed in Chapter 5, however, this method of organizing programs, which uses static scoping, is far from ideal. Therefore, even in languages that allow nested subprograms, they are not used as a primary organizing encapsulation construct.

---

3. In the case of Ada, the package encapsulation can be used for single types, and also for multiple types.

11.6.3 Encapsulation in C

C does not provide strong support for abstract data types, although both abstract data types and multiple-type encapsulations can be simulated.

In C, a collection of related functions and data definitions can be placed in a file, which can be independently compiled. Such a file, which acts as a library, has an implementation of its entities. The interface to such a file, including data, type, and function declarations, is placed in a separate file called a **header file.** Type representations can be hidden by defining them as pointers to struct types in the header file. The complete definitions of such struct types need only appear in the implementation file. This approach has the same drawbacks as the use of pointers as abstract data types in Ada packages, namely, the inherent problems of pointers and the potential confusion with assignment and comparisons of pointers.

The header file, in source form, and the compiled version of the implementation file are furnished to clients. When such a library is used, the header file is included in the client code, using an #include preprocessor specification, so that references to functions and data in the client code can be type checked. The #include specification also documents the fact that the client program depends on the library implementation file. This approach effectively separates the specification and implementation of an encapsulation.

Although these encapsulations work, they create some insecurities. For example, a user could simply cut and paste the definitions from the header file into the client program, rather than using #include. This would work, because #include simply copies the contents of its operand file into the file in which the #include appears. However, there are two problems with this approach. First, the documentation of the dependence of the client program on the library (and its header file) is lost. Second, the author of the library could change the header file and the implementation file, but the client could attempt to use the new implementation file (without ever knowing it had changed) but the old header file, which the user had copied into his or her client program. For example, a variable x could have been defined to be **int** type in the old header file, which the client code still uses, although the implementation code has been recompiled with the new header file, which defines x to be **float.** So, the implementation code was compiled with x as an **int** and the client code was compiled with x as a **float.** The linker does not detect this error.

Thus it is the user's responsibility to ensure that both the header and implementation files are up-to-date. This is often done with a make utility.

11.6.4 Encapsulation in C++

Encapsulation in C++ is similar to that of C. Header files are used to provide the interface to the resources of the encapsulation. In fact, because of the complex interplay of C++ templates and separate compilation, the header files of C++ template libraries often include complete definitions of resources, rather than just data declarations and subprogram protocols; this is due in part to the use of the C linker for C++ programs.

One language design problem that results from having classes but no generalized encapsulation construct is that it is not always natural to associate object operations with single objects. For example, suppose we have an abstract data type for matrices and one for vectors, and need a multiplication operation between a vector and a matrix. The multiplication code must have access to the data members of both the vector and the matrix classes, but neither of those classes is the natural home for the code. Furthermore, regardless of which is chosen, access to the members of the other is a problem. In C++, these kinds of situations can be handled by allowing nonmember functions to be "friends" of a class. Friend functions have access to the private entities of the class where they are declared to be friends. For the matrix/vector multiplication operation, one C++ solution is to define the operation outside both the matrix and the vector classes, but define it to be a friend of both. The following skeletal code illustrates this scenario:

```
class Matrix;  //** A class declaration
class Vector {
  friend Vector multiply(const Matrix&, const Vector&);
  ...
};
class Matrix {  //** The class definition
  friend Vector multiply(const Matrix&, const Vector&);
  ...
};
//** The function that uses both Matrix and Vector objects
Vector multiply(const Matrix& m1, const Vector& v1) {
  ...
}
```

In addition to functions, whole classes can be defined to be friends of a class; then all the private members of the class are visible to all of the members of the friend class.

11.6.5 Ada Packages

Ada specification packages can include any number of data and subprogram declarations in their public and private sections. Therefore, they can include interfaces for any number of abstract data types, as well as any other program resources. So, the package is a multiple-type encapsulation construct.

Ada packages can be compiled separately. The two package parts, specification and body, can also be compiled separately if the specification package is compiled first. An entire program that uses any number of external packages can be compiled separately, as long as the specifications of all of the used packages have been compiled. The bodies of the used packages can be compiled after the client program.

Consider the situation described in Section 11.6.4 of the vector and matrix types and the need for methods with access to the private parts of both, which is handled in C++ with friend functions. In Ada, both the matrix and the vector types could be defined in a single Ada package, which obviates the need for friend functions.

11.6.6 C# Assemblies

C# includes a larger encapsulation construct than the class. In this case, the construct is the one used by all of the .NET programming languages: the assembly. An **assembly** is a collection of one or more files that appears to application programs to be a single dynamic link library or an executable (EXE). Each file defines a module, which can be separately developed. A **dynamic link library** (DLL) is a collection of classes and methods that are individually linked to an executing program when needed during execution. Therefore, although a program has access to all of the resources in a particular DLL, only the parts that are actually used are ever loaded and linked to the program. DLLs have been part of the Windows programming environment since Windows first appeared. In addition to the object code for its resources, a .NET assembly includes a manifest, which has type definitions for every class it contains, definitions of other resources of the assembly, a list of all assemblies referenced in the assembly, and an assembly version number.

In the .NET world, the assembly is the basic unit of deployment of software. Assemblies can be private, in which case they are available to just one application, or public, which means any application can use them.

As mentioned previously, C# has an access modifier, `internal`. An `internal` member of a class is visible to all classes in the assembly in which it appears.

Because an assembly is a self-contained executable unit, it can have only one entry point.

11.7 Naming Encapsulations

We have considered encapsulations to be syntactic containers for logically related software resources—in particular, abstract data types. The purpose of these encapsulations is to provide a way to organize programs into logical units for compilation. This step allows parts of programs to be recompiled after isolated changes. There is another kind of encapsulation that is necessary for constructing large programs: a naming encapsulation.

A large program may be written by many developers, working somewhat independently, perhaps even in different geographic locations. This requires the logical units of the program to be independent, while still able to work together. It also creates a naming problem: How can independently working developers create names for their variables, methods, and classes without accidentally using names already in use by some other programmer developing a different part of the same software system?

Libraries are the origin of the same kind of naming problems. Over the past two decades, large software systems have become progressively more dependent on libraries of supporting software. Nearly all software written in contemporary programming languages requires the use of large and complex standard libraries, in addition to application-specific libraries. This widespread use of multiple libraries has necessitated new mechanisms for managing names. For example, when a developer adds new names to an existing library or creates a new library, he or she must not use a new name that conflicts with a name already defined in a client's application program or in some other library. Without some linguistic assistance, this is virtually impossible, because there is no way for the library author to know what names a client's program uses or what names are defined by the other libraries the client program might use.

Naming encapsulations define name scopes that assist in avoiding these name conflicts. Each library can create its own naming encapsulation to prevent its names from conflicting with the names defined in other libraries or in client code. Each logical part of a software system can create a naming encapsulation with the same purpose.

Naming encapsulations are logical encapsulations, in the sense that they need not be contiguous. Several different collections of code can be placed in the same namespace, even though they are stored in different places. In the following discussion, we briefly describe the uses of naming encapsulations in C++, Java, Ada, and Ruby.

11.7.1 C++ Namespaces

C++ includes a specification, **namespace,** that helps programs manage the problem of global namespaces. One can place each library in its own namespace and qualify the names in the program with the name of the namespace when they are used outside that namespace. For example, suppose there is an abstract data type header file that implements stacks. If there is concern that some other library file may define a name that is used in the stack abstract data type, the file that defines the stack could be placed in its own namespace. This is done by placing all of the declarations for the stack in a namespace block, as in

```
namespace MyStack {
  // Stack declarations
}
```

The implementation file for the stack abstract data type could reference the names declared in the header file with the scope resolution operator, ::, as in

```
MyStack::topPtr
```

The implementation file could also appear in a namespace block specification identical to the one used on the header file, which would make all of the names declared in the header file directly visible. This is definitely simpler, but slightly less readable, because it is less obvious where a specific name in the implementation file is declared.

Client code can gain access to the names in the namespace of the header file of a library in three different ways. One way is to qualify the names from the library with with the name of the namespace. For example, a reference to the variable topPtr could appear as

```
MyStack::topPtr
```

which is exactly the way the implementation code could reference it.

The other two approaches use the **using** directive. This directive can be used to qualify individual names from a namespace, as with

```
using MyStack::topPtr;
```

which makes topPtr visible, but not any other names from the MyStack namespace.

The **using** directive can also be used to qualify all of the names from a namespace, as in the following:

```
using namespace MyStack;
```

Code that includes this directive can directly access the names defined in the namespace, as in

```
p = topPtr;
```

Be aware that namespaces are a complicated feature of C++, and we have mentioned only the simplest part of the story here.

C# includes namespaces that are much like those of C++.

11.7.2   Java Packages

Java includes a naming encapsulation construct: the package. Packages can contain more than one class definition, and the classes in a package are partial friends of one another. *Partial* here means that the entities defined in a class in a package that either are public or protected (see Chapter 12) or have no access specifier are visible to all other classes in the package. A package can have only one public class definition.

Entities without access modifiers are said to have **package scope,** because they are visible throughout the package. Java therefore has less need for explicit friend declarations and does not include the friend functions or friend classes of C++.

The resources defined in a file are specified to be in a particular package with a package declaration, as in

```
package myStack;
```

The package declaration must appear as the first line of the file. The resources of every file that does not include a package declaration are implicitly placed in the same unnamed package.

The clients of a package can reference the names defined in the package using fully qualified names. For example, if the package myStack defines a variable named topPtr, that variable can be referenced in a client of myStack as myStack.topPtr. Because this procedure can quickly become cumbersome when packages are nested, Java provides the **import** declaration, which allows shorter references to names defined in a package. For example, suppose the client includes the following:

```
import myStack.*;
```

Now, the variable topPtr, as well as other names defined in the myStack package, can be referenced by just their names. To access only one name from the package, the specific name can be given on the import declaration, as in

```
import myStack.topPtr;
```

Note that Java's **import** is only an abbreviation mechanism. No otherwise hidden external resources are made available with **import.** In fact, in Java nothing is implicitly hidden if it can be found by the compiler or class loader (using the package name and the CLASSPATH environment variable).

Java's **import** documents the dependencies of the package in which it appears on the packages named in the **import.** These dependencies are less obvious when **import** is not used.

11.7.3 Ada Packages

Ada packages, which often contain libraries, are defined in hierarchies, which correspond to file hierarchies. For example, if subPack is a package defined as a child of the package pack, the subPack code file would appear in a subdirectory of the directory that stored the pack package. The standard class libraries of Java are also defined in a hierarchy of packages, and are stored in a corresponding hierarchy of directories.

As discussed in Section 11.4.1, packages also define namespaces. Visibility to a package from a program unit is gained with the **with** clause. For example,

```
with Ada.Text_IO;
```

makes the resources and namespace of the package `Ada.Text_IO` available. Access to the names defined in the namespace of `Ada.Text_IO` must be qualified. For example, the `Put` procedure from `Ada.Text_IO` must be accessed as

```
Ada.Text_IO.Put
```

To access the names in `Ada.Text_IO` without qualification, the **use** clause can be used, as in

```
use Ada.Text_IO;
```

With this clause, the `Put` procedure from `Ada.Text_IO` can be accessed simply as `Put`. Ada's **use** is closely related to Java's **import**.

11.7.4 Ruby Modules

Ruby classes serve as namespace encapsulations, as do the classes of other languages that support object-oriented programming. Ruby has an additional naming encapsulation, called a *module*. Modules typically define collections of methods and constants. So, modules are convenient for encapsulating libraries of related methods and constants, whose names are in a separate namespace so there are no name conflicts with other names in a program that uses the module. Modules are unlike classes in that they cannot be instantiated or subclassed and do not define variables. Methods that are defined in a module include the module's name in their names. For example, consider the following skeletal module definition:

```
module MyStuff
  PI = 3.114159265
  def MyStuff.mymeth1(p1)
  ...
  end
  def MyStuff.mymeth2(p2)
  ...
  end
end
```

Assuming the `MyStuff` module is stored in its own file, a program that wants to use the constant and methods of `MyStuff` must first gain access to the module. This is done with the `require` method, which takes the file name as a string literal as a parameter. Then the constants and methods of the module can be accessed through the module's name. Consider the following code that uses our example module, `MyStuff`, which is stored in the file named `myStuffMod`:

```
require 'myStuffMod'
...
MyStuff.mymeth1(x)
...
```

Modules are further discussed in Chapter 12.

SUMMARY

The concept of abstract data types and their use in program design was a milestone in the development of programming as an engineering discipline. Although the concept is relatively simple, its use did not become convenient and safe until languages were designed to support it.

The two primary features of abstract data types are the packaging of data objects with their associated operations and information hiding. A language may support abstract data types directly or simulate them with more general encapsulations.

Ada provides encapsulations—packages—that can be used to simulate abstract data types. Packages normally have two parts: a specification, which presents the client interface, and a body, which supplies the implementation of the abstract data type. Data type representations can appear in the specification package but be hidden from clients by putting them in the private clause of the package. The abstract type itself is defined to be private in the public part of the specification package. Private types have built-in operations for assignment and comparison for equality and inequality.

C++ data abstraction is provided by classes. Classes are types, and instances can be either stack- or heap-dynamic. A member function (method) can have its complete definition appear in the class, or have only the protocol given in the class and the definition placed in another file, which can be separately compiled. C++ classes can have three clauses, each prefixed with an access modifier: private, public, or protected. Both constructors and destructors can be given in class definitions. Heap-allocated objects must be explicitly deallocated with **delete.**

Java data abstractions are similar to those of C++, except all Java objects are allocated from the heap and are accessed through reference variables. Also, all objects are garbage collected. Rather than having access modifiers attached to clauses, in Java the modifiers appear on individual declarations (or definitions).

C# supports abstract data types with both classes and structs. Its structs are value types and do not support inheritance. Otherwise, C# classes are similar to those of Java.

Ruby supports abstract data types with its classes. Ruby's classes differ from those of most other languages in that they are dynamic—members can be added, deleted, or changed during execution.

Ada, C++, Java 5.0, and C# 2005 allow their abstract data types to be parameterized; Ada through its generic packages, C++ through its templated classes, and Java 5.0 and C# 2005 with their collection classes.

To support the construction of large programs, some contemporary languages include multiple-type encapsulation constructs, which can contain a collection of logically related types. An encapsulation may also provide access control to its entities. Encapsulations provide the programmer with a method of organizing programs that also facilitates recompilation.

C++, C#, Java, Ada, and Ruby provide naming encapsulations. For Ada and Java, they are named packages; for C++ and C#, they are namespaces; for Ruby, they are modules. Partially because of the availability of packages, Java does not have friend functions or friend classes. In Ada, packages can be used as naming encapsulations.

REVIEW QUESTIONS

1. Define *abstract data type*.
2. What are the advantages of the two parts of the definition of *abstract data type*?
3. What are the language design requirements for a language that supports abstract data types?
4. What are the language design issues for abstract data types?
5. Explain how information hiding is provided in an Ada package.
6. What is the difference between **private** and **limited private** types in Ada?
7. What is in an Ada specification package? What about a body package?
8. What is the fundamental difference between a C++ class and an Ada package?
9. In what different places can the definition of a C++ member function appear?
10. What is the purpose of a C++ constructor?
11. Where are all Java methods defined?
12. How are C++ class objects created?
13. Where are Java class objects created?
14. Why does Java not have destructors?

15. What is a friend function? What is a friend class?

16. What is one reason Java does not have friend functions or friend classes?

17. Why does Java not have destructor methods?

18. Describe the fundamental differences between C# structs and its classes.

19. How is a struct object in C# created?

20. Explain the three reasons accessors to private types are better than making the types public.

21. What are the differences between a C++ struct and a C# struct?

22. Why does Java not need a **use** clause, such as in Ada?

23. What is the name of all Ruby constructors?

24. What is the fundamental difference between the classes of Ruby and those of C++ and Java?

25. How are instances of Ada generic classes created?

26. How are instances of C++ template classes created?

27. Describe the two problems that appear in the construction of large programs that led to the development of encapsulation constructs.

28. What problems can occur using C to define abstract data types?

29. What is a C++ namespace and what is its purpose?

30. Describe the purposes of the **with** and **use** clauses.

31. What is a Java package and what is its purpose?

32. Describe a .NET assembly.

33. What elements can appear in a Ruby module?

PROBLEM SET

1. Some software engineers believe that all imported entities should be qualified by the name of the exporting program unit. Do you agree? Support your answer.

2. Suppose someone designed a stack abstract data type in which the function, `top`, returned an access path (or pointer) rather than returning a copy of the top element. This is not a true data abstraction. Why? Give an example that illustrates the problem.

3. Write an analysis of the similarities of and differences between Java packages and C++ namespaces.

4. What are the disadvantages of designing an abstract data type to be a pointer?

5. Why must the structure of nonpointer abstract data types be given in Ada specification packages?

6. What dangers are avoided in Java by having implicit garbage collection, relative to C++?

7. Discuss the advantages of C# properties, relative to writing accessor methods in C++ or Java.

8. Explain the dangers of C's approach to encapsulation.

9. Why didn't C++ eliminate the problems discussed in Problem 8?

10. Explain why naming encapsulations are important for developing large programs.

11. Describe the three ways a client can reference a name from a namespace in C++.

12. The namespace of the C# standard library, **System**, is not implicitly available to C# programs. Do you think this is a good idea? Defend your answer.

PROGRAMMING EXERCISES

1. Design the example abstract stack type in Fortran using a single subprogram with multiple entries for the type definition and the operations.

2. How does the Fortran implementation of Programming Exercise 1 compare with the Ada implementation in this chapter in terms of reliability and flexibility?

3. Design an abstract data type for a matrix abstraction in a language that you know, including operations for addition, subtraction, and matrix multiplication.

4. Design a queue abstract data type in a language you know, including operations for enqueue, dequeue, and empty.

5. Modify the C++ class for the abstract stack type to use a linked list representation and test it with the same code that appears in this chapter.

6. Write an abstract data type for complex numbers, including operations for addition, subtraction, multiplication, division, extraction of each of the parts of a complex number, and construction of a complex number from two floating-point constants, variables, or expressions. Use Ada, C++, Java, C#, or Ruby.

7. Write an abstract data type for queues whose elements store 10-character names. The queue elements must be dynamically allocated from the heap. Queue operations are enqueue, dequeue, and empty. Use either Ada, C++, Java, C#, or Ruby.

8. Write an abstract data type for a queue whose elements can be any primitive type. Use C++ or Ada.

Support for Object-Oriented Programming

T his chapter begins with a brief introduction to object-oriented programming, followed by an extended discussion of the primary design issues for inheritance and dynamic binding. Next, we discuss the support for object-oriented programming in Smalltalk, C++, Java, C#, Ada 95, and Ruby. Then the object model of JavaScript is briefly described. The chapter concludes with a short overview of the implementation of dynamic bindings of method calls to methods in object-oriented languages.

12.1 Introduction

Languages that support object-oriented programming now are firmly entrenched in the mainstream. From COBOL to LISP, including virtually every language in between, dialects that support object-oriented programming have appeared. C++ and Ada 95 support procedural and data-oriented programming, in addition to object-oriented programming. CLOS, an object-oriented version of LISP (Bobrow et al., 1988), also supports functional programming. Some of the newer languages that were designed to support object-oriented programming do not support other programming paradigms, but still employ some of the basic imperative structures and have the appearance of the older imperative languages. Among these are Java and C#. Ruby is a bit challenging to categorize: It is a pure object-oriented language in the sense that all data are objects, but it is a hybrid language in that one can use it for procedural programming. Finally, there is the pure object-oriented language that is quite unconventional: Smalltalk. Smalltalk was the first language to offer complete support for object-oriented programming. The details of support for object-oriented programming vary widely among languages, and that is the primary topic of this chapter.

This chapter relies heavily on Chapter 11. It is in a sense a continuation of that chapter. This relationship reflects the reality that object-oriented programming is in essence an application of the principle of abstraction to abstract data types. Specifically, in object-oriented programming, the commonality of a collection of similar abstract data types is factored out and put in a new type. The members of the collection inherit these common parts from that new type. This feature is **inheritance,** which is at the center of object-oriented programming and the languages that support it.

12.2 Object-Oriented Programming

12.2.1 Introduction

The concept of **object-oriented programming** has its roots in SIMULA 67 but was not fully developed until the evolution of Smalltalk resulted in Smalltalk 80 (in 1980, of course). Indeed, some consider Smalltalk to be the only purely object-oriented programming language. A language that is object oriented must provide support for three key language features: abstract data types, inheritance, and dynamic binding of method calls to methods. Abstract data types were discussed in detail in Chapter 11, so this chapter focuses on inheritance and dynamic binding.

12.2.2 Inheritance

There has long been pressure on software developers to increase their productivity. This pressure has been intensified by the continuing reduction in the cost of computer hardware. By the middle to late 1980s, it became apparent to many software developers that one of the most promising opportunities for increased productivity in their profession was in software reuse. Abstract data types, with their encapsulation and access controls, are obviously candidates for reuse. The problem with the reuse of abstract data types is that, in nearly all cases, the features and capabilities of the existing type are not quite right for the new use. The old type requires at least some minor modifications. Such modifications can be difficult, for they require the person doing the modification to understand part, if not all, of the existing code. Furthermore, in many cases the modifications require changes to all client programs.

A second problem with programming with abstract data types is that the type definitions are all independent and are at the same level. This design often makes it impossible to organize a program to match the problem space being addressed by the program. In many cases, the underlying problem has categories of objects that are related, both as siblings (being similar to each other) and as parents and children (having a descendant relationship).

Inheritance offers a solution to both the modification problem posed by abstract data type reuse and the program organization problem. If a new abstract data type can inherit the data and functionality of some existing type, and is also allowed to modify some of those entities and add new entities, reuse is greatly facilitated without requiring changes to the reused abstract data type. Programmers can begin with an existing abstract data type and design a modified descendant of it to fit a new problem requirement. Furthermore, inheritance provides a framework for the definition of hierarchies of related classes that can reflect the descendant relationships in the problem space.

The abstract data types in object-oriented languages, following the lead of SIMULA 67, are usually called **classes.** As with instances of abstract data types, class instances are called **objects.** A class that is defined through inheritance from another class is a **derived class** or **subclass.** A class from which the new class is derived is its **parent class** or **superclass.** The subprograms that define the operations on objects of a class are called **methods.** The calls to methods are sometimes called **messages.** The entire collection of methods of an object is called the **message protocol,** or **message interface,** of the object. Computations in an object-oriented program are specified by messages sent from objects to other objects, or in some cases, to classes.

In the simplest case, a derived class inherits all of the entities (variables and methods) of its parent class. This can be complicated by access controls on the entities in a parent class. For example, as we saw in the abstract data type definitions in Chapter 11, some of the entities are classified as public and others as private. These access controls allow the program designer to hide parts of the abstract data type from clients. Derived classes are another kind of client to which access may be granted or withheld. To take this possibility into account, some object-oriented languages include a third category of access control, often called **protected,** that is used to provide access to derived classes while withholding it from clients. The issue of whether all of the entities of a parent class are visible in its subclasses is addressed in more detail in Section 12.3.2.

In addition to inheriting entities from its parent class, a derived class can add new entities and modify inherited methods. A modified method has the same name, and often the same protocol, as the one of which it is a modification. The new method is said to **override** the inherited version, which is then called an **overridden method.** The most common purpose of an overriding method is to provide an operation that is specific for objects of the derived class but is not appropriate for objects of the parent class.

Classes can have two kinds of methods and two kinds of variables. The most commonly used methods and variables are called **instance methods** and **instance variables.** Every object of a class has its own set of instance variables, which store the object's state. The only difference between two objects of the same class is the state of their instance variables. Instance methods operate only on the objects of the class. **Class variables** belong to the class, rather than its object, so there is only one copy for the class. **Class methods** can perform operations on the class, and possibly also on the objects of the class.

If a new class is a subclass of a single parent class, then the derivation process is called **single inheritance.** If a class has more than one parent class, the process is called **multiple inheritance.** When a number of classes are related through single inheritance, their relationships to each other can be shown in a derivation tree. The class relationships in a multiple inheritance can be shown in a derivation graph.

One disadvantage of inheritance as a means of increasing the possibility of reuse is that it creates a dependency among the classes in an inheritance hierarchy. This result works against one of the advantages of abstract data types, which is that they are independent of each other. Of course, not all abstract data types must be completely independent. But in general the independence of abstract data types is one of their strongest positive characteristics. However, it may be difficult, if not impossible, to increase the reusability of abstract data types without creating dependencies among some of them. Furthermore, in many cases the dependencies naturally mirror dependencies in the problem space.

12.2.3   Dynamic Binding

The third characteristic of object-oriented programming languages is a kind of polymorphism provided by the dynamic binding of messages to method definitions. Consider the following situation: There is a base class, A, that defines a method that performs an operation on objects of the base class. A second class, B, is defined as a subclass of A. Objects of this new class need an operation that is like that provided by A, but a bit different because the subclass objects are slightly different. So, the subclass overrides the inherited method. If a client of A and B has a reference or pointer to class A's objects, that reference or pointer also could point at class B's objects, making it a **polymorphic** reference or pointer. If the method, which is defined in both classes, is called through the polymorphic reference or pointer, the run-time system must determine, during execution, which method should be called, A's or B's (by determining which type object is currently referenced by the pointer or reference). An example of dynamic binding in C++ is given in Section 12.5.3.

One purpose of this dynamic binding is to allow software systems to be more easily extended during both development and maintenance. For example, suppose a class defines objects that represent birds and its subclasses define specific birds. Further, suppose that each subclass redefines a method that it inherits from the base class that displays its specific bird. These methods can all be called through a reference or pointer to the base bird class. So, if client code created an array of base-class pointers that referenced objects of the specific bird subclasses and needed to display each bird referenced in the array, the display method for each bird could be called with the same call (in a loop) through the base-class pointers in the array. The advantage of this for maintenance is that adding a new subclass (for a bird that is new to the system) would not require a change to the code that called the display methods.

In some cases, the design of an inheritance hierarchy results in one or more classes that are so high in the hierarchy that an instantiation of them would not make sense. For example, suppose a program defined a `building` class and a collection of subclasses for specific types of buildings, for instance, a `French_Gothic`. It probably would not make sense to have an implemented `draw` method in `building`. But because all of its descendant classes should have such an implemented method, the protocol (but not the body) of that method is included in `building`. This method is often called an **abstract method** (*pure virtual method* in C++). A class that includes at least one abstract method is called an **abstract class** (*abstract base class* in C++). Such a class usually cannot be instantiated, because not all of its methods have bodies. Any subclass of an abstract class that is to be instantiated must provide implementations of all of the inherited abstract methods.

12.3 Design Issues for Object-Oriented Languages

A number of issues must be considered when designing the programming language features to support inheritance and dynamic binding. Those that we consider most important are discussed in this section.

12.3.1 The Exclusivity of Objects

A language designer who is totally committed to the object model of computation designs an object system that absorbs all other concepts of type. Everything, from the smallest integer to a complete software system, is an object in this mind-set. The advantage of this choice is the elegance and pure uniformity of the language and its use. The primary disadvantage is that simple operations must be done through the message-passing process, which often makes them slower than similar operations in an imperative model, where single machine instructions implement such simple operations. For example, in Smalltalk, adding 7 to a variable named x is accomplished by sending the object 7 as a parameter to the + method of the x object. In this purest model of object-oriented computation, all types are classes. There is no distinction between predefined and user-defined classes. In fact, all classes are treated the same way and all computation is accomplished through message passing.

One alternative to the exclusive use of objects that is common in imperative languages to which support for object-oriented programming has been added is to retain a complete imperative typing model and simply add the object model. This approach results in a larger language whose type structure is confusing to all but expert users.

Another alternative to the exclusive use of objects is to have an imperative-style type structure for the primitive scalar types, but implement all structured types as objects. This choice provides the speed of operations on primitive values that is comparable to those expected in the imperative model. Unfortunately, this alternative also leads to complications in the language. Invariably, nonobject values must be mixed with objects. This creates a need for so-called *wrapper classes* for the nonobject types, so that some commonly needed operations can be sent to objects with nonobject type values. In Section 12.6.1, we will discuss an example of this usage in Java.

12.3.2 Are Subclasses Subtypes?

The issue here is relatively simple: Does an "is-a" relationship hold between a derived class and its parent class? From a purely semantics point of view, if a derived class is-a parent class, then objects of the derived class must expose all of the members that are exposed by objects of the parent class. At a less abstract level, an is-a relationship guarantees that in a client a variable of the derived class type could appear anywhere a variable of the parent class type was legal, without causing a type error. Moreover, the derived class objects must be behaviorally equivalent to the parent class objects.

The subtypes of Ada are examples of this simple form of inheritance for data. For example,

```
subtype Small_Int is Integer range -100..100;
```

Variables of `Small_Int` type have all of the operations of `Integer` variables but can store only a subset of the values possible in `Integer`. Furthermore, every `Small_Int` variable can be used anywhere an `Integer` variable can be used. That is, every `Small_Int` variable is, in a sense, an `Integer` variable.

There are a wide variety of ways in which a subclass could differ from its base or parent class. For example, the subclass could have additional methods, it could have fewer methods, the types of some of the parameters could be different in one or more methods, the return type of some method could be different, the number of parameters of some method could be different, or the body of one or more of the methods could be different. Most programming languages severly restrict the ways in which a subclass can differ from its base class. In most cases, the language rules restrict the subclass to be a subtype of its parent class.

As stated previously, a derived class is called a subtype if it has an is-a relationship with its parent class. The characteristics of a subclass that ensure that it is a subtype are as follows: The methods of the subclass that override parent class methods must be type compatible with their corresponding overriden methods. *Compatible* here means that a call to an overriding method can replace any call to the overridden method in any appearance in the client program without causing type errors. That means that every overriding method must have the same number of parameters as the overriden method and the types of the parameters and the return type must be compatible with those of the parent class. Having an identical number of parameters and identical parameter types and return type would, of course, guarantee compliance of a method. Less severe restrictions are possible, however, depending on the type compatibility rules of the language.

Our definition of subtype clearly disallows having public entities in the parent class that are not also public in the subclass. So, the derivation process for subtypes must require that public entities of the parent class are inherited as public entities in the subclass.

It may appear that subtype relationships and inheritance relationships are nearly identical. However, this conjecture is far from correct. An explanation of this incorrect assumption, along with a C++ example, is given in Section 12.5.2.

12.3.3   Type Checking and Polymorphism

In Section 12.2, polymorphism in the object-oriented realm is defined to be the use of a polymorphic pointer or reference to access a method whose name is overridden in the class hierarchy that defines the object to which the pointer or reference is defined to point. The polymorphic variable is the type of the base class, and the base class defines at least the protocol of a method that is overridden by the derived classes. The polymorphic variable can reference objects of the base class and the descendant classes, so the class of the object to which it points cannot always be statically determined. The binding of messages to methods that are sent through polymorphic variables must be dynamic. The issue here is when the type checking of this binding takes place.

This issue is important, for it aligns with the fundamental nature of the programming language. It would be best if this type checking could be statically done, because dynamic type checking costs execution time and delays type error detection. Requiring static type checking forces some important restrictions on the relationship between polymorphic messages and methods.

There are two kinds of type checking that must be done between a message and a method in a strongly typed language: The message's parameter types must be checked against the method's formal parameters, and the return type of the method must be checked against the message's expected type. If these types must match exactly, then an overriding method must have the same number and types of parameters and return type as the overridden method. One relaxation of this rule could be to allow assignment compatibility between actual and formal parameters and between the returned type and the type expected by the message.

The obvious alternative to static type checking is to delay type checking until the polymorphic variable is used to call a method.

12.3.4 Single and Multiple Inheritance

Another simple issue is: Does the language allow multiple inheritance (in addition to single inheritance)? Or maybe it's not so simple. The purpose of multiple inheritance is to allow a new class to inherit from two or more classes.

Because multiple inheritance is sometimes highly useful, why would a language designer not include it? The reasons lie in two categories: complexity and efficiency. The additional complexity is illustrated by several problems. First, note that if a class has two unrelated parent classes and neither defines a name that is defined in the other, there is no problem. However, suppose a subclass named C inherits from both class A and class B and both A and B define an inheritable method named display. If C needs to reference both versions of display, how can that be done? This ambiguity problem is further complicated when the two parent classes both define identically named methods and one or both of them must be overriden in the subclass.

Another issue arises if both A and B are derived from a common parent, Z, and C has both A and B as parent classes. This situation is called **diamond** or **shared** inheritance. In this case, both A and B should include Z's inheritable variables. Suppose Z includes an inheritable variable named sum. The question is whether C should inherit both versions of sum or just one, and if just one, which one? There may be programming situations in which just one of the two should be inherited, and others in which both should be inherited. Section 12.10 includes a brief look at the implementation of these situations. Diamond inheritance is shown in Figure 12.1.

Figure 12.1

An example of diamond inheritance

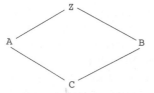

The question of efficiency may be more perceived than real. In C++, for example, supporting multiple inheritance requires just one additional array access and one extra addition operation for each dynamically bound method call, at least with some machine architectures (Stroustrup, 1994, p. 270). Although this operation is required even if the program does not use multiple inheritance, it is a small additional cost.

The use of multiple inheritance can easily lead to complex program organizations. Many who have attempted to use multiple inheritance have found that designing the classes to be used as multiple parents is difficult. Maintenance of systems that use multiple inheritance can be a more serious problem, for multiple inheritance leads to more complex dependencies among classes. It is not clear to some that the benefits of multiple inheritance are worth the added effort to design and maintain a system that uses it.

12.3.5 Allocation and Deallocation of Objects

There are two design questions concerning the allocation and deallocation of objects. The first of these is the place from which objects are allocated. If they behave like the abstract data types, then perhaps they can be allocated from anywhere. This means they could be allocated from the run-time stack, or explicitly created on the heap with an operator or function, such as **new**. If they are all heap-dynamic, there is the advantage of having a uniform method of creation and access through pointer or reference variables. This design simplifies the assignment operation for objects, making it in all cases only a pointer or reference value change. It also allows references to objects to be implicitly dereferenced, simplifying the access syntax.

If objects are stack-dynamic, there is a problem with regard to subtypes. If class B is a child of class A and B is a subtype of A, then an object of B type can be assigned to a variable of A type. For example, if b1 is a variable of B type and a1 is a variable of A type, then

```
a1 = b1;
```

is a legal statement. If a1 and b1 are references to heap-dynamic objects, there is no problem—the assignment is a simple pointer assignment. However, if a1 and b1 are stack-dynamic, then they are value variables in which the value of the object must be copied to the space of the target object. If B adds a data field to what it inherited from A, then a1 will not have sufficient space on the stack for all of b1. The excess will simply be truncated, which could be confusing to programmers who write or use the code.

The second question here is concerned with those cases where objects are allocated from the heap. The question is whether deallocation is implicit or explicit or both. If deallocation is implicit, some implicit method of storage reclamation is required. If deallocation can be explicit, that raises the issue of whether dangling pointers or references can be created.

12.3.6 Dynamic and Static Binding

As we have already discussed, dynamic binding of messages to methods in an inheritance hierarchy is an essential part of object-oriented programming. The question here is whether all binding of messages to methods is dynamic. The alternative is to allow the user to specify whether a specific binding is to be dynamic or static. The advantage of this is that static bindings are faster. So if a binding need not be dynamic, why pay the price?

12.3.7 Nested Classes

One of the primary motivations for nesting class definitions is information hiding. If a new class is needed by only one class, there is no reason to define it so it can be seen by other classes. In this situation, the new class can be nested inside the class that uses it. In some cases, the new class is nested inside a subprogram, rather than directly in another class.

The class in which the new class is nested is called the **nesting class.** The most obvious design issues associated with class nesting are related to visibility. Specifically, one issue is: Which of the facilities of the nesting class are visible in the nested class? The other main issue is the opposite: Which of the facilities of the nested class are visible in the nesting class?

12.4 Support for Object-Oriented Programming in Smalltalk

Many think of Smalltalk as the definitive object-oriented programming language. It was the first language to include complete support for that paradigm. Therefore, it is natural to begin a survey of language support for object-oriented programming with Smalltalk.

12.4.1 General Characteristics

A program in Smalltalk consists entirely of objects, so the concept of an object therefore is truly universal. Virtually everything, from items as simple as the integer constant 2 to a complex file-handling system, is an object. As objects, they are treated uniformly. They all have local memory, inherent processing ability, the capability to communicate with other objects, and the possibility of inheriting methods and instance variables from ancestors.

Messages can be parameterized with variables that reference objects. Replies to messages have the form of objects and are used to return requested information or only to confirm that the requested service has been completed.

All Smalltalk objects are allocated from the heap and are referenced through reference variables, which are implicitly dereferenced. There is no explicit deallocation statement or operation. All deallocation is implicit, using a garbage collection process for storage reclamation.

Unlike hybrid languages such as C++ and Ada 95, Smalltalk was designed for just one software development paradigm—object-oriented. Furthermore, it adopts none of the appearance of the imperative languages. Its purity of purpose is reflected in its simple elegance and uniformity of design.

12.4.2 Type Checking and Polymorphism

The dynamic binding of messages to methods in Smalltalk operates as follows: A message to an object causes the class to which the object belongs to be searched for a corresponding method. If the search fails, it is continued in the superclass of that class, and so forth, up to the system class, Object, which has no superclass. Object is the root of the class derivation tree on which every class is a node. If no method is found anywhere in that chain, an error occurs. It is important to remember that this method search is dynamic—it takes place when the message is sent. Smalltalk does not, under any circumstances, bind messages to methods statically.

The only type checking in Smalltalk is dynamic, and the only type error occurs when a message is sent to an object that has no matching method, either locally or through inheritance. This is a different concept of type checking than that of most other languages. Smalltalk type checking has the simple goal of ensuring that a message matches some method.

Smalltalk variables are not typed; any name can be bound to any object. As a direct result, Smalltalk supports dynamic polymorphism. All Smalltalk code is generic in the sense that the types of the variables are irrelevant, as long as they are consistent. The meaning of an operation (method or operator) on a variable is determined by the class of the object to which the variable is currently bound.

The point of this discussion is that as long as the objects referenced in an expression have methods for the messages of the expression, the types of the objects are irrelevant. This means that no code is tied to a particular type.

12.4.3 Inheritance

A Smalltalk subclass inherits all of the instance variables, instance methods, and class methods of its superclass. The subclass can also have its own instance variables, which must have names that are distinct from the variable names in its ancestor classes. Finally, the subclass can define new methods and redefine methods that already exist in an ancestor class. When a subclass has a method whose name and protocol are the same as an ancestor class, the subclass method hides that of the ancestor class. Access to such a hidden method is provided by prefixing the message with the pseudovariable **super.** The prefix causes the method search to begin in the superclass rather than locally.

Because entities in a parent class cannot be hidden from subclasses, all subclasses are subtypes. An is-a relationship holds between every subclass object and an object of its parent class.

Smalltalk supports single inheritance; it does not allow multiple inheritance.

12.4.4 Evaluation of Smalltalk

Smalltalk is a small language, although the Smalltalk system is large. The syntax of the language is simple and very regular. It is a good example of the power that can be provided by a small language if that language is built around a simple but powerful concept. In the case of Smalltalk, that concept is that all programming can be done employing only a class hierarchy built using inheritance, objects, and message passing.

In comparison with conventional compiled imperative-language programs, equivalent Smalltalk programs are significantly slower. Although it is theoretically interesting that array indexing and loops can be provided within the message-passing model, efficiency is an important factor in the evaluation of programming languages. Therefore, efficiency will clearly be an issue in most discussions of the practical applicability of Smalltalk.

Smalltalk's dynamic binding allows type errors to go undetected until run time. A program can be written and compiled that includes messages to nonexistent methods, which causes a great deal more error repair later in the development than would occur in a static-typed language.

Overall, the design of Smalltalk consistently came down on the side of language elegance and strict adherence to the principles of object-oriented programming support, often without regard for practical matters, in particular execution efficiency. This is most obvious in the exclusive use of objects and the typeless variables.

The Smalltalk user interface has had an important impact on computing: The integrated use of windows, mouse-pointing devices, and pop-up or pull-down menus, all of which first appeared in Smalltalk, dominate contemporary software systems.

Perhaps the greatest impact of Smalltalk is the advancement of object-oriented programming, now the most widely used design and coding methodology.

12.5 Support for Object-Oriented Programming in C++

Chapter 2 describes how C++ evolved from C and SIMULA 67, with the design goal of support for object-oriented programming. C++ classes, as they are used to support abstract data types, are discussed in Chapter 11. C++ support for the other essentials of object-oriented programming is explored in this section. The whole collection of details of C++ classes, inheritance, and dynamic binding is large and complex. This section discusses only the most important among these topics, specifically, those directly related to the design issues described in Section 12.3.

C++ was the first widely used object-oriented programming language, and is still among the most popular. So, naturally, it is the one with which other languages are often compared. For both of these reasons, our coverage of C++ here is more detailed than that of the other example languages discussed in this chapter.

12.5.1 General Characteristics

Because one of the primary design considerations of C++ was that it be backward-compatible with C, it retains the type system of C and adds classes to it. Therefore, C++ has both traditional imperative-language types and the class structure of an object-oriented language. It also supports both methods and functions that are not related to specific classes. This makes it a hybrid language, supporting both procedural programming and object-oriented programming.

The objects of C++ can be static, stack-dynamic, or heap-dynamic. Explicit deallocation using the **delete** operator is required for heap-dynamic objects, because C++ does not include implicit storage reclamation.

All C++ classes include at least one constructor method, which is used to initialize the data members of the new object. Constructor methods are implicitly called when an object is created. If any of the data members are pointers to heap allocated data, the constructor allocates that storage. If no constructor is included in a class definition, the compiler includes a trivial constructor. This default constructor calls the constructor of the parent class, if there is a parent class (see Section 12.5.2).

Many class definitions include a destructor method, which is implicitly called when an object of the class ceases to exist. The destructor is used to delete heap-allocated memory that is referenced by data members. It may also be used to record part or all of the state of the object just before it dies, usually for debugging purposes.

12.5.2 Inheritance

A C++ class can be derived from an existing class, which is then its parent, or base, class. Unlike Smalltalk, a C++ class can also be stand-alone, without a superclass.

On Paradigms and Better Programming

BJARNE STROUSTRUP

Bjarne Stroustrup is the designer and original implementer of C++ and the author of *The C++ Programming Language* and *The Design and Evolution of C++*. His research interests include distributed systems, simulation, design, programming, and programming languages. Dr. Stroustrup is the College of Engineering Professor in Computer Science at Texas A&M University. He is actively involved in the ANSI/ISO standardization of C++. After more than two decades at AT&T, he retains a link with AT&T Labs, doing research as a member of the Information and Software Systems Research Lab. He is an ACM Fellow, an AT&T Bell Laboratories Fellow, and an AT&T Fellow. In 1993, Stroustrup received the ACM Grace Murray Hopper award "for his early work laying the foundations for the C++ programming language. Based on the foundations and Dr. Stroustrup's continuing efforts, C++ has become one of the most influential programming languages in the history of computing."

I. PROGRAMMING PARADIGMS

Your thoughts on the object-oriented paradigm: Its pluses and minuses. Let me first say what I mean by OOP—too many people think that "object-oriented" is simply a synonym for "good." If so, there would be no need for other paradigms. The key to OO is the use of class hierarchies providing polymorphic behavior through some rough equivalent of virtual functions. For proper OO, it is important to avoid directly accessing the data in such a hierarchy and to use only a well-designed functional interface.

In addition to its well-documented strengths, object-oriented programming also has obvious weaknesses. In particular, not every concept naturally fits into a class hierarchy, and the mechanisms supporting object-oriented programming can impose significant overheads compared to alternatives. For many simple abstractions, classes that do not rely on hierarchies and run-time binding provide a simpler and more efficient alternative. Furthermore, where no run-time resolution is needed, generic programming relying on (compile-time) parametric polymorphism is a better behaved and more efficient approach.

So, C++: Is it OO or other? C++ supports several paradigms—including OOP, generic programming, and procedural programming—and combinations of these paradigms define multiparadigm programming as supporting more than one programming style ("paradigm") and combinations of those styles.

Do you have a mini-example of multiparadigm programming? Consider this variant of the classic "collection of shapes" examples (originating from the early days of the first language to support object-oriented programming: Simula67):

```
void draw_all(const vector<Shape*>& vs)
{
    for (int i = 0; i<vs.size(); ++i)
        vs[i]->draw();
}
```

Here, I use the generic container `vector` together with the polymorphic type `Shape`. The `vector` provides static type safety and optimal run-time performance. The `Shape` provides the ability to handle a `Shape` (i.e., any object of a class derived from `Shape`) without recompilation.

We can easily generalize this to any container that meets the C++ standard library requirements:

```
template<class C>
        void draw_all(const C& c)
{
    typedef typename C::
        const_iterator CI;
    for (CP p = c.begin();
        p!=c.end(); ++p)
        (*p)- >draw();
}
```

Using iterators allows us to apply this `draw_all()` to containers that do not support subscripts, such as a standard library list:

```
vector<Shape*> vs;
list<Shape*> ls;
// . . .
draw_all(vs);
draw_all(ls);
```

We can even generalize this further to handle any sequence of elements defined by a pair of iterators:

```
template<class Iterator> void
draw_all(Iterator b, Iterator e)
{
    for_each(b,e,mem_fun(Shape::Draw));
}
```

To simplify the implementation, I used the standard library algorithm `for_each`.

We might call this last version of `draw_all()` for a standard library list and an array:

```
list<Shape*> ls;
Shape* as[100];
// . . .
draw_all(ls.begin(),ls.end());
draw_all(as,as+100);
```

II. SELECTING THE "RIGHT" LANGUAGE FOR THE JOB

How useful is it to have this background in numerous paradigms? Or would it be better to invest time in becoming even more familiar with OO languages rather than learning these other paradigms? It is essential for anyone who wants to be considered a professional in the areas of software to know several languages and several programming paradigms. Currently, C++ is the best language for multi-paradigm programming and a good language for learning various forms of programming. However, it's not a good idea know just C++, let alone to know just a single-paradigm language. That would be a bit like being colorblind or monoglot: You would hardly know what you were missing. Much of the inspiration to good programming comes from having learned and appreciated several programming styles and seen how they can be used in different languages.

Furthermore, I consider programming of any non-trivial program a job for professionals with a solid and broad education, rather than for people with a hurried and narrow "training."

Recall that the data defined in a class definition are called *data members* of that class, and the functions defined in a class definition are called *member functions* of that class (member functions in other languages are often called methods). Some or all of the data member functions and member functions of the base class may be inherited by the derived class, which can also add new data members and member functions and modify inherited member functions.

Recall from Chapter 11 that class members can be private, protected, or public. Private members are accessible only by member functions and friends of the class. Both functions and classes can be declared to be friends of a class and thereby be given access to its private members. Public members are visible everywhere. Protected members are like private members, except in derived classes, whose access is described next. Derived classes can modify accessibility for their inherited members. The syntactic form of a derived class is

class derived_class_name : derivation_mode base_class_name
 {data member and member function declarations}**;**

The derivation_mode can be either **public** or **private**.[1] (Do not confuse public and private derivation with public and private members.) The public and protected members of a base class are also public and protected, respectively, in a public-derived class. In a private-derived class, both the public and protected members of the base class are private. So in a class hierarchy, a private-derived class cuts off access to all members of all ancestor classes to all successor classes, and protected members may or may not be accessible to subsequent subclasses (past the first). Private members of a base class are inherited by a derived class, but they are not visible to the members of that derived class and are therefore of no use there. Consider the following example:

```
class base_class {
  private:
    int a;
    float x;
  protected:
    int b;
    float y;
  public:
    int c;
    float z;
};

class subclass_1 : public base_class { ... };
class subclass_2 : private base_class { ... };
```

---

1. It can also be **protected**, but that option is not discussed here.

In subclass_1, b and y are protected, and c and z are public. In subclass_2, b, y, c, and z are private. No derived class of subclass_2 can have members with access to any member of base_class. The data members a and x in base_class are not accessible in either subclass_1 or subclass_2.

Note that private-derived subclasses cannot be subtypes. For example, if the base class has a public data member, under private derivation that data member would be private in the subclass. Therefore, if an object of the subclass were substituted for an object of the base class, accesses to that data member would be illegal on the subclass object. The is-a relationship would be broken.

Under private class derivation, no member of the parent class is implicitly visible to the instances of the derived class. Any member that must be made visible must be reexported in the derived class. This reexportation in effect exempts a member from being hidden even though the derivation was private. For example, consider the following class definition:

```
class subclass_3 : private base_class {
  base_class :: c;
  ...
}
```

Now, instances of subclass_3 can access c. As far as c is concerned, it is as if the derivation had been public. The double colon (::) in this class definition is a scope resolution operator. It specifies the class where its following entity is defined.

The example in the following paragraphs illustrates the purpose and use of private derivation.

Consider the following example of C++ inheritance, in which a general linked-list class is defined and then used to define two useful subclasses:

```
class single_linked_list {
  private:
    class node {
      public:
        node *link;
        int contents;
    };
    node *head;
  public:
    single_linked_list() {head = 0};
    void insert_at_head(int);
    void insert_at_tail(int);
    int remove_at_head();
    int empty();
};
```

The nested class, node, defines a cell of the linked list to consist of an integer variable and a pointer to a cell. The node class is in the private clause, which hides it from all other classes. Its members are public, however, so they are visible to the nesting class, single_linked_list. If they were private, node would need to declare the nesting class to be a friend to make them visible in the nesting class. Note that nested classes have no special access to members of the nesting class. Only static data members of the nesting class are visible to methods of the nested class.[2]

The enclosing class, single_linked_list, has just a single data member, a pointer to act as the list's header. It contains a constructor function, which simply sets head to the null pointer value. The four member functions allow nodes to be inserted at either end of a list object, nodes to be removed from one end of a list, and lists to be tested for empty.

The following definitions provide stack and queue classes, both based on the single_linked_list class:

```
class stack : public single_linked_list {
  public:
    stack() {}
    void push(int value) {
      single_linked_list :: insert_at_head(value);
    }
    int pop() {
      return single_linked_list :: remove_at_head();
    }
};
class queue : public single_linked_list {
  public:
    queue() {}
    void enqueue(int value) {
      single_linked_list :: insert_at_tail(value);
    }
    int dequeue() {
      single_linked_list :: remove_at_head();
    }
};
```

Note that objects of both the stack and queue subclasses can access the empty function defined in the base class, single_linked_list (because it is a public derivation). Both subclasses define constructor functions that do nothing. When an object of a subclass is created, the proper constructor in the subclass is implicitly called. Then any applicable constructor in the base

---

2. A class can also be defined in a method of a nesting class. The scope rules of such classes are the same as those for classes nested directly in other classes, even for the local variables declared in the method in which they are defined.

class is called. So in our example, when an object of type stack is created, the stack constructor is called, which does nothing. Then the constructor in single_linked_list is called, which does the necessary initialization.

The classes stack and queue both suffer from the same serious problem: Clients of both can access all of the public members of the parent class, single_linked_list. A client of a stack object could call insert_at_tail, thereby destroying the integrity of its stack. Likewise, a client of a queue object could call insert_at_head. These unwanted accesses are allowed because both stack and queue are subtypes of single_linked_list. Public derivation is used where the one wants the subclass to inherit the entire interface of the base class. The alternative is to permit derivation in which the subclass inherits only the implementation of the base class. Our two example derived classes can be written to make them not subtypes of their parent class by using **private**, rather than **public**, derivation.[3] Then both will also need to reexport empty, because it will become hidden to their instances. This situation illustrates the need for the private-derivation option. The new definitions of the stack and queue types, named stack_2 and queue_2, are shown in the following:

```
class stack_2 : private single_linked_list {
  public:
    stack_2() {}
    void push(int value) {
      single_linked_list :: insert_at_head(value);
    }
    int pop() {
      return single_linked_list :: remove_at_head();
    }
    single_linked_list:: empty;
};
class queue_2 : private single_linked_list {
  public:
    queue_2() {}
    void enqueue(int value) {
      single_linked_list :: insert_at_tail(value);
    }
    int dequeue() {
      single_linked_list :: remove_at_head();
    }
    single_linked_list:: empty;
};
```

---

3. They would not be subtypes because the public members of the parent class can be seen in a client, but not in a client of the subclass, where those members are private.

The two versions of stack and queue illustrate the difference between subtypes and derived types that are not subtypes. The linked list is a generalization of both stacks and queues, because both can be implemented as linked lists. So, it is natural to inherit from a linked-list class to define stack and queue classes. However, neither is a subtype of the linked-list class. Rather, the linked list is actually a subtype of the other two.

One of the reasons why friends are necessary is that sometimes a subprogram must be written that can access the members of two different classes. For example, suppose a program uses a class for vectors and one for matrices, and a subprogram is needed to multiply objects of these two classes. In C++, the multiply function is simply made a friend of both classes.

C++ provides multiple inheritance, which allows more than one class to be named as the parent of a new class. For example,

```
class A { ... };
class B { ... };
class C : public A, public B { ... };
```

Class C inherits all of the members of both A and B. If both A and B happen to include members with the same name, they can be unambiguously referenced in objects of class C by using the scope resolution operator (::). Some problems with the C++ implementation of multiple inheritance are discussed in Section 12.10.

Overriding methods in C++ must have exactly the same parameter profile as the overridden method. If there is any difference in the parameter profiles, the method in the subclass is considered a new method that is unrelated to the method with the same name in the ancestor class. The return type of the overriding method either must be the same as that of the overridden method or must be a publicly derived type of the return type of the overridden method.

12.5.3 Dynamic Binding

All of the member functions we have defined thus far are statically bound; that is, a call to one of them is statically bound to a function definition. A C++ object could be manipulated through a value variable, rather than a pointer or a reference. (Such an object would be static or stack-dynamic.) However, in that case the object's type is known and static, so dynamic binding is not needed. On the other hand, a pointer variable that has the type of a base class can be used to point to any heap-dynamic objects of any class publicly derived from that base class, making it a polymorphic variable. Privately derived subclasses are not subtypes. A pointer to a base class cannot be used to reference a method in a subclass that is not a subtype.

C++ does not allow value variables (as opposed to pointers or references) to be polymorphic. When a polymorphic variable is used to call a member function defined in one of the derived classes, the call must be dynamically bound to the correct member function definition. Member functions that must be dynamically bound must be declared to be virtual functions by preceding their headers with the reserved word **virtual,** which can appear only in a class body.

Consider the situation of having a base class named shape, along with a collection of derived classes for different kinds of shapes, such as circles, rectangles, and so forth. If these shapes need to be displayed, then the displaying member function, draw, must be unique for each subclass, or kind of shape. These versions of draw must be defined to be virtual. When a call to draw is made with a pointer to the base class of the derived classes, that call must be dynamically bound to the member function of the correct derived class. The following example has the definitions of the example situation just described:

```
public class shape {
  public:
    virtual void draw() = 0;
  ...
}
public class circle : public shape {
  public:
    void draw() { ... }
  ...
}
public class rectangle : public shape {
  public:
    void draw() { ... }
  ...
}
public class square : public rectangle {
  public:
    void draw() { ... }
  ...
}
```

Given these definitions, the following code has examples of both statically and dynamically bound calls:

```
square* sq = new square;
rectangle* rect = new rectangle;
shape* ptr_shape;
ptr_shape = sq;          // Now ptr_shape points to a
                         //  square object
ptr_shape->draw();       // Dynamically bound to the draw
                         //  in the square class
rect->draw();            // Statically bound to the draw
                         //  in the rectangle class
```

Notice that the draw function in the definition of the base class shape is set to 0. This peculiar syntax is used to indicate that this member function is a **pure virtual function,** meaning that it has no body and it cannot be called. It must be redefined in derived classes if they call the function. The purpose of a pure virtual function is to provide the interface of a function without giving any of its implementation. Pure virtual functions are usually defined when an actual member function in the base class would not be useful. Such a situation was discussed in Section 12.2.3.

Any class that includes a pure virtual function is an **abstract class.** It is illegal to instantiate an abstract class. In a strict sense, an abstract class is one that is used only to represent the characteristics of a type. C++ provides abstract classes to model these truly abstract classes. If a subclass of an abstract class does not redefine a pure virtual function of its parent class, that function remains as a pure virtual function in the subclass and the subclass is also an abstract class.

Abstract classes and inheritance together support a powerful technique for software development. They allow types to be hierarchically defined so that related types can be subclasses of truly abstract types that define their common abstract characteristics.

Dynamic binding allows the code that uses members like draw to be written before all or even any of the versions of draw are written. New derived classes could be added years later, without requiring any change to the code that uses such dynamically bound members. This is a highly useful feature of object-oriented languages.

Reference assignments for stack-dynamic objects are different from pointer assignments for heap-dynamic objects. For example, consider the following code, which uses the same class hierarchy as the last example:

```
square sq;          // Allocate a square object on the stack
rectangle rect;     // Allocate a rectangle object on
                    //   the stack
rect = sq;          // Copies the data member values from
                    //   the square object
rect.draw();        // Calls the draw from the rectangle
                    //   object
```

In the assignment, rect = sq, the member data from the object referenced by sq would be assigned to the data members of the object referenced by rect, but rect would still reference the rectangle object. Therefore, the call to draw through the object referenced by rect would be that of the rectangle class. If rect and sq were pointers to heap-dynamic objects, the same assignment would be a pointer assignment, which would make rect point to the square object, and a call to draw through rect would be bound dynamically to the draw in the square object.

12.5.4 Evaluation

It is natural to compare the object-oriented features of C++ with those of Smalltalk. The inheritance of C++ is more intricate than that of Smalltalk in terms of access control. By using both the access controls within the class definition and the derivation access controls, and also the possibility of friend functions and classes, the C++ programmer has highly detailed control over the access to class members. Furthermore, although there is some debate over its real value, C++ provides multiple inheritance, whereas Smalltalk allows only single inheritance.

In C++, the programmer can specify whether static binding or dynamic binding is to be used. Because static binding is faster, this is an advantage for those situations where dynamic binding is not necessary. Furthermore, even the dynamic binding in C++ is fast when compared with that of Smalltalk. Binding a virtual member function call in C++ to a function definition has a fixed cost, regardless of how distant in the inheritance hierarchy the definition appears. Calls to virtual functions require only five more memory references than statically bound calls (Stroustrup, 1988). In Smalltalk, however, messages are always dynamically bound to methods, and the farther away in the inheritance hierarchy the correct method is, the longer it takes. The disadvantage of allowing the user to decide which bindings are static and which are dynamic is that the original design must include these decisions, which may have to be changed later.

The static type checking of C++ is an advantage over Smalltalk, where all type checking is dynamic. A Smalltalk program can be compiled with messages to nonexistent methods, which are not discovered until the program is executed. A C++ compiler finds such errors. Compiler-detected errors are less expensive to repair than those found in testing.

Smalltalk is essentially typeless, meaning that all code is effectively generic. This provides a great deal of flexibility, but static type checking is sacrificed. C++ provides generic classes through its template facility (as described in Chapter 11), which retains the benefits of static type checking.

The primary advantage of Smalltalk lies in the elegance and simplicity of the language that results from the single philosophy of its design. It is purely and completely devoted to the object-oriented paradigm, devoid of compromises necessitated by the whims of an entrenched user base. C++, on the other hand, is a large and complex language with no single philosophy as its foundation, except to support object-oriented programming and include the C user base. One of its most significant goals was to preserve the efficiency and flavor of C while providing the advantages of object-oriented programming. Some people feel that the features of this language do not always fit well together and that much of the complexity is unnecessary.

According to Chambers and Ungar (1991), Smalltalk ran a particular set of small C-style benchmarks at only 10 percent of the speed of optimized C. C++ programs require only slightly more time than equivalent C programs (Stroustrup, 1988). Given the great efficiency gap between Smalltalk and C++, it is little wonder that the commercial use of C++ is far more widespread than that of Smalltalk. Of course, there are other factors in this difference, but efficiency is clearly a strong argument in favor of C++.

12.6 Support for Object-Oriented Programming in Java

Because Java's design of classes, inheritance, and methods is similar to that of C++, in this section we focus only on those areas in which Java differs from C++.

12.6.1 General Characteristics

As with C++, Java supports both objects and nonobject data. However, in Java only values of the primitive scalar types (Boolean, character, and the numeric types) are not objects. Java's enumerations and arrays are objects. The reason to have nonobjects is efficiency. However, as discussed in Section 12.3.1, having two type systems leads to some cumbersome situations. One of these in Java is that the predefined container classes, such as `ArrayList`, can contain only objects. To put a primitive type value into an `ArrayList`, the value must first be placed in an object. In versions of Java prior to 5.0, this can be done by creating a new object of the wrapper class for the primitive type. Such a class has an instance variable of that primitive type and a constructor that takes a value of the primitive type as a parameter and assigns it to its instance variable. For example, to put `10` into the `ArrayList` object referenced by the variable `myArray`, the following statement could be used:

```
myArray.add(new Integer(10));
```

where `add` is a method of `ArrayList` that inserts a new element and `Integer` is the wrapper class for `int`. Furthermore, when a value is removed from `myArray` and assigned to an `int` variable, it must be cast back to `int` type.

This situation is alleviated in Java 5.0 by the implicit coercion of primitive values when they are put in object context, such as being sent as a parameter to the `add` method of `ArrayList`. This coercion converts the primitive value to an object of the wrapper class of the primitive value's type. For example, putting an `int` value or variable into object context causes the creation of an `Integer` object with the value of the `int` primitive. This coercion is called **boxing**. For example, in Java 5.0, the following is legal

```
myArray.add(10);
```

The compiler furnishes the boxing of the `int` value to an `Integer` object.

In addition to the boxing, when an element is removed from `myArray` and assigned to an `int` variable, it is implicitly cast to `int`.

Whereas C++ classes can be defined to have no parent, that is not possible in Java. All Java classes must be subclasses of the root class, `Object`, or some class that is a descendant of `Object`. One reason to have a single root class is that there are some operations that are universally needed. Among these is a method for comparing objects for equality.

All Java objects are explicit heap-dynamic. Most are allocated with the **new** operator, but there is no explicit deallocation operator. Garbage collection is used for storage reclamation. Like many other language features, although garbage collection avoids some serious problems, such as dangling pointers, it can cause other problems. One such difficulty arises because the garbage collector deallocates, or reclaims the storage occupied by an object, but it does no more. For example, if an object has access to some resource other than heap memory, such as a file or a lock on a shared resource, the garbage collector does not reclaim these. For these situations, Java allows the inclusion of a special method, **finalize**, which is related to a C++ destructor function.

A **finalize** method is implicitly called when the garbage collector is about to reclaim the storage occupied by the object. The problem with **finalize** is that the time it will run cannot be forced or even predicted. The alternative to using **finalize** to reclaim resources held by an object about to be garbage collected is to include a method that does the reclamation. The only problem with this is that all clients of the objects must be aware of this method and remember to call it.

12.6.2 Inheritance

In Java, a method can be defined to be **final,** which means that it cannot be overridden in any descendant class. When the **final** reserved word is specified on a class definition, it means the class cannot be the parent of any subclass. It also means that the bindings of method calls to the methods of the subclass can be statically bound.

Java directly supports only single inheritance. However, it includes a kind of abstract class, called an **interface,** which provides partial support for multiple inheritance. An interface definition is similar to a class definition, except that it can contain only named constants and method declarations (not definitions). It cannot contain constructors or nonabstract methods. So an interface is no more than what its name indicates—it defines only the specification of a class. (Recall that a C++ abstract class can have instance variables and all but one of the methods can be completely defined.) A class does not inherit an interface; it implements it. In fact, a class can implement any number of interfaces. To implement an interface, the class must implement all of the methods whose specifications appear in the interface definition.

An interface can be used to simulate multiple inheritance. A class can be derived from a class and implement an interface, with the interface taking the place of a second parent class. This is sometimes called mix-in inheritance, because the constants and methods of the interface are mixed in with the methods and data inherited from the superclass, as well as any new data and/or methods defined in the subclass.

One more interesting capability of interfaces is that they provide another kind of polymorphism. This is because interfaces can be treated as types. For example, a method can specify a formal parameter that is an interface. Such a formal parameter can accept an actual parameter of any class that implements the interface, making the method polymorphic.

A nonparameter variable also can be declared to be of the type of an interface. Such a variable can reference any object of any class that implements the interface.

One of the problems with multiple inheritance occurs when a class is derived from two parent classes and both define a public method with the same name and protocol. This problem is avoided with interfaces, because a class that implements an interface must provide definitions for *all* of the methods specified in the interface. So, if the parent class and the interface both include methods with the same name and protocol, the subclass must reimplement that method. So, the name conflicts that can occur with multiple inheritance cannot occur with single inheritance and interfaces.

An interface is not a replacement for multiple inheritance, because in multiple inheritance there is code reuse, while interfaces provide no code reuse. This is an important difference, because code reuse is one of the primary benefits of inheritance.

As an example of an interface, consider the `sort` method of the standard Java class, `Arrays`. Any class that uses this method must provide an implementation of a method to compare the elements to be sorted. The `Comparable` interface provides the protocol for this comparing method, which is named `compareTo`. The code for the `Comparable` interface is as follows:

```java
public interface Comparable {
    public int compareTo(Object b);
}
```

The `compareTo` method must return a negative integer if the object through which it is called belongs before the parameter object, zero if they are equal, and a positive integer if the parameter belongs before the object through which `compareTo` was called. A class that implements the `Comparable` interface can sort the contents of any array, as long as the implemented `compareTo` method provides the appropriate value.

Chapter 14 illustrates the use of interfaces in Java event handling.

12.6.3 Dynamic Binding

In C++, a method must be defined as virtual to allow dynamic binding. In Java, all method calls are dynamically bound unless the called method has been defined as **final**, in which case it cannot be overridden and all bindings are static. Static binding is also used if the method is **static** or **private,** both of which disallow overriding.

12.6.4 Nested Classes

Java has several varieties of nested classes, all of which have the advantage of being hidden from all classes in their package, except for the nesting class. Nonstatic classes that are nested directly in another class have an implicit pointer to the nesting class that gives the methods of the nested class access to all of the members of the nesting class. Static nested classes do not have this pointer, so they cannot access members of the nesting class. Therefore, static nested classes in Java are like the nested classes of C++.

Nested classes can also be anonymous. Anonymous classes have complex syntax, but are really only an abbreviated way to define a class that is used from just one location.

A local nested class is defined in a method of its nesting class. Local nested classes are never defined with an access specifier (**private** or **public**). Their scope is always limited to their nesting class. A method in a local nested class can access the variables defined in its nesting class and the **final** variables defined in the method in which the local nested class is defined. Only the method in which it is defined can see the members of a local nested class.

12.6.5 Evaluation

Java's design for supporting object-oriented programming is similar to that of C++, but employs more consistent adherence to object-oriented principles. Because of its lack of functions, Java does not support procedural programming. Also, Java does not allow parentless classes and uses dynamic binding as the "normal" way to bind method calls to method definitions. Access control for the contents of a class definition are rather simple when compared with the jungle of access controls of C++, ranging from derivation controls to friend functions. Finally, Java uses interfaces to provide a simple form of support for multiple inheritance, whereas C++ includes complete but complex support for it.

12.7 Support for Object-Oriented Programming in C#

C#'s support for object-oriented programming is similar to that of Java.

12.7.1 General Characteristics

As discussed in Chapter 11, C# includes both classes and structs, with the classes being very similar to Java's classes and the structs being somewhat less powerful stack-dynamic constructs.

12.7.2 Inheritance

C# uses the syntax of C++ for defining classes. For example,

```
public class NewClass : ParentClass { ... }
```

A method inherited from the parent class can be replaced in the derived class by marking its definition in the subclass with **new**. The **new** method hides the method of the same name in the parent class to normal access. However, the parent class version can still be called by prefixing the call with **base**. For example,

```
base.Draw();
```

C#'s support for interfaces is the same as that of Java.

12.7.3 Dynamic Binding

To allow dynamic binding of method calls to methods in C#, both the base method and its corresponding methods in derived classes must be specially marked. The base class method must be marked with **virtual**, as in C++. To avoid accidental overriding, the corresponding methods in derived classes must be marked **override**. The inclusion of **override** makes it clear that the method is a new version of an inherited method. For example, the C# version of the C++ shape class that appears in Section 12.5.3 is

```
public class Shape {
  public virtual void Draw() { ... }
  ...
}
public class Circle : Shape {
  public override void Draw() { ... }
  ...
}
public class Rectangle : Shape {
  public override void Draw() { ... }
  ...
}
public class Square : Rectangle {
  public override void Draw() { ... }
  ...
}
```

C# includes abstract methods similar to those of C++, except that they are specified with different syntax. For example, the following is a C# abstract method:

```
abstract public void Draw();
```

A class that includes at least one abstract method is an abstract class, and every abstract class must be marked **abstract.** Abstract classes cannot be instantiated. It follows that any subclass of an abstract class that will be instantiated must implement all abstract methods that it inherits.

As with Java, all C# classes are ultimately derived from a single root class, `Object`. The `Object` class defines a collection of methods, including `ToString`, `Finalize`, and `Equals`, which are inherited by all C# types.

12.7.4 Nested Classes

A C# class that is directly nested in a nesting class behaves like a Java static nested class (which is like a nested class in C++). C# does not support nested classes that behave like the nonstatic nested classes of Java.

12.7.5 Evaluation

Because C# is the most recently designed C-based object-oriented language, one should expect that its designers learned from their predecessors and duplicated the successes of the past and remedied some of the problems. One result of this, coupled with the few problems with Java, is that the differences between C#'s support for object-oriented programming and that of Java are relatively minor.

12.8 Support for Object-Oriented Programming in Ada 95

Ada 95 was derived from Ada 83, with some significant extensions. This section presents a brief look at the extensions that were designed to support object-oriented programming. Because Ada 83 already included constructs for building abstract data types, which are discussed in Chapter 11, the necessary additional features for Ada 95 were those for supporting inheritance and dynamic binding. The design objectives were to require minimal changes to the type and package structures of Ada 83 and retain as much static type checking as possible.

12.8.1 General Characteristics

Ada 95 classes are a new category of types called **tagged types,** which can be either records or private types. They are defined in packages, which allows them to be separately compiled. Tagged types are so named because each object of a tagged type implicitly includes a system-maintained tag that indicates its type. The subprograms that define the operations on a tagged type appear in the same declaration list as the type declaration. Consider the following example:

```
package Person_Pkg is
  type Person is tagged private;
  procedure Display(P : in Person);
  private
    type Person is tagged
      record
        Name : String(1..30);
        AddressS : String(1..30);
        Age : Integer;
      end record;
end Person_Pkg;
```

This package defines the type Person, which is useful by itself and can also serve as the parent class of derived classes.

Unlike C++, there is no implicit calling of constructor or destructor subprograms in Ada 95. These subprograms can be written, but they must be explicitly called by the programmer.

12.8.2 Inheritance

Ada 83 supports only a very narrow form of inheritance with its derived types and subtypes. In both of these, a new type can be defined on the basis of an existing type. But the only modification allowed is to restrict the range of values of the new type. This is not the kind of full inheritance required for object-oriented programming, which is supported by Ada 95.

Derived types in Ada 95 are based on tagged types. New entities are added to the inherited entities by placing them in a record definition. Consider the following example:

```
with Person_Pkg; use Person_Pkg;
package Student_Pkg is
  type Student is new Person with
    record
      Grade_Point_Average : Float;
      Grade_Level : Integer;
    end record;
  procedure Display(St : in Student);
end Student_Pkg;
```

In this example, the derived type Student is defined to have the entities of its parent class, Person, along with the new entities Grade_Point_Average and Grade_Level. It also redefines the procedure Display. This new class is defined in a separate package to allow it to be changed without requiring recompilation of the package containing the definition of the parent type.

This inheritance mechanism does not allow one to prevent entities of the parent class from being included in the derived class. Consequently, derived classes can only extend parent classes, and are therefore subtypes. However, child library packages, which are discussed briefly next, can be used to define subclasses that are not subtypes.

Suppose we have the following definitions:

```
P1 : Person;
S1 : Student;
Fred : Person:= ("Fred", "321 Mulberry Lane", 35);
Freddie : Student:=
    ("Freddie", "725 Main St.", 20, 3.25, 3);
```

Because `Student` is a subtype of `Person`, the assignment

```
P1 := Freddie;
```

should be legal, and it is. The `Grade_Point_Average` and `Grade_Level` entities of `Freddie` are simply ignored in the required coercion.

The obvious question now is whether an assignment in the opposite direction is legal; that is, can we assign a `Person` to a `Student`? In Ada 95, this action is legal in a form that includes the entities in the subclass. In our example, the following is legal:

```
S1 := (Fred, 3.05, 2);
```

To derive a class that does not include all of the parent class's entities, child library packages are used. A child library package is simply a package whose name is prefixed with that of a parent package. Child library packages can also be used in place of the friend definitions in C++. For example, if a subprogram must be written that can access the members of two different classes, the parent package can define one of the classes and the child package can define the other. Then a subprogram in the child package can access the members of both.

Ada 95 does not provide multiple inheritance. Although generic classes and multiple inheritance are only distantly related concepts, there is a way to achieve an effect similar to multiple inheritance using generics. However, it is not as elegant as the C++ approach, and it is not discussed here.

12.8.3 Dynamic Binding

Ada 95 provides both static binding and dynamic binding of procedure calls to procedure definitions in tagged types. Dynamic binding is forced by using a classwide type, which represents all of the types in a class hierarchy rooted at a particular type. Every tagged type implicitly has a classwide type. For a tagged type `T`, the classwide type is specified with `T'class`. If `T` is a tagged type, a variable of type `T'class` can store an object of type `T` or any type derived from `T`.

Consider again the `Person` and `Student` classes defined in Section 12.8.2. Suppose we have a variable of type `Person'class`, `Pcw`, which sometimes references a `Person` object and sometimes references a `Student` object. Further suppose we want to display the object referenced by `Pcw`, regardless of whether it is referencing a `Person` object or a `Student` object. This result requires the call to `Display` to be dynamically bound to the correct version of `Display`. We could use a new procedure that takes the `Person` type parameter and sends it to `Display`. Following is such a procedure:

```
procedure Display_Any_Person(P: in Person) is
  begin
  Display(P);
  end Display_Any_Person;
```

This procedure can be called with both of the following calls:

```
with Person_Pkg; use Person_Pkg;
with Student_Pkg; use Student_Pkg;
P : Person;
S : Student;
Pcw : Person'class;
...
Pcw := P;
Display_Any_Person(Pcw);  -- call the Display in Person
Pcw := S;
Display_Any_Person(Pcw);  -- call the Display in Student
```

Ada 95 also supports polymorphic pointers. They are defined to have the classwide type, as in

```
type Any_Person_Ptr is access Person'class;
```

Purely abstract base types can be defined in Ada 95 by including the reserved word **abstract** in the type definitions and the subprogram definitions. Furthermore, the subprogram definitions cannot have bodies. Consider this example:

```
package Base_Pkg is
  type T is abstract tagged null record;
  procedure Do_It (A : T) is abstract;
end Base_Pkg;
```

12.8.4 Child Packages

Packages can be nested directly in other packages, in which case they are called **child packages.** The problem with this design is that if a package has a significant number of child packages and they are large, the nesting package becomes too large to be an effective compilation unit. The solution is relatively simple: Child packages are allowed to be separate units, which are separately compilable. The name of a child package is the nesting package's name with the child package's individual name attached with a period. For example, if the nesting package's name is `Binary_Tree` and the child's individual name is `Traversals`, the child's whole name is `Binary_Tree.Traversals`.

Child packages can be either public (default) or private. The logical position of a public child package is at the end of the declarations in the specification package of the nesting package. Therefore, all of the entities declared in the specification package of the nesting package are visible to the child package. However, any declarations that appear in the body of the nesting package are hidden from the child package. If there is more than one child package, they are not logically in sequential order. Hence, a child package cannot see the declarations of another child package unless it includes a **with** clause with the other child's name.

A child package is declared to be private by preceding the reserved word **package** with the reserved word **private.** The logical position of a private child package is at the beginning of the declarations in the specification package of the nesting package. The declarations of the private child package are not visible to the nesting package body, unless the nesting package includes a **with** clause with the child's name.

12.8.5 Evaluation

Ada offers complete support for object-oriented programming, although users of other object-oriented languages may find that support to be weak. Although packages can be used to build abstract data types, they are actually more generalized encapsulation constructs. Unless child library packages are used, there no way to restrict inheritance, in which case all subclasses are subtypes. This form of access restriction is limited in comparison to that offered by C++, Java, and C#.

C++ clearly offers a better form of multiple inheritance than Ada 95. However, the use of child library units to control access to the entities of the parent class seems to be a cleaner solution than the friend functions and classes of C++. For example, if the need for a friend is not known when a class is defined, it will need to be changed and recompiled when such a need is discovered. In Ada 95, new classes in new child packages are defined without disturbing the parent package, because every name defined in the parent package is visible in the child package.

The inclusion in C++ of constructors and destructors for initialization of objects is good, but Ada 95 includes no such capabilities.

Another difference between these two languages is that the designer of a C++ root class must decide whether a particular member function will be statically or dynamically bound. If the choice is made in favor of static binding, but a later change in the system requires dynamic binding, the root class must be changed. In Ada 95, this design decision need not be made with the design of the root class. Each call can itself specify whether it will be statically or dynamically bound, regardless of the design of the root class.

A more subtle difference is that dynamic binding in the C-based object-oriented languages is restricted to pointers and/or references to objects, rather than the objects themselves. Ada 95 has no such restriction, so in this case Ada 95 is more orthogonal.

12.9 Support for Object-Oriented Programming in Ruby

As stated previously, Ruby is a pure object-oriented programming language in the sense of Smalltalk. Virtually everything in the language is an object and all computation is accomplished through message passing. Although programs have expressions that use infix operators and therefore have the same appearance as expressions in languages like Java, those expressions actually are evaluated through message passing. When one writes `a + b`, it is executed as sending the message + to the object referenced by `a`, passing a reference to the object `b`.

12.9.1 General Characteristics

Recall from Chapter 11 that Ruby class definitions differ from those of languages such as C++ and Java in that they are executable. That they are executable allows them to remain open during execution. This permits a program to add to a class any number of times, simply by providing secondary definitions of the class that include new members. During execution, the current definition of a class is the union of all definitions of the class that have been executed. Method definitions are also executable, which allows a program to choose between two versions of a method definition during execution, simply by putting the two definitions in the then and else clause of a selection construct.

All variables in Ruby are references to objects, and all are typeless. Recall that the names of all instance variables begin with an at sign (@).

In a clear departure from the other common programming languages, access control in Ruby is different for access to data than it is for access to methods. All instance data has private access by default, and that cannot be changed. If external access to an instance variable is required, access methods must be defined. For example, consider the following skeletal class definition:

```ruby
class MyClass

# A constructor

  def initialize
    @one = 1
    @two = 2
  end
```

```
# A getter for @one

  def one
    @one
  end

# A setter for @one

  def one=(my_one)
    @one = my_one
  end

end  # of class MyClass
```

The equal sign (=) attached to the name of the setter method means that its variable is assignable. So, all setter methods have equal signs attached to their names. The body of the one getter method illustrates the Ruby design of methods returning the value of the last expression evaluated when there is no return statement. In this case, the value of @one is returned.

Because getter and setter methods are so frequently needed, Ruby provides shortcuts for both. If one wants a class to have getter methods for two instance variables, @one and @two, those getters can be specified with the single statement in the class:

```
attr_reader :one, :two
```

attr_reader is actually a function call, using :one and :two as the actual parameters. Preceding a variable with a colon (:) causes the variable name to be used, rather than dereferencing it to the object to which it refers.

The function that similarly creates setters is called attr_writer. This function has the same parameter profile as attr_reader.

The functions for creating getter and setter methods are so named because they provide the protocol for objects of the class, which in Ruby are called **attributes.** So, the attributes of a class is the data interface (the public data) to objects of the class.

Access control for methods in Ruby is dynamic, so access violations are detected only during excution. The default method access is public, but it can also be protected or private. There are two ways to specify the access control, both of which use functions with the same names as the access levels, **private, protected,** and **public.** One way is to call the appropriate function without parameters. This resets the default access for subsequently defined methods in the class. For example,

```
class MyClass
  def meth1
  ...
```

```
        end
        ...
    private
      def meth7
      ...
      end
      ...
    protected
      def meth11
      ...
      end
      ...
    end   # of class MyClass
```

The alternative is to call the access control functions with the names of the specific methods as parameters. For example, the following is semantically equivalent to the previous class definition:

```
class MyClass
  def meth1
  ...
  end
  ...
  def meth7
  ...
  end
  ...
  def meth11
  ...
  end
  ...
  private :meth7, ...
  protected :meth11, ..
  end   # of class MyClass
```

Class variables, which are specified by preceding their names with two at signs (@@), are private to the class and its instances. That privacy cannot be changed. Also, unlike global and instance variables, class variables must be initialized before they are used.

12.9.2   Inheritance

Subclasses are defined in Ruby using the less-than symbol (<), rather than the colon of C++. For example,

```
class MySubClass < BaseClass
```

One distinct thing about the method access controls of Ruby is that they can be changed in a subclass, simply by calling the access control functions. This means that two subclasses of a base class can be defined so that objects of one of the subclasses can access a method defined in the base class, but objects of the other subclass cannot. Also, this allows one to change the access of a publically accessible method in the base class to a privately accessible method in the subclass. Such a subclass obviously cannot be a subtype.

Recall that Ruby modules were discussed in Chapter 11. They provide a naming encapsulation that is often used to define libraries of functions. Perhaps the most interesting aspect of modules, however, is that their functions can be accessed directly from classes. Access to the module in a class is specified with an **include** statement, such as

```
include Math
```

The effect of including a module is that the class gains a pointer to the module and effectively inherits the functions defined in the module. In fact, when a module is included in a class, the module becomes a proxy superclass of the class. Such a module is called a **mixin,** because its functions get mixed into the methods defined in the class. Mixins provide a way to include the functionality of a module in any class that needs it. And, of course, the class still has a normal superclass from which it inherits members. So, mixins provide the benefits of multiple inheritance, without the naming collisions that could occur if modules did not require module names on their functions.

12.9.3   Dynamic Binding

Support for dynamic binding in Ruby is the same as it is in Smalltalk. Variables are not typed; rather, they are all references to objects of any class. So, all variables are polymorphic and all bindings of method calls to methods are dynamic.

12.9.4   Evaluation

Because Ruby is an object-oriented programming language in the purest sense, its support for object-oriented programming is adequate. However, access control to class members is weaker than that of C++. Also, multiple inheritance is not supported. Finally, Ruby does not support abstract classes or interfaces, although mixins are closely related to interfaces.

12.10 The Object Model of JavaScript

Although JavaScript does not have classes and supports neither inheritance nor dynamic binding, it uses an object model that is loosely based on the objects of C++ and Java. The design of JavaScript is therefore an interesting alternative to the traditional concepts of language support for objects.

12.10.1   General Characteristics

JavaScript was originally designed by Netscape as a scripting language for use in programming Web servers. It has since grown and evolved to a prominent position as a language for augmenting HTML documents, in which it is used to provide computational capability to those documents. JavaScript is also used to define dynamic HTML documents and to validate form data before it is sent to a Web server. Because of these applications, JavaScript has become a popular language.

In spite of the first part of its name, JavaScript has little in common with Java. It is, however, true to the last part of its name—it is a scripting language. Snippets of JavaScript code can be scattered in various parts of an HTML document. When a browser encounters JavaScript code in a document that it is reading and displaying, the code is immediately interpreted.

JavaScript is similar to Java only in that it uses a similar syntax. There are many fundamental differences. Java is a statically typed object-oriented language; JavaScript is dynamically typed. JavaScript does not have classes. Its objects serve as both objects and models of objects. Without classes, JavaScript cannot support class-based inheritance. Without class-based inheritance, JavaScript cannot support polymorphism. Although JavaScript has objects, they are quite different from those of the object-oriented languages.

As is the case with most languages that support object-oriented programming, JavaScript has two categories of variables, those that reference objects and those that directly store values of primitive types. Variables can be declared, but no type is implied by the declaration. The type of a variable can change every time a value is assigned to it. The new type is the type of the assigned value. Any variable can be used to store any primitive type value or refer to any object.

12.10.2   JavaScript Objects

In JavaScript, objects are collections of properties, which correspond to the members of classes in Java and C++. Each property is either a data property or a method property.

JavaScript objects appear as Perl hashes (see Chapter 6), both internally and externally. Each object is a list of property-value pairs. The properties are names; the values are data values or references to objects, some of which are methods. All functions and methods are objects and are referenced through variables. The only difference between a function and a method is that a method is referenced through an object property.

As is the case with a Perl hash, the collection of properties of a JavaScript object is dynamic—properties can be added or deleted at any time. This makes JavaScript objects very different from the objects of languages such as

C++ and Java. Every object is characterized by its collection of properties, although objects do not have types in any formal sense. JavaScript includes a **typeof** operator, but it returns the string `"object"` for every object.

12.10.3 Object Creation and Modification

Objects are often created with a **new** expression, which must include a call to a constructor method. The constructor that is called in the **new** expression creates the properties that characterize the new object. In an object-oriented language, the **new** operator creates a particular object, meaning an object with a type and a specific collection of members. Constructors in such languages initialize members but do not create them. In JavaScript, the **new** operator creates a blank object, or one with no properties. The constructor both creates and initializes the properties.

The following statement creates an object using the constructor for the predefined `Object` object, which creates no properties:

```
var my_object = new Object();
```

The variable `my_object` now references the new object. Constructors are further discussed later.

The properties of an object are accessed using dot notation, in which the first word is the object name and the second is the property name. Properties are not actually variables. They are keys into a hash, so as with Perl hash keys, they have no values of their own. They are used with object variables to access property values. Because they are not variables, properties are never declared.

As stated previously, at any time during interpretation, properties can be added to or deleted from an object. A property for an object is created by assigning a value to that property. Consider the following example:

```
var my_car = new Object();  // Create a blank object
my_car.make = "Ford";  // Create and initialize the make
                       // property
my_car.model = "Contour SVT";  // Create and initialize
                               // model
```

This code creates a new object, `my_car`, with two properties, `make` and `model`. Because objects can be nested, we can create a new object that is a property of `my_car` with properties of its own. For example,

```
my_car.engine = new Object();
my_car.engine.config = "V6";
my_car.engine.hp = 200;
```

If an attempt is made to access a property of an object that does not exist, the value **undefined** is used. A property can be deleted with **delete.** For example,

```
delete my_car.model;
```

JavaScript constructors are special methods that create and initialize the properties for newly created objects. As previously stated, every **new** expression must include a call to a constructor. Constructors are actually called by the **new** operator, which immediately precedes their names in the **new** expression.

A constructor obviously must be able to reference the object on which it is to operate. JavaScript has a predefined reference variable for this purpose, named **this.** When the constructor is called, **this** is a reference to the newly created object. The **this** variable is used to create and initialize the properties of the object. For example, consider the following constructor:

```
function car(new_make, new_model, new_year) {
    this.make = new_make;
    this.model = new_model;
    this.year = new_year;
}
```

This constructor could be used as follows:

```
my_car = new car("Ford", "Contour SVT", "2000");
```

If a method is to be included in the object, it is initialized the same way as if it were a data property. For example, suppose we created a method for car objects that displayed the property values, named display_car. The display_car method is added to the object being created with **new** and the call to the constructor by adding the following line to the constructor:

```
this.display = display_car;
```

The only concept of categories of objects in JavaScript that is related to the concept of class in an object-oriented programming language is the collection of objects created by use of the same constructor. All such objects would have the same set of properties and methods, at least initially. However, there is no convenient way to determine in the script whether two objects have the same set of properties and methods.

12.10.4 Evaluation

JavaScript is effective at what it is designed to be, a scripting language. If it were meant for large-scale software systems, its object model would be wholly inadequate. Without the encapsulation capability of classes, large programs in JavaScript could not be effectively organized. Without inheritance, reuse would be much more difficult. So, although the object model of JavaScript is interesting, it does not address the needs that motivated the development of object-oriented programming languages.

12.11 Implementation of Object-Oriented Constructs

There are at least two parts of language support for object-oriented programming that pose interesting questions for language implementers: storage structures for instance variables and the dynamic bindings of messages to methods. In this section, we take a brief look at these two.

12.11.1 Instance Data Storage

In C++, classes are defined as extensions of C's record structures—structs. This similarity suggests a storage structure for the instance variables of class instances—that of a record. We call this form of this structure a **class instance record (CIR).** The structure of a CIR is static, so it is built at compile time and used as a template for the creation of the data of class instances. Every class has its own CIR. When a derivation takes place, the CIR for the subclass is a copy of that of the parent class, with entries for the new instance variables added at the end.

Because the structure of the CIR is static, access to all instance variables can be done as it is in records, using constant offsets from the beginning of the CIR instance. This makes these accesses as efficient as those for the fields of records.

12.11.2 Dynamic Binding of Method Calls to Methods

Methods in a class that are statically bound need not be involved in the CIR for the class. However, methods that will be dynamically bound must have entries in this structure. Such entries could simply have a pointer to the code of the method, which must be set at object creation time. Calls to a method could then be connected to the corresponding code through this pointer in the CIR. The drawback to this technique is that every instance would need to store pointers to all dynamically bound methods that could be called from the instance.

Notice that the list of dynamically bound methods that can be called from an instance of a class is the same for all instances of that class. Therefore, the list of such methods must be stored only once. So the CIR for an instance needs only a single pointer to that list to enable it to find called methods. The storage structure for the list is often called a **virtual method table (vtable).** Method calls can be represented as offsets from the beginning of the vtable. Polymorphic variables of an ancestor class always reference the CIR of the correct type object, so getting to the correct version of a dynamically bound method is assured. Consider the following Java example, in which all methods are dynamically bound:

```java
public class A {
  public int a, b;
  public void draw() { ... }
  public int area() { ... }
}
public class B extends A {
  public int c, d;
  public void draw() { ... }
  public void sift() { ... }
}
```

The CIRs for the A and B classes, along with their vtables, are shown in Figure 12.2. Notice that the method pointer for the area method in B's vtable points to the code for A's area method. The reason is that B does not override A's area method, so if a client of B calls area, it is the area method inherited from A. On the other hand, the pointers for draw and sift in B's vtable point to B's draw and sift. The draw method is overriden in B and sift is defined as an addition in B.

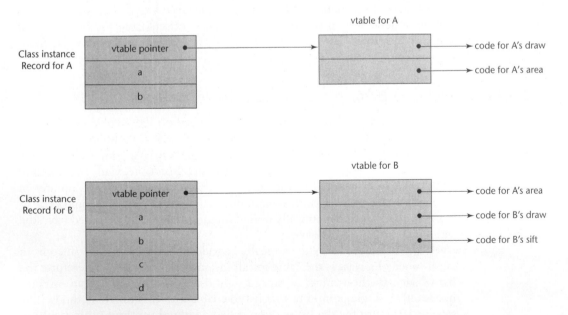

Figure 12.2

An example of the CIRs with single inheritance

Suppose a class named C creates objects of both class A and class B, with references named aObj and bObj, respectively. Further suppose that there is an assignment statement in C

```
aObj = bObj;
```

Now, if there is a call

```
aObj.draw();
```

and the assignment statement only copies bObj's pointer to aObj, A's draw method would be called, which would be incorrect. This example illustrates that the assignment of the reference bObj to aObj must have the side effect of changing the vtable pointer of aObj to point to the vtable of class B.

Multiple inheritance complicates the implementation of dynamic binding. Consider the following three C++ class definitions:

```
class A {
  public:
    int a;
    virtual void fun() { ... }
    virtual void init() { ... }
class B {
  public:
    int b;
    virtual void sum() { ... }
};
class C : public A, public B {
  public:
    int c;
    virtual void fun() { ... }
    virtual void dud() { ... }
};
```

The C class inherits the variable a and the init method from the A class. It redefines the fun method, although both its fun and that of the parent class A are potentially visible through a polymorphic variable (of type A). From B, C inherits the variable b and the sum method. C defines its own variable, c, and defines an uninherited method, dud. A CIR for C must include A's data, B's data, and C's data, as well as some means of accessing all visible methods. Under single inheritance, the CIR would include a pointer to a vtable that has the addresses of the code of all visible methods. With multiple inheritance, however, it is not that simple. There must be at least two different views available in the CIR—one for each of the parent classes, one of which includes the view for the subclass, C. This inclusion of the view of the subclass in the parent class's view is just as in the implementation of single inheritance.

There must also be two vtables: one for the A and C view and one for the B view. The first part of the CIR for C in this case can be the C and A view, which begins with a vtable pointer for the methods of C and those inherited from A, and includes the data inherited from A. Following this in C's CIR is the B view part, which begins with a vtable pointer for the virtual methods of B, which is followed by the data inherited from B and the data defined in C. The CIR for C is shown in Figure 12.3.

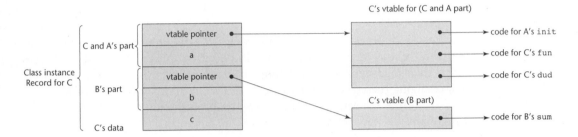

Figure 12.3

An example of a subclass CIR with multiple parents

SUMMARY

Object-oriented programming involves three fundamental concepts: abstract data types, inheritance, and dynamic binding. Object-oriented programming languages support the paradigm with classes, methods, objects, and message passing.

The discussion of object-oriented programming languages in this chapter revolves around seven design issues: exclusivity of objects, subclasses and subtypes, type checking and polymorphism, single and multiple inheritance, dynamic binding, explicit or implicit deallocation of objects, and nested classes.

Smalltalk is a pure object-oriented language—everything is an object and all computation is accomplished through message passing. In Smalltalk, all subclasses are subtypes. All type checking and binding of messages to methods is dynamic, and all inheritance is single. Smalltalk has no explicit deallocation operation.

C++ provides support for data abstraction, inheritance, and optional dynamic binding of messages to methods, along with all of the conventional features of C. This means that it has two distinct type systems. While Smalltalk's dynamic type binding provides somewhat more programming flexibility than the hybrid language, C++, it is far less efficient. C++ provides multiple inheritance and explicit object deallocation. C++ includes a variety of access controls for the entities in classes, some of which prevent subclasses from being subtypes. Both constructor and destructor methods can be included in classes; both are implicitly called.

Java is not a hybrid language like C++; it is meant to support only object-oriented programming. As with C++, Java has both primitive scalar types and classes. All objects are allocated from the heap and are accessed through reference variables. There is no explicit object deallocation operation. The only subprograms are methods, and they can be called only through objects or classes. Only single inheritance is directly supported, although a kind of multiple inheritance is possible using interfaces. All binding of messages to methods is dynamic, except in the case of methods that cannot be overridden. In addition to classes, Java includes packages as a second encapsulation construct.

Ada 95 provides support for object-oriented programming through tagged types, which can support inheritance. Dynamic binding is possible by using classwide types. Derived types are extensions to parent types, unless they are defined in child library packages, in which case entities of the parent type can be eliminated in the derived type. Outside child library packages, all subclasses are subtypes.

C#, which is based on C++ and Java, supports object-oriented programming. Objects can be instantiated from either classes or structs. The struct objects are stack-dynamic and do not support inheritance. Methods in a derived class can call the hidden methods of the parent class by including **base** on the method name. Methods that can be overridden must be marked **virtual,** and the overriding methods must be marked with **override.** All classes (and all primitives) are derived from Object.

Ruby is a scripting language in which all data are objects. As with Smalltalk, all objects are heap allocated and all variables are typeless references to objects. All constructors are named initialize. All instance data is private, but getter and setter methods can be easily included. The collection of all instance variables for which access methods have been provided forms the public interface to the class. Such instance methods are called attributes. Ruby classes are dynamic in the sense that they are executable and can be changed at any time. Ruby supports only single inheritance and subclasses are not necessarily subtypes.

Although JavaScript is not an object-oriented language, it includes an interesting variation on the concept of object. Dynamic binding of method calls to methods can be implemented using class instance records and virtual tables of method addresses. This approach can be extended to include support for multiple inheritance.

REVIEW QUESTIONS

1. Describe the three characteristic features of object-oriented languages.
2. What is the difference between a *class variable* and an *instance variable*?
3. What is an *overriding method*?

4. Describe a situation where dynamic binding is a great advantage over its absence.

5. What is a virtual method?

6. Describe briefly the six design issues used in this chapter for object-oriented languages.

7. What is the message protocol of an object?

8. Why is it that classes of Smalltalk can respond to messages?

9. Explain how Smalltalk messages are bound to methods. When does this take place?

10. What type checking is done in Smalltalk? When does it take place?

11. What kind of inheritance, single or multiple, does Smalltalk support?

12. What are the two most important effects that Smalltalk has had on computing?

13. In essence, all Smalltalk variables are of a single type. What is that type?

14. From where can C++ objects be allocated?

15. How are C++ heap-allocated objects deallocated?

16. Are all C++ subclasses subtypes?

17. Under what circumstances is a C++ method call statically bound to a method?

18. What drawback is there to allowing designers to specify which methods can be statically bound?

19. Explain the difference between the two uses of **private** in C++.

20. What is a **friend** function in C++?

21. How is the type system of Java different from that of C++?

22. From where can Java objects be allocated?

23. How are Java objects deallocated?

24. Are all Java subclasses subtypes?

25. Under what circumstances is a Java method call statically bound to a method?

26. In what way do overriding methods in C# syntactically differ from their counterparts in C++?

27. How can the parent version of an inherited method that is overridden in a subclass be called in that subclass in C#?

28. Are all Ada 95 subclasses subtypes?

29. How is a call to a subprogram in Ada 95 specified to be dynamically bound to a subprogram definition? When is this decision made?

30. How does Ruby implement primitive types, such as those for integer and floating-point data?

31. How are getter methods defined in a Ruby class?

32. What access controls does Ruby support for instance variables?
33. What access controls does Ruby support for methods?
34. Are all Ruby subclasses subtypes?
35. Does Ruby support multiple inheritance?
36. In what fundamental ways do JavaScript objects differ from Java objects?
37. What is the primary difference between a JavaScript constructor and one in Java?

PROBLEM SET

1. Compare the dynamic binding of C++ and Java.
2. Compare the class entity access controls of C++ and Java.
3. Compare the class entity access controls of C++ and Ada 95.
4. Compare the multiple inheritance of C++ with that provided by interfaces in Java.
5. Compare the generic capabilities of Java 5.0 with those of C++.
6. What is one programming situation where multiple inheritance has a significant advantage over interfaces?
7. Explain the two problems with abstract data types that are ameliorated by inheritance.
8. Describe the categories of changes that a subclass can make to its parent class.
9. Explain one disadvantage of inheritance.
10. Explain the advantages and disadvantages of having all values in a language be objects.
11. What exactly does it mean for a subclass to have an is-a relationship with its parent class?
12. Describe the issue of how closely the parameters of an overriding method must match those of the method it overrides.
13. The designers of Java obviously thought it was not worth the additional efficiency of allowing any method to be statically bound, as is the case with C++. What are the arguments for and against the Java design?
14. What is the primary reason why all Java objects have a common ancestor?
15. What is the purpose of the `finalize` clause in Java?
16. What would be gained if Java allowed stack-dynamic objects, as well as heap-dynamic objects? What would be the disadvantage of having both?
17. Compare the way Ada 95 provides polymorphism with that of C++, in terms of programming convenience.

18. Study and explain the issue of why C# does not include Java's nonstatic nested classes.

19. Can you define a reference variable for an abstract class? What use would such a variable be?

20. Compare the access controls for instance variables in Java and Ruby.

21. Compare the type error detection for instance variables in Java and Ruby.

PROGRAMMING EXERCISES

1. Rewrite the `single_linked_list`, `stack_2`, and `queue_2` classes in Section 12.5.2 in Java and compare the result with the C++ version in terms of readability and ease of programming.

2. Repeat Programming Exercise 1 using Ada 95.

3. Repeat Programming Exercise 1 using Ruby.

4. Design and implement a program that defines a base class A, which has a subclass B, which itself has a subclass C. The A class must implement a method, which is overriden in both B and C. You must also write a test class that instantiates A, B, and C, and includes three calls to the method. One of the calls must be statically bound to A's method. One call must be dynamically bound to B's method, and one must be dynamically bound to C's method. All of the method calls must be through a pointer to class A.

13

Concurrency

This chapter begins with introductions to the various kinds of concurrency at the subprogram, or unit level, and at the statement level. Included is a brief description of some common kinds of multiprocessor computer architectures. Next, a lengthy discussion on unit-level concurrency is presented. This begins with a description of the fundamental concepts that must be understood before discussing unit-level concurrency, including competition and cooperation synchronization. Next, the design issues for providing language support for concurrency are described. Following this is a detailed discussion, including code examples, of the three major approaches to language support for concurrency: semaphores, monitors, and message passing. A pseudocode example program is used to demonstrate how semaphores can be used. Ada and Java are used to illustrate monitors; for message passing, Ada is used. The Ada features that support concurrency are described in some detail. These include tasks, protected objects (which are effectively monitors), and asynchronous message passing. Support for unit-level concurrency in Java and C# is then discussed. The last section of the chapter has a discussion of statement-level concurrency, including a short description of part of the language support provided for it in High-Performance Fortran.

13.1 Introduction

Concurrency in software execution can occur at four different levels: instruction level (executing two or more machine instructions simultaneously), statement level (executing two or more source language statements simultaneously), unit level (executing two or more subprogram units simultaneously), and program level (executing two or more programs simultaneously). Because no language design issues are involved with them, we do not discuss instruction-level and program-level concurrency in this chapter. Concurrency at both the subprogram and the statement levels is discussed, with most of the discussion focused on the subprogram level.

Concurrent execution of subprograms can occur either physically, on separate processors, or logically, by sharing a single processor. At first glance, concurrency may appear to be a simple concept, but it presents a significant challenge to the programming language designer.

Concurrent control mechanisms increase programming flexibility. They were originally invented to be used for particular problems faced in operating systems, but they are required for a variety of other programming applications. For example, many software systems are designed to simulate actual physical systems, and many of these physical systems consist of multiple concurrent subsystems. For these applications, the traditional restricted form of subprogram control is inadequate.

Statement-level concurrency is quite different from concurrency at the unit level. From a language designer's point of view, statement-level concurrency is largely a matter of specifying how data should be distributed over multiple memories and which statements can be executed concurrently.

The intention of this chapter is to discuss the aspects of concurrency that are most relevant to language design issues, rather than to present a definitive study of all of the issues of concurrency. That would clearly be inappropriate for a book on programming languages.

13.1.1 Multiprocessor Architectures

A large number of different computer architectures have more than one processor and can support some form of concurrent execution. Before beginning to discuss concurrent execution of programs and statements, we briefly describe some of these architectures.

The first computers that had multiple processors had one general-purpose processor and one or more other processors, often called peripheral processors, that were used only for input and output operations. This architecture allowed these computers, which appeared in the late 1950s, to execute one program while concurrently performing input or output for other programs. Because this kind of concurrency does not require language support, we will not consider it further.

By the early 1960s, there were machines that had multiple complete processors. These processors were used by the job scheduler of the operating system, which distributed separate jobs from a batch-job queue to the separate processors. Systems with this structure supported program-level concurrency.

In the mid-1960s, machines appeared that had several identical partial processors that were fed certain instructions from a single instruction stream. For example, some machines had two or more floating-point multipliers, while others had two or more complete floating-point arithmetic units. The compilers for these machines were required to determine which instructions could be executed concurrently and to schedule these instructions accordingly. Systems with this structure supported instruction-level concurrency.

There are now many different kinds of multiprocessor computers; the most common two categories of these are described in the following two paragraphs.

Computers that have multiple processors that execute the same instruction simultaneously, each on different data, are called Single-Instruction Multiple-Data (SIMD) architecture computers. In an SIMD computer, each processor has its own local memory. One processor controls the operation of the other processors. Because all of the processors, except the controller, execute the same instruction at the same time, no synchronization is required in the software. Perhaps the most widely used SIMD machines are a category of machines called **vector processors.** They have groups of registers that store the operands of a vector operation in which the same instruction is executed on the whole group of operands simultaneously. The kinds of programs that can most benefit from this architecture are common in scientific computation, an area of computing that is often the target of multiprocessor machines.

Computers that have multiple processors that operate independently but whose operations can be synchronized are called Multiple-Instruction

Multiple-Data (MIMD) computers. Each processor in an MIMD computer executes its own instruction stream. MIMD computers can appear in two distinct configurations: distributed and shared memory systems. The distributed MIMD machines, in which each processor has its own memory, can be either built in a single box or distributed, perhaps over a large area. The shared-memory MIMD machines obviously must provide some means of synchronization to prevent memory access clashes. Even distributed MIMD machines require synchronization to operate together on single programs. MIMD computers, which are more expensive and more general than SIMD computers, clearly support unit-level concurrency.

13.1.2   Categories of Concurrency

There are two distinct categories of concurrent unit control. The most general category of concurrency is that in which, assuming that more than one processor is available, several program units from the same program literally execute simultaneously. This is **physical concurrency.** A slight relaxation of this concept of concurrency allows the programmer and the application software to assume that there are multiple processors providing actual concurrency, when in fact, the actual execution of programs is taking place in interleaved fashion on a single processor. This is **logical concurrency.** It is similar to the illusion of simultaneous execution that is provided to different users of a multiprogramming computer system. From the programmer's and language designer's points of view, logical concurrency is the same as physical concurrency. It is the language implementor's task, using the capabilities of the underlying operating system, to map the logical concurrency to the host hardware. Both logical and physical concurrency allow the concept of concurrency to be used as a program design methodology. For the remainder of this chapter, the discussion will apply to both physical and logical concurrency.

One useful technique for visualizing the flow of execution through a program is to imagine a thread laid on the statements of the source text of the program. Every statement reached on a particular execution is covered by the thread representing that execution. Visually following the thread through the source program traces the execution flow through the executable version of the program. Of course, in all but the simplest of programs, the thread follows a highly complex path. A **thread of control** in a program is the sequence of program points reached as control flows through the program.

Programs that have coroutines (see Chapter 9), though they are sometimes called **quasi-concurrent,** have a single thread of control. Programs executed with physical concurrency can have multiple threads of control. Each processor can execute one of the threads. Although logically concurrent program execution may actually have only a single thread of control, such programs can be designed and analyzed only by imagining them as having multiple threads of control. A program designed to have more than one thread of control is said to be **multithreaded.** When a multithreaded program executes on a single-processor machine, its threads are mapped onto a single thread. It becomes, in this case, a virtually multithreaded program.

Statement-level concurrency is a relatively simple concept. Loops that include statements that operate on array elements are unwound so that the processing can be distributed over multiple processors. For example, a loop that executes 500 repetitions and includes a statement that operates on one of 500 array elements may be unwound so that each of 10 different processors can simultaneously process 50 of the array elements.

13.1.3 Motivations for Studying Concurrency

The primary reason to study concurrency is that it provides a method of conceptualizing program solutions to problems. Many problem domains lend themselves naturally to concurrency in much the same way that recursion is a natural way to design the solution to some problems. Many programs are written to simulate physical entities and activities. In many cases, the system being simulated includes more than one entity, and the entities do whatever they do simultaneously—for example, aircraft flying in a control area, relay stations in a communications network, and the various machines in a manufacturing facility. To simulate such systems accurately with software, languages that support concurrency are required.

The second reason to discuss concurrency is that multiple-processor computers currently are being used, although that use is not widespread. This creates the need for software to make effective use of that hardware capability. Because of the importance of both statement-level and unit-level concurrency, facilities to provide them must be developed and included in contemporary programming languages.

13.2 Introduction to Subprogram-Level Concurrency

Before we can discuss language support for concurrency, we must introduce the underlying concepts of concurrency and the requirements for it to be useful. Then we can discuss the language design issues for languages that support concurrency.

13.2.1 Fundamental Concepts

A **task** is a unit of a program, similar to a subprogram, that can be in concurrent execution with other units of the same program. Each task in a program can provide one thread of control. Tasks are sometimes called **processes.**

Three characteristics of tasks distinguish them from subprograms. First, a task may be implicitly started, whereas a subprogram must be explicitly called. Second, when a program unit invokes a task, it need not wait for the task to complete its execution before continuing its own. Lastly, when the execution of a task is completed, control may or may not return to the unit that started that execution.

Tasks fall into two general categories, heavyweight and lightweight. Simply stated, each **heavyweight task** executes in its own address space. **Lightweight tasks** all run in the same address space. It is easier to implement lightweight tasks than heavyweight tasks.

A task can communicate with other tasks through shared nonlocal variables, through message passing, or through parameters. If a task does not communicate with or affect the execution of any other task in the program in any way, it is said to be **disjoint.** Because tasks often work together to create simulations or solve problems and therefore are not disjoint, they must use some form of communication to either synchronize their executions or share data or both.

Synchronization is a mechanism that controls the order in which tasks execute. Two kinds of synchronization are required when tasks share data: cooperation and competition. **Cooperation synchronization** is required between task A and task B when task A must wait for task B to complete some specific activity before task A can continue its execution. **Competition synchronization** is required between two tasks when both require the use of some resource that cannot be simultaneously used. Specifically, if task A needs to access shared data location x while task B is accessing x, task A must wait for task B to complete its processing of x, regardless of what that processing is. So, for cooperation synchronization, tasks may need to wait for the completion of specific processing on which their correct operation depends, whereas for competition synchronization, tasks may need to wait for the completion of any other processing by any task currently occurring on specific shared data.

A simple form of cooperation synchronization can be illustrated by a common problem called the **producer-consumer problem.** This problem originated in the development of operating systems, in which one program unit produces some data value or resource and another uses it. Produced data are usually placed in a storage buffer by the producing unit and removed from that buffer by the consuming unit. The sequence of stores to and removals from the buffer must be synchronized. The consumer unit must not be allowed to take data from the buffer if the buffer is empty. Likewise, the producer unit cannot be allowed to place new data in the buffer if the buffer is full. This is called the **problem of cooperation synchronization** because the users of the shared data structure must cooperate if the buffer is to be used correctly.

Competition synchronization prevents two tasks from accessing a shared data structure at exactly the same time—a situation that could destroy the integrity of that shared data. To provide competition synchronization, mutually exclusive access to the shared data must be guaranteed.

To clarify the competition problem, consider the following scenario: Suppose task A must add 1 to the shared integer variable TOTAL, which has an initial value of 3. Furthermore, suppose task B must multiply the value of

TOTAL by 2. Each task accomplishes its operation on TOTAL with the following three-step process:

1. Fetch the value of TOTAL.
2. Perform the arithmetic operation.
3. Put the new value back in TOTAL.

Without competition synchronization, four different values could result from these operations. If task A completes its operation before task B begins, the value will be 8, which is assumed here to be correct. But if both A and B fetch the value of TOTAL before either task puts its new value back, the result will be incorrect. If A puts its value back first, the value of TOTAL will be 6. This case is shown in Figure 13.1. If B puts its value back first, the value of TOTAL will be 4. Finally, if B completes its operation before task A begins, the value will be 7. A situation that leads to these problems is sometimes called a **race condition,** because two or more tasks are racing to use the shared resource and the behavior of the program depends on which task arrives first. The importance of competition synchronization should now be clear.

One general method for providing mutually exclusive access (to support competition synchronization) to a shared resource is to consider the resource to be something that a task can possess and allow only a single task to possess it at a time. To gain possession of a shared resource, a task must request it. When a task is finished with a shared resource that it possesses, it must relinquish that resource so it can be made available to other tasks.

Three methods of providing for mutually exclusive access to a shared resource are semaphores, which are discussed in Section 13.3; monitors, which are discussed in Section 13.4; and message passing, which is discussed in Section 13.5.

Mechanisms for synchronization must be able to delay task execution. Synchronization imposes an order of execution on tasks that is enforced with these delays. To understand what happens to tasks through their lifetimes, we must consider how task execution is controlled. Regardless of whether a machine has a single processor or more than one, there is always the possibility of there being more tasks than there are processors. A program called a **scheduler** manages the sharing of processors among the tasks. If there were never any interruptions and tasks all had the same priority, the scheduler could simply give each task a time slice, such as 0.1 seconds, and when a task's turn came, the scheduler could let it execute on a processor for that amount of time. Of course, there are several events that complicate this: for example, delays for synchronization and waits for input or output operations.

Tasks can be in several different states, which are:

1. *New:* A task is in the new state when it has been created but has not yet begun its execution.

2. *Ready:* A ready task is ready to run but is not currently running. Either it has not been given processor time by the scheduler, or it had run previously but was blocked in one of the ways described in paragraph 4

Figure 13.1

The need for
competition
synchronization

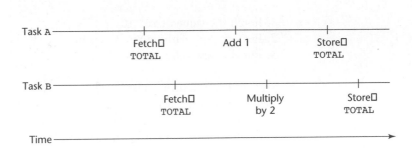

of this subsection. Tasks that are ready to run are stored in a queue that is often called the **task ready queue.**

3. *Running:* A running task is one that is currently executing; that is, it has a processor and its code is being executed.

4. *Blocked:* A task that is blocked has been running, but that execution was interrupted by one of several different events, the most common of which is an input or output operation. Because input and output operations are much slower than program execution, a task that starts an input or output operation is blocked from using the processor while it waits until the input or output operation is completed. In addition to these kinds of blocking, some languages provide operations for the user program to specify that a task be blocked.

5. *Dead:* A dead task is no longer active in any sense. A task dies when its execution is completed or it is explicitly killed by the program.

One important issue in task execution is the following: How is a ready task chosen to move to the running state when the task currently running has become blocked or whose time slice has expired? Several different algorithms have been used for this choice, some based on specifiable priority levels. The algorithm that does the choosing is implemented in the scheduler.

Associated with the concurrent execution of tasks and the use of shared resources is the concept of liveness. In the environment of sequential programs, a program has the characteristic of **liveness** if it continues to execute, eventually leading to completion. In more general terms, liveness means that if some event—say, program completion—is supposed to occur, it will occur, eventually. That is, progress is continually made. In the environment of concurrency and the use of shared resources, the liveness of a task can cease to exist, meaning that the program cannot continue and thus will never terminate.

For example, suppose task A and task B both need the shared resources X and Y to complete their work. Further suppose that task A gains possession of X and task B gains possession of Y. After some execution, task A needs resource Y to continue, so it requests Y but must wait until B releases it. Likewise, task B requests X but must wait until A releases it. Neither relinquishes the resource it possesses, and as a result, both lose their liveness, guaranteeing that execution of the program will never complete normally. This particular kind of loss of liveness is called **deadlock.** Deadlock is a serious threat to the reliability of a program, and therefore its avoidance demands serious consideration in both language and program design.

We are now ready to discuss some of the linguistic mechanisms for providing concurrent unit control.

13.2.2 Language Design for Concurrency

A number of languages have been designed to support concurrency, beginning with PL/I in the middle 1960s and including the contemporary languages Ada 95, Java, C#, Python, and Ruby.

13.2.3 Design Issues

The most important design issues for language support for concurrency have already been discussed at length: competition and cooperation synchronization. In addition to these, there are several design issues of secondary importance. Prominent among them is how to control task scheduling. Also, there are the issues of how and when tasks start and end executions, and how and when they are created.

Keep in mind that our discussion of concurrency is intentionally incomplete, and only the most important of the language design issues related to support for concurrency are discussed.

The following sections discuss three alternative answers to the design issues for concurrency: semaphores, monitors, and message passing.

> **history note**
>
> PL/I was the first programming language to include concurrent tasks. It allowed user programs to execute any subprogram concurrently with the unit that called it. The mechanism for synchronization of these concurrent executions was, however, wholly inadequate. It consisted of only binary semaphores, which were called *events*, and the ability to detect when a task had completed its execution.
>
> ALGOL 68, which allowed compound statement-level concurrency, included a semaphore data type named sema.

13.3 Semaphores

A semaphore is a simple mechanism that can be used to provide synchronization of tasks. In the following paragraphs, we describe semaphores and discuss how they can be used for this purpose.

13.3.1 Introduction

In an effort to provide competition synchronization through mutually exclusive access to shared data structures, Edsger Dijkstra devised semaphores in 1965 (Dijkstra, 1968b). Semaphores can also be used to provide cooperation synchronization.

A **semaphore** is a data structure consisting of an integer and a queue that stores task descriptors. A **task descriptor** is a data structure that stores all of the relevant information about the execution state of a task. The concept of a semaphore is that, to provide limited access to a data structure, guards are placed around the code that accesses the structure. A **guard** is a linguistic device that allows the guarded code to be executed only when a specified condition is true. A guard can be used to allow only one task to access a shared data structure at a time. A semaphore is an implementation of a guard. An integral part of a guard mechanism is a procedure for ensuring that all attempted executions of the guarded code eventually take place. The typical procedure is to have requests for access that occur when access cannot be granted be stored in the task descriptor queue, from which they are later allowed to leave and execute the guarded code. This is the reason a semaphore must have both a counter and a task descriptor queue.

The only two operations provided for semaphores were originally named P and V by Dijkstra, after the two Dutch words *passeren* (to pass) and *vrygeren* (to release) (Andrews and Schneider, 1983). We will refer to these as *wait* and *release* in the remainder of this section.

The process by which semaphores provide guards is described in terms of the most common applications in the following subsection.

13.3.2 Cooperation Synchronization

Through much of this chapter, we use the example of a shared buffer to illustrate the different approaches to providing cooperation and competition synchronization. For cooperation synchronization, such a buffer must have some way of recording both the number of empty positions and the number of filled positions in the buffer (to prevent buffer underflow and overflow). The counter component of a semaphore variable can be used for this purpose. One semaphore variable—for example, `emptyspots`—can be used to store the number of empty locations in a shared buffer, and another—say, `fullspots`—can be used to store the number of filled locations in the buffer. The task queues of these two semaphores store tasks that have been blocked by the delay operation of the semaphore.

Our example buffer is designed as an abstract data type in which all data enters the buffer through the subprogram `DEPOSIT`, and all data leaves the buffer through the subprogram `FETCH`. Then the `DEPOSIT` subprogram needs only to check with the `emptyspots` semaphore to see whether there are any empty positions. If there is at least one, it can go ahead with the `DEPOSIT`, which must include decrementing the counter of `emptyspots`. If the buffer is full, the caller to DEPOSIT must be made to wait in the emptyspots queue for an empty spot to become available. When the DEPOSIT is complete, the DEPOSIT subprogram increments the counter of the fullspots semaphore to indicate that there is one more filled location in the buffer.

The FETCH subprogram has the opposite sequence of DEPOSIT. It checks the fullspots semaphore to see whether the buffer contains at least one item. If it does, an item is removed and the emptyspots semaphore has its counter incremented by 1. If the buffer is empty, the calling process is put in the fullspots queue to wait until an item appears. When FETCH is finished, it must increment the counter of emptyspots.

The operations on semaphore types often are not direct—they are done through the wait and release subprograms. Therefore, the DEPOSIT operation just described is actually accomplished in part by calls to wait and release. Note that wait and release must be able to access the task-ready queue.

The wait subprogram is used to test the counter of a given semaphore variable. If the value is greater than zero, the caller can carry out its operation. In this case, the counter value of the semaphore variable is decremented to indicate that there are now one fewer of whatever it counts. If the value of the counter is zero, the caller must be placed on the waiting queue of the semaphore variable, and the processor must be given to some other ready task.

The release operation is used by a task to allow some other task to have one of whatever the counter of the specified semaphore variable counts. If the queue of the specified semaphore variable is empty, which means no task is waiting, release increments its counter (to indicate there is one more of whatever is being controlled that is now available). If one or more tasks are waiting, release moves one of them from the semaphore queue to the ready queue.

The following are concise pseudocode descriptions of wait and release:

```
wait(aSemaphore)
if aSemaphore's counter > 0 then
    decrement aSemaphore's counter
else
    put the caller in aSemaphore's queue
    attempt to transfer control to some ready task
    (if the task ready queue is empty, deadlock occurs)
end if
```

```
release(aSemaphore)
if aSemaphore's queue is empty (no task is waiting) then
    increment aSemaphore's counter
else
    put the calling task in the task-ready queue
    transfer control to a task from aSemaphore's queue
end
```

We can now present an example program that implements cooperation synchronization for a shared buffer. In this case, the shared buffer stores integer values and is a logically circular structure. It is designed for use by possibly multiple producer and consumer tasks.

The following pseudocode shows the definition of the producer and consumer tasks. Two semaphores are used to ensure against buffer underflow or overflow, thus providing cooperation synchronization. Assume that the buffer has length BUFLEN, and the routines that actually manipulate it already exist as FETCH and DEPOSIT. Accesses to the counter of a semaphore are specified by dot notation. For example, if fullspots is a semaphore, its counter is referenced by fullspots.count.

```
semaphore fullspots, emptyspots;
fullspots.count = 0;
emptyspots.count = BUFLEN;
task producer;
  loop
  -- produce VALUE --
  wait(emptyspots);    { wait for a space }
  DEPOSIT(VALUE);
  release(fullspots);  { increase filled spaces }
  end loop;
end producer;

task consumer;
  loop
  wait(fullspots);     { make sure it is not empty }
  FETCH(VALUE);
  release(emptyspots); { increase empty spaces }
  -- consume VALUE --
  end loop;
end consumer;
```

The semaphore fullspots causes the consumer task to be queued to wait for a buffer entry if it is currently empty. The semaphore emptyspots causes the producer task to be queued to wait for an empty space in the buffer if it is currently full.

13.3.3 Competition Synchronization

Our buffer example does not provide competition synchronization. Access to the structure can be controlled with an additional semaphore. This semaphore need not count anything, but can simply indicate with its counter whether the buffer is currently being used. The wait statement allows the access only if the semaphore's counter has the value 1, which indicates that the shared buffer is not currently being accessed. If the semaphore's counter has a value of 0, there is a current access taking place, and the task is placed on the queue of the semaphore. Notice that the semaphore's counter must be initialized to 1. The queues of semaphores must always be initialized to empty.

A semaphore that requires only a binary-valued counter, like the one used to provide competition synchronization in the following example, is called a **binary semaphore.**

The example pseudocode that follows illustrates the use of semaphores to provide both competition and cooperation synchronization for a concurrently accessed shared buffer. The `access` semaphore is used to ensure mutually exclusive access to the buffer. Note again that there may be more than one producer and more than one consumer.

```
semaphore access, fullspots, emptyspots;
access.count = 1;
fullspots.count = 0;
emptyspots.count = BUFLEN;

task producer;
  loop
  -- produce VALUE --
  wait(emptyspots);      { wait for a space }
  wait(access);          { wait for access }
  DEPOSIT(VALUE);
  release(access);       { relinquish access }
  release(fullspots);    { increase filled spaces }
  end loop;
end producer;

task consumer;
  loop
  wait(fullspots);       { make sure it is not empty }
  wait(access);          { wait for access }
  FETCH(VALUE);
  release(access);       { relinquish access }
  release(emptyspots);   { increase empty spaces }
  -- consume VALUE --
  end loop
end consumer;
```

A brief look at this example may lead one to believe there is a problem with it. Specifically, suppose that while a task is waiting at the `wait(access)` call in `consumer` another task takes the last value from the shared buffer. Fortunately, this cannot happen, because the `wait(fullspots)` reserves a value in the buffer for the task that calls it by decrementing the `fullspots` counter.

There is one crucial aspect of semaphores that thus far has not been discussed. Recall the earlier description of the problem of competition synchronization: Operations on shared data must not be overlapped. If a second operation can be begun while an earlier operation is still in progress, the shared data can become corrupted. A semaphore is itself a shared data object, so the operations on semaphores are also susceptible to the same problem. It is therefore essential that semaphore operations be uninterruptible. Many computers have uninterruptible instructions that were designed specifically for semaphore operations. If such instructions are not available, then using semaphores to provide competition synchronization is a serious problem with no simple solution.

13.3.4   Evaluation

Using semaphores to provide cooperation synchronization creates an unsafe programming environment. There is no way to statically check for the correctness of their use, which depends on the semantics of the program in which they appear. In the buffer example, leaving the `wait(emptyspots)` statement out of the `producer` task would result in buffer overflow. Leaving the `wait(fullspots)` statement out of the `consumer` task would result in buffer underflow. Leaving out either of the releases would result in deadlock. These are cooperation synchronization failures.

The reliability problems that semaphores cause in providing cooperation synchronization also arise when using them for competition synchronization. Leaving out the `wait(access)` statement in either task can cause insecure access to the buffer. Leaving out the `release(access)` statement in either task results in deadlock. These are competition synchronization failures. Noting the danger in using semaphores, Per Brinch Hansen wrote, "The semaphore is an elegant synchronization tool for an ideal programmer who never makes mistakes" (Brinch Hansen, 1973). Unfortunately, programmers of that kind are rare.

13.4 Monitors

One solution to some of the problems of semaphores in a concurrent environment is to encapsulate shared data structures with their operations and hide their representations—that is, to make shared data structures abstract data types. This solution can provide competition synchronization without semaphores by transferring responsibility for synchronization to the run-time system.

13.4.1   Introduction

When the concepts of data abstraction were being formulated, the people involved in that effort applied the same concepts to shared data in concurrent programming environments to produce monitors. According to Per Brinch Hansen (Brinch Hansen, 1977, p. xvi), Edsger Dijkstra suggested in 1971 that all synchronization operations on shared data be gathered into a single program unit. Brinch Hansen formalized this concept in the environment of operating systems (Brinch Hansen, 1973). The following year, Hoare named these structures *monitors* (Hoare, 1974).

The first programming language to incorporate monitors was Concurrent Pascal (Brinch Hansen, 1975). Modula (Wirth, 1977), CSP/k (Holt et al., 1978), and Mesa (Mitchell et al., 1979) also provide monitors. Among contemporary languages, monitors are supported by Ada, Java, and C#, all of which are discussed in this chapter.

13.4.2 Competition Synchronization

One of the most important features of monitors is that shared data is resident in the monitor rather than in any of the client units. Thus the programmer does not synchronize mutually exclusive access to shared data through the use of semaphores or other mechanisms. Because all accesses are resident in the monitor, the monitor implementation can be made to guarantee synchronized access by allowing only one access at a time. Calls to monitor procedures are implicitly queued if the monitor is busy at the time of the call.

13.4.3 Cooperation Synchronization

Although mutually exclusive access to shared data is intrinsic with a monitor, cooperation between processes is still the task of the programmer. In particular, the programmer must guarantee that a shared buffer does not experience underflow or overflow. Different languages provide different ways of programming cooperation synchronization, all of which are related to semaphores.

A program containing four tasks and a monitor that provides synchronized access to a concurrently shared buffer is shown in Figure 13.2. In this figure, the interface to the monitor is shown as the two boxes labeled `insert` and `remove` (for the insertion and removal of data).

13.4.4 Evaluation

Monitors are a better way to provide competition synchronization than are semaphores, primarily because of the problems of semaphores, as discussed in Section 13.3. The cooperation synchronization is still a problem with monitors, as will be clear when Ada and Java implementations of monitors are discussed in the following sections.

Semaphores and monitors are equally powerful at expressing concurrency control—semaphores can be used to implement monitors and monitors can be used to implement semaphores.

Ada provides two ways to implement monitors. Ada 83 includes a general tasking model that can be used to support monitors. Ada 95 added a cleaner

Figure 13.2

A program using a
monitor to control
access to a shared
buffer

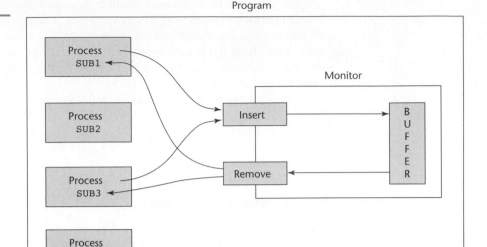

and more efficient way of constructing monitors, called *protected objects*. Both
of these approaches use message passing as a basic model for supporting
concurrency. The message-passing model allows concurrent units to be
distributed, which monitors do not allow. Message passing is described in
Section 13.5; Ada support for message passing is discussed in Section 13.6.

13.5 Message Passing

This section introduces the fundamental concept of message passing. Section
13.6 describes the details of Ada support for the message-passing approach.

13.5.1   Introduction

The first efforts to design languages that provide the capability for message
passing among concurrent tasks were those of Brinch Hansen (1978) and
Hoare (1978). The pioneer developers of message passing also developed a
technique for handling the problem of what to do when multiple simultaneous requests were made by other tasks to communicate with a given task. It
was decided that some form of nondeterminism was required to provide fair-
ness in choosing which among those requests would be taken first. This fair-
ness can be defined in various ways, but in general it means that all requesters
are provided an equal chance of communicating with a given task (assuming
that every requester has the same priority). Nondeterministic constructs for
statement-level control, called *guarded commands*, were introduced by Dijkstra

(1975). (Guarded commands are discussed in Chapter 8.) Guarded commands are the basis of the construct designed for controlling message passing.

13.5.2 The Concept of Synchronous Message Passing

Message passing can be either synchronous or asynchronous. The asynchronous message passing of Ada 95 is described in Section 13.6.8. Here we describe synchronous message passing. The basic concept of synchronous message passing is that tasks are often busy, and when busy, cannot be interrupted by other units. Suppose task A and task B are both in execution, and A wishes to send a message to B. Clearly, if B is busy, it is not desirable to allow another task to interrupt it. That would disrupt B's current processing. Furthermore, messages usually cause associated processing in the receiver, which might not be sensible if other processing is incomplete. The alternative is to provide a linguistic mechanism that allows a task to specify to other tasks when it is ready to receive messages. This approach is somewhat like an executive who instructs his or her secretary to hold all incoming calls until another activity, perhaps an important conversation, is completed. Later, the executive tells the secretary that he or she is now willing to talk to one of the callers who has been placed on hold.

A task can be designed so that it can suspend its execution at some point, either because it is idle or because it needs information from another unit before it can continue. This is like a person who is waiting for an important call. In some cases, there is nothing else to do but sit and wait. In this situation, if task A wants to send a message to B, and B is willing to receive a message, the message can be transmitted. This actual transmission is called a **rendezvous.** Note that a rendezvous can occur only if both the sender and receiver want it to happen. The information of the message can be transmitted in either or both directions.

Both cooperation and competition synchronization of tasks can be conveniently handled with the message-passing model, as described in the following section.

13.6 Ada Support for Concurrency

This section describes the support for concurrency provided by Ada. Ada 83 supports only synchronous message passing; Ada 95 adds support for asynchronous message passing.

13.6.1 Fundamentals

The Ada design for tasks is partially based on the work of Brinch Hansen and Hoare in that message passing is the design basis and nondeterminism is used to choose among competing message-sending tasks.

The full Ada tasking model is complex, and the following discussion of it must be limited. The focus here will be on the Ada version of the synchronous message-passing mechanism.

Ada tasks can be more active than monitors. Monitors are passive entities that provide management services for the shared data they store. They provide their services, though only when those services are requested. When used to manage shared data, Ada tasks can be thought of as managers that can reside with the resource they manage. They have several mechanisms, some deterministic and some nondeterministic, that allow them to choose among competing requests for access to their resources.

The form of Ada tasks is similar to that of Ada packages. There are two parts—a specification part and a body part—both with the same name. The interface of a task is its entry points, or locations where it can accept messages from other tasks. It is natural that these be listed in the specification part of a task. Because a rendezvous can involve an exchange of information, messages can have parameters; therefore, task entry points must also allow parameters, which must also be described in the specification part. In appearance, a task specification is very similar to the package specification for an abstract data type.

As an example of an Ada task specification, consider the following code, which includes a single entry point named `Entry_1`, which has an in-mode parameter:

```ada
task Task_Example is
  entry Entry_1(Item : in Integer);
end Task_Example;
```

A task body must include some syntactic form of the entry points that correspond to the **entry** clauses in that task's specification part. In Ada, these task body entry points are specified by **accept** clauses, which are introduced by the **accept** reserved word. An **accept clause** is defined as the range of statements beginning with the **accept** reserved word and ending with the matching **end** reserved word. **accept** clauses are themselves relatively simple, but other constructs in which they can be embedded can make their semantics complex. A simple **accept** clause has the form

```ada
accept entry_name (formal parameters) do
  ...
end entry_name;
```

The **accept** entry name matches the name in an **entry** clause in the associated task specification part. The optional parameters provide the means of communicating data between the caller and the called task. The statements between the **do** and the **end** define the operations that take place during the rendezvous. These statements are together called the **accept clause body.** During the actual rendezvous, the sender task is suspended.

Whenever an **accept** clause receives a message that it is not ready to accept, for whatever reason, the sender task must be suspended until the **accept** clause in the receiver task is ready to accept the message. Of course, the **accept** clause must also remember the sender tasks that have sent messages that were not accepted. For this purpose, each **accept** clause in a task has a queue associated with it that stores a list of other tasks that have unsuccessfully attempted to communicate with it.

The following is the skeletal body of the task whose specification was given previously:

```
task body Task_Example is
  begin
  loop
    accept Entry_1(Item : in Integer) do
      ...
    end Entry_1;
  end loop;
end Task_Example;
```

The **accept** clause of this task body is the implementation of the **entry** named Entry_1 in the task specification. If the execution of Task_Example begins and reaches the Entry_1 **accept** clause before any other task sends a message to Entry_1, Task_Example is suspended. If another task sends a message to Entry_1 while Task_Example is suspended at its **accept,** a rendezvous occurs and the **accept** clause body is executed. Then, because of the loop, execution proceeds back to the **accept.** If no other task has sent a message to Entry_1, execution is again suspended to wait for the next message.

A rendezvous can occur in two basic ways in this simple example. First, the receiver task, Task_Example, can be waiting for another task to send a message to the Entry_1 entry. When the message is sent, the rendezvous occurs. This is the situation described earlier. Second, the receiver task can be busy with one rendezvous, or with some other processing not associated with a rendezvous, when another task attempts to send a message to the same entry. In that case, the sender is suspended until the receiver is free to accept that message in a rendezvous. If several messages arrive while the receiver is busy, the senders are queued to wait their turn for a rendezvous.

The two rendezvous just described are illustrated with the timeline diagrams in Figure 13.3.

Tasks need not have entry points. Such tasks are called **actor tasks** because they do not wait for a rendezvous in order to do their work. Actor tasks can rendezvous with other tasks by sending them messages. In contrast to actor tasks, a task can have **accept** clauses but not have any code outside those **accept** clauses, so it can only react to other tasks. Such a task is called a **server task.**

An Ada task that sends a message to another task must know the entry name in that task. However, the opposite is not true: A task entry need not

Figure 13.3

Two ways a rendezvous
with `Task_Example`
can occur

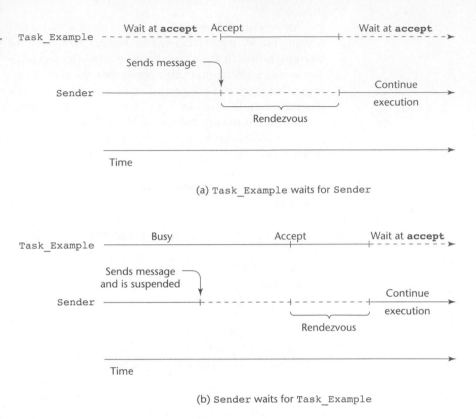

(a) `Task_Example` waits for `Sender`

(b) `Sender` waits for `Task_Example`

know the name of the task from which it will accept messages. This asymmetry is in contrast to the design of the language known as CSP, or Communicating Sequential Processes (Hoare, 1978). In CSP, which also uses the message-passing model of concurrency, tasks accept messages only from explicitly named tasks. The disadvantage of this is that libraries of tasks cannot be built for general use.

The usual graphical method of describing a rendezvous in which task A sends a message to task B is shown in Figure 13.4.

Ada tasks are types, and as such they can be either anonymous or named. An Ada task with a named type can be dynamically created using the **new** operator and referenced through a pointer. For example, consider the following:

```
task type Buffer is
  entry Deposit(Value : in Integer);
  entry Fetch(Value : out Integer);
end;
type Buf_Ptr is access Buffer;
...
Buf : Buf_Ptr;
Buf := new Buffer;
```

Figure 13.4

Graphical
representation of a
rendezvous caused by a
message sent from task
A to task B

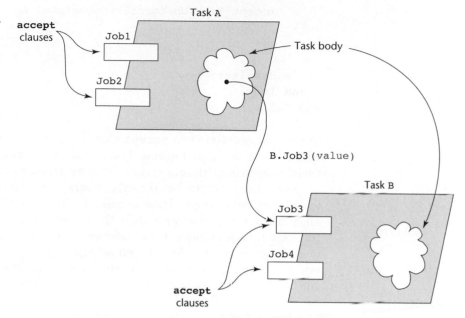

Tasks are declared in the declaration part of a package, subprogram, or block. Statically created tasks begin executing at the same time as the statements in the code to which that declarative part is attached. For example, a task declared in a main program begins execution at the same time as the first statement in the code body of the main program. Tasks created with **new** begin executing immediately. Task termination, which is a complex issue, is discussed later in this section.

Tasks may have any number of entries. The order in which the associated **accept** clauses appear in the task dictates the order in which messages can be accepted. If a task has more than one entry point and requires them to be able to receive messages in any order, the task uses a **select** statement to enclose the entries. For example, suppose a task models the activities of a bank teller, who must serve customers at a walk-up station inside the bank and also serve customers at a drive-up window. The following skeletal teller task illustrates a **select** construct:

```
task body Teller is
  loop
    select
      accept Drive_Up(formal parameters) do
        ...
      end Drive_Up;
      ...
    or
```

```
            accept Walk_Up(formal parameters) do
               ...
            end Walk_Up;
               ...
         end select;'
      end loop;
   end Teller;
```

In this task, there are two **accept** clauses, Walk_Up and Drive_Up, each of which has an associated queue. The action of the **select**, when it is executed, is to examine the queues associated with the two **accept** clauses. If one of the queues is empty, but the other contains at least one waiting message (customer), the **accept** clause associated with the waiting message or messages has a rendezvous with the task that sent the first message that was received. If both **accept** clauses have empty queues, the **select** waits until one of the entries is called. If both **accept** clauses have nonempty queues, one of the **accept** clauses is nondeterministically chosen to have a rendezvous with one of its callers. The loop forces the **select** statement to be executed repeatedly, forever.

The **end** of the **accept** clause marks the end of the code that assigns or references the formal parameters of the **accept** clause. The code, if there is any, between an **accept** clause and the next **or** (or the **end select**, if the **accept** clause is the last one in the **select**) is called the **extended accept clause.** The extended **accept** clause is executed only after the associated (immediately preceding) **accept** clause is executed. This execution of the extended **accept** clause is not part of the rendezvous and can take place in parallel with the execution of the calling task. The sender is suspended during the rendezvous, but it is restarted (put back in the ready queue) when the end of the **accept** clause is reached. If an **accept** clause has no formal parameters, the **do-end** is not required, and the **accept** clause can consist entirely of an extended **accept** clause. Such an **accept** clause would be used exclusively for synchronization. Extended **accept** clauses are illustrated in the Buf_Task task in Section 13.6.3.

13.6.2   Cooperation Synchronization

Each **accept** clause can have a guard attached, in the form of a **when** clause, that can delay rendezvous. For example,

```
when not Full(Buffer) =>
  accept Deposit(New_Value) do
```

An **accept** clause with a **when** clause is either open or closed. If the Boolean expression of the **when** clause is currently true, that **accept** clause is called **open;** if the Boolean expression is false, the **accept** clause is called **closed.**

An **accept** clause that does not have a guard is always open. An open **accept** clause is available for rendezvous; a closed **accept** clause cannot rendezvous.

Suppose there are several guarded **accept** clauses in a **select** clause. Such a **select** clause is usually placed in an infinite loop. The loop causes the **select** clause to be executed repeatedly, with each **when** clause evaluated on each repetition. Each repetition causes a list of open **accept** clauses to be constructed. If exactly one of the open clauses has a nonempty queue, a message from that queue is taken and a rendezvous takes place. If more than one of the open **accept** clauses have nonempty queues, one queue is chosen nondeterministically, a message is taken from that queue, and a rendezvous takes place. If the queues of all open clauses are empty, the task waits for a message to arrive at one of those **accept** clauses, at which time a rendezvous will occur. If a **select** is executed and every **accept** clause is closed, a run-time exception or error results. This possibility can be avoided either by making sure one of the **when** clauses is always true or by adding an **else** clause in the **select**. An **else** clause can include any sequence of statements, except an **accept** clause.

A **select** clause may have a special statement, **terminate**, that is selected only when it is open and no other **accept** clause is open. A **terminate** clause, when selected, means that the task is finished with its job but is not yet terminated. Task termination is discussed later in this section.

13.6.3   Competition Synchronization

The features described so far provide for cooperation synchronization and communication among tasks. We next discuss how mutually exclusive access to shared data structures can be enforced in Ada.

If access to a data structure is to be controlled by a task, then mutually exclusive access can be achieved by declaring the data structure within a task. The semantics of task execution usually guarantees mutually exclusive access to the structure, because only one **accept** clause in the task can be active at a given time. The only exceptions to this occur when tasks are nested in procedures or other tasks. For example, if a task that defines a shared data structure has a nested task, that nested task can also access the shared structure, which could destroy the integrity of the data. Thus, tasks that are meant to control access to a shared data structure should not define tasks.

The following is an example of an Ada task to provide a monitor for a buffer. The buffer behaves very much like the buffer in Section 13.3, in which sychronization is controlled with semaphores.

```
task Buf_Task is
  entry Deposit(Item : in Integer);
  entry Fetch(Item : out Integer);
end Buf_Task;
```

```
task body Buf_Task is
  Bufsize : constant Integer := 100;
  Buf    : array (1..Bufsize) of Integer;
  Filled : Integer range 0..Bufsize := 0;
  Next_In,
  Next_Out : Integer range 1..Bufsize := 1;
  begin
  loop
    select
      when Filled < Bufsize =>
        accept Deposit(Item : in Integer) do
          Buf(Next_In) := Item;
        end Deposit;
        Next_In := (Next_In mod Bufsize) + 1;
        Filled := Filled + 1;
    or
      when Filled > 0 =>
        accept Fetch(Item : out Integer) do
          Item := Buf(Next_Out);
        end Fetch;
        Next_Out := (Next_Out mod Bufsize) + 1;
        Filled := Filled - 1;
      end select;
    end loop;
  end Buf_Task;
```

In this example, both **accept** clauses are extended. These extended clauses can be executed concurrently with the tasks that called the associated **accept** clauses.

The tasks for the producer and consumer that could use Buf_Task have the following form:

```
task Producer;
task Consumer;
task body Producer is
  New_Value : Integer;
  begin
    loop
      -- produce New_Value --
      Buf_Task.Deposit(New_Value);
    end loop;
  end Producer;

task body Consumer is
  Stored_Value : Integer;
  begin
```

```
      loop
        Buf_Task.Fetch(Stored_Value);
        -- consume Stored_Value --
      end loop;
  end Consumer;
```

13.6.4   Task Termination

We now address the issue of task termination. We must first define task completion. The execution of a task is **completed** if control has reached the end of its code body. This may occur because an exception is raised for which there is no handler (Ada exception handling is described in Chapter 14). If a task has not created any other tasks, called *dependents*, it is terminated when its execution is completed. A task that has created dependent tasks is terminated when the execution of its code is completed and all of its dependents are terminated. A task may end its execution by waiting at an open **terminate** clause. In this case, the task is terminated only when its master (the block, subprogram, or task that created it) and all of the tasks that depend on that master have either completed or are waiting at an open **terminate** clause. In that case, all of these tasks are terminated simultaneously. A block or subprogram is not exited until all of its dependent tasks are terminated.

13.6.5   Priorities

Both named and anonymous task types can be assigned priorities. This is done with a pragma, as in

pragma Priority(expression);

The value of the expression specifies the relative priority for the task or task type definition in which it appears. The possible range of priority values is implementation-dependent. The highest priority possible can be specified with the Last attribute, the priority type, which is defined in System (System is a predefined package). For example, the following line specifies the highest priority in any implementation:

pragma Priority(System.Priority'Last);

When tasks are assigned priorities, those priorities are used by the task scheduler to determine which task to choose from the task-ready queue when the currently executing task is either blocked, reaches the end of its allocated time, or completes its execution. Furthermore, if a task with a higher priority than that of the currently executing task enters the task-ready queue, the lower-priority task that is executing is preempted and the higher-priority task begins its execution (or resumes its execution if had previously been in execution). A preempted task loses the processor and is placed in the task-ready queue.

13.6.6 Binary Semaphores

If access to a data structure is to be controlled and the data structure is not encapsulated in a task, another means must be used to provide mutually exclusive access. One way is to build a binary semaphore task to use with the task that references the data structure. Such a binary semaphore task could be defined as follows:

```
task Binary_Semaphore is
  entry Wait;
  entry Release;
end Binary_Semaphore;

task body Binary_Semaphore is
  begin
  loop
    accept Wait;
    accept Release;
  end loop;
  end Binary_Semaphore;
```

The purpose of this task is to guarantee that the Wait and Release operations occur in alternating fashion.

The Binary_Semaphore task illustrates the simplifications that are possible when Ada messages are passed only for synchronization, rather than to also pass data. Specifically, notice the simple form of **accept** clauses that do not need bodies.

Use of the Binary_Semaphore task to provide mutually exclusive access to a shared data structure would take place exactly as with the use of semaphores in the example program in Section 13.3. Of course, this use of semaphores suffers all of the potential problems discussed there.

Like semaphores, monitors can be simulated with the Ada tasking capability. Tasks provide implicit mutually exclusive access, exactly as do monitors. So the Ada tasking model supports both semaphores and monitors.

13.6.7 Protected Objects

As we have seen, access to shared data can be controlled by enclosing the data in a task and allowing access only through task entries, which implicitly provide competition synchronization. One problem with this method is that it is difficult to implement the rendezvous mechanism efficiently. Ada 95 protected objects provide an alternative method of providing competition synchronization that need not involve rendezvous.

A protected object is not a task; it is more like a monitor, as described in Section 13.4. Protected objects can be accessed either by protected subprograms or by entries that are syntactically similar to the **accept** clauses in tasks.[1] The protected subprograms can be either protected procedures, which provide mutually exclusive read-write access to the data of the protected object, or protected functions, which provide concurrent read-only access to that data. Within the body of a protected procedure, the current instance of the enclosing protected unit is defined to be a variable; within the body of a protected function, the current instance of the enclosing protected unit is defined to be a constant, which allows concurrent read-only access.

Entry calls to a protected object provide synchronous communication with one or more tasks using the same protected object. These entry calls provide access similar to that provided to the data enclosed in a task.

The buffer problem that is solved with a task in the previous subsection can be more simply solved with a protected object. Note that this example does not include protected subprograms.

```
protected Buffer is
   entry Deposit(Item : in Integer);
   entry Fetch(Item : out Integer);
private
   Bufsize : constant Integer := 100;
   Buf     : array (1..Bufsize) of Integer;
   Filled : Integer range 0..Bufsize := 0;
   Next_In,
   Next_Out : Integer range 1..Bufsize := 1;
   end Buffer;


protected body Buffer is
   entry Deposit(Item : in Integer) when Filled < Bufsize is
     begin
     Buf(Next_In) := Item;
     Next_In := (Next_In mod Bufsize) + 1;
     Filled := Filled + 1;
     end Deposit;
   entry Fetch(Item : out Integer) when Filled > 0 is
     begin
     Item := Buf(Next_Out);
     Next_Out := (Next_Out mod Bufsize) + 1;
     Filled := Filled - 1;
     end Fetch;
   end Buffer;
```

---

1. Entries in protected object bodies use the reserved word entry, rather than the accept used in task bodies.

13.6.8   Asynchronous Message Passing

The rendezvous mechanism we have described so far in this section is strictly synchronous; both the sender and the receiver must be ready for communication before they actually communicate through the rendezvous.

A task can have a special **select** clause, called an **asynchronous select,** which can react immediately to messages from other tasks. Such a clause can have either of two different triggering alternatives: an entry call or a **delay** statement. In addition to the triggering part, the asynchronous select clause has an abortable part, which could contain any sequence of Ada statements. The semantics of an asynchronous select clause is that it executes just one of its two parts. If the triggering event occurs (either the **entry** call is received or the **delay** timer terminates), it executes that part. Otherwise, it executes the abortable clause. The following two examples of asynchronous **select** clauses appear in the Ada 95 reference manual (ARM, 1995). In the first code segment, the abortable clause is executed repeatedly (because of the loop) until the call to Terminal.Wait_For_Interrupt is received. In the second code segment, the function called in the abortable clause executes for at least five seconds. If it is not finished by then, the **select** is exited.

```
-- Main command loop for a command interpreter
loop
  select
    Terminal.Wait_For_Interrupt;
    Put_Line("Interrupted");
  then abort
    -- This will be abandoned upon terminal interrupt
    Put_Line("-> ");
    Get_Line(Command, Last);
    Process_Command(Command (1..Last));
  end select;
end loop;
```

```
-- A time-limited calculation
select
  delay 5.0;
  Put_Line("Calculation does not converge");
then abort
  -- This calculation should finish in 5.0 seconds;
  -- if not, it is assumed to diverge.
  Horribly_Complicated_Recursive_Function(X, Y);
end select;
```

13.6.9   Evaluation

Using the general message-passing model of concurrency to construct monitors is like using Ada packages to support abstract data types—both are tools that are more general than is needed. Protected objects are a better way to provide synchronized shared data.

In the absence of distributed processors with independent memories, the choice between monitors and tasks with message passing as a means of implementing shared data in a concurrent environment is somewhat a matter of taste. However, in the case of Ada, protected objects are clearly better than tasks for supporting concurrent access to shared data. Not only is the code simpler; it is also much more efficient.

For distributed systems, message passing is a better model for concurrency, because it naturally supports the concept of separate processes executing in parallel on separate processors.

13.7 Java Threads

The concurrent units in Java are methods named run, whose code can be in concurrent execution with other such methods (of other objects) and with the main method. The process in which the run methods execute is called a **thread.** Java's threads are lightweight tasks, which means that they all run in the same address space. This is different from Ada tasks, which are heavyweight threads (they run in their own address spaces). One important result of this difference is that threads require far less overhead than Ada's tasks.

There are two ways to define a class with a run method. One of these is to define a subclass of the predefined class Thread and override its run method. However, if the new subclass has a necessary natural parent, then defining it as a subclass of Thread obviously will not work. In these situations, a subclass that inherits from its natural parent and implements the Runnable interface is defined. Runnable provides the run method protocol. This approach still requires a Thread object, as will be seen in Section 13.7.4.

Java's threads can be used to implement monitors, as discussed in Section 13.7.3.

13.7.1 The Thread Class

The Thread class is not the natural parent of any other classes. It provides some services for its subclasses, but it is not related in any natural way to their computational purposes. Nevertheless, Thread is the only *class* available to the programmer for creating concurrent Java programs. As previously stated, Section 13.7.4 will briefly discuss the use of the Runnable interface.

The bare essentials of Thread are two methods named run and start. The run method is always overridden by subclasses of Thread. The code of the run method describes the actions of the thread. The start method of Thread starts its thread as a concurrent unit by calling its run method.[2] The call to

---

2. Calling the run method directly does not always work, because initialization that is sometimes required is included in the start method.

start is unusual in that control returns immediately to the caller, which then continues its execution, in parallel with the newly started run method.

Following is a skeletal subclass of Thread and a code fragment that creates an object of the subclass and starts the run method's execution in the new thread:

```
class MyThread extends Thread {
  public void run() { ... }
}
...
Thread myTh = new MyThread();
myTh.start();
```

When a Java application program (as opposed to an applet) begins execution, a new thread is created (in which the **main** method will run) and **main** is called. Applets also run in their own threads. Therefore, all Java programs run in threads.

When a program has multiple threads, a scheduler must determine which thread or threads will run at any given time. In most cases, there is only a single processor, so only one thread actually runs at a time. It is difficult to give a precise description of how the Java scheduler works, because the different implementations (Solaris, Windows, and so on) do not necessarily schedule threads in exactly the same way. Typically, however, the scheduler gives equal-size time slices to each ready thread in round-robin fashion, assuming all of these threads have the same priority. Section 13.7.2 describes how different priorities can be given to different threads.

The Thread class provides several methods for controlling the execution of threads. The yield method, which takes no parameters, is a request from the running thread to voluntarily surrender the processor. The thread is immediately put in the task-ready queue, making it ready to run. The scheduler then chooses the highest-priority thread from the task-ready queue. If there are no other ready threads with priority higher than the one that just yielded the processor, it may also be the next thread to get the processor.

The sleep method has a single parameter, which is the integer number of milliseconds that the caller of sleep wants the thread to be blocked. After the specified number of milliseconds has passed, the thread will be put in the task-ready queue. Because there is no way to know how long a thread will be in the task-ready queue before it runs, the parameter to sleep is the minimum amount of time the thread will *not* be in execution. The sleep method can throw an InterruptedException, which must be handled in the method that calls sleep. Exceptions are described in detail in Chapter 14.

The join method is used to force a method to delay its execution until the run method of another thread has completed its execution. join is used when the processing of a method cannot continue until the work of the other thread is complete. For example, we might have the following run method:

```
public void run() {
   ...
   Thread myTh = new Thread();
   myTh.start();
   // do part of the computation of this thread
   myTh.join();  // Wait for myTh to complete
   // do the rest of the computation of this thread
}
```

The join method puts the thread that calls it in the blocked state, which can be ended only by the completion of the thread on which join was called. If that thread happens to be blocked, there is the possibility of deadlock. To prevent this, join can be called with a parameter, which is the time limit in milliseconds of how long the calling thread will wait for the called thread to complete. For example,

```
myTh.join(2000);
```

will cause the calling thread to wait two seconds for myTh to complete. If it has not completed its execution after two seconds have passed, the calling thread is put back in the ready queue, which means that it will continue its execution as soon as it is scheduled.

Early versions of Java included three more Thread methods: stop, suspend, and resume. All three of these have been deprecated because of safety problems. The stop method is sometimes overridden with a simple method that destroys the thread by setting its reference variable to **null**.

The normal way a run method ends its execution is by reaching the end of its code. However, in many cases threads run until told to terminate. Regarding this, there is the question of how a thread can determine whether it should continue or end. The interrupt method is one way to communicate to a thread that it should stop. This method does not stop the thread; rather, it sends the thread a message that actually just sets a bit in the thread, which can be checked by the thread. The bit is checked with the predicate method, isInterrupted. This is not a complete solution, because the thread one is attempting to interrupt may be sleeping or waiting at the time the interrupt method is called, which means that it will not be checking to see if it has been interrupted. For these situations, the interrupt method also throws an exception, InterruptedException, which also causes the thread to awaken (from sleeping or waiting). So, a thread can periodically check to see whether it has been interrupted and if so, whether it can terminate. The thread cannot miss the interrupt, because if it was asleep or waiting when the interrupt occurred, it will be awakened by the interrupt. Actually, there are more details to the actions and uses of interrupt, but they are not covered here (Arnold et al., 2006).

13.7.2 Priorities

The priorities of threads need not all be the same. A thread's default priority is the same as the thread that created it. If main creates a thread, its default priority is the constant NORM_PRIORITY, which is usually 5. Thread defines two other priority constants, MAX_PRIORITY and MIN_PRIORITY, whose values are usually 10 and 1, respectively.[3] The priority of a thread can be changed with the method setPriority. The new priority can be any of the predefined constants or any other number between MIN_PRIORITY and MAX_PRIORITY. The getPriority method returns the current priority of a thread.

When there are threads with different priorities, the scheduler's behavior is controlled by those priorities. When the executing thread is blocked or killed or the time slice for it expires, the scheduler chooses the thread from the task-ready queue that has the highest priority. A thread with lower priority will run only if one of higher priority is not in the task-ready queue when the opportunity arises.

13.7.3 Competition Synchronization

In Java, competition synchronization is implemented by specifying that the methods that access shared data are run completely before another method is executed on the same object. In other words, we can specify that once a particular method begins its execution, that execution will be completed before any other method begins its execution on the same object. Such methods place a lock on the object, which prevents other synchronized methods from executing on the object. This is specified on a method by adding the **synchronized** modifier to the method's definition, as in the following skeletal class definition:

```
class ManageBuf {
  private int [100] buf;
  ...
  public synchronized void deposit(int item) { ... }
  public synchronized int fetch() { ... }
  ...
}
```

The two methods defined in ManageBuf are both defined to be **synchronized,** which prevents them from interfering with each other while executing on the same object, even if they are called by separate threads.

---

3. The number of priorities is implementation-dependent, so there may be fewer or more than 10 levels in some implementations.

An object whose methods are all synchronized is effectively a monitor. Note that an object may have one or more synchronized methods, as well as one or more unsynchronized methods.

In some cases, the number of statements that deal with the shared data structure is significantly less than the number of other statements in the method in which it resides. In these cases, it is better to synchronize the code segment that accesses or changes the shared data structure rather than the whole method. This can be done with a so-called *synchronized statement*, whose general form is

synchronized(expression)
    statement

where the expression must evaluate to an object and the statement can be a single statement or a compound statement. The object is locked during execution of the statement or compound statement, so the statement or compound statement is executed exactly as if it were the body of a synchronized method.

An object that has synchronized methods defined for it must have a queue associated with it that stores the synchronized methods that have attempted to execute on it while it was being operated upon by another synchronized method. When a synchronized method completes its execution on an object, a method that is waiting in the object's waiting queue, if there is such a method, is put in the task-ready queue.

13.7.4 Cooperation Synchronization

Cooperation synchronization in Java is accomplished by using the wait, notify, and notifyAll methods that are defined in Object, the root class of all Java classes. All classes except Object inherit these methods. Every object has a wait list of all of the threads that have called wait on the object. The notify method is called to tell one waiting thread that the event it was waiting for has happened. The specific thread that is awakened by notify cannot be determined, because the Java Virtual Machine (JVM) chooses one from the wait list of the thread object at random. Because of this, along with the fact that the waiting threads may all be waiting for different conditions, the notifyAll method is often used, rather than notify. The notifyAll method awakens all of the threads on the object's wait list, starting their execution just after their call to wait.

The methods wait, notify, and notifyAll can be called only from within a synchronized method, because they use the lock placed on an object by such a method. The call to wait is usually put in a **while** loop that is controlled by the condition for which the method is waiting. Because of the use of notifyAll, some other thread may have changed the condition to false since it was last tested.

The wait method can throw InterruptedException, which is a descendant of Exception (Java's exception handling is discussed in Chapter 14). Therefore, any code that calls wait must also catch InterruptedException. Assuming the condition for which we wait is called theCondition, the conventional way to use wait is as follows:

```
try {
  while (!theCondition)
    wait();
  -- Do whatever is needed after theCondition comes true
}
catch(InterruptedException myProblem) { ... }
```

The following program implements a circular queue for storing **int** values. It illustrates both cooperation and competition synchronization.

```
// Queue
// This class implements a circular queue for storing int
// values. It includes a constructor for allocating and
// initializing the queue to a specified size. It has
// synchronized methods for inserting values into and
// removing values from the queue.

class Queue {
  private int [] que;
  private int nextIn,
              nextOut,
              filled,
              queSize;

  public Queue(int size) {
    que = new int [size];
    filled = 0;
    nextIn = 1;
    nextOut = 1;
    queSize = size;
  }   //** end of Queue constructor

  public synchronized void deposit (int item) {
    try {
      while (filled == queSize)
        wait();
      que [nextIn] = item;
      nextIn = (nextIn % queSize) + 1;
      filled++;
      notifyAll();
```

```
      }  //** end of try clause
      catch(InterruptedException e) {}
   }  //** end of deposit method

   public synchronized int fetch() {
     int item = 0;
     try {
       while (filled == 0)
         wait();
       item = que [nextOut];
       nextOut = (nextOut % queSize) + 1;
       filled--;
       notifyAll();
     }  //** end of try clause
     catch(InterruptedException e) {}
     return item;
   }  //** end of fetch method
}  //** end of Queue class
```

Notice that the exception handler (**catch**) does nothing here.

Classes to define producer and consumer objects that could use the Queue class can be defined as follows:

```
class Producer extends Thread {
  private Queue buffer;
  public Producer(Queue que) {
    buffer = que;
  }
  public void run() {
    int new_item;
    while (true) {
      //-- Create a new_item
      buffer.deposit(new_item);
    }
  }
}

class Consumer extends Thread {
  private Queue buffer;
  public Consumer(Queue que) {
    buffer = que;
  }
  public void run() {
    int stored_item;
    while (true) {
      buffer.fetch(stored_item);
```

```
        //-- Consume the stored_item
    }
  }
}
```

The following code creates a Queue object, and a Producer and a Consumer object, both attached to the Queue object, and starts their execution:

```
Queue buff1 = new Queue(100);
Producer producer1 = new Producer(buff1);
Consumer consumer1 = new Consumer(buff1);
producer1.start();
consumer1.start();
```

We could define one or both of the Producer and the Consumer as implementations of the Runnable interface rather than as subclasses of Thread. The only difference is in the first line, which would now appear as

```
class Producer implements Runnable {
```

To create and run an object of such a class, it is still necessary to create a Thread object that is connected to the object. This is illustrated in the following code:

```
Producer producer1 = new Producer(buff1);
Thread producerThread = new Thread(producer1);
producerThread.start();
```

13.7.5 Evaluation

Java's support for concurrency is relatively simple but effective. Because they are heavyweight threads, Ada's tasks easily can be distributed to different processors, in particular different processors with different memories, which could be on different computers in different places. These kinds of systems are not possible with Java's lightweight threads.

13.8 C# Threads

Although C#'s threads are loosely based on those of Java, there are significant differences. Following is a brief overview of C#'s threads.

13.8.1 Basic Thread Operations

Rather than just methods named run, as in Java, any C# method can run in its own thread. A C# thread is created by creating a Thread object. The Thread constructor must be sent an instantiation of a predefined delegate class, `ThreadStart`,[4] to which must be sent the method that implements the actions of the thread. For example, we might have

```
public void MyRun1() { ... }
...
Thread myThread = new Thread(new ThreadStart(MyRun1));
```

As with Java, creating a thread does not start its concurrent execution. Once again, execution must be requested through a method, in this case named `Start`, as in

```
myThread.Start();
```

As in Java, a thread can be made to wait for another thread to finish its execution before continuing, using the similarly named method `Join`.

A thread can be suspended for a specified amount of time with `Sleep`, which is a public static method of `Thread`. The parameter to `Sleep` is an integer number of milliseconds. Unlike its Java relative, C#'s `Sleep` does not raise any exceptions, so it need not be called in a **try** block.

A thread can be terminated with the `Abort` method, although it does not literally kill the thread. Instead, it throws the `ThreadAbortException`, which the thread can catch. When the thread catches this exception, it usually deallocates any resources it allocated, and then ends (by getting to the end of its code).

13.8.2 Synchronizing Threads

There are three different ways that C# threads can be synchronized: the `Interlock` class, the `lock` statement, and the `Monitor` class. Each of these mechanisms is designed for a specific need. The `Interlock` class is used when the only operations that need to be synchronized are the incrementing and decrementing of an integer. These operations are done atomically with the two methods of `Interlock`, `Increment` and `Decrement`, which take a reference to an integer as the parameter. For example, to increment a shared integer named `counter` in a thread, we could use

```
Interlocked.Increment(ref counter);
```

The `lock` statement is used to mark a critical section of code in a thread. The syntax of this is as follows:

```
lock(expression) {
```

---

4. A C# delegate is an object-oriented version of a function pointer. In this case, it literally points to the method we want to run in the new thread.

```
    // The critical section
}
```

The expression, which looks like a parameter to lock, is usually a reference to the object on which the thread is running, **this.**

The Monitor class has four methods, Enter, Wait, Pulse, and Exit, that can be used to provide more sophisticated synchronization of threads. The Enter method, which takes an object reference as its parameter, marks the beginning of synchronization of the thread on that object. The Wait method suspends execution of the thread and instructs the Common Language Runtime (CLR) of .NET that this thread wants to resume its execution the next time there is an opportunity. The Pulse method, which also takes an object reference as its parameter, notifies waiting threads they now have a chance to run again. Pulse is similar to Java's notifyAll. Threads that have been waiting are run in the order in which they called the Wait method. The Exit method ends the critical section of the thread.

13.8.3 Evaluation

C#'s threads are a slight improvement over those of its predecessor, Java. For one thing, any method can be run in its own thread. Recall that in Java, only methods named run can run in their own threads. Thread termination is also cleaner with C# (calling a method (Abort) is more elegant than setting the thread's pointer to null). Synchronization of thread execution is more sophisticated in C#, because C# has several different mechanisms, each for a specific application. C# threads, like those of Java, are lightweight, so they cannot be as versatile as Ada's tasks.

13.9 Statement-Level Concurrency

In this section, we take a brief look at language design for statement-level concurrency. From the language design point of view, the objective of such designs is to provide a mechanism that the programmer can use to inform the compiler of ways it can map the program onto a multiprocessor architecture.[5]

In this section, we discuss only one collection of linguistic constructs from one language for statement-level concurrency. Furthermore, we will describe the constructs and their objectives in terms of SIMD architecture machines (see Section 13.1.1), although they were designed to be useful for a variety of architectural configurations.

The problem addressed by the language constructs we discuss is that of minimizing the communication required among processors and the memories

---

5. Although ALGOL 68 included a semaphore type that was meant to deal with statement-level concurrency, we do not discuss that application of semaphores here.

of other processors. The assumption is that it is faster for a processor to access data in its own memory than that of some other processor. Well-designed compilers can do a great deal in this process, but much more can be done if the programmer is able to provide information to the compiler about the possible concurrency that could be employed.

13.9.1 High-Performance Fortran

High-Performance Fortran (HPF; ACM, 1993b) is a collection of extensions to Fortran 90 that are meant to allow programmers to specify information to the compiler to help it optimize the execution of programs on multiprocessor computers. HPF includes both new specification statements and intrinsic, or built-in, subprograms. This section discusses only some of the new statements.

The primary specification statements of HPF are for specifying the number of processors, the distribution of data over the memories of those processors, and the alignment of data with other data in terms of memory placement. The HPF specification statements appear as special comments in a Fortran program. Each of them is introduced by the prefix !HPF$, where ! is the character used to begin lines of comments in Fortran 90. This prefix makes them invisible to Fortran 90 compilers but easy for HPF compilers to recognize.

The PROCESSORS specification has the form

```
!HPF$ PROCESSORS procs (n)
```

This statement is used to specify to the compiler the number of processors that can be used by the code generated for this program. This information is used in conjunction with other specifications to tell the compiler how data is to be distributed to the memories associated with the processors.

The DISTRIBUTE statement specifies what data is to be distributed and the kind of distribution that is to be used. Its form is

```
!HPF$ DISTRIBUTE (kind) ONTO procs :: identifier_list
```

In this statement, kind can be either BLOCK or CYCLIC. The identifier list is the names of the array variables that are to be distributed. A variable that is specified to be BLOCK distributed is divided into n equal groups, where each group consists of contiguous collections of array elements evenly distributed over the memories of all the processors. For example, if an array with 500 elements named LIST is BLOCK distributed over five processors, the first 100 elements of LIST will be stored in the memory of the first processor, the second 100 in the memory of the second processor, and so forth. A CYCLIC distribution specifies that individual elements of the array are cyclically stored in the memories of the processors. For example, if LIST is CYCLIC distributed, again over five processors, the first element of LIST will be stored in the memory of the first processor, the second element in the memory of the second processor, and so forth.

The form of the `ALIGN` statement is

`ALIGN  array1_element WITH  array2_element`

`ALIGN` is used to relate the distribution of one array with that of another. For example,

`ALIGN list1(index) WITH list2(index+1)`

specifies that the `index` element of `list1` is to be stored in the memory of the same processor as the `index+1` element of `list2`, for all values of `index`. The two array references in an `ALIGN` appear together in some statement of the program. Putting them in the same memory (which means the same processor) ensures that the references to them will be as close as possible.

Consider the following example code segment:

```
    REAL list_1 (1000), list_2 (1000)
    INTEGER list_3 (500), list_4 (501)
!HPF$ PROCESSORS proc (10)
!HPF$ DISTRIBUTE (BLOCK) ONTO procs :: list_1, list_2
!HPF$ ALIGN list_3 (index) WITH list_4 (index+1)
    ...
    list_1 (index) = list_2 (index)
    list_3 (index) = list_4 (index+1)
```

In each execution of these assignment statements, the two referenced array elements will be stored in the memory of the same processor.

The HPF specification statements actually only provide information for the compiler that it may or may not use to optimize the code it produces. What the compiler actually does depends on its level of sophistication and the particular architecture of the target machine.

The `FORALL` statement specifies a collection of statements that may be executed concurrently. For example,

`FORALL (index = 1:1000) list_1 (index) = list_2 (index)`

specifies the assignment of the elements of `list_2` to the corresponding elements of `list_1`. Conceptually, it specifies that the right side of all 1000 assignments can be evaluated first, before any assignments take place. This permits concurrent execution of all of the assignment statements. The HPF `FORALL` statement is included in Fortran 95 and Fortran 2003.

We have briefly discussed only a part of the capabilities of HPF. However, it should be enough to provide the reader with an idea of the kinds of language extensions that are useful for programming computers with possibly large numbers of processors.

SUMMARY

Concurrent execution can be at the instruction, statement, or subprogram level. We use the phrase *physical concurrency* when multiple processors are actually used to execute concurrent units. If concurrent units are executed on a single processor, we use the term *logical concurrency*. The underlying conceptual model of all concurrency can be referred to as *logical concurrency*.

Most multiprocessor computers fall into one of two categories—SIMD or MIMD. MIMD computers can be distributed.

Two of the primary facilities that languages that support subprogram-level concurrency must provide are mutually exclusive access to shared data structures (competition synchronization) and cooperation among tasks (cooperation synchronization).

Tasks can be in any one of five different states: new, ready, running, blocked, or dead.

A semaphore is a data structure consisting of an integer and a task description queue. Semaphores can be used to provide both competition and cooperation synchronization among concurrent tasks. It is easy to use semaphores incorrectly, resulting in errors that cannot be detected by the compiler, linker, or run-time system.

Monitors are data abstractions that provide a natural way of allowing mutually exclusive access to data shared among tasks. They are supported by several programming languages, among them Ada, Java, and C#. Cooperation synchronization in languages with monitors must be provided with some form of semaphores.

Ada provides complex but effective constructs, based on the message-passing model, for concurrency. Ada's tasks are heavyweight tasks. Tasks communicate with each other through the rendezvous mechanism, which is synchronous message passing. A rendezvous is the action of a task accepting a message sent by another task. Ada includes both simple and complicated methods of controlling the occurrences of rendezvous among tasks.

Ada 95 includes additional capabilities for the support of concurrency, primarily protected objects, and asynchronous message passing. Ada 95 supports monitors in two ways, with tasks and with protected objects.

Java provides lightweight concurrent units in a rather simple but effective way. Any class that either inherits from `Thread` or implements `Runnable` can override an inherited method named `run` and have that method's code executed concurrently with other such methods and with the main program. Competition synchronization is specified by defining methods that access shared data to be synchronized. Small sections of code can also be synchronized. A class whose methods are all synchronized is a monitor. Cooperation synchronization is implemented with the methods `wait`, `notify`, and `notifyAll`. The `Thread` class also provides the `sleep`, `yield`, `join`, and `interrupt` methods.

C#'s support for concurrency is based on that of Java, but is more sophisticated. Any method can be run in a thread. Three kinds of thread synchronization are supported with the `Interlock` and `Monitor` classses and the `lock` statement.

High-Performance Fortran includes statements for specifying how data is to be distributed over the memory units connected to multiple processors. Also included are statements for specifying collections of statements that can be executed concurrently.

BIBLIOGRAPHIC NOTES

The general subject of concurrency is discussed at great length in Andrews and Schneider (1983), Holt et al. (1978), and Ben-Ari (1982).

The monitor concept is developed and its implementation in Concurrent Pascal is described by Brinch Hansen (1977).

The early development of the message-passing model of concurrent unit control is discussed by Hoare (1978) and Brinch Hansen (1978). An in-depth discussion of the development of the Ada tasking model can be found in Ichbiah et al. (1979). Ada 95 is described in detail in ARM (1995). High-Performance Fortran is described in ACM (1993b).

REVIEW QUESTIONS

1. What are the three possible levels of concurrency in programs?
2. Describe the logical architecture of an SIMD computer.
3. Describe the logical architecture of an MIMD computer.
4. What level of program concurrency is best supported by SIMD computers?
5. What level of program concurrency is best supported by MIMD computers?
6. What is the difference between physical and logical concurrency?
7. What is a thread of control in a program?
8. Define *task*, *disjoint task*, *synchronization*, *competition* and *cooperation synchronization*, *liveness*, *race condition*, and *deadlock*.
9. What kind of tasks do not require any kind of synchronization?
10. Describe the five different states in which a task can be.
11. What is the purpose of a task-ready queue?
12. What are the design issues for language support for concurrency?
13. Describe the actions of the wait and release operations for semaphores.

14. What is a binary semaphore? What is a counting semaphore?

15. What are the primary problems with using semaphores to provide synchronization?

16. What advantage do monitors have over semaphores?

17. Define *rendezvous*, **accept** *clause*, **entry** *clause*, *actor task*, *server task*, *extended* **accept** *clause*, *open* **accept** *clause*, *closed* **accept** *clause*, and *completed task*.

18. Which is more general, concurrency through monitors or concurrency through message passing?

19. Are Ada tasks created statically or dynamically?

20. What purpose does an extended **accept** clause serve?

21. How is cooperation synchronization provided for Ada tasks?

22. What is the advantage of protected objects in Ada 95 over tasks for providing access to shared data objects?

23. Describe the Ada 95 asynchronous **select** clause.

24. Specifically, what Java program unit can run concurrently with the main method in an application program?

25. What does the Java `sleep` method do?

26. What does the Java `yield` method do?

27. What does the Java `join` method do?

28. What does the Java `interrupt` method do?

29. What are the two Java constructs that can be synchronized?

30. Describe the actions of the three Java methods that are used to support cooperation synchronization.

31. What kind of Java object is a monitor?

32. Explain why Java includes the `Runnable` interface.

33. What kinds of methods can run in a C# thread?

34. What is different about C#'s `Sleep` method, relative to Java's `sleep`?

35. What exactly does C#'s `Abort` method do?

36. What is the purpose of the `Interlock` class?

37. What does the C# `lock` statement do?

38. What is the objective of the specification statements of High-Performance Fortran?

39. What is the purpose of the `FORALL` statement of High-Performance Fortran?

1. Explain clearly why competition synchronization is not a problem in a programming environment that supports coroutines but not concurrency.

2. What is the best action a system can take when deadlock is detected?

3. Busy waiting is a method whereby a task waits for a given event by continuously checking for that event to occur. What is the main problem with this approach?

4. In the producer-consumer example of Section 13.3, suppose that we incorrectly replaced the `release(access)` in the consumer process with `wait(access)`. What would be the result of this error on execution of the system?

5. From a book on assembly language programming for a computer that uses an Intel Pentium processor, determine what instructions are provided to support the construction of semaphores.

6. Suppose two tasks A and B must use the shared variable `Buf_Size`. Task A adds 2 to `Buf_Size`, and task B subtracts 1 from it. Assume that such arithmetic operations are done by the three-step process of fetching the current value, performing the arithmetic, and putting the new value back. In the absence of competition synchronization, what sequences of events are possible and what values result from these operations? Assume the initial value of `Buf_Size` is 6.

7. Compare the Java competition synchronization mechanism with that of Ada.

8. Compare the Java cooperation synchronization mechanism with that of Ada.

9. What happens if a monitor procedure calls another procedure in the same monitor?

10. Explain the relative safety of cooperation synchronization using semaphores and using Ada's when clauses in tasks.

1. Write an Ada task to implement general semaphores.

2. Write an Ada task to manage a shared buffer such as the one in our example, but use the semaphore task from Programming Exercise 1.

3. Define semaphores in Ada and use them to provide both cooperation and competition synchronization in the shared-buffer example.

4. Write Programming Exercise 3 using Java.

5. Write the shared-buffer example of the chapter in C#.

6. The reader-writer problem can be stated as follows: A shared memory location can be concurrently read by any number of tasks, but when a task must write to the shared memory location, it must have exclusive access. Write a Java program for the reader-writer problem.

7. Write Programming Exercise 6 using Ada.

8. Write Programming Exercise 6 using C#.

Exception Handling and Event Handling

T
his chapter discusses programming language support for two related parts of many contemporary programs: exception handling and event handling. Both exceptions and events can occur at times that cannot be predetermined, and both are best handled with special language constructs and processes. Some of these—for example, propagation—are similar for exception handling and event handling.

We first describe the fundamental concepts of exception handling, including hardware- and software-detectable exceptions, exception handlers, and the raising of exceptions. Then the design issues for exception handling are introduced and discussed, including the binding of exceptions to exception handlers, continuation, default handlers, and exception disabling. This section is followed by a description and an evaluation of the exception-handling facilities of three programming languages: Ada, C++, and Java.

The latter part of this chapter is about event handling. We first present an introduction to the basic concepts of event handling. This topic is followed by a brief discussion of the event-handling approach of Java for its GUI components.

14.1 Introduction to Exception Handling

Most computer hardware systems are capable of detecting certain run-time error conditions, such as floating-point overflow. Early programming languages were designed and implemented in such a way that the user program could neither detect nor attempt to deal with such errors. In these languages, the occurrence of such an error simply causes the program to be terminated and control to be transferred to the operating system. The typical operating system reaction to a run-time error is to display a diagnostic message, which may be meaningful and therefore useful, or highly cryptic. After displaying the message, the program is terminated.

In the case of input and output operations, however, the situation is somewhat different. For example, a Fortran `Read` statement can intercept input errors and end-of-file conditions, both of which are detected by the input device hardware. In both cases, the `Read` statement can specify the label of some statement in the user program that deals with the condition. In the case of the end-of-file, it is clear that the condition is not always considered an error. In most cases, it is nothing more than a signal that one kind of processing is completed and a new kind must begin. In spite of the obvious difference between end-of-file and events that are always errors, such as a failed input process, Fortran handles both situations with the same mechanism. Consider the following Fortran `Read` statement:

```
Read(Unit=5, Fmt=1000, Err=100, End=999) Weight
```

The `Err` clause specifies that control is to be transferred to the statement labeled `100` if an error occurs in the read operation. The `End` clause specifies that control is to be transferred to the statement labeled `999` if the read operation encounters the end of the file. Fortran uses simple branches for both input errors and end-of-file.

There is a category of serious errors that are not detectable by hardware but could be detected by code generated by the compiler. For example, array subscript range errors are almost never detected by hardware,[1] but they lead to fatal errors that often are not noticed until later in the program execution.

Detection of subscript range errors is sometimes required by the language design. For example, Java compilers usually generate code to check the correctness of every subscript expression (they do not generate such code when it can be determined at compile time that a subscript expression cannot have an out-of-range value, for example, if the subscript is a literal). In C, subscript ranges are not checked because the cost of such checking was (and is) not believed to be worth the benefit of detecting such errors. In some compilers for some languages, subscript range checking can be selected (if not turned on by default) or turned off (if it is on by default) as desired in the program or in the command that executes the compiler.

The designers of many contemporary languages have included mechanisms that allow programs to react in a standard way to certain run-time errors, as well as other program-detected unusual events. Programs may also be notified when certain events are detected by hardware or system software, so that they also can react to these events. These mechanisms are collectively called exception handling.

Perhaps the most important reason some languages do not include exception handling is the complexity it adds to the language.

14.1.1   Basic Concepts

We consider both the errors detected by hardware, such as disk read errors, and unusual conditions, such as end-of-file (which is also detected by hardware), as exceptions. We further extend the concept of an exception to include errors or unusual conditions that are software-detectable (by either a software interpreter or the user code itself). Accordingly, we define **exception** to be any unusual event, erroneous or not, that is detectable by either hardware or software and that may require special processing.

The special processing that may be required when an exception is detected is called **exception handling.** This processing is done by a code unit or segment called an **exception handler.** An exception is **raised** when its associated event occurs. In some recent C-based languages, exceptions are said to be *thrown*, rather than *raised*.[2] Different kinds of exceptions require different exception handlers. Detection of end-of-file nearly always requires some specific program action. But, clearly, that action would not also be appropriate for

---

1. In the 1970s, there were some computers that *did* detect subscript range errors in hardware.

2. C++ was the first C-based language that included exception handling. The word *throw* was used, rather than *raise*, because the standard C library includes a function named `raise`.

an array index range error exception. In some cases, the only action is the generation of an error message and an orderly termination of the program.

In some situations, it may be desirable to ignore certain hardware-detectable exceptions—for example, division by zero—for a time. This action would be done by disabling the exception. A disabled exception could be enabled again at a later time.

The absence of separate or specific exception-handling facilities in a language does not preclude the handling of user-defined, software-detected exceptions. Such an exception detected within a program unit is often handled by the unit's caller, or invoker. One possible design is to send an auxiliary parameter, which is used as a status variable. The status variable is assigned a value in the called subprogram according to the correctness and/or normalness of its computation. Immediately upon return from the called unit, the caller tests the status variable. If the value indicates that an exception has occurred, the handler, which may reside in the calling unit, can be enacted. Many of the C standard library functions use a variant of this approach: The return values are used as error indicators.

Another possibility is to pass a label parameter to the subprogram. Of course, this approach is possible only in languages that allow labels to be used as parameters. Passing a label allows the called unit to return to a different point in the caller if an exception has occurred. As in the first alternative, the handler is often a segment of the calling unit's code. This is a common use of label parameters in Fortran.

A third possibility is to have the handler as a separate subprogram whose name is passed as a parameter to the called unit. In this case, the handler subprogram is provided by the caller, but the called unit calls the handler when an exception is raised. One problem with this approach is that one is required to send a handler subprogram with *every* call to *every* subprogram that takes a handler subprogram as a parameter, whether it is needed or not. Furthermore, to deal with several different kinds of exceptions, several different handler routines would need to be passed, complicating the code.

If it is desirable to handle an exception in the unit in which it is detected, the handler is included as a segment of code in that unit.

There are some definite advantages to having exception handling built into a language. First, without exception handling, the code required to detect error conditions can considerably clutter a program. For example, suppose a subprogram includes expressions that contain 10 references to elements of a matrix named `mat`, and any one of them could have an index out-of-range error. Further suppose that the language does not require index range checking. Without built-in index range checking, every one of these operations may need to be preceded by code to detect a possible index range error. For example, consider the following reference to an element of `mat`, which has 10 rows and 20 columns:

```
if (row >= 0 && row < 10 && col >= 0 && col < 20)
  sum += mat[row][col];
```

```
else
  System.out.println("Index range error on mat, row = " +
                     row + " col = " + col);
```

The presence of exception handling in the language would permit the compiler to insert such checks before every array element access, greatly shortening and simplifying the source program.

Another advantage of language support for exception handling results from exception propagation. Exception propagation allows an exception raised in one program unit to be handled in some other unit in its dynamic or static ancestry. This allows a single exception handler to be used for any number of different program units. This reuse can result in significant savings in development cost, program size, and program complexity.

A language that supports exception handling encourages its users to consider all of the events that could occur during program execution and how they can be handled. This approach is far better than not considering such possibilities and simply hoping nothing will go wrong. This advantage is related to requiring a multiple-selector construct to include actions for all possible values of the control expression, as is required by Ada.

Finally, there are programs in which dealing with nonerroneous but unusual situations can be simplified with exception handling, and in which program structure can become overly convoluted without it.

14.1.2 Design Issues

We now explore some of the design issues for an exception-handling system when it is part of a programming language. Such a system might allow both predefined and user-defined exceptions and exception handlers. Note that predefined exceptions are implicitly raised, whereas user-defined exceptions are explicitly raised by user code. Consider the following skeletal subprogram that includes an exception-handling mechanism for an implicitly raised exception:

```
void example() {
  ...
  average = sum / total;
  ...
  return;
/* Exception handlers */
  when zero_divide {
    average = 0;
    printf("Error—divisor (total) is zero\n");
  }
  ...
}
```

The exception of division by zero, which is implicitly raised, causes control to transfer to the appropriate handler, which is then executed.

The first design issue for exception handling is how an exception occurrence is bound to an exception handler. This issue occurs on two different levels. On the unit level, there is the question of how the same exception being raised at different points in a unit can be bound to different handlers within the unit. For example, in the example subprogram, there is a handler for a division-by-zero exception that appears to be written to deal with an occurrence of division by zero in a particular statement (the one shown). But suppose the function includes several other expressions with division operators. For those operators, this handler would probably not be appropriate. So, it should be possible to bind the exceptions that can be raised by particular statements to particular handlers, even though the same exception can be raised by many different statements.

At a higher level, the binding question arises when there is no exception handler local to the unit in which the exception is raised. In this case, the designer must decide whether to propagate the exception to some other unit and, if so, where. How this propagation takes place and how far it goes have an important impact on the writability of exception handlers. For example, if handlers must be local, then many handlers must be written, which complicates both the writing and reading of the program. On the other hand, if exceptions are propagated, a single handler might handle the same exception raised in several program units, which may require the handler to be more general than one would prefer.

An issue that is related to the binding of an exception to an exception handler is whether information about the exception is made available to the handler.

After an exception handler executes, either control can transfer to somewhere in the program outside of the handler code or program execution can simply terminate. We term this the question of control continuation after handler execution, or simply **continuation. Termination** is obviously the simplest choice, and in many error exception conditions, the best. However, in other situations, particularly those associated with unusual but not erroneous events, the choice of continuing execution is best. This design is called **resumption.** In these cases, some conventions must be chosen to determine where execution should continue. It might be the statement that raised the exception, the statement after the statement that raised the exception, or possibly some other unit. The choice to return to the statement that raised the exception may seem like a good one, but in the case of an error exception, it is useful only if the handler somehow is able to modify the values or operations that caused the exception to be raised. Otherwise the exception will simply be reraised. The required modification for an error exception is often very difficult. Even when possible, however, it may not be a sound practice. It allows the program to remove the symptom of a problem without removing the cause.

The two issues of binding of exceptions to handlers and continuation are illustrated in Figure 14.1.

When exception handling is included, a subprogram's execution can terminate in two ways: when its execution is complete or when it encounters an exception. In some situations, it is necessary to complete some computation regardless of how subprogram execution terminates. The ability to specify such a computation is called *finalization*. The choice of whether to support finalization is obviously a design issue for exception handling.

Another design issue is the following: If users are allowed to define exceptions, how are these exceptions specified? The usual answer is to require that they be declared in the specification parts of the program units in which they can be raised. The scope of a declared exception is usually the scope of the program unit that contains the declaration.

In the case where a language provides predefined exceptions, several other design issues follow. For example, should the language run-time system provide default handlers for the built-in exceptions, or should the user be required to write handlers for all exceptions? Another question is whether predefined exceptions can be raised explicitly by the user program. This usage can be convenient if there are software-detectable situations in which the user would like to use a predefined handler.

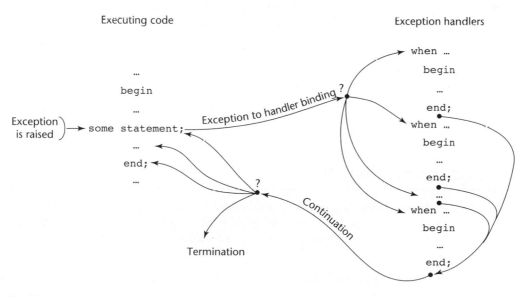

Figure 14.1

Exception-handling control flow

Another issue is whether hardware-detectable errors should be treated as exceptions that could be handled by user programs. If not, all exceptions obviously are software-detectable. A related question is whether there should be any predefined exceptions. Predefined exceptions are implicitly raised by either hardware or system software.

Finally, there is the question of whether exceptions, either predefined or user-defined, can be temporarily or permanently disabled. This question is somewhat philosophical, particularly in the case of predefined error conditions. For example, suppose a language has a predefined exception that is raised when a subscript range error occurs. Many believe that subscript range errors should always be detected, and therefore it should not be possible for the program to disable detection of these errors. Others argue that subscript range checking is too costly for production software, where, presumably, the code is sufficiently error-free that range errors should not occur.

The exception-handling design issues can be summarized as follows:

- How and where are exception handlers specified, and what is their scope?
- How is an exception occurrence bound to an exception handler?
- Can information about an exception be passed to the handler?
- Where does execution continue, if at all, after an exception handler completes its execution? (This is the question of continuation or resumption.)
- Is some form of finalization provided?
- How are user-defined exceptions specified?
- If there are predefined exceptions, should there be default exception handlers for programs that do not provide their own?
- Can predefined exceptions be explicitly raised?
- Are hardware-detectable errors treated as exceptions that may be handled?
- Are there any predefined exceptions?
- Should it be possible to disable predefined exceptions?

We are now prepared to examine the exception-handling facilities of three contemporary programming languages.

14.2 Exception Handling in Ada

Exception handling in Ada is a powerful tool for constructing more reliable software systems. It includes the good parts of the exception-handling design of two earlier languages with exception handling—PL/I and CLU.

14.2.1 Exception Handlers

Ada exception handlers are often local to the code in which the exception can be raised (although they can be propagated to other program units). Because this provides them with the same referencing environment, parameters for handlers are not necessary and are not allowed. Therefore, if an exception is handled in a unit different from the unit that raised the exception, no information about the exception can be passed to the handler.[3]

Exception handlers have the following general form, given here in EBNF:

when exception_choice {| exception_choice} => statement_sequence

Recall that the braces are metasymbols that mean that what they contain may be left out or repeated any number of times. The exception_choice has the form

exception_name | **others**

The exception name indicates the particular exception or exceptions that this handler is meant to handle. The statement sequence is the handler body. The reserved word **others** indicates that the handler is meant to handle any exceptions not named in any other local handler.

Exception handlers can be included in blocks or in the bodies of subprograms, packages, or tasks. Regardless of the block or unit in which they appear, handlers are gathered together in an **exception** clause, which must be placed at the end of the block or unit. For example, the usual form of an exception clause is shown in the following:

```
begin
-- the block or unit body --
exception
    when exception_name_1 =>
        -- first handler --
    when exception_name_2 =>
        -- second handler --
        -- other handlers --
end;
```

Any statement that can appear in the block or unit in which the handler appears is also legal in the handler.

14.2.2   Binding Exceptions to Handlers

When the block or unit that raises an exception includes a handler for that exception, the exception is statically bound to that handler. If an exception is raised in a block or unit that does not have a handler for that particular exception, the exception is propagated to some other block or unit. The way in

---

3. Not quite true. It is possible for the handler to retrieve the exception name, a short description of the exception, and the approximate location where the exception was raised.

which exceptions are propagated depends on the program entity in which the exception occurs.

When an exception is raised in a procedure, whether in the elaboration of its declarations or in the execution of its body, and the procedure has no handler for it, the exception is implicitly propagated to the calling program unit at the point of the call. This policy is reflective of the design philosophy that exception propagation from subprograms should trace back through the control path (dynamic ancestors), not through static ancestors.

If the calling unit to which an exception has been propagated also has no handler for the exception, it is again propagated to that unit's caller. This continues, if necessary, to the main procedure, which is the dynamic root of every Ada program. If an exception is propagated to the main procedure and a handler is still not found, the program is terminated.

In the realm of exception handling, an Ada block is considered to be a parameterless procedure that is "called" by its parent block when execution control reaches the block's first statement. When an exception is raised in a block, in either its declarations or executable statements, and the block has no handler for it, the exception is propagated to the next larger enclosing static scope, which is the code that "called" it. The point to which the exception is propagated is just after the end of the block in which it occurred, which is its "return" point.

When an exception is raised in a package body and the package body has no handler for the exception, the exception is propagated to the declaration section of the unit containing the package declaration. If the package happens to be a library unit (which is separately compiled), the program is terminated.

If an exception occurs at the outermost level in a task body (not in a nested block) and the task contains a handler for the exception, that handler is executed and the task is marked as being completed. If the task does not have a handler for the exception, the task is simply marked as being completed; the exception is not propagated. The control mechanism of a task is too complex to lend itself to a reasonable and simple answer to the question of where its unhandled exceptions should be propagated.

Exceptions can also occur during the elaboration of the declarative sections of subprograms, blocks, packages, and tasks. For example, suppose that a function is called to initialize a variable in its declaration statement, as in the following:

```ada
procedure River is
  Current_Flow : Float := Get_Flow;
  ...
  begin
  ...
 end River;
```

Assume that Get_Flow is a function with no parameters. If Get_Flow raises and propagates an exception to its caller, the exception is reraised in this declaration. Storage allocation during declaration elaboration can also raise an exception. When exceptions are raised during the declaration elaborations of procedures, packages, and blocks, those exceptions are propagated exactly as if the exception were raised in the associated code section. In the case of a task, the task is marked as being completed, no further elaboration takes place, and the built-in exception `Tasking_Error` is raised at the point of activation for the task.

14.2.3 Continuation

In Ada, the block or unit that raises an exception, along with all units to which the exception was propagated but that did not handle it, is always terminated. Control never returns implicitly to the raising block or unit after the exception is handled. Control simply continues after the exception clause, which is always at the end of a block or unit. This causes an immediate return to a higher level of control.

When deciding where execution would continue after exception handler execution was completed in a program unit, the Ada design team had little choice, because the requirements specification for Ada (Department of Defense, 1980a) clearly states that program units that raise exceptions cannot be continued or resumed. However, in the case of a block, a statement can be retried after it raises an exception and that exception is handled. For example, suppose a statement that can raise an exception and a handler for that exception are both enclosed in a block, which is itself enclosed in a loop. The following example code segment, which gets four integer values in the desired range from the keyboard, illustrates this kind of structure:

```
...
type Age_Type is range 0..125;
type Age_List_Type is array (1..4) of Age_Type;
package Age_IO is new Integer_IO (Age_Type);
use Age_IO;
Age_List : Age_List_Type;
...
begin
for Age_Count in 1..4 loop
  loop  -- loop for repetition when exceptions occur
  Except_Blk:
    begin  -- compound to encapsulate exception handling
    Put_Line("Enter an integer in the range 0..125");
    Get(Age_List(Age_Count));
    exit;
    exception
      when Data_Error =>  -- Input string is not a number
    Put_Line("Illegal numeric value");
    Put_Line("Please try again");
```

```
      when Constraint_Error =>  -- Input is < 0 or > 125
   Put_Line("Input number is out of range");
   Put_Line("Please try again");
   end Except_Blk;
 end loop;  -- end of the infinite loop to repeat input
              -- when there is an exception
end loop;  -- end of for Age_Count in 1..4 loop
...
```

Control stays in the inner loop, which contains only the block, until a valid input number is received.

14.2.4 Other Design Choices

There are four exceptions that are defined in the default package, `Standard`:

```
Constraint_Error
Program_Error
Storage_Error
Tasking_Error
```

Each of these is actually a category of exceptions. For example, the exception `Constraint_Error` is raised when an array subscript is out of range, when there is a range error in a numeric variable that has a range restriction, when a reference is made to a record field that is not present in a discriminated union, and in many other situations.

In addition to the exceptions defined in `Standard`, other predefined packages define other exceptions. For example, `Ada.Text_IO` defines the `End_Error` exception.

User-defined exceptions are defined with the following declaration form:

exception_name_list : **exception**

Such exceptions are treated exactly as predefined exceptions, except that they must be raised explicitly.

There are default handlers for the predefined exceptions, all of which result in program termination.

Exceptions are explicitly raised with the **raise** statement, which has the general form

raise [exception_name]

The only place a **raise** statement can appear without naming an exception is within an exception handler. In that case, it reraises the same exception that caused execution of the handler. This has the effect of propagating the exception according to the propagation rules stated previously. A **raise** in an exception handler is useful when one wishes to print an error message where an exception is raised but handle the exception elsewhere.

An Ada **pragma** is a directive to the compiler. Certain run-time checks that are parts of the built-in exceptions can be disabled in Ada programs by use of the Suppress **pragma,** the simple form of which is

pragma Suppress(check_name)

where check_name is the name of a particular exception check. Examples of such checks are given later in this chapter.

The Suppress **pragma** can appear only in declaration sections. When it appears, the specified check may be suspended in the associated block or program unit of which the declaration section is a part. Explicit raises are not affected by Suppress. Although it is not required, most Ada compilers implement the Suppress **pragma.**

Examples of checks that can be suppressed are the following: Index_Check and Range_Check specify two of the checks that are normally done in an Ada program; Index_Check refers to array subscript range checking; Range_Check refers to checking such things as the range of a value being assigned to a subtype variable. If either Index_Check or Range_Check is violated, Constraint_Error is raised. Division_Check and Overflow_Check are suppressible checks associated with Numeric_Error. The following **pragma** disables array subscript range checking:

pragma Suppress(Index_Check);

There is an option of Suppress that allows the named check to be further restricted to particular objects, types, subtypes, and program units.

14.2.5 An Example

The following example program illustrates some simple uses of exception handlers in Ada. The program computes and prints a distribution of input grades by using an array of counters. The input is a sequence of grades, terminated by a negative number, which raises a Constraint_Error exception because the grades are Natural type (non-negative integers). There are 10 categories of grades (0–9, 10–19, ... , 90–100). The grades themselves are used to compute indexes into an array of counters, one for each grade category. Invalid input grades are detected by trapping indexing errors in the counter array. A grade of 100 is special in the computation of the grade distribution because the categories all have 10 possible grade values, except the highest, which has 11 (90, 91, ... , 100). (The fact that there are more possible A grades than Bs or Cs is conclusive evidence of the generosity of teachers.) The grade of 100 is also handled in the same exception handler that is used for invalid input data.

```
-- Grade Distribution
--   Input: A list of integer values that represent
```

```ada
--              grades, followed by a negative number
-- Output: A distribution of grades, as a percentage for
--              each of the categories 0-9, 10-19, ...,
--              90-100.
with Ada.Text_IO, Ada.Integer.Text_IO;
use Ada.Text_IO, Ada.Integer.Text_IO;
procedure Grade_Distribution is
  Freq: array (1..10) of Integer := (others => 0);
  New_Grade : Natural;
  Index,
  Limit_1,
  Limit_2 : Integer;
begin
Grade_Loop:
  loop
    begin  -- A block for the negative input exception
    Get(New_Grade);
    exception
      when Constraint_Error =>  -- for negative input
        exit Grade_Loop;
  end;  -- end of negative input block
   Index := New_Grade / 10 + 1;
      begin  -- A block for the subscript range handler
      Freq(Index) := Freq(Index) + 1;
      exception
        when Constraint_Error =>  -- for index range errors
          if New_Grade = 100 then
            Freq(10) := Freq(10) + 1;
          else
              Put("ERROR -- new grade: ");
              Put(New_Grade);
              Put(" is out of range");
              New_Line;
          end if;
      end;  -- end of the subscript range block
    end loop;
-- Produce output
    Put("Limits   Frequency");
    New_Line; New_Line;
    for Index in 0..9 loop
      Limit_1 := 10 * Index;
      Limit_2 := Limit_1 + 9;
      if Index = 9 then
        Limit_2 := 100;
      end if;
      Put(Limit_1);
```

```
            Put(Limit_2);
            Put(Freq(Index + 1));
            New_Line;
         end loop;  -- for Index in 0..9 ...
      end Grade_Distribution;
```

Notice that the code to handle invalid input grades is in its own local block. This allows the program to continue after such exceptions are handled, as in our earlier example that reads values from the keyboard. The handler for negative input is also in its own block. The reason for this block is to restrict the scope of the handler for `Constraint_Error` when it is raised by negative input.

14.2.6 Evaluation

As is the case in some other language constructs, Ada's design of exception handling represents something of a consensus, at least at the time of its design (the late 1970s and early 1980s), of ideas on the subject. It is clearly a significant advance over the exception handling of PL/I (see the history sidebar in Section 14.1.2). For some time, Ada was the only widely used language that included exception handling.

There are several problems with Ada's exception handling. One problem is the propagation model, which allows exceptions to be propagated to an outer scope in which the exception is not visible. Also, it is not always possible to determine the origin of propagated exceptions.

Another problem is the inadequacy of exception handling for tasks. For example, a task that raises an exception but does not handle it simply dies.

Finally, when support for object-oriented programming was added in Ada 95, its exception handling was not extended to deal with the new constructs. For example, when several objects of a class are created and used in a block and one of them propagates an exception, it is impossible to determine which one raised the exception.

The problems of Ada's exception handling are discussed in Romanovsky and Sander (2001).

14.3 Exception Handling in C++

The exception handling of C++ was accepted by the ANSI C++ standardization committee in 1990 and subsequently found its way into C++ implementations. The design is based in part on the exception handling of CLU, Ada, and ML. One major difference between the exception handling of C++ and that of Ada is the absence of predefined exceptions in C++ (other than in its standard libraries). Thus, in C++, exceptions are user- or library-defined and explicitly raised.

14.3.1   Exception Handlers

In Section 14.2, we saw that Ada uses program units or blocks to specify the scope for exception handlers. C++ uses a special construct that is introduced with the reserved word **try** for this purpose. A **try** construct includes a compound statement called the **try** clause and a list of exception handlers. The compound statement defines the scope of the following handlers. The general form of this construct is

```
try {
//** Code that is expected to raise an exception
}
catch(formal parameter) {
//** A handler body
}
...
catch(formal parameter) {
//** A handler body
}
```

Each **catch** function is an exception handler. A **catch** function can have only a single formal parameter, which is similar to a formal parameter in a function definition in C++, including the possibility of it being an ellipsis (**...**). A handler with an ellipsis formal parameter is the catch-all handler; it is enacted for any raised exception if no appropriate handler was found. The formal parameter also can be a naked type specifier, such as **float,** as in a function prototype. In such a case, the only purpose of the formal parameter is to make the handler uniquely identifiable. When information about the exception is to be passed to the handler, the formal parameter includes a variable name that is used for that purpose. Because the class of the parameter can be any user-defined class, the parameter can include as many data members as are necessary. Binding exceptions to handlers is discussed in Section 14.3.2.

In C++, exception handlers can include any C++ code.

14.3.2   Binding Exceptions to Handlers

C++ exceptions are raised only by the explicit statement **throw**, whose general form in EBNF is

```
throw [expression];
```

The brackets here are metasymbols used to specify that the expression is optional. A **throw** without an operand can appear only in a handler. When it appears there, it reraises the exception, which is then handled elsewhere. This effect is exactly as with Ada.

The type of the **throw** expression selects the particular handler, which of course must have a "matching" type formal parameter. In this case, *matching* means the following: A handler with a formal parameter of type T, **const** T, T& (a reference to an object of type T), or **const** T& matches a **throw** with an expression of type T. In the case where T is a class, a handler whose parameter is type T or any class that is an ancestor of T matches. There are more complicated situations in which a **throw** expression matches a formal parameter, but they are not described here.

An exception raised in a **try** construct causes an immediate end to the execution of the code in that **try** construct. The search for a matching handler begins with the handlers that immediately follow the **try** construct. The matching process is done sequentially on the handlers until a match is found. This means that if any other match precedes an exactly matching handler, the exactly matching handler will not be used. Therefore, handlers for specific exceptions are placed at the top of the list, followed by more generic handlers. The last handler is often one with an ellipsis (...) formal parameter, which matches any exception. This guarantees that all exceptions are caught, if that is preferred.

If an exception is raised in a **try** clause and there is no matching handler associated with that **try** clause, the exception is propagated. If the **try** clause is nested inside another **try** clause, the exception is propagated to the handlers associated with the outer **try** clause. If none of the enclosing **try** clauses yields a matching handler, the exception is propagated to the caller of the function in which it was raised. If the call to the function was not in a **try** clause, the exception is propagated to that function's caller. If no matching handler is found in the program through this propagation process, the default handler is called. This handler is further discussed in Section 14.3.4.

14.3.3 Continuation

After a handler has completed its execution, control flows to the first statement following the **try** construct (the statement immediately after the last handler in the sequence of handlers of which it is an element). A handler may reraise an exception, using a **throw** without an expression, in which case that exception is propagated.

14.3.4 Other Design Choices

In terms of the design issues summarized in Section 14.1.2, the exception handling of C++ is simple. There are *only* user-defined exceptions, and they are not specified (though they might be declared as new classes). There is a default exception handler, unexpected, whose only action is to terminate the program. This handler catches all exceptions not caught by the program. It can be replaced by a user-defined handler. The replacement handler must be a function that returns **void** and takes no parameters. The replacement function is set by assigning its name to set_terminate. Exceptions cannot be disabled.

A C++ function can list the types of the exceptions (the types of the **throw** expressions) that it could raise. This is done by attaching the reserved word **throw,** followed by a parenthesized list of these types, to the function header. For example,

```
int fun() throw (int, char *) { ... }
```

specifies that the function fun could raise exceptions of type **int** and **char *** but no others. The purpose of the **throw** clause is to specify to users of the function what exceptions might be raised by the function. The **throw** clause is in effect a contract between the function and its callers. It guarantees that no other exception will be raised in the function. If the function does throw some unlisted exception, the program will be terminated. Note that the compiler ignores **throw** clauses.

If the types in the **throw** clause are classes, then the function can raise any exception that is derived from the listed classes. If a function header has a **throw** clause and raises an exception that is not listed in the **throw** clause and is not derived from a class listed there, the default handler is called. Note that this error cannot be detected at compile time. The list of types in the list may be empty, meaning that the function will not raise any exceptions. If there is no **throw** specification on the header, the function can raise any exception. The list is not part of the function's type.

If a function overrides a function that has a **throw** clause, the overriding function cannot have a **throw** clause with more exceptions than the overriden function.

When an exception terminates a **try** construct, all stack-dynamic and heap-dynamic variables that were allocated by code executed in the **try** construct before the exception occurred are deallocated. Therefore, the handler can never access such variables.

Although C++ has no predefined exceptions, the standard libraries define and throw exceptions, such as out_of_range, which can be thrown by library container classes, and overflow_error, which can be thrown by math library functions.

14.3.5 An Example

The following example has the same intent and use of exception handling as the Ada program shown in Section 14.2.5. It produces a distribution of input grades by using an array of counters for 10 categories. Illegal grades are detected by checking for invalid subscripts used in incrementing the selected counter.

```
// Grade Distribution
//  Input: A list of integer values that represent
//         grades, followed by a negative number
// Output: A distribution of grades, as a percentage for
```

```cpp
//          each of the categories 0-9, 10-19, ...,
//          90-100.
#include <iostream.h>
void main() {    //* Any exception can be raised
  int new_grade,
      index,
      limit_1,
      limit_2,
      freq[10] = {0,0,0,0,0,0,0,0,0,0};
// The exception definition to deal with the end of data
class NegativeInputException {
  public:
    NegativeInputException() {   //* Constructor
      cout << "End of input data reached" << endl;
    }  //** end of constructor
}  //** end of NegativeInputException class
  try {
    while (1) {
      cout << "Please input a grade" << endl;
      if ((cin >> new_grade) < 0)  //* Terminating condition
        throw new NegativeInputException();
      index = new_grade / 10;
      {try {
        if (index > 9)
          throw new_grade;
        freq[index]++;
      }  //* end of inner try compound
      catch(int grade) {  //* Handler for index errors
        if (grade == 100)
          freq[9]++;
        else
          cout << "Error -- new grade: " << grade
               << " is out of range" << endl;
      }  //* end of catch(int grade)
    }  //* end of the block for the inner try-catch pair
    }  //* end of while (1)
  }  //* end of outer try block
  catch(NegativeInputException e) {  //** Handler for
                                     //** negative input
    cout << "Limits    Frequency" << endl;
    for (index = 0; index < 10; index++) {
      limit_1 = 10 * index;
      limit_2 = limit_1 + 9;
      if (index == 9)
        limit_2 = 100;
      cout << limit_1 << limit_2 << freq[index] << endl;
```

```
      } //* end of for (index == 9)
    } //* end of catch (short int)
  } //* end of main
```

This program is meant to illustrate the mechanics of C++ exception handling. Note that the index range exception is often handled in C++ by overloading the indexing operation, which could then raise the exception, rather than the direct detection of the indexing operation with the selection construct used in our example.

14.3.6   Evaluation

In some ways, the C++ exception-handling mechanism is similar to that of Ada. For example, unhandled exceptions in functions are propagated to the function's caller. But in other ways, the C++ design is quite different: There are no predefined hardware-detectable exceptions that can be handled by the user, and exceptions are not named. Exceptions are connected to handlers through a parameter type in which the formal parameter may be omitted. The type of the formal parameter of a handler determines the condition under which it is called but may have nothing whatsoever to do with the nature of the raised exception. Therefore, the use of predefined types for exceptions certainly does not promote readability. It is much better to define classes for exceptions with meaningful names in a meaningful hierarchy that can be used for defining exceptions. The exception parameter provides a way to pass information about an exception to the exception handler.

14.4 Exception Handling in Java

In Chapter 13, the Java example program includes the use of exception handling with little explanation. This section describes the details of Java's exception-handling capabilities.

Java's exception handling is based on that of C++, but it is designed to be more in line with the object-oriented language paradigm. Furthermore, Java includes a collection of predefined exceptions that are implicitly raised by the Java Virtual Machine (JVM).

14.4.1   Classes of Exceptions

All Java exceptions are objects of classes that are descendants of the `Throwable` class. The Java system includes two predefined exception classes that are subclasses of `Throwable`, `Error` and `Exception`. The `Error` class and its descendants are related to errors that are thrown by the JVM, such as running out of heap memory. These exceptions are never thrown by user programs, and they should never be handled there. There are two system-defined direct descendants of `Exception`, `RuntimeException` and `IOException`.

As its name indicates, IOException is thrown when an error has occurred in an input or output operation, all of which are defined as methods in the various classes defined in the package java.io.

There are predefined classes that are descendants of RuntimeException. In most cases, RuntimeException is thrown (by the JVM) when a user program causes an error. For example, ArrayIndexOutOfBoundsException, which is defined in java.util, is a commonly thrown exception that descends from RuntimeException. Another commonly thrown exception that descends from RuntimeException is NullPointerException.

User programs can define their own exception classes. The convention in Java is that user-defined exceptions are subclasses of Exception.

14.4.2 Exception Handlers

The exception handlers of Java have the same form as those of C++, except that every **catch** must have a parameter and the class of the parameter must be a descendant of the predefined class Throwable.

The syntax of the **try** construct in Java is exactly as that of C++, except for the **finally** clause described in Section 14.4.6.

14.4.3 Binding Exceptions to Handlers

Throwing an exception is quite simple. An instance of the exception class is given as the operand of the **throw** statement. For example, suppose we define an exception named MyException as

```
class MyException extends Exception {
  public MyException() {}
  public MyException(String message) {
    super (message);
  }
}
```

This exception can be thrown with

```
throw new MyException();
```

The creation of the instance of the exception for the **throw** could be done separately from the **throw** statement, as in

```
MyException myExceptionObject = new MyException();
...
throw myExceptionObject;
```

One of the two constructors we have included in our new class has no parameter and the other has a String object parameter that it sends to the

The Birth of Java

JAMES GOSLING

James Gosling is a Fellow and Vice President at Sun Microsystems, the creator of the Java programming language, and he is one of the computer industry's most noted programmers. He was the 1996 recipient of Software Development's Programming Excellence Award. He developed NeWS, Sun's network-extensible window system, and was a principal in the Andrew project at Carnegie-Mellon University, from which he holds a Ph.D. in computer science.

PERSONAL HISTORY/ DOWN MEMORY LANE

How did you get involved with computing? When I was 14 years old a friend of my dad's took me on a tour of the computing facilities at the University of Calgary. I got hooked. Simply put, it was love at first sight. I then taught myself how to program, got a job at the physics department when I was in high school, and it snowballed from there.

What was your first computing job? Writing ground software for the ISIS-II satellite for the physics department at the University of Calgary.

What was your favorite job? My first job was pretty special. But I like my current one a lot too: being a researcher at Sun's research labs. Officially, I am "VP and Fellow."

JAVA: THE BIRTH OF A LANGUAGE

Lots of languages were born as a sort of by-product of a separate goal. I've heard this was the case with Java and the Green Project. Can you tell us the story? A group of us were investigating future trends that might have an impact on Sun. We pretty quickly focused in on the spread of digital systems into devices not normally thought of as computers (such as cell phones, televisions, control systems), coupled with the growth of networking. We started building a prototype device to help us learn about the space. Problems were encountered that stemmed from the base programming tools we were using. My part of the project ended up being to solve the tool problem. The result was Java.

Why create a language? Nothing else worked. The first prototype was done in C++, but we thought about and discarded many others. They were [all] too tied to specific CPU architectures (at the binary level) with little regard for security. Not to mention, they had some reliability issues.

You've talked about Simula as Java's predecessor. Why Simula? It was the original OO language. I used Simula a lot in years past. Over C and C++, it had single inheritance and tight memory mode.

What couple of features distinguished Java from the popular languages out there? Productivity, reliability, security, portability.

How much did these features and the current development trends in hardware and software play into the immediate success of Java? A lot.

JAVA: THE NAME GAME

Why was the original project called Green? No good reason. Apple had a research project called "Pink," so colors were in. We got ours from the door to the suite of offices we worked in: It was green. [Java] was originally called "oak," because that was growing outside my office window when I had to pick a name and was staring out the window. That original name had all kinds of trademark conflicts. The lawyers made us find a name that was clear of issues.

Are you tired of the name Java? No.

If you could name Java something else today, what name would you give it? Gak! That's too hard a question. Picking names is really tough.

JAVA: PAST, PRESENT, FUTURE

If you could go back and change two features of Java, or rework them, what might they be? Lightweight objects and switch statements.

Do you think about these things? Yes.

Looking back at what you were trying to build on Project Green, do such devices exist today? Were you "barking up the right tree" at the time? Yes. Palm Pilots and modern, fancy cell phones are directly in line with what we were trying to do.

If you were assigned to a Project Green–type goal today, on what user functionality would you focus your efforts? Or better said, if the Internet and

> 66 *[Java] was originally called "oak," because that was growing outside my office window when I had to pick a name and was staring out the window.* 99

Java were the "wow" tools of the early 1990s, what will be the next "wow" tool? The next "wow" tool hasn't changed—it still is the Internet. We've hardly begun exploiting it.

Jump forward 15 years: What functionality may programming languages offer then that they do not offer now? Reasoning/verification.

If you weren't doing this, what would you be doing? Anything that involves building stuff.

superclass (`Exception`), which displays it. So our new exception could be thrown with

```
throw new MyException
        ("a message to specify the location of the error");
```

The binding of exceptions to handlers in Java is similar to that of C++. If an exception is thrown in the compound statement of a **try** construct, it is bound to the first handler (**catch** function) immediately following the **try** clause whose parameter is the same class as the thrown object, or an ancestor of it. If a matching handler is found, the **throw** is bound to it and it is executed.

Exceptions can be handled and then rethrown by including a **throw** statement without an operand at the end of the handler. The newly thrown exception will not be handled in the same **try** where it was originally thrown, so looping is not a concern. This rethrowing is usually done when some local action is useful, but further handling by an enclosing **try** clause or a caller is necessary. A **throw** statement in a handler could also throw some exception other than the one that transferred control to this handler.

To ensure that exceptions that can be thrown in a **try** clause are always handled in a method, a special handler can be written that matches all exceptions that are derived from `Exception` simply by defining the handler with an `Exception` type parameter, as in

```
catch (Exception genericObject) {
  ...
}
```

Because a class name always matches itself or any ancestor class, any class derived from `Exception` matches `Exception`. Of course, such an exception handler should always be placed at the end of the list of handlers, for it will block the use of any handler that follows it in the **try** construct in which it appears. This occurs because the search for a matching handler is sequential, and the search ends when a match is found.

14.4.4 Other Design Choices

During program execution, the Java run-time system stores the class name of every object in the program. The method `getClass` can be used to get an object that stores the class name, which itself can be gotten with the `getName` method. So we can retrieve the name of the class of the actual parameter from the **throw** statement that caused the handler's execution. For the handler shown earlier, this is done with

```
genericObject.getClass().getName()
```

In addition, the message associated with the parameter object, which is created by the constructor, can be gotten with

```
genericObject.getMessage()
```

Furthermore, in the case of user-defined exceptions, the thrown object could include any number of data fields that might be useful in the handler.

The **throws** clause of Java has the appearance and placement (in a program) that is similar to that of the **throw** specification of C++. However, the semantics of **throws** is somewhat different from that of the C++ **throw** clause.

The appearance of an exception class name in the **throws** clause of a Java method specifies that that exception class or any of its descendant exception classes can be thrown but not handled by the method. For example, when a method specifies that it can throw IOException, it means it can throw an IOException object or an object of any of its descendant classes, such as EOFException, and it does not handle the exception it throws.

Exceptions of class Error and RuntimeException and their descendants are called **unchecked exceptions.** All other exceptions are called **checked exceptions.** Unchecked exceptions are never a concern of the compiler. However, the compiler ensures that all checked exceptions a method can throw are either listed in its **throws** clause or handled in the method. Note that checking this at compile time is in contrast with C++, in which it is done at run time. The reason why exceptions of the classes Error and RuntimeException and their descendants are unchecked is that any method could throw them. A program can catch unchecked exceptions, but it is not required.

As is the case with C++, a method cannot declare more exceptions in its **throws** clause than the method it overrides, though it may declare fewer. So if a method has no **throws** clause, neither can any method that overrides it. A method can throw any exception listed in its **throws** clause, along with any of its descendant classes.

A method that does not directly throw a particular exception, but calls another method that could throw that exception, must list the exception in its **throws** clause. This is the reason the buildDist method (in the example in the next subsection), which uses the readLine method, must specify IOException in the **throws** clause of its header.

A method that does not include a **throws** clause cannot propagate any checked exception. Recall that in C++, a function without a **throws** clause can throw *any* exception.

A method that calls a method that lists a particular checked exception in its **throws** clause has three alternatives for dealing with that exception: First, it can catch the exception and handle it. Second, it can catch the exception and throw an exception that is listed in its own **throws** clause. Third, it could declare the exception in its own **throws** clause and not handle it, which effectively propagates the exception to an enclosing **try** clause, if there is one, or to the method's caller, if there is no enclosing **try** clause.

There are no default exception handlers, and it is not possible to disable exceptions. Continuation in Java is exactly as in C++.

14.4.5   An Example

Following is the Java program with the capabilities of the C++ program in Section 14.3.5:

```java
// Grade Distribution
//   Input: A list of integer values that represent
//          grades, followed by a negative number
// Output: A distribution of grades, as a percentage for
//          each of the categories 0-9, 10-19, ...,
//          90-100.
import java.io.*;
// The exception definition to deal with the end of data
class NegativeInputException extends Exception {
  public NegativeInputException() {
    System.out.println("End of input data reached");
  }  //** end of constructor
}  //** end of NegativeInputException class

class GradeDist {
  int newGrade,
      index,
       limit_1,
       limit_2;
  int [] freq = {0, 0, 0, 0, 0, 0, 0, 0, 0, 0};

  void buildDist() throws IOException {
    DataInputStream in = new DataInputStream(System.in);
    try {
      while (true) {
        System.out.println("Please input a grade");
        newGrade = Integer.parseInt(in.readLine());
        if (newGrade < 0)
          throw new NegativeInputException();
        index = newGrade / 10;
        try {
          freq[index]++;
        }  //** end of inner try clause
        catch(ArrayIndexOutOfBoundsException) {
          if (newGrade == 100)
            freq [9]++;
          else
            System.out.println("Error - new grade: " +
                    newGrade + " is out of range");
```

```
      }  //** end of catch (ArrayIndex...
    }  //** end of while (true) ...
  }  //** end of outer try clause
  catch(NegativeInputException) {
    System.out.println ("\nLimits     Frequency\n");
    for (index = 0; index < 10; index++) {
      limit_1 = 10 * index;
      limit_2 = limit_1 + 9;
      if (index == 9)
        limit_2 = 100;
      System.out.println("" + limit_1 + " - " +
                    limit_2 + "        " + freq [index]);
    }  //** end of for (index = 0; ...
  }  //** end of catch (NegativeInputException ...
}  //** end of method buildDist
```

The exception for a negative input, NegativeInputException, is defined in the program. Its constructor displays a message when an object of the class is created. Its handler produces the output of the method. ArrayIndexOutOfBoundsException is a predefined unchecked exception that is thrown by the JVM. In both of these cases, the handler does not include an object name in its parameter. In neither case would a name serve any purpose. Although all handlers get objects as parameters, but they often are not useful.

14.4.6   The `finally` Clause

There are some situations in which a process must be executed regardless of whether a **try** clause throws an exception and regardless of whether a thrown exception is caught in a method. One example of such a situation is a file that must be closed. Another is if the method has some external resource that must be freed in the method regardless of how the execution of the method terminates. The **finally** clause was designed for these kinds of needs. A **finally** clause is placed at the end of the list of handlers just after a complete **try** construct. In general, the **try** construct and its **finally** clause appear as

```
try {
  ...
}
catch (...) {
  ...
}
... //** More handlers
finally {
  ...
}
```

The semantics of this construct is as follows: If the **try** clause throws no exceptions, the **finally** clause is executed before execution continues after the **try** construct. If the **try** clause throws an exception and it is caught by a following handler, the **finally** clause is executed after the handler completes its execution. If the **try** clause throws an exception but it is not caught by a handler following the **try** construct, the **finally** clause is executed before the exception is propagated.

A **try** construct with no exception handlers can be followed by a **finally** clause. This makes sense, of course, only if the compound statement has a **break, continue,** or **return** statement. Its purpose in these cases is the same as when it is used with exception handling. For example, consider the following:

```
try {
  for (index = 0; index < 100; index++) {
    ...
    if (... ) {
      return;
    }  //** end of if
    ...
  }  //** end of for
}  //** end of try clause
finally {
  ...
}  //** end of try construct
```

The **finally** clause here will be executed, regardless of whether the **return** terminates the loop or it ends normally.

14.4.7 Assertions

In the discussion of Plankalkül in Chapter 2, we mentioned its inclusion of assertions. Assertions were added to Java in version 1.4, although in that version they were disabled by default.[4] To use them, it was necessary to enable them by running the program with the enableassertions (or ea) flag, as in

```
java -enableassertions MyProgram
```

The two possible forms of the **assert** statement are:

```
assert condition;
assert condition : expression;
```

---

4. In Java 5.0, they are enabled by default.

In the first case, the condition is tested when execution reaches the **assert.** If the condition evaluates to true, nothing happens. If it evaluates to false, the AssertionError exception is thrown. In the second case, the action is the same, except that the value of the expression is passed to the AssertionError constructor as a string and becomes debugging output.

The **assert** statement is used for defensive programming. A program may be written with many **assert** statements, which ensure that the program's computation is on track to produce correct results. Many programmers put in such checks when they write a program, as an aid to debugging, even though the language they are using does not support assertions. When the program is sufficiently tested, these checks are removed. The advantage of **assert** statements, which have the same purpose, is that they can be disabled without removing them from the program. This saves the effort of removing them, and also allows their use during subsequent program maintenance.

14.4.8   Evaluation

The Java mechanisms for exception handling are an improvement over the C++ version on which they are based.

First, a C++ program can throw any type defined in the program or by the system. In Java, only objects that are instances of Throwable or some class that descends from it can be thrown. This separates the objects that can be thrown from all of the other objects (and nonobjects) that inhabit a program. What significance can be attached to an exception that causes an **int** value to be thrown?

Second, a C++ program unit that does not include a **throws** clause can throw any exception, which tells the reader nothing. A Java method that does not include a **throws** clause cannot throw any checked exception that it does not handle. Therefore, the reader of a Java method knows from its header what exceptions it could throw but does not handle. A C++ compiler ignores **throws** clauses, but a Java compiler ensures that all exceptions that a method can throw are listed in its **throws** clause.

Third, the addition of the **finally** clause is a great convenience in certain situations. It allows cleanup kinds of actions to take place regardless of how a compound statement terminated.

Finally, the JVM implicitly throws a variety of predefined exceptions, such as for array indices out of range and null reference variable accesses, which can be handled by any user program. A C++ program can handle only those exceptions that it explicitly throws (or that are thrown by library classes it uses).

Relative to the exception handling of Ada, Java's facilities are roughly comparable. The presence of the **throws** clause in a Java method is a good aid to readability, whereas Ada has no corresponding feature. Java is certainly closer to Ada than it is to C++ in one area, that of allowing programs to deal with system-detected exceptions.

C# includes exception-handling constructs that are very much like those of Java, except that C# does not have a **throws** clause.

14.5 Introduction to Event Handling

Event handling is similar to exception handling. In both cases, the handlers are implicitly called by the occurrence of something, either an exception or an event. While exceptions can be created either explicitly by user code or implicitly by hardware or a software interpreter, events are created by external actions, such as user interactions through a graphical user interface (GUI). In this section, the fundamentals of event handling, which are substantially less complex than those of exception handling, are introduced.

In conventional (non-event-driven) programming, the code itself specifies the order in which that code is executed, although the order is usually affected by the program's input data. In event-driven programming, parts of the program are executed at completely unpredictable times, often triggered by user interactions with the executing program.

The particular kind of event handling discussed in this chapter is related to GUIs. Therefore, most of the events are caused by user interactions through graphical objects or components, often called *widgets*. The most common widgets are buttons. Implementing reactions to user interactions with GUI components is the most common form of event handling.

An **event** is a notification that something specific has occurred, such as a mouse click on a graphical button. Strictly speaking, an event is an object that is implicitly created by the run-time system in response to a user action, at least in the context in which event handling is being discussed here.

An **event handler** is a segment of code that is executed in response to the appearance of an event. Event handlers enable a program to be responsive to user actions.

Although event-driven programming was being used long before GUIs appeared, it has become a widely used programming methodology only in response to the popularity of these interfaces. As an example, consider the GUIs presented to users of Web browsers. Many Web documents presented to browser users are now dynamic. Such a document may present an order form to the user, who chooses the merchandise by clicking buttons. The required internal computations associated with these button clicks are performed by event handlers that react to the click events.

Another common use of event handlers is to check for simple errors and omissions in the elements of a form, either when they are changed or when the form is submitted to the Web server for processing. Using event handling on the browser to check the validity of form data saves the time of sending that data to the server, where its correctness then must be checked by a server-resident program or script before it can be processed. This kind of event-driven programming is often done using a client-side scripting language, such as JavaScript.

14.6 Event Handling with Java

Java supports two different approaches to presenting interactive displays to users, either from application programs or from applets. Both use the same classes to define the GUI components and the event handlers that provide the interactivity. Although we discuss only applets, this section also applies to application programs.

The initial version of Java provided a somewhat primitive form of support for GUI components. In version 1.2 of the language, a new collection of components were added. These were collectively called Swing.

14.6.1 Java Swing GUI Components

The Swing package, defined in `javax.swing`, includes a collection of GUI components. Because our interest here is event handling, not GUI components, we discuss only two kinds of widgets, text boxes and radio buttons.

A text box is an object of class `JTextField`. The simplest `JTextField` constructor takes a single parameter, the length of the box in characters. For example,

```
JTextField name = new JTextField(32);
```

The `JTextField` constructor can also take a literal string as an optional first parameter. This string parameter, when present, is displayed as the initial contents of the text box.

Radio buttons are special buttons that are placed in a button group. A button group is an object of class `ButtonGroup`, whose constructor takes no parameters. In a radio button group, only one button can be pressed at a time. If any button in the group becomes pressed, the previously pressed button is implicitly unpressed. The `JRadioButton` constructor, used for creating radio buttons, takes two parameters: the label and the initial state of the radio button (`true` or `false`, for pressed and not pressed, respectively). After the radio buttons are created, they are put in their button group with the `add` method of the group object. Consider the following example:

```
ButtonGroup payment = new ButtonGroup();
JRadioButton box1 = new JRadioButton("Visa", true);
JRadioButton box2 = new JRadioButton("Master Charge",
                                      false);
JRadioButton box3 = new JRadioButton("Discover", false);
payment.add(box1);
payment.add(box2);
payment.add(box3);
```

An applet's display is actually a frame, which is a multilayered structure. We are interested in just one of those layers, the content pane. The content pane is where applets put their output. User programs do not place anything directly in the content pane; rather, they place graphical objects in a panel and then add the panel to the content pane. For applications, a frame is created and the constructed panel is added to that frame's content pane.

A content pane is created as a `Container` object, using the `getContent-Pane` method, as in

```
Container contentPane = getContentPane();
```

Predefined graphic objects, such as GUI components, can be placed directly in a panel that is created in the applet and then added to the applet's content pane. The following creates the panel object we use in the following discussion of components:

```
JPanel myPanel = new JPanel();
```

After the components have been created with constructors, they must be placed in the panel with the `add` method, as in

```
myPanel.add(button1);
```

14.6.2   The Java Event Model

User interactions with GUI components create events that can be caught by event handlers, which provide the associated computations. GUI components are considered event generators; they all generate events. In Java, event handlers are called **event listeners.** Event listeners are connected to event generators through event listener registration. Listener registration is done with a method of the class that implements the listener interface, as described later in this section. The panel object into which the components are placed can be the event listener for those components. Only event listeners that are registered for a specific event are notified when that event occurs.

An event generator tells a listener of an event by sending a message to the listener (in other words, by calling one of the listener's methods). The listener method that receives the message implements an event handler. To make the event-handling methods conform to a standard protocol, an interface is used. An interface prescribes standard method protocols but does not provide implementations of those methods. This protocol could be specified by forcing the event generator to be a subclass of a class from which it would inherit the protocol. However, the `JApplet` class already has a superclass, and in Java, a class can have just one parent class. Therefore, the protocol must come from an interface. A class cannot be instantiated unless it provides definitions for all methods in the interfaces that it implements.

A class that needs to implement a listener must implement an interface for that listener. There are many classes of events and listener interfaces. One class of events is `ItemEvent`, which is associated with the event of selecting a checkbox, radio button, or list item. The `ItemListener` interface prescribes a method, `itemStateChanged`, which is the handler for `ItemEvent` events. So, to provide an action that is triggered by a radio button action, the interface `ItemListener` must be implemented, which requires a definition of the method, `itemStateChanged`.

As stated previously, the connection of a component to an event listener is made with a method of the class that implements the listener interface. For example, because `ItemEvent` is the class name of event objects created by user actions on radio buttons, the `addItemListener` method is used to register a listener for radio buttons. The listener for button events created in a panel in an applet could be implemented in the panel. So, for a radio button named `button1` in a panel named `myPanel` that implements the `ItemEvent` event handler for buttons, we would register the listener with the following statement:

```
button1.addItemListener(this);
```

Each event handler method receives an event parameter, which provides information about the event. Event classes have methods to access that information. For example, when called through a radio button, `isSelected` returns true or false, depending on whether the button was on or off (pressed or not pressed), respectively.

All the event related classes are in the `java.awt.event` package, so it is usually imported to any applet class that uses events.

The following is an example applet, `RadioB`, that illustrates the use of events and event handling to display dynamic content in an applet. This applet constructs radio buttons that control the font style of the contents of a text field. It creates a `Font` object for each of four font styles. Each of these has a radio button to enable the user to select the style. The applet then creates a text string, whose font style will be controlled by the user through the radio buttons. Then it sets the font style of the text string accordingly.

```
/* RadioB.java
   An applet to illustrate event handling with interactive
   radio buttons that control the font style of a
   textfield
   */
import java.awt.*;
import java.awt.event.*;
import java.applet.*;
import javax.swing.*;

public class RadioB extends JApplet implements
                                    ItemListener {
```

```
// Make most of the variables class variables, because
//   both init and the event handler must see them

    private Container contentPane = getContentPane();
    private JTextField text;
    private Font plainFont, boldFont, italicFont,
                boldItalicFont;
    private JRadioButton plain, bold, italic, boldItalic;
    private ButtonGroup radioButtons = new ButtonGroup();
    private JPanel myPanel = new JPanel();

// The init method is where the document is initially
//   built

    public void init() {

// Set the background color of the panel

        myPanel.setBackground(Color.cyan);

// Create the fonts

        plainFont = new Font("Serif", Font.PLAIN, 16);
        boldFont = new Font("Serif", Font.BOLD, 16);
        italicFont = new Font("Serif", Font.ITALIC, 16);
        boldItalicFont = new Font("Serif", Font.BOLD +
                                  Font.ITALIC, 16);

// Create the test text string, set its font, and add it
//   to the panel

        text = new JTextField(
            "In what font style should I appear?", 30);
        myPanel.add(text);
        text.setFont(plainFont);

// Create radio buttons for the fonts and add them to
//    the panel

        plain = new JRadioButton("Plain", true);
        bold = new JRadioButton("Bold");
        italic = new JRadioButton("Italic");
        boldItalic = new JRadioButton("Bold Italic");
        radioButtons.add(plain);
```

```
            radioButtons.add(bold);
            radioButtons.add(italic);
            radioButtons.add(boldItalic);

    // Register the event handlers to myPanel

            plain.addItemListener(this);
            bold.addItemListener(this);
            italic.addItemListener(this);
            boldItalic.addItemListener(this);

    // Add the buttons to the panel

            myPanel.add(plain);
            myPanel.add(bold);
            myPanel.add(italic);
            myPanel.add(boldItalic);

    // Add the panel to the content pane for the applet

            contentPane.add(myPanel);

        }   // End of init()

    // The event handler

        public void itemStateChanged (ItemEvent e) {

    // Determine which button is on and set the font
    //   accordingly

            if (plain.isSelected())
               text.setFont(plainFont);
            else if (bold.isSelected())
               text.setFont(boldFont);
            else if (italic.isSelected())
               text.setFont(italicFont);
            else if (boldItalic.isSelected())
               text.setFont(boldItalicFont);

        } // End of itemStateChanged

} // End of RadioB applet
```

The `RadioB` applet produces the screen shown in Figure 14.2.

Figure 14.2

Output of the `RadioB`
applet

SUMMARY

Exception handling now has been incorporated into several widely used languages, although many experimental languages designed since the mid-1970s have had such facilities.

Ada provides extensive exception-handling facilities and a small but comprehensive collection of built-in exceptions. The handlers are attached to the program entities, although exceptions can be implicitly or explicitly propagated to other program entities if no local handler is available.

C++ includes no predefined exceptions (except those defined in the standard library). C++ exceptions are objects of a primitive type, a predefined class, or a user-defined class. Exceptions are bound to handlers by connecting the type of the expression in the **throw** statement to that of the formal parameter of the handler. Handlers all have the same name—**catch**. The C++ **throw** clause of a method lists the types of exceptions that the method could throw.

Java exceptions are objects whose ancestry must trace back to a class that descends from the `Throwable` class. There are two categories of exceptions—checked and unchecked. Checked exceptions are a concern for the user program and the compiler. Unchecked exceptions can occur anywhere and are often ignored by user programs.

The Java **throws** clause of a method lists the checked exceptions that it could throw and does not handle. It must include exceptions that methods it calls could raise and propagate back to its caller.

The Java **finally** clause provides a mechanism for guaranteeing that some code will be executed regardless of how the execution of a **try** compound terminates.

Java now includes an **assert** statement, which facilitates defensive programming.

An event is a notification that something has occurred that requires handling. Events are often created by user interactions with a program, usually through a graphical user interface. Java event handlers are called event listeners. An event listener must be registered for an event if it is to be notified when the event occurs. Two of the most commonly used event listeners are `actionPerformed` and `itemStateChanged`, whose protocols are provided by associated interfaces.

BIBLIOGRAPHIC NOTES

One of the most important papers on exception handling that is not connected with a particular programming language is the work by Goodenough (1975). The problems with the PL/I design for exception handling are covered in MacLaren (1977). The CLU exception-handling design is clearly described by Liskov and Snyder (1979). Exception-handling facilities of the Ada language are described in ARM (1995) and are critically evaluated in Romanovsky and Sander (2001). Exception handling in C++ is described by Stroustrup (1997). Exception handling in Java is described by Campione et al. (2001).

REVIEW QUESTIONS

1. Define *exception, exception handler, raising an exception, disabling an exception, continuation*, and *built-in exception*.

2. What are the design issues for exception handling?

3. What does it mean for an exception to be bound to an exception handler?

4. What are the possible frames for exceptions in Ada?

5. Where are unhandled exceptions propagated in Ada if raised in a subprogram? A block? A package body? A task?

6. Where does execution continue after an exception is handled in Ada?

7. How can an exception be explicitly raised in Ada?

8. How is a user-defined exception defined in Ada?

9. How can an exception be suppressed in Ada?

10. What is the name of all C++ exception handlers?

11. How can exceptions be explicitly raised in C++?

12. How are exceptions bound to handlers in C++?

13. How can an exception handler be written in C++ so that it handles any exception?

14. Where does execution control go when a C++ exception handler has completed its execution?

15. Does C++ include built-in exceptions?

16. What is the root class of all Java exception classes?

17. What is the parent class of most Java user-defined exception classes?

18. How can an exception handler be written in Java so that it handles any exception?

19. What are the differences between a C++ **throw** specification and a Java **throws** clause?

20. What is the difference between checked and unchecked exceptions in Java?

21. Can you disable a Java exception?

22. What is the purpose of the Java **finally** clause?

PROBLEM SET

1. What run-time errors or conditions, if any, can Pascal programs detect and handle?

2. From textbooks on the PL/I and Ada programming languages, look up the respective sets of built-in exceptions. Do a comparative evaluation of the two, considering both completeness and flexibility.

3. From ARM (1995), determine how exceptions that take place during rendezvous are handled.

4. From a textbook on COBOL, determine how exception handling is done in COBOL programs.

5. In languages without exception-handling facilities, it is common to have most subprograms include an "error" parameter, which can be set to some value representing "OK" or some other value representing "error in procedure." What advantage does a linguistic exception-handling facility like that of Ada have over this method?

6. In a language without exception-handling facilities, we could send an error-handling procedure as a parameter to each procedure that can detect errors that must be handled. What disadvantages are there to this method?

7. Compare the methods suggested in Problems 5 and 6. Which do you think is better and why?

8. Compare the exception-handling facilities of C++ with those of Ada. Which design, in your opinion, is the most flexible? Which makes it possible to write more reliable programs?

9. Consider the following C++ skeletal program:

```
class Big {
  int i;
  float f;
void fun1() throw int {
  ...
  try {
    ...
    throw i;
```

```
      ...
      throw f;
      ...
   }
   catch(float) { ... }
      ...
}
class Small {
   int j;
   float g;
   void fun2() throw float {
      ...
      try {
      ...
         try {
           Big.fun1();
           ...
           throw j;
           ...
           throw g;
           ...
         }
      catch(int) { ... }
      ...
      }
   catch(float) { ... }
}
```

In each of the four **throw** statements, where is the exception handled? Note that fun1 is called from fun2 in class Small.

10. Write a detailed comparison of the exception-handling capabilities of C++ and those of Java.

11. Summarize the arguments in favor of the temination and resumption models of continuation.

PROGRAMMING EXERCISES

1. Write an Ada code segment that retries a call to a procedure, Tape_Read, that reads input from a tape drive and can raise the Tape_Read_Error exception.

2. Suppose you are writing an Ada procedure that has three alternative methods for accomplishing its requirements. Write a skeletal version of this procedure so that if the first alternative raises any exception, the second is tried, and if the second alternative raises any exception, the third is

executed. Write the code as if the three methods were procedures named `Alt1`, `Alt2`, and `Alt3`.

3. Write an Ada program that inputs a list of integer values in the range of −100 to 100 from the keyboard and computes the sum of the squares of the input values. This program must use exception handling to ensure that the input values are in range and are legal integers, to handle the error of the sum of the squares becoming larger than a standard `Integer` variable can store, and to detect end-of-file and use it to cause the output of the result. In the case of overflow of the sum, an error message must be printed and the program terminated.

4. Write a C++ program for the specification of Exercise 3.

5. Write a Java program for the specification of Exercise 3.

Functional Programming Languages

T his chapter introduces functional programming and some of the programming languages that have been designed for this approach to software development. Because these languages are based on mathematical functions, we begin by reviewing the fundamental ideas of these. Next, the idea of a functional programming language is introduced, followed by a look at the first functional language, LISP, and its list data structures and functional syntax, which is based on lambda notation. The next, somewhat lengthy section is devoted to an introduction to Scheme, including some of its primitive functions, special forms, functional forms, and some examples of simple functions written in Scheme. Next, we provide brief introductions to COMMON LISP, ML, and Haskell. A section follows that describes some of the applications of functional programming languages. Finally, we present a short comparison of functional and imperative languages.

15.1 Introduction

The first 14 chapters of this book have been concerned primarily with the imperative and object-oriented programming languages. With the exception of Smalltalk, the object-oriented languages we have discussed have had forms that are similar to the imperative languages.

The high degree of similarity among the imperative languages arises in part from one of the common bases of their design: the von Neumann architecture, as discussed in Chapter 1. We can think of the imperative languages collectively as a progression of developments to improve the basic model, which was Fortran I. All have been designed to make efficient use of von Neumann architecture computers. Although the imperative style of programming has been found acceptable by most programmers, its heavy reliance on the underlying architecture is thought by some to be an unnecessary restriction on the process of software development.

Other bases for language design exist, some of them oriented more to particular programming paradigms or methodologies than to efficient execution on a particular computer architecture. Thus far, however, only a small minority of programs are written in nonimperative languages.

The functional programming paradigm, which is based on mathematical functions, is the design basis for one of the most important nonimperative styles of languages. This style of programming is supported by functional, or applicative, programming languages.

LISP began as a purely functional language but soon acquired some important imperative features that increased its execution efficiency. It is still the most important of the functional languages, at least in the sense that it is the only one that has achieved widespread use. Scheme is a small, static-scoped dialect of LISP. COMMON LISP is an amalgam of several early 1980s dialects of LISP. ML and Haskell are strongly typed functional languages with more conventional syntax than LISP and Scheme.

The 1977 ACM Turing Award was given to John Backus for his work in the development of Fortran. Each recipient of this award presents a lecture when the award is formally given, and the lecture is subsequently published in the *Communications of the ACM.* In his Turing Award lecture (Backus, 1978), Backus made a case that purely functional programming languages are better than imperative languages because they result in programs that are more readable, more reliable, and more likely to be correct. The crux of his argument was that purely functional programs are easier to understand, both during and after development, largely because the meanings of expressions are independent of their context (one characterizing feature of a pure functional programming language is that neither expressions nor functions have side effects).

In this lecture, Backus proposed a pure functional language, FP(*functional programming*), which he used to frame his argument. Although the language did not succeed, at least in terms of achieving widespread use, his idea motivated debate and research on pure functional programming languages. The point here is that some well-known computer scientists have attempted to promote the concept that functional programming languages are superior to the traditional imperative languages, though those efforts have obviously fallen short of their goals.

One objective of this chapter is to provide an introduction to functional programming using the core of Scheme, intentionally leaving out its imperative features. Sufficient material on Scheme is included to allow the reader to write some simple but interesting programs. It is difficult to acquire an actual feel for functional programming without some actual programming experience, so that is strongly encouraged.

15.2 Mathematical Functions

A mathematical function is a mapping of members of one set, called the domain set, to another set, called the range set. A function definition specifies the domain and range sets, either explicitly or implicitly, along with the mapping. The mapping is described by an expression or, in some cases, by a table. Functions are often applied to a particular element of the domain set, given as a parameter to the function. Note that the domain set may be the cross product of several sets (reflecting that there can be more than one parameter). A function yields, or returns, an element of the range set.

One of the fundamental characteristics of mathematical functions is that the evaluation order of their mapping expressions is controlled by recursion and conditional expressions, rather than by the sequencing and iterative repetition that are common to the imperative programming languages.

Another important characteristic of mathematical functions is that because they have no side effects, they always define the same value given the same set of arguments.[1] Side effects in programming languages are connected to variables that model memory locations.

---

1. Note that mathematical functions *define* values, whereas programming language functions *produce* values.

In mathematics, there is no such thing as a variable that models a memory location. Local variables in functions in imperative programming languages maintain the state of the function. In mathematics, there is no concept of the state of a function.

A mathematical function defines a value, rather than specifying a sequence of operations on values in memory to produce a value. There are no variables in the sense of imperative languages, so there can be no side effects.

15.2.1   Simple Functions

Function definitions are often written as a function name, followed by a list of parameters in parentheses, followed by the mapping expression. For example,

cube(x) ≡ x * x * x, where x is a real number

In this definition, the domain and range sets are the real numbers. The symbol ≡ is used to mean "is defined as." The parameter x can represent any member of the domain set, but it is fixed to represent one specific element during evaluation of the function expression. This is how the parameters of mathematical functions differ from the variables in imperative languages.

Function applications are specified by pairing the function name with a particular element of the domain set. The range element is obtained by evaluating the function-mapping expression with the domain element substituted for the occurrences of the parameter. For example, cube(2.0) yields the value 8.0. Once again, it is important to note that during evaluation, the mapping of a function contains no unbound parameters, where a bound parameter is a name for a particular value. Every occurrence of a parameter is bound to a value from the domain set and is considered a constant during evaluation.

Early theoretical work on functions separated the task of defining a function from that of naming the function. Lambda notation, as devised by Alonzo Church (Church, 1941), provides a method for defining nameless functions. A **lambda expression** specifies the parameter and the mapping of a function. The lambda expression is the function itself, which is nameless. For example, consider

λ(x)x * x * x

As stated earlier, before evaluation, a parameter represents any member of the domain set, but during evaluation it is bound to a particular member. When a lambda expression is evaluated for a given parameter, the expression is said to be applied to that parameter. The mechanics of such an application are the same as for any function evaluation. Application of the example lambda expression is denoted, as in the following example:

(λ(x)x * x * x)(2)

which results in the value 8.

Lambda expressions, like other function definitions, can have more than one parameter.

15.2.2   Functional Forms

A higher-order function, or **functional form,** is one that either takes functions as parameters or yields a function as its result, or both. One common kind of functional form is **function composition,** which has two functional parameters and yields a function whose value is the first actual parameter function applied to the result of the second. Function composition is written as an expression, using $°$ as an operator, as in

$h \equiv f \; °g$

For example, if

$f(x) \equiv x + 2$
$g(x) \equiv 3 \; * \; x$

then h is defined as

$h(x) \equiv f(g(x))$, or $h(x) \equiv (3 \; * \; x) + 2$

Apply-to-all is a functional form that takes a single function as a parameter. If applied to a list of arguments, apply-to-all applies its functional parameter to each of the values in the list argument and collects the results in a list or sequence. Apply-to-all is denoted by α. Consider the following example:

Let
$h(x) \equiv x \; * \; x$

then

$\alpha(h, (2, 3, 4))$ yields $(4, 9, 16)$

There are many other functional forms, but these two examples illustrate their characteristics.

15.3 Fundamentals of Functional Programming Languages

The objective of the design of a functional programming language is to mimic mathematical functions to the greatest extent possible. This objective results in an approach to problem solving that is fundamentally different from approaches used with imperative languages. In an imperative language, an expression is evaluated and the result is stored in a memory location, which is represented as a variable in a program. This necessary attention to memory cells results in a relatively low-level programming methodology. A program in an assembly language often must also store the results of partial evaluations of expressions. For example, to evaluate

$(x + y)/(a - b)$

the value of $(x + y)$ is computed first. That value must then be stored while $(a - b)$ is evaluated. The compiler handles the storage of intermediate results of expression evaluations in high-level languages. The storage of intermediate results is still required, but the details are hidden from the programmer.

A purely functional programming language does not use variables or assignment statements, thus freeing the programmer from concerns about the memory cells of the computer on which the program is executed. Without variables, iterative constructs are not possible, for they are controlled by variables. Repetition must be done by recursion rather than by repetition. Programs are function definitions and function application specifications, and executions consist of evaluating the function applications. Without variables, the execution of a purely functional program has no state in the sense of operational and denotational semantics. The execution of a function always produces the same result when given the same parameters. This feature is called **referential transparency.** It makes the semantics of purely functional languages far simpler than the semantics of the imperative languages (and the functional languages that include imperative features).

A functional language provides a set of primitive functions, a set of functional forms to construct complex functions from those primitive functions, a function application operation, and some structure or structures for representing data. These structures are used to represent the parameters and values computed by functions. If a functional language is well defined, it requires only a relatively small number of primitive functions.

Although functional languages are often implemented with interpreters, they can also be compiled.

Imperative languages usually provide only limited support for functional programming. The most serious drawback to using an imperative language to do functional programming is that functions in imperative languages have restrictions on the types of values that can be returned. In some languages—for example, Fortran—only scalar type values can be returned. More important, imperative languages typically cannot return a function. Such restrictions limit the kinds of functional forms that can be provided. Another serious problem with the functions of imperative languages is the possibility of functional side effects. As we saw in Chapter 7, functional side effects complicate the readability and lower the reliability of expressions.

15.4 The First Functional Programming Language: LISP

A number of functional programming languages have been developed. The oldest and most widely used is LISP. Studying functional languages through LISP is somewhat akin to studying the imperative languages through Fortran: LISP was the first functional language, but although it has steadily evolved over the last 40 years, it no longer represents the latest design concepts for functional languages. In addition, with the exception of the first version, all LISP dialects include imperative-language features, such as imperative-style variables, assignment statements, and iteration. (Imperative-style variables are used to name memory cells, whose values can change many times during program execution.) Despite this and their somewhat odd form, the descendants of the original LISP represent well the fundamental concepts of functional programming and are therefore worthy of study.

15.4.1 Data Types and Structures

There were only two types of data objects in the original LISP: atoms and lists.[2] They are not types in the sense that imperative languages have types. In fact, the original LISP was a typeless language. Atoms are either symbols, in the form of identifiers, or numeric literals.

Recall from Chapter 2 that LISP originally used lists as its data structure because they were thought to be an essential part of list processing. As it eventually developed, however, LISP rarely requires the general list operations of insertion and deletion.

Lists are specified in LISP by delimiting their elements within parentheses. The elements of **simple lists** are restricted to atoms, as in

(A B C D)

Nested list structures are also specified by parentheses. For example, the list

(A (B C) D (E (F G)))

is a list of four elements. The first is the atom A; the second is the sublist (B C); the third is the atom D; the fourth is the sublist (E (F G)), which has as its second element the sublist (F G).

Internally, lists are usually stored as single-linked list structures in which each node has two pointers and represents an element. A node for an atom has its first pointer pointing to some representation of the atom, such as its symbol or numeric value. A node for a sublist element has its first pointer pointing to the first node of the sublist. In both cases, the second pointer of a node points to the next element of the list. A list is referenced by a pointer to its first element.

The internal representations of our two example lists are shown in Figure 15.1. Note that the elements of a list are shown horizontally. The last element of a list has no successor, so its link is NIL. Sublists are shown with the same structure.

---

2. Actually, lists are the most commonly used form of a more general data structure, the dotted pair. We will ignore dotted pairs, except to explain in Section 15.5.8 how one can be accidentally created.

Figure 15.1

Internal representation
of two LISP lists

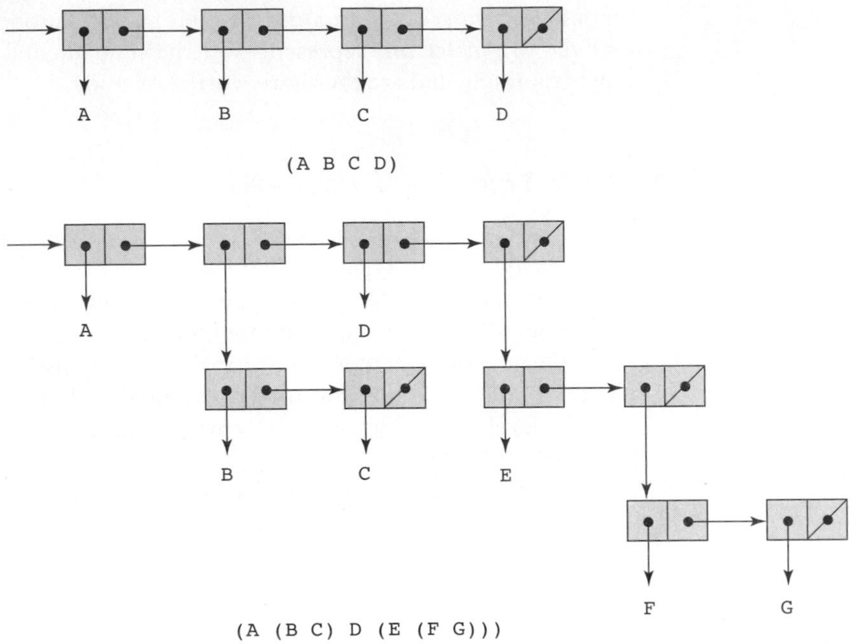

(A B C D)

(A (B C) D (E (F G)))

15.4.2 The First LISP Interpreter

The original intent of LISP's design was to have a notation for programs that
would be as close to Fortran's as possible, with additions when necessary.
This notation was called M-notation, for meta-notation. There was to be a
compiler that would translate programs written in M-notation into semantically equivalent machine code programs for the IBM 704.

Early in the development of LISP, McCarthy decided to write a paper
that would promote list processing as an approach to general symbolic processing. McCarthy believed that list processing could be used to study computability, which at the time was usually studied using Turing machines.
McCarthy thought that the processing of symbolic lists was a more natural
model of computation than Turing machines were. One of the common
requirements of the study of computation is that one must be able to prove
certain computability characteristics of the whole class of whatever model of
computation is being used. In the case of the Turing machine model, one can
construct a universal Turing machine that can mimic the operations of any
other Turing machine. From this concept came the idea of constructing a
universal LISP function that could evaluate any other function in LISP.

The first requirement for the universal LISP function was a notation that
allowed functions to be expressed in the same way data was expressed. The
parenthesized list notation described in Section 15.4.1 had already been
adopted for LISP data, so it was decided to invent conventions for function

definitions and function calls that could also be expressed in list notation. Function calls were specified in a prefix list form called Cambridge Polish, as in the following:

(function_name   argument_1 ... argument_n)

For example, if + is a function that takes two numeric parameters,

(+ 5 7)

evaluates to 12.

The lambda notation described in Section 15.2.1 was chosen to specify function definitions. It had to be modified, however, to allow the binding of functions to names so that functions could be referenced by other functions and by themselves. This name binding was specified by a list consisting of the function name and a list containing the lambda expression, as in

(function_name (LAMBDA (arg_1 ... arg_n) expression))

If you have had no prior exposure to functional programming, it may seem odd to even consider a nameless function. However, nameless functions are sometimes useful in functional programming (as well as in mathematics). For example, consider a function whose action is to produce a function for immediate application to a parameter list. The produced function has no need for a name, for it is applied only at the point of its construction. Such an example is given in Section 15.5.10.

LISP functions specified in this new notation were called S-expressions, for symbolic expressions. Eventually, all LISP structures, both data and code, were called S-expressions. An S-expression can be either a list or an atom. We will usually refer to S-expressions simply as expressions.

McCarthy successfully developed a universal function that could evaluate any other function. This function was named EVAL and was itself in the form of an expression. Two of the people in the AI Project, Stephen B. Russell and Daniel J. Edwards, noticed that an implementation of EVAL could serve as a LISP interpreter, and they promptly constructed such an implementation (McCarthy et al., 1965).

There were several important results of this quick, easy, and unexpected implementation. First, all early LISP systems copied EVAL and were therefore interpretive. Second, the definition of M-notation, which was the planned programming notation for LISP, was never completed or implemented, so S-expressions became LISP's only notation. The use of the same notation for data and code has important consequences, one of which will be discussed in Section 15.5.12. Third, much of the original language design was effectively frozen, keeping certain odd features in the language, such as the conditional expression form and the use of ( ) for both the empty list and logical false.

Another feature of early LISP systems that was apparently accidental was the use of dynamic scoping. Functions were evaluated in the environments of their callers. No one at the time knew much about scoping, and it is doubtful that much thought was given to the choice. Dynamic scoping was used for most dialects of LISP before 1975. Contemporary dialects either use static scoping or allow the programmer to choose between static and dynamic scoping.

15.5 An Introduction to Scheme

In this section, we describe a part of Scheme (Dybvig, 2003). We have chosen Scheme because it is relatively simple, it is popular in colleges and universities, and Scheme interpreters are readily available for a wide variety of computers. The version of Scheme described in this section is Scheme 4. Note that this section covers only a small part of Scheme, and it includes none of Scheme's imperative features.

15.5.1   Origins of Scheme

The Scheme language, which is a dialect of LISP, emerged from MIT in the mid-1970s (Sussman and Steele, 1975). It is characterized by its small size, its exclusive use of static scoping, and its treatment of functions as first-class entities. As first-class entities, Scheme functions can be the values of expressions, elements of lists, assigned to variables, and passed as parameters. Early versions of LISP did not provide all of these capabilities.

As a small language with simple syntax and semantics, Scheme is well-suited to educational applications, such as courses in functional programming, and also to general introductions to programming.

Note that most of the Scheme functions in the following sections would require only minor modifications to be rewritten as LISP functions.

15.5.2   The Scheme Interpreter

The Scheme interpreter is a read-evaluate-write infinite loop. It repeatedly reads an expression typed by the user (in the form of a list), interprets the expression, and displays the resulting value. Expressions are interpreted by the function EVAL. Literals evaluate to themselves. So, if you type a number to the interpreter, it simply displays the number. Expressions that are calls to primitive functions are evaluated in the following way: First, each of the parameter expressions is evaluated, in no particular order. Then the primitive function is applied to the parameter values, and the resulting value is displayed.

15.5.3   Primitive Numeric Functions

This subsection introduces Scheme by discussing its primitive functions that deal with only numeric atoms, as opposed to symbolic atoms and lists.

Scheme includes primitive functions for the basic arithmetic operations. These are +, −, *, and /, for add, subtract, multiply, and divide. * and + can have zero or more parameters. If * is given no parameters, it returns 1; if + is given no parameters, it returns 0. + adds all of its parameters together. * multiplies all its parameters together. / and – can have two or more parameters. In the case of subtraction, all but the first parameter are subtracted from the first. Division is similar to subtraction. Some examples are:

Expression	*Value*
42	42
(* 3 7)	21
(+ 5 7 8)	20
(– 5 6)	–1
(– 15 7 2)	6
(– 24 (* 4 3))	12

SQRT returns the square root of its numeric parameter, if the parameter's value is not negative.

15.5.4 Defining Functions

A Scheme program is a collection of function definitions. Consequently, knowing how to define these functions is a prerequisite to writing the simplest program. Recall from Section 15.2.1 that the form of Scheme functions is based on lambda notation. In Scheme, a nameless function actually includes the word LAMBDA, and is called a **lambda expression.** For example,

```
(LAMBDA (x) (* x x))
```

is a nameless function that returns the square of its given numeric parameter. This function can be applied in the same way that named functions are: by placing it in the beginning of a list that contains the actual parameters. For example, we could have

```
((LAMBDA (x) (* x x)) 7)
```

which yields 49. Here, x is called a **bound variable** within the lambda expression. A bound variable never changes in the expression after being bound to an actual parameter value at the time evaluation of the lambda expression begins.

The Scheme special form function DEFINE serves two fundamental needs of Scheme programming: to bind a name to a value and to bind a name to a lambda expression. The former use may sound like DEFINE can be used to create imperative language–style variables. However, these name bindings create named constants, not variables.

DEFINE is called a special form because it is interpreted (by EVAL) in a different way than the normal primitives like the arithmetic functions, as we shall soon see.

The simplest form of DEFINE is one used to bind a name to the value of an expression. This form is

(DEFINE symbol expression)

For example,

(DEFINE pi 3.14159)
(DEFINE two_pi (* 2 pi))

If these two expressions have been typed to the Scheme interpreter and then pi is typed, the number 3.14159 will be displayed; when two_pi is typed, 6.28318 will be displayed. In both cases, the numbers may have more digits than are shown here.

Names in Scheme can consist of letters, digits, and special characters except parentheses; they are case-insensitive and must not begin with a digit.

The second use of the DEFINE function is to bind a lambda expression to a name. In this case, the lambda expression is abbreviated by removing the word LAMBDA. To bind a name to a lambda expression, DEFINE takes two lists as parameters. The first parameter is the prototype of a function call, with the function name followed by the formal parameters, together in a list. The second list contains an expression to which the name is to be bound. The general form of such a DEFINE is[3]

(DEFINE (function_name parameters)
    (expression)
)

The following example call to DEFINE binds the name square to the expression that follows it, which takes one parameter:

(DEFINE (square number) (* number number))

After the interpreter evaluates this function, it can be used, as in

(square 5)

which displays 25.

To illustrate the difference between primitive functions and the DEFINE special form, consider

(DEFINE x 10)

---

3. Actually, the general form of DEFINE has as its body a list containing a sequence of one or more expressions, although in most cases only one is included. We include only one for simplicity's sake.

If DEFINE were a primitive function, EVAL's first action on this expression would be to evaluate the two parameters of DEFINE. If x were not already bound to a value, this would be an error. Furthermore, if x were already defined, it would also be an error, because this DEFINE would attempt to redefine x, which is illegal.

Following is another example of a function. It computes the length of the hypotenuse of a right triangle, given the lengths of the two other sides.

```
(DEFINE (hypotenuse side1 side2)
    (SQRT(+(square side1)(square side2)))
)
```

Notice that hypotenuse uses square, which was defined earlier.

15.5.5 Output Functions

Scheme includes a few simple output functions, such as

(DISPLAY expression)

and

(NEWLINE)

with the obvious semantics. Most output from Scheme programs, however, is the normal output from the interpreter, displaying results of applying EVAL to top-level functions.

15.5.6 Numeric Predicate Functions

A predicate function is one that returns a Boolean value (either true or false). Scheme includes a collection of predicate functions for numeric data. Among them are the following:

Function	Meaning
=	Equal
<>	Not equal
>	Greater than
<	Less than
>=	Greater than or equal to
<=	Less than or equal to
EVEN?	Is it an even number?
ODD?	Is it an odd number?
ZERO?	Is it zero?

Notice that the names for all predefined predicate functions that have words for names end with question marks. In Scheme, the two Boolean values are #T and #F. The Scheme predefined predicate functions return the empty list, (), instead of #F (the two are equivalent). Any non-null list returned by a predicate function is interpreted as #T. In the interest of readability, all of our example predicate functions in this chapter return #F, rather than ().

15.5.7　Control Flow

Scheme uses three different constructs for control flow, one modeled on the selection construct of the imperative languages and two based on the evaluation control used in mathematical functions.

The Scheme two-way selector, named IF, has three parameters: a predicate expression, a then expression, and an else expression. A call to IF has the form

```
(IF predicate then_expression else_expression)
```

For example,

```
(DEFINE (factorial n)
  (IF (= n 0)
    1
    (* n (factorial (- n 1)))
))
```

Notice how closely the form of this function relates to that of the mathematical definition of factorial given previously.

Control flow in mathematical function definitions is quite different from that in programs in imperative programming languages. Whereas functions in imperative languages are defined as collections of statements that may include several kinds of sequence control flow, mathematical functions do not have multiple statements and use only recursion and conditional expressions for evaluation flow control. For example, the factorial function can be defined with these two operations as

$$f(n) \equiv \begin{cases} 1 \text{ if } n = 0 \\ n * f(n-1) \text{ if } n > 0 \end{cases}$$

A mathematical conditional expression is in the form of a list of pairs, each of which is a guarded expression. Each guarded expression consists of a predicate guard and an expression. The value of such a conditional expression is the value of the expression associated with the predicate that is true. Only one of the predicates can be true for a given parameter or parameter list.

The Scheme multiple selector, which is based on mathematical conditional expressions, is a special form named COND. COND is a slightly generalized version of the mathematical conditional expression; it allows more than one predicate to be true at the same time. Because different mathematical conditional expressions have different numbers of parameters, COND does not require a fixed number of actual parameters. Each parameter to COND is a pair of expressions in which the first is a predicate.

The general form of COND is

```
(COND
    (predicate_1 expression)
    (predicate_2 expression)
    ...
    (predicate_n expression)
    [ (ELSE expression) ]
)
```

where the ELSE clause is optional.

The semantics of COND is as follows: The predicates of the parameters are evaluated one at a time, in order from the first, until one evaluates to #T. The expression that follows the first predicate that is found to be #T is then evaluated, and its value is returned as the value of COND. If none of the predicates is true and there is an ELSE, its expression is evaluated and the value is returned. If none of the predicates is true and there is no ELSE, the value of COND is unspecified. Therefore, all COND's should include an ELSE.

Notice the similarity between a COND and the multiple-selection statement with an "otherwise" clause at the end, such as an Ada **case** statement.

Following is an example of a simple function that uses COND:

```
(DEFINE (compare x y)
    (COND
        ((> x y) "x is greater than y")
        ((< x y) "y is greater than x")
        (ELSE "x and y are equal")
)
```

The following subsections contain additional examples of the use of COND.

The third Scheme control mechanism is recursion, which is used, as in mathematics, to control repetition. Most of the example functions in Section 15.5.10 use recursion.

15.5.8 List Functions

The most common use of the LISP-based programming languages—indeed, the most common use of functional languages—is list processing. This subsection introduces the Scheme functions for dealing with lists.

The first Scheme primitive we describe is a utility function required by the nature of the Scheme function application operation, EVAL. It is called to handle the evaluate part of the read-evaluate-write action of the Scheme interpreter. When applied to a primitive function, EVAL first evaluates the parameters of the given function. This action is necessary when the actual parameters in a function call are themselves function calls, which is frequently the case. In some calls, however, the parameters are data elements rather than function references. When a parameter is not a function reference, it obviously should not be evaluated. We were not concerned with this earlier, because numeric literals cannot be mistaken for function names.

Suppose we have a function that has two parameters, an atom and a list, and the purpose of the function is to determine whether the given atom is in the given list. Neither the atom nor the list should be evaluated; they are literal data to be examined. To avoid evaluating a parameter, it is first given as a parameter to the primitive function QUOTE, which simply returns it without change. The following examples illustrate QUOTE:

```
(QUOTE A) returns A
(QUOTE (A B C)) returns (A B C)
```

In the remainder of this chapter, we use the common abbreviation of the call to QUOTE, which is done simply by preceding the expression to be quoted by an apostrophe ('). Thus, instead of (QUOTE (A B)), we will use '(A B).

A programming language for list processing must include primitives for manipulating lists. In particular, it must provide operations for selecting parts of a list, which in a sense dismantle the list, and at least one operation for constructing lists. There are two primitive list selectors in Scheme: CAR and CDR (pronounced "could-er"). The CAR function returns the first element of a given list. The following examples illustrate CAR:

```
(CAR '(A B C)) returns A
(CAR '((A B) C D)) returns (A B)
(CAR 'A) is an error because A is not a list
(CAR '(A)) returns A
(CAR '()) is an error
```

The CDR function returns the remainder of a given list after its CAR has been removed:

```
(CDR '(A B C)) returns (B C)
(CDR '((A B) C D)) returns (C D)
(CDR 'A) is an error
(CDR '(A)) returns ()
(CDR '()) is an error
```

The names of the CAR and CDR functions are peculiar at best. The origin of these names lies in the first implementation of LISP, which was on an IBM 704 computer. The 704's memory words had two fields, named *decrement* and *address*, that were used in various operand addressing strategies. Each of these fields could store a machine memory address. The 704 also included two machine instructions, named CAR (contents of address register) and CDR (contents of decrement register), that extracted the associated fields. It was natural to use the two fields to store the two pointers of a list node so that a memory word could neatly store a node. Using these conventions, the CAR and CDR instructions of the 704 provided efficient list selectors. The names carried over into the primitives of all dialects of LISP.

As another example of a simple function, consider

```
(DEFINE (second lst) (CAR (CDR lst)))
```

Once this function is evaluated, it can be used, as in

```
(second '(A B C))
```

which returns B.

CONS is a primitive list constructor. It builds a list from its two arguments, the first of which can be either an atom or a list; the second is usually a list. CONS inserts its first parameter as the new CAR of its second parameter. Consider the following examples:

```
(CONS 'A '()) returns (A)
(CONS 'A '(B C)) returns (A B C)
(CONS '() '(A B)) returns (() A B)
(CONS '(A B) '(C D)) returns ((A B) C D)
```

The results of these CONS operations are shown in Figure 15.2. Note that CONS is, in a sense, the inverse of CAR and CDR. CAR and CDR take a list apart, and CONS constructs a new list from given list parts. The two parameters to CONS become the CAR and CDR of the new list. Thus, if lis is a list, then

```
(CONS (CAR lis) (CDR lis))
```

returns a list identical to lis.

Dealing only with the relatively simple problems and programs discussed in this chapter, it is unlikely one would ever intentionally apply CONS to two atoms. However, that is legal and commonly happens accidentally. The result of such an application is a dotted pair, so named because of the way it is displayed by Scheme. For example, consider the following call:

```
(CONS 'A 'B)
```

If the result of this is displayed, it would appear as

```
(A . B)
```

Figure 15.2

The result of several
CONS operations

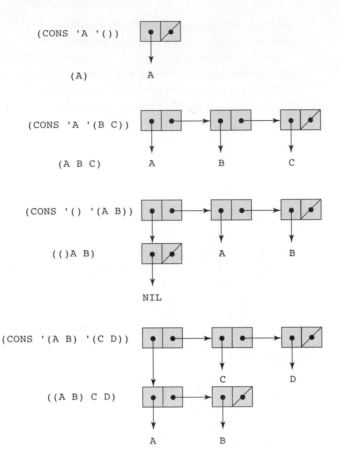

This dotted pair indicates that instead of an atom and a pointer or a pointer and a pointer, this cell has two atoms.

LIST is a function that constructs a list from a variable number of parameters. It is a shorthand version of nested CONS functions, as illustrated in

```
(LIST 'apple 'orange 'grape) returns (apple orange grape)
```

15.5.9   Predicate Functions for Symbolic Atoms and Lists

Scheme has three funcamental predicate functions, EQ?, NULL?, and LIST?, for symbolic atoms and lists.

The EQ? function takes two symbolic atoms as parameters. It returns #T if both parameters are atoms and the two are the same; otherwise, it returns (). Consider the following examples:

```
(EQ? 'A 'A) returns #T
(EQ? 'A 'B) returns #F
```

```
(EQ? 'A '(A B)) returns #F
(EQ? '(A B) '(A B)) returns #F or #T
```

As the last case indicates, the result of comparing lists with EQ? is implementation-dependent—some yield #T and some yield #F. The reason for this difference is that EQ? is often implemented as a pointer comparison (do two given pointers point to the same place?), and two lists that are exactly the same are often not duplicated in memory. At the time the Scheme system creates a list, it checks to see whether there is already such a list. If there is, the new list is nothing more than a pointer to the existing list. In these cases, the two lists will be judged equal by EQ?. However, in some cases, it may be difficult to detect the presence of an identical list, in which case a new list is created. In this scenario, EQ? yields #F.

Note that EQ? works for symbolic atoms but does not necessarily work for numeric atoms. The = predicate works for numeric atoms but not symbolic atoms. As discussed previously, EQ? also does not work reliably for list parameters.

Sometimes it is convenient to be able to test two atoms for equality when it is not known whether they are symbolic or numeric. For this purpose, Scheme has a different predicate, EQV?, which works on both numeric and symbolic atoms. The primary reason to use EQ? or = rather than EQV? when it is possible is that EQ? and = are faster than EQV?.

The LIST? predicate function returns #T if its single argument is a list and #F otherwise, as in the following examples:

```
(LIST? '(X Y)) returns #T
(LIST? 'X) returns #F
(LIST? '()) returns #T
```

The NULL? function tests its parameter to determine whether it is the empty list and returns #T if it is. Consider the following examples:

```
(NULL? '(A B)) returns #F
(NULL? '()) returns #T
(NULL? 'A) returns #F
(NULL? '(())) returns #F
```

The last call yields #F because the parameter is not the empty list. Rather, it is a list containing a single element, the empty list.

15.5.10 Example Scheme Functions

This section contains several examples of function definitions in Scheme. These programs solve simple list-processing problems.

Consider the problem of membership of a given atom in a given list that does not include sublists. Such a list is called a **simple list.** If the function is named member, it could be used as follows:

```
(member 'B '(A B C)) returns #T
(member 'B '(A C D E)) returns #F
```

Thinking in terms of iteration, the membership problem is simply to compare the given atom and the individual elements of the given list, one at a time in some order, until either a match is found or there are no more elements in the list to be compared. A similar process can be accomplished using recursion. The function can compare the given atom with the CAR of the list. If they match, the value #T is returned. If they do not match, the CAR of the list should be ignored and the search continued on the CDR of the list. This can be done by having the function call itself with the CDR of the list as the list parameter and return the result of this recursive call. This process will end if the given atom is found in the list. If the atom is not in the list, the function will eventually be called (by itself) with a null list as the actual parameter. That event must force the function to return #F. In this process, there are two ways out of the recursion: Either the list is empty on some call and #F is returned, or a match is found and #T is returned.

Altogether, there are three cases that must be handled in the function: an empty input list, a match between the atom and the CAR of the list, or a mismatch between the atom and the CAR of the list, which causes the recursive call. These three are the three parameters to COND, with the last being the default case that is triggered by an ELSE predicate. The complete function follows:

```
(DEFINE (member atm lis)
  (COND
    ((NULL? lis) #F)
    ((EQ? atm (CAR lis)) #T)
    (ELSE (member atm (CDR lis)))
))
```

This form is typical of simple Scheme list-processing functions. In such functions, the data in lists are processed one element at a time. The individual elements are specified with CAR, and the process is continued using recursion on the CDR of the list.

Notice that the null test must precede the equal test, because applying CAR to an empty list is an error.

As another example, consider the problem of determining whether two given lists are equal. If the two lists are simple, the solution is relatively easy, although some programming techniques with which the reader may not be familiar are involved. A predicate function, equalsimp, for comparing simple lists is shown here:

```
(DEFINE (equalsimp lis1 lis2)
  (COND
    ((NULL? lis1) (NULL? lis2))
    ((NULL? lis2) #F)
    ((EQ? (CAR lis1) (CAR lis2))
          (equalsimp (CDR lis1) (CDR lis2)))
    (ELSE #F)
))
```

The first case, which is handled by the first parameter to COND, is for when the first list parameter is the empty list. This can occur in an external call if the first list parameter is initially empty. Because a recursive call uses the CDRs of the two parameter lists as its parameters, the first list can be empty in such a call if the first list has had all of its elements removed by previous recursive calls. When the first list is empty, the second list must be checked to see whether it is also empty. If so, they are equal (either initially or the CARs were equal on all previous recursive calls), and NULL? correctly returns #T. If the second list is not empty, it is larger than the first list and #F should be returned, as it is by NULL?. Recall that any nonempty list that is returned by a predicate function is interpreted as #T.

The next case deals with the second list being empty when the first list is not. This situation occurs only when the first list is larger than the second. Only the second list must be tested, because the first case catches all instances of the first list being empty.

The third case is the recursive step that tests for equality between two corresponding elements in the two lists. It does this by comparing the CARs of the two nonempty lists. If they are equal, then the two lists are equal up to that point, so recursion is used on the CDRs of both. This case fails when two unequal atoms are found. When this occurs, the process need not continue, so the default case ELSE is selected, which returns #F.

Note that equalsimp expects lists as parameters and does not operate correctly if either or both parameters are atoms.

The problem of comparing general lists is slightly more complex than this, because sublists must be traced completely in the comparison process. In this situation, the power of recursion is uniquely appropriate, because the form of sublists is the same as that of the given lists. Any time the corresponding elements of the two given lists are lists, they are separated into their two parts, CAR and CDR, and recursion is used on them. This is a perfect example of the usefulness of the divide-and-conquer approach. If the corresponding elements of the two given lists are atoms, they can simply be compared using EQ?.

The definition of the complete function follows:

```
(DEFINE (equal lis1 lis2)
  (COND
    ((NOT (LIST? lis1)) (EQ? lis1 lis2))
```

```
      ((NOT (LIST? lis2)) #F)
      ((NULL? lis1) (NULL? lis2))
      ((NULL? lis2) #F)
      ((equal (CAR lis1) (CAR lis2))
             (equal (CDR lis1) (CDR lis2)))
      (ELSE #F)
))
```

The first two cases of the COND handle the situation where either of the parameters is an atom instead of a list. The third and fourth cases are for the situation where one or both lists are empty. These cases also prevent subsequent cases from attempting to apply CAR to an empty list. The fifth COND case is the most interesting. The predicate is a recursive call with the CARs of the lists as parameters. If this recursive call returns #T, then recursion is used again on the CDRs of the lists. This algorithm allows the two lists to include sublists to any depth.

This definition of equal works on any pair of expressions, not just lists. equal is equivalent to the system predicate function EQUAL?. Note that EQUAL? should be used only when necessary (the forms of the actual parameters are not known), because it is much slower than EQ? and EQV?.

Another commonly needed list operation is that of constructing a new list that contains all of the elements of two given list arguments. This is usually implemented as a Scheme function named append. The result list can be constructed by repeated use of CONS to place the elements of the first list argument into the second list argument, which becomes the result list. To clarify the action of append, consider the following examples:

```
(append '(A B) '(C D R)) returns (A B C D R)
(append '((A B) C) '(D (E F))) returns ((A B) C D (E F))
```

The definition of append is

```
(DEFINE (append lis1 lis2)
  (COND
    ((NULL? lis1) lis2)
    (ELSE (CONS (CAR lis1) (append (CDR Lis1) lis2)))
))
```

The first COND case is used to terminate the recursive process when the first argument list is empty, returning the second list. In the second case (the ELSE), the CAR of the first parameter list is CONSed onto the result returned by the recursive call, which passes the CDR of the first list as its first parameter.

Consider the following Scheme function, named guess, which uses the member function described in this section. Try to determine what it does before reading the description that follows it. Assume the parameters are simple lists.

```
(DEFINE (guess lis1 lis2)
  (COND
    ((NULL? lis1) '())
    ((member (CAR lis1) lis2)
            (CONS (CAR lis1) (guess (CDR lis1) lis2)))
    (ELSE (guess (CDR lis1) lis2))
))
```

guess yields a simple list that contains the common elements of its two parameter lists. So if the parameter lists represent sets, guess computes a list that represents the intersection of those two sets.

LET is a function that allows names to be temporarily bound to the values of subexpressions. It is often used to factor out the common subexpressions from more complicated expressions. These names can then be used in the evaluation of another expression. Its general form is

```
(LET (
  (name_1 expression_1)
  (name_2 expression 2)
  ...
  (name_n expression_n))
  expression {expression}
)
```

The semantics of LET is that the first *n* expressions are evaluated and the resulting values are bound to their associated names. Then the expressions in the body, which consists of the remaining parameters, are evaluated. The result of LET is the value of the last expression in its body. The following example illustrates the use of LET. It computes the roots of a given quadratic equation, assuming the roots are real.[4]

```
(DEFINE (quadratic_roots a b c)
  (LET (
    (root_part_over_2a
            (/ (SQRT (- (* b b) (* 4 a c))) (* 2 a)))
    (minus_b_over_2a (/ (- 0 b) (* 2 a)))
    )
  (LIST (+ minus_b_over_2a root_part_over_2a)
          (- minus_b_over_2a root_part_over_2a))
)
```

This example uses LIST to create the list of the two values that make up the result.

---

4. Some versions of Scheme include "complex" as a data type and will compute the roots of the equation, regardless of whether they are real or complex.

LET creates a new local static scope in much the same way as Ada's **declare.** New variables can be created, used, and then discarded when the end of the new scope is reached. The named components of LET are like assignment statements, but they can be used only in LET's new scope. Furthermore, they cannot be rebound to new values in LET.

LET is actually just shorthand for a LAMBDA expression. The following two expressions are equivalent:

```
(LET ((alpha 7))(* 5 alpha))
((LAMBDA (alpha) (* 5 alpha)) 7)
```

In the first expression, 7 is bound to alpha with LET; in the second, 7 is bound to alpha through the parameter of the LAMBDA expression.

15.5.11 Functional Forms

This section describes two common mathematical functional forms that are provided by Scheme: composition and apply-to-all. Both of these are mathematically defined in Section 15.2.2.

15.5.11.1 Functional Composition

Functional composition is the only primitive functional form provided by the original LISP. All subsequent LISP dialects, including Scheme, also provide it. Functional composition is the essence of how EVAL works. All nonquoted lists are assumed to be function calls, which requires their parameters to be evaluated first. This applies recursively to the smallest list in any expression, which is precisely what functional composition means. The following examples illustrate functional composition:

```
(CDR (CDR '(A B C))) returns (C)
(CAR (CAR '((A B) B C))) returns A
(CDR (CAR '((A B C) D))) returns (B C)
(NULL? (CAR '(() B C))) returns #T
(CONS (CAR '(A B)) (CDR '(A B))) returns (A B)
```

Notice that the function names in inner calls are not quoted because they must be evaluated rather than treated as literal data.

Some of the most commonly used functional compositions in Scheme are built in as single functions. For example, (CAAR x) is equivalent to (CAR (CAR x)), (CADR x) is equivalent to ((CAR (CDR x)), and (CADDAR x) is equivalent to (CAR (CDR (CDR (CAR x)))). Any combination of As and Ds, up to four, are legal between the 'C' and the 'R' in the function's name.

15.5.11.2 An Apply-to-All Functional Form

The most common functional forms provided in common functional programming languages are variations of mathematical apply-to-all functional forms. The simplest of these is mapcar, which has two parameters, a function and a list. mapcar applies the given function to each element of the given list, and it returns a list of the results of these applications. A Scheme definition of mapcar follows:

```
(DEFINE (mapcar fun lis)
  (COND
    ((NULL? lis) '())
    (ELSE (CONS (fun (CAR lis)) (mapcar fun (CDR lis))))
))
```

Note the simple form of mapcar, which expresses a complex functional form. This function is testament to the great expressive power of Scheme.

As an example of the use of mapcar, suppose we want all of the elements of a list cubed. We can accomplish this with

```
(mapcar (LAMBDA (num) (* num num num)) '(3 4 2 6))
```

This call returns (27 64 8 216).

Note that in this example, the first parameter to mapcar is a LAMBDA expression. When EVAL evaluates the LAMBDA expression, it constructs a function that has the same form as any predefined function except that it is nameless. In the example expression, this nameless function is immediately applied to each element of the parameter list and the results are returned in a list.

15.5.12 Functions That Build Code

The fact that programs and data have the same structure can be exploited in constructing programs. Recall that the Scheme interpreter is a function named EVAL. The Scheme system applies EVAL to every expression typed at the Scheme prompt. The EVAL function can also be called directly by Scheme programs. This provides the possibility of a Scheme program creating expressions and calling EVAL to evaluate them.

One of the simplest examples of this process involves numeric atoms. Scheme includes a function named +, which takes any number of numeric atoms as arguments and returns their sum. For example, (+ 3 7 10 2) returns 22.

Our problem is the following: Suppose that in a program we have a list of numeric atoms and need the sum. We cannot apply + directly on the list, because + can take only atomic parameters, not a list of numeric atoms. We could, of course, write a function that repeatedly adds the CAR of the list to the sum of its CDR, using recursion to go through the list. Such a function follows:

```
(DEFINE (adder lis)
  (COND
    ((NULL? lis) 0)
    (ELSE (+ (CAR lis) (adder (CDR lis))))
))
```

An alternative solution to the problem is to write a function that builds a call to + with the proper parameter forms. This can be done by using CONS to insert the atom + into the list of numbers. This new list can then be submitted to EVAL for evaluation, as in the following:

```
(DEFINE (adder lis)
  (COND
    ((NULL? lis) 0)
    (ELSE (EVAL (CONS '+ lis)))
))
```

Note that the + function's name is quoted to prevent EVAL from evaluating it in the evaluation of CONS. As an example, consider that the call

```
(adder '(3 4 6))
```

causes adder to build the list

```
(+ 3 4 6)
```

The list is then submitted to EVAL, which invokes + and returns the result, 13.

In all earlier versions of Scheme, the EVAL function evaluates its expression in the outermost scope of the program. The latest version of Scheme, Scheme 4, requires a second parameter to EVAL that specifies the scope in which the expression is to be evaluated. For simplicity's sake, we left the scope parameter out of our example, and we do not discuss scope names here.

15.6 COMMON LISP

COMMON LISP (Steele, 1984) was created in an effort to combine the features of several early 1980s dialects of LISP, including Scheme, into a single language. Being something of a union of languages, it is quite large and complex. Its basis, however, is the original LISP, so its syntax, primitive functions, and fundamental nature come from that language.

Recognizing the occasional flexibility provided by dynamic scoping, as well as the simplicity of static scoping, COMMON LISP allows both. The default scoping for variables is static, but by declaring a variable to be "special," that variable becomes dynamically scoped.

The list of features of COMMON LISP is long: a large number of data types and structures, including such things as records, arrays, complex numbers, and character strings; powerful input and output operations; a form of packages for modularizing collections of functions and data, and also for providing access control.

In a sense, Scheme and COMMON LISP are opposites. Scheme is far smaller and semantically simpler, in part because of its exclusive use of static scoping. COMMON LISP was meant to be a commercial language and has succeeded in being a widely used language for AI applications. Scheme, on the other hand, is more frequently used in college courses on functional programming. It is also more likely to be studied as a functional language because of its relatively small size. An important design criterion of COMMON LISP that caused it to be a very large language was the desire to make it compatible with several of the dialects of LISP from which it was derived.

15.7 ML

ML (Milner et al., 1990) is a static-scoped functional programming language, like Scheme. However, it differs from LISP and its dialects, including Scheme, in a number of significant ways. Perhaps the most important difference is that ML is a strongly typed language, whereas Scheme is essentially typeless. ML has type declarations, although because of its type inferencing, which is discussed briefly in Chapter 5, they are often not used. The type of every variable and expression can be determined at compile time. Another important difference between Scheme and ML is that ML uses a syntax that is more closely related to that of an imperative language than that of LISP. For example, arithmetic expressions are written in ML using infix notation.

ML has exception handling and a module facility for implementing abstract data types. A brief history of the development and primary features of ML are given in Chapter 2.

Function declarations in ML appear in the general form

fun function_name (formal_parameters) = function_body_expression;

For example,

fun square (x : **int**) = x * x;

The type of the return value can be specified after the parameter list, as in

fun square(x : **int**) : **int** = x * x;

Of course, in this function the type of the return value need not be explicitly specified.

The following line,

fun square (x) = x * x;

defines the same function as the last function definition, because ML assumes the **int** type, given that the operator in the expression (x * x) indicates that x is some numeric type. So functions that use arithmetic operators cannot be polymorphic. The same is true for functions that use relational operators, except = and <>, and Boolean operators. However, functions that use only list operations, =, <>, and tuple operators (those for forming tuples and for component selection) can be polymorphic.

If we wanted a square function for **real** type values and we had already defined square for **int** values, we would need to define it with a different name, because user-defined overloaded functions are not allowed. Furthermore, if we defined square for **real** parameters, it could not be called with an integer actual parameter, because ML, like Ada, does not coerce integer values to **real** type.

The ML selection control flow construct is similar to that of the imperative languages. It has the general form

if expression **then** then_expression **else** else_expression

where the first expression must evaluate to a Boolean value.

The conditional expressions of Scheme can appear at the function definition level in ML. In Scheme, the COND function is used to determine the value of the given parameter, which in turn specifies the value returned by COND. In ML, the computation performed by a function can be defined for different forms of the given parameter. This feature is meant to mimic the form and meaning of conditional function definitions in mathematics. In ML, the particular expression that defines the return value of a function is chosen by pattern matching against the given parameter. For example, without using this pattern matching, a function to compute factorial could be written as:

```
fun fact(n : int): int = if n = 0 then 1
                         else n * fact(n - 1);
```

Multiple definitions of a function can be written using parameter pattern matching. The different function definitions that depend on the form of the parameter are separated by an OR symbol (|). For example, using pattern matching, the factorial function could be written as

```
fun fact(0) = 1
|   fact(n : int): int = n * fact(n - 1);
```

If fact is called with the actual parameter 0, the first definition is used; if an **int** value that is not zero is sent, the second definition is used.

ML has lists and list operations, although their appearance is not like those of Scheme. Lists are specified in square brackets, with the elements separated by commas, as in the following list of integers:

```
[5, 7, 9]
```

[ ] is the empty list, which could also be specified with `nil`.

The Scheme CONS function is a binary infix operator in ML, represented as `::`. For example,

```
3 :: [5, 5, 9]
```

evaluates to [3, 5, 7, 9].

The elements of a list must be of the same type, so the following list would be illegal:

```
[5, 7.3, 9]
```

ML has functions that correspond to Scheme's CAR and CDR, named hd (head) and t1 (tail). For example,

```
hd [5, 7, 9] is 5
tl [5, 7, 9] is [7, 9]
```

Because of the availability of patterned function parameters, the hd and t1 functions are much less frequently used in ML than in Scheme. For example, in a formal parameter, the expression

```
(h :: t)
```

is actually two formal parameters, the head and tail of given list parameter, while the corresponding actual parameter is a list. For example, the number of elements in a given list can be computed with the following function:

```
fun length([]) = 0
|   length(h :: t) = 1 + length(t);
```

As another example of these concepts, consider the append function, which does what the Scheme APPEND function does:

```
fun append([], lis2) = lis2
|   append(h :: t, lis2) = h :: append(t, lis2);
```

The first case in this function handles the situation of the function being called with an empty list as the first parameter. This case also terminates the recursion when the initial call has a nonempty first parameter. The second case of the function breaks the first parameter list into its head and tail (CAR and CDR). The head is CONSed onto the result of the recursive call, which uses the tail as its first parameter.

In ML, names can be bound to values with value declaration statements of the form

```
val new_name = expression;
```

For example,

```
val distance = time * speed;
```

Do not get the idea that this statement is exactly like the assignment statements in the imperative languages, for it is not. The **val** statement binds a name to a value, but the name cannot be later rebound to a new value. Well, in a sense it can. Actually, if you do rebind a name with a second **val** statement, it causes a new entry in the environment that is not related to the previous version of the name.[5] In fact, after the new binding, the old environment entry (for the previous binding) is no longer visible. Also, the type of the new binding need not be the same as that of the previous binding. **val** statements do not have side effects. They simply add a name to the current environment and bind it to a value, like the LET special form of Scheme. The normal use of **val** is in a **let** expression, whose general form is

```
let val new_name = expression_1  in  expression_2 end
```

For example,

```
let
  val pi = 3.14159
in
  pi * radius * radius
end;
```

There are no type coercions in ML; the types of the operands of an operator or assignment simply must match to avoid syntax errors.

ML also has enumerated types, arrays, and tuples, which are similar to records.

15.8 Haskell

Haskell (Thompson, 1999) is similar to ML in that it uses a similar syntax, is static scoped, is strongly typed, and uses the same type inferencing method. There are two characteristics of Haskell that set it apart from ML. First, functions in Haskell can be polymorphic (most functions in ML cannot). Second, nonstrict semantics are used in Haskell, whereas in ML (and most other programming languages) strict semantics are used. Both nonstrict semantics and polymorphism are further discusssed later in this section.

The code in this section is written in version 1.4 of Haskell.

---

5. The environment can be thought of as a symbol table that stores names, and also the values to which the names are bound, during execution.

Consider the following definition of the factorial function, which uses pattern matching on its parameters:

```
fact 0 = 1
fact n = n * fact (n - 1)
```

Note the differences in syntax between this definition and its ML version in Section 15.7. First, there is no reserved word to introduce the function definition (fun in ML). Second, parentheses are not used to delimit the formal parameters.[6] Third, alternative definitions of functions (with different formal parameters) all have the same appearance.

Using pattern matching, we can define a function for computing the nth Fibonacci number with the following:

```
fib 0 = 1
fib 1 = 1
fib (n + 2) = fib (n + 1) + fib n
```

Guards can be added to lines of a function definition to specify the circumstances under which the definition can be applied. For example,

```
fact n
  | n == 0 = 1
  | n > 0 = n * fact(n - 1)
```

This definition of factorial is more precise than the previous one, for it restricts the range of actual parameter values to those for which it works. Pattern matching would of course fail in this use, for the parameter pattern is n for both value expressions. This form of a function definition is called a *conditional expression*, after the mathematical expressions on which it is based.

An **otherwise** can appear as the last condition in a conditional expression, with the obvious semantics. For example,

```
sub n
  | n < 10     = 0
  | n > 100    = 2
  | otherwise  = 1
```

Notice the similarity between the guards here and the guarded commands discussed in Chapter 8.

Consider the following function definition, whose purpose is the same as the corresponding ML function in Section 15.7:

```
square x = x * x
```

---

6. The parentheses are actually optional in ML.

In this case, however, because of Haskell support for polymorphism, this function can take a parameter of any numeric type.

As with ML, lists are written in brackets in Haskell, as in

```
colors = ["blue", "green", "red", "yellow"]
```

Haskell includes a collection of list operators. For example, lists can be catenated with ++, : serves as an infix version of CONS, and .. is used to specify arithmetic series. For example,

```
5:[2, 7, 9]  results in [5, 2, 7, 9]
[1, 3..11] results in [1, 3, 5, 7, 9, 11]
[1, 3, 5] ++ [2, 4, 6] results in [1, 3, 5, 2, 4, 6]
```

Notice that the : operator is just like ML's :: operator.[7] Using : and pattern matching, we can define a simple function to compute the product of a given list of numbers:

```
product [] = 1
product (a:x) = a * product x
```

Using product, we can write a factorial function in the simpler form

```
fact n = product [1..n]
```

Haskell includes a **let** construct that is similar to ML's **let** and **val**. For example, we could write

```
quadratic_root a b c =
    let
     minus_b_over_2a = - b / (2.0 * a)
     root_part_over_2a =
               sqrt(b ^ 2 - 4.0 * a * c) / (2.0 * a)
    in
     [minus_b_over_2a - root_part_over_2a,
      minus_b_over_2a + root_part_over_2a]
```

List comprehensions provide a method of describing lists that represent sets. The syntax of a list comprehension is the same as that often used to describe sets in mathematics, the general form of which is

```
[body | qualifiers]
```

---

7. It is interesting that ML uses : for attaching a type name to a name and :: for cons, while Haskell uses these two operators in exactly opposite ways.

For example,

```
[n * n * n | n <- [1..50]]
```

defines a list of the cubes of the numbers from 1 to 50. It is read as "a list of all n*n*n such that n is taken from the range of 1 to 50." In this case, the qualifier is in the form of a **generator.** It generates the numbers from 1 to 50. In other cases, the qualifiers are in the form of Boolean expressions, in which case they are called **tests.** This notation can be used to describe algorithms for doing many things, such as finding permutations of lists and sorting lists. For example, consider the following function, which when given a number n returns a list of all its factors:

```
factors n = [ i | i <-  [1..n `div` 2], n `mod` i == 0]
```

The list comprehension in `factors` creates a list of numbers, each temporarily bound to the name i, ranging from 1 to n/2, such that n `mod` i is zero. This is indeed a very exacting and short definition of the factors of a given number. The backticks (backward apostrophes) surrounding **div** and **mod** are used to specify the infix use of these functions. When they are called in functional notation, as in **div** n 2, the backticks are not used.

Next, consider the concision of Haskell shown in the following implementation of the quicksort algorithm:

```
sort [] =  []
sort (h:t) = sort [b | b <- t, b ≤ h]
             ++ [h] ++
             sort [b | b <- t, b > h]
```

In this program, the set of list elements that are smaller or equal to the list head are sorted and catenated with the head element, then the set of elements that are greater than the list head are sorted and catenated onto the previous result. This definition of quicksort is significantly shorter and simpler than the same algorithm coded in an imperative language.

A programming language is **strict** if it requires all actual parameters to be fully evaluated, which ensures that the value of a function does not depend on the order in which the parameters are evaluated. A language is **nonstrict** if it does not have the strict requirement. Nonstrict languages can have several distinct advantages over strict languages. First, nonstrict languages are generally more efficient, because some evaluation is avoided.[8] Second, some interesting capabilities are possible with nonstrict languages that are not possible with strict languages. Among these are infinite lists. Nonstrict langugages can

---

8. Notice how this is related to short-circuit evaluation of Boolean expressions, which is done in some imperative languages.

use an evaluation form called **lazy evaluation,** which means that expressions are evaluated only if and when their values are needed.

Recall that in Scheme the parameters to a function are fully evaluated before the function is called, so it has strict semantics. Lazy evaluation means that an actual parameter is evaluated only when its value is necessary to evaluate the function. So if a function has two parameters, but on a particular execution of the function the first parameter is not used, the actual parameter passed for that execution will not be evaluated. Furthermore, if only a part of an actual parameter must be evaluated for an execution of the function, the rest is left unevaluated. Finally, actual parameters are evaluated only once, if at all, even if the same actual parameter appears more than once in a function call.

As stated earlier, lazy evaluation allows one to define infinite data structures. For example, consider the following:

```
positives = [0..]
evens = [2, 4..]
squares = [n * n | n <- [0..]]
```

Of course, no computer can actually represent all of the numbers of these lists, but that does not prevent their use if lazy evaluation is used. For example, if we wanted to know if a particular number was a perfect square, we could check the squares list with a membership function. Suppose we had a predicate function named `member` that determined whether a given list contained a given atom. Then we could use it as in

```
member squares 16
```

which would return `True`. The `squares` definition would be evaluated until the 16 was found. The `member` function would need to be carefully written. Specifically, suppose it were defined as follows:

```
member [] b = False
member (a:x) b = (a == b) || member x b
```

The second line of this definition breaks the first parameter into its head and tail. Its return value is true if either the head matches the element for which it is searching (b) or if the recursive call with the tail of the list returns `True`.

This definition of `member` would work correctly with `squares` only if the given number were a perfect square. If not, `squares` would keep generating squares forever, or until some memory limitation was reached, looking for the given number in the list. The following function performs the membership test of an ordered list, abandoning the search and returning `False` if a number greater than the searched-for number is found.

```
member2 (m:x) n
  | m < n     = member2 x n
```

```
| m == n     = True
| otherwise = False
```

Lazy evaluation sometimes provides a modularization tool. Consider functional composition. Suppose that in a program there is a call to function f and the parameter to f is the return value of a function g.[9] So, we have f(g(x)). Further suppose that g produces a large amount of data, a little at a time, and that f must then process this data, a little at a time. With lazy evaluation, the executions of f and g implicitly will be tightly synchronized. Function g will execute only long enough to produce enough data for f to begin its processing. When f is ready for more data, g will be restarted to produce more, while f waits. If f terminates without getting all of g's output, g is aborted, thereby avoiding useless computation. Also, g need not be a terminating function, perhaps because it produces an infinite amount of output. g will be forced to terminate when f terminates. So, under lazy evaluation, g runs as little as possible. This evaluation process supports the modularization of programs into generator units and selector units, where the generator produces a large number of possible results and the selector chooses the appropriate subset.

Lazy evaluation is not without its costs. It would certainly be surprising if such expressive power and flexibility came free. In this case, the cost is in a far more complicated semantics, which results in much slower speed of execution.

15.9 Applications of Functional Languages

Over the past 45 years in the history of high-level programming languages, only a few functional languages have gained widespread use. Most prominent among these is LISP.

LISP is a versatile and powerful language. For its first 15 years, it was thought of, mostly by nonusers, as a strange-looking and odd-behaving language that was very costly to use. Indeed, it was common in the 1960s and early 1970s to think of two categories of languages, one containing LISP and one with all of the other programming languages.

LISP was developed for symbolic computation and list-processing applications, which lie mainly in the AI realm of computing. In many AI applications, LISP and its derivatives are still the standard languages.

Within AI, a number of areas have been developed, primarily through the use of LISP; although other kinds of languages can be used—primarily, logic programming languages. Most existing expert systems, for example, were developed in LISP. LISP also dominates in the areas of knowledge representation, machine learning, intelligent training systems, and the modeling of speech.

---

9. This example appears in Hughes (1989).

Outside AI, LISP has also been successful for some applications. For example, the Emacs text editor is written in LISP, as is the symbolic mathematics system MACSYMA, which does symbolic differentiation and integration, among other things. The LISP machine was a personal computer whose entire systems software was written in LISP. LISP has also been successfully used to construct experimental systems in a variety of application areas.

Scheme is widely used to teach functional programming. It is also used in some universities to teach introductory programming courses. Use of ML and Haskell has been, for the most part, restricted to research laboratories and universities.

15.10 A Comparison of Functional and Imperative Languages

Functional languages can have a very simple syntactic structure. The list structure of LISP, which is used for both code and data, clearly illustrates this. The syntax of the imperative languages is much more complex.

The semantics of functional languages can also be simple compared to that of the imperative languages. For example, in the denotational semantics description of an imperative loop construct given in Section 3.5.3, the loop is converted from an iterative construct to a recursive construct. This conversion is unnecessary in a pure functional language, in which there is no iteration. Furthermore, we assumed there were no expression side effects in all of the denotational semantic descriptions of imperative constructs in Chapter 3. This restriction is unrealistic, because all of the C-based languages include expression side effects. This restriction is not needed for the denotational descriptions of pure functional languages.

Some in the functional programming community have claimed that the use of functional programming results in an order-of-magnitude increase in productivity, largely due to functional programs being only 10 percent as large as their imperative counterparts. While such numbers have been actually shown for certain problem areas, for other problem areas, functional programs are more like 25 percent as large as imperative solutions to the same problems (Wadler, 1998). These factors allow proponents of functional programming to claim productivity advantages over imperative programming of 4 to 10 times. However, program size alone is not necessarily a good measure of productivity. Certainly not all lines of source code have equal complexity, nor do they take the same amount of time to produce. In fact, because of the necessity of dealing with variables, imperative programs have many trivially simple lines for initializing and making small changes to variables.

Execution efficiency is another basis for comparison. When functional programs are interpreted, they are of course much slower than their compiled imperative counterparts. However, there are now compilers for most functional languages, so that execution speed disparities between functional languages and compiled imperative languages are no longer so great. One might be tempted to say that because functional programs are significantly smaller than equivalent imperative programs, they should execute much faster than the imperative programs. However, this often is not the case, because of a collection of language characteristics of the functional languages that have a strong negative impact on execution efficiency. Considering the relative efficiency of functional and imperative programs, it is reasonable to estimate that an average functional program will execute in about twice the time of its imperative counterpart (Wadler, 1998). This may sound like a significant difference, one that would often lead one to dismiss the functional languages for a given application. However, this factor-of-two difference is important only in situations where execution speed is of the utmost importance. There are many situations where a factor of two in execution speed is not considered important. For example, consider that many programs written in imperative languages, such as the Web software written in JavaScript, PHP, and as Java applets, are interpreted and therefore are much slower than equivalent compiled versions. For these applications, execution speed is not the first priority.

Another potential advantage of functional languages is readability. In many imperative programs, the details of dealing with variables obscure the logic of the program. Consider a function that computes the sum of the cubes of the first n positive integers. In C, such a function would be similar to the following:

```
int sum_cubes(int n){
  int sum = 0;
  for(int index = 1; index <= n; index++)
    sum += index * index * index;
  return sum;
}
```

In Haskell, the function could be:

```
sumCubes n = sum (map (^3) [1..n])
```

This version simply specifies three steps:
  1. Build the list of numbers ([1..n]).
  2. Create a new list by mapping a function that computes the third power onto each number in the list.
  3. Sum the new list.
Because of the lack of details of variables and iteration control, this version is more readable than the C version.

Concurrent execution in the imperative languages is difficult to design and difficult to use. For example, consider the tasking model of Ada, in which cooperation among concurrent tasks is the responsibility of the programmer. Functional programs can be executed by first translating them into graphs. These graphs can then be executed through a graph reduction process, which can be done with a great deal of concurrency that was not specified by the programmer. The graph representation naturally exposes many opportunities for concurrent execution. Cooperation synchronization in this process is not the concern of the programmer. A detailed description of this process is beyond the scope of this book.

In an imperative language, the programmer must make a static division of the program into its concurrent parts, which are then written as tasks. This can be a complicated process. Programs in functional languages can be divided into concurrent parts dynamically by the execution system, making the process highly adaptable to the hardware on which it is running. Understanding concurrent programs in imperative languages is much more difficult.

It is not a simple matter to determine precisely why functional languages have not attained great popularity. The inefficiency of the early implementations was clearly a factor then, and it is likely that at least some contemporary imperative programmers believe that programs written in functional languages are still very slow. In addition, the vast majority of programmers begin with imperative languages, which makes functional programs appear to them to be strange and difficult to understand. For many who are comfortable with imperative programming, the switch to functional programming is an unattractive and potentially difficult move. On the other hand, those who begin with a functional language never notice anything strange about functional programs.

There are those, obviously imperative programmers, who believe that because they are at ease with imperative programming, that imperative programming is somehow an intrinsically more natural way to program. Some functional programmers feel the same way about functional programs. Of course, no one has determined an effective way to measure "naturalness." One last thought: Perhaps the closeness of functional programming to mathematics, while resulting in conciseness and elegance, may in fact make them less accessible to many programmers, especially those who are not overly comfortable with mathematics.

SUMMARY

Mathematical functions are named or unnamed mappings that use only conditional expressions and recursion to control their evaluations. Complex functions can be built using functional forms, in which functions are used as parameters, returned values, or both.

Functional programming languages are modeled on mathematical functions. In their pure form, they do not use variables or assignment statements to produce results; rather, they use functional applications, conditional expressions, and recursion for execution control, and functional forms to construct complex functions. LISP began as a purely functional language but soon had a number of imperative-language features added in order to increase its efficiency and ease of use.

The first version of LISP grew out of the need for a list-processing language for AI applications. LISP is still the most widely used language for that area.

The first implementation of LISP was serendipitous: The original version of EVAL was developed solely to demonstrate that a universal LISP function could be written.

Because LISP data and LISP programs have the same form, it is possible to have a program build another program. The availability of EVAL allows such programs to be executed immediately.

Scheme is a relatively simple dialect of LISP that uses static scoping exclusively. Like LISP, Scheme's primary primitives include functions for constructing and dismantling lists, functions for conditional expressions, and simple predicates for numbers, symbols, and lists. Scheme includes some imperative operations, such as for changing an element of a given list.

COMMON LISP is a large LISP-based language that was designed to include most of the features of the LISP dialects of the early 1980s. It allows both static- and dynamic-scoped variables and includes many imperative features.

ML is a static-scoped and strongly typed functional programming language that uses a syntax that is more similar to that of an imperative language than to LISP. It includes a type-inferencing system, exception handling, a variety of data structures, and abstract data types.

Haskell is similar to ML, except that all expressions in Haskell are evaluated using a lazy method, which allows programs to deal with infinite lists. Haskell also supports list comprehensions, which provide a convenient and familiar syntax for describing sets.

Although LISP's primary area of application is AI, it has been successfully used for a number of different areas of problem solving.

Although there may be advantages to purely functional languages over their imperative relatives, their lower efficiency of execution on von Neumann machines has prevented them from being considered by many as replacements.

BIBLIOGRAPHIC NOTES

The first published version of LISP can be found in McCarthy (1960). A widely used version from the mid-1960s until the late 1970s is described in McCarthy et al. (1965) and Weissman (1967). COMMON LISP is described in Steele (1984). The Scheme language, along with some of its innovations and advantages, is discussed in Rees and Clinger (1986).

Dybvig (2003) is a good source of information on programming in Scheme. ML is defined in Milner et al. (1990). Ullman (1998) is an excellent introductory textbook for ML. Programming in Haskell is introduced in Thompson (1996).

A rigorous discussion of functional programming in general can be found in Henderson (1980). The process of implementing functional languages through graph reduction is discussed in detail in Peyton Jones (1987).

1. Define *functional form* and *referential transparency*.
2. What data types were part of the original LISP?
3. What are the differences between =. EQ?, EQV?, and EQUAL?
4. What are the differences between the evaluation method used for the Scheme special form DEFINE and that used for its primitive functions?
5. What are the two forms of DEFINE?
6. Describe the syntax and semantics of COND.
7. Describe the syntax and semantics of LET.
8. Why were imperative features added to most dialects of LISP?
9. In what ways are COMMON LISP and Scheme opposites?
10. What scoping rule is used in Scheme? In COMMON LISP? In ML? In Haskell?
11. What are three ways that ML is significantly different from Scheme?
12. What is type inferencing, as used in ML? (See Chapter 5.)
13. What are three features of Haskell that make it significantly different from Scheme?
14. What does *lazy evaluation* mean?
15. What are the differences between CONS, LIST, and APPEND?

1. Read John Backus's paper on FP (Backus, 1978) and compare the features of Scheme discussed in this chapter with the corresponding features of FP.
2. Find definitions of the Scheme functions EVAL and APPLY, and explain their actions.
3. One of the most modern and complete programming environments for any language is the INTERLISP system for LISP, as described in "The INTERLISP Programming Environment," by Teitelmen and Masinter (*IEEE Computer*, Vol. 14, No. 4, April 1981). Read this article carefully and compare the difficulty of writing LISP programs on your system with

that of using INTERLISP (assuming that you do not normally use INTERLISP).

4. Refer to a book on LISP programming and determine what arguments support the inclusion of the PROG feature in LISP.

5. A functional language could use some data structure other than the list. For example, it could use sequences of symbols. What primitives would such a language have in place of the CAR, CDR, and CONS primitives of Scheme?

6. What does the following Scheme function do?

```
(define (y s lis)
  (cond
    ((null? lis) '() )
    ((equal? s (car lis)) lis)
    (else (y s (cdr lis)))
))
```

7. What does the following Scheme function do?

```
(define (x lis)
  (cond
    ((null? lis) 0)
    ((not (list? (car lis)))
      (cond
        ((eq? (car lis) nil) (x (cdr lis)))
        (else (+ 1 (x (cdr lis))))))
    (else (+ (x (car lis)) (x (cdr lis))))
))
```

PROGRAMMING EXERCISES

1. Write a Scheme function that computes the volume of a sphere, given its radius.

2. Write a Scheme function that computes the real roots of a given quadratic equation. If the roots are complex, the function must display a message indicating that. This function must use an IF function. The three parameters to the function are the three coefficients of the quadratic equation.

3. Repeat Programming Exercise 2 using a COND function, rather than an IF function.

4. Write a Scheme function that returns the number of zeros in a given simple list of numbers.

5. Write a Scheme function that deletes all top-level instances of a given atom from a given list.

6. Write a Scheme function that removes the last element from a given list.

7. Repeat Programming Exercise 5, except that the atom can be either an atom or a list.

8. Write a Scheme function that takes two atoms and a list as parameters and replaces all occurrences of the first given atom in the list with the second given atom, no matter how deeply the first atom is nested.

9. Write a Scheme function that returns the reverse of its simple list parameter.

10. Write a Scheme predicate function that tests for the structural equality of two given lists. Two lists are structurally equal if they have the same list structure, although their atoms may be different.

11. Write a Scheme function that returns the union of two simple list parameters that represent sets.

12. Write a Scheme function with two parameters, an atom and a list, that returns the list with all occurrences, no matter how deep, of the given atom deleted. The returned list cannot contain anything in place of the deleted atoms.

13. Write a Scheme function that takes a list as a parameter and returns it with the second top-level element removed. If the given list does not have two elements, the function should return ().

14. Write a Scheme function that takes a simple list of numbers as its parameter and returns the list with the numbers in ascending order.

15. Write a Scheme function that takes a simple list of numbers as its parameter and returns the largest and smallest numbers in the list.

16. Write a Scheme function that takes a simple list as its parameter and returns a list of all permutations of the given list.

16

Logic Programming Languages

T he objectives of this chapter are to introduce the concepts of logic programming and logic programming languages, including a brief description of a subset of Prolog. We begin with an introduction to predicate calculus, which is the
basis for logic programming languages. This is followed by a discussion of how predicate calculus can be used for automatic theorem-proving systems. We then present a
general overview of logic programming. Next, a lengthy section introduces the basics
of the Prolog programming language, including arithmetic, list processing, and a
trace tool that can be used to help debug programs and also to illustrate how the
Prolog system works. The final two sections describe some of the problems of Prolog
as a logic language and some of the application areas in which Prolog has been used.

16.1 Introduction

Chapter 15 discusses the functional programming paradigm, which is significantly different from the software development methodologies used with the
imperative languages. In this chapter, we describe another different programming methodology. In this case, the approach is to express programs in a form
of symbolic logic and use a logical inferencing process to produce results.
Logic programs are declarative rather than procedural, which means that only
the specifications of the desired results are stated rather than detailed procedures for producing them.

Programming that uses a form of symbolic logic as a programming language is often called **logic programming,** and languages based on symbolic
logic are called **logic programming languages,** or **declarative languages.**
We have chosen to describe the logic programming language Prolog, because
it is the only widely used logic language.

The syntax of logic programming languages is remarkably different from
that of the imperative and functional languages. The semantics of logic programs also bears little resemblance to that of imperative-language programs.
These observations should lead the reader to some curiosity about the nature
of logic programming and declarative languages.

16.2 A Brief Introduction to Predicate Calculus

Before we can discuss logic programming, we must briefly investigate its
basis, which is formal logic. This is not our first contact with formal logic in
this book; it was used extensively in the axiomatic semantics described in
Chapter 3.

A **proposition** can be thought of as a logical statement that may or may
not be true. It consists of objects and the relationships of objects to each
other. Formal logic was developed to provide a method for describing propositions, with the goal of allowing those formally stated propositions to be
checked for validity.

Symbolic logic can be used for the three basic needs of formal logic: to express propositions, to express the relationships between propositions, and to describe how new propositions can be inferred from other propositions that are assumed to be true.

There is a close relationship between formal logic and mathematics. In fact, much of mathematics can be thought of in terms of logic. The fundamental axioms of number and set theory are the initial set of propositions, which are assumed to be true. Theorems are the additional propositions that can be inferred from the initial set.

The particular form of symbolic logic that is used for logic programming is called **first-order predicate calculus** (though it is a bit imprecise, we will usually refer to it as predicate calculus). In the following subsections, we present a brief look at predicate calculus. Our goal is to lay the groundwork for a discussion of logic programming and the logic programming language Prolog.

16.2.1   Propositions

The objects in logic programming propositions are represented by simple terms, which are either constants or variables. A constant is a symbol that represents an object. A variable is a symbol that can represent different objects at different times, although in a sense that is far closer to mathematics than the variables in an imperative programming language.

The simplest propositions, which are called **atomic propositions,** consist of compound terms. A **compound term** is one element of a mathematical relation, written in a form that has the appearance of mathematical function notation. Recall from Chapter 15 that a mathematical function is a mapping, which can be represented either as an expression or as a table or list of tuples. Compound terms are elements of the tabular definition of a function.

A compound term is composed of two parts: a **functor,** which is the function symbol that names the relation, and an ordered list of parameters, which together represent an element of the relation. A compound term with a single parameter is a 1-tuple; one with two parameters is a 2-tuple, and so forth. For example, we might have the two propositions

man(jake)
like(bob, steak)

which state that {jake} is a 1-tuple in the relation named man, and that {bob, steak} is a 2-tuple in the relation named like. If we added the proposition

man(fred)

to the two previous propositions, then the relation man would have two distinct elements, {jake} and {fred}. All of the simple terms in these propositions —man, jake, like, bob, and steak—are constants. Note that these propositions have no intrinsic semantics. They mean whatever we want them to mean. For example, the second example may mean that bob likes steak, or that steak likes bob, or that bob is in some way similar to a steak.

Propositions can be stated in two modes: one in which the proposition is defined to be true, and one in which the truth of the proposition is something that is to be determined. In other words, propositions can be stated to be facts or queries. The example propositions could be either.

Compound propositions have two or more atomic propositions, which are connected by logical connectors, or operators, in the same way compound logic expressions are constructed in imperative languages. The names, symbols, and meanings of the predicate calculus logical connectors are as follows:

Name	Symbol	Example	Meaning
negation	$\neg$	$\neg a$	not a
conjunction	$\cap$	$a \cap b$	a and b
disjunction	$\cup$	$a \cup b$	a or b
equivalence	$\equiv$	$a \equiv b$	a is equivalent to b
implication	$\supset$	$a \supset b$	*a implies b*
	$\subset$	$a \subset b$	*b implies a*

The following are examples of compound propositions:

$a \cap b \supset c$
$a \cap \neg b \supset d$

The $\neg$ operator has the highest precedence. The operators $\cap$, $\cup$, and $\equiv$ all have higher precedence than $\supset$ and $\subset$. So the second example is equivalent to

$(a \cap (\neg b)) \supset d$

Variables can appear in propositions but only when introduced by special symbols called *quantifiers*. Predicate calculus includes two quantifiers, as described below, where X is a variable and P is a proposition:

Name	Example	Meaning
universal	$\forall X.P$	For all X, P is true.
existential	$\exists X.P$	There exists a value of X such that P is true.

The period between X and P simply separates the variable from the proposition. For example, consider the following:

$\forall X.(\text{woman}(X) \supset \text{human}(X))$
$\exists X.(\text{mother}(\text{mary}, X) \cap \text{male}(X))$

The first of these propositions means that for any value of X, if X is a woman, then X is a human. The second means that there exists a value of X such that mary is the mother of X and X is a male; in other words, mary has a son. The scope of the universal and existential quantifiers is the atomic propositions to which they are attached. This scope can be extended using parentheses, as in the two compound propositions just described. So the universal and existential quantifiers have higher precedence than any of the operators.

16.2.2   Clausal Form

We are discussing predicate calculus because it is the basis for logic programming languages. As with other languages, logic languages are best in their simplest form, meaning that redundancy should be minimized.

One problem with predicate calculus as we have described it thus far is that there are too many different ways of stating propositions that have the same meaning; that is, there is a great deal of redundancy. This is not such a problem for logicians, but if predicate calculus is to be used in an automated (computerized) system, it is a serious problem. To simplify matters, a standard form for propositions is desirable. Clausal form, which is a relatively simple form of propositions, is one such standard form. Without loss of generality, all propositions can be expressed in clausal form. A proposition in clausal form has the following general syntax:

$$B_1 \cup B_2 \cup ... \cup B_n \subset A_1 \cap A_2 \cap ... \cap A_m$$

in which the As and Bs are terms. The meaning of this clausal form proposition is as follows: If all of the As are true, then at least one B is true. The primary characteristics of clausal form propositions are the following: Existential quantifiers are not required; universal quantifiers are implicit in the use of variables in the atomic propositions; and no operators other than conjunction and disjunction are required. Also, conjunction and disjunction need appear only in the order shown in the general clausal form: disjunction on the left side and conjunction on the right side. All predicate calculus propositions can be algorithmically converted to clausal form. Nilsson (1971) gives proof that this can be done, as well as a simple conversion algorithm for doing it.

The right side of a clausal form proposition is called the **antecedent.** The left side is called the **consequent** because it is the consequence of the truth of the antecedent. As examples of clausal form propositions, consider the following:

likes(bob, trout) $\subset$ likes(bob, fish) $\cap$ fish(trout)

father(louis, al) $\cup$ father(louis, violet) $\subset$ father(al, bob) $\cap$ mother(violet, bob) $\cap$ grandfather(louis, bob)

The English version of the first of these states that if bob likes fish and a trout is a fish, then bob likes trout. The second states that if al is bob's father and violet is bob's mother and louis is bob's grandfather, then louis is either al's father or violet's father.

16.3 Predicate Calculus and Proving Theorems

Predicate calculus provides a method of expressing collections of propositions. One use of collections of propositions is to determine whether any interesting or useful facts can be inferred from them. This is exactly analogous to the work of mathematicians, who strive to discover new theorems that can be inferred from known axioms and theorems.

The early days of computer science (the 1950s and early 1960s) saw a great deal of interest in automating the theorem-proving process. One of the most significant breakthroughs in automatic theorem proving was the discovery of the resolution principle by Alan Robinson at Syracuse University (Robinson, 1965).

Resolution is an inference rule that allows inferred propositions to be computed from given propositions, thus providing a method with potential application to automatic theorem proving. Resolution was devised to be applied to propositions in clausal form. The concept of resolution is the following: Suppose there are two propositions with the forms

$$P_1 \subset P_2$$
$$Q_1 \subset Q_2$$

Their meaning is that P_2 implies P_1 and Q_2 implies Q_1. Further suppose that P_1 is identical to Q_2, so that we could rename P_1 and Q_2 as T. Then, we could rewrite the two propositions as

$$T \subset P_2$$
$$Q_1 \subset T$$

Now, because P_2 implies T and T implies Q_1, it is logically obvious that P_2 implies Q_1, which we could write as

$$Q_1 \subset P_2$$

The process of inferring this proposition from the original two propositions is resolution.

As another example, consider the two propositions:

older(joanne, jake) $\subset$ mother(joanne, jake)
wiser(joanne, jake) $\subset$ older(joanne, jake)

From these propositions, the following proposition can be constructed using resolution:

wiser(joanne, jake) ⊂ mother(joanne, jake)

The mechanics of this resolution construction are simple: The terms of the left sides of the two propositions are ANDed together to make the left side of the new proposition. Then the same thing is done to get the right side of the new proposition. Next, any term that appears on both sides of the new proposition is removed from both sides. The process is exactly the same when the propositions have multiple terms on either or both sides. The left side of the new inferred proposition initially contains all of the terms of the left sides of the two given propositions. The new right side is similarly constructed. Then the term that appears in both sides of the new proposition is removed. For example, if we have

father(bob, jake) ∪ mother(bob, jake) ⊂ parent(bob, jake)
grandfather(bob, fred) ⊂ father(bob, jake) ∩ father(jake, fred)

resolution says that

mother(bob, jake) ∪ grandfather(bob, fred) ⊂
    parent(bob, jake) ∩ father(jake, fred)

which has all but one of the atomic propositions of both of the original propositions. The one atomic proposition that allowed the operation father(bob, jake) in the left side of the first and in the right side of the second is left out. In English, we would say

if: bob is the parent of jake implies that bob is either the
      father or mother of jake
and: bob is the father of jake and jake is the father of fred implies that
      bob is the grandfather of fred
then: *if* bob is the parent of jake and jake is the father of fred
      then: either bob is jake's mother or bob is fred's grandfather

Resolution is actually more complex than these simple examples illustrate. In particular, the presence of variables in propositions requires resolution to find values for those variables that allow the matching process to succeed. This process of determining useful values for variables is called **unification.** The temporary assigning of values to variables to allow unification is called **instantiation.**

It is common for the resolution process to instantiate a variable with a value, fail to complete the required matching, and then be required to backtrack and instantiate the variable with a different value. We will discuss unification and backtracking more extensively in the context of Prolog.

A critically important property of resolution is its ability to detect any inconsistency in a given set of propositions. This property allows resolution to be used to prove theorems, which can be done as follows: We can envision a theorem proof in terms of predicate calculus as a given set of pertinent propositions, with the negation of the theorem itself stated as a new proposition. The theorem is negated so that resolution can be used to prove the theorem by finding an inconsistency. This is proof by contradiction. Typically, the original propositions are called the **hypotheses,** and the negation of the theorem is called the **goal.**

Theoretically, this process is valid and useful. The time required for resolution, however, can be a problem. Although resolution is a finite process when the set of propositions is finite, the time required to find an inconsistency in a large database of propositions may be huge.

Theorem proving is the basis for logic programming. Much of what is computed can be couched in the form of a list of given facts and relationships as hypotheses, and a goal to be inferred from the hypotheses, using resolution.

When propositions are used for resolution, only a restricted kind of clausal form can be used, which further simplifies the resolution process. The special kinds of propositions, called **Horn clauses,** can be in only two forms: They have either a single atomic proposition on the left side or an empty left side.[1] The left side of a clausal form proposition is sometimes called the *head*, and Horn clauses with left sides are called *headed Horn clauses*. Headed Horn clauses are used to state relationships, such as

likes(bob, trout) ⊂ likes(bob, fish) ∩ fish(trout)

Horn clauses with empty left sides, which are often used to state facts, are called *headless Horn clauses*. For example,

father(bob, jake)

Most, but not all, propositions can be stated as Horn clauses.

16.4 An Overview of Logic Programming

Languages used for logic programming are called *declarative languages*, because programs written in them consist of declarations rather than assignments and control flow statements. These declarations are actually statements, or propositions, in symbolic logic.

One of the essential characteristics of logic programming languages is their semantics, which is called **declarative semantics.** The basic concept of this semantics is that there is a simple way to determine the meaning of each

---

1. Horn clauses are named after Alfred Horn, who studied clauses in this form (Horn, 1951).

statement, and it does not depend on how the statement might be used to solve a problem. Declarative semantics is considerably simpler than the semantics of the imperative languages. For example, the meaning of a given proposition in a logic programming language can be concisely determined from the statement itself. In an imperative language, the semantics of a simple assignment statement requires examination of local declarations, knowledge of the scoping rules of the language, and possibly even examination of programs in other files just to determine the types of the variables in the assignment statement. Then, assuming the expression of the assignment contains variables, the execution of the program prior to the assignment statement must be traced to determine the values of those variables. The resulting action of the statement, then, depends on its run-time context. Comparing this semantics with that of a proposition in a logic language, with no need to consider textual context or execution sequences, it is clear that declarative semantics is far simpler than the semantics of imperative languages. Thus, declarative semantics is often stated as one of the advantages that declarative languages have over imperative languages (Hogger, 1984, pp. 240–241).

Programming in both imperative and functional languages is primarily procedural, which means that the programmer knows *what* is to be accomplished by a program and instructs the computer on exactly *how* the computation is to be done. In other words, the computer is treated as a simple device that obeys orders. Everything that is computed must have every detail of that computation spelled out. Some believe that this is the essence of the difficulty of programming computers.

Programming in a logic programming language is nonprocedural. Programs in such languages do not state exactly *how* a result is to be computed but rather describe the form of the result. The difference is that we assume the computer system can somehow determine *how* the result is to be computed. What is needed to provide this capability for logic programming languages is a concise means of supplying the computer with both the relevant information and a method of inference for computing desired results. Predicate calculus supplies the basic form of communication to the computer, and resolution provides the inference technique.

An example commonly used to illustrate the difference between procedural and nonprocedural systems is sorting. In a language like C++, sorting is done by explaining in a C++ program all of the details of some sorting algorithm to a computer that has a C++ compiler. The computer, after translating the C++ program into machine code or some interpretive intermediate code, follows the instructions and produces the sorted list.

In a nonprocedural language, it is necessary only to describe the characteristics of the sorted list: It is some permutation of the given list such that for each pair of adjacent elements, a given relationship holds between the two elements. To state this formally, suppose the list to be sorted is in an array named list that has a subscript range $1 \dots n$. The concept of sorting the elements of the given list, named old_list, and placing them in a separate array, named new_list, can then be expressed as follows:

sort(old_list, new_list) ⊂ permute(old_list, new_list) ∩ sorted(new_list)
sorted(list) ⊂ ∀j such that 1 ≤ j < n, list(j) ≤ list(j+1)

where permute is a predicate that returns true if its second parameter array is a permutation of its first parameter array.

From this description, the nonprocedural language system could produce the sorted list. That makes nonprocedural programming sound like the mere production of concise software requirements specifications, which is a fair assessment. Unfortunately, however, it is not that simple. Logic programs that use only resolution face serious problems of execution efficiency. Furthermore, the best form of a logic language may not yet have been determined, and good methods of creating programs in logic programming languages for large problems have not yet been developed.

16.5 The Origins of Prolog

As was stated in Chapter 2, Alain Colmerauer and Phillippe Roussel at the University of Aix-Marseille, with some assistance from Robert Kowalski at the University of Edinburgh, developed the fundamental design of Prolog. Colmerauer and Roussel were interested in natural-language processing, and Kowalski was interested in automated theorem proving. The collaboration between the University of Aix-Marseille and the University of Edinburgh continued until the mid-1970s. Since then, research on the development and use of the language has progressed independently at those two locations, resulting in, among other things, two syntactically different dialects of Prolog.

The development of Prolog and other research efforts in logic programming received limited attention outside of Edinburgh and Marseille until the announcement in 1981 that the Japanese government was launching a large research project called the Fifth Generation Computing Systems (FGCS; Fuchi, 1981; Moto-oka, 1981). One of the primary objectives of the project was to develop intelligent machines, and Prolog was chosen as the basis for this effort. The announcement of FGCS aroused in researchers and the governments of the United States and several European countries a sudden strong interest in artificial intelligence and logic programming.

After a decade of effort, the FGCS project was quietly dropped. Despite the great assumed potential of logic programming and Prolog, little of great significance had been discovered. This led to the decline in the interest in and use of Prolog, although it still has its applications and proponents.

16.6 The Basic Elements of Prolog

There are now a number of different dialects of Prolog. These can be grouped into several categories: those that grew from the Marseille group, those that came from the Edinburgh group, and some dialects that have been developed for microcomputers, such as micro-Prolog, which is described by Clark and McCabe (1984). The syntactic forms of these are somewhat different. Rather than attempt to describe the syntax of several dialects of Prolog or some hybrid of them, we have chosen one particular, widely available dialect, which is the one developed at Edinburgh. This form of the language is sometimes called **Edinburgh syntax.** Its first implementation was on a DEC System-10 (Warren et al., 1979). Prolog implementations are available for virtually all popular computer platforms, for example, from the Free Software Organization (http://www.gnu.org).

16.6.1 Terms

As with programs in other languages, Prolog programs consist of collections of statements. There are only a few kinds of statements in Prolog, but they can be complex. All Prolog statements are constructed from terms.

A Prolog **term** is a constant, a variable, or a structure. A constant is either an **atom** or an integer. Atoms are the symbolic values of Prolog and are similar to their counterparts in LISP. In particular, an atom is either a string of letters, digits, and underscores that begins with a lowercase letter or a string of any printable ASCII characters delimited by apostrophes.

A variable is any string of letters, digits, and underscores that begins with an uppercase letter. Variables are not bound to types by declarations. The binding of a value, and thus a type, to a variable is called an **instantiation.** Instantiation occurs only in the resolution process. A variable that has not been assigned a value is called **uninstantiated.** Instantiations last only as long as it takes to satisfy one complete goal, which involves the proof or disproof of one proposition. Prolog variables are only distant relatives, in terms of both semantics and use, to the variables in the imperative languages.

The last kind of term is called a **structure.** Structures represent the atomic propositions of predicate calculus, and their general form is the same:

functor(parameter list)

The functor is any atom and is used to identify the structure. The parameter list can be any list of atoms, variables, or other structures. As discussed at length in the following subsection, structures are the means of specifying facts in Prolog. They can also be thought of as objects, in which case they allow facts to be stated in terms of several related atoms. In this sense, structures are relations, for they state relationships among terms. A structure is also a predicate when its context specifies it to be a query (question).

16.6.2 Fact Statements

Our discussion of Prolog statements begins with those statements used to construct the hypotheses, or database of assumed information—the statements from which new information can be inferred.

Prolog has two basic statement forms; these correspond to the headless and headed Horn clauses of predicate calculus. The simplest form of headless Horn clause in Prolog is a single structure, which is interpreted as an unconditional assertion, or fact. Logically, facts are simply propositions that are assumed to be true.

The following examples illustrate the kinds of facts one can have in a Prolog program. Notice that every Prolog statement is terminated by a period.

```
female(shelley).
male(bill).
female(mary).
male(jake).
father(bill, jake).
father(bill, shelley).
mother(mary, jake).
mother(mary, shelley).
```

These simple structures state certain facts about `jake`, `shelley`, `bill`, and `mary`. For example, the first states that `shelley` is a `female`. The last four connect their two parameters with a relationship that is named in the functor atom; for example, the fifth proposition might be interpreted to mean that `bill` is the `father` of `jake`. Note that these Prolog propositions, like those of predicate calculus, have no intrinsic semantics. They mean whatever the programmer wants them to mean. For example, the proposition

```
father(bill, jake).
```

could mean `bill` and `jake` have the same `father` or that `jake` is the `father` of `bill`. The most common and straightforward meaning, however, is that `bill` is the `father` of `jake`.

16.6.3 Rule Statements

The other basic form of Prolog statement for constructing the database corresponds to a headed Horn clause. This form can be related to a known theorem in mathematics from which a conclusion can be drawn if the set of given conditions is satisfied. The right side is the antecedent, or *if* part, and the left side is the consequent, or *then* part. If the antecedent of a Prolog statement is true, then the consequent of the statement must also be true. Because they are Horn clauses, the consequent of a Prolog statement is a single term, while the antecedent can be either a single term or a conjunction.

Conjunctions contain multiple terms that are separated by logical AND operations. In Prolog, the AND operation is implied. The structures that specify atomic propositions in a conjunction are separated by commas, so one could consider the commas to be AND operators. As an example of a conjunction, consider the following:

```
female(shelley), child(shelley).
```

The general form of the Prolog headed Horn clause statement is

consequence_1 :– antecedent_expression.

It is read as follows: "consequence_1 can be concluded if the antecedent expression is true or can be made to be true by some instantiation of its variables." For example,

```
ancestor(mary, shelley) :- mother(mary, shelley).
```

states that if mary is the mother of shelley, then mary is an ancestor of shelley. Headed Horn clauses are called **rules,** because they state rules of implication between propositions.

As with clausal form propositions in predicate calculus, Prolog statements can use variables to generalize their meaning. Recall that variables in clausal form provide a kind of implied universal quantifier. The following demonstrates the use of variables in Prolog statements:

```
parent(X, Y) :- mother(X, Y).
parent(X, Y) :- father(X, Y).
grandparent(X, Z) :- parent(X, Y) , parent(Y, Z).
sibling(X, Y) :- mother(M, X) , mother(M, Y),
                 father(F, X) , father(F, Y).
```

These statements give rules of implication among some variables, or universal objects. In this case, the universal objects are X, Y, Z, M, and F. The first rule states that if there are instantiations of X and Y such that mother(X, Y) is true, then for those same instantiations of X and Y, parent(X, Y) is true.

16.6.4   Goal Statements

So far, we have described the Prolog statements for logical propositions, which are used to describe both known facts and rules that describe logical relationships among facts. These statements are the basis for the theorem-proving model. The theorem is in the form of a proposition that we want the system to either prove or disprove. In Prolog, these propositions are called

goals, or **queries.** The syntactic form of Prolog goal statements is identical to that of headless Horn clauses. For example, we could have

```
man(fred).
```

to which the system will respond either **yes** or **no.** The answer **yes** means that the system has proved the goal was true under the given database of facts and relationships. The answer **no** means that either the goal was determined to be false or the system was simply unable to prove it.

Conjunctive propositions and propositions with variables are also legal goals. When variables are present, the system not only asserts the validity of the goal but also identifies the instantiations of the variables that make the goal true. For example,

```
father(X, mike).
```

can be asked. The system will then attempt, through unification, to find an instantiation of X that results in a true value for the goal.

Because goal statements and some nongoal statements have the same form (headless Horn clauses), a Prolog implementation must have some means of distinguishing between the two. Interactive Prolog implementations do this by simply having two modes, indicated by different interactive prompts: one for entering fact and rule statements and one for entering goals. The user can change the mode at any time.

16.6.5 The Inferencing Process of Prolog

This section examines Prolog resolution. Efficient use of Prolog requires that the programmer know precisely what the Prolog system does with his or her program.

Queries are called **goals.** When a goal is a compound proposition, each of the facts (structures) is called a **subgoal.** To prove that a goal is true, the inferencing process must find a chain of inference rules and/or facts in the database that connect the goal to one or more facts in the database. For example, if Q is the goal, then either Q must be found as a fact in the database or the inferencing process must find a fact P_1 and a sequence of propositions P_2, $P_3, \ldots, P_n$ such that

$$P_2 \text{ :- } P_1$$
$$P_3 \text{ :- } P_2$$
$$\ldots$$
$$Q \text{ :- } P_n$$

Of course, the process can be and often is complicated by rules with compound right sides and rules with variables. The process of finding the Ps, when they exist, is basically a comparison, or matching, of terms with each other.

Because the process of proving a subgoal is done through a proposition-matching process, it is sometimes called **matching.** In some cases, proving a subgoal is called **satisfying** that subgoal.

Consider the following query:

```
man(bob).
```

This goal statement is the simplest kind. It is relatively easy for resolution to determine whether it is true or false: The pattern of this goal is compared with the facts and rules in the database. If the database includes the fact

```
man(bob).
```

the proof is trivial. If, however, the database contains the following fact and inference rule,

```
father(bob).
man(X) :- father(X).
```

Prolog would be required to find these two statements and use them to infer the truth of the goal. This would necessitate unification to instantiate X temporarily to bob.

Now consider the goal

```
man(X).
```

In this case, Prolog must match the goal against the propositions in the database. The first proposition that it finds that has the form of the goal, with any object as its parameter, will cause X to be instantiated with that object's value. X is then displayed as the result. If there is no proposition having the form of the goal, the system indicates, by saying no, that the goal cannot be satisfied.

There are two opposite approaches to attempting to match a given goal to a fact in the database. The system can begin with the facts and rules of the database and attempt to find a sequence of matches that lead to the goal. This approach is called **bottom-up resolution,** or **forward chaining.** The alternative is to begin with the goal and attempt to find a sequence of matching propositions that lead to some set of original facts in the database. This approach is called **top-down resolution,** or **backward chaining.** In general, backward chaining works well when there is a reasonably small set of candidate answers. The forward chaining approach is better when the number of possibly correct answers is large; in this situation, backward chaining would require a very large number of matches to get to an answer. Prolog implementations use backward chaining for resolution, presumably because its designers believed backward chaining was more suitable for a larger class of problems than forward chaining.

The following example illustrates the difference between forward and backward chaining. Consider the query:

```
man(bob).
```

Assume the database contains

```
father(bob).
man(X) :- father(X).
```

Forward chaining would search for and find the first proposition. The goal is then inferred by matching the first proposition with the right side of the second rule (`father(X)`) through instantiation of `X` to `bob` and then matching the left side of the second proposition to the goal. Backward chaining would first match the goal with the left side of the second proposition (`man(X)`) through the instantiation of `X` to `bob`. As its last step, it would match the right side of the second proposition (now `father(bob)`) with the first proposition.

The next design question arises whenever the goal has more than one structure, as in our example. The question then is whether the solution search is done depth first or breadth first. A **depth-first** search finds a complete sequence of propositions—a proof—for the first subgoal before working on the others. A **breadth-first** search works on all subgoals of a given goal in parallel. Prolog's designers chose the depth-first approach primarily because it can be done with fewer computer resources. The breadth-first approach is a parallel search that can require a large amount of memory.

The last feature of Prolog's resolution mechanism that must be discussed is backtracking. When a goal with multiple subgoals is being processed and the system fails to show the truth of one of the subgoals, the system abandons the subgoal it could not prove. It then reconsiders the previous subgoal, if there is one, and attempts to find an alternative solution to it. This backing up in the goal to the reconsideration of a previously proven subgoal is called **backtracking.** A new solution is found by beginning the search where the previous search for that subgoal stopped. Multiple solutions to a subgoal result from different instantiations of its variables. Backtracking can require a great deal of time and space because it may have to find all possible proofs to every subgoal. These subgoal proofs may not be organized to minimize the time required to find the one that will result in the final complete proof, which exacerbates the problem.

To solidify your understanding of backtracking, consider the following example. Assume that there is a set of facts and rules in a database and that Prolog has been presented with the following compound goal:

```
male(X), parent(X, shelley).
```

This goal asks whether there is an instantiation of X such that X is a `male` and X is a `parent` of `shelley`. As its first step, Prolog finds the first fact in the database with `male` as its functor. It then instantiates X to the parameter of the found fact, say `mike`. Then it attempts to prove that `parent(mike, shelley)` is true. If it fails, it backtracks to the first subgoal, `male(X)`, and attempts to resatisfy it with some alternative instantiation of X. The resolution process may have to find every `male` in the database before it finds the one that is a `parent` of `shelley`. It definitely must find all `males` to prove that the goal cannot be satisfied. Note that our example goal might be processed more efficiently if the order of the two subgoals were reversed. Then, only after resolution had found a `parent` of `shelley` would it try to match that person with the `male` subgoal. This is more efficient if `shelley` has fewer parents than there are `males` in the database, which seems like a reasonable assumption. Section 16.7.1 discusses a method of limiting the backtracking done by a Prolog system.

Database searches in Prolog always proceed in the direction of first to last.

The following two subsections describe Prolog examples that further illustrate the resolution process.

16.6.6 Simple Arithmetic

Prolog supports integer variables and integer arithmetic. Originally, the arithmetic operators were functors, so that the sum of 7 and the variable X was formed with

```
+(7, X)
```

Prolog now allows a more abbreviated syntax for arithmetic with the **is** operator. This operator takes an arithmetic expression as its right operand and a variable as its left operand. All variables in the expression must already be instantiated, but the left-side variable cannot be previously instantiated. For example, in

```
A is B / 17 + C.
```

if B and C are instantiated but A is not, then this clause will cause A to be instantiated with the value of the expression. When this happens, the clause is satisfied. If either B or C is not instantiated or A is instantiated, the clause is not satisfied and no instantiation of A can take place. The semantics of an **is** proposition is considerably different from that of an assignment statement in an imperative language. This difference can lead to an interesting scenario. Because the **is** operator makes the clause in which it appears look like an assignment statement, a beginning Prolog programmer may be tempted to write a statement such as

```
Sum is Sum + Number.
```

which is never useful, or even legal, in Prolog. If Sum is not instantiated, the reference to it in the right side is undefined and the clause fails. If Sum is already instantiated, the clause fails, because the left operand cannot have a current instantiation when **is** is evaluated. In either case, the instantiation of Sum to the new value will not take place. (If the value of Sum + Number is required, it can be bound to some new name.)

Prolog does not have assignment statements in the same sense as imperative languages. They are simply not needed in most of the programming for which Prolog was designed. The usefulness of assignment statements in imperative languages depends on the capability of the programmer to control the execution control flow of the code in which the assignment statement is embedded. Because this type of control is not always possible in Prolog, such statements are far less useful.

As a simple example of the use of numeric computation in Prolog, consider the following problem: Suppose we know the average speeds of several automobiles on a particular racetrack and the amount of time they are on the track. This basic information can be coded as facts, and the relationship between speed, time, and distance can be written as a rule, as in the following:

```
speed(ford, 100).
speed(chevy, 105).
speed(dodge, 95).
speed(volvo, 80).
time(ford, 20).
time(chevy, 21).
time(dodge, 24).
time(volvo, 24).
distance(X, Y) :- speed(X, Speed),
                  time(X, Time),
                  Y is Speed * Time.
```

Now, queries can request the distance traveled by a particular car. For example, the query

```
distance(chevy, Chevy_Distance).
```

instantiates Chevy_Distance with the value 2205. The first two clauses in the right side of the distance computation statement instantiate the variables Speed and Time with the corresponding values of the given automobile functor. After satisfying the goal, Prolog also displays the name Chevy_Distance and its value.

At this point it is instructive to take an operational look at how a Prolog system produces results. Prolog has a built-in structure named trace that displays the instantiations of values to variables at each step during the attempt to satisfy a given goal. trace is used to understand and debug Prolog programs. To understand `trace`, it is best to introduce a different model of the execution of Prolog programs, called the **tracing model.**

The tracing model describes Prolog execution in terms of four events: (1) call, which occurs at the beginning of an attempt to satisfy a goal, (2) exit, which occurs when a goal has been satisfied, (3) redo, which occurs when backtrack causes an attempt to resatisfy a goal, and (4) fail, which occurs when a goal fails. Call and exit can be related directly to the execution model of a subprogram in an imperative language if processes like `distance` are thought of as subprograms. The other two events are unique to logic programming systems. In the following trace example, a trace of the computation of the value for `Chevy_Distance`, the goal requires no redo or fail events:

```
trace.
distance(chevy, Chevy_Distance).

(1) 1 Call: distance(chevy, _0)?
(2) 2 Call: speed(chevy, _5)?
(2) 2 Exit: speed(chevy, 105)
(3) 2 Call: time(chevy, _6)?
(3) 2 Exit: time(chevy, 21)
(4) 2 Call: _0 is 105*21?
(4) 2 Exit: 2205 is 105*21
(1) 1 Exit: distance(chevy, 2205)

Chevy_Distance = 2205
```

Symbols in the trace that begin with the underscore character (_) are internal variables used to store instantiated values. The first column of the trace indicates the subgoal whose match is currently being attempted. For example, in the example trace, the first line with the indication `(3)` is an attempt to instantiate the temporary variable `_6` with a `time` value for `chevy`, where `time` is the second term in the right side of the statement that describes the computation of `distance`. The second column indicates the call depth of the matching process. The third column indicates the current action.

To illustrate backtracking, consider the following example database and traced compound goal:

```
likes(jake, chocolate).
likes(jake, apricots).
likes(darcie, licorice).
likes(darcie, apricots).

trace.
likes(jake, X), likes(darcie, X).
```

```
(1) 1 Call: likes(jake, _0)?
(1) 1 Exit: likes(jake, chocolate)
(2) 1 Call: likes(darcie, chocolate)?
(2) 1 Fail: likes(darcie, chocolate)
(1) 1 Redo: likes(jake, _0)?
(1) 1 Exit: likes(jake, apricots)
(3) 1 Call: likes(darcie, apricots)?
(3) 1 Exit: likes(darcie, apricots)
```

```
X = apricots
```

One can think about Prolog computations graphically as follows: Consider each goal as a box with four ports—call, fail, exit, and redo. Control enters a goal in the forward direction through its call port. Control can also enter a goal from the reverse direction through its redo port. Control can also leave a goal in two ways: If the goal succeeded, control leaves through the exit port; if the goal failed, control leaves through the fail port. A model of the example is shown in Figure 16.1. In this example, control flows through each subgoal twice. The second subgoal fails the first time, which forces a return through redo to the first subgoal.

Figure 16.1

Control flow model for the goal `likes (jake, X), likes (darcie, X)`

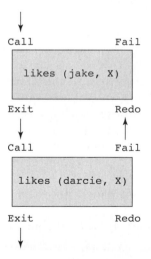

16.6.7   List Structures

So far, the only Prolog data structure we have discussed is the atomic proposition, which looks more like a function call than a data structure. Atomic propositions, which are also called structures, are actually a form of records. The other basic data structure supported is the list, which is similar to the list structure used by LISP. Lists are sequences of any number of elements, where the elements can be atoms, atomic propositions, or any other terms, including other lists.

Prolog uses the syntax of ML and Haskell to specify lists. The list elements are separated by commas, and the entire list is delimited by square brackets, as in

```
[apple, prune, grape, kumquat]
```

The notation `[]` is used to denote the empty list. Instead of having explicit functions for constructing and dismantling lists, Prolog simply uses a special notation. `[X | Y]` denotes a list with head `X` and tail `Y`, where head and tail correspond to CAR and CDR in LISP. This is similar to the notation used in ML and Haskell.

A list can be created with a simple structure, as in

```
new_list([apple, prune, grape, kumquat]).
```

which states that the constant list `[apple, prune, grape, kumquat]` is a new element of the relation named `new_list` (a name we just made up). This statement does not bind the list to a variable named `new_list`; rather, it does the kind of thing that the proposition

```
male(jake)
```

does. That is, it states that `[apple, prune, grape, kumquat]` is a new element of `new_list`. Therefore, we could have a second proposition with a list argument, such as

```
new_list([apricot, peach, pear])
```

In query mode, one of the elements of `new_list` can be dismantled into head and tail with

```
new_list([New_List_Head | New_List_Tail]).
```

If `new_list` has been set to have the two elements as shown, this statement instantiates `New_List_Head` with the head of the first list element (in this case, `apple`) and `New_List_Tail` with the tail of the list (or `[prune, grape, kumquat]`). If this were part of a compound goal and backtracking forced a new evaluation of it, `New_List_Head` and `New_List_Tail` would be reinstantiated to `apricot` and `[peach, pear]`, respectively, because `[apricot, peach, pear]` is the next element of `new_list`.

The | operator used to dismantle lists can also be used to create lists from given instantiated head and tail components, as in

```
[Element_1 | List_2]
```

If `Element_1` has been instantiated with `pickle` and `List_2` has been instantiated with `[peanut, prune, popcorn]`, the sample notation will create, for this one reference, the list `[pickle, peanut, prune, popcorn]`.

As stated previously, the list notation that includes the | symbol is universal: It can specify either a list construction or a list dismantling. Note further that the following are equivalent:

```
[apricot, peach, pear | []]
[apricot, peach | [pear]]
[apricot | [peach, pear]]
```

With lists, certain basic operations are often required, such as those found in LISP, ML, and Haskell. As an example of such operations in Prolog, we examine a definition of `append`, which is related to such a function in LISP. In this example, the differences and similarities between functional and declarative languages can be seen. We need not specify how Prolog is to construct a new list from the given lists; rather, we need specify only the characteristics of the new list in terms of the given lists.

In appearance, the Prolog definition of `append` is very similar to the ML version that appears in Chapter 15, and a kind of recursion in resolution is used in a similar way to produce the new list. In the case of Prolog, the recursion is caused and controlled by the resolution process. As with ML and Haskell, a pattern-matching process is used to choose, based on the actual parameter, between two different definitions of the append process.

The first two parameters to the `append` operation in the following code are the two lists to be appended, and the third parameter is the resulting list:

```
append([], List, List).
append([Head | List_1], List_2, [Head | List_3]) :-
            append(List_1, List_2, List_3).
```

The first proposition specifies that when the empty list is appended to any other list, that other list is the result. This statement corresponds to the recursion-terminating step of the ML `append` function. Note that the terminating proposition is placed before the recursion proposition. This is done because we know that Prolog will match the two propositions in order, starting with the first (because of its use of the depth-first order).

The second proposition specifies several characteristics of the new list. It corresponds to the recursion step in the ML function. The left-side predicate states that the first element of the new list is the same as the first element of the first given list, because they are both named `Head`. Whenever `Head` is instantiated to a value, all occurrences of `Head` in the goal are, in effect, simultaneously instantiated to that value. The right side of the second statement specifies that the tail of the first given list (`List_1`) has the second given list (`List_2`) appended to it to form the tail (`List_3`) of the resulting list.

One way to read the second statement of `append` is as follows: Appending the list [Head | List_1] to any list List_2 produces the list [Head | List_3], but only if the list List_3 is formed by appending List_1 to List_2. In LISP, this would be

```
(CONS (CAR FIRST) (APPEND (CDR FIRST) SECOND))
```

In both the Prolog and LISP versions, the resulting list is not constructed until the recursion produces the terminating condition; in this case, the first list must become empty. Then the resulting list is built using the append function itself; the elements taken from the first list are added, in reverse order, to the second list. The reversing is done by the unraveling of the recursion.

To illustrate how the `append` process progresses, consider the following traced example:

```
trace.
append([bob, jo], [jake, darcie], Family).

(1) 1 Call: append([bob, jo], [jake, darcie], _10)?
(2) 2 Call: append([jo], [jake, darcie], _18)?
(3) 3 Call: append([], [jake, darcie], _25)?
(3) 3 Exit: append([], [jake, darcie], [jake, darcie])
(2) 2 Exit: append([jo], [jake, darcie], [jo, jake,
                   darcie])
(1) 1 Exit: append([bob, jo], [jake, darcie],
                   [bob, jo, jake, darcie])
Family = [bob, jo, jake, darcie]
yes
```

The first two calls, which represent subgoals, have `List_1` nonempty, so they create the recursive calls from the right side of the second statement. The left side of the second statement effectively specifies the arguments for the recursive calls, or goals, thus dismantling the first list one element per step. When the first list becomes empty, in a call, or subgoal, the current instance of the right side of the second statement succeeds by matching the first statement. The effect of this is to return as the third parameter the value of the empty list appended to the second original parameter list. On successive exits, which represent successful matches, the elements that were removed from the first list are appended to the resulting list, `Family`. When the exit from the first goal is accomplished, the process is complete, and the resulting list is displayed.

The `append` propositions can also be used to create other list operations, such as the following, whose effect we invite the reader to determine. Note that `list_op_2` is meant to be used by providing a list as its first parameter and a variable as its second, and the result of list_op_2 is the value to which the second parameter is instantiated.

```
list_op_2([], []).
list_op_2([Head | Tail], List) :-
list_op_2(Tail, Result), append(Result, [Head], List).
```

As you may have been able to determine, list_op_2 causes the Prolog system to instantiate its second parameter with a list that has the elements of the list of the first parameter, but in reverse order. For example, ([apple, orange, grape], Q) instantiates Q with the list [grape, orange, apple].

Once again, although the LISP and Prolog languages are fundamentally different, similar operations can use similar approaches. In the case of the reverse operation, both the Prolog's list_op_2 and LISP's reverse function include the recursion-terminating condition, along with the basic process of appending the reversal of the CDR or tail of the list to the CAR or head of the list to create the result list.

The following is a trace of this process, now named reverse:

```
trace.
reverse([a, b, c], Q).

(1) 1 Call: reverse([a, b, c], _6)?
(2) 2 Call: reverse([b, c], _65636)?
(3) 3 Call: reverse([c], _65646)?
(4) 4 Call: reverse([], _65656)?
(4) 4 Exit: reverse([], [])
(5) 4 Call: append([], [c], _65646)?
(5) 4 Exit: append([], [c], [c])
(3) 3 Exit: reverse([c], [c])
(6) 3 Call: append([c], [b], _65636)?
(7) 4 Call: append([], [b], _25)?
(7) 4 Exit: append([], [b], [b])
(6) 3 Exit: append([c], [b], [c, b])
(2) 2 Exit: reverse([b, c], [c, b])
(8) 2 Call: append([c, b], [a], _6)?
(9) 3 Call: append([b], [a], _32)?
(10) 4 Call: append([], [a], _39)?
(10) 4 Exit: append([], [a], [a])
(9) 3 Exit: append([b], [a], [b, a])
(8) 2 Exit: append([c, b], [a], [c, b, a])
(1) 1 Exit: reverse([a, b, c], [c, b, a])

Q = [c, b, a]
```

Suppose we need to be able to determine whether a given symbol is in a given list. A straightforward Prolog description of this is

```
member(Element, [Element | _]).
member(Element, [_ | List]) :- member(Element, List).
```

The underscore indicates an "anonymous" variable; it is used to mean that we do not care what instantiation it might get from unification. The first statement in the previous example succeeds if Element is the head of the list, either initially or after several recursions through the second statement. The second statement succeeds if Element is in the tail of the list. Consider the following traced examples:

```
trace.
member(a, [b, c, d]).
(1) 1 Call: member(a, [b, c, d])?
(2) 2 Call: member(a, [c, d])?
(3) 3 Call: member(a, [d])?
(4) 4 Call: member(a, [])?
(4) 4 Fail: member(a, [])
(3) 3 Fail: member(a, [d])
(2) 2 Fail: member(a, [c, d])
(1) 1 Fail: member(a, [b, c, d])
no

member(a, [b, a, c]).
(1) 1 Call: member(a, [b, a, c])?
(2) 2 Call: member(a, [a, c])?
(2) 2 Exit: member(a, [a, c])
(1) 1 Exit: member(a, [b, a, c])
yes
```

16.7 Deficiencies of Prolog

Although Prolog is a useful tool, it is neither a pure nor a perfect logic programming language. This section describes some of the problems with Prolog.

16.7.1 Resolution Order Control

Prolog, for reasons of efficiency, allows the user to control the ordering of pattern matching during resolution. In a pure logic programming environment, the order of attempted matches that take place during resolution is nondeterministic, and all matches could be attempted concurrently. However, because Prolog always matches in the same order, starting at the beginning of the database and at the left end of a given goal, the user can profoundly affect efficiency by ordering the database statements to optimize a particular application. For example, if the user knows that certain rules are much more likely to succeed than the others during a particular "execution," then the program can be made more efficient by placing those rules first in the database.

Slow program execution is not the only negative result of user-defined ordering in Prolog programs. It is very easy to write statements in forms that cause infinite loops and thus total program failure. For example, consider the following recursive statement form:

```
f(X, Y) :- f(Z, Y), g(X, Z).
```

Because of Prolog's left-to-right depth-first order of evaluation, regardless of the purpose of the statement, it will cause an infinite loop. As an example of this kind of statement, consider

```
ancestor(X, X).
ancestor(X, Y) :- ancestor(Z, Y), parent(X, Z).
```

In attempting to satisfy the first subgoal of the right side of the second proposition, Prolog instantiates Z to make ancestor true. It then tries to satisfy this new subgoal, coming right back to the definition of ancestor and repeating the same process, leading to unending recursion.

This particular problem is identical to the problem a recursive descent parser has with left recursion in a grammar rule, as discussed in Chapter 3. As was the case with grammar rules in parsing, simply reversing the order of the terms in the right side of the example proposition eliminates the problem. The trouble with this is that a simple change of term ordering should not be crucial to the correctness of the program. After all, the lack of the need for programmer concern for control order is supposedly one of the advantages of logic programming.

In addition to allowing the user to control database and subgoal ordering, Prolog, in another concession to efficiency, allows some explicit control of backtracking. This is done with the cut operator, which is specified by an exclamation point (!). The cut operator is actually a goal, not an operator. As a goal, it always succeeds immediately, but it cannot be resatisfied through backtracking. Thus, a side effect of the cut is that subgoals to its left in a compound goal also cannot be resatisfied through backtracking. For example, in the goal

```
a, b, !, c, d.
```

if both a and b succeed but c fails, the whole goal fails. This goal would be used if it were known that whenever c fails, it is a waste of time to resatisfy b or a.

The purpose of the cut then is to allow the user to make programs more efficient by telling the system when it should not attempt to resatisfy subgoals that presumably could not result in a complete proof.

As an example of the use of the cut operator, consider the `member` rules from Section 16.6.7, which are:

```
member(Element, [Element | _]).
member(Element, [_ | List]) :- member(Element, List).
```

If the list argument to `member` represents a set, then it can be satisfied only once (sets contain no duplicate elements). Therefore, if `member` is used as a subgoal in a multiple subgoal goal statement, there can be a problem. The problem is that if `member` succeeds but the next subgoal fails, backtracking will attempt to resatisfy `member` by continuing a prior match. But because the list argument to `member` has only one copy of the element to begin with, `member` cannot possibly succeed again, which eventually causes the whole goal to fail, in spite of any additional attempts to resatisfy `member`. For example, consider the goal:

```
dem_candidate(X) :- member(X, democrats), tests(X).
```

This goal determines whether a given person is a democrat and is a good candidate to run for a particular position. The `tests` subgoal checks a variety of characteristics of the given democrat to determine the suitability of the person for the position. If the set of democrats has no duplicates, then we do not want to back up to the `member` subgoal if the `tests` subgoal fails, because `member` will search all of the other democrats but fail, because there are no duplicates. The second attempt of `member` subgoal will be a waste of computation time. The solution to this inefficiency is to add a right side to the first statement of the `member` definition, with the cut operator as the sole element, as in

```
member(Element, [Element | _]) :- !.
```

Backtracking will not attempt to resatisfy `member` but instead will cause the entire subgoal to fail.

Cut is particularly useful in a programming strategy in Prolog called **generate and test.** In programs that use the generate-and-test strategy, the goal consists of subgoals that generate potential solutions, which are then checked by later "test" subgoals. Rejected solutions require backtracking to "generator" subgoals, which generate new potential solutions. As an example of a generate-and-test program, consider the following, which appears in Clocksin and Mellish (1997):

```
divide(N1, N2, Result) :- is_integer(Result),
                          Product1 is Result * N2,
```

```
                    Product2 is (Result + 1) * N2,
                    Product1 =< N1, Product2 > N1, !.
```

This program performs integer division, using addition and multiplication. Because most Prolog systems provide division as an operator, this program is not actually useful, other than to illustrate a simple generate-and-test program.

The predicate `is_integer` succeeds as long as its parameter can be instantiated to some non-negative integer. If its argument is not instantiated, `is_integer` instantiates it to the value 0. If the argument is instantiated to an integer, `is_integer` instantiates it to the next larger integer value.

So, in `divide`, `is_integer` is the generator subgoal. It generates elements of the sequence 0, 1, 2, ... , one each time it is satisfied. All of the other subgoals are the testing subgoals—they check to determine whether the value produced by `is_integer` is, in fact, the quotient of the first two parameters, `N1` and `N2`. The purpose of the cut as the last subgoal is simple: It prevents `divide` from ever trying to find an alternative solution once it has found *the* solution. Although `is_integer` can generate a huge number of candidates, only one is the solution, so the cut here prevents useless attempts to produce secondary solutions.

Use of the cut operator has been compared to the use of the goto in imperative languages (Van Emden, 1980). Although it is sometimes needed, it is possible to abuse it. Indeed, it is sometimes used to make logic programs have a control flow that is inspired by imperative programming styles.

The ability to tamper with control flow in a Prolog program is a deficiency, because it is directly detrimental to one of the important advantages of logic programming—that programs do not specify how solutions are to be found. Rather, they simply specify what the solution should look like. This design makes programs easier to write and easier to read. They are not cluttered with the details of how the solutions are to be determined and, in particular, the precise order in which the computations are done to produce the solution. So, while logic programming requires no control flow directions, Prolog programs frequently use them, mostly for the sake of efficiency.

16.7.2 The Closed-World Assumption

The nature of Prolog's resolution sometimes creates misleading results. The only truths, as far as Prolog is concerned, are those that can be proved using its database. It has no knowledge of the world other than its database. Any query about which there is insufficient information in the database to prove absolutely is assumed to be false. Prolog can prove that a given goal is true, but it cannot prove that a given goal is false. It simply assumes that, because it cannot prove a goal true, the goal must be false. In essence, Prolog is a true/fail system, rather than a true/false system.

Actually, the closed-world assumption should not be at all foreign to you—our judicial system operates the same way. Suspects are innocent until proven guilty. They need not be proven innocent. If a trial cannot prove a person guilty, he or she is considered innocent.

The problem of the closed-world assumption is related to the negation problem, which is discussed in the following subsection.

16.7.3   The Negation Problem

Another problem with Prolog is its difficulty with negation. Consider the following database of two facts and a relationship:

```
parent(bill, jake).
parent(bill, shelley).
sibling(X, Y) :- (parent(M, X), parent(M, Y).
```

Now, suppose we typed the query

```
sibling(X, Y).
```

Prolog will respond with

```
X = jake
Y = jake
```

Thus, Prolog "thinks" jake is a sibling of himself. This happens because the system first instantiates M with bill and X with jake to make the first subgoal, parent(M, X), true. It then starts at the beginning of the database again to match the second subgoal, parent(M, Y), and arrives at the instantiations of M with bill and Y with jake. Because the two subgoals are satisfied independently, with both matchings starting at the database's beginning, the shown response appears. To avoid this result, X must be specified to be a sibling of Y only if they have the same parents *and* they are not the same. Unfortunately, stating that they are not equal is not straightforward in Prolog, as we will discuss. The most exacting method would require adding a fact for every pair of atoms, stating that they were not the same. This can, of course, cause the database to become very large, for there is often far more negative information than positive information. For example, most people have 364 more unbirthdays than they have birthdays.

A simple alternative solution is to state in the goal that X must not be the same as Y, as in

```
sibling(X, Y) :- parent(M, X), parent(M, Y), not(X = Y).
```

In other situations, the solution is not so simple.

The Prolog not operator is satisfied in this case if resolution cannot satisfy the subgoal X = Y. Therefore, if the not succeeds, it does not necessarily mean that X is not equal to Y; rather, it means that resolution cannot prove from the database that X is the same as Y. Thus the Prolog not operator is not equivalent to a logical NOT operator, in which NOT means that its operand is provably true. This nonequivalency can lead to a problem if we happen to have a goal of the form

```
not(not(some_goal)).
```

which would be equivalent to

```
some_goal.
```

if Prolog's not operator were a true logical NOT operator. In some cases, however, they are not the same. For example, consider again the member rules:

```
member(Element, [Element | _]) :- !.
member(Element, [_ | List]) :- member(Element, List).
```

To discover one of the elements of a given list, we could use the goal

```
member(X, [mary, fred, barb]).
```

which would cause X to be instantiated with mary, which would then be printed. But if we used

```
not(not(member(X, [mary, fred, barb]))).
```

the following sequence of events would take place: First, the inner goal would succeed, instantiating X to mary. Then Prolog would attempt to satisfy the next goal:

```
not(member(X, [mary, fred, barb])).
```

This statement would fail because member succeeded. When this goal failed, X would be uninstantiated, because Prolog always uninstantiates all variables in all goals that fail. Next, Prolog would attempt to satisfy the outer not goal, which would succeed, because its argument had failed. Finally, the result, which is X, would be printed. But X would not be currently instantiated, so the system would indicate that. Generally, uninstantiated variables are printed in the form of a string of digits preceded by an underscore. So the fact that Prolog's not is not equivalent to a logical NOT can be, at the very least, misleading.

The fundamental reason why logical NOT cannot be an integral part of Prolog is the form of the Horn clause:

$$A :- B_1 \cap B_2 \cap \ldots \cap B_n$$

If all the B propositions are true, it can be concluded that A is true. But regardless of the truth or falseness of any or all of the Bs, it cannot be concluded that A is false. From positive logic, one can conclude only positive logic. Thus the use of Horn clause form prevents any negative conclusions.

16.7.4 Intrinsic Limitations

A fundamental goal of logic programming, as stated in Section 16.4, is to provide nonprocedural programming; that is, a system by which programmers specify what a program is supposed to do but need not specify how that is to be accomplished. The example given there for sorting is rewritten here:

sort(old_list, new_list) ⊂ permute(old_list, new_list) ∩ sorted(new_list)
sorted(list) ⊂ ∀j such that $1 \leq j < n$, list(j) ≤ list(j+1)

It is straightforward to write this in Prolog. For example, the sorted subgoal can be expressed as

```
sorted ([]).
sorted ([x]).
sorted ([x, y | list]) :- x <- y, sorted ([y | list]).
```

The problem with this sort process is that it has no idea of how to sort, other than simply to enumerate all permutations of the given list until it happens to create the one that has the list in sorted order—a very slow process, indeed.

So far, no one has discovered a process by which the description of a sorted list can be transformed into some efficient algorithm for sorting. Resolution is capable of many interesting things, but certainly not this. Therefore, a Prolog program that sorts a list must specify the details of how that sorting can be done, as is the case in an imperative or functional language.

Do all of these problems mean that logic programming should be abandoned? Absolutely not! As it is, it is capable of dealing with many useful applications. Furthermore, it is based on an intriguing concept and is therefore interesting in and of itself. Finally, there is the possibility that new inferencing techniques will be developed that will allow a logic programming language system to efficiently deal with progressively larger classes of problems.

16.8 Applications of Logic Programming

In this section, we briefly describe a few of the larger classes of present and potential applications of logic programming in general and Prolog in particular.

16.8.1 Relational Database Management Systems

Relational database management systems (RDBMSs) store data in the form of tables. Queries on such databases are often stated in Structured Query Language (SQL). SQL is nonprocedural in the same sense that logic programming is nonprocedural. The user does not describe how to retrieve the answer; rather, he or she describes only the characteristics of the answer. The connection between logic programming and RDBMSs should be obvious. Simple tables of information can be described by Prolog structures, and relationships between tables can be conveniently and easily described by Prolog rules. The retrieval process is inherent in the resolution operation. The goal statements of Prolog provide the queries for the RDBMS. Logic programming is thus a natural match to the needs of implementing an RDBMS.

One of the advantages of using logic programming to implement an RDBMS is that only a single language is required. In a typical RDBMS, a database language includes statements for data definitions, data manipulation, and queries, all of which are embedded in a general-purpose programming language, such as COBOL. The general-purpose language is used for processing the data and input and output functions. All of these functions can be done in a logic programming language.

Another advantage of using logic programming to implement an RDBMS is that deductive capability is built in. Conventional RDBMSs cannot deduce anything from a database other than what is explicitly stored in them. They contain only facts, rather than facts *and* inference rules. The primary disadvantage of using logic programming for an RDBMS, compared with a conventional RDBMS, is that the logic programming implementation is slower. Logical inferences simply take longer than ordinary table look-up methods using imperative programming techniques.

16.8.2 Expert Systems

Expert systems are computer systems designed to emulate human expertise in some particular domain. They consist of a database of facts, an inferencing process, some heuristics about the domain, and some friendly human interface that makes the system appear much like an expert human consultant. In addition to their initial knowledge base, which is provided by a human expert, expert systems learn from the process of being used, so their databases must be capable of growing dynamically. Also, an expert system should include the capability of interrogating the user to get additional information when it determines that such information is needed.

One of the central problems for the designer of an expert system is dealing with the inevitable inconsistencies and incompleteness of the database. Logic programming appears to be well suited to deal with these problems. For example, default inference rules can help deal with the problem of incompleteness.

Prolog can and has been used to construct expert systems. It can easily fulfill the basic needs of expert systems, using resolution as the basis for query processing, using its ability to add facts and rules to provide the learning capability, and using its trace facility to inform the user of the "reasoning" behind a given result. Missing from Prolog is the automatic ability of the system to query the user for additional information when it is needed.

One of the most widely known uses of logic programming in expert systems is the expert system construction system known as APES, which is described in Sergot (1983) and Hammond (1983). The APES system includes a very flexible facility for gathering information from the user during expert system construction. It also includes a second interpreter for producing explanations to its answers to queries.

APES has been successfully used to produce several expert systems, including one for the rules of a government social benefits program and one for the British Nationality Act, which is the definitive source for rules of British citizenship.

16.8.3   Natural-Language Processing

Certain kinds of natural-language processing can be done with logic programming. In particular, natural-language interfaces to computer software systems, such as intelligent databases and other intelligent knowledge based systems, can be conveniently done with logic programming. For describing language syntax, forms of logic programming have been found to be equivalent to context-free grammars. Proof procedures in logic programming systems have been found to be equivalent to certain parsing strategies. In fact, backward-chaining resolution can be used directly to parse sentences whose structures are described by context-free grammars. It has also been discovered that some kinds of semantics of natural languages can be made clear by modeling the languages with logic programming. In particular, research in logic-based semantics networks has shown that sets of sentences in natural languages can be expressed in clausal form (Deliyanni and Kowalski, 1979). Kowalski (1979) also discusses logic-based semantic networks.

SUMMARY

Symbolic logic provides the basis for logic programming and logic programming languages. The approach of logic programming is to use as a database a collection of facts and rules that state relationships between facts, and to use an automatic inferencing process to check the validity of new propositions, assuming the facts and rules of the database are true. This approach is the one developed for automatic theorem proving.

Prolog is the most widely used logic programming language. The origins of logic programming lie in Robinson's development of the resolution rule for logical inference. Prolog was developed primarily by Colmeraur and Roussel at Marseille, with some help from Kowalski at Edinburgh.

Logic programs should be nonprocedural, which means that the characteristics of the solution are given but the complete process of getting the solution is not.

Prolog statements are facts, rules, or goals. Most are made up of structures, which are atomic propositions, and logic operators, although arithmetic expressions are also allowed.

Resolution is the primary activity of a Prolog interpreter. This process, which uses backtracking extensively, involves mainly pattern matching among propositions. When variables are involved, they can be instantiated to values to provide matches. This instantiation process is called *unification*.

There are a number of problems with the current state of logic programming. For reasons of efficiency, and even to avoid infinite loops, programmers must sometimes state control flow information in their programs. Also, there are the problems of the closed-world assumption and negation.

Logic programming has been used in a number of different areas, primarily in relational database systems, expert systems, and natural-language processing.

BIBLIOGRAPHIC NOTES

The Prolog language is described in several books. Edinburgh's form of the language is covered in Clocksin and Mellish (2003). The microcomputer implementation is described in Clark and McCabe (1984).

Hogger (1991) is an excellent book on the general area of logic programming. It is the source of the material in this chapter's section on logic programming applications.

REVIEW QUESTIONS

1. What are the three primary uses of symbolic logic in formal logic?
2. What are the two parts of a compound term?
3. What is the general form of a proposition in clausal form?
4. Give general (not rigorous) definitions of *resolution* and *unification*.
5. What are the forms of Horn clauses?
6. What is the basic concept of declarative semantics?
7. What are the three forms of a Prolog term?
8. What are the syntactic forms and usage of fact and rule statements in Prolog?

9. Explain the two approaches to matching goals to facts in a database.

10. Explain the difference between a depth-first and a breadth-first search when discussing how multiple goals are satisfied.

11. Explain how backtracking works in Prolog.

12. Explain what is wrong with the Prolog statement K **is** K + 1.

13. What are the two ways a Prolog programmer can control the order of pattern matching during resolution?

14. Explain the generate-and-test programming strategy in Prolog.

15. Explain the closed-world assumption used by Prolog. Why is this a limitation?

16. Explain the negation problem with Prolog. Why is this a limitation?

17. Explain the connection between automatic theorem proving and Prolog's inferencing process.

18. Explain the difference between procedural and nonprocedural languages.

19. Explain why Prolog systems must do backtracking.

20. What is the relationship between resolution and unification in Prolog?

PROBLEM SET

1. Compare the concept of data typing in Ada with that of Prolog.

2. Describe how a multiple-processor machine could be used to implement resolution. Could Prolog, as currently defined, use this method?

3. Write a Prolog description of your family tree (based only on facts), going back to your grandparents and including all descendants. Be sure to include all relationships.

4. Write a set of rules for family relationships, including all relationships from grandparents through two generations. Now add these to the facts of Problem 3, and eliminate as many of the facts as you can.

5. Write the following English conditional statements as Prolog headed Horn clauses:

   a. If Fred is the father of Mike, then Fred is an ancestor of Mike.

   b. If Mike is the father of Joe and Mike is the father of Mary, then Mary is the sister of Joe.

   c. If Mike is the brother of Fred and Fred is the father of Mary, then Mike is the uncle of Mary.

6. Explain two ways in which the list-processing capabilities of Scheme and Prolog are similar.

7. In what way are the list-processing capabilities of Scheme and Prolog different?

8. Write a comparison of Prolog with ML, including two similarities and two differences.

9. From a book on Prolog, learn and write a description of an occur-check problem. Why does Prolog allow this problem to exist in its implementation?

PROGRAMMING EXERCISES

1. Write a Prolog program that finds the maximum of a list of numbers.

2. Write a Prolog program that succeeds if the intersection of two given list parameters is empty.

3. Write a Prolog program that returns a list containing the union of the elements of two given lists.

4. Write a Prolog program that returns the final element of a given list.

Bibliography

ACM. (1979) "Part A: Preliminary Ada Reference Manual" and "Part B: Rationale for the Design of the Ada Programming Language." SIGPLAN Notices, Vol. 14, No. 6.

ACM. (1993a) History of Programming Language Conference Proceedings. ACM SIGPLAN Notices, Vol. 28, No. 3, March.

ACM. (1993b) "High Performance FORTRAN Language Specification Part 1." FORTRAN Forum, Vol. 12, No. 4.

Aho, A. V., R. Sethi, and J. D. Ullman. (1986) Compilers: Principles, Techniques, and Tools. Addison-Wesley, Reading, MA.

Aho, A. V., B. W. Kernighan, and P. J. Weinberger. (1988) The AWK Programming Language. Addison-Wesley, Reading, MA.

Andrews, G. R., and F. B. Schneider. (1983) "Concepts and Notations for Concurrent Programming." ACM Computing Surveys, Vol. 15, No. 1, pp. 3–43.

ANSI. (1966) American National Standard Programming Language FORTRAN. American National Standards Institute, New York.

ANSI. (1976) American National Standard Programming Language PL/I. ANSI X3.53–1976. American National Standards Institute, New York.

ANSI. (1978a) American National Standard Programming Language FORTRAN. ANSI X3.9–1978. American National Standards Institute, New York.

ANSI. (1978b) American National Standard Programming Language Minimal BASIC. ANSI X3.60–1978. American National Standards Institute, New York.

ANSI. (1985) American National Standard Programming Language COBOL. ANSI X3.23–1985. American National Standards Institute, New York.

ANSI. (1989) American National Standard Programming Language C. ANSI X3.159–1989. American National Standards Institute, New York.

ANSI. (1992) American National Standard Programming Language FORTRAN 90. ANSI X3.198–1992. American National Standards Institute, New York.

Arden, B. W., B. A. Galler, and R. M. Graham. (1961) "MAD at Michigan." Datamation, Vol. 7, No. 12, pp. 27–28.

ARM. (1995) Ada Reference Manual. ISO/IEC/ANSI 8652:19. Intermetrics, Cambridge, MA.

Arnold, K., J. Gosling, and D. Holmes (2006) The Java (TM) Programming Language, 4e. Addison-Wesley, Reading, MA.

Backus, J. (1954) "The IBM 701 Speedcoding System." J. ACM, Vol. 1, pp. 4–6.

Backus, J. (1959) "The Syntax and Semantics of the Proposed International Algebraic Language of the Zurich ACM-GAMM Conference." Proceedings International Conference on Information Processing. UNESCO, Paris, pp. 125–132.

Backus, J. (1978) "Can Programming Be Liberated from the von Neumann Style? A Functional Style and Its Algebra of Programs." Commun. ACM, Vol. 21, No. 8, pp. 613–641.

Backus, J., F. L. Bauer, J. Green, C. Katz, J. McCarthy, P. Naur, A. J. Perlis, H. Rutishauser, K. Samelson, B. Vauquois, J. H. Wegstein, A. van Wijngaarden, and M. Woodger. (1963) "Revised Report on the Algorithmic Language ALGOL 60." Commun. ACM, Vol. 6, No. 1, pp. 1–17.

Balena, F. (2003) Programming Microsoft Visual Basic .NET Version 2003, Microsoft Press, Redmond, WA.

Ben-Ari, M. (1982) Principles of Concurrent Programming. Prentice-Hall, Englewood Cliffs, NJ.

Birtwistle, G. M., O.-J. Dahl, B. Myhrhaug, and K. Nygaard. (1973) Simula BEGIN. Van Nostrand Reinhold, New York.

Bobrow, D. G., L. DeMichiel, R. Gabriel, S. Keene, G. Kiczales, and D. Moon. (1988) "Common Lisp Object System Specification X3J13 Document 88-002R." ACM SIGPLAN Notices, Vol. 17, No. 6, pp. 216–229.

Bodwin, J. M., L. Bradley, K. Kanda, D. Litle, and U. F. Pleban. (1982) "Experience with an Experimental Compiler Generator Based on Denotational Semantics." ACM SIGPLAN Notices, Vol. 17, No. 6, pp. 216–229.

Bohm, C., and G. Jacopini. (1966) "Flow Diagrams, Turing Machines, and Languages with Only Two Formation Rules." Commun. ACM, Vol. 9, No. 5, pp. 366–371.

Bolsky, M., and D. Korn. (1995) The New KornShell Command and Programming Language. Prentice-Hall, Englewood Cliffs, NJ.

Booch, G. (1987) Software Engineering with Ada, 2e. Benjamin/Cummings, Redwood City, CA.

Bradley, J. C. (1989) QuickBASIC and QBASIC Using Modular Structures. W. C. Brown, Dubuque, IA.

Brinch Hansen, P. (1973) Operating System Principles. Prentice-Hall, Englewood Cliffs, NJ.

Brinch Hansen, P. (1975) "The Programming Language Concurrent-Pascal." IEEE Transactions on Software Engineering, Vol. 1, No. 2, pp. 199–207.

Brinch Hansen, P. (1977) The Architecture of Concurrent Programs. Prentice-Hall, Englewood Cliffs, NJ.

Brinch Hansen, P. (1978) "Distributed Processes: A Concurrent Programming Concept." Commun. ACM, Vol. 21, No. 11, pp. 934–941.

Brown, J. A., S. Pakin, and R. P. Polivka. (1988) APL2 at a Glance. Prentice-Hall, Englewood Cliffs, NJ.

Campione, M., K. Walrath, and A. Huml. (2001) The Java Tutorial, 3e. Addison-Wesley, Reading, MA.

Cardelli, L., J. Donahue, L. Glassman, M. Jordan, B. Kalsow, and G. Nelson. (1989) Modula-3 Report (revised). Digital System Research Center, Palo Alto, CA.

Chambers, C., and D. Ungar. (1991) "Making Pure Object-Oriented Languages Practical." SIGPLAN Notices, Vol. 26, No. 1, pp. 1–15.

Chomsky, N. (1956) "Three Models for the Description of Language." IRE Transactions on Information Theory, Vol. 2, No. 3, pp. 113–124.

Chomsky, N. (1959) "On Certain Formal Properties of Grammars." Information and Control, Vol. 2, No. 2, pp. 137–167.

Church, A. (1941) Annals of Mathematics Studies. Volume 6: Calculi of Lambda Conversion. Princeton Univ. Press, Princeton, NJ. Reprinted by Klaus Reprint Corporation, New York, 1965.

Clark, K. L., and F. G. McCabe. (1984) Micro-PROLOG: Programming in Logic. Prentice-Hall, Englewood Cliffs, NJ.

Clarke, L. A., J. C. Wileden, and A. L. Wolf. (1980) "Nesting in Ada Is for the Birds." ACM SIGPLAN Notices, Vol. 15, No. 11, pp. 139–145.

Cleaveland, J. C. (1986) An Introduction to Data Types. Addison-Wesley, Reading, MA.

Cleaveland, J. C., and R. C. Uzgalis. (1976) Grammars for Programming Languages: What Every Programmer Should Know About Grammar. American Elsevier, New York.

Clocksin, W. F., and C. S. Mellish. (2003) Programming in Prolog, 5e. Springer-Verlag, New York.

Cohen, J. (1981) "Garbage Collection of Linked Data Structures." ACM Computing Surveys, Vol. 13, No. 3, pp. 341–368.

Converse, T., and J. Park. (2000) PHP 4 Bible. IDG Books, New York.

Conway, M. E. (1963). "Design of a Separable Transition-Diagram Compiler." Commun. ACM, Vol. 6, No. 7, pp. 396–408.

Conway, R., and R. Constable. (1976) "PL/CS—A Disciplined Subset of PL/I." Technical Report TR76/293. Department of Computer Science, Cornell University, Ithaca, NY.

Cornell University. (1977) PL/C User's Guide, Release 7.6. Department of Computer Science, Cornell University, Ithaca, NY.

Correa, N. (1992) "Empty Categories, Chain Binding, and Parsing." pp. 83–121, Principle-Based Parsing. Eds. R. C. Berwick, S. P. Abney, and C. Tenny. Kluwer Academic Publishers, Boston.

Dahl, O.-J., E. W. Dijkstra, and C. A. R. Hoare. (1972) Structured Programming. Academic Press, New York.

Dahl, O.-J., and K. Nygaard. (1967) "SIMULA 67 Common Base Proposal." Norwegian Computing Center Document, Oslo.

Deitel, H. M., D. J. Deitel, and T. R. Nieto. (2002) Visual BASIC .Net: How to Program, 2e. Prentice-Hall, Inc. Upper Saddle River, NJ.

Deliyanni, A., and R. A. Kowalski. (1979) "Logic and Semantic Networks." Commun. ACM, Vol. 22, No. 3, pp 184–192.

Department of Defense. (1960) "COBOL, Initial Specifications for a Common Business Oriented Language." U.S. Department of Defense, Washington, D.C.

Department of Defense. (1961) "COBOL—1961, Revised Specifications for a Common Business Oriented Language." U.S. Department of Defense, Washington, D.C.

Department of Defense. (1962) "COBOL—1961 EXTENDED, Extended Specifications for a Common Business Oriented Language." U.S. Department of Defense, Washington, D.C.

Department of Defense. (1975a) "Requirements for High Order Programming Languages, STRAWMAN." July. U.S. Department of Defense, Washington, D.C.

Department of Defense. (1975b) "Requirements for High Order Programming Languages, WOODENMAN." August. U.S. Department of Defense, Washington, D.C.

Department of Defense. (1976) "Requirements for High Order Programming Languages, TINMAN." June. U.S. Department of Defense, Washington, D.C.

Department of Defense. (1977) "Requirements for High Order Programming Languages, IRONMAN." January. U.S. Department of Defense, Washington, D.C.

Department of Defense. (1978) "Requirements for High Order Programming Languages, STEELMAN." June. U.S. Department of Defense, Washington, D.C.

Department of Defense. (1980a) "Requirements for High Order Programming Languages, STONEMAN." February. U.S. Department of Defense, Washington, D.C.

Department of Defense. (1980b) "Requirements for the Programming Environment for the Common High Order Language, STONEMAN." U.S. Department of Defense, Washington, D.C.

DeRemer, F. (1971) "Simple LR(k) Grammars." Commun. ACM, Vol. 14, No. 7, pp. 453–460.

DeRemer, F. and T. Pennello. (1982) "Efficient Computation of LALR(1) Look-Ahead Sets." ACM TOPLAS, Vol. 4, No. 4, pp. 615–649.

Deutsch, L. P., and D. G. Bobrow. (1976) "An Efficient Incremental Automatic Garbage Collector." Commun. ACM, Vol. 11, No. 3, pp. 522–526.

Dijkstra, E. W. (1968a) "Goto Statement Considered Harmful." Commun. ACM, Vol. 11, No. 3, pp. 147–149.

Dijkstra, E. W. (1968b) "Cooperating Sequential Processes." In Programming Languages, F. Genuys (ed.). Academic Press, New York, pp. 43–112.

Dijkstra, E. W. (1972) "The Humble Programmer." Commun. ACM, Vol. 15, No. 10, pp. 859–866.

Dijkstra, E. W. (1975) "Guarded Commands, Nondeterminacy, and Formal Derivation of Programs." Commun. ACM, Vol. 18, No. 8, pp. 453–457.

Dijkstra, E. W. (1976). A Discipline of Programming. Prentice-Hall, Englewood Cliffs, NJ.

Dybvig, R. K. (2003) The Scheme Programming Language, 3e. MIT Press, Boston.

Ellis, M. A., and B. Stroustrup (1990) The Annotated C++ Reference Manual. Addison-Wesley, Reading, MA.

Farber, D. J., R. E. Griswold, and I. P. Polonsky. (1964) "SNOBOL, a String Manipulation Language." J. ACM, Vol. 11, No. 1, pp. 21–30.

Farrow, R. (1982) "LINGUIST 86: Yet Another Translator Writing System Based on Attribute Grammars." ACM SIGPLAN Notices, Vol. 17, No. 6, pp. 160–171.

Fischer, C. N., G. F. Johnson, J. Mauney, A. Pal, and D. L. Stock. (1984) "The Poe Language-Based Editor Project." ACM SIGPLAN Notices, Vol. 19, No. 5, pp. 21–29.

Fischer, C. N., and R. J. LeBlanc. (1977) "UW-Pascal Reference Manual." Madison Academic Computing Center, Madison, WI.

Fischer, C.N., and R. J. LeBlanc. (1980) "Implementation of Runtime Diagnostics in Pascal." IEEE Transactions on Software Engineering, SE-6, No. 4, pp. 313–319.

Fischer, C. N., and R. J. LeBlanc. (1991) Crafting a Compiler in C. Benjamin/Cummings, Menlo Park, CA.

Flanagan, D. (2002) JavaScript: The Definitive Guide, 4e. O'Reilly Media, Sebastopol, CA

Floyd, R. W. (1967) "Assigning Meanings to Programs." Proceedings Symposium Applied Mathematics. Mathematical Aspects of Computer Science Ed. J. T. Schwartz. American Mathematical Society, Providence, RI.

Frege, G. (1892) "Über Sinn und Bedeutung." Zeitschrift für Philosophie und Philosophisches Kritik, Vol. 100, pp. 25–50.

Friedl, J. E. F. (2006) Mastering Regular Expressions, 3e. O'Reilly Media, Sebastopol, CA.

Friedman, D. P., and D. S. Wise. (1979) "Reference Counting's Ability to Collect Cycles Is Not Insurmountable." Information Processing Letters, Vol. 8, No. 1, pp. 41–45.

Fuchi, K. (1981) "Aiming for Knowledge Information Processing Systems." Proceedings of the International Conference on Fifth Generation Computing Systems. Japan Information Processing Development Center, Tokyo. Republished (1982) by North-Holland Publishing, Amsterdam.

Gehani, N. (1983) Ada: An Advanced Introduction. Prentice-Hall, Englewood Cliffs, NJ.

Gilman, L., and A.J. Rose. (1976) APL: An Interactive Approach, 2e. J. Wiley, New York.

Goldberg, A., and D. Robson. (1983) Smalltalk-80: The Language and Its Implementation. Addison-Wesley, Reading, MA.

Goldberg, A., and D. Robson. (1989) Smalltalk-80: The Language. Addison-Wesley, Reading, MA.

Goodenough, J. B. (1975) "Exception Handling: Issues and Proposed Notation." Commun. ACM, Vol. 18, No. 12, pp. 683–696.

Goos, G., and J. Hartmanis (eds.) (1983) The Programming Language Ada Reference Manual. American National Standards Institute. ANSI/MIL-STD-1815A–1983. Lecture Notes in Computer Science 155. Springer-Verlag, New York.

Gordon, M. (1979) The Denotational Description of Programming Languages, An Introduction. Springer-Verlag, Berlin–New York.

Graham, P. (1996) ANSI Common LISP. Prentice-Hall, Englewood Cliffs, NJ.

Gries, D. (1981) The Science of Programming. Springer-Verlag, New York.

Griswold, R. E., and M. T. Griswold. (1983) The ICON Programming Language. Prentice-Hall, Englewood Cliffs, NJ.

Griswold, R. E., F. Poage, and I. P. Polonsky. (1971) The SNOBOL 4 Programming Language, 2e. Prentice-Hall, Englewood Cliffs, NJ.

Hammond, P. (1983) APES: A User Manual. Department of Computing Report 82/9. Imperial College of Science and Technology, London.

Henderson, P. (1980) Functional Programming: Application and Implementation. Prentice-Hall, Englewood Cliffs, NJ.

Hoare, C. A. R. (1969) "An Axiomatic Basis of Computer Programming." Commun. ACM, Vol. 12, No. 10, pp. 576–580.

Hoare, C. A. R. (1972) "Proof of Correctness of Data Representations." Acta Informatica, Vol. 1, pp. 271–281.

Hoare, C. A. R. (1973) "Hints on Programming Language Design." Proceedings ACM SIGACT/ SIGPLAN Conference on Principles of Programming Languages. Also published as Technical Report STAN-CS-73-403, Stanford University Computer Science Department.

Hoare, C. A. R. (1974) "Monitors: An Operating System Structuring Concept." Commun. ACM, Vol. 17, No. 10, pp. 549–557.

Hoare, C. A. R. (1978) "Communicating Sequential Processes." Commun. ACM, Vol. 21, No. 8, pp. 666–677.

Hoare, C. A. R. (1981) "The Emperor's Old Clothes." Commun. ACM, Vol. 24, No. 2, pp. 75–83.

Hoare, C. A. R., and N. Wirth. (1973) "An Axiomatic Definition of the Programming Language Pascal." Acta Informatica, Vol. 2, pp. 335–355.

Hogger, C. J. (1984) Introduction to Logic Programming. Academic Press, London.

Hogger, C. J. (1991) Essentials of Logic Programming. Oxford Science Publications, Oxford, England.

Holt, R. C., G. S. Graham, E. D. Lazowska, and M. A. Scott. (1978) Structured Concurrent Programming with Operating Systems Applications. Addison-Wesley, Reading, MA.

Horn, A. (1951) "On Sentences Which Are True of Direct Unions of Algebras." J. Symbolic Logic, Vol. 16, pp. 14–21.

Hudak, P., and J. Fasel. (1992) "A Gentle Introduction to Haskell, ACM SIGPLAN Notices, 27(5), May 1992, pp. T1–T53.

Hughs, (1989) "Why Functional Programming Matters", The Computer Journal, Vol. 32, No. 2 pp. 98–107.

Huskey, H. K., R. Love, and N. Wirth. (1963) "A Syntactic Description of BC NELIAC." Commun. ACM, Vol. 6, No. 7, pp. 367–375.

IBM. (1954) "Preliminary Report, Specifications for the IBM Mathematical FORmula TRANslating System, FORTRAN." IBM Corporation, New York.

IBM. (1956) "Programmer's Reference Manual, The FORTRAN Automatic Coding System for the IBM 704 EDPM." IBM Corporation, New York.

IBM. (1964) "The New Programming Language." IBM UK Laboratories.

Ichbiah, J. D., J. C. Heliard, O. Roubine, J. G. P. Barnes, B. Krieg-Brueckner, and B. A. Wichmann. (1979) "Rationale for the Design of the Ada Programming Language." ACM SIGPLAN Notices, Vol. 14, No. 6, Part B.

IEEE. (1985) "Binary Floating-Point Arithmetic." IEEE Standard 754, IEEE, New York.

INCITS/ISO/IEC (1997) 1539-1-1997 Information Technology—Programming Languages—FORTRAN Part 1: Base Language. American National Standards Institute, New York.

Ingerman, P. Z. (1967). "Panini-Backus Form Suggested." Commun. ACM, Vol. 10, No. 3, p. 137.

Intermetrics. (1993) Programming Language Ada, Draft, Version 4.0. Cambridge, MA.

ISO. (1982) Specification for Programming Language Pascal. ISO7185–1982. International Organization for Standardization, Geneva, Switzerland.

ISO/IEC (1996) 14977:1996, Information Technology—Syntactic Metalanguage—Extended BNF. International Organization for Standardization, Geneva, Switzerland.

ISO. (1998) ISO14882-1, ISO/IEC Standard – Information Technology—Programming Language—C++. International Organization for Standardization, Geneva, Switzerland.

ISO. (1999) ISO/IEC 9899:1999, Programming Language C. American National Standards Institute, New York.

ISO/IEC (2002) 1989:2002 Information Technology—Programming Languages—COBOL. American National Standards Institute, New York.

Iverson, K. E. (1962) A Programming Language. John Wiley, New York.

Jensen, K., and N. Wirth. (1974) Pascal Users Manual and Report. Springer-Verlag, Berlin.

Johnson, S. C. (1975) "Yacc—Yet Another Compiler Compiler." Computing Science Report 32. AT&T Bell Laboratories, Murray Hill, NJ.

Jones, N. D. (ed.) (1980) Semantic-Directed Compiler Generation. Lecture Notes in Computer Science, Vol. 94. Springer-Verlag, Heidelberg, FRG.

Kay, A. (1969) The Reactive Engine. Ph.D. Thesis. University of Utah, September.

Kernighan, B. W., and D. M. Ritchie. (1978) The C Programming Language. Prentice-Hall, Englewood Cliffs, NJ.

Knuth, D. E. (1965) "On the Translation of Languages from Left to Right." Information & Control, Vol. 8, No. 6, pp. 607–639.

Knuth, D. E. (1967) "The Remaining Trouble Spots in ALGOL 60." Commun. ACM, Vol. 10, No. 10, pp. 611–618.

Knuth, D. E. (1968a) "Semantics of Context-Free Languages." Mathematical Systems Theory, Vol. 2, No. 2, pp. 127–146.

Knuth, D. E. (1968b) The Art of Computer Programming, Vol. I, 2e. Addison-Wesley, Reading, MA.

Knuth, D. E. (1974) "Structured Programming with GOTO Statements." ACM Computing Surveys, Vol. 6, No. 4, pp. 261–301.

Knuth, D. E. (1981) The Art of Computer Programming, Vol. II, 2e. Addison-Wesley, Reading, MA.

Knuth, D. E., and L. T. Pardo. (1977) "Early Development of Programming Languages." In Encyclopedia of Computer Science and Technology, Vol. 7. Dekker, New York, pp. 419–493.

Kowalski, R. A. (1979) Logic for Problem Solving. Artificial Intelligence Series, Vol. 7. Elsevier-North Holland, New York.

Laning, J. H., Jr., and N. Zierler. (1954) "A Program for Translation of Mathematical Equations for Whirlwind I." Engineering memorandum E-364. Instrumentation Laboratory, Massachusetts Institute of Technology, Cambridge, MA.

Ledgard, H. (1984) The American Pascal Standard. Springer-Verlag, New York.

Ledgard, H. F., and M. Marcotty. (1975) "A Genealogy of Control Structures." Commun. ACM, Vol. 18, No. 11, pp. 629–639.

Lischner, R. (2000) Delphi in a Nutshell. O'Reilly Media, Sebastopol, CA.

Liskov, B., R. L. Atkinson, T. Bloom, J. E. B. Moss, C. Scheffert, R. Scheifler, and A. Snyder (1981) "CLU Reference Manual." Springer, New York.

Liskov, B., and A. Snyder. (1979) "Exception Handling in CLU." IEEE Transactions on Software Engineering, Vol. SE-5, No. 6, pp. 546–558.

Lomet, D. (1975) "Scheme for Invalidating References to Freed Storage." IBM J. of Research and Development, Vol. 19, pp. 26–35.

Lutz, M., and D. Ascher. (2004) Learning Python, 2e. O'Reilly Media, Sebastopol, CA.

MacLaren, M. D. (1977) "Exception Handling in PL/I." ACM SIGPLAN Notices, Vol. 12, No. 3, pp. 101–104.

Marcotty, M., H. F. Ledgard, and G. V. Bochmann. (1976) "A Sampler of Formal Definitions." ACM Computing Surveys, Vol. 8, No. 2, pp. 191–276.

Mather, D. G., and S. V. Waite (eds.) (1971) BASIC. 6e. University Press of New England, Hanover, NH.

McCarthy, J. (1960) "Recursive Functions of Symbolic Expressions and Their Computation by Machine, Part I." Commun. ACM, Vol. 3, No. 4, pp. 184–195.

McCarthy, J., P. W. Abrahams, D. J. Edwards, T. P. Hart, and M. Levin. (1965) LISP 1.5 Programmer's Manual, 2e. MIT Press, Cambridge, MA.

McCracken, D. (1970) "Whither APL." Datamation, Sept. 15, pp. 53–57.

Metcalf, M., J. Reid, and M. Cohen. (2004) Fortran 95/2003 Explained, 3e. Oxford University Press, Oxford, England.

Meyer, B. (1990) Introduction to the Theory of Programming Languages. Prentice-Hall, Englewood Cliffs, NJ.

Meyer, B. (1992) Eiffel: The Language. Prentice-Hall, Englewood Cliffs, NJ.

Microsoft. (1991) Microsoft Visual Basic Language Reference. Document DB20664-0491, Redmond, WA.

Milner, R., M. Tofte, and R. Harper. (1990) The Definition of Standard ML. MIT Press, Cambridge, MA.

Milos, D., U. Pleban, and G. Loegel. (1984) "Direct Implementation of Compiler Specifications." ACM Principles of Programming Languages 1984, pp. 196–202.

Mitchell, J. G., W. Maybury, and R. Sweet. (1979) Mesa Language Manual, Version 5.0, CSL-79-3. Xerox Research Center, Palo Alto, CA.

Moss, C. (1994) Prolog++: The Power of Object-Oriented and Logic Programming. Addison-Wesley, Reading, MA.

Moto-oka, T. (1981) "Challenge for Knowledge Information Processing Systems." Proceedings of the International Conference on Fifth Generation Computing Systems. Japan Information Processing Development Center, Tokyo. Republished (1982) by North-Holland Publishing, Amsterdam.

Naur, P. (ed.) (1960) "Report on the Algorithmic Language ALGOL 60." Commun. ACM, Vol. 3, No. 5, pp. 299–314.

Newell, A., and H. A. Simon. (1956) "The Logic Theory Machine—A Complex Information Processing System." IRE Transactions on Information Theory, Vol. IT-2, No. 3, pp. 61–79.

Newell, A., and F. M. Tonge. (1960) "An Introduction to Information Processing Language V." Commun. ACM, Vol. 3, No. 4, pp. 205–211.

Nilsson, N. J. (1971) Problem Solving Methods in Artificial Intelligence. McGraw-Hill, New York.

Ousterhout, J. K. (1994) Tcl and the Tk Toolkit. Addison-Wesley, Reading, MA.

Pagan, F. G. (1981) Formal Specifications of Programming Languages. Prentice-Hall, Englewood Cliffs, NJ.

Papert, S. (1980) MindStorms: Children, Computers and Powerful Ideas. Basic Books, New York.

Perlis, A., and K. Samelson. (1958) "Preliminary Report—International Algebraic Language." Commun. ACM, Vol. 1, No. 12, pp. 8–22.

Peyton Jones, S. L. (1987) The Implementation of Functional Programming Languages. Prentice-Hall, Englewood Cliffs, NJ.

Pratt, T. W. (1984) Programming Languages: Design and Implementation, 2e. Prentice-Hall, Englewood Cliffs, NJ.

Pratt, T. W., and M. V. Zelkowitz (2001) Programming Languages: Design and Implementation, 4e. Prentice-Hall, Englewood Cliffs, NJ.

Raymond, E. (2004) Art of UNIX Programming. Addison Wesley, Boston.

Rees, J., and W. Clinger. (1986) "Revised Report on the Algorithmic Language Scheme." ACM SIGPLAN Notices, Vol. 21, No. 12, pp. 37–79.

Remington-Rand. (1952) "UNIVAC Short Code." Unpublished collection of dittoed notes. Preface by A. B. Tonik, dated October 25, 1955 (1 p.); Preface by J.R. Logan, undated but apparently from 1952 (1 p.); Preliminary exposition, 1952? (22 pp., where in which pp. 20–22 appear to be a later replacement); Short code supplementary information, topic one (7 pp.); Addenda #1, 2, 3, 4 (9 pp.).

Richards, M. (1969) "BCPL: A Tool for Compiler Writing and Systems Programming." Proc. AFIPS SJCC, Vol. 34, pp. 557–566.

Robinson, J. A. (1965) "A Machine-Oriented Logic Based on the Resolution Principle." Journal of the ACM, Vol. 12, pp. 23–41.

Romanovsky, A. and B. Sandin (2001) "Except for Exception Handling," Ada Letters, Vol. 21, No. 3, September 2001, pp. 19–25.

Roussel. P. (1975) "PROLOG: Manual de Reference et D'utilisation." Research Report. Artificial Intelligence Group, Univ. of Aix-Marseille, Luming, France.

Rubin, F. (1987) "'GOTO Statement Considered Harmful' considered harmful" (letter to editor). Commun. ACM, Vol. 30, No. 3, pp. 195–196.

Rutishauser, H. (1967) Description of ALGOL 60. Springer-Verlag, New York.

Sammet, J. E. (1969) Programming Languages: History and Fundamentals. Prentice-Hall, Englewood Cliffs, NJ.

Sammet, J. E. (1976) "Roster of Programming Languages for 1974–75." Commun. ACM, Vol. 19, No. 12, pp. 655–669.

Schneider, D. I. (1999) An Introduction to Programming Using Visual BASIC 6.0. Prentice-Hall, Englewood Cliffs, NJ.

Schorr, H., and W. Waite. (1967) "An Efficient Machine Independent Procedure for Garbage Collection in Various List Structures." Commun. ACM, Vol. 10, No. 8, pp. 501–506.

Scott, D. S., and C. Strachey. (1971) "Towards a Mathematical Semantics for Computer Language." In Proceedings, Symposium on Computers and Automation, J. Fox (ed.). Polytechnic Institute of Brooklyn Press, New York, pp. 19–46.

Scott, M. (2000) Programming Language Pragmatics, Morgan Kaufman, San Francisco, CA.

Sebesta, R. W. (1991) VAX Structured Assembly Language Programming, 2e. Benjamin/ Cummings, Redwood City, CA.

Sergot, M. J. (1983) "A Query-the-User Facility for Logic Programming." In Integrated Interactive Computer Systems, P. Degano and E. Sandewall (eds.). North-Holland Publishing, Amsterdam.

Shaw, C. J. (1963) "A Specification of JOVIAL." Commun. ACM, Vol. 6, No. 12, pp. 721–736.

Sommerville, I. (2005) Software Engineering, 7e. Addison-Wesley, Reading, MA.

Steele, G. L., Jr. (1984) Common LISP. Digital Press, Burlington, MA.

Stoy, J. E. (1977) Denotational Semantics: The Scott–Strachey Approach to Programming Language Semantics. MIT Press, Cambridge, MA.

Stroustrup, B. (1983) "Adding Classes to C: An Exercise in Language Evolution." Software—Practice and Experience, Vol. 13, pp. 139–161.

Stroustrup, B. (1984) "Data Abstraction in C." AT&T Bell Laboratories Technical Journal, Vol. 63, No. 8.

Stroustrup, B. (1986) The C++ Programming Language. Addison-Wesley, Reading, MA.

Stroustrup, B. (1988) "What Is Object-Oriented Programming?" IEEE Software, May 1988, pp. 10–20.

Stroustrup, B. (1991) The C++ Programming Language, 2e. Addison-Wesley, Reading, MA.

Stroustrup, B. (1994) The Design and Evolution of C++. Addison-Wesley, Reading, MA.

Stroustrup, B. (1997) The C++ Programming Language, 3e. Addison-Wesley, Reading, MA.

Sussman, G. J., and G. L. Steele, Jr. (1975) "Scheme: An Interpreter for Extended Lambda Calculus." MIT AI Memo No. 349 (December, 1975).

Suzuki, N. (1982) "Analysis of Pointer 'Rotation.'" Commun. ACM, Vol. 25, No. 5, pp. 330–335.

Tanenbaum, A. S. (2005) Structured Computer Organization, 5e. Prentice-Hall, Englewood Cliffs, NJ.

Tenenbaum, A. M., Y. Langsam, and M. J. Augenstein. (1990) Data Structures Using C. Prentice-Hall, Englewood Cliffs, NJ.

Teitelbaum, T., and T. Reps. (1981) "The Cornell Program Synthesizer: A Syntax-Directed Programming Environment." Commun. ACM, Vol. 24, No. 9, pp. 563–573.

Teitelman, W. (1975) INTERLISP Reference Manual. Xerox Palo Alto Research Center, Palo Alto, CA.

Thomas, D., C. Fowler, and A. Hunt. (2005) Ruby: The Progmatic Programmers Guide, 2e, The Pragmatic Bookshelf, Raleigh, NC.

Thompson, S. (1999) Haskell: The Craft of Functional Programming, 2e. Addison-Wesley, Reading, MA.

Turner, D. (1986) "An Overview of Miranda." ACM SIGPLAN Notices, Vol. 21, No. 12, pp. 158–166.

Ullman, J. D. (1998) Elements of ML Programming. ML97 Edition. Prentice-Hall, Englewood Cliffs, NJ.

van Emden, M.H. (1980) "McDermott on Prolog: A Rejoinder." SIGART Newsletter, No. 72, August, pp. 19–20.

van Wijngaarden, A., B. J. Mailloux, J. E. L. Peck, and C. H. A. Koster. (1969) "Report on the Algorithmic Language ALGOL 68." Numerische Mathematik, Vol. 14, No. 2, pp. 79–218.

Wadler, P. (1998) "Why No One Uses Functional Languages." ACM SIGPLAN Notices, Vol. 33, No. 2, February 1998, pp. 25–30.

Wall, L., J. Christiansen, and J. Orwant. (2000) Programming Perl, 3e. O'Reilly & Associates, Sebastopol, CA.

Warren, D. H. D., L. M. Pereira, and F. C. N. Pereira. (1979) "User's Guide to DEC System-10 Prolog." Occasional Paper 15. Department of Artificial Intelligence, Univ. of Edinburgh, Scotland.

Watt, D. A. (1979) "An Extended Attribute Grammar for Pascal." ACM SIGPLAN Notices, Vol. 14, No. 2, pp. 60–74.

Wegner, P. (1972) "The Vienna Definition Language." ACM Computing Surveys, Vol. 4, No. 1, pp. 5–63.

Weissman, C. (1967) LISP 1.5 Primer. Dickenson Press, Belmont, CA.

Wexelblat, R. L. (ed.) (1981) History of Programming Languages. Academic Press, New York.

Wheeler, D. J. (1950) "Programme Organization and Initial Orders for the EDSAC." Proc. R. Soc. London, Ser. A, Vol. 202, pp. 573–589.

Wilkes, M. V. (1952) "Pure and Applied Programming." In Proceedings of the ACM National Conference, Vol. 2. Toronto, pp. 121–124.

Wilkes, M. V., D. J. Wheeler, and S. Gill. (1951) The Preparation of Programs for an Electronic Digital Computer, with Special Reference to the EDSAC and the Use of a Library of Subroutines. Addison-Wesley, Reading, MA.

Wilkes, M. V., D. J. Wheeler, and S. Gill. (1957) The Preparation of Programs for an Electronic Digital Computer, 2e. Addison-Wesley, Reading, MA.

Wilson, P. R. (2005) "Uniprocessor Garbage Collection Techniques." Available at http://www.cs.utexas.edu/users/oops/papers.html#bigsurv.

Wirth, N. (1971) "The Programming Language Pascal." Acta Informatica, Vol. 1, No. 1, pp. 35–63.

Wirth, N. (1973) Systematic Programming: An Introduction. Prentice-Hall, Englewood Cliffs, NJ.

Wirth, N. (1975) "On the Design of Programming Languages." Information Processing 74 (Proceedings of IFIP Congress 74). North Holland, Amsterdam, pp. 386–393.

Wirth, N. (1977) "Modula: A Language for Modular Multi-Programming." Software—Practice and Experience, Vol. 7, pp. 3–35.

Wirth, N. (1985) Programming in Modula-2, 3e. Springer-Verlag, New York.

Wirth, N. (1988) "The Programming Language Oberon." Software—Practice and Experience, Vol. 18, No. 7, pp. 671–690.

Wirth, N., and C. A. R. Hoare. (1966) "A Contribution to the Development of ALGOL." Commun. ACM, Vol. 9, No. 6, pp. 413–431.

Wulf, W. A., D. B. Russell, and A. N. Habermann. (1971) "BLISS: A Language for Systems Programming." Commun. ACM, Vol. 14, No. 12, pp. 780–790.

Zuse, K. (1972) "Der Plankalkül." Manuscript prepared in 1945, published in Berichte der Gesellschaft für Mathematik und Datenverarbeitung, No. 63 (Bonn, 1972); Part 3, 285 pp. English translation of all but pp. 176–196 in No. 106 (Bonn, 1976), pp. 42–244.

Index